NATIONAL GEOGRAPHIC

T R A V E L E R

france

# NATIONAL GEOGRAPHIC

# T R A V E L E R

# france

by Rosemary Bailey
photography by Gilles Mingasson

National Geographic
Washington, D.C.

# CONTENTS

**Pages 2–3: The Thiou canal reflects the charming town of Annecy—in the Alps.**
**Opposite: At the Louvre in Paris, architect I. M. Pei's pyramids offer modern counterpoint.**

# TRAVELING WITH EYES OPEN

Alert travelers go with a purpose and leave with a benefit. If you travel responsibly, you can help support wildlife conservation, historic preservation, and cultural enrichment in the places you visit. You can enrich your own travel experience as well.

To be a geo-savvy traveler:

- Recognize that your presence has an impact on the places you visit.

- Spend your time and money in ways that sustain local character. (Besides, it's more interesting that way.)

- Value the destination's natural and cultural heritage.

- Respect the local customs and traditions.

- Express appreciation to local people about things you find interesting and unique to the place: its nature and scenery, music and food, historic villages and buildings.

- Vote with your wallet: Support the people who support the place, patronizing businesses that make an attempt to celebrate and protect what's special there. Seek out shops, local restaurants, inns, and tour operators who love their home—who love taking care of it and showing it off. Avoid businesses that detract from the character of the place.

- Enrich yourself, taking home memories and stories to tell, knowing that you have contributed to the preservation and enhancement of the destination.

That is the type of travel now called geotourism, defined as "tourism that sustains or enhances the geographical character of a place—its environment, culture, aesthetics, heritage, and the well-being of its residents." To learn more, visit National Geographic's Center for Sustainable Destinations at *www.nationalgeographic.com/travel/sustainable*.

# france

## ABOUT THE AUTHOR & THE PHOTOGRAPHER

**Rosemary Bailey** fell in love with France 20 years ago when she stayed on a rose farm in Provence. Since then she has traveled all over France and has written and edited a number of guides to the country and its regions, including the Côte d'Azur, Burgundy, the Loire Valley, and southwest France. She has written many travel articles and three travel memoirs, including *Love and War in the Pyrenees*. Rosemary Bailey's website is *www.rosemarybailey.com*.

Photographer **Gilles Mingasson,** who grew up in Grenoble, France, moved to Paris to pursue photojournalism. After, he was sent to the United States on assignment. He traveled through Latin America, then made Los Angeles his base. His photography can be seen in the *Panama* and *Dominican Republic National Geographic Traveler* guidebooks. Gilles Mingasson's website is *www.mingasson.com*.

With contributions by:

**Professor Colin Jones,** professor of history at London University:
pages 20–30

**Elizabeth Carter,** restaurant critic and author: pages 32–35

**Dr. Julian Petley,** lecturer in sociology, Brunel University:
pages 36–50

**Jo Sturgis,** editor of a number of travel guides, author of a *Guide to France for Children*: pages 51–104

**Helen Varley,** travel writer and journalist, founder of *Time Out* city guides, and author of *Weekends Across the Channel*: pages 105–136

# Charting Your Trip

Europe's third largest country (after Russia and Ukraine), France is the world's most popular travel destination. Layers of its long, dramatic history can be seen everywhere. Celebrated for its art, culture, fashion, and, of course, food and wine, France rewards the traveler on a wealth of levels. It could take a lifetime to discover it all, but even in a short visit it is possible to experience its riches.

## How to Get Around

Traveling in France is easy. Between cities it is most expedient to travel by train *www .raileurope.com).* The TGV (Train à Grand Vitesse high-speed train) network means you can travel between most of the big cities in two or three hours. Smaller places will take a bit longer on an SCNF train, which are frequent and comfortable. If you prefer to drive, the autoroutes are excellent, though car rentals are expensive. But if you want to explore the countryside, you will need a car. Buses are sometimes an option, though in really remote areas there may be only one or two buses a day. There are a few scenic small trains, especially in mountain regions, which offer a splendid way to see the scenery. Cyclists are well respected, and you can take bikes on most trains or rent them at your destination. In Paris and the provinces, cycle routes are increasingly common.

## How to Visit

France is not easily covered in a whistle-stop tour. It is best to be selective and focus on appreciating a few chosen places. If you only have a week or so, it would be best to concentrate on a city or two and add on a trip to the coast or countryside. No visitor to France can miss **Paris,** but even a day or two is enough to absorb the flavor of this very special capital city, which is really quite easy to walk around; Parisians do it all the time. The Métro is easy and safe, as are the buses. Taxis can be expensive, and you need to stand at a taxi stand to get a cab.

If you base yourself in Paris, you can make day visits by train to the great cathedral of **Chartres,** the palace of **Versailles,** or the gardens at **Giverny,** painted by Impressionist artist Claude Monet. Or spend a day or two a little farther afield. Less than 100 miles (161 km) from Paris is **Reims,** known for the or the stained glass of its magnificent Gothic cathedral and its fine Champagne. It's about 145 miles (234 km) north to **Normandy,** where highlights include the Bayeux tapestry and the World War II landing beaches. **Mont-St.-Michel** and its glorious abbey is 175 miles (283 km) west of Paris. Another option is the **Loire Valley:**

**A towering symbol of Paris since 1889**

Head for **Tours** (126 miles/202 km southwest of Paris) by train or car and take in the finest châteaus: Chambord, Amboise, and Chenonceau.

Alternatively, from Paris you could head south to **Avignon** by fast TGV (2 hours and 15 minutes); from there it is 122 miles (196 km) south to **Nice** and 65 miles (104 km) to **Marseille.** Or go to the gastronomic paradise of **Lyon** (a two-hour train trip south from Paris). You can also add in a trip into the **Alps,** about 60 miles (97 km) east.

## If You Have More Time

To appreciate fine food and architecture—and the quality of life of which the French are so proud— explore the **Loire Valley** via a boat trip along the river. Or plan a stay in one of the many private châteaus (see p. 187). Another elegant option would be **Bordeaux** with its incomparable wines, fine restaurants, superb classical architecture, and museums. Wine-lovers should also consider **Burgundy,** including a visit to the elegant towns of **Dijon** and **Beaune** plus a trip to the **Côte d'Or** to learn about and sample its legendary Pinot Noirs and Chardonnays. For a taste of the real *France profonde*—deep France—go to the southwest. Start in **Toulouse** (5 hours by train from Paris), a lively city of brick mansions and Romanesque cathedrals, or the preserved medieval citadel of **Carcassonne** (also about 5 hours by train from Paris). Stay in a small château (see pp. 363–370) and enjoy the myriad preparations of duck, goose, and foie gras. Don't miss the **Dordogne**—out of season preferably, because it has become so popular—which offers beautiful landscapes, rich stews, and good wine. The river is flanked by splendid castles and important caves with prehistoric paintings.

## Visitor Information

The official French Government Tourist Office website (*www.franceguide.com*) offers a wealth of information in English as well as in other languages on all aspects of travel to France, with excellent photographs and comprehensive descriptions of all regions and cities. You'll find practical trip-planning advice on driving, trains, buses, shopping, food, entertainment, special events, outdoor activities, and even details on the weather. For a mine of information on Paris, go to *www.paris.org*. For train information, schedules, bookings, and sightseeing suggestions, go to *www.raileurope.com*.

Given the popularity of France, a cornucopia of websites exists to assist travelers and those considering making France their home. Here is a list of good English-language sites: *www.anglophone-direct.com*, *www.france.angloinfo.com*, *www.frenchentree.com*, *www.informationfrance.com*, and *www.francethisway.com*.

## When France Closes

The French lunch hour remains a hallowed tradition, especially in rural areas and the south, so expect most shops, banks, and offices to close between 12 and 1:30 or 2 p.m. Given that lunch usually starts at noon in traditional restaurants, you need to be fairly prompt to be sure of being fed. Evening meals are not usually served until 7:30 or 8 p.m.

Most towns have one closing day, often Monday, and shut down completely after midday on Sunday. Be aware of specific holidays (see p. 341), during which shops, post offices, and sometimes museums will be closed.

For more dramatic countryside and especially for those with a taste for skiing, hiking, or horseback riding, head for the **Massif Central** (central France; about 200 miles/322 km south of Paris) and the nearby volcanic region of the **Auvergne** or the dramatic canyons of the **Gorges du Tarn.** The **Alps** (some 100 miles/160 km east of the Massif Central) offer plenty of opportunities for the *sportif,* from winter skiing to summer hiking through flowery mountain meadows. In the southwest of the country, on the border with Spain, the **Pyrenees** can also be enjoyed at all seasons.

For a classic seaside holiday, go to the northwest. The coast of **Normandy** or **Brittany** (roughly two hours by train from Paris) delight with their fishing ports and deserted rocky coves. Farther down the Atlantic coast are the **Île de Re** and **La Rochelle,** favorite summer destinations for Parisians in the know. Even farther south is **Biarritz,** with its dramatic waves and popular surfing beaches.

For many, **Provence** and the **Côte d'Azur** (the TGV train from Paris to **Nice** takes about 6 hours) remain the supreme pleasure of a visit to France, and it is true that the lavender-scented southern hinterland of olive groves and sleepy villages is very beguiling. Roman sites here include the great amphitheaters of **Nîmes** and **Arles,** and the Pont du Gard, a bridge still standing after 2,000 years.

The Mediterranean coast, loved by Picasso and Matisse, is a treasure trove, with its palm-fringed beaches, azure sea, glitzy nightlife, and fabulous art museums. A string of legendary hotels re-create the glamorous heyday of this land of vacations. To get from Paris to the popular resort of **Cannes,** via **Marseille,** takes about six hours—most of them quite scenic.

## Cultural Etiquette

The French can seem quite formal. They expect to kiss or shake hands on greeting. The numbers of kisses remains a vexed question even to the French themselves, but generally speaking they will kiss twice (once on each cheek) in Paris and the north, and three or even four times in the south. It also depends on the level of familiarity. When you enter a shop, it is normal to wish the other customers and shopkeeper *bonjour*—and *au revoir* when you leave. It is always polite to address older people as *madame* or *monsieur,* even if the French today are much more casual.

While the French can be passionately argumentative among themselves—a good French argument is well worth observing—they are also discreet. It is rare in a French restaurant to be able to hear the conversation at a nearby table. There is, however, one area in which manners fall away: Be sure to stand your ground when you are in line for a taxi or in a busy market waiting to pay.

Just imagine the rich, bracing fragrance of lavender flowers rising from this Provençal field.

Geography aside, a great way to really appreciate France and its culture would be to attend one of the many festivals that take place throughout the year. You can sample Celtic culture in **Brittany,** theater in **Avignon,** photography in **Arles,** dance in **Montpellier,** jazz in **Nice,** and **Menton**'s annual celebration of the lemon (see Travelwise, pp. 383–386).

Indeed, you could simply revel in one or more of the many local food festivals that take place all year round, celebrating wine, oysters, chestnuts, cherries, apples, honey—all the glories that France produces. Or plan your travel based on market days. Wherever you plan to visit, first find out when and where markets are held (see Travelwise pp. 378–382).

There is nothing more authentically and enjoyably French than to wander around the stalls of local vegetables and fruit, regional products, and bric-a-brac, perhaps buying lunch and gifts, but most definitely watching the French in their habitat, going about their daily lives.

### Eurotunnel

The rail system has two main tunnels under the English Channel. Eurostar trains, each up to a quarter mile (0.4 km) long and powered by 16,000-horsepower cars at each end, can go 186 mph (300 kph) and carry more than 6 million passengers a year. Paris to London takes two and a half hours, while the trip from both Brussels and Lille to London takes an hour and 40 minutes. *www.eurostar.com.*

# History & Culture

A date adorns a St. Guilhem-le-Désert
abbey, built in the ninth century.
Opposite page: In northern France,
a procession follows Sunday Mass at
the Reims cathedral.

# France Today

**The boundaries of France are largely natural: the English Channel and the Ardennes hills in the north; the Atlantic Ocean in the west; the Pyrenees in the southwest; the Mediterranean in the south; the Alps in the southeast; and the Jura and Vosges Mountains and the Rhine River in the east. To these striking features add the Massif Central and its huge extinct volcanoes.**

## The Land

France is the largest country in western Europe at 211,150 square miles (547,020 sq km) and the 37th largest in the world; at the same time, it is actually slightly smaller than the state of Texas. Although twice the size of the United Kingdom, it has roughly the same population—62 million. It is a largely rural country: 56 percent of the land is farmed and 25 percent forested. Agriculture, the country's largest industry, has been described as France's *pétrole vert* (green oil). France has by far the largest cultivatable area, and the biggest agricultural output, of any state in the European Union. Big cities are few and far between; Paris is the largest, with a population of 2.1 million, followed by Lyon (1.3 million) and Marseille (1.1 million)—all of them small cities by European standards.

> **For all the splendors of Paris, and of provincial cities such as Lille and Nice, France is predominantly a country of villages.**

## Regional Diversity

The first feature that strikes any visitor traveling through France, aside from its rurality, is its remarkable regional diversity. France is the only European country that spreads into both the north and south of the continent. Significant regional differences in climate, geology, geography, and culture have given rise to the extremely varied and rich agriculture that contributes so strikingly to the diversity of the French landscape—and, of course, produces France's fabled cuisines and wines. Again, these are above all regional: The cuisine of Périgord is as unlike that of Normandy as the wines of Champagne differ from those of Bordeaux.

## Village Life

For all the splendors of Paris, and of provincial cities such as Lille and Nice, France is predominantly a country of villages. There are 33,000 communes (the smallest administrative unit in France), each embracing a number of villages. Again, these vary from region to region—from the gray, granite fishermen's cottages of Brittany shielding against the rolling Atlantic breakers, to the thatched and half-timbered Normandy hamlets nestling among apple orchards dotted with cows, to the flat, Roman-tiled, red roofs of Provençal hill villages clinging in terraces to steep slopes.

At first sight, many of these villages and their rural surroundings may appear to have changed little over the centuries. But changes there most certainly have been. In 1789, the population of France was 27 million, 22 million of whom lived in the countryside. Since the middle of the 19th century, there has been a steady flight from the land and, since 1945, 6 million people have left for the towns and cities, driven away by dramatic changes in farming practice. In 1939, 35 percent of France's active population worked on the land; now the proportion is down to about 5 percent and expected to fall further. Hardest hit of all has been the smallest farmer, the *paysan* or peasant—unknown in America, already extinct in many European countries, and in almost certain terminal

**Paris has become more casual over the years, but romance and style remain hallmarks.**

decline in France. In the brave new world of agribusiness and European Union farm subsidies, the peasant farmer and his tiny, much-divided smallholding is simply being modernized out of existence. Subsidy farming and the remote, absentee landlord-businessperson have become unattractive but increasingly common features of the French countryside. The evidence can be seen in the vast, eerie prairies that now clothe parts of the north and center, unbroken by the outline of a single house, let alone a village. This is less an empty countryside than an emptied one. Traveling through France, and especially through poorer parts such as the Auvergne or the Ariège, it is hard not to be struck by the number of ruined houses left as the visible sign of this exodus.

But, while it is important to understand the forces that have made the French countryside what it is, one should also beware of romanticizing the peasant past—a considerable body of French literature exists to suggest that most of us would actually have loathed to have lived in it! And in recent times French villages have undergone something of a revival, as French people and foreigners have bought rural vacation houses or even set up small businesses, thus bringing new forms of work and encouraging fresh varieties of rural economic activity.

## The People

As with the French landscape, the keynotes here are again diversity and regionality. Although the French are famously patriotic (Chauvin was a Frenchman, after all), a French person referring to *mon pays* may very well mean the area in which he or she lives rather than France as a whole. It can be quite disconcerting to discover just how little acquainted some French people are with parts of the country other than their own. In its most pronounced form, this identification with region over country has led to separatist demands—largely peaceful (albeit illegal)—in Brittany, Corsica, and the Basque region of the Pyrenees. Language is also a symbol of regional independence—Breton in Brittany (see p. 154), and Occitan in Provence and Languedoc (as in "tongue of oc," see p. 315), are both experiencing a revival.

It is impossible to visit France without immediately becoming aware of the importance of style. Looking good really matters.

Nothing illustrates so clearly the enormous diversity of France as the differences among its peoples. The Celtic Bretons are dramatically distinct not only from the Mediterranean people of Provence and Languedoc but also from their Norman neighbors—and so on all around France. A gulf still exists between Parisians and the rest of France. Parisians may think of themselves as urban sophisticates, but there are those outside the capital who regard them as arrogant. Parisians may enjoy having their *maisons secondaires* (second houses) deep in rural France, but for some the word "provincial" is still virtually a term of abuse. Even celebrated writers such as François Mauriac (Bordeaux) and Gustave Flaubert (Normandy) frequently seem to have harbored distinctly ambivalent feelings about their own provincial backgrounds. There can be few more poisonous portrayals of small town bourgeois life than Flaubert's *Madame Bovary* (which makes it all the more surprising that various Normandy villages vie with each other in claiming to be the model for Flaubert's suffocating town of Yonville).

## À la Mode

Paris is still considered the fashion capital of the world, as it has been since the 17th century. Haute couture (a legally protected term in France) developed during the early 20th century with designers such as Elsa Schiaparelli, Paul Poiret, Madeleine Vionnet, and Coco Chanel and returned after the deprivations of World War II with Christian Dior's "new look" and the *prêt-a-porter* (ready-to-wear) line of Yves Saint Laurent.

Increasing competition is challenging the French dominance of the industry, and many foreign designers now head up Paris fashion houses, such as German Karl Lagerfeld at Chanel and American Marc Jacobs at Louis Vuitton.

Avenue Montaigne, the high-fashion street of the 16th arrondissement, has recently seen the opening of Ralph Lauren's flagship store.

Nevertheless, the twice-yearly Paris fashion week in the Carrousel de Louvre are highlights of the fashionista's calendar, and many of the world's top designers have their headquarters in Paris.

In the end, there is still no better place in the world to sit than in a Paris café to observe the natural fashion chic of the French.

Not surprisingly, given its colonial past (in Algeria, Morocco, Indochina, French West Africa, and so on), France also has many communities of different ethnic origins. From the mid-1950s to the mid-1970s, furthermore, labor shortages led to massive recruitment campaigns not only in North Africa but also in poorer European countries such as Greece, Spain, and southern Italy. Many of these foreign workers chose to settle permanently. In spite of that famous French saying, "*Vive la différence!*" France is not free of racism. It has been exploited by the overtly racist Front National political party, with considerable success in some areas. Tourists are unlikely to encounter this side of France, however, unless they visit the run-down housing projects on the fringes of cities.

France remains a deeply civilized country, nevertheless, and the liberal majority are disgusted by this particular blot on their nationhood. Indeed, no one can visit France and fail to notice the role that courtesy, decorum, and good manners play in everyday life (except, unfortunately, behind the wheel of a car). Shaking hands and kissing on the cheeks—two, three, or even four times, depending on the region and how well those kissing know each other—are indispensable and graceful social rituals. Anyone entering a store, café, restaurant, or waiting room will greet the assembled company with a "*Bonjour Messieurs-Dames*," and "*Monsieur*" and "*Madame*" are routinely added to any conversational remark, even if it is only "*merci*" or "*pardon*." Understandably, foreign tourists often do not realize how important these niceties are to the French.

It is impossible to visit France without immediately becoming aware of the importance of style. Looking good really matters. This is the case not only in super-fashionable Paris. Chairs outside French bars and cafés often face outward, not toward each other: You are there to watch the passersby. People don't spend all that money and time on their images simply to be ignored!

Immensely stylish, too, is the presentation of food. One of the many joys of walking down just about any French street is not simply the sheer variety of small shops but also the virtuoso window displays, particularly of food—mouth-watering works of art in their own right. And even in the simplest of restaurants, dishes are frequently presented with a style and flair—and taste—that completely belie the modest prices charged for them.

The French are extremely proud of their rich cultural heritage. Intellectuals and artists are listened to and even revered. A significant number of politicians are writers, too—and not simply of the usual turgid, self-serving memoirs.

In this increasingly global era, the French do tend to feel that their very Frenchness is at risk, be it from American films and hamburgers, or the conditions for European monetary union, and they are quite prepared to take to the streets to defend it. In France, with its revolutionary tradition, direct action is seen not as inimical to democracy, but rather as an integral part of it. This was seen recently in dramatic countrywide protests against new youth employment laws, which were perceived to threaten the basis of French society, and proposed changes to the pension entitlement. There is particular concern that French culture—be it food, fashion, film, or even the very language itself—is under threat from an Anglo-Saxon invasion. On the other hand, no European country has done more than France to celebrate the best of American culture: its jazz in the twenties and thirties, "hard-boiled" crime writing in the forties, Hollywood in the fifties, and so on. And it is France—not, as might be expected, English-speaking Great Britain—which plays host to the European Disneyland.

> Given the importance that the French accord to culture, it is hardly surprising that the country abounds in cultural festivals.

## Festivals

France has a large number of public holidays (for details see p. 341) when everything is closed. Seven of these are religious ones. As France has been a secular state since 1905, the existence of so many religious holidays may seem curious. Only about 14 percent of the French go regularly to Mass, and although this may rise to 80 percent in traditionalist rural areas, it drops to 10 percent in Paris and 4 to 5 percent in certain industrial centers. The flight from the land has contributed significantly to the decline of religious observance. On the other hand, a majority of French people are still nominally Christian, and about half of all children are baptized. Furthermore, the organized church is still a formidable force. A Socialist government discovered this to its cost when in 1984 it tried to integrate Catholic schools into the state system, thus sparking off one of the biggest demonstrations ever seen in postwar Paris.

Aside from the national holidays, there is a myriad of local religious festivities. Perhaps the most striking is the Gypsy Pilgrimage held every year on May 24–25 at Stes.-Maries-de-la-Mer in the Camargue (see p. 309).

Given the importance that the French accord to culture, it is hardly surprising that the country abounds in cultural festivals. Best known is the Cannes film festival, but enlightened local, regional, and national attitudes to what the French call the *septième art* insure funding for a whole host of smaller (and many would say better) film festivals.

Every form of art is catered to in France's festivals: classical music at Aix-en-Provence, Montpellier, Orange, and Prades; jazz at Juan-les-Pins and Marciac; rock at Bordeaux and Rennes; graphic art at Angoulême and St.-Malo; theater at Avignon. And these are but a fraction of the hundreds of festivals that take place each year, especially in summer. ■

**The annual pre-Lent carnival in Nice rocks with fun, food, and fabulous floats.**

# History of France

**The distinctive style associated with France and Frenchness is rooted in an extraordinarily rich history that is full of contrasts. Contemporary France stands as an object lesson in state centralization, its carefully honed administrative procedures an example to the world. Yet it has always been a bastion of resistance to bureaucracy and of regional diversity, localism, and individualism.**

France's past has often seemed inextricably linked with the peasant, rural orientation of its society. Yet at the same time, this apparent rootedness belies the extent to which the country has been built up through a gradual accretion of other peoples. As much as other richly diverse states, such as the United States, France is a melting pot on whose history a dazzling succession of peoples have left their mark:

**Prehistoric artists used the contours of the Lascaux caves to make animals more lifelike.**

Celts and Romans in earliest times, Germans and Scandinavians in the Middle Ages, Africans and Asians in the 20th century, and spasmodically the English, the Spanish and Portuguese, the Jews, and many other groupings have all affected the composition and temperament of French society.

Although France is sometimes seen as a supremely land-based state, its destiny linked intrinsically with that of continental Europe, it is in reality an amphibious power, as much at home at sea as on land. Its naval and commercial strengths have made it a crucial player in the fates of parts of North America, Africa, India, Southeast Asia, and the Pacific.

> **At every stage of its history, France's role in the development of Western civilization ... has been crucial.**

## Prehistory

At every stage of its history, France's role in the development of Western civilization and culture has been crucial. The prehistoric cave art found in the Dordogne area and in the Pyrenees, dating back 20,000 years or so, is among the richest in Europe.

### The Romans

The Romans infused a sense of collective identity into the diverse and belligerent Celtic tribes who had developed a powerful Iron Age culture. The Roman Empire had brought the Mediterranean fringe of France under control in 125–121 B.C., but it was Julius Caesar who conquered the warlike Celts. Though the last resisting chieftain, Vercingétorix, defeated by Caesar at Alésia in Burgundy in 52 B.C., was to become something of a national hero, the establishment of the *pax romana* brought new wealth and prosperity to the region.

### The Franks

With the collapse of the Roman Empire in the fourth and fifth centuries, Roman Gaul gave way to Francia the kingdom of the Franks. The Franks were originally just one among a tribal swarm of Germanic societies outside the Roman Empire whom the Romans dubbed "barbarians." They were well placed to benefit from the slow crumbling of imperial power. In the late fourth and fifth centuries, one Frankish grouping, the Merovingians, took over northern France and extended its power south. Their ruler, Clovis, chose Paris as his capital, and in A.D. 496 became a Christian, thus assisting the spread of Frankish power over the Christian south.

### Charlemagne

In the eighth century, the Frankish prince Charlemagne founded the Carolingian dynasty, building up a European

Louis XII (R. 1489–1515) graces the pages of
*Le Voyage de Gêby* by Jean Marot.

power bloc centered on what would later be France and Germany. In 800, he was crowned emperor (the first since Roman times) by the pope. The centrifugal tendencies within feudalism, together with new incursions by Saracens from northern Italy, by Magyars from central Europe, and by Norsemen (or Vikings) from Scandinavia, cut short the life of the Carolingian Empire. In the Treaty of Verdun of 843, the empire was divided into three units: the Germanic kingdom of the East Franks; the kingdom of the West Franks, which was to become the historic core of France; and an intermediary state, Lotharingia.

In 987, West Francia, or simply Francia as it was increasingly called, passed into the hands of Hugh Capet, founder of the Capetian dynasty. Branches of this family provided the French ruling house to the 19th century. His authority was initially meager—he ruled over a tiny region in the Île-de-France around Paris, a power base dwarfed by the territory and war bands possessed by feudal lords throughout France. One of his vassals, William, Duke of Normandy, became king of England after a successful invasion in 1066. The English kings built an empire stretching from the Scottish border to the Pyrenees. But the Capetians gradually—through a combination of military force, diplomacy, skillful marriage alliances, and outright chicanery—rolled back the power of the English and their other overmighty subjects.

## The Crusades

From the 11th century to the 13th, French kings were in the forefront of the West's Crusades to rescue the Holy Land from the infidel. One monarch, St. Louis (Louis IX), even died on a Crusade. The extension of Capetian power into southwest France into the 13th century came through an internal Crusade authorized by the pope against the so-called Albigensian heresy. Now the authority of kings of France was imposed, almost for the first time, in the Mediterranean as well as in the northern zones.

The increasing political power of the Capetian monarchy was accompanied by considerable economic prosperity. Much newfound wealth was channeled into cathedral building, and the Gothic style that Capetian rulers sponsored was widely copied throughout Europe. The towns also saw the emergence of the first universities. The university in Paris, where Pierre Abélard and Thomas Aquinas taught, soon achieved wide renown and respect.

## The Hundred Years' War

But by the early 14th century, there were already signs that the economy was failing, and the Black Death of 1348 came as a final hammer blow. The disease killed perhaps one-third of France's population, which in many regions took centuries to rise again to pre-plague levels. The epidemic caused unparalleled damage to the economy, though the ensuing labor shortage did lead to the erosion of feudalism, as lords were obliged to lessen the feudal burden on their serfs. At this critical moment, English claims to French lands triggered the Hundred Years' War (1337–1453), with the English forming an alliance with the dukes of Burgundy, who were angling for autonomy from France.

The wars frequently went badly for the French. English feats of arms—most famously at the Battle of Agincourt in 1415—humiliated the French kings. By the early 15th century, the power of the latter was negligible, and the country seemed on the verge of partition. With the charismatic Jeanne d'Arc at the helm, though—notably in 1429–1430—the French king fought back. Despite sacrificing Jeanne d'Arc to the Anglo-Burgundians, Charles VII drove the English back to the Channel. He and his successors also brought Burgundy to heel. Its integration into the French kingdom in 1477 was complemented by that of Provence in 1481 and Brittany in 1491.

> **Despite sacrificing Jeanne d'Arc to the Anglo-Burgundians, Charles VII drove the English back to the Channel.**

## The Renaissance

In 1494, Charles VIII invaded the Italian peninsula, thus inaugurating the Italian wars that would last to 1559. Though they were fought on Italian soil, the main targets of French aggression were the Habsburg rulers who held the title of Holy Roman emperor in Germany and who also ruled Spain. The struggle, eventually a stalemate, marked a period of cultural and economic vitality as well as political recovery in France. Italian Renaissance masters such as Leonardo da Vinci and Benvenuto Cellini worked for the French king, François I, and the spectacular court culture that François developed gave rise to important building projects. The most outstanding of those were in the Loire Valley, resulting in a dazzling spread of both new châteaus such as Chambord, Chenonceau, and Azay-le-Rideau and up-to-date additions to older ones, like Blois.

## The Wars of Religion

The Renaissance was accompanied by religious reformation. France was split between two antagonistic camps, as Protestants and Catholics fought no fewer than eight Wars of Religion between 1562 and 1598. The struggle was marked by terrible bloodshed—most notoriously in the infamous St. Bartholomew's Eve Massacre of 1572. In Paris alone, 2,700 Protestants were slaughtered (more than the Revolutionary Tribunal was to manage in two years of the Terror, between 1792 and 1794), with as many as 20,000 more deaths in other cities throughout France. Only the conversion from Protestantism to Catholicism of Henri IV—first of the Bourbons—accompanied by the military defeat of his ultra-Catholic enemies and his erstwhile Protestant allies, was to bring the religious struggles to a conclusion.

The Edict of Nantes in 1598 established an uneasy truce between the two sides.

By rallying his subjects around the notion of religious tolerance and social welfare after the horrors of civil war—his ideal of every peasant having a "chicken in the pot" was an enduring propaganda image—Henri IV sealed his reputation as Good King Henry. But from the 1620s on, the cardinal ministers, Richelieu and Mazarin, who successively wielded great power, sought to defeat the Austrian Habsburg monarchy in Europe and to establish a centralized absolutist state. This placed severe strains on French society—the tax burden rose threefold between 1630 and 1648—and the discontent of the poor, amplified by the grievances of nobles and religious dissidents, exploded in riots and rebellions.

## The Sun King

Despite these alarms, the groundwork for a strong centralized monarchy had been laid by 1661, when Louis XIV achieved his majority and began his personal rule. The reign of the "Sun King" was to be one of the longest in French history, mingling glory and ingloriousness in equal measure. The elaborate court society that Louis installed and led in his new palace at Versailles became the envy of Europe. It was also the base from which Louis pursued European power and a colonial empire, notably in Canada.

**Behind the Apollo Basin stands the largest and most opulent palace in France: Versailles.**

This was the period in which some of the greatest creative talents in French cultural history—Descartes, Corneille, Racine, Molière—flourished and lent luster to France's *Grand Siècle* (Great Age), when France was Europe's greatest power. From the 1680s on, however, Louis lurched into an increasingly desperate struggle against an alliance of his principal European foes, the English and the Dutch. He added to his problems by revoking the Edict of Nantes in 1685 and launching a repressive campaign against France's Protestants.

> **The Enlightenment fostered a widespread taste for freedom, which the monarchy did little to satisfy.**

## The Enlightenment

If the cultural achievements of 17th-century France centered on Versailles, those of the 18th-century Enlightenment largely flowed through the network of organs and institutions that characterized the bourgeois society now emerging as trade and manufacturing increased. Salons, coffeehouses, academies, novels, periodicals and newspapers, masonic lodges, and political clubs all now proliferated. Thus developed an urbane and humane culture that did not shrink from criticism of hidebound court-based hierarchy. There was an international, pacifist flavor to the French Enlightenment, too—English and Scottish philosophers were honorary members, as were Americans Benjamin Franklin and Thomas Jefferson. In contrast, the dynastic wars of kings seemed both primitive and cruel.

The Enlightenment fostered a widespread taste for freedom, which the monarchy did little to satisfy. The crown became increasingly indebted, even though for most of the century the economy boomed. Foreign policy was directed for the most part against France's commercial rival England; this antagonism was to remain the fulcrum of European relations from the last wars of Louis XIV in 1688 to the overthrow of Napoleon in 1815. For most of the century, France was losing the struggle. The only significant success it managed—when French armed forces helped England's American colonies achieve independence (1775–1783)—bankrupted the state. Financial crisis, combined with a social crisis caused by several poor harvests in the late 1780s, drove the state toward something more drastic than reform: revolution.

## The French Revolution

The French Revolution was to provide the seeds of European liberal democratic traditions. The values of liberty, equality, and fraternity, enshrined in the Declaration of the Rights of Man of 1789, established an ideal both for political action and for the political culture within which most European states have evolved. The decade from 1789 to 1799 saw a kind of fast-forward scramble through five types of government: absolutist monarchy of the Ancien Régime type, constitutional monarchy, authoritarian republicanism (and "the Terror"), liberal republicanism, and finally—with the advent of Napoleon Bonaparte—military dictatorship.

It was probably asking too much of the well-meaning but ineffectual Louis XVI to mutate from an absolute monarch to a liberal ruler working within strict constitutional limits. His queen, the implacably anti-Revolutionary Austrian Marie-Antoinette, did not help, encouraging him to view his principal duty as lying more toward the old nobility than the new political nation.

The king's tireless efforts to sit on the political fence were doomed following the declaration of war against Austria. His failure to give his full support to the national war effort led to his overthrow in August 1792 (he was executed the following January) and to the establishment of a republic that became increasingly authoritarian as the war became more desperate.

By early 1793, France was fighting virtually the whole of Europe. The Enlightenment had put religious tolerance on the agenda, so it was perhaps surprising that religion became a major bone of contention, too, with the church supporting the Ancien Régime and the Revolutionaries tempted into ever more anticlerical policies.

### Off with Their Heads!

The guillotine remains the bloody emblem of the French Revolution, with the horror of heads rolling into baskets and enraptured mobs howling for blood. The executions took place at the Place de la Revolution in Paris, now Place de la Concorde; during the Reign of Terror, up to 40,000 people were executed in this fashion. However, the guillotine was actually devised as a more humane method of execution, a substitute for traditional beheadings, hangings, or burning at the stake. It remained the legal method of execution in France until 1981, when the death penalty was abolished.

## The Terror

The Committee of Public Safety, with Maximilien de Robespierre as its mouthpiece, set out to assure the defense of the Republic against internal and external enemies through policies of internal terror (combined with radical social legislation aimed at eliciting support from peasants and urban workers) and national mobilization. The so-called levée en masse of August 1793 was the closest that any state came to total warfare prior to the 20th century.

However, Robespierre and his faction seemed to want to intensify the Terror even as the war threat receded. In July 1794, his fellow deputies in the National Assembly deposed him in order to move toward a more liberal republic, enshrined in the Constitution of 1795. The period known as the Directory failed to impose internal harmony on warring factions or to bring the external war to a successful conclusion. In November 1799, the regime fell to a coup d'état by the Revolutionary Corsican general, Napoleon

Bonaparte. A new constitution was organized, but within a couple of years Napoleon's de facto dictatorship had become a de jure imperial regime.

## The Napoleonic Empire

To a considerable degree, Napoleon only continued what the Revolutionaries had already started. Through brilliant generalship and astute diplomacy, he built an empire encompassing a good deal of western and central Europe. He also famously redrew the map of Europe in order to provide sufficient new states for the members of his extensive family to rule.

The spread of French power under Napoleon was far from a victory for the Rights of Man. Though he accepted and consolidated some of the gains of the Revolution—notably equality before the law, religious tolerance, economic freedom, and the abolition of feudalism—in many respects he represented an absolutism even more absolute than that of his Bourbon predecessor. The Napoleonic Civil Code was a signal achievement, though it demonstrated that the emperor was concerned even less with the rights of women than with the Rights of Man.

As long as he could insure that the costs of warfare fell on his enemies rather than on the people of France, Napoleon remained popular. After his disastrous Moscow campaign of 1811–12, however, he was always on the run. The main European states combined forces against him and encouraged dissent within territories under French rule. By 1814, he had been deposed, and though he made a brief return from exile, he was defeated definitively by the Duke of Wellington at the Battle of Waterloo (in Belgium) in 1815.

François Gérard painted Napoleon in the robes in which he crowned himself emperor in 1805.

## After Napoleon

The factionalism and acrimony of French politics in the Revolutionary and Napoleonic periods did not go away after 1815. The restoration of the Bourbon dynasty in 1815 failed to satisfy all but dyed-in-the-wool enthusiasts for "Throne and Altar" since they had learned nothing from the preceding 25 years. The revolution of 1830 brought a more liberal regime under a cadet Bourbon branch, the Orléanists. But this, too, failed to find general favor.

A further revolution in 1848 brought a flirtation with more radical policies, but the president of the new Second Republic—Louis Bonaparte—stayed true to his uncle's political sympathies. He seized power in a coup d'état in 1851, and in 1852 installed the Second Empire. This, too, failed to put down strong enough roots to survive defeat by the

Prussians in 1870–71, along with the loss of Alsace and Lorraine, which were incorporated into the new Germany.

## Social & Political Change

A republican regime seemed to be the type of government that divided the country least, though in the early days of the Third Republic many believed that it would preface the restoration of the monarchy. Fearing this, the people of Paris seized power and set up the Commune to rule the city. Its brief rule ended in massive loss of life as the communards fought the government forces street by street for the city. The monarchy was not restored, but French political life remained venomously divided. The emergence of organized working-class parties, some of which proudly laid claim to a revolutionary tradition, brought fresh lines of division.

While politics oscillated wildly, French society was rapidly changing under the impact of industrialization. The process was slower than in neighboring England, but less painful, too. The growth of towns and the development of industry neither spelled the end of peasant farming nor utterly transformed the countryside. By the last years of the century, moreover, industrialization was bearing fruit for a large proportion of the population. Writing on the eve of World War I, the writer Charles Péguy claimed—with a certain amount of accuracy—that the world had been transformed more radically since his own school days in the 1880s than it had been between then and the time of the Romans.

## Paris Renewed

Paris was the beacon of the new, with its Tour Eiffel constructed in 1889 for the international exhibition to commemorate the centenary of the Revolution, towering over the city. The city enjoyed wide new boulevards and was famed for fashion houses, department stores, and glamorous sites of all imaginable pleasures. The elegant belle epoque had its dark and pessimistic side, however. As realist novelists such as Émile Zola showed, working-class conditions were appalling, and yet the Third Republic took little interest in social questions.

> **While politics oscillated wildly [in the late 19th century], French society was rapidly changing under the impact of industrialization.**

## Conflict with Germany

France had lost its colonial empire to England during the Revolutionary and Napoleonic wars. In 1830, it conquered Algeria and began to amass a new one. The bulk of imperial acquisitions were made after the 1870s, amplifying tensions with other European powers, notably Great Britain. Nevertheless, the prime target for French aggression was now Germany, which in economic and military terms seemed to be outstripping France down to the outbreak of World War I in 1914.

France benefited from being on the winning side of that war. Alsace and Lorraine were restored to the Third Republic with the Treaty of Versailles in 1919, but the victory was won at a massive price. France lost more men in the war—1.3 million—than any other nation. Much of the northern part of the country was devastated by the passage of the Allied and German armies, as first one side and then the other gained a few miles of country in the fruitless struggle of trench warfare. Modernization meant not only more consumer goods and more elegant lifestyles but also murderous new forms of mechanized and mass warfare.

French men and women still found it difficult to sleep soundly at night, moreover. The German call for revenge became ever more threatening in the interwar years, as Hitler and the Nazis came to power in Germany in 1933. France had its own Fascist movement, too, against which was pitted a revolutionary Communist movement linked to the Soviet regime established in Russia in 1917.

The Third Republic still had its charms: Foreigners such as writers Gertrude Stein, Ernest Hemingway, F. Scott Fitzgerald, and Ezra Pound; black jazz musicians; and a variegated range of painters and sculptors found Paris in particular a welcoming center of cultural dynamism. But the Third Republic's political compromise would not be sufficient to deal with the new challenge of war in 1939.

Gen. Charles de Gaulle, shown here in French Equatorial Africa in 1941, led the Free French forces during World War II.

## Occupation & Decolonization

In the middle decades of the 20th century, France had to cope with two profound traumas: World War II and the process of decolonization. The French defeat at the hands of Nazi Germany in 1940 brought German occupation, at first in the northern half of the country and then, from 1942 on, throughout all of France. It also involved collaboration with the Nazis. Under Marshal Pétain, a World War I hero, Jews and Communists became the prime targets of the Vichy regime's collaborationist zeal.

Resistance was at first directed from London by the self-exiled Gen. Charles de Gaulle, and from the early 1940s was spearheaded by a wide range of political activists, with Communists to the fore. The Allied landings on the Normandy beaches in 1944 found Resistance movements coming out into the open to mop up the retreating German forces. After the war, France united around the new Fourth Republic (which granted women the vote for the first time). Yet painful memories of collaboration remained, rising spasmodically to haunt the national conscience.

The process of decolonization had a similar effect. From the early 1950s, the liberation movements in North Africa and Indochina elicited a military response from the French. Their defeat at the battle of Dien Bien Phu in Indochina (which Vietnam was then part of) in 1954 by the Communist Viet Minh led to the withdrawal of the French from the Far East. Civil war flared up in Algeria and threatened political stability within France itself. Political crisis triggered by events in Algeria brought General de Gaulle to power as president of the new Fifth Republic. His solution to the crisis—complete independence of Algeria plus repatriation of the colonists—left lasting rancor on both sides of the Mediterranean.

## The "May Events"

Political scars should not blind us to the way in which France came to terms with some of its thorniest problems in the late 20th century. Most notably, it has achieved an almost undreamed-of political stability. During de Gaulle's lifetime, many political thinkers suspected that the structure of the Fifth Republic was such that only a right-wing figure could operate effectively within it. The regime, however, has proved able to accommodate the death of its founder; the election of a Socialist president, François Mitterrand, in 1981; and since then an acceptance of the principle of alternation (*alternance*) between left- and right-wing governments and presidents. The only time the regime appeared to be in danger was during the "May Events" of 1968, when protests almost brought down de Gaulle's government. With its 40th birthday now behind it, however, the Fifth Republic has become the second longest-enduring regime in French history since the 18th century, after the much-underestimated Third Republic.

> **Political scars should not blind us to the way in which France has come to terms with some of its thorniest problems in the late 20th century.**

## European Cooperation

Another specter exorcised from French political life since World War II was that of an aggressive Germany. From the 1860s to the 1940s, French foreign policy was constructed around hostility to Germany. But Germany's defeat in war led farsighted individuals in both countries to work toward cooperation. Starting with the Coal and Steel Union of 1951, France and Germany have been at the forefront of every stage of European cooperation.

This is a situation in which France has generally prospered. The end of World War II in 1945 initiated the Thirty Glorious Years, which saw the French economy modernizing and expanding at a faster rate than ever before. Impressive economic growth and an unparalleled baby boom combined with a shake-up in infrastructure and services, the widespread diffusion of consumer durables and other commodities, the growth of mass leisure, and a new affluence that put a question mark against hallowed customs and conventions.

France is one of the world's richest countries, though unemployment and taxes are high, and its general health and pension benefits are under threat. Despite international tensions, France remains a popular tourist destination, with more than 80 million visitors annually. Paris, beneficiary of a policy of cultural grandeur (as exemplified by the Centre Pompidou, the Opéra National de Paris-Bastille, the Musée d'Orsay, and the Musée du Quai Branly), is still outstanding among cities. Equally striking has been the dynamism of provincial cities such as Lyon, Montpellier, Lille, Toulouse, Rennes, and Nantes. A growing concern for regionalism, multiculturalism, and gender issues is leading to a broadening of political and cultural options and greater respect for the country's heritage.

In 2007 Nicolas Sarkozy was elected president. His administration has weathered worldwide recession and growing protests about threatened state benefits and educational reform, with civil unrest in many areas. Nevertheless, despite rising racial tensions France remains one of the most tolerant countries in the world. ∎

**In an annual tradition, May Day demonstrators in Paris speak out on critical social issues.**

# Food & Drink—French Ways

**Gastronomy—the art and science of good eating and drinking—is not simply a pastime: The population spends more of its income on the pleasures of the table than on anything else. In 2010, UNESCO added French cuisine to its list of intangible cultural treasures.**

France's gastronomic and regional diversity is probably greater than that of any other country. An exasperated Charles de Gaulle once famously remarked, "How can anyone be expected to govern a country that produces 265 different cheeses?" (The official tally is now closer to 400.) And a gastronomic pilgrim traveling the south-west coast from La Rochelle to the Spanish border (a distance of some 300 miles, or

**Parisians and visitors flock to the Latin Quarter's Rue Mouffetard outdoor market.**

480 km) could encounter more than 500 different seafood dishes.

The French pleasure in food is perhaps most apparent at the ubiquitous street markets. For the visitor, a tour of a French market is an education in the nature of Gallic society. Established food shops are also busiest on market days. French butchers and fishmongers are masters of their craft who can be counted on to dispense verbal recipes and banter with each purchase, while sellers of cheese, fruits, and vegetables will ask if your purchase is meant for that evening or for the next day, and then select accordingly.

Although daily marketing at local shops and markets is still the general rule in France, giant supermarkets filled with prepackaged bread, vegetables, diet cuisine, and frozen foods are hugely popular, and there is concern that individual shops will eventually find it hard to compete. *Boulangeries* (bakeries) are a case in

**INSIDER TIP:**

**A major Burgundy event since the 19th century, the annual November Beaune wine auction is a gala three-day affair. The auction itself is traditionally candlelit.**

—ROSEMARY BAILEY
*National Geographic author*

point. The traditional French baguette goes stale in a matter of hours. As bakers become increasingly reluctant to bake twice a day (early morning and again in the afternoon), so the French have changed their habits, buying their bread once a day instead of, as was customary, twice. And so the baguette seems to get flabbier as preservatives are added. The faster-paced lifestyle of modern France is fueled by microwaveable meals and chains of fast-food restaurants (McDonalds is known as Macdo).

Curnonsky, the famous French gastronome and author of the 32-volume *La France gastronomique,* described four distinct types of French cookery: "la Haute Cuisine, la Cuisine Bourgeoise, la Cuisine Régionale, et la Cuisine Improvisée." Half a century later, these categories still stand.

*Haute cuisine* is professional cooking by chefs of the highest achievement. In current terms, it describes accurately the cooking of multi-Michelin-starred chefs such as Guy Savoy and Alain Ducasse. *Nouvelle cuisine* is (or was)

In the Alsatian town of Colmar, *saucissons* form a tempting still life in a shop window.

a modern interpretation of haute cuisine. Top chefs reconstructed classic French dishes in response to the demand for lighter dishes containing less butter and cream and fewer heavily reduced sauces. In its original form, the style was short lived, but nouvelle cuisine has left its mark on French haute cuisine; classic dishes are prepared in a much lighter vein than 20 years ago. By contrast, *cuisine improvisée* is peasant in origin. This cuisine comprises farmhouse dishes of hams, sausages, stews, and omelettes.

But it is the two remaining categories that have most shaped the culinary map of France. *Cuisine bourgeoise* is the simple and unbeatable ordinary middle-class French cookery. *Cuisine régionale* consists of the great regional specialties of France in classic dishes such as bouillabaisse from Provence, coq au vin from Burgundy, and *cassoulet* from Toulouse.

Restaurants vary greatly. At their simplest, they are small, family-run affairs offering home-style cooking, with local cheeses and desserts probably brought in from the local patisserie.

Wine is offered by the carafe, with a small selection available by the bottle.

Then come *brasseries,* lively restaurants serving a limited menu at any time of day and often fairly late at night. Beer remains a feature (*brasserie* means brewery), with some brasseries offering an extensive selection. Typical dishes include *steak pommes frites* (frequently described as the national dish of France); *estouffade de boeuf;* and *blanquette de veau,* as well as cold meats and cheeses.

Most distinguished are top-flight restaurants offering classic haute cuisine in a refined setting. Prices are higher, but often there will be a fixed-price menu representing surprisingly good value, especially at lunchtime. Some specialize in creative, modern cooking, others in seafood or regional classics, and all will offer an extensive wine list, possibly with a sommelier to give advice on what to order.

And then there are cafés, those picture windows for observing everyday life, as French as the baguette. No village is complete without one. To adopt the café lifestyle, just learn how to nurse a beer or coffee for hours.

Regional differences are marked, and defended vigorously and with pride. In the cool north, where dairy produce is paramount, butter, cream, and cheese form the basis of a rich cuisine. Traveling south, the emphasis shifts, with chestnuts, walnuts, and truffles dominating dishes that rely on duck and goose fat. The market gardens of the Mediterranean provide the olive oil, garlic, tomatoes, and peppers for dishes reflecting the influence of Spain to the southwest and of Italy to the east.

## Wine

Climatic differences also distinguish French wine. Thousands of properties all over the country make wines of all complexions, though, in general, northern vineyards produce the stunning white wines, and those farther south make the great reds. In the United States, the names of a handful of grape varieties such as Chardonnay and Merlot are used as the ready reference for wine. But in France, more complex traditions prevail: Wine is usually known by its place of origin, rather than by the grape.

## Cider & Beer

Not all French people drink wine with their meals. In Normandy and Brittany, farmers brew a range of ciders. Beer, too, is popular throughout northern France and neighboring Belgium.

---

## EXPERIENCE: How to Eat in France

A favorite French pastime is strolling around a town or seaside resort, checking the menus of lots of restaurant before deciding—after a great deal of excited discussion—where to eat. Most restaurants display a list of variously priced menus outside. They are obliged to offer at least one set menu, and this is usually the cheapest option, particularly at lunch, when many French people have their main meal of the day. The menu will normally consist of a starter (hors d'oeuvres), main course (entrée), and dessert. Sometimes there is a lower price for just two of the courses. Usually a restaurant will offer one or two specials (the *plat du jour*—dish of the day), which may be based on what the chef has found in the market that morning. Wine or coffee may also be included in the price, and bread (usually sliced baguette) is brought to the table at no extra charge.

You can ask for bottled water, but if you are happy to drink local water, simply ask for *l'eau de robinet* (tap water) or *une carafe d'eau*. The service charge is nearly always included (it will say *service compris* on your bill), but you can always leave a bit extra if you are pleased with the food and/or the service.

If you do not want a complete menu, you can order à la carte and simply choose what you want. If you can communicate in French, always ask the waiter or waitress for advice; servers are usually happy to tell you what looks good in the kitchen. (But address them as monsieur, madame, or mademoiselle, not *garçon*). You can order wine by the bottle, but it is often offered in carafes and by the quarter or half liter. In a wine-producing area, this will be a good—and the best priced—option. If you order coffee—*café*—you will get simple black espresso. If you want coffee with milk, ask for café au lait, *café crème*, or a *noisette*, which is espresso with a bit of milk added. You may be offered herbal teas or tisanes, which can be delicious especially if made fresh. Classics include chamomile, vervain, mint, and lime flower (tilleul), the tea in which Proust dipped his famous madeleines.

# The Arts

Hardly surprisingly, given all the riches, the French are extremely proud of their cultural heritage. Education is highly valued, and discussion of artistic and intellectual matters is taken for granted as part of everyday life.

### Roman Era (56 B.C.–A.D. 476)

It was with the Romans that the first signs of "modern" civilization appeared in France. Their architecture symbolized the power of their empire, and it can still be seen to striking effect in the amphitheaters at Arles and Nîmes, the temples at Nîmes and Vienne, and the aqueduct of the Pont du Gard.

In Paris, visitors climb the floating staircase in I. M. Pei's glass pyramid at the Louvre.

## Romanesque Period (11th–12th Centuries)

After the fall of the Roman Empire, France plunged into the Dark Ages until the coming of the Carolingian dynasty in the eighth century. This period has left few visible remains: For these one looks to the flowering of Romanesque ecclesiastical architecture in the 11th century. Here timber roofs give way to stone vaulting, buttresses take the increased weight, and the use of decoration grows.

The Romanesque style spread throughout France and developed regional features—especially in Burgundy, where you can appreciate an excellent example of the Romanesque at Vézelay (see p. 200).

> **In 13th-century France, courtly romances were preoccupied with the Arthurian legend.**

Fortresses were the other major buildings to survive from the Romanesque era, but most have been either reduced to ruins, modified, or rebuilt. Angers (see p. 184) retains

its massive curtain wall, and Langeais still has a medieval exterior (see p. 188).

The main themes of this period's literature, which was mostly in verse, are faith and chivalry. Particularly important are the *chansons de geste* or heroic songs. A favorite theme was Charlemagne's wars against the infidel, as in the *Chanson de Roland* (circa 1098), which recounts the death of the Carolingian hero while defending the pass at Roncesvalles against the Saracens.

The first courtly romances appeared in the 12th century—narrative poems concerned with idealized and chivalrous conceptions of love. The classical influence was strong, and the most famous romance writer, Chrétien de Troyes (died circa 1183), saw himself and his contemporaries as inheritors of the literary traditions of the Greeks and Romans. In 13th-century France, courtly romances were preoccupied with the Arthurian legend; the genre also produced the most influential work of the Middle Ages, the *Roman de la Rose*, a dream-allegory of courtly love. The same theme dominated the lyric poetry of the Provençal troubadours, who made a significant contribution to the development of French music.

## Gothic Period (12th–15th Centuries)

Gothic architecture had strong upward aspirations (see pp. 116–117). Gothic churches and cathedrals have high, pointed arches, flying buttresses, and large traceried windows filled with stained glass, which reach their apogee in the rose window, as at Chartres cathedral (see pp. 100–101). Interiors became more highly decorated and elaborate, with rood and choir screens, altarpieces, and statuary.

**It was Louis XV who had the Panthéon built in Paris in the late 18th century.**

Book decoration and illustration, known as illumination and best represented by the books of hours, containing prayers to be said at the canonical hours, reached its zenith in the 14th century. At the same time, easel painting arrived. In its attention to detail and concern with representing space convincingly, French art of this period shows the influence of the more developed Italian and Flemish schools. The major figure is Jean Fouquet (circa 1420–circa 1481), painter to Louis XI.

Medieval France's main contribution to music was through the monasteries, which preserved the tradition of the plainchant and elaborated it into polyphony. The Burgundian court also had a key musical role, employing a huge number of musicians, and composers such as Guillaume Dufay (circa 1400–1474) flourished under its patronage.

The 15th century saw France's most outstanding medieval lyric poet, François Villon, who used conventional verse forms but invested them with the spirit of the *fabliaux* (bawdy popular tales) to draw a vivid picture of low life in 15th-century Paris.

The most interesting prose writers of the time are the chroniclers, of whom the best known is Jean Froissart, the chief historian of the Hundred Years' War; in particular he compiled a remarkable eyewitness account of the Battle of Crécy (1346).

## The Renaissance (16th–17th Centuries)
French campaigns in northern Italy at the end of the 15th century brought the aesthetics of the Italian Renaissance to the attention of French artists and architects and their patrons. This can be seen most clearly in the building of châteaus by the royal family and nobility that marked the final stages of the castle's progression from fortification to elaborate residence. Living quarters were extended, windows became larger, and moats, keeps, and turrets became purely decorative as opposed to defensive features. The castle descended from hilltop to riverside, where its watery reflection further enhanced its splendor. The château was supposed to harmonize with its natural surroundings, but formal grounds were integrated into

the grand design more and more. The Renaissance influence made for increasingly regular and symmetrical architectural designs. Nonetheless, châteaus exhibit a number of different styles. Thus Cheverny, built in 1634, is classical in its purity of line, while Blois (see p. 169), built between the 13th and 17th centuries, reflects the development of secular French architecture from feudalism to classicism. Chambord (see pp. 170–171), the largest of the Loire châteaus, is a superb example of Italian Renaissance style.

The spirit of the Renaissance began to permeate literature in the 16th century, as scholars rediscovered the classical Greek and Latin writers. Under their renewed influence, a broader outlook began to challenge the rigid theological thinking of the late medieval period. The first printing press was established in Paris in 1470, and by 1515 some 100 operated in France. This had a huge impact on the development of vernacular literature. The work of François Rabelais is the supreme expression of this newfound freedom, vitality, and enthusiasm. His *Gargantua* and *Pantagruel* were parodies of chivalric romances, but also addressed serious philosophical issues.

Equally a Renaissance man, but far more methodical and rationalist, was Michel de Montaigne, whose three books of *essais* (literally "tryings out") gave the form its name. Montaigne's remark that "each man bears the complete stamp of the human condition" perfectly sums up the humanist spirit of Renaissance thought.

The key poet of the 16th century, and the leader of a group of writers known as the Pléiade, was Pierre de Ronsard (1524–1584). The Pléiade broke with medieval poetic forms and looked to Greece and Rome for models. The 12-syllable line—the Alexandrine—began its long dominance of French poetry.

### Classicism (17th Century)

Classicism started during the reign of Louis XIII and reached its apogee with his successor, Louis XIV. The absolutism of the age is expressed in its architecture by grandiosity, stress on order and symmetry, and evocation of the glory of Greece and Rome. The zenith of the early Louis XIV style is undoubtedly the château of Vaux-le-Vicomte, built in 1656–1661 for Nicolas Fouquet, finance minister in Mazarin's time. Louis XIV was so envious that he hired the same design team (led by Louis le Vau) to build a château a hundred times bigger—Versailles.

> **The spirit of the Renaissance began to permeate literature in the 16th century, as scholars rediscovered the classical Greek and Latin writers.**

In 1648, the Royal Academy of Painting and Sculpture, a key instrument for imposing "official" standards and principles of taste, was founded. It enshrined the classical idea that the practice and appreciation of art are rational activities that can be reduced to rules and precepts, and thus be taught and learned.

**Italian Influence:** In painting, Italy was the influential center of Europe. Especially important was Caravaggio for his rich colors, deep shadows, and dramatic compositions, and his introduction of a realism into conventional religious subjects as in his "Death of the Virgin" (in the Louvre). His influence is visible in the work of leading French 17th-century painters like Moïse Valentin, Georges de La Tour, and

Simon Vouet. The two 17th-century French painters who best express the classical spirit are Claude Lorraine and Nicolas Poussin. Lorraine's landscapes are Arcadian, evoking the pastoral serenity of a golden age bathed in a glorious light. Poussin dealt with noble themes from classical mythology treated in a pastoral mood, but developed a more austere classicism in works that exude monumental simplicity, lucidity, and calm.

Elaborate ballets were the main form of musical entertainment at court, and a young Florentine, Jean-Baptiste Lully, became one of the principal dancers and compos-ers. More popular than Italian opera were *tragédies lyriques* (a form of sung play with balletic elements). Lully composed a large number of these; he also greatly influenced church music and wrote solemn motets for the royal chapel, with soloists, chorus, and orchestra. This form was also developed by Gustave Charpentier, François Couperin, and Michel-Richard Delalande with strict counterpoint enriched by sonorous harmonies.

**Literature:** French classical literature was built on the foundations laid by Montaigne. He saw literature as a part of the enlightened study of human nature, a search for its universal features, inseparable from what we would now think of as philosophy. Furthermore, Descartes's conception of man as essentially rational, endowed by the Creator with reason to be used in the pursuit of truth, had a massive impact on all forms of intellectual life. Their literary followers were preoc-cupied with the purity of language and style, and the dramatic unities of time and place. They divided litera-ture into discrete genres such as comedy and tragedy and founded the Académie Française in 1634 to safe-guard French language and literature. The century also saw the growth of salons, hosted by noblewomen such as the Marquise de Rambouillet, in which literary matters were discussed.

> **The two 17th-century French painters who best express the classical spirit are Claude Lorraine and Nicolas Poussin.**

Some of the most interesting writers of the age dealt in nonfiction. For example, La Rochefoucauld's *maximes*—such as "Hypocrisy is the homage which vice pays to virtue" and "We are all strong enough to bear other people's misfor-tunes"—give off a certain sense of cynicism and moral pessimism. Madame de Sévigné's *Lettres* paints a lively picture of daily happenings. Finally, the *Lettres Provinciales* and *Pensées* by Blaise Pascal provide a welcome antidote to the narrow, overly neat, and self-confi-dent rationalism of much 17th-century thought. His famous saying, "The heart has its reasons of which Reason knows nothing," marks him as a precursor of Romanticism.

**Drama:** The chief poetry of the 17th century is in its drama (although one should not forget the sly and sometimes cynical *Fables* of Jean de La Fontaine, which bor-rows heavily from Greek fabulist Aesop's originals). The plays of Pierre Corneille and Jean Racine ensured that tragedy was the supreme genre. Corneille's tragedies such as *Le Cid* and *Polyeucte* are highly formal, concentrated dramas about passion versus moral duty, peopled by superhuman figures who are less three-dimensional, psychological characters than symbols of nobility and heroism. Racine took the theme of duty versus desire to even greater heights in *Andromaque*, *Phèdre*, and other classically inspired plays, but he was the greater poet; his characters are not just ciphers but passion-filled human beings, the language has an incantatory power, and the dramatic action has a remorseless intensity.

**Comedy:** Comedy flourished at the same time, thanks to Jean-Baptiste Molière. The first French playwright to use the genre for social commentary, he is, along with William Shakespeare and Ben Jonson, a key figure in the development of European comedy.

Molière's plays mingle farce, ballet, and the comedy of manners, and they have a satirical edge that sometimes caused trouble with the authorities. His attack on intellectual pretension, *Les Précieuses ridicules*, offended the habitués of the salons and earned him enemies there. *Tartuffe* attacked religious hypocrisy, but was taken as an attack on religion and banned for five years. But his masterpiece, *Le Misanthrope*, shows that Molière was not simply a deft satirist but also a master of the comedy of character who knew that the line between comedy and tragedy was indeed a fine one.

## French Rococo (18th Century)

Molière posed for "La Mort de Pompée," painted by Pierre Mignard (1612–1695).

Inevitably there was a reaction against the austere grandeur of the Louis XIV style. In architectural terms, interiors became smaller, more intimate, and highly decorated, with elaborate furniture to match. There was an abundance of curved lines, exotic woods, lacquered paneling, and gilt.

The paintings of Antoine Watteau, François Boucher, and Jean Honoré Fragonard best express the rococo spirit. Watteau may have been influenced by Rubens, but he is quintessentially 18th-century French. Painting in colors that are rich, yet also soft and light, he depicts an exquisitely delicate and artificial world of *fêtes galantes* in dreamy, pastoral settings. After this, Boucher, Madame de Pompadour's favorite artist—several of his most famous paintings are of Louis XV's mistress—and the epitome of the elegant superficiality of the mid-18th-century French court, seems rather frivolous. His pupil, Fragonard, painted lightly erotic works such as "The Progress of Love"—full of rococo verve, sparkle, color, and wit—for Madame du Barry, a later mistress of Louis XV.

## Neoclassicism & the Enlightenment (18th Century)

After the frivolity of the rococo, there was a return to the classical. In painting, the Académie Française insisted on seriousness, reviving heroic themes from antiquity. The most notable exponent of the new manner was Jacques-Louis David, whose subjects displayed self-sacrifice and moral duty in a suitably severe style. He had strong Revolutionary sympathies, later becoming Napoleon's official painter and, indeed, the principal artist of the Revolution. One of his best known works, "The Death of Marat" (1793), depicts the Revolutionary hero assassinated in his bath.

In philosophy and literature, the spirit of free, rational inquiry was predominant, and there was a widespread belief in progress through enlightenment. This was the century of the *philosophe*, the progressive-minded individual involved in cultural and artistic activity as well as social and scientific thinking. In literary terms, the treatise and the essay were equally as important as the novel, play, or poem—marking the beginnings of a literature of thought.

**Philosophical Thought:** Montesquieu epitomized the Enlightenment spirit. In his *Considérations sur les Causes de la Grandeur des Romains et de Leur Décadence* he laid down a rational, theoretical approach to the study of history, arguing that "it is not chance that dominates the world, but general causes, either moral or physical." Similarly *L'Esprit des Lois* attempts to explain why the laws of different countries vary; characteristically it enthrones reason as "the most noble, the most perfect, the most exquisite of our senses."

**Rousseau:** The 18th century also saw a reaction against rationalism and a foreshadowing of Romanticism. Nobody illustrates this better than the philosopher Jean-Jacques Rousseau, who proclaims the natural over the civilized, emotion over reason, the individual over society. Largely self-taught, Rousseau exerted an enormous influence on every field he entered. His *Discours sur les Sciences et les Arts* elaborated the theory of natural goodness, the *Discours sur l'Inégalité* the virtue of primitive society. The novel *La Nouvelle Héloïse* is the key work of the "sentimental revolution," which dethroned reason and reestablished the claims of the heart. It was the century's publishing sensation, going through 70 editions in its first 40 years. *Émile*, part novel, part treatise, and wholly a defense of nature as the greatest educator, was a key text of progressive education, as *Le Contrat Social* was of democracy. Finally, Rousseau's devastatingly intimate *Confessions* virtually defined the modern autobiography.

**Empire dresses illustrated in the *Journal des Dames et des Modes* likely inspired many a dressmaker.**

The sentimental revolution is also expressed in novels concerned with libertinage. Typical is *Manon Lescaut* by the Abbé Prévost. The novel's ostensible purpose is to show "the disastrous effects of the passions," but it is so ambiguous and bizarre that it is almost a celebration of *l'amour fou*. Similarly, Pierre Choderlos de Laclos's much-adapted *Les Liaisons Dangereuses* poses as a moral lessons but what emerges is the seductive fascination of evil. In the novels of the Marquis de Sade, the idea of presenting libertinage so as to deliver a moral message is taken to such pornographic extremes that it has the opposite result.

## Romanticism (19th Century)

French Romanticism was at its height from 1820 to 1850, but cultural movements are never neat. A reaction against the rationalism of the Enlightenment and its attendant classicism, French Romanticism proposed the primacy of unfettered, individual imagination. Romantics rejected external reality to seek solace and inspiration within themselves or in exotic or imaginary locales. Particularly via the writer Madame de Staël, who spent much time in Germany, interest grew in German writers such as Goethe, Schiller, and Novalis. Meanwhile, English influence ceased to be philosophical and rationalist and became lyrical and picturesque, thanks to such writers and artists as Byron, Scott, Constable, Turner, and the hitherto neglected Shakespeare.

**Painting:** Théodore Géricault was the archetypal Romantic, even dying young (at 33). His "Raft of the Medusa" is typical in its macabre subject (dying castaways on a raft), Romantic brio, movement, and energetic handling of paint. Even more important, however, was Eugène Delacroix. Influenced by Rubens and the English painters Bonington, Gainsborough, and Constable, he specialized in emotionally charged and often exotic subjects; his technical virtuosity, freedom of brushwork, and richness of color were extraordinarily influential, way beyond the confines of Romanticism.

**Music & Opera:** The rigid institutionalization of music in France made it difficult for outsiders to break in, and the Romantics were outsiders by temperament. But German composer Christoff Gluck had helped to pave the way for Romanticism when he worked on his operas in Paris in the 1770s, and in the next century the French, no longer musically insular, welcomed the arch-Romantics Franz Liszt and Frédéric Chopin.

France produced a key Romantic composer, indeed Romanticism personified, in the

### In the Words of Voltaire and His Contemporaries

Voltaire (1694–1778) wrote *Lettres Philosophiques* based on two years' exile in England. These writings show an admiration (shared by Montesquieu) for tolerance and liberalism, as epitomized by English political and religious institutions. Voltaire's *Essai sur les moeurs*, a survey of world history, shows peoples' slow progress from superstition to rationality.

Voltaire is best known for his satirical philosophical tales. The most famous, *Candide*, hilariously satirizes the then influential philosopher Leibniz and his idea that what God had created was indeed the best of all possible worlds.

Voltaire made social thinking popular—even fashionable. The key product of the Enlightenment is the 17-volume *Encyclopédie*, edited by Denis Diderot and his assistant Jean d'Alembert. It laid out the latest positions in science and philosophy and aimed to "change the general manner of thinking."

In the theater, the *drame bourgeois*, with contemporary characters, began to replace the outmoded classical forms. This was first attempted by Beaumarchais, whose fame rests on the plays *Le Barbier de Séville* and *Le Mariage de Figaro*, the latter being the box office hit of the 18th century. These topical comedies, tinged with risqué democratic sentiment, restored a vitality to the genre that had been missing since Molière.

**Kitsch with a French accent: Montmartre's Moulin Rouge is pure Paris entertainment.**

shape of Hector Berlioz. A composer with the grandest of ideas and a formidable sense of drama, his *Symphonie Fantastique*, with its evocations of a violent storm, a march to the scaffold, and a climactic witches' sabbath, broke all the bounds of what a symphony was "supposed" to be. Berlioz's *Mass* and *Te Deum* are works on a truly gargantuan scale, and had he completed *Les Troyens,* it would have been the equivalent of Richard Wagner's *Ring* cycle. His *Memoirs* is one of the great heroic expressions of the Romantic era, but it would be a mistake to regard its author simply as the archetypal Romantic rebel and outsider, disdaining all formal procedures. Berlioz also wrote one of the definitive treatises on orchestration and introduced the finest Romantic music to France. He was not only a key Romantic but also a pioneer of modern music.

Romanticism had a longer life in music than elsewhere. Charles Gounod's *Faust* was for many years the best loved French opera. Jules Massenet, the most popular opera composer of the second half of the century, specialized in grand but rather prettified and sentimental Romantic spectacles such as *Manon*. In orchestral music, the influence of Liszt was clearly felt in the symphonic poems of Camille Saint-Saëns and César Franck.

For example, Saint-Saëns in *Danse Macabre* portrays Death playing his violin in a churchyard at midnight whilst skeletons dance around, while Franck's *Le Chasseur Maudit* paints a noisy picture of a huntsman doomed to be chased forever by the hounds of Hell as punishment for hunting on the Sabbath. After 1880, the German Romantic influence was further intensified by the seemingly irresistible lure of Wagner, which tends sometimes to make itself felt in a rather un-French grandiosity. However, French classical restraint, albeit tinged with Romantic feeling, reasserted itself in the work of Gabriel Fauré and Henri Duparc who, among other things, transformed the drawing room *mélodie* into an art song that can stand comparison with the great German lieder.

**Literature of Romanticism:** Some of the finest expressions of French Romanticism can be found in the poetry of Lamartine, de Vigny, Hugo, and de Musset. Here, poetry is the expression of primarily personal feelings and emotions. Intensely lyrical and introspective, it allows the imagination full play, and uses the outside world, especially nature, as a reflection of inner feelings. This kind of Romantic poetry helped to establish the image of the poet as the tortured artist.

In the theater, Romanticism is best exemplified by the historical verse dramas of Victor Hugo. In prose, Alexandre Dumas *père* leads the way. Hugo rejected the classical unities of time and place, attacked the artificial separation of the tragic and the comic, and demanded more natural language and local color. His picturesque historical dramas *Hernani* and *Ruy Blas* feature noble characters battling against all odds.

The confessional tales of Chateaubriand, *Atala* and *René*, clearly prefigure the doomed Romantic hero, and Benjamin Constant's *Adolphe* is a bleakly Romantic story of *le mal du siècle*. But it is in the historical novel that the Romantic impulse is clearest: Alfred de Vigny's *Cinq Mars*, Hugo's *Notre-Dame de Paris*, and the colorfully exotic works of Prosper Mérimée, whose *Carmen* was the source of Georges Bizet's opera. However, it was Dumas *père* who developed the Romantic past into something really popular in his Musketeers trilogy and *The Count of Monte Cristo*.

Nineteenth-century French culture can be seen as a dialogue between Romanticism and realism, and the novels of Stendhal (Marie-Henri Beyle) and Honoré de Balzac straddle both. Stendhal was a Romantic in his fascination with Italy, his championship of Shakespeare, his interest in the theme of love, and his novels' proud, young, egotistical heroes. The ambitious Julien Sorel in *Le Rouge et le Noir* enters the priesthood in order to climb the social ladder, and Fabrice

> **In the theater, Romanticism is best exemplified by the historical verse dramas of Victor Hugo.**

in *La Chartreuse de Parme* becomes embroiled in the intrigues of the court at Parma. But society is portrayed with a profundity, irony, and sharpness that is more realist than Romantic. Meanwhile, Balzac's vast *Comédie Humaine*, which includes 80-odd novels and stories and covers French life from the Revolution until 1840, has an extraordinary, even obsessive, realism of detail. At the same time, the novels often seem to be infused by a shadowy, Romantic aura.

## Realism (19th Century)

In art, an interest in unadorned nature and ordinary people began to appear in the middle of the century. There is still something of the Arcadian in Camille Corot's misty, soft-edged paintings, but he did attempt to represent nature without idealization or romanticization. Théodore Rousseau, Charles Daubigny, Jean-François Millet, and others painted direct from nature and formed the Barbizon school, named after the village in the Fontainebleau forest in which they painted. Millet's scenes from rural life emphasize its tough side, and he invested ordinary people with weight and dignity. His "Angélus" was the most frequently reproduced painting of the century, but because of the religious nature of its subject matter, it also earned him an unjust reputation for pious sentimentality.

The chief realist painter is undoubtedly Gustave Courbet. A Socialist who was imprisoned for his part in the 1871 Commune, he concentrated on the tangible reality of things and people. Conventional opinion regarded his pictures as crude and ugly, but his influence was tremendous, not least on the cubists.

**Monet immortalized his gardens in Giverny in paintings now known the world over.**

The Impressionists also belong under the realist banner. They were not a unified school, but a loose association of artists with a certain community of outlook. They came together between 1860 and 1886 for the purposes of exhibiting in a largely hostile environment. Monet, Renoir, Sisley, Pissarro, Degas, Manet, and others, though often interested in different subject matter, shared the rejection of the Romantic ideal. In particular, they wanted to capture immediate, fleeting impressions of color and light rather than the permanent aspects of a subject. Thus, for example, Monet's series of paintings of poplars, haystacks, and the west front of the cathedral at Rouen, in which he tried to capture the impression of the same subject under different climatic conditions and times of day.

**The year 1889 saw the opening of the Tour Eiffel, which demonstrated grandly the architectural potential of steel.**

**Realist Literature:** Gustave Flaubert's *Madame Bovary*, published in 1857, marks the arrival of the realist novel, although formally it also prefigures modernism. However, his notion that the author should be like God, omnipresent but invisible, is certainly realist. Flaubert's hostility to Romanticism is underlined in the novel by Madame Bovary immersing herself in escapist Romantic fantasies as compensation for the ghastliness of provincial Normandy life. The Normandy countryside is also the setting for many of the best stories of Guy de Maupassant, the acknowledged master of the realist short story.

In Émile Zola, realism developed into naturalism. He believed that the novel should be an illustration of the laws of scientific determinism that govern human nature through heredity and the environment. He put this theory into practice in his huge *Rougon-Macquart* series of 20 novels—a vivid and imaginative panorama of the whole Second Empire.

In musical terms, Bizet's *Carmen*, based on a novel by Mérimée and, almost unbelievably, a flop at its first performance in 1875, is an interesting mix of realism and Romanticism. The Spanish setting may have exotic connotations, but its treatment of passionate (as opposed to simply romantic) feelings is realistic, as is the inclusion of speech between the music.

## Modern Times

In the first half of the 20th century, France became a hotbed of artistic modernism, and its culture was further enriched by the novelists, poets, artists, and composers who flocked there from across the world. These included Aaron Copland, Ernest Hemingway, Henry Miller, Ezra Pound, and Gertrude Stein. However, modernism's roots lie firmly in 19th-century France.

**Architecture:** During the Second Empire, Baron Haussmann laid the basis of modern Paris. He replaced the ancient narrow streets with wide boulevards, a move that went well beyond quality of life and aesthetics. Paris had seen three uprisings in 50 years; in any future trouble, the boulevards would facilitate rapid troop movements and provide clear fields for artillery fire. The year 1889 saw the opening of the Tour Eiffel, which demonstrated grandly the architectural potential of steel. It helped to usher in the modern era.

In classic Renaissance style, the Hôtel de Ville—City Hall—in Paris is awash in statuary.

Today we tend to blame modern architects for creating inhuman, alienating environments. But one of the founding figures of architectural modernism, the Swiss Le Corbusier, was almost utopian in his vision of the social benefits of a rationally planned urban environment, with iskyscrapers, gridlike street systems, open spaces, and rings of satellite towns. That vision is exemplified by the Cité Radieuse in Marseille (see p. 299). Also worth visiting are La Roche Villa (now the Le Corbusier Foundation, *10 square du Docteur-Blanche*) in Paris and the extraordinary Chapelle de Notre-Dame-du-Haut in Ronchamp in the Jura (see p. 210), one of the few great modernist religious buildings.

Even in these supposedly postmodernist times, France has never shied from promoting unapologetically modern architecture; nor has it been afraid to use considerable public funds in doing so. Indeed, elected officials regard bold architectural commissions as an excellent means of leaving a mark and encouraging tourism. Consequently, no visitor to France can ignore its modern architecture.

**Modern Art:** In the early 20th century, Paris was the world center of contemporary art. The Impressionists and other painters of the time had begun to liberate art from the merely representational, and photography had made the straightforward copying of reality redundant. The founding figure of modern art is undoubtedly Paul Cézanne, who was concerned above all with the underlying structural forms of nature. His influence is incalculable, but can be seen at its clearest in the cubism of Picasso, Braque, Léger, Delaunay, and others. A key precursor of later abstract art, cubism abandoned the traditional notions of perspective and tried to represent objects not as they appear from a particular angle, but analytically and from all sides at once, as it were, as if the eye could take in simultaneously every facet and plane.

Non- and indeed antinaturalism was the order of the day. Paul Gauguin and Vincent van Gogh had been influential, in their different ways, in nonnaturalistic use of color. Further, van Gogh had taken to its extreme the use of the external world to express the inner; not only do his strong colors and bold lines communicate the artist's tortured state, but the thickly laid-on paint pushes ever closer toward abstract patterns and shapes. The influence of the way these artists used color is visible in the *fauves* (literally, wild beasts), including Henri Matisse, André Derain, Georges Braque, and Georges Rouault.

**Music:** Musical modernism also owes a great deal to France. In Paris in 1913, the émigré Igor Stravinsky's ballet *The Rite of Spring* caused one of modernism's great scandals. But just as important is Claude Debussy, and especially his *Prélude à l'Après-Midi d'un Faune* (1894). Though deceptively easy on the ear it actually marks the beginnings of modern music. The piece is by no means atonal, but already conventional harmonic relationships are giving way. Debussy does not take a clear-cut theme and develop it in consecutive, goal-directed fashion; rather the overall impression is improvisatory. There are fluctuating tempi and irregular rhythms, and orchestral color is no longer an ornament but increasingly an end in itself. Debussy was to develop these ideas much further, but, without this seemingly innocuous piece, it would be hard to envisage the more obviously modern compositions of the great 20th-century French composers Olivier Messiaen and his pupil Pierre Boulez.

**Surrealism:** One modernist movement that spread across all the arts, and still has an influence on much contemporary culture, is surrealism. Again, this has its roots in the 19th century—in the extraordinary symbolist paintings of Odilon Redon and Gustave Moreau (whose Parisian house is now a gallery devoted to his art). It can also be seen in the hallucinatory, transgressive writings of Joris Karl Huysmans, Gérard de Nerval, and Lautréamont (the pseudonym of Isidore Ducasse) and especially in the intensely subjective, language-stretching poetry of Charles Baudelaire, Arthur Rimbaud, and Paul Verlaine.

## Bienvenue Chez les Ch'tis

This film, which is all about the French laughing at themselves, is the most successful film ever made in France, a runaway box office smash in 2008, and one of the highest grossing movies of all time in any language. In France they laugh at the "lazy" Southerners, the "mean" Normans and Auvergnats, and most especially the inhabitants of the North, the Ch'tis, whose accent they find impossible to understand. ("Ch'tis" is supposed to be how they render the word *petit*.)

The film, starring Dany Boon, recounts the adventures of a post office manager from Provence who is assigned to French Flanders in the north (home of les Ch'tis). When he arrives in the medieval town of Bergues, he is involved in a collision with the local postman. He is convinced the man must have fractured his jaw in the crash, but finally realizes that it is his accent that makes him sound so odd.

A third of the population of France howled with laughter at the film during the first 20 weeks of its appearance. And it has put Bergues on the map, too. Now you can take a guided tour of the town and the film locations *(www.bergues.fr)*.

Surrealists were fascinated by the unconscious, the bizarre, and the irrational. Clearly influenced by Freud, they wanted to challenge the dominance of reason and the conscious mind. Two of the key French poets of the 20th century—Louis Aragon and Paul Éluard—emerged from surrealism, and it also left a distinct mark on the scriptwriter Jacques Prévert and the films of Jean Cocteau, particularly *Le Sang d'un Poète*.

**Cinema:** Cocteau brings us to cinema, the quintessentially modern medium, which the French christened *le septième art*, the seventh art. Pioneers Étienne Marey and Felix-Louis Regnault played key roles in the prehistory of the cinema, while the Lumière brothers laid the basis for the documentary and Georges Méliès for fantasy genres.

Film might have been regarded early as an art in France, but its commercial possibilities, too, were rapidly realized by Gaumont and Pathé. After World War I, however, France, like other European countries, felt the effects of Hollywood imports. Nevertheless, French cinema managed to thrive, as evidenced by the immensely varied work of directors such as Marcel L'Herbier, Jean Epstein, René Clair, Jacques Feyder, Jean Renoir (the painter's son), and Marcel Carné, among many others.

**Best known for his 1960 film *Breathless*, Jean-Luc Godard helped pioneer French New Wave cinema.**

After World War II, and in spite of the country's economic difficulties, interesting new figures such as Henri-Georges Clouzot, Jean-Pierre Melville, Jacques Tati, and Georges Franju appeared. By the early fifties, a number of critics grouped around the journal *Cahiers du Cinéma* argued for a more personal and contemporary form of cinema. They reexamined Hollywood cinema and argued that the works of Alfred Hitchcock, John Ford, and Harold Hawks, among others, were *authored* movies, with strong personal content.

Soon *Cahiers* critics such as Jean-Luc Godard, Claude Chabrol, François Truffaut, and others were putting their ideas into practice by making their own highly personal movies. This *Nouvelle Vague* (New Wave), as it was called, rapidly became the new French art cinema, envied and imitated around the world. Indeed, by inspiring directors like Scorsese, Coppola, and De Palma, it later helped to revitalize the American cinema, which had helped to give birth to it in the first place.

By the end of the sixties, the filmmakers of the Nouvelle Vague had largely dispersed, although they carried on making distinctive films, Godard in particular. Today it would be difficult to isolate any one trend or school. However, thanks to its enlightened system of state support, France remains one of the key filmmaking countries. ∎

The country's core—the Île-de-France—at whose heart is Paris, the pivot around which the fortunes of France have turned for 15 centuries

# Paris & the Île-de-France

The icon of a city—and a nation

# Paris

Paris has a well-earned reputation for being one of the most beautiful, exciting, and romantic cities in the world. Often called the City of Dreams, Paris has been a mecca for aspiring artists, writers, thinkers, and adventurers since the earliest times. Stroll down almost any street in central Paris and you pass evidence of its past in the narrow, twisting medieval byways and awe-inspiring churches; in the ornate 17th-century Renaissance palaces that flaunt incredible wealth; in Napoleon's classically inspired monuments; and in the sweeping tree-lined boulevards of Baron Haussmann's 19th-century revamp of Paris.

Packed into the center of the grand city on the Seine are some of the greatest museums in the world, the most beautiful buildings in France, and all possible luxuries. Indeed, Paris continues to be an elegant, sophisticated, vibrant, living city, the economic and cultural center of France.

The creativity of today is evident in the exciting new buildings and modern painting and sculpture that sit harmoniously along-side the treasures of the past. With dozens of museums and stylish galleries, a wealth of beautiful parks, stunning stores displaying the fashions of world-famous designers, unparalleled people-watching, and

## NOT TO BE MISSED:

Area of map detail

irresistible cafés and restaurants at every turn, the visitor can happily occupy every moment.

Over the centuries, the city has played host to a procession of performing artists. Kings and nobles acted as patrons to playwrights, musicians, and actors. Today, the capital still offers a vast choice of entertainment: theaters, rock venues, nightclubs, and bars—although just wandering the streets of so lively a city can be entertainment enough. ■

# Île de la Cité

**The oldest and most celebrated part of Paris is the Île de la Cité, an island in the Seine, little more than half a mile (1 km) long. Here, on a sandbank at a crossing point on the river, the Parisii, or boat people, had built a fortified town by the third century B.C.**

The jewel in the crown that is the Île de la Cité remains the high Gothic Cathédrale Notre-Dame. In the south tower is "Emmanuel," the only cathedral bell to escape destruction in the Revolution.

Under Roman rule, the settlement, called Lutetia Parisiorum, prospered, becoming the hub of a network of roads that crossed the northern portion of the Roman Empire. In the third century A.D. it was destroyed by barbarians, so when the Parisii restored it, they built a thick stone wall to create an island fortress.

By A.D. 508, Paris was the seat of the kings of the Franks. When Hugh Capet was declared King of France in 987 (see p. 22), Paris—as the capital city—became ever more important.

The Île de la Cité was the residence of the French kings from the 10th to the 14th centuries. In a display of wealth and power by the Church, the medieval streets were overshadowed by the new Gothic cathedral of Notre-Dame, built in the 12th and 13th centuries. Royal power was equally evident in the huge palace, so vast that it now forms the Conciergerie, the Palais de Justice, and Ste.-Chapelle. When the court left in the 14th century, the Île lost its significant place in French affairs.

The island, connected to the mainland by bridges that crossed the Seine, was later linked to the nearby Île St.-Louis. In the 16th and 17th centuries, the Île St.-Louis became fashionable and noblemen built their beautiful mansions here. ■

# Notre-Dame

On a site that has been occupied since Roman times, the Cathédrale Notre-Dame is the essence of the city. Between 1163 and 1375, armies of craftsmen labored to create a masterpiece of Gothic architecture. The cathedral became a meeting place for the craftsmen's guilds and a place of education renowned throughout Europe. On these foundations, Paris's world-famous university, the Sorbonne, was based.

Changing fashions, neglect, and vandalism took their toll on the cathedral, particularly in the 18th century. The Revolution saw carvings removed and statues beheaded. By the time Napoleon crowned himself emperor here in 1804, the cathedral had fallen into a sorry state.

Victor Hugo's 1831 novel *Notre-Dame de Paris* was instrumental in prompting restoration plans, and work by historian-architect Eugène Viollet-le-Duc began in 1844, bringing back the cathedral's past splendor. Today, Notre-Dame remains a masterpiece of French Gothic style. It displays several steps in the development of Gothic cathedrals (see pp. 116–117).

towers, the west facade has three imposing portals. In the Middle Ages the statues and sculptures here would have been brightly painted. The central portal depicts the Last Judgment, with Christ and the celestial court. The cathedral's oldest sculptures (1165–1175), on the right-hand portal, show the life of St. Anne, and include one of the Virgin Mary showing Jesus to a kneeling King Louis VII (who consecrated the cathedral in the 12th century) and to the founder, Bishop Sully. The Virgin's portal, on the left, depicts her coronation, resurrection, and assumption, surrounded by saints, angels, and signs of the zodiac.

## Cathédrale Notre-Dame

- 🅰 53 D2
- ✉ place du Parvis Notre-Dame, Île de la Cité
- ☎ 01 42 34 56 10, towers; 01 53 10 07 00, information
- 💲 $$
- 🚇 Métro: Cité

**www.notredame deparis.com**

## Place du Parvis Notre-Dame

Medieval houses and streets were swept away in a 19th-century scheme to enlarge the square overlooked by Notre-Dame's west front. People could stand here to see the biblical carvings on the facade—a valuable introduction to Bible stories in an age when congregations were largely illiterate.

## West Facade

Crowned by two early Gothic

### Paris-Plages

Grab your sunscreen and head to the beach—not far from Notre-Dame. For a month, from mid-July to mid-August, Paris-Plages help define summer in the city. The quaysides of the Seine, closed to car traffic, sport free beaches with all the trimmings: sand, parasols, deck chairs, and palm trees. All sorts of leisure activities, sports, and concerts are available. The beaches stretch on the right bank from the Louvre to Pont de Sully, and on the left bank from Pont du Tolbiac to the Simone de Beauvoir footbridge.

Above the portals is the Galerie des Rois (Gallery of Kings). The 21 statues of Old Testament kings are reconstructions. The originals, damaged by revolutionaries who mistook them for French monarchs, were rediscovered in a 1977 excavation. Fragments are in the Musée de Cluny (see p. 61). Higher still, above the rose window, is the Galerie des Chimères, a balustrade embellished with grotesque stone figures of demons, birds, and weird beasts. The gargoyles, together with Quasimodo, the hunchback of Notre-Dame, feature in Victor Hugo's *Notre-Dame de Paris*. Redesigned by Viollet-le-Duc, the gargoyles were intended to drain water from the roof (and, perhaps, to deter evil spirits).

## Towers

Originally designed to be surmounted by spires, the towers are 226 feet (69 m) high. Climbing the 238 steps to the north tower is hard work; a further 140 steps lead to the top of the south tower, but the spectacular

Clerestory

Rose window

South tower

Portals

Triforium

Nave

views over the city make the climb well worthwhile. The 13-ton bell in the south tower is famous for its pure tone.

## Flying Buttresses

The famous flying buttresses, so typical of a high Gothic cathedral, were built between 1220 and 1230. Each incorporates a channel to allow rainwater to run off. Those at the east end have a span of 49 feet (15 m). The chapels between the buttresses date from 1250–1325.

## Interior

The traditional Gothic layout consists of a nave of ten bays flanked by double aisles continuing around the choir. The walls are lined with 37 chapels, added during the 13th and 14th centuries. Stand at the crossing of the transepts for the best view of the rose windows.

**Windows:** The cathedral has three magnificent rose windows. The north window measures an amazing 69 feet (21 m) across. Almost all its medieval glass remains. It depicts the Virgin encircled by figures from the Old Testament. The west window, above the main door, was completed in the 1490s, but restored in the 19th century. It also portrays the Virgin. The south rose window, with some original 13th-century glass, shows Christ surrounded by angels, saints, and the 12 Apostles.

The original stained glass of the nave windows survived until 1771, when Louis XV, declaring stained glass outmoded, had it replaced with clear panes. These were changed in 1965 to modern abstract stained glass by Jacques Le Chevallier.

**Great Organ:** With 110 stops and 6,000 pipes, this is the largest organ in France. Some pipes survive from the late Middle Ages, but most are 18th century. In 1868 the master organ-builder Aristide Cavaillé-Coll improved the instrument to make it as expressive and versatile as a symphony orchestra. Free organ concerts are given on Sunday afternoons.

**Chancel & Choir:** At one time a carved 14th-century stone screen shut off the nave from the chancel; only parts survive, in front of the first three north and south bays. Inside the chancel are the choir stalls, with scenes from the life of the Virgin. Bishops lie in their tombs around the ambulatory and below the choir. The sacristy, on the south side of the choir, houses the treasury of medieval manuscripts, sacred dishes, and caskets for the relics of saints. ■

Flying buttress

**Notre-Dame**

# Strolling the Islands

The Île de la Cité and the Île St.-Louis are the oldest parts of Paris. This walk takes you around both islands—past their most historically memorable features—and offers wonderful views up and down the river.

Bustling capital city or serene river-punctuated countryside? Yes, it's Paris—the Île de la Cité.

**NOT TO BE MISSED:**

Ste.-Chapelle • Conciergerie • Notre-Dame

Begin at Place Louis-Lépine, whose colorful flower market (one of Paris's last remaining) makes way for the Marché aux Oiseaux (bird market) on Sundays. Walk along Rue de Lutèce to the ornate gates of the vast **Palais de Justice** ❶ *(tel 01 44 32 50 00)*. Since the 16th century the palace has been the seat of the *parlement* (law court). After repeated fires and damage during the Revolution, most of the palace was rebuilt in the 19th century.

Before turning left along Boulevard du Palais, look up for a glimpse of the spire of **Ste.-Chapelle** *(tel 01 53 40 60 80)*. This lovely Gothic chapel, built for Louis IX (St. Louis, R. 1226–1270) in 1248, is tucked away in a courtyard within the precincts of the Palais de Justice. The entrance is on Boulevard du Palais. Take binoculars for close-up views of the stained-glass windows, which depict more than 1,000 biblical scenes in an area of almost 7,000 square feet (620 sq m).

At Pont St.-Michel turn right along Quai des Orfèvres. Turn right again to cross quaint Place Dauphine, whose huge trees shade a *boules* pitch. A narrow medieval street, Rue Henri Robert, leads to Pont Neuf. Beyond the bridge is a fine

## Boats on the Seine

Many of the most memorable views of Paris are from the river. Sightseeing trips in glass-roof boats take in the stretch of the Seine between the Tour Eiffel and the Île St.-Louis, passing the Grand Palais, the Louvre, the Musée d'Orsay, Notre-Dame, and other top landmarks.

Most trips last about an hour, departing half-hourly in summer (hourly in winter) from 10 a.m. Some of the larger boats offer longer lunch or dinner trips.

The large *Bateaux-Mouches (tel 01 42 25 96 10)* vessels depart from Pont de l'Alma (Right Bank), while Bateaux Parisiens Tour Eiffel *(tel 08 25 01 01 01)* uses the quay near the Tour Eiffel. Vedettes du Pont-Neuf *(tel 01 46 33 98 38)* operates smaller boats, departing from the western tip of the Île de la Cité near Pont Neuf. Vedettes de Paris *(tel 01 44 18 19 50, vedettesde paris.com)* has one-hour cruises.

You can even swim on the river. The Josephine Baker floating pool *(21 quai François Mauriac, tel 01 56 61 96 50)* is moored on the Seine. The pool complex includes saunas and steam baths.

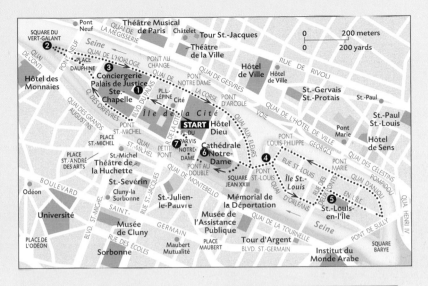

equestrian **statue of Henri IV.** Steps lead down to **Square du Vert-Galant ②**. This little park, a peninsula in the Seine, offers marvelous views, especially at sunset. Picasso's 1943 painting of this view is in the Musée Picasso (see p. 76).

Walk east along Quai de l'Horloge, in the shadow of the turreted **Conciergerie ③** (tel 01 53 40 60 80). The oldest part of the former royal palace, it was rebuilt in about 1300. The Salle des Gens d'Armes, the largest hall in medieval Europe, could hold the entire palace staff—some 2,000 people. In 1358 the palace was stormed and the king was forced to move the royal residence. An important noble was appointed *concierge* (caretaker). From 1391 until 1914 the building was a prison. Prisoners here during the Revolution included the queen, Marie-Antoinette. Her cell is one of several that have been reconstructed and can be visited.

At the far end of Quai de l'Horloge, notice the Conciergerie's famous clock tower; the clock dates from 1370 and still works today. Continue along Quai de la Corse and Quai aux Fleurs, where typical Parisian stalls, *bouquinistes*, sell books and artworks. Across the river is the 1882 neo-Renaissance **Hôtel de Ville** building.

Cross **Pont St.-Louis ④** to the Île St.-Louis. Follow Quai d'Orléans past magnificent

⬛ See area map p. 53
➤ Place Louis-Lépine (Métro: Cité)
↔ 2.5 miles (4 km)
⏱ 2 hours
➤ Place Louis-Lépine

17th-century town houses—look for superb courtyards, wrought iron, and carved heads. The Île St.-Louis has long been a sought-after residential area of Paris. Turn left onto Rue des Deux Ponts, then right onto Rue St.-Louis-en-l'Île. Pass the island's richly decorated church, **St.-Louis-en-l'Île ⑤**, and turn left on Quai d'Anjou. Continue along Quai de Bourbon then, at Pont Louis-Philippe, turn left and recross Pont St.-Louis to approach **Notre-Dame ⑥** (see pp. 55–57) through a small park. Walk to **Place du Parvis Notre-Dame ⑦**, at the west end of the cathedral. Here a bronze star marks the official center of Paris, from where all distances on French roads are measured. Below the parvis, in the **Crypte Archéologique** (tel 01 55 42 50 10), lie the remains of 16th- and 18th-century houses, the church of St.-Étienne, and fragments from Lutetia, the Gallo-Roman city. From the parvis, take Rue de la Cité back to Place Louis-Lépine.

# Left Bank

The Left Bank—the famous Rive Gauche—is a lively area south of the Seine. Stretching from the Jardin des Plantes to the Champ de Mars, it encompasses the narrow streets of St.-Germain in the Latin Quarter (Quartier Latin)—until the Revolution teaching at the Sorbonne was in Latin), the quieter, grander areas around the Panthéon and the Palais du Luxembourg, the Musée d'Orsay, and the Assemblée Nationale.

With its mix of fashionable locals and wide-eyed visitors, worn-smooth cobblestone streets and charming old buildings with flower boxes, the Latin Quarter is Paris at its most atmospheric.

For both visitors and local Parisians there is an endless attraction to the cozy, medieval streets of St.-Germain. The popular area possesses a wealth of little shops and cafés frequented by writers, artists, and students from the Sorbonne and the École des Beaux-Arts.

The Latin Quarter, right alongside the Île de la Cité, is where Paris first spilled onto the mainland. Scattered Roman remains show how extensive the city then became. The Latin Quarter also boasts several institutions of higher learning.

The Musée de Cluny houses a stunning collection of Roman and medieval artifacts, while the Roman-style Panthéon nearby serves as a mausoleum for many of France's most revered historical figures. Napoleon Bonaparte, perhaps the greatest, is close by; he was laid to rest a little farther west, in the magnificent Église du Dôme in Les Invalides.

Finally, soaring over central Paris, is la Tour Eiffel—the Eiffel Tower—a monument to the Parisian flair for innovation. The steel icon is flanked by the Musée du Quai Branly, which opened in 2006. ■

# Museums on the Left Bank

Truly an embarrassment of riches, the Left Bank of Paris is home to several world-class museums. The Musée d'Orsay and the Musée Rodin, great destinations in their own right, showcase French art from the 19th and 20th centuries. Celebrated at Musée de Cluny is France's medieval history, while the Musée du Quai Branly spotlights ethnic art from many corners of the world.

## Musée de Cluny

Built for visiting Benedictine monks from Cluny, in Burgundy, in the late 15th century, the former Hôtel de Cluny stands beside the remains of Paris's oldest Roman baths, off Boulevard St.-Michel.. The mansion, one of France's finest examples of Gothic domestic architecture, was owned after the Revolution by art collector Alexandre de Sommerard. His acquisitions form the basis of the Musée National du Moyen Age et des Thermes de Cluny. Don't miss this unique combination of Gallo-Roman ruins, medieval mansion, and one of the world's finest collections of medieval art and crafts.

On display are medieval furniture, clothes, and accessories; textiles, including examples of Byzantine and Coptic work as well as European; and some magnificent tapestries. One series, "La Vie Seigneuriale," illustrates the life of a noble household in the Middle Ages. Also in the museum are the 21 mutilated stone heads of the Kings of Judah, carved around 1220 for the west front of Notre-Dame but defaced and then lost during the Revolution.

**Roman Baths:** On the ground floor are the remains of second-century baths: three stone chambers for steam, tepid, and cold baths, and a gymnasium. The vaulted ceiling of the cold bath (*frigidarium*) rises over 45 feet (14 m). The capitals of the supporting pillars are ships' prows, which suggests that the baths were built for the Nautae, the wealthy corporation of Paris boatmen.

**Hôtel de Cluny:** On the first floor is the abbot's chapel, with fan-vaulting radiating from a central pillar. One room has been restored as a medieval living room with wooden

*(continued on p. 65)*

### Musée de Cluny
- 53 D2
- 6 place Paul-Painlevé
- 01 53 73 78 16
- Closed Tues.
- $$
- Métro: St.-Michel, Odéon

**www.musee-moyenage.fr**

---

## EXPERIENCE:
## Culture After Dark

For a truly romantic experience of Paris by night, take part in the **Nuit Blanche**, on the first Saturday in October. From 7 p.m. until dawn, the city is illuminated with amazing creations, and you can spend the whole night immersing yourself in the creative, free concerts, live shows, and contemporary design sites. The **Nuit des Musées—** Museum Night— is another increasingly popular event that takes place usually in May, with museums staying open until midnight, with special events and chance encounters at no extra charge. Details for both events: *www.paris.fr.*

# Latin Quarter Walk

Enjoy the special buzz of this enticing Paris neighborhood by strolling through its student-thronged streets and quiet backwaters.

Stately, elegant, and serene, the Luxembourg Garden invites strolling and relaxation.

Starting from the Pont au Double beside Notre-Dame, cross the Quai Montebello. Walk through the small garden facing you; a false acacia here is reputedly the oldest tree in Paris. Pass beside the little 13th-century church of **St.-Julien-le-Pauvre** ❶.

Turn right down Rue St.-Jacques and cross to Rue de la Huchette. Once the heart of the Latin Quarter, the street is now dominated by Greek restaurants but still retains the famous Caveau de la Huchette jazz club at No. 5. At the end of the street, turn left onto Rue de la Harpe, with its cafés and clubs. This area is at its most vibrant when crowded with students on a warm evening.

Cross Boulevard St.-Germain and walk up the hill on Boulevard St.-Michel, past the remains of some Roman baths. Turn left into

## NOT TO BE MISSED:

Musée de Cluny • St.-Étienne-du-Mont • Panthéon • Jardin du Luxembourg • Hôtel des Monnaies

Place Paul-Painlevé for the **Musée de Cluny** ❷ (see p. 61).

From the museum, cross the small square and walk up to Rue des Écoles. Turn left past the buildings of the **Sorbonne,** Paris's world-famous university, founded in 1253.

At the junction of Rue des Écoles and Rue de la Montagne de Ste.-Geneviève, turn right and walk up the steep hill. Named after the patron saint of Paris, the street was part of the

Roman road that linked Lutetia (Paris) with Italy.

At the fork, take Rue Descartes. Turn right into Rue Clovis, named after the king of the Franks who defeated the Romans and founded France. On your right is the charming church of **St.-Étienne-du-Mont** ❸, well worth a brief visit to see the intricately carved 16th-century rood screen, flanked by spiral staircases. Rue Clovis opens onto the Place du Panthéon. Walk around the square to go inside the **Panthéon** ❹ *(tel 01 44 32 18 00)*, burial place of Voltaire, Rousseau, Hugo, and other French luminaries. Walk down Rue Soufflot to the

**Jardin du Luxembourg** ❺. The 17th-century promenades offer some relaxing strolls.

Leave the gardens to the right of the **Palais du Luxembourg** (seat of the French Senate) to reach the 18th-century Odéon-Théâtre de

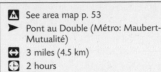

🅐 See area map p. 53
▶ Pont au Double (Métro: Maubert-Mutualité)
3 miles (4.5 km)
🕐 2 hours
▶ Pont au Double

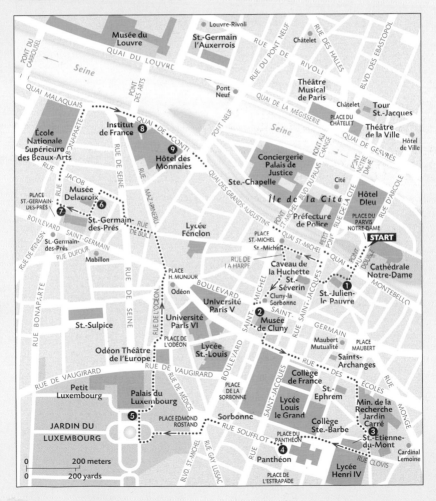

l'Europe. Continue downhill to Boulevard St.-Germain and cross to Rue de l'Ancienne Comédie. On the right is **Le Procope** *(13 rue de l'Ancienne Comédie, tel 01 40 46 79 00),* Paris's first café (see p. 70), now a restaurant.

Turn left on Rue de Buci and right on Rue de Seine. The area is full of small stores, many selling antiques and art. Turn left on Rue Jacob and left again on Rue Furstemberg. In a corner of elegant Place Furstemberg is the **Musée National Eugène Delacroix 6** *(tel 01 44 41 86 50, closed Tues.),* based in the last home of the major Romantic artist, who died in 1836.

Turn right from Rue Furstemberg and continue to Place St.-Germain-des-Prés. Beside the old abbey church of **St.-Germain-des-Prés 7**, a little garden contains Picasso's sculpture "L'Hommage à Apollinaire."

Place St.-Germain-des-Prés offers the chance of a reviving drink at one of Paris's best known cafés, including the atmospheric **Les Deux Magots** and the **Café de Flore** (see p. 71). From the square, go down Rue Bonaparte, lined with interesting little stores and galleries. On the left you will see the École Nationale Supérieure des Beaux-Arts (School of Fine Art).

Having reached the Seine—and the splendid view of the enormous Louvre—turn right on Quai Malaquais and walk past the **Institut de France 8**. This is where the historic French academies, including the exclusive Académie Française, carry out their research.

Farther along, in the former mint—the 18th-century **Hôtel des Monnaies 9**—is the Musée de la Monnaie *(tel 01 40 46 56 66, closed Mon.),* which traces the history of coinage from 300 B.C. Limited-edition coins are still made here.

Go down steps from Quai des Grands-Augustins to the lower embankment of the Seine, away from the busy road (but usually closed at night). Return to Pont au Double.

**The immense—and immensely impressive—Panthéon is an 18th-century engineering feat.**

shutters, candelabra, armor, and tapestries. Also on this floor is a superb collection of goldwork and jewelry, including belts, bracelets, rare votive Visigoth crowns, and two 13th-century double gold crosses.

## INSIDER TIP:

See more of the Roman baths' underground ruins on a guided tour, offered by the Musée de Cluny at 2 p.m. on Wednesdays.

—BARBARA NOE
*National Geographic Books
senior editor*

The most famous of the treasures are the six allegorical tapestries "La Dame à la Licorne" ("The Lady with the Unicorn"), displayed in a circular room. Exquisitely woven, they are in 15th-century millefleurs style, noted for its graceful depiction of plants, animals, and people. Five of the tapestries show the lady acting out the five senses, while the enigmatic sixth presents her in front of the motto "À Mon Seul Désir" (To My Only Desire).

## Musée d'Orsay

Opened in 1986, the Musée d'Orsay (about a 20-minute walk from Musée de Cluny along Boulevard St.-Germain) soon became one of Europe's top art museums. The unconventional building—a converted hotel and railroad station—lent itself to

imaginative displays, winning wide acclaim. The collections cover the period from 1848 to 1914, an exciting time for the art world, with Paris very much at the helm. All the great names are here.

**The Station:** The original hotel and station were built for the 1900 Universal Exhibition on the site of the Palais d'Orsay, burned down in the Commune uprising of 1871. Functional iron-and-glass railway architecture would have looked wrong in this elegant part of Paris, so a monumental stone facade was built, effectively concealing the building's purpose. The ornate belle epoque reception areas, restaurant, and ballroom are still intact.

Within 10 years, the station was obsolete, its platforms too short for modern trains. Temporary uses for the building included a mailing center, film set, and hostel for prisoners of war. By the 1960s, demolition plans were well advanced when the present innovative conversion was proposed. This allowed various important art collections to be regrouped, including famous Impressionist works from the overcrowded Jeu de Paume across the Seine. The Musée d'Orsay thus filled a gap between the Louvre and the contemporary art of the Centre Georges Pompidou (Beaubourg).

**Ground Floor:** Visitors in a hurry may be tempted to head for the Impressionist works upstairs. Resist, if you have time: The ground floor, mostly covering the period 1848–1870, traces some of the developments that paved the

**Musée d'Orsay**

🗺 53 C3

✉ rue de la Legion d'Honneur

☎ 01 40 49 48 14

🕐 Closed Mon.

💲 $$

🚇 Métro: Solférino, Musée d'Orsay

**www.musee-orsay.fr**

way for 20th-century painting and sculpture. In the central gallery, devoted to sculpture, look especially at the work of the influential Jean-Baptiste Carpeaux (1827–1875), whose bronze group "Count Ugolino" gave Rodin ideas he used in "The Thinker."

Mid-19th-century paintings occupy the side galleries on this floor. To the right (as you enter) are later works by the conservative Ingres, devotee of classical ideas and technical precision, and the Romantic Delacroix, for whom imagination and the use of color became more important.

Highlights of the galleries on the opposite (north) side include pictures by realists Millet and Courbet. Note Millet's deliberately mundane portrayal of three peasant women, "The Gleaners," and Courbet's "Burial at Ornans," considered vulgar when it was first shown.

Many such paintings illustrate the important move away from heroic, stylized subject matter toward depictions of ordinary people and everyday themes. Equally revolutionary approaches to color and light characterize the pre-1870 works of art by painters such as Monet, Pissarro, Manet, and Renoir that can be found toward the northeastern end of this floor of the museum.

**Upper Level:** The core of the museum's world-famous Impressionist collection is on the Upper Level. Many familiar images include Manet's "Déjeuner sur l'Herbe," Monet's "Poppies," and Whistler's portrait of his mother. All the great artists of the period are well represented; there

## EXPERIENCE: Artistic Paris

Paris has always been the city of creativity, so what better place to try to express your own artistic talents? **Paris Loisirs Culturels** *(11 rue St.-Maur, tel 01 81 29 25 76, www.pdizian.com)* offers painting classes at every level. Teaching, available in French and English, concentrates on various painting techniques, composition, and pictorial construction. The great French masters are studied, notably Matisse, and once a month there is a group visit to the Musée d'Orsay or the Louvre. Personalized courses allow you to develop and advance at your own rhythm—in your own choice of subject matter and materials.

For weeklong courses or just an outdoor Sunday class in drawing, painting, or watercolors, consider **Atelier Alupi** *(tel 06 78 26 82 94, www.atelieralupi.com)*.

For art classes en plein air you can learn to paint in Monet's garden and in his beloved village of Giverny, outside Paris. English-language artistic retreats are run by **ArtStudy/Giverny** *(www.giverny.org/artists/schools/artstudy.com)*, with hands-on workshops taught by professional artists.

**Even ethereal works of art can't mask the Musée d'Orsay's rail terminal past.**

are works by Renoir, Cézanne, Pissarro, and Degas. Some fine van Gogh paintings are here, including "Bedroom at Arles," "Church at Auvers," and several self-portraits. Van Gogh was in Paris from 1886 to 1888, meeting and exchanging ideas with all the major artists.

Some of the rooms at the western end of this floor show pictures by the Pont-Aven school, a breakaway group led by Gauguin. They emphasized two-dimensional patterns from memory rather than nature. A nearby room is devoted to the *nabis,* another genre of late 19th-century painters including Bonnard and Vuillard, named for the Hebrew word *nabi* (prophet). Their flat, linear forms and arbitrary use of color paved the way for early 20th-century abstract art.

**Middle Level:** Make time, if you can, to visit the varied collections

here. Some—such as the early photographs, the art nouveau glass and ceramics, or the sumptuous ballroom of the former hotel  offer a complete contrast with exhibits on other levels. Other galleries return to themes already explored. There are larger works by the nabis (such as Bonnard's "The Croquet Party"), some sculptures by Rodin, and rooms of naturalist and symbolist paintings.

## Musée du Quai Branly

The Musée du Quai Branly, located on the Seine near the Tour Eiffel, opened in June 2006. Its vast collection, comprising 3,500 pieces from the Musée de l'Homme and the Musée National des Arts d'Afrique et d'Océanie, showcases ethnic art from all over the world. Jean Nouvel designed the glass-fronted structure, which echoes the shadow of the neighboring Tour Eiffel and is surrounded by a park

**Musée du Quai Branly**

🅰 52 B3

✉ Entrances on rue de l'Université or Quai Branly

☎ 01 56 61 70 00

🕒 Closed Mon

💲 $$$

Ⓜ Métro: Iena, Alma-Marceau. Or take the river shuttle.

**www.quaibranly.fr**

## Musée Rodin

- 🅰 52 B3
- ✉ 77 rue de Varenne
- ☎ 01 44 18 61 10
- 🕐 Closed Mon.
- 💲 $
- 🚇 Métro: Varenne, Invalides

**www.musee-rodin.fr**

of paths, a pool, and trees. One of its most curious features is a *mur végétal,* a wall with 150 species of plants.

## Musée Rodin

Sculptor Auguste Rodin (1840–1917) spent his last nine years in the Hôtel Biron, an elegant rococo mansion near Les Invalides. Built in 1730, the house and its lovely garden were owned by a horticulturist, Maréchal de Biron, who died on the guillotine.

The house became artists' studios in 1908. Rodin stayed here from then until his death, paying the rent with his works. After he died, the house became a museum for the collection he left to the nation.

Rodin gained fame only in his forties, but his output was prolific, and the museum possesses several thousand sculptures and fragments

as well as many drawings. Works from Rodin's youth include a bust of his father, and the charming terra-cotta "Young Woman in a Flowered Hat" (circa 1865). The sculptor's first major commission, in 1880, was "The Gates of Hell." Intended as a bronze door for the planned Musée des Arts Décoratifs, the work was not cast until 1929, after Rodin's death, but many of the figures that he made for this project developed into independent sculptures.

Alongside Rodin's own works in the museum are works by his contemporaries, notably his talented but tragic mistress, Camille Claudel. She never recovered from Rodin's rejection in 1898, spending her last years in a mental institution.

With their roses, well-placed seats, and summer café, the gardens make an agreeable end to a visit to the museum. ■

Sometimes you just have to sit down and think. Where better than at the Rodin Museum?

# Tour Eiffel

**Rising from the green expanse of the Champ de Mars, a former military parade ground established 140 years before its construction, the Tour Eiffel (Eiffel Tower) is Paris's most enduring symbol. Built for the centenary of the Revolution in 1889, it was feted by half a million people at its own centenary celebrations in 1989.**

When plans for the Tour Eiffel won first prize in a competition organized for the 1889 Universal Exhibition, Gustave Eiffel pronounced that France would be the only nation with a 300-meter flagpole. The precision of his plans, with exact measurements for more than 15,000 metallic parts, enabled 300 workers to complete the tallest structure in the world in just over two years (January 1887 to March 1889). A staggering 2.5 million rivets were used.

An immediate success, it was visited by almost two million people during the exhibition. Within a year it had recouped most of its building cost. The tower was due to be pulled down in 1909, but by then it had become indispensable in the world of telecommunications, particularly for the first transatlantic radio telephone service.

You can reach the first platform by 360 steps or by one of four elevators that travel diagonally up the legs (one serves only the restaurant). A small museum on the first floor runs a short film about the tower's history. A video gives additional details and statistics..

The panorama from the top platform is breathtaking. On a very clear day, the horizon can

The grand tower is the spot for bird's-eye-view Paris photos.

extend to 45 miles (72 km). Directly below is the Seine and, on the opposite bank, the Palais de Chaillot. At night the tower is lit from within for ten minutes every hour, making a glittering spectacle so evocative of Paris's romantic image. ∎

**Tour Eiffel**

- 32 A3
- Champ de Mars
- 01 44 11 23 23
- $$
- Métro: Bir-Hakeim

**www.tour-eiffel.fr**

## Paris Icon: Facts & Stats

- Height (including antenna): 1,051 feet (319 m)
- Height increase on hot days from metal expansion: up to 6 inches (15 cm)
- First platform at 187 feet (57 m)
- Second platform at 377 feet (115 m)
- Top platform at 905 feet (276 m)
- 1,585 steps
- 6 million visitors per year

# Café Life

For Parisians, the café has a special place in their lives: It is here that they meet friends, discuss the affairs of the day, and watch the world go by. For some, the café is virtually a second home. Many Parisian cafés have famous histories as melting pots for artists and intellectuals to exchange and develop ideas. Traditional café culture remains strong, though the number of cafés in Paris has dropped significantly in recent years.

Paris in a nutshell: Folks lingering at a café, with waiters in black and white carrying cups of coffee.

## Historic Haunts

The first café to open its doors in Paris, in 1686, was **Le Procope,** on the Left Bank. It soon became the meeting place of actors from the Comédie-Française and later of philosophers Voltaire and Rousseau, revolutionaries Danton, Robespierre, and Marat, and 19th-century writers, including Balzac and Hugo. Le Procope still exists, but as a classic restaurant (13 rue de l'Ancienne Comedie, tel 01 40 46 79 00, www.procope .com) with mirrors, banquettes, chandeliers, and several rooms.

The broad, sweeping grands boulevards of the 19th century moved café life onto the sidewalks. One of the first of these places was **Café de la Paix** (12 boulevard des Capucines, tel 01 40

07 36 36), which retains much of its Second Empire glory. Parisians delight in sitting outside where they can watch the passing street life. In the summer, as would be expected, the streets buzz with people crowded at outdoor café tables. But even in the gray winter, people can be seen happily muffled up at tables set up on the sidewalk.

By the 1920s, café society had moved to Montparnasse, where the likes of revolutionary photographer Man Ray and controversial novelist Henry Miller—both American expatriates—frequented a trio of neighborhood spots. **La Rotonde** (105 boulevard du Montparnasse, tel 01 43 26 48 26, www.rotondemontparnasse .com), overlooking the Opéra, remains a traditional brasserie with a huge terrace, velvet banquettes, and perfect service. Starring on the menu are steak tartare and fresh oysters. **Le Dôme** (*108 boulevard du Montparnasse, tel 01 40 47 04 91*), another Paris institution, has a famous glass-fronted terrace tailor-made for people-watching. The third legendary hangout of Lost Generation Americans is **Le Select** (*99 boulevard du Montparnasse, tel 01 42 22 65 27*), perfect for brunch enjoyed with a newspaper.

In 1939, Picasso was a regular at **Café de Flore** (*172 boulevard St.-Germain, tel 01 45 48 55 26, www.cafe-de-flore.com*), likely setting the pace for Jean-Paul Sartre and Simone de Beauvoir. Sartre developed the philosophy of existentialism during the many hours he and de Beauvoir spent here—from 9 a.m. until well into the night. It's still a popular hangout, with plays performed upstairs.

Nearby is **Les Deux Magots** (*6 place St. Germain, tel 01 45 48 55 25, www.lesdeuxmagots .com*), named for its two statues of Chinese mandarins, *magots*, which sit inside on a pillar—a reminder of the café's original function, selling silks. Les Deux Magots attracted the key figures of a whole postwar generation of philosophers and writers, including Ernest Hemingway, André Breton, and André Gide. It is still a favorite among Parisians and travelers.

## The New Crop

Modern cafés are keeping tradition alive. Many of the new spots still attract an artistic clientele while acting as a showcase for superb design. The **Café Beaubourg** (*100 rue de St.-Martin, 01 48 87 64 96*), on the square outside the Centre Pompidou, was designed by Christian de Pontzamparc and is a fashionable rendezvous for artists, critics, and gallery owners.

On the Left Bank, **La Palette** (*43 rue de Seine, tel 01 43 26 68 15, www.cafelapaletteparis .com*) is very popular with students from the École des Beaux-Arts. Retired Parisians and the fashionable elite also go there—to "be seen." Its pretty tree-shaded terrace is a wonderful refuge in summer.

One very popular café for people-watching is the **Café Marly** (*93 rue de Rivoli, tel 01 49 26 06 60*), with its arcaded courtyard terrace overlooking the famous pyramid of the Louvre. It's expensive but delightful. Note: It must boast the most stylish rest rooms ever seen in a café.

At the other end of the spectrum are the local cafés. Newly fashionable for its cafés and nightlife is the Rue Oberkampf, leading up to Belleville. Try the belle epoque **Café Charbon** (*109 rue Oberkampf, tel 01 43 57 55 13*) or the fashionable **Cannibale Café** (*93 rue Oberkampf, tel 01 49 29 95 59*).

## Café Nuts & Bolts

Some cafés are low-profiles local places where working people eat a quick snack at lunchtime and neighborhood residents meet in the evening. You can find plenty of these around Montmartre and Pigalle.

In general, cafés open early in the morning, in time to serve the traditional *grand crème* (large cup of coffee with milk) with croissants to people on their way to work.

Throughout the day they also serve wine, beer, *pastis*—a strong aniseed spirit diluted with water—and, of course, espresso coffee (Parisians traditionally add milk to their coffee only in the morning). Drinks are cheaper *au bar* (standing at the bar) than *en salle* (sitting at a table inside). They are even more expensive if you sit at a table outside, but this increase in price never seems to worry anyone who is intent on soaking up the atmosphere and lingering a while. This archetypal Paris experience is worth every euro.

# Hôtel des Invalides

Monumental even by the standards of the Sun King, the Hôtel des Invalides was founded by Louis XIV to care for his veteran soldiers, many of them sick or disabled and desperately poor. The impressive classical building, with its huge severe facade, was completed in 1676. The Église du Dôme, whose commanding gilded and painted cupola stands directly over Napoleon's tomb, was added in 1706.

captured regimental standards.

The **Église du Dôme** alongside is a mausoleum to the military heroes of France. Directly under the dome is the centerpiece, the **tomb of Napoleon I.** At its center, a red porphyry sarcophagus stands on a green granite base, with Napoleon's ashes inside.

## INSIDER TIP:

**Nearby Cour du Commerce St.-André, still a cobblestone passageway, is where you'll find café/restaurant Le Procope (see p. 70). Marat and others who planned the revolution met here in the 1700s.**

—EMILIE C. HARTING
Intelligent Travel *blog writer*

In Paris a military hospital gets grand architectural treatment.

**Hôtel des Invalides**

🗺 52 B3
✉ esplanade des Invalides
☎ 08 10 11 33 99
Guided tours: 01 44 42 37 72
💲 $$
Ⓜ Métro: Varenne, Latour Maubourg

www.invalides.org

The huge **Cour d'Honneur** is lined with two-story arcades. "The Little Corporal," a statue of Napoleon I, stands above the south side. Trophies, flags, guns, and heraldic symbols adorn four pavilions and, at roof level, carved horses trample emblems of war. At the end is the entrance to the soldiers' church, **St.-Louis-des-Invalides,** its interior hung with

The **Musée de l'Armée** is one of the world's largest military collections. The **Musée des Plans-Reliefs** displays scale models of fortified towns and fortresses in France and along the borders. Also visit the **Musée de l'Ordre de la Libération,** devoted to World War II and partially under renovation. ∎

# More Places to Visit on the Left Bank

## Les Catacombes

The world's largest depository of human bones has over six million skeletons in many miles of former Montparnasse quarry tunnels. 🅰 53 C1 ✉ 1 avenue Colonel Rol Tanguy ☎ 01 43 22 47 63 🕐 Closed Mon. 💲 $ 🚇 Métro: Denfert-Rochereau

## Cimetière du Montparnasse

Montparnasse in its heyday drew literary and artistic figures. Baudelaire, Saint-Saëns, Sartre, Ionesco, and many others are buried here. 🅰 53 C1 ✉ 3 boulevard E. Quinet ☎ 01 44 10 86 50 🚇 Métro: Edgar Quinet, Raspail

## Docks en Seine

The old warehouses of the quai d'Austerlitz, next to the Bibliotheque François Mitterrand, are being transformed. Between Charles de Gaulle and Bercy bridges is the Cité de la Mode et du Design (dubbed Docks en Seine), housing the Institut Français fashion college. The green steel and glass structure, with a terrace overlooking the Seine, will house shops and restaurants. 🅰 53 E1 ✉ 34 quai d'Austerlitz 🚇 Métro: Gare d'Austerlitz

## Les Égouts (Paris Sewers)

Haussmann's vast 1850 network of sewers has become a popular tourist attraction, especially among children. 🅰 53 B3 ✉ opposite 93 quai d'Orsay ☎ 01 47 05 10 29 🕐 Closed Thurs., Fri., & Jan. 💲 $ 🚇 Métro: Alma Marceau

## Institut du Monde Arabe

An innovative 1987 building, with light-sensitive windows and transparent elevators. A museum displays Islamic metalwork, ceramics, and carpets. 🅰 53 E2 ✉ 1 rue des Fossés St.-Bernard ☎ 01 40 51 38 38 🕐 Closed Mon. 💲 $ 🚇 Métro: Jussieu, Cardinal Lemoine

**The Institut du Monde Arabe**

## Jardin des Plantes

The splendidly restored botanical gardens, with avenues of trees, a zoo, and grand greenhouses, includes the Natural History Museum with its Grand Galerie of Evolution in a 19th-century glass-domed building. 🅰 53 E2 ✉ 57 rue Cuvier 🕐 Museum closed Tues. ☎ 01 40 79 56 01 💲 $ 🚇 Métro: Monge, Gare d'Austerlitz

## Jardin Tino-Rossi

Relax among trees, lawns, and sculpture in this peaceful area beside the Seine, with views across to the Île St.-Louis. Avoid after dark. 🅰 53 E2 ✉ quai St.-Bernard 🚇 Métro: Gare d'Austerlitz

## La Mosquée

The courtyards of this mosque, inspired by the Alhambra, hide a *hammam*, or Turkish bath. 🅰 53 D2–E2 ✉ 2 place du Puits-de-l'Ermite ☎ 01 43 31 18 14 🕐 Closed Fri. 🚇 Métro: Monge

## Tour Montparnasse

The 688-foot (210 m) tower offers panoramic views from its 58th floor. 🅰 53 C2 ✉ place Rault-Dautry 💲 $$ 🚇 Métro: Montparnasse-Bienvenue

# Right Bank

The wealthy have favored this area north of the Seine ever since Charles V moved the royal residence here in the late 14th century. Palaces, elegant squares and gardens, sweeping boulevards, and grand town houses are their legacy. Recent decades have brought imaginative rejuvenation schemes to areas such as Les Halles, Beaubourg, and the Marais. Cultural life on the Right Bank (Rive Droite) ranges from the Opéra Garnier to a series of museums, including the Louvre, the largest museum in the world.

At the Palais-Royal, conceptual artist Daniel Buren's striped columns set the stage for fun.

As Paris grew in importance, so did its grand buildings—including the Tuileries, built for Catherine de Médicis but destroyed by fire in 1871, and the Palais-Royal, which began life as the residence of Cardinal Richelieu. Napoleon encouraged neoclassic schemes such as La Madeleine and the imposing Arc de Triomphe to glorify his growing empire.

The *grands projets* of the 19th century swept away earlier housing to create broad vistas along the *grands boulevards* in Baron Haussmann's major exercise in town planning.

The well-known Champs-Élysées excels as a powerful setting for state occasions, from General de Gaulle's 1944 return to Paris, to the procession celebrating the 1989 Bicentennial.

Among the Right Bank's art enclaves, dominated by the imposing Louvre, the much smaller Musée Picasso stands out for its works of art as well the building that houses them. The ornate elegance of the Hôtel Salé, built for a salt tax collector in 1656, makes a perfect backdrop for the works of this great 20th-century master. The very modern Beauborg is yet another don't-miss museum.

For elegance and style of the up-to-the-minute variety, look no further than the designer shops, jewelers, and galleries that line handsome Rue St.-Honoré and Place Vendôme. This remains the hallowed center of the world of high fashion. Indeed, the Right Bank can be seriously chic. ∎

# Champs-Élysées & the Arc de Triomphe

From an unpaved, swampy track, the Champs-Élysées has evolved into one of the world's grandest and best known avenues. In civic planner Baron Haussmann's 19th-century modernizing transformation of the city, the monumental Arc de Triomphe became the central point of 12 radiating avenues.

## Champs-Élysées

Marie de Médicis began the process of creating a sophisticated byway in 1616, and by the time landscape designer André Le Nôtre planted trees to frame the westward vista from the Louvre, her avenue was a fashionable carriage drive.

### INSIDER TIP:

**Try classic Guerlain fragrances (including Shalimar) at the company's 68 Champs-Élysées flagship shop.**

—SHEILA BUCKMASTER
National Geographic Traveler
magazine editor at large

By 1836, when the view was crowned by the Arc de Triomphe, the Champs-Élysées was firmly established as an elegant promenade.

After years of overcommercialization, the Champs-Élysées is currently undergoing a face-lift, with new stylish restaurants, several dramatic architectural projects, and the newly restored Publicis Drugstore, long a Paris landmark and now home to a bookstore, wine shop, brasserie, fancy food market, cigar store, boutiques, and two movie theaters.

## Arc de Triomphe

This great Paris landmark dominates the axis leading east down the Champs-Élysées and west down the Avenue de la Grande Armée toward La Défense. Now known as the Place Charles-de Gaulle, it is a perpetual maelstrom of swirling traffic.

Napoleon I commissioned the triumphal arch in 1806 as a tribute to his Grande Armée. It was finally completed in 1836, and Napoleon's remains passed under the arch on their way to Les Invalides in 1840.

The arch is 164 feet (50 m) high and has four massive sculptures carved on its main facades. The sculptures portray victories achieved during the 1789 Revolution and the First Empire. Inside the arch, an elevator and stairs lead up to the viewing platform with panoramas in all directions over the city. A small museum in the crosspiece has video displays about the arch.

The Unknown Soldier was buried beneath the arch in 1920. A flame is relit daily at 6:30 p.m. in a remembrance ceremony. ■

**Champs-Élysées**
- 52 B4
- Métro: Champs-Élysées Clemenceau, Franklin Roosevelt, George V

**Arc de Triomphe**
- 52 A4–B4
- place Charles de Gaulle
- 01 55 37 73 77
- $$
- Métro: Charles de Gaulle-Étoile

# Musée Picasso

An outstanding 17th-century town house in the Marais has been established as a showcase for the world's largest Picasso collection. The paintings, collages, sculptures, drawings, and ceramics are complemented by letters, photographs, and other archival material. Picasso's collection of works by his contemporaries, including Cézanne and Matisse, is also on show here.

**Musée Picasso**

⚠ 53 E3

✉ Hotel Salé, 5 rue de Thorigny

☎ 01 42 71 25 21

🕐 Closed Tues. **Note:** The entire museum is closed for renovations until 2012.

💲 $$

🚇 Métro: Chemin Vert

**www.musee-picasso .fr**

Though Picasso (1881–1973) was born in Spain, his adult life was spent almost entirely in France. During his long career he had kept many of his own works, resulting in a huge inheritance tax liability when he died. The French state claimed this in the form of works of art amounting to a quarter of the artist's collection, and then undertook a lavish refurbishment of the Hôtel Salé as a museum for them.

**INSIDER TIP:**

**Don't miss the joyful ceramics Picasso made in Provence. He crafted literally thousands of pots, jugs, plates, and figures.**

—ROSEMARY BAILEY
*National Geographic author*

With more than 250 paintings, 3,000 drawings, and 100,000 archival items, the collection is much too big to be displayed all at once. A selection representing Picasso's hugely varied output over some 70 years is always on show. The sequence is broadly chronological, so visitors can trace the artist's development .

The collection begins with works produced after Picasso's first visit to Paris from Spain in 1900, among them the bleak "Self Portrait" (1901), a masterpiece of his famous Blue Period, and "Celestine" (1904). Poignant sadness continued to pervade Picasso's work in his so-called Rose Period (1904–1906), through his harlequins and circus performers.

The rapid developments in Picasso's work during his twenties and thirties were influenced by key events in his life. In Paris, artists of the day such as Matisse, Cézanne, Braque, and Rousseau made a powerful impression on him. He often visited the Louvre. His travels, notably to Rome, Spain, and the Meditteranean, brought new themes. Primitive art from French colonies in Africa and the South Seas was becoming the object of serious interest.

In his mid-twenties, Picasso, with Georges Braque and Juan Gris, began to develop cubism, a style that aimed to depict the complete structure of an object from different angles by breaking it down into geometrical units.

Picasso's work in ceramics began with traditional techniques and moved on to ever bolder artistic experiments—a familiar trend in the work of this great genius of 20th-century art. ∎

# Beaubourg

"This will cause a stir," said President Georges Pompidou about the museum and cultural center that officially bears his name. When the project was completed by architects Renzo Piano and Richard Rogers in 1977, its design was compared to a factory.

Getting from one floor to another at the Beaubourg is a great-views experience.

Today, the Centre Georges Pompidou—generally called the Beaubourg by locals—is a familiar and much loved part of the Paris landscape. With its external glass-walled escalators, colored pipes, and massive steel struts, this icon of high-tech industrial style finally seems to fit right into the center of historic (and evolving) Paris.

A recent revamp has given the center more room to display the fine contemporary art collection of the Musée Nationale d'Art Moderne—the largest modern art museum in Europe, with works by artists including Picasso, Braque, Ernst, Magritte, Chagall, Matisse, Delaunay, Kandinsky, and Klee. Other parts of the building are devoted to temporary exhibitions, industrial design, the performing arts, film, and a vast reference library. There are several restaurants, children's facilities, and a panoramic terrace with a view over the rooftops of Paris.

Next to the museum is the Place Igor Stravinsky, famous for its colorful mobile water-fountain sculptures by Swiss sculptor Jean Tinguely and French artist Nikki de Saint Phalle. It is now a favorite gathering place, where you can listen to music, watch the jugglers and mimes, and visit the Brancusi workshop. ■

**Beaubourg**
- 🗺 53 D3
- ✉ Rue St. Martin
- ☎ 01 44 78 12 33
- 🕐 Closed Tues.
- 💲 $$
- Ⓜ Métro: Rabbouteau

**www.centre pompidou.fr**

# An Art, Park, & Palace Walk

To see Paris at its most supremely elegant, follow this walk from the Opéra to the Champs-Élysées, then through the Jardin des Tuileries to return past the Palais-Royal.

Equally lavish inside and out, Paris's legendary **Opéra Garnier** (newly restored) **1**, opened in 1875, is now devoted to ballet. From the Place de l'Opéra, take Rue de la Paix past glittering jewelry stores to the equally classy Place Vendôme, dominated by the Ritz Hotel.

Cross the square to Rue de Castiglione and turn right on Rue St.-Honoré, celebrated for its designer shops. Fork right on Rue Duphot to Place de la Madeleine. **La Madeleine 2**, with its 52 Corinthian pillars, commands a stunning vista down Rue Royale to Place de la Concorde.

From Rue Royale, turn right on Rue du Faubourg St.-Honoré, past the **Palais de l'Élysée 3**, the French president's official residence since 1873 (not open to the public). Turn left on Avenue de Marigny and walk across the Champs-Élysées to Avenue Winston Churchill, between the **Grand Palais 4** and the **Petit Palais** (tel 01 44 51 19 31, closed Mon.), both built for the 1900 Universal Exhibition. The Petit Palais houses the art collections of the City of Paris in a beautifully renovated building. In the west wing of the Grand Palais is the **Palais de la Découverte,** a science museum and planetarium (tel 01 44 13 17 17, closed Mon.).

Cross Cours la Reine to view the Seine from the elaborate Pont Alexandre III. Turn left along the embankment to **Place de la Concorde 5**, which witnessed thousands of executions during the Reign of Terror (1793–1794). The ancient Egyptian obelisk in the center overlooks eight statues representing the major French cities.

Go through the iron gates into the **Jardin des Tuileries,** originally landscaped for Catherine de Médicis's palace here in 1564. The palace was destroyed by the Communards in 1871, but its gardens have changed little since then.

The octagonal pond is flanked by two art galleries. The **Galerie Nationale du Jeu de Paume 6** (tel 01 47 03 12 50, closed Mon.), built in 1878 as a tennis court, is now a center for photography. The **Musée de l'Orangerie 7**

---

## NOT TO BE MISSED:

La Madeleine • Place de la Concorde • Jardin des Tuileries • Musée de l'Orangerie

(tel 01 44 77 80 07, closed Tues.), built in 1852, has reopened to exhibit Monet's famous "Water Lilies" in a superbly lit space.

Continue through the gardens toward the Arc de Triomphe du Carrousel, built to commemorate Napoleon's victories of 1805. Look back for the vista to the more famous Arc de Triomphe. Cross the gardens and go through the arch beneath the Louvre's north gallery to Rue de Rivoli. Turn right to Place du Palais-Royal, then left into Place des Pyramides, home of the **Comédie-Française,** still the venue for classic French theater. Walk beneath the theater's arcades to reach the **Palais-Royal** 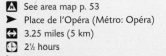. Cardinal Richelieu's palace (now government offices) is not open, but the gardens are a fine

meeting place. Walk past the arcade of shops to the left of the gardens, then turn right and left on Rue Vivienne, passing the former **Bibliothèque Nationale de France Richelieu,** whose 12 million books are now at the TGB (Très Grand Bibliothèque) in Bercy. At Rue du Quatre Septembre, opposite **La Bourse** ❾ (Stock Exchange), turn left to return to the Opéra.

| | |
|---|---|
| 🅰 | See area map p. 53 |
| ► | Place de l'Opéra (Métro: Opéra) |
| ↔ | 3.25 miles (5 km) |
| 🕐 | 2½ hours |
| ► | Place de l'Opéra |

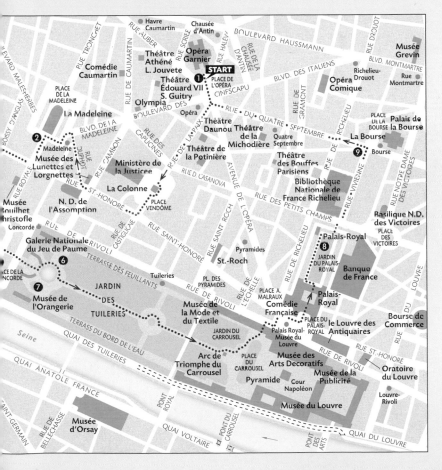

# The Louvre

Once the largest palace in the world, the Louvre was first a showcase for art during the reign of François I, who was eager to display his Italian paintings. Subsequent rulers acquired new works of art, and the Louvre in the end became one of the world's largest museums, with exhibits spanning more than seven millennia.

Controversial when unveiled in 1989, I. M. Pei's glass pyramids are now a Louvre centerpiece.

**The Louvre**

🅰 53 C3–D3

✉ Palais du Louvre

☎ 01 40 20 50 50. Recorded information: 01 40 20 51 51

🕐 Closed Tues.

💲 $$

$ Wed. & Fri. 6 p.m.–9:45 p.m.

🚇 Métro: Palais-Royal–Musée du Louvre

www.louvre.fr

The palace began as a fortress in the medieval city walls. Philippe-Auguste enlarged this tower about 1200, creating a keep surrounded by a moat. Already called the Louvre, his building served as a prison and arsenal. Excavations beneath the Cour Carrée in 1984–85 revealed some of its foundations, now on exhibit in the Sully Wing.

The Louvre's transformation into a palace began in 1385, when Charles V began to turn it into an elegant royal residence with large windows, a grand entrance, and luxurious apartments. The result was a Gothic palace fit for a king.

Succeeding monarchs preferred more fashionable residences in the Marais or on the Loire River. Not until the reign of François I (R. 1515–1547) did the Louvre regain royal favor. The cultured François had begun to collect paintings and sculptures on his travels in Italy, and he encouraged Renaissance artists such as Leonardo da Vinci and Benvenuto Cellini to come to France. Toward the end of his life, he began to plan a rebuilding of the Louvre,

INSIDER TIP:

**In the basement of the Louvre you'll find the remains of the original royal castle—including the dungeon and the base of a huge tower.**

—BARBARA NOE
*National Geographic Books editor*

in Renaissance style, as a fitting home for his collection, which included Leonardo's "Mona Lisa."

François's project was continued by Henri II. After his death in 1559, his widow, Catherine de Médicis, moved the official royal residence from the Hôtel des Tournelles to the Louvre. Between 1595 and 1607 Henri IV realized Catherine's plans for a long gallery beside the Seine, to join the Louvre to the neighboring Tuileries.

Building work in the 17th century included much of the Cour Carrée and the Colonnade at the eastern end. Progress slowed after Louis XIV moved his court to Versailles in 1682, but a great benefit of the Sun King's reign was a tenfold increase in the size of the royal art collections. Many of the Louvre's key works by major artists such as Raphael, Titian, Rubens, and Holbein were acquired during this period.

The 18th century saw the Louvre neglected and lacking a focus. Its apartments were put to various uses, from sheltering homeless artists to housing the French academies. Eventually, in 1793, the Musée Central des Arts was inaugurated at the Louvre,

which soon became the home of many treasures acquired by Napoleon I from his victories in Europe. (A large proportion of them were returned after his defeat.) Napoleon III finally completed the museum's symmetrical "grand design" and created state apartments. The Louvre continues its tradition of change in a radical reorganization and expansion program known as the "Grand Louvre" project. The Salle des États recently reopened with an entire room now dedicated to the "Mona Lisa."

Recent initiatives to support the museum include corporate sponsorship and fund-raising, extensions planned for Lens (France) and Abu Dhabi, and a new wing, with a translucent undulating roof, to house the huge collection of Islamic art.

## Paris Icon: Facts & Stats

- **40 percent of visitors are under 26.**
- **80 percent of people only come to see the "Mona Lisa," "Venus de Milo," or "Winged Victory."**
- **The director of the Louvre estimates it would take a month to see everything in the whole museum.**
- **The Louvre is expected to host 10 million visitors a year by 2014.**

## Finding Your Way

The Louvre's main entrance, in the Cour Napoléon, is through I. M. Pei's ingenious 793-panel glass pyramid. Visitors go down into the gleaming marble underworld of the reception area, known as the Hall Napoléon.

# The Louvre

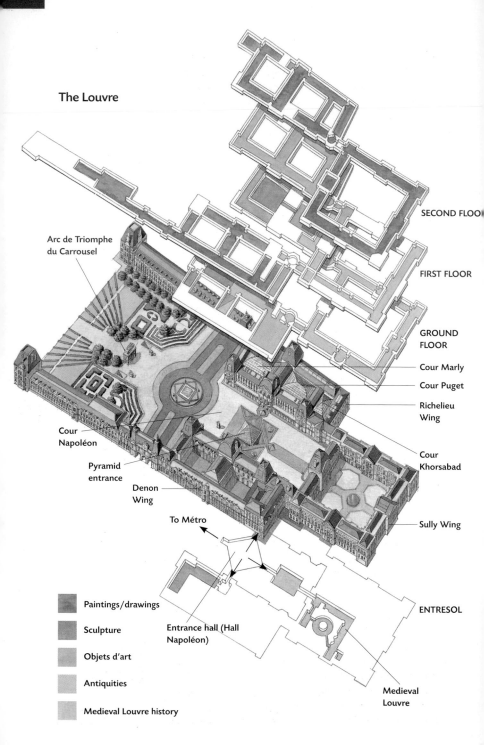

SECOND FLOOR

Arc de Triomphe
du Carrousel

FIRST FLOOR

GROUND
FLOOR

Cour Marly

Cour Puget

Richelieu
Wing

Cour
Napoléon

Cour
Khorsabad

Pyramid
entrance

Denon
Wing

To Métro

Sully Wing

Paintings/drawings

ENTRESOL

Sculpture

Entrance hall (Hall
Napoléon)

Objets d'art

Antiquities

Medieval
Louvre

Medieval Louvre history

The museum's three wings are Sully (enclosing the Cour Carrée), Denon (alongside the Seine), and Richelieu (beside the Rue de Rivoli). Each wing has four levels: entresol, ground floor, first floor, and second floor. Another entrance brings visitors in from the Carrousel du Louvre, a huge underground shopping complex, and the Métro.

With up to 30,000 artworks to choose from, the first thing you need when visiting the Louvre is some idea of what you would like to see. The second thing you need is a floor plan, available from the Information desk in the Hall Napoléon. Audio guides and guided tours are also offered.

The museum has seven departments: Oriental Antiquities; Egyptian Antiquities; Greek, Etruscan, and Roman Antiquities; Objets d'Art; Sculptures; Paintings; and Prints and Drawings. Within each department are several collections. The Sully Wing is a good place to start. Here, at the entresol level are the impressive remains of Philippe-Auguste's medieval fortress. The dungeons, the base of the towers, and the support for the moat drawbridge can be seen, together with displays of pottery and royal artifacts found during excavations.

## Ancient World

The recently expanded galleries of the Egyptian Antiquities department, on the lower floors of the Sully Wing, are easily reached from the Medieval Louvre exhibition through the Crypt of the Sphynx. The collection has two parts: the ground floor, arranged by theme (The Nile; Writing and Scribes; Music and Games), and the first floor, arranged by date. This starts with a 5,000-year-old ceremonial dagger with an intricately carved ivory handle. Room upon room of mummies, friezes, exquisite fabrics, papyrus texts, jewels, and statues make up the largest Egyptian collection outside Cairo.

The main collections representing ancient Greece and Rome are also in the Sully Wing, where you (and many other visitors!) will find the instantly recognizable "Venus de Milo," elegant as ever, on the ground floor. Don't miss the huge collection of Greek terra-cotta vases in the Galerie Campana (first floor) and the Greek and Roman glassware in the Salle des Verres. Not far away, in Napoleon III's former stables (Denon Wing, entresol), is an exciting new gallery devoted to pre-Hellenic Greece. Don't miss the Cycladic sculptures, whose simple shapes belie their early date (2,000–3,000 B.C.). Two floors up is the Louvre's second world-famous Greek statue, the graceful "Winged Victory of Samothrace" (circa 190 B.C.).

**The marble "Winged Victory of Samothrace"**

## Paintings

The Louvre's enormous collection of paintings spreads into all three wings. The second floor of the Richelieu Wing may be the best place to start. It can be reached by Pei's imaginatively designed escalator—a 1990s answer to the grand staircase of bygone days.

### Celebrating Design

To gain a deeper understanding of French interior decor, visit the recently restored **Musée des Arts Decoratifs** (*107 rue de Rivoli, tel 01 44 55 57 50, www.lesartsdecoratifs.fr*), part of the Louvre. It offers a glorious overview of furniture and ornament from the Middle Ages to the present day. Each of its superb rooms is decorated in period style. Notable are the art nouveau and art deco rooms. Also worthy of some time are the exquisite jewelry and glass collections, a reconstruction of novelist Marcel Proust's cork-lined bedroom, and the fabulous marble and bronze bathroom of couturier Jeanne Lanvin.

The northern European paintings, occupying the western part of the wing, include works by important Dutch and Flemish masters such as van Eyck, Rembrandt, the Brueghels, and Vermeer. The large Médici Gallery is a fine setting for the most ambitious work here, Rubens's epic 24-panel sequence depicting scenes from the life of Marie de Médicis, designed to adorn the Palais du Luxembourg.

A broadly chronological sequence of French pictures, from the 14th to 19th centuries, starts at the eastern end of this area and continues clockwise around the entire second floor of the Sully Wing. Worth seeking out are Watteau's enigmatic "Pierrot" (1718–19), Fragonard's "The Bathers" (1764), and paintings by Ingres, including the technically brilliant portrait of publisher Louis-François Bertin (1832) and the well-known "Turkish Bath" (1862). A number of pictures by Corot, including "The Church at Marissel" (1866), show revolutionary developments in subject matter and light, foreshadowing the Impressionist movement.

The Italian collection is based in and around the Grande Galerie on the first floor of the Denon Wing. Be sure to see Botticelli's delicate 15th-century frescoes and Raphael's portrait of his friend Baldassare Castiglione. Titian and Tintoretto are represented not only through their own paintings but also by Veronese, who is said to have depicted his fellow artists among the musicians in "The Wedding Feast at Cana" (1563). Close by is the world's most famous enigmatic smile—that of the "Mona Lisa" (1503–06), known in France as "La Joconde."

## Sculpture

French sculpture is on the lower floors of the Richelieu Wing, where three new glass-roofed courts were laid out during the conversion of the wing from government offices. The Cour Marly is named after the grand château and park that Louis XIV created just outside Paris. Not surprisingly the Sun King commissioned many fine statues

"The Wedding Feast at Cana," at the Louvre, was painted by Veronese in 1563.

for his retreat, including "Fame Riding Pegasus" (1699–1702) by Antoine Coysevox. Exhibits in the nearby Cour Puget include sculptures by Pierre Puget. His most famous work, the dynamic "Milon of Croton" (1671–1682), was commissioned by Louis XIV for Versailles.

Foreign sculpture is displayed on the lower two floors of the Denon Wing. Michelangelo's two powerful (though unfinished) "Slaves" (1513–15) are the most popular exhibits.

## Decorative Arts

The Galerie d'Apollon, on the Denon Wing's first floor, is the site of a glittering display—the crown jewels of France, including the golden scepter made for Charles V in the late 14th century and the coronation crowns of Louis XV and Napoleon.

Also here is one of the word's purest diamonds, the Regent, worn by Louis XV at his coronation in 1722.

For insight into Second Empire style at its peak, visit the sumptuously decorated and lavishly furnished state apartments of Napoleon III, at the west end of the Richelieu Wing's first floor.

Multimedia guides are now available at the Louvre, with commentaries from conservators, to help you appreciate the history of the art.

## Beyond the Louvre

Three more museums in the area, accessible from the rue de Rivoli, are the **Musée de la Mode et du Textile,** the **Musée des Arts Decoratifs** (see sidebar p. 84), and the **Musée de la Publicité,** devoted to advertising. ∎

# A Walk Around the Marais

Architectural gems of the 17th and 18th centuries—several of them now museums—highlight this stroll through a recently rejuvenated area of the city.

Pretty Place des Vosges has seen pedestrian traffic for some 400 years.

## NOT TO BE MISSED:

Place des Vosges • Musée Carnavalet • Musée Cognacq-Jay • Musée Picasso • Hôtel de Sens

The Marais (marsh), a swampy area on the Right Bank, was enclosed by King Philippe-Auguste's great wall of Paris. In the 1200s, the marsh was drained and building began. Today the area is a medley of narrow medieval streets, grand 17th-century *hôtels,* and chic little shops, galleries, and bars.

Begin at the **Place de la Bastille ❶,** famous as the site where the Bastille fort was stormed on July 14, 1789, marking the start of the French Revolution. In the 1980s, the **Opéra National de Paris-Bastille** was built in the southeast corner. Its appearance and its cost provoked much criticism. The 164-foot (50-m) column towering above the square commemorates the July 1830 Revolution.

Walk west along the busy Rue St.-Antoine and turn right on Rue de Birague for the spectacular Square Louis XIII, better known as **Place des Vosges ❷.** Commissioned by Henri IV, with two royal pavilions, the square was completed in 1612. It quickly attracted new residents such as Cardinal Richelieu and the playwright Molière. **Maison de Victor Hugo ❸** at No. 6 is a museum in memory of the writer who lived here in 1832–1848 *(tel 01 42 72 10 16, closed Mon.).* On the southwest corner is an entrance to the **Hôtel de Sully,** perhaps the most magnificent private palace in the Marais, dating from about 1630; its courtyards are open to the public. Stroll farther around the square to admire its symmetry, perhaps stopping to browse in galleries or shops, or to have lunch or a drink under the arcades of Ma Bourgogne (No. 19).

Leave the square on Rue des Francs-Bourgeois. Turn right on Rue de Sévigné for the **Musée Carnavalet ❹** *(tel 01 44 59 58 58, closed Mon.).* Part of the museum occupies the Hôtel Carnavalet, a 16th-century mansion that was the home of aristocratic writer Madame de Sévigné (1626–1696), who penned vivid accounts of life in the era of Louis XIV. The museum brings to life the history of Paris, from Roman times to the early 20th century. The extravagant decor of the 17th and 18th centuries can be seen in the beautifully renovated interiors. Some were rescued from buildings demolished by Baron Haussmann in his 19th-century remodeling of Paris.

Continue north up Rue de Sévigné. Turn left on Rue du Parc Royal and take the second left, on Rue Elzévir, to visit the remarkable **Musée Cognacq-Jay ❺** *(tel 01 40 27 07 21, closed Mon.).* Here, in the exquisite Hôtel Denon, is a superb collection of 18th-century paintings, furniture, and decorative items. Retrace your steps to Rue de Thorigny and the Hôtel Salé, now the **Musée Picasso ❻** (see p. 76).

Turn left onto Rue des Coutures-St.-Gervais

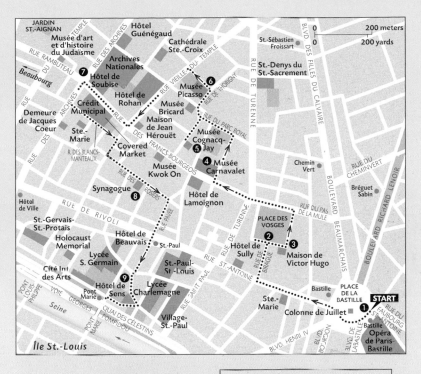

JARDIN ST.-AIGNAN
Musée d'art et d'histoire du Judaïsme
RUE RAMBUTEAU
Beaubourg
Hôtel Guénégaud
Cathédrale Ste.-Croix
Archives Nationales
Hôtel de Soubise **7**
Crédit Municipal
Demeure de Jacques Coeur
Hôtel de Rohan
Ste.-Marie
R. DES BLANCS-MANTEAUX
Covered Market
Musée Picasso **6**
Musée Bricard
Maison de Jean Hérouët
Musée Kwok On
Synagogue **8**
RUE DES ROSIERS
St.-Sébastien Froissart
St.-Denys du St.-Sacrement
BLVD. DES FILLES DU CALVAIRE
Musée Cognacq-Jay **5**
Musée Carnavalet **4**
Hôtel de Lamoignon
Chemin Vert
RUE DU CHEMINVERT
Bréguet Sabin
BOULEVARD RICHARD LENOIR
Hôtel de Ville
RUE DE RIVOLI
RUE PAVÉE
St.-Gervais-St.-Protais
Holocaust Memorial
Lycée S. Germain
Cité Int des Arts
Hôtel de Sens **9**
Pont Marie
Hôtel de Beauvais
St.-Paul
Lycée Charlemagne
St.-Paul-St.-Louis
RUE ST.-ANTOINE
RUE SAINT PAUL
PLACE DES VOSGES **2** **3**
Hôtel de Sully
RUE DE TURENNE
Maison de Victor Hugo
Bastille
PLACE DE LA BASTILLE
**START** **1**
Ste.-Marie
Colonne de Juillet
Village-St.-Paul
Île St.-Louis
Seine
QUAI DES CÉLESTINS
BLVD HENRI IV
Bastille
Opéra de Paris Bastille
RUE DU FAUBOURG ST.-ANTOINE

0 ——— 200 meters
0 ——— 200 yards

and left again down Rue Vieille-du-Temple. Pass the gates of the Hôtel de Rohan and, on the corner of Rue des Francs-Bourgeois, the pretty turret of the Maison de Jean Hérouët (private).

Turn right on Rue des Francs-Bourgeois, known for its eclectic shops, elegant mansions, and the Crédit Municipal (municipal pawnshop) at No. 55. Across the street is the impressive courtyard of the **Hôtel de Soubise 7**. This sumptuous building houses the Musée de l'Histoire de France and the National Archives (tel 01 40 27 60 96, closed Tues.). Rebuilt in 1709 from a 14th-century manor for the Princesse de Soubise, the interiors were decorated by the most talented artists of the day. On Rue du Temple, the **Musée d'art et d'histoire du Judaïsme** (71 rue du Temple, tel 01 53 01 86 53, closed Sat.) commemorates Jewish culture.

Turn left down Rue des Archives, then left on Rue des Blancs-Manteaux to the covered market. On the far side of the market, take Rue des Rosiers. This is the city's central Jewish

| | |
|---|---|
| 🗺 | See also area map p. 53 |
| ▶ | Place de la Bastille (Métro: Bastille) |
| 🚶 | 2.25 miles (3.5 km) |
| 🕐 | 2 hours |
| ▶ | Quai des Célestins (Métro: Pont Marie) |

quarter, full of specialist shops as far as Rue Pavée. Walk past the **Synagogue 8** designed in 1913 by Hector-Germain Guimard, known for his art nouveau Métro stations, then turn right at Rue Pavée. Cross Rue St.-Antoine and follow Rue du Figuier to the 15th-century **Hôtel de Sens 9** near the Pont Marie, which houses the Bibliothèque Forney, a decorative arts library (tel 01 42 78 14 60, closed Sun. & Mon.). Nearby, on Rue Geoffroy l'Asnier, is the **Holocaust Memorial,** a deeply moving testimony to the fate of the Jews in World War II, with its Wall of Names, photographs, private letters, and documentary films (tel 01 42 77 44 72, closed Sat.).

# Montmartre & Sacré-Coeur

Thirty windmills once dotted the Montmartre skyline. The steep hill that Parisians call "La Butte" now has an even more distinctive landmark: the great white Basilique du Sacré-Coeur. Although tourists flock to Montmartre today, it is still possible to stroll in quiet backwaters where streets and squares have retained a village atmosphere.

Above it all in bustling Montmartre is the stately white dome of Sacré-Coeur.

Its commanding position over-looking Paris ensured Montmartre's importance from early times. The Roman temple here probably gave the district its name (from Mons Martis, "Hill of Mars"). The 12th-century Benedictine abbey church **St.-Pierre-de-Montmartre,** one of Paris's oldest; still overlooks the Place du Tertre.

Quarries and vineyards supported Montmartre, and it remained a separate village until the quarries (and their associated windmills) had to close because of collapsing tunnels. By 1860, the Montmartre area had become the 18th *arrondissement* of the city of Paris.

The late 19th century saw Montmartre as it is most often pictured now—a focus of the exciting, if lurid, bohemian life, enjoyed by resident poets and painters. Many great names from this period can be seen on the gravestones in the **Cimetière de Montmartre** on Avenue Rachel. They include composers Hector

## INSIDER TIP:

**Instead of climbing the 200-plus steep stairs from Montmartre to Sacré-Coeur, take the small funicular.**

—MARGIE GOLDSMITH
National Geographic Traveler
*magazine writer*

Berlioz and Jacques Offenbach (who wrote the famous cancan), writers Stendhal and Émile Zola, and painter Edgar Degas. Film director François Truffaut and Russian dancer Vaslav Nijinsky are also buried here.

Today the creative ferment of the belle epoque has been replaced by the engaging street artists at work on the **Place du Tertre,** a prime stop on the sightseeing circuit.

Visible from almost anywhere in Paris, the stark white **Basilique du Sacré-Coeur** was started in 1876 by the French government to honor the 58,000 killed in the Franco-Prussian War and to atone for the "crimes" of the Commune. Pillars had to be driven deep into unstable rock to support the enormous church, which was finally consecrated in 1919. Inside the basilica, the chancel vaulting is decorated with a colossal square mosaic (1912–1922) by Luc-Olivier Merson. It depicts the French nation worshiping the Sacred Heart of Christ.

Steep spiral stairs lead to the dome, where an exterior gallery—the second highest point in the city, after the Tour Eiffel—commands a spectacular panorama of Paris. Given the high elevation of the street, views at ground level are almost as stunning. ■

**Basilique du Sacré-Coeur**

🅰 53 D5
✉ place du Parvis du Sacré-Coeur
☎ 01 53 41 89 00
💲 Crypt & dome $
Ⓜ Métro: Abbesses, Anver, Caulaincourt

**www.sacre-coeur -montmartre.com**

## Artists in Montmartre

Paris has long been an inspirational magnet for artists, both French and foreign, who have come here and made it their home. With its picturesque streets, bohemian ways, and cheap lodging houses, Montmartre began to attract impoverished artists in the 19th century. Legendary cafés and clubs—Le Chat Noir, Au Lapin Agile, La Nouvelle Athènes—became known as literary and artistic meeting places.

The Moulin Rouge, the famous night spot on Boulevard de Clichy, opened its doors in 1889. Henri de Toulouse-Lautrec was a regular visitor, often sketching and painting as he sat in the dance hall. Dancers and cabaret *artistes* of the louche Montmartre world, such as Aristide

Bruant, Jane Avril, and Yvette Guilbert, were immortalized in his posters. Another Montmartre dance hall, the Moulin de la Galette, was the subject of paintings by Renoir, Bonnard, and others.

Montmartre's streets are peppered with memories of famous artists. Boulevard de Clichy, painted by van Gogh and Renoir, was a focal point. Seurat, Signac, and, later, Picasso all had studios here. Degas died at No. 6 in 1917. The squalid Bateau-Lavoir building, where Picasso lived from 1904 to 1909, was shared by 30 other residents, many of them artists. The building (at No. 13 Place Émile-Goudeau) is gone now—but the clowns and harlequins of the Montmartre circus world live on in Picasso's paintings.

# La Défense

Paris has frequently hit the headlines for its daring new architectural exploits, such as the Opéra-Bastille and the Beaubourg (see p. 77). But of all of these *grands travaux,* none has been more ambitious than the controversial space-age development at La Défense, dominated by the truly monumental Grande Arche.

The Grande Arche majestically dominates La Défense.

**Grande Arche**

- 🗺 52 A4
- ✉ esplanade de La Défense
- ☎ 01 49 07 27 27
- 💲 $$
- 🚇 Métro: Grande Arche de la Défense

**www.grande arche.com**

**Dôme Imax**
- ☎ 08 36 67 06 06

The entirely modern district of La Défense, located to the west of Paris across the Pont de Neuilly, takes its name from a statue in the central square, symbolizing the defense of Paris in the 1870 Franco-Prussian War.

A broad pedestrian avenue, the Esplanade du Général de Gaulle, rises in steps from the Pont de Neuilly to give access to office towers, apartment blocks, the vast shopping complex of Les Quatre-Temps, and the CNIT. The oldest building on the site (1958), the triangular CNIT building is now an international business and conference center. Roads and railroads run beneath the buildings, leaving the main areas traffic free. More

than 70 works of contemporary sculpture punctuate the concrete landscape.

The focal point of La Défense is the colossal **Grande Arche.** Designed by Danish architect Johann Otto von Spreckilsen, it was completed for the Bicentennial of the Revolution in 1989. Shaped like a huge hollow cube and faced with glass and white marble, this "window on the world" is so vast that Notre-Dame would easily fit beneath it. The walls of the arch contain government and company offices. External glass elevators can take visitors up to the roof to admire the views over Paris from a height of more than 300 feet (100 m). Be sure to look to the southeast, where a dramatic corridor cuts a swath straight across the city. Stretching to the Arc de Triomphe and beyond, it continues along the same axis to the Place de la Concorde and the Bastille. The Grande Arche was deliberately aligned on this historic "Triumphal Way."

At the base of the arch, fountains and cafés enliven the square of La Défense. Beside the Grande Arche, the spherical grid-covered **Dôme IMAX** encloses one of the world's largest cinema screens. There are fountains and sculptures by artists including Miró, Serra, Calder, and César. ∎

# Parc de la Villette & Cité des Sciences

An astonishing transformation has taken place in northeast Paris. The former livestock market and slaughterhouses of La Villette are now a futuristic cultural park and interactive science museum. Allow a full day to make the most of a visit—there is lots to see and do.

Adults and children alike will be enthralled by the Parc de la Villette's star attraction, the **Cité des Sciences et de l'Industrie.** This vast science museum occupies a former cattle auction hall, innovatively converted by Adrien Fainsilber. Notice how his designs play with the light reflected off water, steel, and glass.

### INSIDER TIP:

**To get to this part of Paris, rent a bicycle (see p. 94) and follow the canal de l'Ourcq. Enjoy the views!**

—CHRISTEL CHERQAOUI
*National Geographic Books
promotion director*

**Explora,** the main exhibition, invites visitors to find out about the universe, from space to volcanoes and the oceans, through its range of interactive presentations. Greenhouses and the aquarium focus on the living world.

To see the stars, make your way up to the **Planétarium** on the second floor. Its 10,000-lens astronomical projector throws images of some 5,000 stars onto the impressive 68-foot (21 m) hemispherical dome.

Children will love the robots and rockets, the sound bubble, and the room of optical illusions. In addition, the **Cité des Enfants** (ages 3–12) encourages children to experiment with scientific theories and techniques, for example, building houses and programming computers.

Reflecting sky and water in front of the building is the shiny steel of the **Géode,** which contains an enormous curved IMAX cinema screen *(tel 08 92 68 45 40, closed Mon.).* Next to the Géode lies the submarine *Argonaute,* built in 1957, and the Cinaxe *(tel 01 40 05 79 99, www.lageode.fr),* a mobile projection room simulating high-speed flight.

Bridges across the Canal de l'Ourcq lead into the landscaped southern area, with playgrounds and cafés. From mid-July to the end of August there is a free open-air cinema, which includes English-language films.

A portion of the original cattle market, the Grande Halle, is now an exhibition and concert hall, while the Zénith is a venue for rock concerts. The **Cité de la Musique** *(tel 01 44 84 45 00)* is a resource center for music and dance. ■

**Parc de la Villette**
- 53 E5
- 01 40 03 75 75
- Métro: Porte de la Villette

www.villette.fr

**Cité des Sciences et de l'Industrie**
- 30 avenue Corentin Cariou
- 01 40 05 70 00
- Closed Mon.
- $$$
- Métro: Porte de la Villette

www.cites-sciences.fr

# A Shoppers' Paradise

From tiny boutiques in medieval streets to elegant, world-famed department stores, Paris is a shopper's paradise. Whatever you wish for is here in this Aladdin's cave of a city—at a price! If your purse does not stretch to haute couture or diamond necklaces, it is still fun to browse through the arcades and hunt for bargains in markets or among the stalls alongside the Seine.

The giant glass dome of Galeries Lafayette lights three floors of enticing merchandise.

## Specialty Shopping

Some streets and areas have particular specialties. On the Île St.-Louis you will find unusual boutiques and restaurants (and the capital's best ice cream, at Berthillon). The *bouquinistes*, booksellers, with their ramshackle stalls along Quai de Montebello, are a particular Parisian delight. Flowers, birds, and animals are for sale in Place Louis-Lépine and on Quai de la Mégisserie.

The area around the chic Boulevard St.-Germain brims with galleries and antiques, especially on Rue Bonaparte and Rue des Sts.-Pères. Collectors of first editions head for Rue Jacob.

In the Marais, the Rue du Temple and the parallel Rue des Archives are known for leather goods and jewelry, while the arcaded shops of the Place des Vosges sell antiques, art, fashions, and books.

## Fashion Capital

For centuries the world has been influenced by fashion trends from Paris. It is still home to the most prestigious couturiers and a mecca for the design-conscious. Serious haute-couture seekers head for Avenue Montaigne, where nearly all the top names have their premises. Chanel, Givenchy, Dior, Cartier, and now Ralph Lauren are all here. Fabergé maintains a long tradition of displaying jewelry at astronomical prices.

Rue du Faubourg St.-Honoré is ultra-fashionable and high end. Expensive antiques galleries, furriers, perfumeries, crystal and caviar shops, and designers Gucci, Hermès, Lagerfeld, and Lacroix all encourage the well-heeled to

## EXPERIENCE: Browsing the Flea Markets

The *puces* or flea markets located at the gates *(portes)* of Paris are a treasure trove for anyone who likes hunting for bargains, searching out antiques or vintage clothing, or simply enjoying the constantly changing panorama of a Parisian market. Most famous is the **Saint Ouen** *(avenue de la Porte de Clignancourt, tel 08 92 70 57 65, Sat.–Mon. 10 a.m.–5 p.m.)*, which is huge, with more than 2,000 exhibitors offering a range of quality antiques, clothing, and objets d'art. Although the main drag tends to be full of tourists and T-shirts, the warren of narrow passages around the market remains as intriguing as a Moroccan souk. **Montreuil** *(avenue de la Porte de Montreuil, Sat. & Sun. 7 a.m.–8 p.m.)* is the place for knickknacks, secondhand bikes, furniture, and clothes. Vanves *(Porte de Vanves & avenue Georges-Lafenestre, Sat. & Sun. 7 a.m.–5 p.m.)* is essentially a secondhand market overflowing with a huge variety of stuff, from old toys to paintings.

Carry cash, and by all means exercise your bargaining skills—it's all part of the fun! For more market options: *www.parispuces.com*. You can also visit the city's vintage boutiques with the help of Ooh la la Vintage *(www.oohlalavintage.com)*.

part with their euros. Exclusive jewelers, such as Van Cleef et Arpels, line Rue de la Paix and Place Vendôme. Less expensive are the dress shops on Rue de Rivoli, which is unfortunately also crammed with tacky souvenir shops.

### Galleries & Arcades

In the 19th century, fashionable Parisians shopped in the 140 covered galleries of the Right Bank. Fewer than 30 remain. Hardly changed since they were built, the Galerie Véro-Dodat, Galerie Colbert, and Galerie Vivienne make harmonious settings for restaurants, galleries, and antiques and contemporary design shops.

The area between Rue de Rivoli and Boulevard de Sébastopol is crisscrossed with glass-roofed walkways, such as the passages Molière, des Princes, des Panoramas, and du Claire. Also relics of a veritable warren of 19th-century arcades, they now shelter a host of specialty shops and unusual eating places.

### Department Stores & Shopping Centers

Paris's celebrated department stores offer clothes, accessories, and household goods. Printemps and the Galeries Lafayette are

near the Opéra district, known as the *quartier des grands magasins*. Bazar de l'Hôtel de Ville (BHV), good for household and do-it-yourself items, is on Rue de Rivoli. Au Bon Marché, on the Left Bank, has a fine food section.

Covered shopping continues to be popular, and there are modern underground complexes at Forum des Halles (site of the former central market, undergoing major renovation) and the Carrousel du Louvre, off Avenue du Général Lemonnier. The Galeries des Champs-Élysées are worth exploring for their elegant boutiques, while Les Quatre-Temps at La Défense is one of the largest shopping centers in Europe.

There are also designer outlets in Serris *(www.lavalleevillage.com)*, a 35-minute drive from the center of Paris (shuttle service available).

# More Places to Visit on the Right Bank

## Bois de Boulogne

This huge expanse of parkland, forest, and lakes offers boating, fishing, cycling, horseback riding, horse racing, and a popular children's playground, the Jardin d'Acclimatation. 52 A4 Métro: Porte d'Auteuil (south), Les Sablons, Porte Maillot (north)

---

## EXPERIENCE:
## Paris by Bike

**Vélib** *(www.velib.paris.fr)*, a hugely successful self-service bike-rental company, offers more than 20,000 bikes at more than 1,450 locations in Paris. There are 231 miles (371 km) of bicycle routes, with more planned outside the city. Prices start from 1 euro plus a refundable deposit. You will need a credit card to make the deposit.

---

## Château & Bois de Vincennes

Set in a large landscaped park east of Paris, the château has a moated 14th-century keep, a Gothic chapel, and royal apartments. More recent additions include a Buddhist center, a theater complex, and a zoo. 52 F2 $$ Métro: Château de Vincennes

## Cimetière du Père-Lachaise

Located just beyond the city center but worth the trip, this vast, much visited cemetery is full of fantastic tomb designs and memorials to a host of famous people (including Héloïse and Abélard, Chopin, Molière, Victor Hugo, Édith Piaf, Oscar Wilde, and Jim Morrison). *www .pere-lachaise.com* 52 F3 boulevard de Ménilmontant $ Métro: Père Lachaise

## Musée d'Art Moderne de la Ville de Paris

A showcase for living artists, this collection also covers earlier 20th-century art movements, including the École de Paris, cubism, and 1960s pop art. Artists represented here include Bonnard, Soutine, Picasso, Gris, Arp, Matisse, Dufy, and Utrillo. *www.mam. paris.fr* 52 B3 11 avenue du Président Wilson 01 53 67 40 80 Closed Mon. $ Métro: Iéna, Alma Marceau

## Musée Marmottan

Not to be missed, this museum housed in an elegant 19th-century mansion has a fabulous Monet collection; among the works of art are some of the "Water Lilies" paintings. Renoir, Sisley, and Gauguin are also represented. And there are sculptures, furniture, and medieval manuscripts. 52 A3 2 rue Louis-Boilly 01 44 96 50 53 Closed Mon. $$ Métro: La Muette

## INSIDER TIP:

**Beyond the city is the Cimetière des Chiens (Métro stop Mairie de Clichy), where beloved pets are given exquisite tributes.**

—SHEILA BUCKMASTER
National Geographic Traveler *magazine
editor at large*

## Palais de Chaillot

The curved wings and vast terrace of this 1937 edifice form the backdrop of many classic pictures of the Tour Eiffel. Inside are several museums, including the **Musée de l'Homme,** scheduled to reopen in 2013; the **Musée de la Marine** *(tel 01 53 65 69 69),* a maritime museum; and the **Cité de l'Architecture et du Patrimoine,** the new museum of Monuments Français, devoted to the history of architecture and building. *www.citechaillot.fr* 52 A3 place du Trocadéro Closed Tues. $$ Métro: Trocadéro

# Île-de-France

Not literally an island, though largely bounded by rivers, the Île-de-France comprises the region ruled over by Hugh Capet when he was declared King of France in 987. Although his kingdom nominally extended over western and southern Gaul, he only controlled an area of 60 by 120 miles (100 by 200 km). Well populated even then, it is an area rich in art and architecture. St.-Denis, a royal burial place, was the site of the first French cathedral. Sèvres is famous for its 18th-century porcelain factory, and Meudon has a museum with works of Rodin. The elegance of Meaux and the charm of medieval Provins underscore the area's cultural richness.

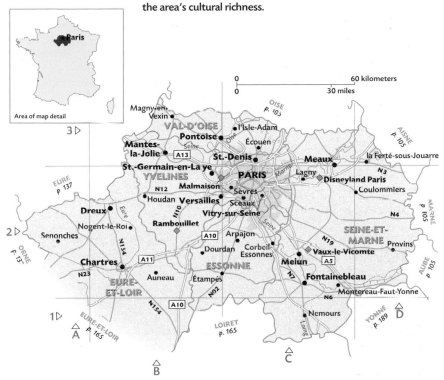

With roots as far back as Roman times, this is France's royal heartland, littered with sumptuous châteaux and gardens. The most grandiose of all, of course, is the 17th-century palace of Versailles, closely followed by its precursor, the magnificent château of Vaux-le-Vicomte, a baroque French masterpiece.

A great number of smaller châteaux testify to the popularity of the area as a country retreat over the centuries. The intimate Malmaison was home to Empress Josephine in her last years, while Champs-sur-Marne belonged to Madame de Pompadour, stylish mistress of Louis XV. The forest and château of Fontaine-bleau have inspired generations of painters.

Just beyond the Île de France is the town of Chartres, best known for the stained-glass windows in its exquisite cathedral. ∎

# Château de Versailles

In 1661, Louis XIV decided to build the ultimate royal residence at Versailles, 12 miles (17 km) from Paris. For nearly 50 years, the greatest artists of the time worked on the château: Louis Le Vau and then Jules Hardouin-Mansart were the architects; André Le Brun supervised the interior decoration; and André Le Nôtre designed the gardens.

Versailles remains a grand testament to wealth, power, and artistic achievement.

**Château de Versailles**

🅰 95 B2
✉ 12 miles (17 km) southwest of Paris
☎ 01 30 83 78 00
🕐 Closed Mon.
💲 $$
🚇 RER line C: Château de Versailles. Or SNCF train from Paris Montparnasse or Paris St.-Lazare

**www.chateau versailles.fr**

The king and his court—some 5,000 people, rising later to 20,000—moved in during 1682. Versailles became the political heart of France until October 1789, when the revolutionary mob invaded the palace and carried Louis XVI and Queen Marie-Antoinette off to captivity in Paris. During the Revolution, the furniture was sold, the paintings sent to the Louvre, and the buildings abandoned. In 1837, Louis-Philippe converted it into a museum of French history; in 1919, the Treaty of Versailles, bringing to an end World War I, was signed in the Hall of Mirrors. Only after that did any serious restoration begin.

The château was built around Louis XIII's small hunting lodge, whose brick front is still visible in the Marble Courtyard. Le Vau built the first enlargement in the 1660s, a series of wings that expanded into a courtyard. Columns were added to the west facade and a great terrace was created on the first floor. In 1678, the huge north and south wings and the Hall of Mirrors were created.

The private apartments of the King and Queen are arranged around the Marble Courtyard. In the north wing the Great Staircase leads visitors up to the Grands Appartements, extravaganzas of colored marble, gilt bronze, silk and velvet drapes, trompe l'oeil murals, and paintings and sculptures. Each state room is dedicated to an Olympian deity. The Salon de Diane, its decor based on the themes of Diana and hunting, once served as a billiard room, a game at which Louis XIV excelled. The Salon de Mars displays the first of a series of beautiful Savonnerie carpets woven in the reign of Louis XVI for the Great Gallery in the Louvre. The Throne Room of Louis XIV, the Sun King, is dedicated (needless to say) to Apollo, god of the sun.

A multimillion-dollar renovation began in 2003 with the cleaning of the Hall of Mirrors. It is supported by the American Friends of Versailles, a nonprofit organization based in Chicago.

## Hall of Mirrors

In 1678, Louis XIV built the Galerie des Glaces, Hall of Mirrors,

**INSIDER TIP:**

Worth a visit for its historic marketplace and Potager du Roi garden, Versailles (the town) is 14 miles (23 km) southwest of Paris.

—DOUG COLLIGAN
National Geographic Traveler
*magazine writer*

to enhance the magnificence of the palace and glorify his stature. Flanked by the ornate salons of "War" and "Peace," this vast, recently restored room, 230 feet (70 m) long, has 17 huge mirrors—an ostentatious display of wealth in the days when mirrors were staggeringly expensive. Further embellishments include

## The Palace Gardens

Landscaping work on some 2,000 acres (815 ha) created an extensive series of formal gardens with statues, fountains, a kitchen garden, a vast artificial lake, and even a zoo. Laid out by André Le Nôtre, 247 acres (100 ha) of gardens radiate from the west facade of the château. The apotheosis of 17th-century French formal style, their rigid symmetry and tamed version of nature reflect the classical ideals of the period.

The Grand Canal serves as the landscape's focal point, with ponds, fountains, sculptures, flower beds, lawns, groves, and shady retreats placed around it. Exquisitely gilded gondolas once plied its waters; today, handsome white-and-red rowboats can be rented.

The most impressive of Versailles's 300 statues grace the Water Garden, the

Pyramid Fountain in the North Garden, and the Apollo Fountain in the Apollo Basin at the end of the Royal Avenue and start of the Grand Canal. Allegorical references to the sun god Apollo pervade the palace's decorative scheme—above all, the superb figure of Apollo rising triumphantly in the Chariot of the Sun.

Beyond the North Garden, the Water Avenue leads to the Basin of Neptune, the central figure bordered by 22 fountains, each with a marble basin supported by charming bronze statues of children.

Within the garden's formal design are a variety of architectural follies, and one grove—decorated with shells, rock gardens, and ornamental lamps—is where the court danced in summer. A marble colonnade provided an elegant setting for palace festivities.

**Fountains**

🕐 The fountains play Sat.–Sun. & some bank holidays April–Oct. 11 a.m.–noon & 3:30–5:30 p.m.

crystal chandeliers and silver furniture (including a throne).

## Bedchambers & Beyond

From 1701, Louis XIV was in the habit of granting private audiences and dining informally in the royal bedchamber. The ceremonies of the king's *levée* (rising) and *couchée* (retiring) were also held here, and it was here that Louis XIV died in September 1715 after reigning for 72 years. The bed alcove is lined with velvet, gold, silver, and brocade; most paintings were chosen by Louis XIV.

The Queen's State Bedchamber, with its balustrade, canopied

the royal family and members of the highest nobility sitting on the upper floor with the courtiers below. The interior of the chapel is gloriously decorated in marble, gilding, and baroque murals.

The Theater was inaugurated in 1770 for the wedding of Marie-Antoinette to Louis XVI. It seated 1,000; today there is room for an audience of about 700 spectators. As was usual with court theaters, it also doubled as a ballroom.

Louis-Philippe's museum, with some 8,000 paintings and sculptures devoted to the history

bed, and silk hangings, has been restored to look as it did when Marie-Antoinette left in 1789, never to return. In this room, in full view of members of the court, various queens of France gave birth to 19 royal children.

The two-story baroque chapel, dedicated to St. Louis and finished in 1710, was Louis XIV's final addition to Versailles. Here, Masses were said for military victories and the baptisms and weddings of princes were celebrated, of France in the 17th and 18th centuries, is housed in the north wing. The huge Battle Gallery is lined with paintings celebrating French feats of arms from 496 to 1809.

## Grand & Petit Trianon

The Italianate Grand Trianon was built for Louis XIV in 1687 as a retreat. The Petit Trianon was for Louis XV's mistress Madame du Barry. Louis XVI gave the neoclassical jewel to Marie-Antoinette. She turned its grounds into an English-style park and built her famous hamlet, complete with a farm, in which she and her court play-acted an idealized form of rural life ■

Grand Canal

Apollo Basin

Latona Basin

Chapel

Theater

Statue of Louis XIV

**Château de Versailles**

# Chartres

The modest town of Chartres, located about 45 miles (75 km) southwest of Paris just outside the Île-de-France, boasts a magnificent cathedral considered one of the greatest surviving examples of 13th-century Gothic architecture. Its asymmetrical spires rise majestically above the town and the surrounding countryside, a perfect monument to the medieval fervor for building to the glory of God.

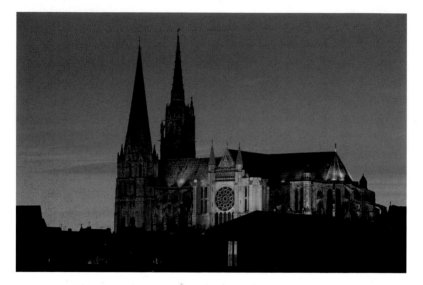

The Chartres cathedral, with its 13th-century stained-glass rose window, is a popular Paris day trip.

**Chartres**

▲ 95 B2

**Visitor information**

✉ place de la Cathédrale

☎ 02 37 18 26 26

www.chartres.com

**Musée des Beaux-Arts**

✉ Cloître Notre-Dame

☎ 02 37 36 41 39

⊕ Closed Sun. a.m. & all Tues.

💲 $

## Cathedral

Dedicated to the Virgin Mary, the first cathedral here was built (reputedly on the site of a Druid temple) to house a precious relic of her veil donated by Charles the Bald in the late ninth century. It is still displayed in the Treasury. Chartres immediately became an important center of pilgrimage, which it remains to this day. Fire destroyed the first shrine and four successive churches, the last in 1194, but contributions to the rebuilding poured in from every side. Completed in a record 30 years,

the new cathedral preserves the Romanesque west front and the south tower of the earlier building. The rest of the cathedral, with its flying buttresses, is pure Gothic. The triple portal of the west front and its recessed statues, devoted to the glory of Christ, are superb examples of Romanesque carving. The sculptures on the north portal (circa 1230) are devoted to the Old Testament, and those on the south (1225–1250) to the New Testament.

The **Clocher Vieux,** at 345 feet (105 m), is the tallest

## INSIDER TIP:

**As you gaze at the cathedral's stained glass, think of how technologically advanced it must have seemed to pilgrims in the Middle Ages.**

—DIANA PARSELL
*National Geographic contributor*

Romanesque steeple in existence; the **Clocher Neuf** has a slightly taller Gothic spire, added after lightning damage in the 16th century. A strenuous 378-step climb up the tower leads to tremendous views from the top.

**Inside:** The breathtaking interior is illuminated by 176 incomparable stained-glass windows, covering a total area of 27,000 square feet (2,500 sq m). Most date from the 13th century, though the west facade contains three that survived the fire of 1194. The rose windows depict the events of the Apocalypse, the life of the Virgin, and the Last Judgment.

The floor of the nave features a circular **labyrinth** (usually obscured by chairs) representing good and evil, with paradise at its center. Medieval pilgrims would crawl the 920-foot-long (280 m) path. The unusually broad choir is surrounded by a stone wall sculpted with a filigree pattern and with scenes from the life of Christ and the Virgin arranged in 41 groups of about 200 figures. Behind the choir, in the Chapelle

St.-Piat, is the **Treasury.** The 11th-century crypt, entered via the Maisons des Clercs, is the largest in France and encloses another crypt dating from the ninth century.

## The Town

The Eure River creates a picturesque backdrop to the quiet town, with old washhouses and drying lofts along its banks. The medieval town has some fine architectural features, particularly on Rue du Cheval Blanc and also at 35 rue des Ecuyers and 12 rue des Grenets. The former bishop's

### Maison Picassiette

✉ 22 rue du Repos
☎ 02 37 90 45 95
🕐 Closed Tues.
&  Sun. a.m. &
Nov.–March

💲 $

---

## Walking Encyclopedia

Malcolm Miller *(e-mail: millerchartres@aol .com)* is the world authority on Chartres—he has devoted his life to the study of this magnificent cathedral. After completing his education in Britain, he began doing tours in 1958; in his late 70s, he is still going strong. For a real appreciation of all aspects of the architecture, particularly the remarkably preserved stained glass, and the world that produced it, join his group tour *(March–Oct., noon and 2:45 p.m., except Sun.; private tours can be arranged).*

---

palace, which still has some state rooms, now houses the **Musée des Beaux-Arts,** with collections including enamels; tapestries; 18th-century French paintings, notably by Chardin and Fragonard; and contemporary works, including a room of Vlamincks. Amateurs of the bizarre will enjoy **Maison Picassiette,** where Raymond Isidore devoted his life to decorating every surface and object with fragments of china and glass. ∎

# Château de Fontainebleau

This lovely château, situated 37 miles (60 km) south of Paris, started life in the tenth century as a hunting lodge in the huge forest of Fontainebleau and quickly became a favorite retreat of the kings of France. Beginning in 1527, François I rebuilt it as a château, importing Italian artists to design the interior. Within a few years, their mannerist style became known as the school of Fontainebleau, subsequently exerting a major influence on French painting.

Once a hunting lodge, Fontainebleau is one of the largest châteaus in France today.

**Fontainebleau**
95 C2

**Château de Fontainebleau**
01 60 71 50 70
Closed Tues. (except gardens)
$$

www.musee-chateau -fontainebleau.fr

Many French monarchs were born at Fontainebleau and several died here. The château also witnessed the fateful revocation of the Edict of Nantes in 1685 (see p. 25) and Napoleon's abdication as Emperor of the French in 1814.

The interior is magnificently decorated with paneling, stucco, and frescoes—most famously in the Galerie François I. Other highlights at the château include the 98-foot-long (30 m) Salle de Bal, the Galerie Henri II, and the salon of Marie de Médicis. The apartments of Napoleon I are in pure Empire style.

The beautiful forest of deciduous woodland offers opportunities for walking, cycling, horseback riding, and rock climbing. ■

## Barbizon School

The mid-1800s saw a move toward greater realism in landscape painting, pioneered by Jean-Baptiste Corot and Gustave Courbet in France, and British artist John Constable. Influenced by their ideas, a group of painters, led by Théodore Rousseau, settled in the village of Barbizon in Fontainebleau forest. Working outdoors and taking scenes from peasant life, they produced shimmering landscapes and touching tableaus. The charming village features several house museums devoted to the artists, including Jean-François Millet's house *(27 Grande Rue, tel 01 60 66 21 55)*, which is jam-packed with his paintings. The Office de Tourism is in Rousseau's former house *(tel 01 60 66 41 87)*.

# Short Excursions from Paris

## Cathedrale St.-Denis

According to legend, St. Denis was beheaded on Montmartre in A.D. 262. He then picked up his head and walked 6,000 paces north before expiring. There the abbey church of St.-Denis was built, his tomb becoming a shrine. Clovis, king of the Franks, was buried here in 511 to be joined the following year by Ste. Geneviève, patron saint of Paris. By 1143, a great Gothic cathedral stood here, the first example of the new style in Europe. Massively damaged during the Revolution, the cathedral was partially restored in the 19th century. Today only the choir and west front authentically reflect the original. The cathedral is the mausoleum of the French monarchy, with some 60 funeral monuments carved by the greatest sculptors from the 13th century onward. Louis IX commissioned monuments for his predecessors, the most remarkable being King Dagobert's tomb. The later graves are very elaborate, particularly the Renaissance monument of Henri II and Catherine de Médicis. The crypt contains the collective grave of the Bourbon dynasty.
🅼 95 C3 ✉ rue de la Légion d'Honneur, St.-Denis ☎ 01 48 09 83 54 💲 $$

## Chantilly

The Chantilly châteaus (see p. 118) make a pleasant day's outing from Paris.

## Château de Malmaison

Empress Joséphine, first wife of Napoleon, bought this elegant château in 1799 and died there in 1814. It houses an extensive collection of Empire paintings and decorative arts. The Château Bois-Préau, next door, is devoted to souvenirs of Napoleon.
🅼 95 B2 ✉ avenue du Château, Rueil-Malmaison ☎ 01 41 29 05 55 🕒 Closed Tues. 💲 $$

## Château de Rambouillet

Since 1897, the château of Rambouillet has been the presidential summer residence, but it is open to the public when the president is not there. Only the round tower of the original 1375 fortress remains. The rest was rebuilt in 1706 for Louis XIV's illegitimate son, the Count of Toulouse. Here Louis XVI bred the noted Rambouillet sheep, known for their resistance to heat and drought, and built a dairy and grotto in the park for the amusement of his wife, Marie-Antoinette.
🅼 95 B2 ☎ 01 34 83 00 25 🕒 Closed Tues. 💲 $$

## Château de Vaux-le-Vicomte

The inspiration for Versailles, this outstanding baroque château built by Nicholas Fouquet, one of Louis XIV's ministers, was the first project on which the formidable team of architect Louis Le Vau, painter Charles Le Brun, and landscape gardener André Le Nôtre worked together. On the château's completion in 1661, Fouquet held a lavish party and banquet, to which he invited Louis XIV. Supper was served on 432 gold plates and 6,000 silver plates; 1,200 fountains framed the entertainment, written and performed by Molière and his troupe; and the evening culminated with spectacular fireworks. Unfortunately, just before the feast, Louis was told that Fouquet had embezzled state funds. Fouquet was arrested and Vaux-le-Vicomte confiscated. The candlelight tours and dinners *(July–Aug.)*, lit by over a thousand flickering candle flames, are breathtaking. Fountain displays 2nd & last Sat, April–Oct. 3–6 p.m. 🅼 95 C2 ✉ Maincy ☎ 01 64 14 41 90 🕒 Closed Jan.–Feb & Wed. except July & Aug. 💲 $$–$$$

## Disneyland Paris

The vast theme park and resort of Disneyland Paris covers nearly 5,000 acres (2,000 ha) at Marne-la-Vallée. RER line

## Resistance Celebrated

A 19th-century villa on the banks of the Marne River houses the Musée de la Résistance Nationale *(Parc Vercors, 88 avenue Marx-Dormoy, Champigney-sur-Marne, tel 01 48 81 00 80, www.musee-resistance.com, closed Mon., Sat.& Sun. a.m, Sept., $)* devoted to the history of the French Resistance. It offers a comprehensive and fascinating overview of France during World War II. A vast array of photographs, films, personal testimonies, and memorabilia, including a railway saboteur's kit, document the story. The exhibitions take you from the pre-war political background to the Fall of France, Nazi occupation and Vichy collaboration, the concentration camps, and the gradual development of internal resistance. Treasures include clandestine publications, the photographs of Robert Doisneau, and the original manuscript of Paul Eluard's famous poem "Liberté."

A4 whisks visitors from the Gare de Lyon in central Paris directly into the park. The Magic Kingdom offers over 50 rides in Fantasyland, Adventureland, Discoveryland, and Frontierland. Pirates, a haunted house, a giant treehouse, and Main Street U.S.A. parades add to the fun. Walt Disney Studios takes you behind the scenes. There are also seven themed hotels, campsites, restaurants, stores, golf, tennis, and nighttime entertainment. *www.disneylandparis.com* ▲ 95 C2 ✉ Marne-la-Vallée, about 20 miles (32 km) east of Paris ☎ 08 25 30 60 30 💲 $$$$$. Entrance fee includes all rides

### Giverny & Monet

The village of Giverny *(Map p. 139 F2)*, in the Seine Valley between Paris and Rouen, contains the house where Claude Monet lived from 1883 until his death in 1926. Gardens (including the famous water garden), studios, and house, lovingly restored as Monet himself designed them, are a delight: the house with its yellow walls and tile floors, Monet's own furniture and Japanese prints, the shutters and garden furniture still painted in the exact green chosen by the master. Maintained by **Fondation Claude Monet** *(84 rue Claude Monet, Giverny, tel 02 32 51 54 18, www.fondationmonet.fr, $$)*

Also in Giverny is the **Musée des Impressionnismes** *(tel 02 32 51 94 65, www.museedesimpressionnismesgiverny.com, closed Nov-March)*—formerly the Musée d'art Americain)—devoted to the colony of Impressionist artists who came here, including Americans Winslow Homer and Mary Cassatt, and to the global impact of Impressionism.

## MAC/VAL Musée d'Art Contemporain du Val-de-Marne

This museum just outside Paris is devoted to French art of the past 50 years, with works by Picasso, Miró, Tinguely, César, and others, in a stunning glass building in a huge park. *www.macval.fr* ✉ Place de la Libération, Vitry-sur-Seine ☎ 01 43 91 64 20 🕐 Closed Mon. 💲 $$

## St.-Germain-en-Laye

Just west of Paris lies this pleasant residential town, where you'll find the fortress of St.-Germain-en-Laye, home of French kings from François I to Louis XIV. Napoleon III restored the Renaissance castle, establishing the **Musée d'Archéologie** *(tel 01 39 10 13 00, closed Tues.)*. The tremendous **Grande Terrasse** gives a sweeping overview of the Seine Valley. Also of interest is **Ste.-Chapelle,** a Gothic masterpiece similar to the chapel of the same name in Paris (see p. 58). Nearby, the **Musée du Prieuré** *(rue Maurice Denis, tel 01 39 73 77 87, closed Mon.)* contains postimpressionist art. You can also visit and attend concerts at the 17th-century residence of musician Claude Debussy *(38 rue au Pain, tel 01 34 51 05 12; open Tues.–Fri. p.m., & 10–12:30 & 2–6 Sat., closed Sun.–Mon.)*. ▲ 95 B2

A land of great Gothic cathedrals, important wine regions (Champagne and Alsace), and, from Flanders to the Marne, sobering mementos of war

# Northern France

Gate detail, Place Stanislas, Nancy

# Northern France

Some of France's greatest wines, earliest and most magnificent Gothic cathedrals, and most valued art collections are to be found in the five northern regions: Nord-Pas-de-Calais, Picardie, Champagne-Ardennes, Alsace, and Lorraine. These are France's borderlands with Germany, Switzerland, Luxembourg, and Belgium, and—mediated by the narrow Manche or English Channel—with Britain.

A mix of languages, cultures, and traditions testifies to the historic impermanence of France's frontiers. Calais, for example, was once English; Alsace and most of Lorraine have intermittently been part of Germany; and Flandre (Flanders), now in the Nord-Pas-de-Calais region, was part of a medieval state that included much of Belgium. It scarcely seems credible that these frontiers were being fought over only half a century ago, in wars that drew the world's greatest nations to battle in northern France.

## Wine Country

Stained-glass windows in Reims's cathedral depict vine cultivation and wine production, for Reims is capital of the Champagne

### NOT TO BE MISSED:

region, where wine has been made since Roman times. It was here that the renowned sparkling wine is thought to have been developed about 300 years ago. Champagne is France's most northerly wine-growing district, and the cool climate is a factor in the success of its great wine.

The main area of production centers on the vineyards around Reims and Épernay, where the major *maisons de champagne* are located. Most invite you to tour their *caves*—the labyrinthine cellars where the wine is fermented, blended, and stored—and taste the champagne before buying (see p. 124).

Another delightful part of a visit to the Champagne region is touring the charming villages, abbeys, churches, and castles of the area along the signposted Route Touristique du Champagne (see pp. 122–123).

Wine has also been made since Roman times in picturesque Alsace. You can follow the signposted Route du Vin for about 130 miles (200 km) along a scenic route that winds through the foothills of the Vosges Mountains, passing tidy vineyards and charming old towns and villages with good places to eat, churches, and castles.

## Cradle of the Gothic Style

Gothic architecture grew up here: Picardie alone has six major cathedrals. The former bishop's palace and medieval abbeys and churches cluster around Strasbourg's cathedral and the early Gothic Cathédrale de Notre-Dame in Laon. The treasuries of these ancient cathedrals preserve centuries-old relics, gold and silverware, art, and church ornaments. The magnificent cathedral of Reims was the coronation cathedral of the kings of France, and its Treasury includes an array of sacred vessels and coronation regalia. ■

Paris ★

Area of map detail

0 —— 60 kilometers
0 —— 30 miles

# Nord & Picardie

The rolling, wooded Nord area includes the French part of what was historically Flanders (the rest is now in Belgium). Flanders resembles the Low Countries, with canals and windmills, and towns with cobbled squares and gabled houses. North from Lille, capital of the region, are the medieval Flemish walled towns of Bergues and Wormhout, surrounded by canals. Fortified towns are a feature. Cambrai, for example, still has its old gatehouse, citadel, and keep. Farther south, Picardie has splendid cathedrals and notable Gothic churches, including the 16th-century abbey church of St. Riquier, near Abbeville.

Picardie is the larger of the two northern regions, with three *départments*. Of these, the peaceful Aisne in the east is a region of open plain crossed by rivers and interspersed with pockets of pastureland, villages, churches, and châteaus. Aisne's capital is the cathedral town of Laon, once a royal city.

The western département, Oise, is heavily wooded, and the fine forests were favorite hunting grounds of the French kings, whose summer palace was at Compiègne. Oise has a wealth of architectural gems, chief among them the Château de Chantilly and the beautifully preserved cathedral town of Senlis with its ancient ramparts.

The Somme to the north will always be associated with the battles of World War I. Its capital, Amiens, is graced by one of the greatest Gothic cathedrals in the country.

The entire area is famed for its church belfries, 17 of which have been awarded UNESCO World Heritage site status. ■

## Insiders' Pas de Calais

Get to know this inviting region like a local by contacting a greeter. The idea, which actually originated in New York City, is for local people with a passion for their area to act as free guides for visitors. They can tailor a tour to your interest, from natural history to architecture, long walks to long lunches, and, if you'd like, take you off the beaten path. Contact them at *www .greeters 62.com.*

One of the few remaining working mills in the Créquoise Valley can be found outside Montreuil.

# Lille

Lille is a frontier town (though France's border with its European Union partner Belgium is scarcely noticeable) and a major transport hub. During its thousand-year history, Lille has belonged variously to Flanders, Burgundy, the Spanish Netherlands, France, and Germany. One of its best-preserved buildings is the star-shaped Citadelle, a great fort designed by Louis XIV's military engineer Vauban in 1667, for protection against the Spanish Netherlands when Lille became part of France.

Lille's Palais des Beaux-Arts museum showcases fine European paintings.

From the visitors gallery high up in the 345-foot (105 m) belfry of the 1930s **Hôtel de Ville,** a UNESCO World Heritage site, you get a notion of the scale of the largest industrial city in northern France. Its spreading suburbs embrace surrounding towns all the way to the Belgian border, 6 miles (10 km) away. The charming **Place Général de Gaulle** in the heart of the city, surrounded by old, steep-gabled Flemish houses, comes as a pleasant surprise. One of its most attractive buildings, the **Vieille Bourse** (Old Stock Exchange) was built in 1652–1653 in Flemish Renaissance style. The nearby **Palais des Beaux-Arts** displays art works by Flemish, French, Dutch, Italian, and Spanish

masters from the 15th century to the 20th, including a renowned collection of works by Goya.

Lille is a lively regional center with excellent shopping, theater, music, and cinema. It brightened its image with renovations and a major cleanup upon being designated the European City of Culture in 2004; the Opéra reopened, and many buildings became art and performance spaces. Lille has become known for art, with an art fair held in the spring.

**Villeneuve-d'Ascq,** a suburb northeast of Lille, has the **Musée d'Art Moderne** *(1 allée de Musée, closed Tues.),* with a respected cubist collection, and at **Roubaix,** the **Musée d'Art et d'Industrie** has opened in a converted art deco swimming pool. ∎

## Lille

 106 B4

**Visitor information**

✉ 42 Palais Rihour, place Rihour

☎ 03 59 57 94 00
Ask for a permit to visit the Citadelle at the tourist office.

**www.lilletourisme.com**

### Hôtel de Ville & belfry

✉ place Roger Salergro

☎ 03 20 49 50 00

🕐 Closed Mon. Apply to tourist office for guided tours.

### Palais des Beaux-Arts

✉ place de la République

☎ 03 20 06 78 00

🕐 Closed Tues., & Mon. a.m.

💲 $$

**www.pba-lille.fr**

### Musée d'Art et d'Industrie

✉ 24 rue de l'Espérance, Roubaix

☎ 03 20 69 23 60

🕐 Closed Mon.

# Battlefields

The map of northern France, from Dunkerque to Verdun and from Cambrai to beyond the Somme River, is a map of battlefields now buried beneath towns and villages, woods and fields. The most recent saw action not much more than half a century ago—it was only in 1940 that hundreds of thousands of retreating British troops evacuated the beaches of Dunkerque. Six centuries earlier in 1346, Edward III's English soldiers vanquished Philippe VI's army at Crécy-en-Ponthieu. Memorials, cemeteries, and museums all over the region explain the actions in these wars, recent and long gone.

Many monuments, some of great artistic distinction—Edwin Lutyens's British monument at Thiepval in the Somme; Walter Seymour Allward's **Canadian War Memorial on Vimy Ridge** near Vimy—mark the battle sites where more than a million young soldiers were killed in 1914–18. World War I laid waste to the entire region, from Amiens to Alsace and Reims to Belgium, and it is scattered with trenches, cemeteries, and memorials to French, British, Australian, New Zealand, American, Moroccan, Indian, Nepalese, and Chinese troops.

Many visitors make the journey to see the site of a particular battle, or to visit a certain graveyard or a memorial to a division. Alternatively, you might follow one of the signposted memorial routes that trace the line of a front or the battles in a campaign, or visit one of several very moving

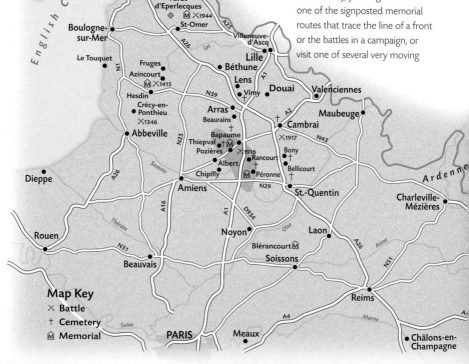

Map Key
× Battle
† Cemetery
Ⓜ Memorial

museums of the wars. Here are some of the fields and wartime sites most worth visiting:

## Arras

Beneath the Grand'Place in Arras (see p. 114) are **Les Boves,** a network of caves thought to have been dug out more than 1,000 years ago. They have provided a refuge for locals during the region's frequent conflicts. During World War I, British troops were sheltered and their wounds dressed in Les Boves, now a memorial with guided tours.

## Cambrai

The first full-scale tank battle occurred in 1917 near Cambrai. The military cemetery here has a fine memorial.

## La Coupole

The Nazi Germans built their first factory and launch base for V2 missiles aimed at London during World War II in the Forêt d'Éperlecques northwest of **St.-Omer.** The bunker, now

---

### EXPERIENCE:
## Wilfred Owen Memorial

Follow in the footsteps of the revered World War I poet Wilfred Owen in his last hours. Visit the **Forester's House** outside Ors, near Cambrai. Here he hid out in the cellar and wrote his last letter to his mother, now being transformed into a monumental artwork. See the **Bois Leveque forest,** the canal where he was killed on November 4, 1918—a day that is now commemorated every year—and the village of **Ors,** where the library bears his name. He is buried in the cemetery in Ors. For more details, *www.wilfredowen.com*

---

a museum called La Coupole, shows everything from the liquid oxygen factory to the launch pad, accompanied by audiovisual displays.

## Hundred Years' War

The lookout tower at the site of the Battle of Crécy in 1346 displays an orientation table showing the battle plan. A small museum focuses on the Battle of Agincourt in **Azincourt** village *(closed Wed.).* An orientation table and model archers and horsemen on the field of battle itself enable visitors to follow the battle of 1415, in which the English soldiers of Henry V overcame superior French forces.

## The Somme

A Tour of Remembrance follows the front lines of the two World War I battles

---

**Vimy**

🗺 106 B4

**Canadian War Memorial, Vimy Ridge**

☎ 03 21 50 68 68 (museum)

🕒 Open daily. Guided tours: May–Nov.

**St.-Omer**

🗺 106 B5

**La Coupole**

✉ Forêt d'Éperlecques

☎ 03 21 12 27 27

💲 $$

www.lacoupole-france.com

BELGIUM
dan
LUXEMBOURG
GERMANY
Lorraine
Thionville
Meuse
Verdun
1916
Metz
0    40 kilometers
0    20 miles
A31

**Somme Regional
Tourism**

- ✉ 21 rue Ernest
  Cauvin, Amiens
- ☎ 03 22 71 22 71
- www.somme
  -tourisme.com

**Historial de la
Grande Guerre,
Péronne**

- ✉ place du Château
- ☎ 03 22 83 14 18
- 🕐 Closed Mon. in
  winter & mid-
  Dec.–mid-Jan.
- www.historial.org

**Memorial de
Verdun**

-  107 D3

**Visitor information**

- ✉ 1 avenue du
  Corps Européen
  Fleury devant
  Douaumont, Verdun
- ☎ 03 29 84 35 34
- 🕐 Closed Jan.
- 💲 $$
- www.memorial-de
  -verdun.fr

of the Somme *(information from
the Somme tourist office)*. Among
the signposted sights are two
blockhouses at **Pozières** taken
by Australian divisions, the Brit-
ish memorial at **Thiepval,** the
French cemetery at **Rancourt,**
and the memorial at **Bellicourt**

---

### The End of the Fighting

On May 7, 1945, the Ger-
mans surrendered to the
Allies in Reims (see pp.
120–121), in the school-
room headquarters of Gen.
Eisenhower. The **Musée de
Reddition** *(12 rue Franklin
Roosevelt, Reims, tel 03
26 47 84 19, closed Tues.)*
preserves the space exactly
as it was at that dramatic
moment, with the table,
chairs, and huge wall maps
detailing the progress of
the conflict.

---

The information cen-
ter in Suippes *(www
.marne14-18.fr)* offers
fascinating documen-
tation from soldiers
and their families.

—ROSEMARY BAILEY
*National Geographic author*

to American soldiers. The tour
encompasses trenches, shelters,
and the rail supply line. The
**Historial de la Grande Guerre**
is a museum beside Péronne's
medieval fortress.

### Verdun

The 17th-century citadel now
holds a museum commemorat-
ing the 1916 German attack
that destroyed this barracks
town. There are tours of the
battlefield in summer *(ask at
the tourist office)*. ■

Cemeteries with World War II graves dot the area. This one is in Chatillon-sur-Marne.

# EXPERIENCE: Take to the Water (and Sand)

The Channel coast between Calais and the Somme estuary is called the Côte d'Opale due to the misty horizon of sea and sky visible from the white chalk cliffs stretching down to Boulogne-sur-Mer, the other side of the Channel from the White Cliffs of Dover. It was from this coast that Julius Caesar launched his invasion of England and that the rescue of the French and British troops by little boats from Britain took place after the fall of France. Today, the Côte d'Opale is the best place in northern France for water sports.

From Cap Blanc Nez and Cap Gris-Nez are terrific views of the Channel. On a clear day, you might be able to see all the way to England.

The coast offers numerous opportunities to experience the beach and sea by taking part in an activity, maybe even one that's dependent on the winds that blow this way.

At low tide, the sea retreats so far that vast swaths of pale sandy beach are left exposed, making it an ideal location for sand yachting, also known as land sailing, a racing sport that's actually been around since the 1950s.

You can also sign up for kitesurfing, a sailing outing in a catamaran or small dinghy, kayaking, and sea fishing on board a former trawler. Beginners' group lessons and private courses are available. Waterproof clothing and helmets can be provided by most clubs, but having your own rubber-sole footwear is advisable.

If you want more of a spectator water experience, head to the **Nausicaá aquarium** (9 Parvis de Nausicaá, Boulogne-sur-Mer, tel 03 21 10 88 10, www .nausicaa.fr).

Enjoy the coast without even getting wet. The sport of sand yachting has a wealth of practitioners along the English Channel.

### Kayaking
**Base de Voile et de Loisirs** (RD 940, Sangatte, tel 03 21 17 70 60, www.capcalais.fr)

### Kitesurfing
**Wimkite** (boulevard Thiriez, Wimereux, tel 06 81 76 82 05, www.wimkite.com)

### Sailing
**Centre Régionale de Voile** (Club Nautique, Digue de Mer, Wimereux, tel 03 21 83 18 54, www.club-nautique -wimereux.com)

**Dunkerque Plaisance** (Centre Regional de Voile, Quai d'Armement Nord, Dunkerque, tel 03 28 66 38 72, www.lesdunesdeflandre.fr)

### Sand Yachting
**Char à Voile Club de la Côte d'Opale** (272 boulevard Sainte Beuve, Boulogne sur Mer, tel 03 21 83 25 48, www.cvcco.com)

**École de Char à Voile** (boulevard Pouget Base Nautique Sud, Le Touquet-Paris-Plage, tel 03 21 05 33 51, www.letou quet.com)

### Sea Fishing
**Étaples Tourist Office** (boulevard Bigot Descelers, Étaples, tel 03 21 09 56 94, www.etaplestourisme.com)

# From Arras to the Coast

West of Arras, the Picardie plain slopes gently to the coast. The countryside is patched with woodland and threaded by rivers: the picturesque Authie, the majestic Somme, and the Canche, overlooked by the medieval hill town of Montreuil. Le Touquet on the Canche estuary is the most sophisticated of the resorts clustering along the sandy north-coast beaches.

Quaint Montreuil was once Europe's wealthiest port town.

**Arras**
🅰 106 B4
**Visitor information**
✉ Hôtel de Ville, place des Héros
☎ 03 21 51 26 95

**Le Touquet**
🅰 106 A4
**Visitor information**
✉ Palais de l'Europe
☎ 03 21 06 72 00
**www.letouquet.com**

With its underground shelters (see p. 111) and moving memorial to the many French Resistance members who were shot here during World War II, Arras is an important site on any battlefield tour. The late Gothic **Hôtel de Ville** overlooks the **Place des Héros,** one of Arras's two great central squares. You can look down on it from the town hall's 250-foot (80 m) belfry, but you get a better sense of its scale from within.

During the 1914–1918 fighting, bombardments destroyed the

Hôtel de Ville and many of the 16th-century houses surrounding the squares. After the war they were faithfully reconstructed.

Halfway between Arras and Lille is the ancient university town of **Douai** *(visitor information, place d'Armes, tel 03 27 88 26 79),* with 18th-century houses, narrow streets, and a famous 62-bell carillon in the belfry above the town hall.

Don't miss the **Musée Matisse Palais Fenelon Cateau Cambresis** *(tel 03 27 84 64 50, www.cg59.fr),* near Cambrai. In the artist's birthplace, more than 170 paintings and sculptures cover Matisse's entire career.

A trip to **Le Touquet**, an elegant resort town, makes a pleasant morning's drive from Arras. Take the N39 via the pretty town of **Hesdin** (near the site of the Battle of Agincourt, see p. 111) and the D340 along the Canche River to the hill town of **Montreuil** with its well-preserved ramparts. Le Touquet was fashionable when the Prince of Wales (later King Edward VIII) brought his guests there. Today it is an art nouveau and art deco period piece, albeit one with a casino, horse racing, golf, hotels, fine restaurants, boutiques, nightlife, great beaches, and, nearby, Bagatelle, an amusement park. ∎

# Amiens

Amiens, on the Somme River, was heavily bombed in 1918, and shelling in 1940 destroyed much of its ancient heart. But the grand cathedral has survived centuries of war and revolution. A classic model of the French Gothic style, it is the main reason to visit Amiens.

The **Cathédrale de Notre-Dame** (place Notre-Dame, tel 03 22 71 60 50) is France's tallest cathedral. Its nave, built between 1220 and 1236, was then the highest in France, at 139 feet (42 m). Stand at the west end of the nave and look toward the altar. Instantly, the soaring piers and pointed arches sweep your gaze heavenward, fulfilling one of the ideals of Gothic architecture.

The dramatic interior of this vast church is illuminated by windows that seem to replace the upper walls of the nave, choir, and chapels of the apse. The rose window in the west front still has its 16th-century glass, but much of the ancient glass was shattered during World War II bombings. Local woodcarvers at the beginning of the 16th century decorated the 110 oak choir stalls with more than 400 scenes. The

west front's three great portals are masterpieces of stonecarving. The "weeping angel," a hugely popular putto crying on a tomb, is by local sculptor Nicolas Blasset.

The streets around the cathedral contain painstakingly restored buildings, such as the medieval belfry; the **Musée de Picardie** (48 rue de la République, tel 03 22 97 14 00, closed Mon.); the 17th-century **Hôtel de Berny** (36 rue Victor Hugo, tel 03 22 97 14 00, closed Mon.), now a museum with local decorative arts displayed in period settings; and the **Maison à la Tour,** the home of author Jules Verne (2 rue Charles Dubois, tel 03 22 45 45 75).

Waterways flow around the city's St.-Leu district, and you can stroll the towpaths and bridges or tour around by boat. The son et lumière in the evening is a wonderful way to end a day. ∎

**Amiens**
- 106 B4

**Visitor information**
- 6 bis rue Dusevel
- 03 22 71 60 50
- Closed Sun.

## EXPERIENCE: Looking for Birds in the Somme

Exploring the bay of the Somme is a fine way to discover the bird life in the **Parc Regional du Nord-Pas-de-Calais** (Maison de la Baie de Somme et de l'Oiseau, Carrefour du Hourdel, Lanchères, tel 03 22 26 93 93, www.baiedesomme.fr). You can walk the coastal path that stretches from the Belgian border to south of Le Touquet to glimpse migrating birds such as divers, grebes, ducks, and herons (best in spring or autumn), or make your way to the

**Marquenterre Bird Park** on the edge of the bay at St.-Quentin-en-Tourmont. Hire a boat or take a guided open boat trip around the salt marshes. Another means of exploration is by bike. You can rent one and explore for yourself. In spring, a festival of birds and nature (www.festival-oiseau-nature .com) in Abbeville offers guided nature trips on foot, bike, horseback, and boat, plus photographic exhibitions and special events for kids.

# Gothic Cathedrals

The towers and spires of the Gothic cathedrals of northern France rise high above its spreading plains and cities, like spiritual landmarks. This is the birthplace of Gothic architecture—the style dates from circa 1140–44, when the choir of the abbey church of St.-Denis, north of Paris (see p. 103), was built.

The Cathedrale St.-Étienne went up in the 13th century, when Metz was an important frontier city.

Notre-Dame in Paris, begun in 1163, was the next monumental church to be built in the new style, with a nave 109 feet (33 m) high. In a burst of cathedral building within a 100-mile (160-km) radius of Paris, the style evolved from the simplicity of Laon (see p. 117) to the dramatic vertical lines of the mature Gothic style at Amiens (see p. 115) and Chartres (see pp. 100–101) and to the late or high Gothic style of Reims (see pp. 120–121), with its complex system of flying buttresses. Strasbourg cathedral (see p. 126), begun in the 13th century and

finished in the 15th, reflects this evolution from the Romanesque style (see pp. 322–323) all the way through to the flamboyant, the ornate late form of high Gothic.

## Cathedral Tour

A round-trip of 240 miles (380 km) will take you to six of France's most magnificent Gothic cathedrals. Begin at the cathedral of **Amiens,** whose interior is the supreme example of the mature French Gothic style. Follow the D934 southeast to **Noyon,**

**INSIDER TIP:**

In the hilltop town of Laon is a well-preserved octagonal chapel built in the late 12th century by the Knights Templar.

—SHEILA BUCKMASTER
National Geographic Traveler
*magazine editor at large*

A formal procession follows a Sunday Mass inside the high Gothic Reims cathedral.

whose lovely cathedral, begun around 1150, is transitional in style between Romanesque and Gothic. Take the N32 and N44 across the Aisne *département* to **Laon,** once the royal city of the Carolingian kings. Here the 12th-century cathedral of Notre-Dame, begun in the 1160s and completed in 1230, is a fine example of early Gothic style. It has beautiful rose windows and captivating sculptures of exotic animals—a hippopotamus gargoyle, for instance—on its facade. Clustered around it are the bishop's palace and the Dauphin's court, medieval abbeys, and streets of charming old town houses.

From Laon, it is a short journey southeast along the N44 (or the A26) to **Reims,** with its high Gothic cathedral. Then take the N31 west to **Soissons** to admire its cathedral, restored after shelling in 1918. Started in the 12th and not finished until the 14th century, it shows the evolution of the Gothic style.

Continue westward along the N31 via Compiègne to **Beauvais,** whose cathedral was

a daring attempt to build the tallest such edifice ever. In 1284, 12 years after its completion, the choir collapsed and had to be rebuilt with reinforcing buttresses. However, this grand project overstretched the town's resources, and the cathedral was never finished; today you see the choir and transepts built onto the tiny, early 11th century Romanesque nave, which the new cathedral was intended to replace. From Beauvais the A16 returns you to Amiens.

## Anatomy of a Gothic Cathedral

The classic, three-stage structural system of the Gothic cathedral consists of a nave arcade at ground level, a triforium (arcaded passage) above it, and a clerestory (upper wall zone, pierced by windows) above that. The high walls are buttressed for stability. In order to raise the nave roof to unprecedented heights, the builders constructed flying buttresses to transmit the thrust of the brick or stone vaults down to the sturdy main vertical buttresses.

The pointed arches characteristic of Gothic architecture take the thrust from the vaults downward, so buildings could have thin walls pierced by large windows. These windows were divided by a tracery of delicate stonework, which reached astonishing heights of complexity in the round rose windows.

# Royal Forests

The forests still surviving in the south of Picardie are just remnants of those that originally covered much of northern France. Kings and nobles came here from Paris and built hunting lodges, palaces, and châteaus in and around the forests.

**Chantilly**

Ⓜ 106 B3

**Visitor information**

✉ 60 avenue du Maréchal Joffre

☎ 03 44 67 37 37

www.chantilly
-tourisme.com

**Chantilly
château**

✉ route national 924A

☎ 03 44 27 31 80

🕐 Closed Tues.

💲 $$

www.chateau
dechantilly.com

**Senlis**

Ⓜ 106 B3

**Visitor information**

✉ parvis Notre-Dame

☎ 03 44 53 06 40

**Compiègne**

Ⓜ 106 B3

**Visitor information**

✉ place Hôtel de Ville

☎ 03 44 40 01 00

🕐 Closed Mon. a.m. Oct.–March

## Chantilly

Once famous for its lace, the town of Chantilly is now best known for its châteaus set on an island in a lake and surrounded by handsome gardens designed by André Le Nôtre. The Petit Château and the adjoining Grand Château form the **Musée Condé,** a collection of fine and decorative arts, and a priceless library, all assembled by the Duc d'Aumale in the 19th century. Treasures include the *Très Riches Heures du Duc de*

**INSIDER TIP:**

## In Senlis, have a nice lunch at Le Scaramouche *(4 place Notre-Dame, tel 03 44 53 01 26),* facing the cathedral. The seafood is a good choice here.

—SHEILA BUCKMASTER
National Geographic Traveler
*magazine editor at large*

*Berry,* a 15th-century book of hours (not always on display), and paintings by Raphael and French masters. The beautiful 18th-century stables now house the **Musée Vivant du Cheval** (Living Museum of the Horse; *tel 03 44 57 40 40).*

## Senlis

One of the most ancient towns in France, Senlis was founded before the Romans conquered Gaul. Its Gallo-Roman walls thread through the town; 16 of the 28 towers still stand, though hidden by houses.

**Cathédrale Notre-Dame,** begun in 1155, is on a more modest scale than many such Gothic edifices. It has a 13th-century spire and, inside, superb sculptures of the Virgin.

From the cathedral, it is easy to explore the old town, castle remains, and ancient walls. The 18th-century **Château de Raray** nearby so enraptured Jean Cocteau that he set his film *La Belle et la Bête* (1945) in it.

## Compiègne

Set on the edge of the forest, Compiègne is dominated by the palace built in 1754 for Louis XV. Inside are the apartments of Napoleon I and his wife Marie-Louise and the Hunting Gallery decked with Gobelins tapestries.

A clearing in the Forêt de Laigue, 4 miles (6 km) east of Compiègne off the N31, is the site of the **Musée de l'Armistice** *(tel 03 44 85 14 18, closed Tues.).* The museum is housed in a reconstruction of the railroad car in which the armistice that ended World War I was signed. ∎

# Champagne

The vineyards of the Champagne region carpet the wide river valleys and climb gentle slopes to wooded escarpments that overlook some of the most beautiful countryside in northern France. Venerable villages with Romanesque churches and medieval market towns dot the countryside. Reims, the northern, and Troyes, the southern capital of Champagne, have superb Gothic cathedrals and splendid museums. Both are little more than an hour's drive or train ride from Paris.

In Épernay—Champagne central—many a shop window is dressed for celebration.

The size and splendor of the half-timbered medieval merchants' houses that survive in the old towns testify to Champagne's past prosperity. During the Middle Ages, it lay at the crossroads of northern Europe's trade routes. From the 14th to 16th centuries, cloth from Italy, Flanders, and the German states, furs from Scandinavia, leather from Catalonia, and costly woods, spices, and gold from the Mediterranean were traded in six-week-long summer fairs in Troyes, Lagny, Bar-sur-Aube, and Provins.

History has left a legacy of castles and fortifications, built in strong defensive positions high on the edges of escarpments right across the region to repel invaders. From the fifth century, when Attila the Hun's army was routed near Châlons-en-Champagne, to the Nazi invasions of 1940, this part of France has been an entry point for armies marching on Paris.

Grapes have been cultivated in the chalky soils of Champagne for some 2,000 years. In the late 17th century, Pierre Pérignon, cellarer at the Benedictine abbey of Hautvillers near Épernay, is said to have discovered how to make wine sparkle. Wine historians debunk this myth, but they recognize the part played by Dom Pérignon in the evolution of Champagne. He made progress in controlling the wine's fermentation, and he blended wines from different vineyards to make richer, more subtle wines. ∎

# Reims

In 498, in Reims's first cathedral, St. Rémi baptized Clovis, king of the conquering Frankish tribe from the upper Rhine. Subsequently, almost every king of France was crowned here. Reims has always been an important French city and is now only 45 minutes away from Paris by TGV.

**Reims**

🅰 107 C3

**Visitor information**

✉ 2 rue Guillaume de Machault

☎ 03 26 77 45 00

**www.reims-tourisme.com**

The fittingly majestic **Cathédrale Notre-Dame,** begun in 1211 after a fire destroyed the previous cathedral, was designed for coronations. To create room for the ceremonies, the nave and choir were broadened to embrace the transepts, so that the interior appears luxuriously spacious, and the nave, with its avenues of piers, seems to soar. No expense was spared in its construction or its decoration—Reims was intended to surpass in concept and ornament even the great cathedrals at Chartres and Amiens. Much of its old glass was lost as a result of World War II bombing; the modern windows of the Lady Chapel are by Marc Chagall.

Although built in stages between the 13th and 15th centuries, Reims has a unity of style representing the pinnacle of mature French Gothic. Its flying buttresses are daringly thin and light, an expression of the confidence medieval architects had achieved by the 13th century. One of its glories is the wealth of sculpture on its facade, though some are copies of originals damaged beyond repair. The central doorway is devoted to the Virgin. The statue of the coronation of the Virgin that used to grace the central gable is now in the Palais du Tau. Above the rose window on the west front, look for the statues of the kings of France, and by the left-hand portal the smiling "Angel of Reims."

The bishop's palace next to the cathedral, the **Palais du Tau,** displays coronation regalia, carvings and statues rescued from

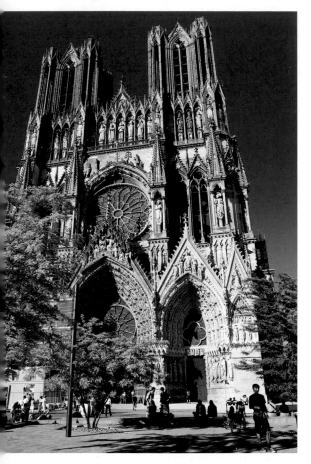

The Cathédrale de Notre-Dame showcases Gothic detailing.

## Charles de Gaulle Museum

From the June 18 "call to Resistance" in 1940 to the final caricatures grafittied on the streets of Paris in 1968, de Gaulle is undoubtedly the most famous Frenchman of the 20th century. The Charles de Gaulle Memorial Museum *(tel 03 25 30 90 80, www.memorial-charlesde gaulle.fr, $$)* opened in 2008 in Colombey-les-deux-Eglises, a small village in Haute Marne (one of the smallest departments of France), where de Gaulle lived for much of his life. The museum nestles into the hillside, already dominated by a vast marble cross of Lorraine, and was designed by architects Jacques Millet and Jean-Côme Chilou, also responsible for the Memorial Museum of Caen. Almost a third is tucked into the mountainside, part of it with an eco-conscious grass roof. A grand staircase leads up to the cross, and a broad terrace offers an almost 180-degree view of the misty countryside de Gaulle revered. Using photographs, films, and reconstructions (including a World War I trench), the museum is a fascinating journey through 20th-century history. All the texts are in German, French, and English, and though it is an unstinting tribute to one patriotic Frenchman, it offers a moving sense of the deep necessity for European unity. You can also visit La Boisserie, de Gaulle's family home in the village. Stroll the gardens and see the splendid library de Gaulle designed for himself with three windows opening to grand views.

---

the war-damaged cathedral, and several tapestries.

**Musée-Chapelle Foujita** *(33 rue de Champs de Mars, tel 03 26 40 06 96)* was created in 1966 by Japanese artist Leonard Foujita to express his gratitude for the mystical enlightenment he experienced in Reims cathedral. His designs for ironwork, sculptures, frescoes, and stained glass are exquisite, and this is his chosen burial place.

At the south end of town, the **Basilique St.-Rémi** *(place du Chanoine Ladaine),* founded in the 11th century, is the largest Romanesque church in northern France, though with later additions. It was built over the chapel of St. Christophe, where St. Rémi was buried.

These great ecclesiastical buildings are reason enough to visit Reims, but the city has much more to offer. Beneath its streets are the foundations of Durocortier, the metropolis of a Gaulish tribe called the Remes that in 55 B.C. made an alliance with Julius Caesar. You can visit the **Cryptoporticus** *(place du Forum, tel 03 26 50 13 M, closed a.m. mid-June–mid-Sept, & all mid-Sept.–mid-June)*—vaulted galleries, perhaps a former temple—and the **Porte de Mars,** the largest triumphal arch in the Roman world. Limestone for these edifices and for aqueducts, roads, and homes was cut from beneath the city. Centuries later, these subterranean quarries make ideal storage cellars for maturing wine.

In medieval times, Reims was primarily a textile town. During the 15th century, wine overtook cloth in importance. Today Reims, at the heart of the vineyards, is home to more than 20 top Champagne houses, many of which offer tours and tastings (see sidebar p. 124). ∎

**Cathédrale Notre-Dame**

- ⊠ place du Cardinal Luçon
- ☎ 03 26 17 55 34
- 🕐 Mass at 9:30 a.m. & 11 a.m. Sun., 8 a.m. daily

www.cathedrale-reims.com

**Palais du Tau**

- ⊠ place du Cardinal Luçon
- ☎ 03 26 47 81 79
- 🕐 Closed Mon.
- 💲 $$

www.palais-tau.mon uments-nationaux.fr

# Champagne Country

Minor roads crisscrossing the Champagne region connect the many pretty wine villages. A leisurely drive is the best way to experience Champagne, with stops here and there to stroll the villages and to visit the *vignerons*—small independent wine producers—to taste their distinctive, often excellent champagnes.

Lush vineyards and charming villages catch the traveler's attention at every turn.

### Épernay

 107 C3

**Visitor information**

✉ 7 avenue de Champagne

☎ 03 26 53 33 00

🕐 Closed Sun. in winter

**www.epernay.fr**

**Centre Inter-professionel des Vins de Champagne, Épernay**

☎ 03 26 51 19 30

## Exploring the Champagne Countryside

Meandering east from Reims around the Parc Naturel de la Montagne de Reims, the 40-mile (70 km) Route Touristique weaves through the heart of the Champagne countryside. Road-trippers can pause at vineyards and historical villages filled with architectural marvels and charming outposts of everyday life. The vines you see along the way primarily bear the Pinot Noir grape, the mainstay of Champagne.

Begin by taking the D380 southwest out of Reims and follow the signposts; soon you'll be driving east along the D26. The route rises to magnificent viewpoints at the St.-Lie chapel beyond Jouy-lès-Reims. Farther east, climb the woodsy path above Verzy to an observation point at **Mont Sinai** for a marvelous view of the vineyards. The road drops down to the Vallée de la Marne in the southwest corner of the Champagne region. Here the grapes are Pinot Meunier, which impart a spiciness to the wine.

**INSIDER TIP:**

The Union of Champagne Houses (1 rue Marie-Stuart, Reims, tel 03 26 47 26 89) is a fine info source on dozens of producers.

—ROSEMARY BAILEY
*National Geographic author*

Soon you'll come to the quiet town of **Épernay**, the capital of Champagne country. The prestigious **Avenue de Champagne** is lined with sumptuous Champagne houses, including industry giant **Moët & Chandon** (see p. 383), founded in 1743. Opposite is the **Trianon Palace**—two pavilions and a lovely orangery surrounded by typically French formal gardens—built in the early 1800s by Jean-Rémy Moët to entertain his friend Napoleon Bonaparte.

The impressive **Château Perrier**, built in the 19th century by Charles Perrier, a former mayor of Épernay, now accommodates the town museum, a good place to learn more about Champagne production. Another museum is housed in the **Maison de Castellane**, identifiable by its ornate tower. The **Maison Pol Roger** is headquarters of the eponymous firm founded in 1849; its Champagne was Winston Churchill's favorite.

### Other Routes

West from Épernay, you can follow another "route touristique" along the Marne River, flanked on both sides with Meunier grapevines. On the way to Dormans, a peaceful riverside town, it passes through Hautvillers, where you can visit the abbey where Dom Pérignon (see p. 119) was a monk. Another interesting town en route is Boursault, with a 19th-century castle built for the enterprising Madame Clicquot, who sold her Champagne to the Russian court.

A different tourist route heads south of Épernay to Vertus, through a region called the **Côte des Blancs** for the white Chardonnay grapes that are almost exclusively planted here. ■

## How Champagne Is Made

After the grapes are pressed, the juice, or "must," is put in vats until the following spring, when the wine is blended and bottled. Blending is what makes Champagne the drink it is; there are many sparkling wines made by the Champagne method (*méthode champenoise*), but the blenders of Champagne marry wines from the current vintage with reserve wines from other vintages. Once blended, sugar and yeast mixed with reserve wine are added to each bottle, which is then corked and stored in a V-shaped rack called a *pupitre*. The yeast converts the sugar into carbon dioxide, which dissolves in the wine, forming tiny bubbles. Bottles are turned daily and gradually tilted, a process known as *remuage*. When the cork is removed, escaping gas expels the residue and a small amount of wine, to be replaced by a mix of Champagne and sugar. Champagne must be aged for at least a year, and a fine vintage may be aged for a decade or more.

# More Places to Visit in Champagne

## Châlons-en-Champagne

The third, with Reims and Épernay, in Champagne's triangle of wine towns, Châlons is has picturesque canals and half-timbered houses. The town gate, the Porte Ste.-Croix, was erected in 1770 for Marie-Antoinette to pass through on her way to marry Louis XVI. In 1791, during the Revolution, the royal couple were recognized and arrested in Ste.-Ménéhould, 15 miles (25 km) east, on their flight from Paris. The queen's prayer book is displayed in Châlons's public library. *www.chalons-tourisme.com* ▲ 107 C3 **Visitor information** ✉ 3 quai des Arts ☎ 03 26 65 17 89 ⏱ Closed Sun.

## Langres

You enter the town through 17th-century gateways. Built on a hill, Langres was the first town fortified by the Romans and has a triumphal arch embedded in its curtain wall. The old town has several beautiful stone Renaissance mansions with courtyards that can be visited. *www.tourisme-langres.com* ▲ 107 D2 **Visitor information** ✉ place O. Lahalle ☎ 03 25 87 67 67 ⏱ Closed Sun. Oct.–April

## Sedan

The impressive **Château Fort** *(1 place du Château, tel 03 24 27 73 73)*, begun in 1424 on the site of 11th-century fortifications, still dominates this border town. Vast and towering, it is one of the largest castles in Europe, still containing its sinister *oubliette* dungeons (the name comes from the French *oublier*, to forget) and lord's living quarters. Southeast of Sedan is **Fort La-Ferté**, the northernmost fort on the Maginot Line, which was overrun in 1940. *www.tourisme-langres.com* ▲ 107 D3

## Troyes

Half-timbered 16th-century houses overlook cobbled streets in the atmospheric St.-Jean district. The European Center of Hebraic Study commemorates a medieval center of Jewish learning here. The **Cathédrale St.-Pierre-et-St.-Paul** has beautifully preserved stained glass, some from the 13th century. Other attractions include the **Musée d'Art Moderne** with a collection of fauvist artworks. *www.tourism-troyes.com* ▲ 105 C2 **Visitor information** ✉ 16 boulevard Carnot ☎ 03 25 82 62 70

---

# EXPERIENCE: Going to the Champagne Houses

Among the Reims Champagne houses offering tours and tastings are **Veuve Clicquot** *(1 place de Droits-de-l'Homme, tel 03 26 89 53 90, www.veuve-cliquot.com)*, whose *chef de caves*, Antoine Müller, perfected the technique of *remuage* (see p. 123) in 1818; **Charles Heidsieck** *(4 boulevard Henry Vasnier, tel 03 26 84 43 50, www.charlesheidsieck.com)*, which first exported Champagne to the United States in 1851; **Pommery** *(5 place du Général Gouraud, tel 03 26 61 62 63, www.pommery .com)*, producer of the first brut or dry Champagne, popular in England;

**Roederer** *(21 boulevard Lundy, tel 03 26 40 42 11)*, maker of Cristal; and **Ruinart** *(4 rue des Crayères, tel 03 26 77 51 51, www.ruinart .com)*, Champagne's oldest *maison*. **Maison Mumm** *(34 rue du Champ de Mars, tel 03 26 49 59 70, www.mumm.com)*, founded in 1827 by two Protestant winemakers from the Rheingau region, runs guided tours of its cellars, followed by tastings, and has a small museum and an impressive archive of vintages, with bottles dating back to the late 19th century. Ask at the Reims tourist office (see p. 120) for details of tour times, duration, and charges.

# Alsace & Lorraine

Half plateau and half forested mountain range, half French and half German, Alsace and Lorraine share a history, landscape, and cultural identity that are unique in France. Along their eastern edge, they follow the German border, marked by the Rhine River, from Lauterbourg in the northwest to Basel in the southeast, where France, Germany, and Switzerland meet.

They have a common history, having been part of a German state since the ninth century, entering the kingdom of France only in the 17th and 18th centuries, respectively. Several times since then, they have been conquered by Germany and later returned to France, making for an interesting mix in architecture, culture, and food.

Lorraine's southern *département* is the mountainous, forested Vosges, an ancient, low massif that spreads eastward into Alsace. In winter there is skiing at St.-Maurice-sur-Moselle, la Bresse-le-Hohneck, Bussang, and Gérardmer.

**INSIDER TIP:**

Try a glass of dry white Gewurztraminer—lush and aromatic—with a slice of onion pie, quiche, or country pâté.

—SHEILA BUCKMASTER
National Geographic Traveler *magazine editor at large*

Among the peaks and valleys of Alsace, glacial Lac des Truites is the highest lake in the Vosges.

The highest peak of the Vosges, the 4,672-foot (1,424 m) Grand Ballon, is in Alsace, with vineyards blanketing the foothills of the massif. Few visitors can resist following the Route du Vin through wine villages that are among the prettiest in France, and most visitors take time to explore Colmar and other towns.

Strasbourg, one of the largest ports on the Rhine, has a world-class cathedral. And, like Brussels, it holds many European institutions, such as the European Parliament.

Stretching between the region's two great capitals, Metz and Nancy, the Parc Naturel Régional de Lorraine, a quiet countryside crossed by rivers, is dotted by ancient fortifications and sites associated with past wars. Growing numbers of visitors now come to follow the traces of these conflicts. ∎

# Strasbourg

Strasbourg is France's biggest river port and its sixth largest city, yet it has extraordinary charm and beauty. Founded more than 2,000 years ago, the city grew on marshy ground around branches of the Ill River, which threads through its picturesque old quarter. The Rhine port and outlying districts are busily industrial, but the city has all the vitality of a student town—its university, founded in 1566, is one of the oldest in France. Strasbourg faces Germany, just a bus ride away across the Rhine, and with some of Europe's most powerful institutions in its northeast quarter, it feels more like the capital of Europe than the old capital of Alsace.

The old quarter of Strasbourg, accented with half-timbered houses, is punctuated by a branch of the Ill River.

**Strasbourg**

🅐 107 F2

**Visitor information**

✉ 17 place de la Cathédrale

☎ 03 88 52 28 28

**www.ot-strasbourg .fr**

**Cathédrale Notre-Dame**

✉ place de la Cathédrale

💲 $; Astronomical clock $

**www.cathedrale-strasbourg.fr**

"I have seen many magnificent buildings in Switzerland, France, Italy and Greece. But the most beautiful thing of all is the interior of the Strasbourg cathedral with its great jewels, the miracle of its stained-glass windows." Thus wrote sculptor Hans Jean Arp (1887–1966), who was born in a house near the **Cathédrale Notre-Dame.** The glass, dating from the 12th to 13th centuries and set in two rose windows with beautiful tracery, was removed and hidden for safekeeping during World War II.

In the 1220s, when construction of the cathedral began, Strasbourg was an independent city.

The cathedral's transept was built first in Romanesque style. Little more than a decade later, the nave was rebuilt in the French Gothic style. The plans show that the architect modeled the building on Notre-Dame in Paris, but because it was built in stages until the 15th century, it perfectly reflects the progression from Romanesque to high Gothic styles. It is worth climbing to the platform on top of the tower to admire the statuary that decorates the spire.

The west front is remarkable for its medieval sculptures, especially the figures of the Wise and Foolish Virgins in the right portal. Many, however, are copies of those disfigured during the Revolution: The originals are displayed in the **Musée de l'Oeuvre de Notre-Dame** (tel 03 88 52 50 00, closed Mon.), opposite the cathedral.

In the cathedral transept is an astronomical clock. Made in the 16th century, it was given a new movement in the 19th. Its crowd of little figures can be seen in action every day at 12:30 p.m.

Notre-Dame and the medieval streets around it survived terrible bombardments in 1944. Across the Place du Château next to the cathedral, the 18th-century

Palais Rohan *(tel 03 88 52 50 00)*, once the archbishop's palace, now houses the city's principal museums, the Musée des Beaux-Arts and the Musée des Arts Décoratifs et d'Archéologie. Close by is the 13th-century **Pharmacie du Cerf** (closed since 2000) in the Place de la Cathédrale. West of the city center in Place Hans Jean Arp stands the **Musée d'Art Contemporain** *(tel 03 88 23 31 31)*, with works by Arp among others. The **Musée Alsacien** *(tel 03 88 52 50 01)*, on the Quai St.-Nicolas, displays regional costumes and furniture.

Take time to stroll around Strasbourg's old quarter built around canals once used by tanners and fishermen. The Ponts Couverts (the name means "covered bridges," but they lost their tops in the 18th century) cross

## EXPERIENCE: Tradition-Rich Holiday Shopping

The famous Christmas market in Strasbourg (www.noel-strasbourg.com), held November 29 to December 24, is filled with holiday magic. This is one of the biggest Christmas markets in France, centered around the magnificent cathedral. It has been a local tradition since 1570, with hundreds of stalls offering an array of festive products and crafts. The warming food on offer is hard to resist and includes dense and spicy gingerbread, mulled wine, and Bredle cakes—delicious little morsels traditionally prepared during the Advent period. There is also a skating rink and Christmas music performed at various locations around the city.

the canals under the restored 14th century city wall. Tall houses line the quays, and the area is full of restaurants and bars ∎

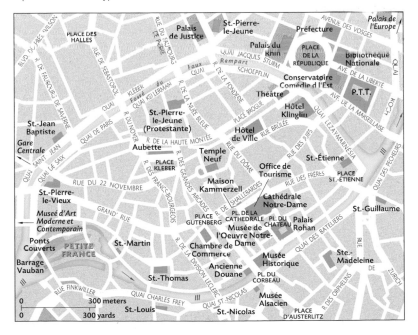

# Drive Along the Alsace Wine Route

**The Route du Vin winds through the Vosges foothills, threading between the valley floor and the fringes of woods blanketing higher slopes.**

The Alsace vineyards stretch for over 130 miles (200 km) across the foothills of the wooded Vosges Mountains from Marlenheim in the north to Thann in the south. Alsace wines were not widely known before World War II and were sold mainly as *vin ordinaire*; today, these dry, full-bodied wines have a reputation for quality, and Alsace now boasts 51 *grands crus* vineyards.

Mainly white wines are produced in Alsace, varying from bone-dry Rieslings to the sweet dessert wines labeled Vendanges Tardives, made from very late harvested grapes. Most independent producers (who sell wines made from grapes grown in their own vineyards) offer wine tastings and vineyard tours; their cellars and wineries are signposted along the way. You can also try wines at the many wine fairs and festivals (*www.tourisme-alsace.com, alsace-routes-des-vins.com*).

The Route du Vin passes ancient castles such as Eguisheim in the south, and abbeys farther north such as Andlau, whose ninth-century church was part of a convent. Towns and villages have cobbled streets, overhanging

## NOT TO BE MISSED:

Turckheim • Riquewihr • Ribeauvillé • Château d'Haut-Koenigsbourg • Rosheim

eaves, fountains, wells, and hanging baskets of flowers. The whole route takes days to enjoy, but the section between Colmar and Rosheim makes a fine day trip.

From Colmar (see pp. 132–133), take the D417 west to **Wintzenheim** ❶ and turn north onto the minor road that leads across the pretty Fecht River to **Turckheim,** with its three medieval gateways. From here, follow the Route du Vin signposts along mountain roads, climbing through vineyards to the flower-decked village of **Niedermorschwihr;** then go east and back west to Katzenthal, known for its Rieslings; and north to the village of **Ammerschwihr.**

From here, follow the N415 north to **Kaysersberg** ❷—birthplace of the missionary

## Grapes of the Region

Alsace wines are varietal (pressed from one grape variety) and are identified by grape and the maker's name. Most are made from one of four "noble" grapes. However, rosé and red wines are also produced from the **Pinot Noir** grape in a few vineyards around Ottrott in the north of Alsace and Herrenweg in the south. Crémant d'Alsace is a sparkling wine made by the Champagne method (see p. 123) from a blend of wines.

The white wine grapes and the characteristics of the wine they make:
**Gewurztraminer**—powerful, aromatic, with a fruity, spicy bouquet
**Muscat**—citrusy, slightly aromatic, and essentially dry
**Pinot Blanc**—fresh, harmonious
**Pinot Gris**—richly flavored with complex aromas
**Riesling**—fruity, floral, but delicate
**Sylvaner**—light, refreshing

doctor and Nobel Prize winner Albert
Schweitzer—set among woods.

Turn eastward through vineyards along
the D28 and then left onto the D1B. A detour
along the D3 takes you to the popular walled
village of **Riquewihr** ❸ (see p. 136). Then
follow the D1B north through medieval
**Ribeauvillé** ❹. Still on the D1B, continue
to Bergheim, where a Wednesday market is
held in the cobbled square, and **St.-Hippolyte**
❺, whose medieval ramparts are overlooked
by the spectacular towers of **Château d'Haut-
Koenigsbourg** (see p. 136).

From St.-Hippolyte, the D35 then
meanders north through a string of wine
villages—**Orschwiller**, with a small wine
museum; Riesling-producing **Scherwiller** ❻;
the old commune of **Dambach-la-Ville** ❼,
**Ottrott** ❽, which makes red wine from its
Pinot Noir grapes; and finally to **Rosheim**
❾, whose Maison des Païens may be the oldest domestic dwelling in Alsace (circa 1170).

| | |
|---|---|
| 🅰 | See also map pp. 106–107 |
| ▶ | Colmar |
| ⓘ | 52 miles (85 km) |
| 🕒 | One day |
| ▶ | Rosheim |

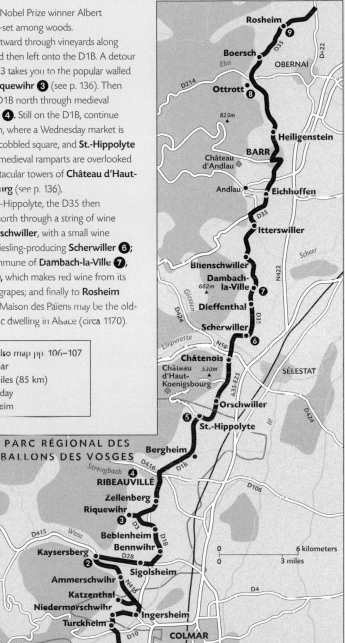

# Metz

The immense scale of the defenses of Metz convey something of the importance of this city, once one of the great frontier fortresses of France. A fortified bridge connects the Porte des Allemands, with its crenellations and lofty 13th-century towers, to the two huge bastions on the opposite bank of the Seille River.

**Metz**
- ⛰ 107 E3
- **Visitor information**
- ✉ place d'Armes
- ☎ 03 87 55 53 76

**St.-Pierre-aux-Nonnains**
- ✉ just off boulevard Poincaré

**Cathédrale St.-Étienne**
- ✉ place d'Armes

**Musée d'Art et d'Histoire**
- ✉ 2 rue de Haut-Poirier
- ☎ 03 87 20 13 20
- 🕐 Closed Tues.
- 💲 $$

Metz was already an old capital when the Romans invaded Gaul; it was the capital of the Frankish Merovingian dynasty before becoming a free city under the Holy Roman Empire. Water was brought in via an aqueduct whose remains can be seen at Jouy-aux-Arches, some 4 miles (7 km) southwest on the N57.

Set at the strategic confluence of the Seille and Moselle Rivers, the city center is crisscrossed by old bridges. **St.-Pierre-aux-Nonnains,** built on the site of a fourth-century Roman basilica, is thought to be France's earliest Christian church. The **Cathédrale St.-Étienne** was built between the 13th and 16th centuries. At 138 feet (42 m), its nave is the third highest of any French cathedral, lit by great windows with their original medieval glass.

The Petits-Carmes convent, between the cathedral and an arm of the Moselle River, became a museum in 1839. During a 1930s expansion, remains of the city's Roman baths were found. You can see them at the **Musée d'Art et d'Histoire.** The beaux arts collection here includes works by Rembrandt and Titian.

Though Metz is an easy day trip from Nancy or Strasbourg, the medieval houses, Moselle Valley views, nightlife, and entertainment make it a delightful place to stay. It is a good base for excursions to the battlefields of Verdun (see p. 112) and the Maginot Line forts at Fermont, Entrange, and Hackenberg. ∎

## Pompidou Metz

The Centre Pompidou in Metz (*1 parvis des Droits de l'Homme, tel 03 87 15 39 39, www .centrepompidou-metz.fr, $$*), which opened in 2010, is the first regional outpost of the Paris Pompidou (Beaubourg), putting the capital of Lorraine on the cultural map of Europe. Only 80 minutes from Paris with a new TGV rail connection, the museum expects to attract up to 400,000 visitors a year—a boost for the local economy, which has suffered in recent times due to industrial decline. The extraordinary modern building, designed by Japanese architect Shigeru Ban and his French colleague Jean de Gastines, is a light and airy structure, with an exposed wooden frame and undulating fiberglass roof, rather like a Chinese hat, with a large atrium and adjoining public garden. There is no permanent collection; major works will be borrowed from the vast collection of the Paris Pompidou. The inaugural exhibition featured masterpiece artworks by Georges Braque, Pablo Picasso, Jackson Pollock, Wassily Kandinsky, and Joan Miró.

# Nancy

The capital of Lorraine, on the Meurthe River, may be an up-to-date manufacturing city, but its historic heart is still caught in the 18th century. Nancy grew up in the 12th century around the stronghold of the dukes of Lorraine, but its transformation came in the 18th, when it was elegantly replanned and rebuilt under Stanislas Leszczynski, the dethroned king of Poland. In 1738 Leszczynski was created Duke of Lorraine by Louis XV, his son-in-law, and he made Nancy the seat of his brilliant court.

This charming town is green with parks and gardens. **Place Stanislas,** focus of the 18th-century town planning, has been recognized as a UNESCO World Heritage site. In the middle, a statue of Stanislas is flanked by two ornate fountains and enclosed by magnificent gilded wrought-iron railings. Surrounding the square are several 18th-century palaces and the Hôtel de Ville by Emmanuel Héré, a student of Gabriel Boffrand, leading architect of French rococo style.

The Place Stanislas gates were crafted by a master: Lamour.

A hotel occupies the palace on one side of the square; the **Musée des Beaux-Arts,** the other. The 18th-century facade remains, but the building has been extended to accommodate its collection of works by 19th- and 20th-century artists as well as decorative arts, including glassware from Cristalleries Daum.

The 16th-century ducal palace, west of Parc de la Pepinière, now holds the **Musée Lorrain,** featuring jewelry, arms, armor, and illuminated manuscripts, and a section devoted to the furniture, textiles, and even tombstones of the city's Jewish community.

Walking is the best way to appreciate the vistas from Place Stanislas along the tree-lined Place de la Carrière, flanked by gracious 18th-century residences, to the Palais du Gouvernement.

As if Nancy's fine baroque town planning were not enough, a group of artists led by glass craftsman Émile Gallé helped found the celebrated school of art nouveau here. Look for the artists' work on the west side of town, ranging from the 1903 Maison Huot by architect Émile André to the 1910 interior of the Brasserie Excelsior. Southwest of the railroad station, the **Musée de l'École de Nancy** (36–38 rue du Sergent-Blandan, tel 03 83 40 14 86, closed Mon.–Tues., $) displays the art nouveau style, with an emphasis on furniture, ceramics, and glassware. ■

**Nancy**
- 107 E2

**Visitor information**
- ✉ 1 place Stanislas
- ☎ 03 83 35 22 41

**www.ot-nancy.fr**

**Musée des Beaux-Arts**
- ✉ 3 place Stanislas
- ☎ 03 83 85 30 72
- 🕐 Closed Tues.
- $ $

**Musée Lorrain**
- ✉ 64 Grande Rue
- ☎ 03 83 32 18 74
- 🕐 Closed Mon.
- $ $$

# Colmar

An important fortified town in the Middle Ages, Colmar has kept many of its ancient churches and much of its medieval center. Half-timbered houses sport colored roof tiles and, in the Petite Venise quarter of the town, winding streets cross the canals that link to the Ill River, which in turn joins Colmar to the Rhine.

The second driest city in France, Colmar has perfected the art of outdoor dining.

**Colmar**

🗺 107 E2

**Visitor information**

✉ rue d'Unterlinden

☎ 03 89 20 68 92

**www.colmar.com**

**Musée d'Unterlinden**

✉ 1 rue d'Unterlinden

☎ 03 89 20 15 50

🕐 Closed Tues. Nov.–April

💲 $$

**www.musee-unter linden.com**

## Isenheim Altarpiece

One of France's most visited buildings is the former Dominican convent of Unterlinden (named after its linden trees), founded in the 13th century and still retaining its arcaded cloister. Converted into the **Musée d'Unterlinden** in 1849, it became the repository for works of art from surrounding religious institutions. The convent's most celebrated exhibit is the remarkable altarpiece originally painted

for the convent at Isenheim, 14 miles (22 km) south of Colmar. This inspirational work is one of the few extant paintings by the great 16th-century artist Mathias Grünewald, court painter at Mainz. Plans are under way for an ambitious modern extension to the building.

Southwest of the Unterlinden Museum, the 13th- to 14th-century **Basilique St.-Martin** contains some beautiful 14th-century stained glass. The

Dominican church nearby boasts the exquisite "Virgin in the Rose Bower," painted by 16th-century Colmar artist Martin Schongauer.

Cars are banned in old Colmar, so it is pleasant to stroll around, past some of ancient Colmar's superb buildings. The **Maison Adolphe,** built around 1350, and the former **Corps de Garde,** with a Renaissance balcony, are on Rue Mercerie, close to the St.-Martin basilica. The **Maison des Têtes** on Rue des Têtes, near the Unterlinden Museum, has a carved oriel window. The **Ancienne Douane** (Old Customs House) is 15th century and stands on the Grand'Rue, appropriately by a canal. La Petite Venise is the former leather-tanners' district, where the Lauch River and its canals are overlooked by picturesque old town houses, hung with flower baskets in summer.

The birthplace of master sculptor Frédéric-Auguste

**Underscoring fashion and style, Colmar's lavishly decorated architectural gem known as the Pfister House was built in 1537—for a hat maker.**

—MARGUERITE THOMAS
National Geographic Traveler
*magazine writer*

Bartholdi is now the **Musée Bartholdi** (*30 rue des Marchands, tel 03 89 41 90 60, closed Tues.*), a local history museum, where his studies for the Statue of Liberty are displayed. The **Fontaine du Vigneron,** a fountain dedicated to Alsatian vineyard owners, adorns the streets of Colmar. To the west, vineyards climb the slopes of the Vosges Mountains. As the capital of the Alsace wine district, Colmar hosts its August wine fair. ∎

## Routes des Crêtes

The most spectacular drive in northern France scales the Route des Crêtes (*www.massif-des-vosges.com*), literally the Road of the Crests, a strategic route cut across the peaks of the Vosges by French army engineers during World War I. On a clear day, vistas from the summit of 4,672-foot (1,424 m) Grand Ballon embrace the entire Vosges range—all the way to the Black Forest in Germany, south to the Jura, and across the Alps to Mont Blanc. (Check the weather forecast before setting out; low clouds, not unusual, will obscure views.)

The Route des Crêtes begins at Cernay, about 5 miles (9 km) west of Mulhouse.

Take the D5 north to Uffholtz and turn west on the D431. The road twists and turns its way up the steep sides of the Grand Ballon, the highest peak in the Vosges, its name said to be a corruption of *bois long* (long forest—the mountaintops were once clothed with trees).

Past the Grand Ballon the road forks: Follow the D430 to Le Hohneck (4,467 feet/1,362 m), where the grassy summit affords lovely views across wooded mountainsides. Continue on the D430 to its junction with the D417, then take the D61 northward past Lac Noir and Lac Blanc, mountain lakes in extinct volcanic craters, surrounded by woods.

# Food & Drink—Rich and Tasty

Alsace and Lorraine are the gastronomic giants of the north, home of quiche Lorraine, foie gras, suckling pig, and free-range goose. Alsatian cooks bring French elegance to such German staples as sauerkraut, dumplings, and stews—try the traditional *baeckenoffe*, a stew with beef and lamb. Lorraine has wonderful preserves and fruit tarts, such as bilberry, mirabelle plum, and red currant, and *jambon d'Ardennes* is one of the world's great cured hams.

Sunshine, seafood, *frites,* and friends. This casually convivial scene plays out all over the northern reaches of France in the warmer months.

Along the northern coast of France and in Flanders, along the Belgian border, you find delicious winter stews: *hochepot* (meat and root vegetable stew), *waterzooi* (fish stew), and *carbonnade de boeuf à la flamande* (beef stewed in beer). In summer there are light fish dishes to search out, such as herring around Boulogne (look for *craquelot*—a dish using grilled, smoked herring). Marvelous vegetables come from the market gardens of the marshy Somme and Flanders,

including endive and the raw ingredients for *flamiches* (leek, onion, or pumpkin tarts made with a pizza crust). Champagne offers extraordinarily imaginative cabbage dishes, and the Ardennes and the forests of the Vosges Mountains yield an equally astonishing array of mushrooms.

Amiens is famous for duck pie and pastry-encased pâtés; Arras and Troyes for *andouillettes*—spicy chitterling sausages. Pork is a specialty of Troyes; Ste.-Ménéhould

## INSIDER TIP:

Colmar's popular bakery Helmstetter *(11 rue des Serruriers)* has been making bread since 1776. Just look for the large wrought-iron sign of a pretzel—the traditional symbol of Alsatian bakers.

—MARGUERITE THOMAS
National Geographic Traveler *magazine writer*

is celebrated for pig's trotters slow-cooked for 48 hours. Expect to find rabbit, hare, partridge, venison, wild boar, and truffles on menus in the Ardennes, as well as in the Vosges Mountains.

Visitors touring the Champagne vineyards may be surprised to find still wines produced there, too. Bouzy, for example, is a still red made from the Pinot Noir grapes grown on the Montagne de Reims; Rosé des Riceys is a still rosé from Les Riceys in the southern vineyard area.

France's reputation for great wines overshadows its tradition of beer (see sidebar below) and cider. Cider, though typically a Norman and Breton drink, is also produced in Champagne and by the Cidrerie Georges Maeyaert in Milly-sur-Thérain by Beauvais.

Food with sense of place: traditional kugelhof, sweet and rich, and the famous quiche Lorraine, savory and rich. Both grace food-shop windows all through the region.

## The Other Bubbly

Northern France and Belgium share a long-established tradition of beer brewing, but only about three dozen nonindustrialized breweries are left in France. A French pressure group for traditional beer, Les Amis de la Bière, works hard to support these enterprises. Although Strasbourg is northern France's great brewing city, the best beer is actually brewed around Lille in the heart of Flanders. You could make a satisfying *brasserie* (brewery) tour of Nord and

Picardie, including the brasseries of St.-Sylvestre, near Steenvoorde; Lepers at Annoeullin and Castelain at Bénifontaine, both near Lens; the Brasserie Duyck at Jenlain, near Valenciennes; and Les Enfants de Guyant in Douai.

Alsace still has a few independent breweries, notably Fischer in Schiltigheim, which also produces Adelscott beer, flavored with malt whiskey, and Meteor, which makes a rustic, unpasteurized pilsner beer.

# More Places to Visit in Alsace & Lorraine

### Alsace-Moselle Memorial Museum

This dramatic modern museum sits on the site of the Schirmeck internment camp. It reveals the history of this region, which has changed nationalities four times since 1870, and illustrates the history of the camp and the wartime evacuations. Also visible is the site of Struthof, the only Nazi concentration camp on French soil. ✉ Schirmeck ☎ 03 88 47 45 50 🕐 Closed Mon. & most of Jan. 💲 $$

### Château d'Haut-Koenigsbourg

The D159 loops its way up from St.-Hippolyte toward this castle, giving startling vistas across the Alsace plain, 2,500 feet (750 m) below. The present castle is a 19th-century restoration of 15th-century fortifications around a 12th-century keep. Guides in period dress describe the building and its defenses. 🗺 107 E2 ☎ 03 88 82 50 60 💲 $$

**INSIDER TIP:**

**The best way to get to Château d'Haut-Koenigsbourg is via shuttle bus from the rail station in the pretty town of Selesrat.**

—ROSEMARY BAILEY
*National Geographic author*

### Domrémy-la-Pucelle

This Vosges village about 45 miles (74 km) southwest of Nancy boasts the modest house where Jeanne d'Arc was born in 1412. In the surrounding fields, she heard the voices of saints who urged her to deliver France from English domination and restore the Dauphin Charles to the French throne. In the chapel of **Notre-Dame de Bermont**

*(1 mile/1.5 km north in Brixey, open first Sat. of month)* where she prayed, a fresco has been dated to the 15th century. It shows a teenage girl with blond hair and blue eyes in peasant dress and may be a portrait of the warrior saint. 🗺 107 D2

### Mulhouse

A medieval town that was once a free city attached to the Swiss Confederation, Mulhouse saw some action in World War II. The 16th-century Hôtel de Ville survived and is now a museum of local history. The **Musée de l'Automobile** *(avenue de Colmar, tel 03 89 33 23 23, www.collection-schlumpf.com)* displays the Schlumpf collection, including Juan Fangio's Maserati and Charlie Chaplin's 1937 Rolls-Royce Phantom III. *www.tourisme-mulhouse.com* 🗺 107 E1 **Visitor information** ✉ 9 Hôtel de Ville, place de la Reunion ☎ 03 89 35 48 48

### Riquewihr

Layers of fortifications still protect the 16th-century houses and courtyards of this picturesque little wine town. The main street is defended by a medieval fortified gate, now a museum of archaeology. The Cour des Bergers is the original town gate, complete with portcullis and a prison with torture chamber. *www.ribeau-riquewihr.com* 🗺 107 E2 **Visitor information** ✉ rue 1ère Armée ☎ 03 89 73 23 23 🕐 Closed Sun.

### Wissembourg

On the Alsace–Germany border, Wissembourg has a beautiful old center, partly enclosed by ramparts and encircled by the Lauter River. The 13th-century **Église de St.-Paul-et-St.-Pierre** *(avenue de la Sous-Préfecture)* was built on the site of a seventh-century Benedictine abbey. 🗺 107 F3 **Visitor information** ✉ 9 Place de la République ☎ 03 38 89 41 10 11

Northern European provinces, historically more influenced by
Norsemen and Celts than by Romans—and by the artists drawn here

# Normandy &
Brittany

In Normandy, Rouen's old quarter
boasts a work-of-art outdoor clock.

# Normandy & Brittany

Normandy and Brittany together form the northwestern corner of France and combine a largely agricultural hinterland with a coast that has long been popular with both French and foreign vacationers. Both regions are major agricultural producers: Normandy is particularly famous for its dairy products and apples and Brittany for its vegetables, though both now also produce substantial quantities of meat and grains.

In Brittany, walls built in the 13th century were the first of Fougère's fortifications.

The extensive coastline has made fishing an important industry, along with the cultivation of mussels and oysters. The shoreline of northern Normandy and northern Brittany is edged by the English Channel (la Manche), while to the south, Brittany's coast juts out into the Atlantic Ocean.

All along the coast, fishing harbors and ferry ports see constant traffic between France and Britain. The entire shoreline offers a wonderful variety of landscape: rugged granite headlands or chalky cliffs interspersed with sandy beaches.

The climate is relatively gentle, affected by the Gulf Stream and warmed by west winds that bring humidity and mild winters. However, harsher winds from the northwest and west can lower the temperatures and create sudden storms, especially along the coast. Brittany has some of the highest tides in the world around the bay of Mont-St.-Michel.

Southern Normandy and Brittany cover what is known as the Armorican Massif, ancient granite mountains that have eroded into gently rolling hills. In the west, the hard granite produces the dramatic coastline of Brittany. To the east the granite gives way to the limestone of the Paris basin, the source of the pale, easily carved Caen stone used to build many cathedrals and churches, and the chalk cliffs of the upper Normandy Channel coast.

The Seine is the main river of the region, looping its way through Normandy from Paris to Le Havre, a major communications route that has carried trade (and occasionally invading armies) for thousands of years. The main cities of the area are Rouen and Caen, both of which are regional capitals of Normandy, and Rennes, the capital of Brittany. Brest is a great naval port, while Nantes and Le Havre are important commercial ports.

Despite their proximity, the histories of Normandy and Brittany have been very different, resulting in very distinct regional identities.

Normandy, on the Seine River and on the way to Paris, has always been an easy target for invaders. The Vikings began their raids up the Seine in the ninth century and eventually settled and colonized the land that took its name from these Norsemen. Traffic with Britain, and the success of William the Conqueror's 1066 invasion, meant significant cultural exchange, exemplified in the many churches in the Romanesque style (referred to as Norman style in England) on both sides of the English Channel.

British Celts colonized the Armorican Peninsula in the sixth century, and it became known as "la Petite Bretagne" (Little Britain), a designation eventually shortened to Bretagne (Brittany is the anglicized version

of Bretagne). They established a culture and spoke a language utterly different from those of the rest of France and these endure to this day. ■

## NOT TO BE MISSED:

Rouen cathedral's west front 141

A drive on the Route des Abbayes 142–143

The Bayeux tapestry's stunning details 144–145

Sipping cider in the pays d'Auge 147

The sea-lashed Mont St.-Michel 150–151

The parish closes of Finistère 160

Carnac's superb Neolithic remains 162–163

Area of map detail

# Normandy

Sheer variety of landscape is Normandy's most striking feature. The craggy grandeur of the coastline on the Cotentin Peninsula in the west gives way to the sands of the Calvados area, the elegance of Deauville and Trouville-sur-Mer, and the cliffs of the Côte d'Albâtre. Inland are rich rural landscapes with cheese producers, Calvados distilleries, and small restaurants. And everywhere, pretty stone villages, manors, and farmhouses evince an architectural heritage that has managed to survive even the devastation of World War II.

Normandy's steep chalk cliffs are being steadily eroded by the sea.

The scenes of picturesque rural contentment that typify Normandy today belie the region's momentous and often somber history. Conflicts of many ages are made tangible in the great cathedral city of Rouen and in the majestically ruined medieval abbeys studded along the meandering course of the Seine River.

Most awe inspiring of all is the Abbaye de Mont-St.-Michel, a place of pilgrimage for ten centuries on its perilous rocky island above the sea. Bayeux still treasures its astonishing tapestry, a priceless record of William the Conqueror's invasion of Britain from these shores in 1066. Nearby, the Allied landing beaches mark a more recent story of invasion, serving as a permanent reminder of a period of heroism and extreme suffering.

Other, gentler, images of Normandy are owed to the Impressionist artists who sought inspiration in its seascapes and watery skies. Eugène Boudin's windblown dresses on the beach at Trouville and Raoul Dufy's gaily bobbing yachts at Le Havre elegantly capture these aspects of Normandy. Above them all, however, towers Claude Monet, who, in his exquisite gardens at Giverny (see p. 104), created compositions of light, reflections, and color that no visitor to Normandy should willingly miss. ■

# Rouen

The ancient capital of the duchy of Normandy, founded as a Roman settlement on the Seine, Rouen today is a huge industrial city and port. The old city to the north of the river has been sensitively restored after the widespread destruction of World War II, and a stroll here will reveal a mass of museums, fine churches, and half-timbered Norman houses.

Start as Monet did, at the **Cathédrale Notre-Dame,** the glorious Gothic west front of which he painted in many different lights. Springing from 12th-century foundations are soaring Gothic arches, intricate Flamboyant carving, and two mismatched towers flanking the facade. Above the doorways, delicate openwork gables top rows of statues. The interior is a cool retreat of tall columns, luminous stained glass, and ancient tombs, including that of Rollo, first Duke of Normandy.

To find the heart of old Rouen, head along pedestrians-only Rue du Gros-Horloge, lined with fine half-timbered buildings, passing under the medieval clock set in a Renaissance arch. At the western end is **Place du Vieux-Marché,** where Jeanne d'Arc was burned at the stake in 1431. At the site of her pyre is a modern church built in her honor. The **Musée Jeanne d'Arc** (33 place du Vieux-Marché, tel 02 35 88 02 70) contains one of the few known portraits of Joan, a sketch from 1429.

Back toward the cathedral, the **Palais de Justice** is a remarkable example of 16th-century Gothic Flamboyant architecture, delicate and exuberant. West of Place du Vieux-Marché lies the **Hôtel-Dieu,** Rouen's old hospital,

where novelist Gustave Flaubert was born in 1821. It is now the **Musée Flaubert et Histoire de la Médecine** (tel 02 35 15 59 95, closed Sun.–Mon.), devoted to his life and to medical history. Flaubert used to be a regular visitor at the **Natural History Museum** (rue Beauvoisine, tel 02 35 71 41 50, closed Mon.), now refurbished.

## INSIDER TIP:

**Rouen's soaring Cathédrale Notre-Dame is magnificently detailed. Bring along binoculars to see the architectural elements way up high.**

—JANE SUNDERLAND
*National Geographic contributor*

To the north on Square Verdrel, the **Musée des Beaux-Arts** (tel 02 35 71 28 40, closed Tues.) houses an excellent collection of European paintings, including one of Monet's Rouen cathedral series.

Beyond the cathedral are the beautifully restored **Église de St.-Ouen** and another Flamboyant Gothic masterpiece, the **Église de St.-Maclou.** ∎

**Rouen**
🅼 139 E3
**Visitor information**
✉ 25 place de la Cathédrale
☎ 02 32 08 32 40
**www.rouen tourisme.com**

**Cathédrale Notre-Dame**
✉ place de la Cathédrale

# Seine Valley Drive: Rouen to the Coast

Beyond Rouen, the Seine River snakes its way slowly to the sea past wooded valleys, chalk cliffs, and apple orchards. This lovely drive along the north bank is also known as the Route des Abbayes, after the string of abbeys founded on the banks of the river in the seventh century, which were to become powerful centers of learning.

Follow the D982 west from Rouen to the village of **St.-Martin-de-Boscherville ①**, whose **Abbaye de St.-Georges** *(tel 02 35 32 10 82)* is on the site of Roman temples. Begun in 1050, it escaped destruction during the Revolution because the villagers adopted it as their parish church. Today it is one of the best preserved examples of Norman Romanesque architecture.

Continue on the D982 to **Duclair,** with fine views of the river. Fork left to detour along the D65, following a great meander of the Seine past the orchards around Le

---

**NOT TO BE MISSED:**

Abbaye de St.-Georges • Abbaye de Jumièges • Abbaye de St.-Wandrille • Musée Victor-Hugo • Pont de Tancarville

---

Mesnil-sous-Jumièges. After the village, the white towers of the **Abbaye de Jumièges ②** *(tel 02 35 37 24 02)* soon loom into sight above the distant trees. These ruins, the most

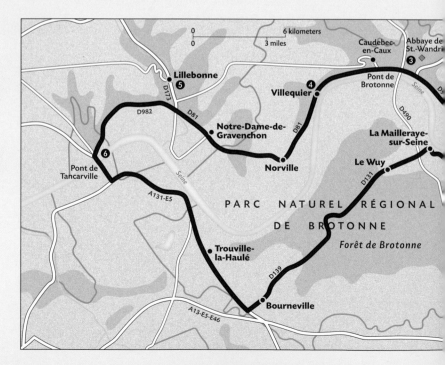

majestic in Normandy, bear witness to a turbulent past. Founded in 654, the abbey was sacked in the ninth century by the Vikings, then refounded in 1067 in the presence of William the Conqueror. At its height, in the 13th and 14th centuries, the monastery housed over 2,000 monks and lay brothers. Only small portions of the abbey survived the Revolution.

Proceed along the D143 back to the D982, and go northwest to the Fontenelle Valley and the **Abbaye de St.-Wandrille** ❸ *(tel 02 35 96 23 11, under restoration)*, a Benedictine community revived in 1931. Founded in the seventh century, then sacked by the Vikings, the abbey was refounded in the tenth century and flourished until the Revolution. The church, dating from the 13th and 14th centuries, remains in ruins, but the 14th-century cloister has been restored. The monks founded a new church in the 1960s in an ancient wooden tithe barn, brought here

from 30 miles (48 km) away and lovingly rebuilt piece by piece. Try to time your visit to attend a sung Mass of Gregorian chant *(weekdays 9:25 a.m., Sun. 10 a.m.)*.

Drive on to Caudebec-en-Caux on the D982, then take the D81 to **Villequier** ❹, where the **Musée Victor-Hugo** *(quai Victor-Hugo, tel 02 35 56 78 31, closed Sun. a.m. & Tues.)* tells of the drowning of the writer's daughter, which inspired some of his most poignant poetry. **Lillebonne** ❺, farther west along the D81 and D173, has impressive Roman remains. Return to the D982 and cross the Seine on the **Pont de Tancarville** ❻, a stunning feat of engineering offering great views of the estuary.

From here, take the A131 to the D139 turnoff to Bourneville. Follow the D139 and D131 to La Mailleraye-sur-Seine and then take the D65 south through the Forêt de Brotonne to Jumièges via the ferry *(free, leaves every 20 minutes)* and return to Rouen.

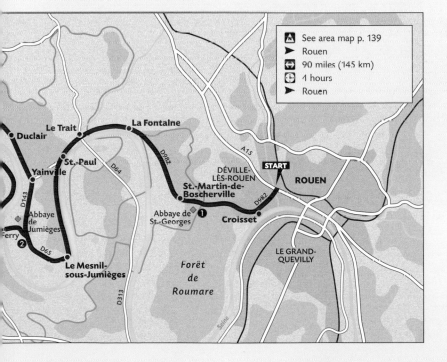

# Bayeux

Even without the Bayeux Tapestry, the historic town of Bayeux would merit a leisurely visit for its beautifully preserved medieval center and impressive cathedral. But it is, of course, the world-famous tapestry (actually an embroidery on linen) that makes Bayeux so irresistible.

The tower of the mainly 13th-century Gothic Cathédrale Notre-Dame in Bayeux was a late 15th-century addition. Within the cathedral are fine 15th-century frescoes.

**Bayeux**

🗺 139 D3

**Visitor information**

✉ Pont St.-Jean

☎ 02 31 51 28 28

**www.bessin-normandie.com**

Recounting the 1066 Norman invasion of England under William the Conqueror, the 230-foot-long (70 m) **Tapisserie de la reine Mathilde** is an extraordinary historical document as well as a staggering work of art. Age has dimmed some of the dyes (green in particular), but the wit and vigor of its execution are still superb. Panel by panel (58 in all), it tells a dramatic story rich in incident and amusing detail, from the original meeting of Harold

and William, to the blessing of William's invasion fleet, the appearance of Halley's comet, and the fatal arrow that felled King Harold of England, ensuring victory for the Normans. The minutiae of medieval and military life are graphically detailed: Suits of chain mail are carried on portable hangers; soldiers picnic off their shields, while dukes dine at a table on roast chicken and kabobs.

Protected behind bulletproof glass in the **Centre**

**Guillaume-le-Conquérant,** this medieval forerunner of the strip cartoon was probably commissioned by William's half brother, Bishop Odo of Bayeux, for the consecration of the cathedral in 1077—certainly Odo himself figures large in the story. The tapestry may have been the work of French or English embroiderers,

**INSIDER TIP:**

**Walk along the ancient park-edged canal in the center of Bayeux; keep an eye out for the old mill works.**

—BARBARA NOE
*National Geographic Books editor*

but is usually attributed to Saxon weavers or English nuns. Try to allow at least 90 minutes for a visit in order to take full advantage not only of the tapestry itself but also of the highly illuminating audiovisual displays that precede it and set it in context.

Emerging from the exhibition, stroll into the heart of medieval Bayeux. The town was particularly fortunate in being the first to be liberated by the Allies in 1944, thus escaping the devastation suffered by many others.

Overlooking the town are the Gothic spires of the **Cathédrale Notre-Dame** (*rue du Bienvenu*), with its beautiful 11th-century crypt and towers remaining from Bishop Odo's original Romanesque church. The chapels and crypt showcase delightful 15th-century frescoes, and the 12th-century chapter house has a maze depicted in its 15th-century tiled floor. The cobbled streets around the south of Rue St.-Martin contain many fine stone and timber-framed houses dating from the 15th to the 17th centuries. The Aure River runs through the garden-filled town, spanned by a humpback bridge.

Saturday is market day in **Place St.-Patrice,** a huge bustling outdoor event recalling something of the flavor of medieval Bayeux. You can find all kinds of local fruits and vegetables, along with flowers and meat and regional specialties. Traditional Bayeux lace is still made in the town and is worth seeking out.

On the southern edge of the town is the **Musée Mémorial de la Bataille de Normandie** (see p. 148), with a poignant British war cemetery almost opposite it. ∎

**Centre Guillaume-le-Conquérant**
✉ rue de Nesmond
☎ 02 31 51 25 50
$ $$
**www.tapisserie-bayeux.fr**

**Normandie Pass**

If you're planning to see the Bayeux tapestry as well as visit several of the D-Day sights, it is worth buying a Normandie Pass *(www.normandiepass.com)*, which gives a range of discounts for more than three dozen A-list museums and sights in the Normandy area.

Here's how it works: You simply pay an extra 1 euro on top of your first admission charge to cover all the other sights you might visit.

# Food & Drink—Oysters, Etc.

Both Normandy and Brittany rejoice in a long coastline that yields an abundance of fish and shellfish. Combined with the produce of the lush dairy farms and orchards of Normandy and the vegetable farms of Brittany, this rich trawl of seafood has shaped the gastronomy of the region.

A Normandy success story: cheese, bread, wine, friends, a dog, and the pretty outdoors.

Along the coast you can dine sumptuously on all manner of seafood, especially mussels, oysters, and lobster. Fish, particularly sole, is often served with *sauce normande,* containing cream, mussels, shrimps, and mushrooms.

Pork and pork products are also popular, especially the wide range of *andouille* (chitterling) sausages made locally. The lamb here is excellent, acquiring a delicate salty flavor from grazing on the coastal salt marshes *(pré-salé).*

A favorite dish is *tripes à la mode de Caen,* a rich stew of tripe and root vegetables cooked slowly with cider and traditionally enjoyed as a midmorning snack. Other hearty main courses of the region include Rouen duck in a blood-thickened sauce and *pieds de cochon farcis,* stuffed pig's trotters.

Normandy is famous for its dairy products and for the apples that go into cider, traditionally drunk with meals instead of wine, and

Calvados (apple brandy). Apples come sliced, caramelized, in almond cream, fried in fritters, or doused in Calvados. Apples and cream are often combined with Calvados to make delicious sauces for meat. The rich milk of Normandy cows produces France's finest butter and some of its best cheeses, including Camembert, Livarot, and Pont l'Éveque.

Calvados (or affectionately, Calva) is widely used, enhancing the flavor and cutting the richness of the ubiquitous cream sauces. It is often drunk midmeal as a *digestif* known as *le trou Normand* (literally "Norman hole," clearly intended to be filled with more food). Another specialty is Benedictine liqueur, made to an herbal recipe developed by monks.

The harsher landscapes of Brittany yield a gastronomy that is, not surprisingly, less rich. The sea dominates local menus: Among the bewildering variety of fish available, sole, turbot, and whiting come together in the spectacular *cotriade*, a fish soup, often with potatoes or, occasionally, cream.

Moulade—mussel soup—is a local favorite, as is *moules marinières*—mussels cooked in white wine, shallots, onions, and fresh parsley. *Palourdes farcies*, grilled clams on the half shell stuffed with shallots and herbs, is another popular dish.

Most impressive of all Breton dishes is the handsome *plateau de fruits de mer*, a giant spread of seafood, including oysters, crabs, langoustines, prawns, clams, and winkles. (This grand still life is a mainstay in Paris brasseries.) Watch a French family out for Sunday lunch dive into one of these; chances are good that hours later they will still be there, surrounded by picked-clean shells and empty glasses.

Cancale is the center of the Breton oyster industry and worth a visit specifically to sample its fresh-from-the-sea bivalves, usually served raw with a dip of shallot vinegar or just a squeeze of lemon.

In the "turf," category, *gigot d'agneau à la bretonne*—roast lamb with white haricot beans—shows up on many restaurant menus.

Breton food is not all fish, pork, and pré-salé

**Mussels make for a first course that deliciously communicates the taste of the sea.**

lamb. Brittany produces vast quantities of vegetables. Artichokes have now become the symbol of the region (not least when they are used to block the roads to protest European Union agricultural policy).

Crepes (*galettes*), both sweet and savory, are mainstays of the Breton diet, served as a main course—usually with ham or cheese fillings, or with eggs on top—or lacily thin as exquisite desserts, known appropriately as *crêpes dentelles*. And, yes, *crêpes Suzette*—those thin sweet pancakes with orange juice and Grand Marnier—is authentic to the area. Another don't-miss dessert is *Kouign-Amann*: pastry topped with caramelized sugar.

---

## EXPERIENCE: The Circular Cider Route

Enjoy the full flavor of the apples of Normandy by following the Cider Route (*www.calvados-tourisme.com*) through the pays d'Auge. A 25-mile (40 km) well-signposted circular route takes you to cider and Calvados (apple brandy) producers in traditional half-timbered houses. The route passes through tiny villages, cornfields, and, of course, apple orchards. Apples have been grown here since the ninth century; today, some 40 varieties are cultivated. The trees are in bloom from April to May, and harvesting takes place from September to December.

Start at the village of **Cambremer,** where you could have lunch with a glass

of cider, then head to **Calvados Pierre Huet** (*5 avenue des Tilleuls, tel 02 31 63 01 09*) for a guided tour and tastings of cider, Calvados, and *pommeau* (a mixture of apple juice and apple brandy).

Next, visit the pretty village of **Beuvron-en-Auge,** the caves and cemetery at **Beaufour-Druval,** and the little hamlet of **La Roque-Baignard.**

At **Le Domaine de Canon** (*14270 Mezidon-Canon, tel 02 31 90 94 49, www.coupdecanon.fr*), you can participate in the harvest of apples and honey and explore the farm with its sheep, cows, pigs, and llamas. You could even spend the night in a treehouse.

# Normandy Landing Beaches

Early on June 6, 1944—D-Day—an invasion force of thousands of craft landed on the beaches of the Normandy coast. This was Operation Overlord, the meticulously planned and desperately fought Allied offensive to reclaim Normandy and ultimately Europe from its German occupiers. Many of the towns and villages lay largely in ruins, but the Battle of Normandy was won, and the tide of the war turned irrevocably in the Allies' favor.

Among those buried in the Colleville-sur-Mer cemetery are 9,386 American war casualties.

**Musée Mémorial de la Bataille de Normandie**

- ✉ boulevard Fabian-Ware, Bayeux
- ☎ 02 31 51 46 90
- 💲 $$. Free for World War II veterans

**www.normandie memoire.com**

Today, more than 60 years later, the debris of war can still be seen, and some who visit the landing beaches have personal memories of those somber days. To make sense of the deserted bunkers, tangles of barbed wire, and rusting hulks, begin by visiting one of the museums devoted to the subject. Almost every town in the area has its own small museum with a poignant display of mementos, but a useful overview—complete with a wealth of photographs and contemporary uniforms, weapons, and documents—is

presented in the **Musée Mémorial de la Bataille de Normandie** in Bayeux.

All along the beaches, the remains of German bunkers have been converted into memorials, providing a terrifying intimation of the challenge faced by the troops in the landing craft. The vast expanses of sand—at low tide, in particular—make it chillingly clear why it was so critical to time the landing to coincide with high tide.

## Battles and Aftermath

Tales of heroism abound. At the west end of **Omaha Beach** rises the **Pointe du Hoc,** where an advance force of U.S. Rangers scaled the cliffs at dawn to knock out the German batteries. They were fiercely fought and by the end only 65 Rangers, out of the initial 225, survived. **St.-Laurent-sur-Mer** has an Omaha museum *(rue de la Mer, tel 02 31 21 97 44, closed mid-Nov.–mid-Feb.).*

Overlooking Omaha Beach, where nearly 10,000 Americans perished in the face of the most effective German resistance of the battle, is the largest American military cemetery in Normandy at **Colleville-sur-Mer** *(tel 02 31 51 62 00).* Most of the French soldiers who died now lie in their home towns, but the cemeteries for the American, British, Canadian, Polish, and German casualties dot the landscape. Heartrending rows of crosses and Stars of David stretch to the horizon.

The town of **Arromanches** (near the beach code-named Gold) preserves part of the famous Mulberry harbors, perhaps the most striking remains of the hardware of war. The **Musée du Débarquement** *(place du 6 Juin, tel 02 31 22 34 31, closed Jan.)* tells the scarcely believable story of these artificial harbors, towed stealthily across the channel to land 135,000 men, 20,000 vehicles, mountains of ammunition, and stores to support the troops.

## After D-Day

In the days and weeks after D-Day, land was gained inch by inch across Normandy by dint of bitter fighting. Tanks struggled

in the narrow sunken lanes and the thick hedges of Normandy's *bocage* country, and villages caught in the crossfire were pulverized.

Two months of fighting left many historic towns in smoking ruins. St.-Lô and Falaise were the epicenters of the battle and suffered massive damage, but **Caen** (see p. 152) was also ravaged. Its rebuilding, like that of many other ports and towns in Normandy, took years. The town center has been completely reconstructed, and the castle, churches, and two great Romanesque abbeys restored.

### Battlefield Routes

**Eight routes signposted Normandie Terre-Liberté** *(www.normandie memoire .com/NM60Anglais/1_par cours/parcours.htm)* trace some key 1944 battle sites, starting from the famous Pegasus Bridge near Caen, the site of the first airborne assault. The itineraries, in chronological sequence, put the D-Day battle into a geographic perspective, showing how it unfolded in 1944.

Caen's **Le Mémorial,** a museum for peace, opened in 1988. This high-tech building, on the German headquarters site of June 1944, tells the story of D-Day through archive film and audiovisual displays. With its thoughtful tone and emphasis on the sacrifice rather than the glory of war, it is a fitting place to end a tour of the landing beaches. ■

**Arromanches**
- 139 D3

**Visitor information**
- 2 rue du Maréchal Joffre
- 02 31 22 36 45

**www.ot-arromanches.fr**

**Le Mémorial (Musée pour la Paix)**
- 139 D3
- esplanade Eisenhower, Caen
- 02 31 06 06 44 (from abroad) or 08 25 06 06 44 (within France)
- Closed Jan.
- $$. Free for World War II veterans

# Mont St.-Michel

Buffeted by ferocious tides and winds, ringed by treacherous quicksand, and currently accessible only via a narrow causeway, the Abbaye de Mont-St.-Michel rises magnificently from its pinnacle of rock. Symbol of Normandy and now a World Heritage site, described by Guy de Maupassant as a "gigantic granite jewel, delicate as lace, thronged with towers and slender belfries," the abbey has been a place of pilgrimage for well over a thousand years.

First settled in the eighth century, Mont St.-Michel now receives more than 3 million visitors a year.

**Mont St.-Michel**
🗺 139 D2
**Visitor information**
✉ boulevard de l'Avancée
☎ 02 33 60 14 30
💲 $$. Guided tours (1 hour)

**www.ot-montsaint michel.com**

In the eighth century, this was a simple rock in the sea, a Celtic funeral mount covered in woods. Then in 708, according to legend, Aubert, Bishop of Avranches, had a vision of the Archangel Michael who instructed him to build an oratory on this rock, accessible only at low tide. In the church of St. Gervais in Avranches you can see Aubert's skull with a dent where the archangel is said to have tapped him on the head.

Richard I, Duke of Normandy, founded a Benedictine abbey here in the tenth century. Gradually the island became encased in monastic buildings. Through the centuries, these structures have been altered, have expanded, or have fallen down.

Over the original oratory, the monks built the church of Notre-Dame-sous-Terre, which is now the crypt of the Romanesque abbey church, begun in the 11th century. As the monastery increased in importance, the French monarchy took a greater interest in its strategic potential, and more monastic buildings, known as La Merveille, were added in the new Gothic style.

This soaring Gothic masterpiece encompasses three levels. At the top, the monks remained enclosed in the abbey church with its exquisite marble cloisters and the superbly lit refectory. On this level, a terrace on the seaward side gives superb views of the bay. The second story accommodated the abbot, noble guests, and knights: The rib vaulting and capitals of the knights' room are particularly magnificent. Humble pilgrims found succor on the lower level.

Even though medieval pilgrims risked being sucked into the quicksand surrounding the rock or overtaken by the incoming tide, Mont St.-Michel steadily prospered to become one of the most prominent sites of pilgrimage in France. In the 12th century, the influence of the great abbey was ensured when it hosted peace negotiations between Louis VII of France and Henry II of England.

## INSIDER TIP:

**Experience Mont St.-Michel via horseback or by taking a micro-flight. Contact the visitor information office for details.**

—ROSEMARY BAILEY
*National Geographic author*

The **Porte de l'Avancée** gives access to the **Grande Rue,** lined by 15th- and 16th-century houses. It leads steeply up to the abbey's stairway, the **Grand Degré.**

## Visiting Mont St.-Michel

**Access to the island of Mont St.-Michel (www.mont-saint-michel.world-guides.com) is free, but there is a fee for parking. You will be warned if there is any risk of submersion by the tide—Mont St.-Michel has the greatest tidal range in continental Europe. In summer, it is best to park on the mainland and then walk across the causeway. But that option might not be available soon. In the fight to prevent the bay from silting over, a major project due for completion in 2012 is under way. It involves removing the causeway. A river dam and new bridge are under construction. Visitors will then be able to park on the mainland, visit a new visitor center, and take a shuttle to the island.**

During the Revolution, the abbey buildings were turned into a prison, and it was not until the mid-19th century, after a public outcry led by Victor Hugo, that restoration began. In addition to repair work, a spire was added to the church. The architect moved in, along with his maid, who married the baker's son and established a hotel. She was the legendary Mère Poulard. Her restaurant on the lower slopes of the mount remains to this day.

In 1966, monks returned and Mont St.-Michel is once more a Benedictine foundation: Monastic life continues despite the tourists. Visit early or late, or attend the daily lunchtime Mass.

The **Scriptorial** in Avranches, completed in 2007, exhibits thousands of Mont St.-Michel books and medieval manuscripts, most on view for the first time since the French Revolution. ∎

# More Places to Visit in Normandy

It's easy to see why Normandy's port of Honfleur has lured artists over the centuries.

## Caen

Heavily restored after World War II, Caen nevertheless retains magnificent vestiges of its past. This was the site chosen by William the Conqueror for his castle in the 11th century. As penance for their consanguineous marriage, he and his wife, Matilda, endowed the city with two Romanesque jewels, the **Abbaye aux Hommes** and the **Abbaye aux Dames.** The great church of St.-Étienne, in the Abbaye aux Hommes, sheltered hundreds of citizens during the 1944 bombardment; today the abbey houses the fine **Musée des Beaux-Arts.** Also worth visiting is the D-Day museum **Le Mémorial** (see p. 149). *www.tourisme.caen.fr* 139 D3  **Visitor information** ✉ place St.-Pierre ☎ 02 31 27 14 14

## Cherbourg-Octeville

The great port of Cherbourg, on the tip of the Cotentin Peninsula, is famed chiefly for its harbor—and justly so: The building of its great breakwater, 2 miles (3 km) out to sea, was a heroic achievement spanning two centuries. **Fort du Roule,** overlooking the town, offers panoramic views of the harbor.

Cherbourg also saw ferocious German resistance in 1944, and now houses the **Musée de la Guerre et de la Libération.** The **Musée Thomas-Henry** contains works by painter Jean-François Millet, who was born in the nearby village of Gruchy. The biggest attraction is the **Cité de La Mer,** where you can learn about the sea and explore a missile submarine. *www.otcherbourgcotentin.fr* 139 D3  **Visitor information** ✉ 3 quai Alexandre III ☎ 02 33 93 52 02

## Côte Fleurie

The string of sandy beaches and fashionable resorts west of Honfleur, known as the "flowery coast," was popularized in the 19th century by artists and writers. In the 1860s, Napoleon III started bringing his court for summer visits to **Trouville-sur-Mer** *(Map 139 E3, visitor information, boulevard F. Moureaux, tel 02 31 14 60 70).* Fashionable Paris flocked in his wake, the journey facilitated by the new railroad.

Even grander is **Deauville** *(Map 139 E3, visitor information, place de la Mairie, tel 02 31 14 40 00, www.trouvillesurmer.org),* the 19th-century creation of one of Napoleon's dukes, who also built its racecourse. The casino followed, along with the famous esplanade, Les Planches. Both Trouville-sur-Mer and Deauville boast exuberant villas and some very grand hotels.

Farther west is **Cabourg** *(Map 139 E3, visitor information, place Bruno Coquatrix, tel 02 31 91 20 00)*, immortalized in all its belle epoque elegance by Marcel Proust in *À la Recherche du Temps Perdu (Remembrance of Things Past)*, under the pen name Balbec. The glorious beach is still there, as is the astonishing seaside architecture, including the Grand Hôtel, where Proust stayed (and where madeleines are served for breakfast, naturally).

## INSIDER TIP:

**People like to sit around Honfleur's boat-filled harbor, tucking into mussels and fries (mussels are to Normandy what burgers are to America).**

—ALAN RICHMAN
National Geographic Traveler
*magazine writer*

## Dieppe

Dieppe, one of the deepest harbors on the English Channel, prospered through trade in the 16th and 17th centuries, but its heyday was as a 19th-century beach resort, the nearest to Paris and very fashionable. Today, visitors enjoy the seafront esplanade, the casino, amusement parks, seawater pools, and the busy port. *www.dieppetourisme.com* ⚠ 139 E3 **Visitor information** ✉ pont Jehan-Ango ☎ 02 32 14 40 60

## Granville

Visit the childhood home of Christian Dior *(rue d'Estouteville, tel 02 33 61 48 27, closed Oct.-April, www.musee-dior-granville.com)*, a superb pink-and-white belle epoque villa on a cliff overlooking the sea, surrounded by beautiful gardens

originally planned by the fashion designer's mother. The collection includes costumes, hats, and many accessories and artifacts. In summer you can take tea in the garden with views of the sea. ⚠ 139 D2

## Honfleur

This delightful harbor town at the mouth of the Seine has retained much of the charm that attracted artists in the 19th century, among them Boudin and Pissarro. It remains a magnet for artists: Painters perch on the quaysides, and exhibitions of contemporary art are held in the converted 17th-century warehouses around the Vieux Bassin, the old fishing port. The **Musée Eugène-Boudin** tells the story of Honfleur's artistic past, with works by Boudin, Dufy, and Monet. One of Monet's many subjects was the 15th-century **Église Ste.-Catherine,** a structure built of wood and a rare surviving example of the medieval shipwright's craft. *www.ot-honfleur .fr* ⚠ 139 E3 **Visitor information** ✉ quai le Paulmier ☎ 02 31 89 23 30

## Le Havre & the Côte d'Albâtre

Aside from the St. François quarter around the old docks, Le Havre has little to show for its long history as a major port. But the new town built by architect Auguste Perret on the ruins left by World War II is an example of bold 20th-century urban planning and was designated a World Heritage site in 2005. The glass-and-steel **Musée Malraux** *(closed Tues.)* is an outstanding example of modern design, with works by Boudin, Dufy, and others. North of Le Havre and across the estuary now spanned by the vast new Pont de Normandie stretch the dazzling white cliffs of the Côte d'Albâtre (Alabaster Coast). The chic little town of **Étretat**, nestling between huge cliffs, is famous for its rock formations. ⚠ 139 E3 **Visitor information** ✉ 186 boulevard Clemenceau, Le Havre ☎ 02 32 74 04 04

# Brittany

Wave-lashed and windswept, Brittany's breathtaking coastline stretches for over 700 miles (1,100 km), a world of rocky peninsulas and headlands, mist-wreathed islands and tiny harbors, secret coves and hidden inlets. Its strength is in fortified towns such as St.-Malo and Vitré, and its wealth in the ports that shelter its fishing fleet and the old fishing villages that now double as resorts. Its drama lies in the towering cliffs of Finistère and the fantastic—and treacherous—rock formations of the Côte de Granit Rose.

The fine-sand beaches along the old summer resort of Val-André are made for walking.

Here the sea is a force to be treated with respect. But the mild climate, sheltered bays, and magnificent beaches also make Brittany a perfect place for family vacations, and a paradise for bird-watchers. Its clear skies and wild beauty have inspired generations of artists, including Turner, Monet, Picasso, and perhaps most famously Gauguin, who exulted: "I love Brittany. There is something wild and primitive about it. When my wooden clogs strike this granite, I hear the dull, muffled, powerful tone I seek in my painting."

Inland from the Armor, the Celtic name meaning land of the sea, lies the Argoat, or land of forests, the mysterious interior that was the legendary haunt of King Arthur. This is the heart of rural Brittany, a landscape of wild woodland, remote moorland, and fertile fields, threaded by rivers and studded with historic towns and villages. In Brittany, the rich legacy of the past is everywhere apparent, in great Gothic cathedrals and medieval castles, Renaissance manors and solid granite farmhouses, frescoed churches and Finistère's unique parish closes.

Far older in geological terms than the "mainland" of France, Brittany has a timeless quality. Nowhere else in Europe has such a wealth of megalithic monuments, including the mysterious alignments at Carnac. The Celtic legacy of Cornish settlers in the fifth century B.C. still permeates Brittany's language and culture. Independent of France until the 16th century, the province retains a fierce pride in its local traditions: The Breton language is still alive among the old, who remember it, and the young, who are taught it. Visitors may enjoy a taste of Breton culture in the many summer festivals and *pardons* (religious processions). ∎

# Rennes

**The capital of Brittany since 1561, Rennes today is a lively university town and telecommunications research center. Although few of its inhabitants actually speak Breton, it is the focal point for the revival of academic interest in Breton culture. The town is at its most spectacular in early July, when it erupts into a street festival (Les Tombées de la Nuit), celebrating music, poetry, and dance.**

Although Rennes flourished in the Middle Ages, it lost most of its medieval buildings in a disastrous fire in 1720. In rebuilding, its citizens redesigned as well, and the result is a city of fine 18th-century buildings around a small medieval nucleus. Most of the old streets, with charmingly crooked half-timbered houses, are in a relatively small area around the **Place des Lices.** Used for medieval jousting events, this square now has an excellent market on Saturday mornings. Look particularly for the medieval houses around Place Ste. Anne, Rue de la Psalette, Rue St.-Georges, and Rue du Chapitre.

Sadly, the magnificent 17th-century **Palais de Justice** (place du Palais), the parliament building and survivor of the 1720 fire, was almost completely burned during fishermen's riots in 1994, but it is now reopened after major renovation. The **Cathédrale St.-Pierre** (for guided tours, tel 02 99 67 11 11) in the center of old Rennes dates from 1844, but has a 16th-century Flemish altarpiece.

The stately public buildings and grand town houses of Rennes are laid out in a geometric arrangement around the Place de l'Hôtel de Ville. Worth noting are the Hôtel de Ville itself, the superb arcading of the Théâtre, and the Palais du Commerce. To the east lies the **Jardin du Thabor,** a delightful botanical and rose garden. South of the river is the **Musée des Beaux-Arts** (20 quai Émile Zola, tel 02 23 62 17 45, closed Mon.), noted for its Georges de La Tour "Virgin and Child" and works from the Pont-Aven school. The **Musée de Bretagne** (10 cours des Allies, tel 02 23 40 66 00, www.musee-bretagne.fr, closed Mon.) offers a good overview of Breton history and culture. ∎

**Rennes**
◩ 139 C1
**Visitor information**
✉ 11 rue St.-Yves
☎ 02 99 67 11 11
**www.tourisme
.rennes.com**

## Local Art Style

The Pont-Aven school of painting developed in Pont-Aven during the last half of the 19th century, with painters escaping the city for more bucolic spots. The most famous of these artists was Paul Gauguin, whose wild use of color and primitive style—the same savage quality he sought in Brittany—was a rejection of Impressionism that caught on with many other artists. Their first painting exhibition together, at the Universelle Exposition Paris, took place in 1889.

# St.-Malo

This virtually impregnable port was known for centuries as the city of pirates. Its privateers plundered ships in the English Channel, building fine houses with the proceeds. More law-abiding corsairs from St.-Malo explored the distant Falkland Islands, and Jacques Cartier, who began the colonization of Canada in the 16th century, also sailed from here. Novelist Gustave Flaubert described St-Malo's gray granite walls as a "crown of stone above the waves."

Hiking is nice, but the most impressive view of St.-Malo is undoubtedly from the sea.

### St.-Malo
🄰 139 C2
**Visitor information**
✉ esplanade St.-Vincent
☎ 08 25 13 52 00
**www.saint-malo -tourisme.com**

### Musée d'Histoire de la Ville et du Pays Malouin
✉ Château's Great Keep and main tower
☎ 02 99 40 71 57
🕐 Closed Mon. in winter
💲 $$

The first community here was founded on the neighboring island of Aleth (now part of St.-Servan), by the Welsh monk Maclou or Malo in the sixth century. Two centuries later, attacks by Franks drove the population onto the island of St.-Malo, linked to the mainland by a causeway. Behind their fortifications, the townspeople gained a livelihood from the sea.

The narrow streets of the old walled city (the citadel), grouped around the partly 12th-century **Cathédrale St.-Vincent,** are lined with the tall 17th- and 18th-century houses of wealthy shipowners. It is all so authentic that it is hard to believe that they

were largely rebuilt, stone by stone, after the bombardments of World War II. Place Chateaubriand has some fine houses and good cafés, and the elegant dwellings on Rue Chateaubriand include the turreted **Maison de la Duchesse Anne.** The same duchess was responsible for the building of the late 15th-century **Château,** which houses the town museum. A walk around the ramparts provides exhilarating views out to sea and inland across the harbor. At low tide, you can walk out from the beach below the ramparts to the island of Grand-Bé, last resting place of the 19th-century writer Chateaubriand, and to the Fort National, built by Vauban. ∎

# Côte d'Émeraude & Côte de Granit Rose

The Emerald Coast extends from the Pointe de Grouin, west of St.-Malo and north of the oyster port of Cancale, to Val-André to the west, via a string of good beaches, pretty resorts, and headlands with spectacular views. The Côte de Granit Rose is characterized by pink rocks weathered into fantastic shapes.

**Rothéneuf,** just east of St.-Malo, has a rock face of bizarre sculptures, carved by an eccentric 19th-century cleric. Facing St.-Malo across the Rance Estuary is **Dinard,** described at the beginning of the 20th century as "the most aristocratic and elegant seaside resort in northern Europe." In the mid-19th century, this fishing village was adopted by wealthy British and American visitors. They proceeded to make it their own by lining its cliffs and shore with an extravaganza of villas, with turrets, cupolas, verandas, and other belle epoque embellishments. Dinard and St.-Malo are now linked by a road across the **Rance Barrage** *(tel 02 99 16 37 14)*, the dam of the world's first and largest tidal power station, which is open to visitors.

To the west, some splendid beaches and attractive small resorts include **St.-Briac-sur-Mer** with its delightful little coves, the small fishing port of **St.-Jacut-de-la-Mer,** and the sands of **Sables-d'Or-les-Pins** and **Erquy.** The medieval **Fort la Latte** (with two drawbridges) overlooks the bay of La Frenaye, and **Cap Fréhel** offers wonderful views along the coast and over

to the **Île de Bréhat.** The island is accessible by ferry from the Pointe de l'Arcouest. The cliffs here are a bird sanctuary: Keep an eye out for cormorants, razorbills, and guillemots.

**INSIDER TIP:**

**As a rule, the *sentiers des douaniers* (customs agents trails) along the Emerald Coast offer great hiking above the sea. The trail near the town of Val-André is particularly scenic.**

—GILLES MINGASSON
*National Geographic photographer*

Farther west, running from the Pointe de l'Arcouest to Trégastel, is the **Côte de Granit Rose,** where winds and tides erode the pink granite rocks into extraordinary shapes. The most dramatic section is around the resort of **Perros-Guirec.** From here the **Sentier des Douaniers** ("path of customs officers") leads over cliffs to Ploumanac'h, giving views to **Les Sept-Îles,** a wildlife sanctuary. ∎

**Rothéneuf**
🅰 139 C2

**Dinard**
🅰 139 C2
**Visitor information**
✉ 2 boulevard Féart
☎ 02 99 46 94 12
www.ot-dinard.com

**Perros-Guirec**
🅰 138 B2
**Visitor information**
✉ 21 place Hôtel de Ville
☎ 02 96 23 21 15
www.perros-guirec.com

# Breton Customs

The key to the character and traditions of Brittany—so markedly distinct from anything else in France—lies not only in the rugged nature of the land but also, and more significantly, in the influence of the Celts. The Celtic colonizers from Britain of the sixth century B.C. were Druidic nature-worshippers, whose beliefs embraced a world of mystical beings and sorcery. Their monuments were adapted by the Roman invaders who subjugated them, and again by the second wave of British Celts who arrived in the fifth and sixth centuries A.D., bringing Christianity with them.

A traditionally garbed woman and man—a priest—share laughs in a festival performance in Locronan.

From this mix of influences, a distinctive culture developed with its own customs, a strong tradition of music and dance, and a separate language. The Breton language spoken today (by upwards of a quarter of a million people) bears no resemblance whatever to French, but has close links with Welsh, Gaelic, and Cornish.

Against heavy odds, Brittany retained its independence until the 16th century. Only with the death of the formidable Anne, Duchess of Brittany, in 1532 did the French King François I take possession of her daughter and her lands. The province then officially became French, and the Breton language, culture, and customs were suppressed.

## Celtic Spirit

The indomitable Breton spirit survived down the centuries, nevertheless, and the 20th century has seen a great revival of all things Breton (though advocating independence from France remains a criminal offense). The language is taught in schools, and Celtic music has experienced a tremendous upsurge in interest.

To experience Breton fervor at its most intense, you can attend one of several major festivals of Celtic culture. Festivals of music, theater, dance, and poetry are held every year, but the biggest of all is the Interceltic Festival in Lorient (see sidebar p. 159). There are also festivals in Rennes (Les Tombées de la Nuit, the first ten days of July) and Quimper (the festival de Cornouaille, in the week up to the fourth Sunday in July).

## Pardons

Celtic Christians had a particular reverence for nature, and they were content to integrate their faith with other beliefs and religious customs, adopting local saints and holy wells and springs. The pagan figure of Ankou, a grim reaper figure representing death, made unique and vivid appearances in Breton religious imagery, as may be seen in the *danse macabre* in the 13th-century chapel of Kermaria, just off the D786 between St.-Brieuc and Paimpol. The early missionaries were elevated from being dragon-slaying miracle workers to the status of saints, revered within Brittany but largely unknown to the Vatican.

The Breton passion for music and dance, ritual, and religion come together in the *pardons*: annual processions to the shrines of local saints to make a vow or seek forgiveness. A Mass is followed by a procession; participants carry statues and relics and sing hymns, and some wear traditional costume.

These pardons offer an opportunity to admire the men's intricately embroidered vests and the women's headdresses: magnificent confections of lace and starched linen, sometimes

In Lorient, a teenager dons a traditional tall Breton cap crafted of lace.

with holes to let the wind pass through. Each village has a traditional shape and style of headdress. After the procession, the whole village celebrates with traditional music and dancing.

Of the many pardons, some of the most impressive are those of St.-Yves, the patron saint of Brittany, an ecclesiastical lawyer who helped poor clients, at Tréguier *(May 19)*; of Ste.-Anne at Ste. Anne d'Auray *(July 25 & 26)*; and of the Petite Troménie at Locronan *(second Sun. in July)*, when the procession climbs a hill, a place of retreat (Tro Minihy—"Tour of the Retreat"—Iroménie in French). The Grande Troménie, when the procession goes right around the hill, takes place every six years; the next will be on the second and third Sundays of July 2013.

## A Celebration of Brittany's Celtic Past and Present

The Interceltic Festival in Lorient *(www .festival-interceltique.com, tel 02 97 21 24 29)* is the biggest Celtic event in Brittany, attracting people from all seven Celtic countries. The Celts were once the most powerful people in Europe. Distinctive Celtic crosses and symbols survive in many places. Hundreds of names of places, including Paris, have Celtic roots. The Celts were artistic and skilled and had a strong oral tradition of song and story-telling. But they left no written history and have traditionally been relegated to the role of pre-Roman barbarians. Today the countries of what is known as the Celtic triangle, around the Bay of Biscay— Asturias and Galicia in Spain, Cornwall, Wales, and Scotland—all claim their Celtic roots. In a popular celebration of cultural solidarity, well over a quarter of a million people come to Brittany in August and attend more than a hundred different shows, while Scotch and Guinness flow with French and Spanish wines and ciders.

# Parish Closes of Finistère

The *enclos paroissiaux*, or parish closes, of Finistère are a phenomenon unique to Brittany, enshrining in this remotest part of a far-flung region not only the devoutness of traditional Breton Catholicism but also its somber preoccupation with death.

The 16th-century *enclos paroissal* of the Guehénno, which has been restored, depicts the Crucifixion.

## Parish Closes

📍 138 B3

**Visitor information**

✉ 14 avenue Foch, Landivisiau

☎ 02 98 68 33 33

**www.ot-paysdelan divisau.com**

Dating mainly from the 15th century to the 17th, these walled churchyards typically contain, alongside the church and graveyard, a triumphal arch symbolizing entry into paradise, an ossuary, and, most importantly, a calvary. Stone carvings—intricate, sometimes primitive, and often very moving—frequently digress to include local legends, with figures clearly based on local characters. This was a prosperous period in Breton history, and villages made rich by the linen trade vied with each other in the extravagance of their parish closes. Two of the most flamboyant lie close together south of Morlaix, at St.-Thégonnec and Guimiliau.

St.-Thégonnec *(see map on p. 138, B2)* spared no expense in attempting to outdo Guimiliau, its rival, in splendor, employing the finest craftsmen from as far away as England. The result is a rather indigestible but undeniably impressive interior to its vast church, with an especially fine pulpit. The calvary contains a wealth of detail and intriguing figures, including St. Thégonnec himself, shown with the wolves he harnessed to his plow after they consumed his horses. The events surrounding the Crucifixion appear slightly muddled. This is because many of the elements of the calvary, hidden for safekeeping before the Revolution, were put back afterward in the wrong order.

The even more fabulous calvary at **Guimiliau** *(see map on p. 138, B2)*, a few miles away, teems with more than 200 figures depicting scenes from the life of Christ. A riot of other figures include Kate Gollet (Katharine the Damned), who suffered a variety of deaths according to different calvaries. Here she is shown being torn apart at the gates of hell for stealing a holy wafer.

Other fine—and sometimes refreshingly simple—parish closes are to be seen nearby at Sizun, Commana, Ploudiry, La Martyre, and Guehénno near Josselin. ∎

# Quimper

Brittany's oldest city and capital of the ancient duchy of Cornouaille, Quimper has a history that starts in legend. King Gradlon founded Quimper after the flooding of his fabulous city of Ys, off Douarnenez. The spot he chose lay at the confluence (kemper in Breton) of the Odet and Steir Rivers, and the Odet threads through the cobbled streets of the medieval quarter, crossed by low, flower-decked bridges.

The delightful old town, with good shopping on Rue Kéréon, is dominated by the huge 13th-century Gothic **Cathédrale St.-Corentin,** its nave strangely set at an angle to the choir. The **Musée des Beaux-Arts** (40 place St.-Corentin, tel 02 98 95

**INSIDER TIP:**

## Quimper's Rue Kéréon is lined with pretty houses and shops filled with authentic local goods, from handmade faience pottery to cakes.

—SHEILA BUCKMASTER
National Geographic Traveler
magazine editor at large

45 20, www.quimper-tourisme.com, closed Tues. except July & Aug. & Sun a.m. Nov.–March) has an outstanding collection of 19th- and 20th-century works, including some from the school of nearby Pont-Aven, where Paul Gauguin painted his colorful works (see sidebar p. 155).

Quimper is also famous for its distinctive and very pretty faience, a local industry since the 17th century. The **Musée de la Faïence Jules-Verlingue** is currently closed, but there are numerous shops in Quimper where you can buy the traditional folk art porcelain, and you can visit the factory of the oldest of the faienceries, **HB-Henriot** (rue Haute-Locmaria, tel 02 98 52 22 52, closed Dec.–Feb., www.hb-henriot.com) to observe the manufacturing process. ∎

**Quimper**
🔺 138 B1
**Visitor information**
✉ place de la Résistance
☎ 02 98 53 04 05
**www.quimper-tourisme.com**

**Concarneau**
🔺 138 B1
**Visitor information**
✉ quai d'Aiguillon
☎ 02 98 97 01 44
**www.tourisme concarneau.fr**

## Concarneau

A major fishing port 13 miles (22 km) southeast of Quimper and now also a resort, Concarneau's chief attraction is its **Ville Close,** the walled old town on an island in the bay. This rocky perch had been inhabited for centuries before its fortifications were started in the 13th century. The Hundred Years' War increased its strategic importance, and the defenses were strengthened again in the 17th century by Louis XIV's military architect

Vauban. There are wonderful views from the ramparts, and the tiny streets are full of restaurants and souvenir shops. The old barracks now house the **Musée de la Pêche** (3 rue Vauban, tel 02 98 97 10 20), devoted to the local fishing industry. In the second half of August, the Ville Close comes alive with the Fête des Filets Bleus (blue nets), a festival of Breton music and dancing that has developed from the traditional ceremony of blessing the fishing nets.

# Carnac & Its Menhirs

Brittany is strewn with megaliths—menhirs, cairns, passage graves, and dolmens—hewn from solid granite and put in place by a shadowy Neolithic civilization. How or why, no one knows for certain. Of them all, the stone circles and alignments at Carnac, which means "the place where there are piles of stones," are the most staggering in their sheer size, number, and complexity. Possibly dating back as far as 5000 B.C., making them far older than Stonehenge, they are now recognized as the most important prehistoric site in Europe.

Menhirs that date back some 5,000 years continue to weather the elements at Le Ménec.

**Carnac**

⚑ 138 B1

**Visitor information**

✉ 74 avenue des
Druides

☎ 02 97 52 13 52

**www.ot-carnac.fr**

**Musée de Préhistoire**

✉ 10 place de la
Chapelle

☎ 02 97 52 22 04

🕐 Closed Jan. &
Tues. except in
July & Aug.

💲 $$

Some of the lines of stones may originally have been as much as 2.5 miles (4 km) long, containing thousands of menhirs. A construction on this scale was clearly of enormous significance to the civilization that built it. Archaeologists generally favor the theory that it formed a vast astronomical observatory. Visit in the early morning or at dusk to avoid the crowds. To make the leap back in time necessary to set the stones in context, start at the **Musée de Préhistoire** in Carnac.

The stones are in three main locations: The largest, at **Le Ménec,** just north of Carnac beyond the D196, consists of two oval-shaped enclosures, one of which has a medieval village built on top. Here 12 lines of menhirs (with over a thousand stones in the principal alignment) extend for nearly a mile (1.6 km). Access is restricted in order to protect the site from erosion, and plans are under way for long-term protection. The **Maison des Megaliths** provides a viewing platform and audiovisual displays.

The best preserved alignments are at **Kermario.** Over a thousand

**INSIDER TIP:**

## Windsurfers adore St.-Colomban beach in nearby Carnac-Plage. It's a resort town also loved for its oysters.

—JAYNE WISE
National Geographic Traveler
*magazine senior editor*

menhirs are arranged in ten lines, with the giant of Le Manio, at 21 feet (6.5 m) the largest menhir still standing here, surrounded by a smaller stones. **Kerlescan** has another 594 stones, arranged in 13 lines, with a covered passageway.

Just to the east of Carnac rises the **Tumulus St.-Michel,** a tremendously ancient burial ground probably laid out around 4000 B.C. At the summit, the little chapel of St.-Michel has an orientation table overlooking the entire area. **Carnac-Ville** itself is a pretty town of gardens and avenues with a 17th-century church, just inland from the popular resort of Carnac-Plage.

A good way to savor the landscape and sea views is on a **Golfe du Morbihan** boat trip *(tel 02 97 57 19 38).* You can glimpse many of the stones from the sea and visit the tiny island of **Gavrinis—** only accessible by boat and guided tour—with its burial chamber and extraordinary carvings. Trips can be made from Vannes, Locmariaquer, Port Navalo, La Trinité-sur-Mer, or Auray. ∎

**Maison des Megalith (Alignements du Ménec)**
✉ Carnac
☎ 02 97 52 29 81

**GLOSSARY**
*alignment:* row of upright stones
*dolmen:* two uprights roofed with a third; probably the supports of a burial chamber originally covered with earth
*menhir:* upright stone

---

## Menhirs

Marching silently over the land, row after row and mile after mile, Brittany's thousands of megaliths manage to impress us with a sense of deep significance while remaining unfathomably mysterious. As archaeologist R. P. Giot remarked: "We may conclude, simply, that they are religious monuments, and in resorting to this vague, easy description we may attempt to conceal our ignorance."

According to legend, the megaliths are Roman soldiers turned to stone by St. Cornély as they pursued him to the sea. Earlier centuries thought they were part of Roman or Celtic burial rites or that they were intended to help sailors find their bearings. Not until the late 18th century was the astronomical significance of the alignments first noted, and no other theory since has dislodged this one.

Was Carnac an observatory for following the motions of the stars, with a view to predicting the days of the summer solstice and the equinoxes? This would have enabled the designers to establish a calendar for sowing and harvesting.

The gigantic menhir at nearby Locmariaquer—a place best known for oysters—was probably part of the same huge complex. Toppled by an earthquake in the 18th century and now lying in four pieces, this colossus originally stood some 65 feet (20 m) high. Near it stands the famous dolmen known as the Table des Marchands, decorated with graceful spirals and curves.

The same designs cover the burial chamber on the Île de Gavrinis in the Golfe du Morbihan (see above), where many stones are now half engulfed by the waves.

# More Places to Visit in Brittany

Fougère's 13 mighty towers were erected in the 14th and 15th centuries.

## Brest

Brest, one of France's most important naval ports, suffered heavy damage during World War II. But you can still see the remains of the 11th-century château and tour the naval town. Explore the marine world at **Océan-opolis** (Port de Plaisance du Moulin Blanc, tel 02 98 34 40 40, www.oceanopolis.com, closed Mon. Sept.–March, $$$), an important research center with three pavilions that showcase the polar, tropical, and temperate marine ecosystems. Discover the flora and fauna of the underwater world in beautiful settings. The huge variety of extraordinary exhibits includes a colony of 40 penguins and France's biggest seaweed forest. 138 B2 **Visitor information** ✉ place de la Liberté ☎ 02 98 44 24 96

## Crozon Peninsula & Pointe du Raz

The most magnificent spots on the coastline of southern Finistère are the rocky fingers of the Crozon Peninsula and the Pointe du Raz. Cliff paths lead out to the westernmost points: to Pointe du Raz from Lescoff, and to Pointe de Pen-Hir on the Crozon Peninsula from Veryach beyond Camaret. 138 A2

## Dinan

A lovely walled citadel, Dinan has been tactfully restored. Medieval cobbled streets, two splendid churches, and a 14th-century keep lie within its 13th-century defenses. 139 C2 **Visitor information** ✉ 9 rue du Château ☎ 02 96 87 69 76

## Fougères & Vitré

These two fortified frontier towns guarded the old border between Brittany and France. In its spectacular position on a loop of the Nançon River, the stronghold at **Fougères** (Map 139 D2, visitor information, 2 rue Nationale, tel 02 99 94 12 20) is a feudal fortress par excellence. A rocky moat surrounding the 11th-century core was later reinforced by 13 splendid towers.

Standing guard over the Vilaine Valley, the fairy-tale turrets and drawbridge of the castle at **Vitré** (Map 139 D1, visitor information, place du Général-de-Gaulle, tel 02 99 75 04 46) were also begun in the 11th century. The ramparts offer views over a maze of half-timbered houses to the 15th-century Flamboyant Gothic church.

## Josselin

The three slate-roofed turrets of Josselin's mighty castle, rising from a wall of granite that drops straight down into the Oust River, make one of the most famous Breton silhouettes. Built by the powerful Rohan family in the 14th century, it remains their home to this day but is open to the public for tours. 139 C1 **Visitor information** ✉ place de la Congrégation ☎ 02 97 22 36 43

## Tréguier

The hill town of Tréguier is dominated by the spire of its 14th-century cathedral dedicated to dragon-slaying St. Tugdual. The pardon of St. Yves takes place here on May 19. 138 B2 **Visitor information** ✉ 67 rue Ernest Renan ☎ 02 96 92 22 33

Often considered the most quintessentially French region, with mild climate, delicate light, and gentle landscapes

# Loire Valley

Château de Villandry is famed for its stunning Renaissance-style gardens.

# Loire Valley

**The chief glory of the Loire Valley—now a UNESCO World Heritage site—lies in the magnificent châteaus studding the banks of the river and its tributaries like jewels. The playground of medieval kings and nobles, the valley was to become the cradle of the artistic explosion of the French Renaissance. Today these sumptuous palaces and castles and their noble gardens are among France's chief attractions.**

The Loire is France's longest river, flowing some 600 miles (1,000 km) from its source in the Ardèche to its estuary at St.-Nazaire on the Atlantic coast. Most of the time, the river is a wide, slow stream, but sometimes it floods and breaks its banks. Raised embankments, *levées*, have been built up to contain it, but controversy rages over proposals to control it further with barrages and dams. Although the Loire was a crucial trade and communications route for centuries, today much of it is so silted up and shallow that it is barely navigable.

The Loire region is now divided into two administrative areas, Centre and Pays de la Loire. Centre has the great city of Orléans as its capital, and includes Tours in the west and Bourges to the south. Its landscapes encompass vast wheatfields in the Beauce, the area north of the Loire, and the lakes and forests of the Sologne south of the river, historically a favored royal hunting ground. Farther south still, the rolling hills of the Berry region are one of the most deeply rural parts of France.

Touraine, the old name for the area around Tours, is the heart of the Loire Valley, its rich soils producing melons, asparagus, plums, strawberries, and some of the Loire's best wines. Many of the ravishing châteaus are in Touraine.

The Pays de la Loire starts just west of Tours and includes Angers, Le Mans, Nantes (the capital), and the Vendée to the south. Anjou, the old name for the region around Angers, was once a powerful duchy, with lands as far afield as Provence and Sicily. It

4▷

was in the Loire Valley that the English were most memorably defeated by Jeanne d'Arc at Orléans, and her memory is still cherished throughout the region.

Poets have for centuries hymned *la douce vie*, the gentle life, of this great valley straddling the heart of France, neatly dividing the north from the south. The region's fertile alluvial soil and an exceptionally mild climate combine to yield fine wines and a cornucopia of fruit and vegetables.

Most of the great châteaus lie close to the banks of the Loire or its tributaries, and the great river itself runs like a silver thread through any journey here. Crisscrossing it in order to be on the right side at the right time is an art requiring careful planning, especially as the levées sometimes obscure the river from the road. Be prepared to forsake the Loire from time to time to explore its quiet backwaters and tributaries.

Some of the smaller Loire châteaus now offer accommodations, presenting a wonderful opportunity for travelers to experience first-hand *la vie en château*. ■

# Orléans

Because of its strategic but vulnerable position on a great bend of the Loire, Orléans has suffered greatly over the centuries, culminating in the devastation of World War II, when most of the city center was destroyed. Nevertheless, it has fine restaurants, excellent shopping (especially on Rue Royale), and beautiful parks.

**Orléans**

⬛ 167 E3

**Visitor information**

✉ 2 place de l'Étape

☎ 02 38 24 05 05

www.tourisme-orleans.com

**Maison Jeanne d'Arc**

✉ 3 place du Général-de-Gaulle

☎ 02 38 52 99 89

🕐 Closed Mon. & a.m. Nov.–April

💲 $

**Parc Floral de la Source**

✉ Orléans-la-Source

☎ 02 38 49 30 00

💲 Park $. Park & greenhouse $$

Start your visit in Place du Martroi, dominated by a statue of Joan of Arc, and explore the rebuilt medieval streets of the old quarter. On Place du Général-de-Gaulle is the reconstructed **Maison Jeanne d'Arc,** where she spent ten days in 1429 after her defeat of the English and the lifting of the siege of Orléans. **Hôtel Groslot** on Place d'Étape is the best Renaissance building in the city.

**Cathédrale Ste.-Croix** (place Ste.-Croix), built in Gothic style in the 17th and 18th centuries, has always aroused controversy (Proust considered it the ugliest building in France), but it is interesting for its bizarre wedding-cake towers, grand nave, and huge rose window. Museums include the **Musée des Beaux-Arts** (place Ste.-Croix, tel 02 38 79 21 55, closed Mon.), with works by Tintoretto

and Velázquez, and the **Musée Historique et Archéologique** (place de l'Abbé Desnoyers, tel 02 38 79 25 60, call for opening times), whose exhibits include second-century Celtic bronze statues.

Outside Orléans, head south for Olivet, where you can boat on the river and visit the glorious **Parc Floral de la Source,** a 245-acre (100 ha) nature reserve surrounding a 17th-century château. ■

## Jeanne d'Arc

The Maid of Orléans is honored annually in Orléans on May 7 and 8, the anniversary of the days in 1429 when she liberated the city from the besieging English forces, thus becoming one of French history's most potent heroines.

This young peasant girl from Lorraine (see p. 136) was first noticed when she came to Chinon and recognized the Dauphin, Charles VII, among a crowd of courtiers. She claimed that heavenly voices had instructed her to save him. She succeeded in rallying the French troops and relieving Orléans. The English were driven away, and she led Charles to Reims to be crowned. But a series of disasters led to her capture by the English, who tried her as a witch and burned her at the stake in Rouen on May 30, 1431. She was canonized a saint in 1920.

# Blois

Clinging prettily to hills overlooking the Loire, Blois makes a perfect touring base, small enough to be accessible and situated for exploring both up- and downriver. Its steeply winding streets, lined with half-timbered buildings, alleys, and hidden courtyards, have preserved both the architecture and the atmosphere of the town's illustrious past. The surrounding farmland and the game forests of the nearby Sologne area keep restaurants supplied with fine ingredients.

The Château de Blois underscores the power of royal taste and budget.

Blois is still dominated by its magnificent **château** *(place du Château, tel 02 54 70 33 33, www .chateaudeblois.com, $$).* The great 13th century Gothic hall and tower remain from the original fortress. Subsequent additions present an extraordinary mix of architectural styles. Louis XII (R.1498–1515) transformed it into an opulent palace (his emblem, the porcupine, is everywhere). His son, François I (R.1515–1547), created its greatest feature, the octagonal open spiral staircase that forms part of the dazzling François I wing.

The cabinet of Catherine de Médicis is intriguing for its secret closets in which she reputedly hid her poisons. The château is also notorious for the murder of the Catholic Duc de Guise at the instigation of his Protestant brother, Henri III (R.1574–1589), fearful of the growing power of the Catholics. Henri was himself murdered only six months later.

The Louis XII wing of the château houses the **Musée des Beaux-Arts Décoratifs** and **Musée Archéologique;** the terrace gardens offer a good view of the town, the Loire, the 18th-century bridge over the river, and the 12th-century church of St.-Nicolas. A fine restaurant is set in the Orangerie (see p. 357). ∎

### Blois
🅰 167 D3–E3

**Visitor information**
✉ Pavillon Anne de Bretagne, 23 place du Château
☎ 02 54 90 41 41

**www.bloispaysde chambord.com**

### Musée des Beaux-Arts Décoratifs & Musée Archéologique
✉ place du Château
☎ 02 54 70 33 33
💲 Entrance included with château ticket

# Chambord

The largest of the Loire châteaus, Chambord is a Renaissance masterpiece on an enormous scale, with 440 rooms, 85 staircases, and 365 chimneys—a fireplace for every day of the year. It was a simple hunting lodge until 1519, when François I decided to build himself the ultimate château. He was greatly inspired by Italian architecture and had invited Leonardo da Vinci to live at Amboise. It seems more than likely that Leonardo may have drawn the first plans for the château, including a scheme to divert the Loire to flow past it.

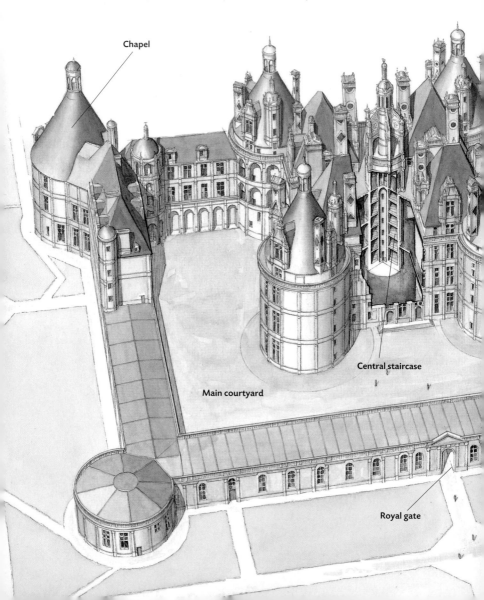

Chapel

Central staircase

Main courtyard

Royal gate

The central keep is flanked by four towers and enclosed by a courtyard. The **Grand Staircase** rises through the keep to a lantern tower that was originally open, though glass was later added. This famous double spiral staircase was designed so that two people—one going up and one going down—could always see each other but would meet only at the top and bottom.

Apartments flank the staircase on four sides, and everywhere you see the image of the salamander, emblem of François I. Grandest of the rooms are the state apartments; in particular, the **bedchamber** hung with richly embroidered velvet, added by Louis XIV, who finished the château in 1685 while he waited for Versailles to be built.

Most extraordinary of all is the roof, a riot of gables, turrets, and spires, likened by Vivian Rowe to an Oriental town, "the skyline of Constantinople on a single building." The roof terraces were designed for the court to watch summer spectacles or herald the king on his return from the hunt. They make a splendid vantage point to survey the vast estate of 13,600 acres (5,550 ha) that surrounds the château. ■

**Chambord**

⚠ 167 E3

**Visitor information**

✉ 78–82 rue Bernard-Palissy

☎ 02 54 40 50 00

🕐 Closed Dec. 25, Jan. 1, & May 1

💲 $$

www.chambord.org

François I tower

Roof terrace

Keep

Chambord

# Food & Drink—Gems of the Soil

**Vineyards flank the Loire along much of its length, though the Loire wines do not rank with those of Burgundy or Bordeaux. But for relaxation between visiting the châteaus and hearing the history of noble pleasures, try the excellent wines and regional dishes so graciously offered today.**

**Sumptuously simple: Farm-fresh salads and fruity red and white wine are Loire Valley staples.**

*"Artichokes and salad greens, asparagus, parsnips and the melons of Touraine, all are more tempting than great mounds of royal meats."*
Pierre de Ronsard (1524–1585)

Vines were first planted in the Loire Valley by the Romans, then grown assiduously by the monks who established important abbeys throughout the region. Their wines were drunk enthusiastically by the kings, queens, and courtiers who made the fertile Loire Valley their playground. In recent years, the Loire vineyards have made great efforts to improve the quality of their wines and to promote those that have always been revered.

Restaurants in the Loire area will have a good list of local wines, and there are signs everywhere for *dégustation*, or wine tasting (and buying, of course), at the vineyards themselves. Ask at a town's *syndicat d'initiative* or tourist office for a list of the nearby vineyards that welcome visitors.

The Loire Valley wines are light, fresh, and sometimes relatively low in alcohol. White wines predominate, based on the Chenin Blanc, Muscadet, and Sauvignon Blanc grapes, perfect with shellfish, to fine Vouvrays and Sancerres farther east. Of the rosé wines, Rosé d'Anjou is the best known, and the Cabernet Franc grape grown here makes a number of good reds. Seek out the fruity reds of Chinon and Bourgeuil. In Saumur, look for the *méthode champenoise* (Champagne method) sparkling wines. Most voluptuous of all are the sweet dessert wines of the Coteaux du Layon.

These local wines go perfectly with the regional cuisine, which, like the climate of the Loire, is gentle, agreeable, and never extreme. The key is simplicity: Local game, fish, vegetables, and fruit are so good they need only a subtle sauce to bring out the flavor.

The Loire Valley is the garden of France: young white asparagus tips in season, salad crops, squashes, mushrooms (grown in caves along the riverside cliffs near Saumur), and tiny potatoes. Raspberries and strawberries flourish in the market gardens, while orchards yield apples, pears, and quinces as well as plums, especially greengages (*reines claudes*).

Fish from the river, spotlighted on many menus, include carp and pike, often served with a sauce of shallots, butter, and vinegar *(beurre blanc)*; salmon is delicious with sorrel sauce; and eel is often made into a succulent red wine stew. Tiny fish, impeccably fresh, are served simply fried, and great platters of seafood are available in profusion near the coast. A popular first course having nothing to so with the sea is the exquisitly rich *rillettes du Mans* (shredded pork or rabbit conserved in its own fat).

In Tours, pork is cooked with prunes, game comes from primarily from the Sologne region south of the Loire, and chicken and fat capons

Tarte tatin, a buttery caramel apple treat, sets the bar high when it comes to desserts.

are the basis for fricassees and casseroles. Among the traditional local main dishes are duck with turnips and chunks of pork cooked until crispy and golden.

Keep an eye out for fresh cheeses, especially goat cheese. You can't go wrong with Valençay, Crottin de Chavignol, Sainte-Maure de Touraine, Crémet de Nantes. Crisp white wines are the best accompaniment for goat cheese.

Traditional desserts include open tarts of apples and plums, fritters flavored with eau-de-vie, puff pastry almond cake, and tarte tatin (see sidebar below).

## Upside Down & Irresistible

Tarte Tatin is a famous French dessert, an upside-down apple tart in which the apples are caramelized in butter and sugar before the tart is baked. The story goes that tarte tatin was created by accident at the Hotel Tatin in Lamotte-Beuvron in 1898 by sisters Stéphanie and Caroline Tatin. Stéphanie, who did most of the cooking, was overworked one day. She started to make a more traditional apple dessert but left the apples cooking in butter and sugar for too long. Smelling the burning, she tried to rescue the dish by putting the pastry base on top of the pan of caramelized apples, quickly finishing the cooking by putting the whole pan in the oven. After turning out the upside-down tart, she served it up and was surprised to find how much the hotel guests liked it.

The tart became the signature dish at the Hotel Tatin, and the recipe spread through the Sologne region. It gained further fame thanks to the restaurateur Louis Vaudable, who tasted the tart on a visit to Sologne and then decided to make the dessert a permanent fixture on the menu at his restaurant Maxim's in Paris.

# Amboise

Although only a fraction now remains of the original Château d'Amboise, its creamy walls and slate roof turrets still make a lovely sight, dominating the Loire River and the charming narrow streets of the old town. For much of the 15th and 16th centuries, Amboise was a favorite residence of French kings, and it was here that the art of the Renaissance first came to France from Italy.

Medieval Amboise sits on the Loire River.

**Amboise**
- 🅜 167 D2

**Visitor information**
- ✉ quai du Général de Gaulle
- ☎ 02 47 57 09 28

www.amboise-valdeloire.com

**Château Royal d'Amboise**
- ☎ 02 47 57 00 98
- 💲 $$

www.chateau-amboise.com

François I established a glittering court life at Amboise, enlivened by tournaments, masked balls, and fireworks designed by none other than Leonardo da Vinci. But in 1560, a Protestant conspiracy to murder the young François II (married to Mary, Queen of Scots) was put down with appalling ferocity, and hundreds of corpses hung from the battlements.

Nowadays, after a great deal of demolition and a period as a jail, this elegant château is again in royal hands, administered by the Comte de Paris, heir to the French throne. Enjoy the view of the Loire Valley from the terrace, visit the royal apartments in the 15th-century Gothic Logis du Roi, and climb the Tour des Minimes with its extraordinary spiral ramp designed for carriages. The jewel of Amboise is the late 15th-century Chapelle St.-Hubert, a dazzling example of Flamboyant Gothic that allegedly contains the tomb of Leonardo da Vinci.

**INSIDER TIP:**

**Amboise is a great château to visit with kids; many royal children grew up here, and there's a tour geared to youngsters.**

—SYLVIE BIGAR
National Geographic Traveler
*magazine writer*

In 1516, Leonardo came to Amboise as painter, engineer, and architect to the king, bringing with him some of his favorite paintings, including the "Mona Lisa." François I installed Leonardo in the elegant **Manoir du Clos-Lucé** (*2 rue du Clos-Lucé, tel 02 47 57 00 73, $$*), just outside Amboise, where you can visit his rooms. A museum dedicated to his technical drawings and experiments has computer-generated models of some of his astonishing inventions. ∎

# Tours

**Louis XI's capital, Tours today is a big, prosperous city, well worth exploring for its museums, stores, restaurants, and handsomely restored old buildings.**

An important city even in Gallo-Roman times, Tours enjoyed great wealth and celebrity in the Middle Ages thanks to the tomb of its famous bishop, St. Martin (now in the crypt of the New Basilica). The town flourished during the Renaissance, becoming famous for its silks, jewels, and arms. But several centuries of decline followed, culminating in the devastation of World War II. In 1959, the city began the process of regeneration that has made it a model of urban development.

The **Quartier St.-Julien,** bordered by the river, is today all trendy restaurants and antique shops. Start with lively Place Plumereau, lined with cafés and restored half-timbered buildings. Nearby is the Hôtel Gouin, a lavishly sculptured Renaissance building that houses the **Musée de l'Hôtel de Gouin** *(currently under renovation).*

On the other side of Rue Nationale (running across the Pont Wilson, a faithful 1978 reconstruction of an 18th-century stone bridge partly washed away by the river), in the former abbey of St.-Julien, is the **Musée des Vins de Touraine.** Equally fascinating is the **Musée du Compagnonnage** next door, devoted to the history of craft guilds and trades.

The **Cathédrale St.-Gatien** *(place de la Cathédrale)* was built from the 13th to the 16th centuries. It is a superb example of the development of the Gothic style. Especially fine are the Gothic facade, the richly colored medieval stained-glass windows, and a 14th-century fresco of St. Martin and the beggar.

Next door, in the 17th- and 18th-century former Bishop's Palace, is the **Musée des Beaux-Arts** *(18 place François-Sicard, tel 02 47 05 68 73, closed Tues.),* which has two parts of a triptych by Andrea Mantegna (1431–1506). ∎

**Tours**

Ⓜ 167 D2
**Visitor information**
✉ 78–82 rue Bernard-Palissy
☎ 02 47 70 37 37

**Musée des Vins de Touraine/ Musée du Compagnonnage**
✉ Cloître St. Julien, 16 rue Nationale
☎ 02 47 21 62 20
🕐 Closed Tues.
💲 $

Cathédrale St.-Gatien boasts flamboyant Gothic intricacies.

# Chenonceau & Villandry

Built by women for women, Chenonceau is perhaps the most romantic château in France. Designed by Catherine Briçonnet in the early 16th century on the foundations of a manor house and watermill, this gem of Renaissance architecture was given by Henri II to his mistress Diane de Poitiers. It was she who in 1556 called in the great architect Philibert Delorme to build a bridge across to the other side of the river, so that she could go hunting more easily. The glory of the Château de Villandry, another star on the château circuit, is its 16th-century-style garden. faithfully re-created in 16th-century Renaissance style.

Chenonceau spans the gentle water of the broad Cher River on a series of graceful arches.

**Château de Chenonceau**

⚐ 167 D2

☎ 02 47 23 90 07

$ $$

## Chenonceau

When Henri II died, Diane de Poitiers was ousted by his jealous wife, Catherine de Médicis, who commissioned Delorme to build a two-story gallery on top of the bridge. These remarkable women were succeeded by the widow of Henri III, Louise, who retired here for an 11-year vigil, hanging her bedchamber with black velvet decorated with symbols of death.

Today, an avenue of plane trees leads to the forecourt of the château. To the right is the 13th-century keep with a carved Renaissance doorway. Within the château, the lavish rooms have painted ceilings, monumental stone fireplaces, gorgeous Flemish tapestries, and fine paintings.

The Cabinet Vert, Catherine de Médicis's delightful study overlooking the river, was originally hung with green velvet and is still sumptuously decorated in fine brocade, while the tragic Queen Louise's bedchamber has been refurbished in funereal black. There is also a little private chapel with stained-glass windows (replaced after being bombed in 1944). Do not miss the extraordinary kitchens, deep in the hollow piers supporting the house.

In the 17th century the château fell into oblivion, resurfacing in the 18th century, when philosopher Jean-Jacques Rousseau stayed here. It escaped damage in the Revolution, and became a military hospital during World War I.

Since 1913, Chenonceau has been owned by the Menier family, chocolate manufacturers, who maintain it impeccably. It is extremely popular, so try to visit early in the day or, even better, out of high season. Try to spend a day here, viewing the château, boating on the river, strolling in the gardens, and perhaps attending a son et lumière performance.

## Villandry

Less than a hundred years ago, the Château de Villandry was closed in by woodland. It was rescued by a Spanish doctor,

Joachim Carvallo, and his wife, Ann, a steel heiress from Philadelphia. After restoring the château, with its moat on three sides, they furnished it in Renaissance style. Then they replanted the gardens as they would have been in the 16th century.

The gardens are on three levels, linked by shady pergolas and fountains. On the upper terrace is the **Jardin d'Eau,** where a huge basin feeds water to the moat and fountains. A linden tree avenue forms the main axis of the gardens. Below is the **Jardin Potager,** or vegetable garden, laid out in geometric patterns, with a variety of fruit trees and herbs. On the south terrace is the **Jardin d'Ornement,** a garden on the theme of love—a confection of geometric box parterres shaped in flames, butterflies, hearts, and daggers, symbolizing the different manifestations of love. The latest addition is the **Sun Garden,** a cloister of greenery around a sun-shaped fountain, with a garden for children. ∎

**Château de Villandry**

Ⓜ 167 D2
☎ 02 47 50 02 09
🕐 Château closed mid-Nov.– mid-Feb., except Christmas holidays
💲 $$

www.chateau villandry.com

---

## French Gardens

The French Renaissance garden—a stylized and beautiful combination of broad avenues and geometrical patterns, terraces and clipped hedges, statues and water gardens, fountains and pools—was heavily influenced by Italian ideas, then so prevalent in all the arts. André Le Nôtre (1613–1700) was the master of this style, creating château gardens all over France, most famously at **Vaux-le-Vicomte** (see p. 103) and **Versailles** (see pp. 96–99). In the 18th century, Marie- Antoinette was largely responsible for the vogue for picturesque and informal gardens à l'anglaise, green spaces loosely inspired by the English landscape tradition. Fine examples of this style can be seen at the Grand Trianon at Versailles and the **Jardin de Bagatelle** at the Bois de Boulogne. Today, interest in French landscape gardening is reviving. An international garden festival takes place at Chaumont-sur-Loire every August, and Blois has a school of landscape gardening.

# A Drive Along the Indre River

This route takes you along the Indre River from Rigny-Ussé as far as Loches. Start at Ussé, picturesquely located to the south of the Indre near its junction with the Loire, between Tours and Saumur.

The **Château d'Ussé** ❶ *(tel 02 47 95 54 05, closed mid-Nov.–mid-Feb.)* on the D7 is a treat: a truly fairy-tale castle of romantic turrets silhouetted against a dark forest. It is the setting of the original *Sleeping Beauty (La Belle au Bois Dormant)*, a 17th-century tale by Charles Perrault. From Rigny-Ussé, the D7 runs parallel to the Indre River, and its great sister the Loire is visible across a fertile floodplain. Flanking the other side of the road is the forest of Chinon. Several turnings into the forest offer a chance for further exploration of its little hamlets.

Just past the village of Rivarennes, turn right on the D17, which follows the Indre and soon passes the little town of **Azay-le-Rideau** ❷ across the water; don't miss the lovely **château** here (see p. 180). Turn south off the D17, to the D57 and the village of

---

## NOT TO BE MISSED:

Château d'Azay-le-Rideau
• Villaines-les-Rochers basket weavers • Cormery • Loches

---

**Villaines-les-Rochers** ❸, famous for its baskets made from rushes that grow beside the Indre. You can buy anything from a bread basket to a baby's crib, and see the basket weavers at work. Return to the river on the D217 and stay south until you reach **Saché** ❹, a small village with a 16th-century manor house set among chestnut trees. In 1835, Balzac wrote *Le Père Goriot* here, having fled from his creditors. It is now a museum *(Château de Saché, tel 02 47 26 86 50)*, with his rooms perfectly preserved

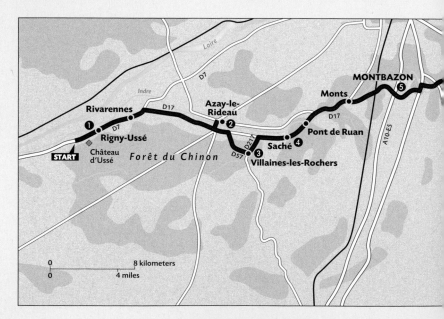

(particularly his bedroom: the bed made up, his coffeepot ready, and his inkwell and quill pen on the little wooden desk). Exhibits include first editions of his works and even his own carefully annotated proofs.

From here to **Montbazon** ❺, both banks of the river are equally rewarding. This is a gentle landscape of little wooded valleys and waterside villages with the river curving past orchards, châteaus, and mills. At Montbazon, the huge 11th-century stone keep now lies in ruins but is well worth climbing for the view. You might also stop at **Château d'Artigny** just outside the town, a luxury hotel and restaurant in an early 20th-century mansion.

The D17 proceeds north of the river to the charming little town of **Cormery** ❻, where the remains of a medieval Benedictine abbey stretch along Rue de l'Abbaye, and the 12th-century Église de Notre-Dame has a wealth of frescoes, statues, and carvings. Cormery is famed for its macaroon cookies. At Azay-sur-Indre, the Indrois River joins the Indre, and a delightful detour on the D10 takes you up beside the Indrois to **Montrésor** ❼,

a peaceful little town beside an ancient château *(tel 02 47 92 60 04, closed Nov.–March except weekend p.m.)*. The walls and towers of the 11th-century fortress enclose a much-restored 16th-century residence overlooking the river.

From Azay-sur-Indre, the main route follows the D17; at Chambourg-sur-Indre cross the river and take the D25 along the valley past the forest of Loches, fronted by orchards and meadows. **Loches** ❽ *(visitor information, place de la Marne, tel 02 47 91 82 82)* itself is a splendid town, its medieval core high on a rock overlooking the river. Stroll around the ramparts, admire the town's fine Renaissance doorways, and explore the 11th-century keep, the dungeons, the manor, and the royal apartments in the **château**. Here Agnès Sorel (1422–1450), the mistress of Charles VII, lived in great luxury; look for her tomb and Jean Fouquet's painting of the Virgin whose face is said to be that of Agnès.

From Loches, you can continue up the river and then return down the D25 to explore the forest, or take the N143 straight back to Tours.

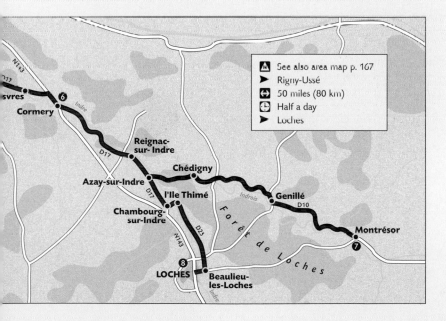

# Azay-le-Rideau

Azay-le-Rideau is one of the loveliest of the Loire châteaus, famously described by Balzac as "a many-faceted diamond set in the Indre." With its delicate turrets and purely decorative fortifications reflected in the peaceful river moat against a background of trees, this is a château unquestionably built for pleasure rather than defense. While the building remains Gothic in its outlines, the delicate decorative work is of Italianate Renaissance inspiration.

**Château d'Azay-le-Rideau**
- 🅰 167 D2
- ✉ rue de Pineau
- ☎ 02 47 45 42 04
- 💲 $$

www.azay-le-rideau.
monuments
-nationaux.fr

Building at Azay started in 1518 for a wealthy financier, Gilles Berthelot (a relation of Catherine Briçonnet, who built Chenonceau), whose wife, Philippa Lesbahy, oversaw the work. It entered royal hands when it was confiscated by François I still unfinished (it did not receive its final touches until the 19th century).

Perhaps the most striking feature of Azay is the harmony achieved between the château and its setting, a virtuoso composition of pale stone, lush greenery, and limpid water. Set on an island between two arms of the Indre River, the château is almost surrounded by water. Azay is also noted for its grand staircase, a major innovation at that time, consisting of three zigzag flights of stairs, with open loggia windows in Italianate style on each landing.

The interior, though luxuriously appointed, has an authentic, somewhat domestic feel. It has been furnished with period pieces, hung with sumptuous brocades, and some fine tapestries. The impressive kitchen is equipped with huge stone fireplaces, oak doors, and an intriguing selection of antique cooking equipment. A son et lumière show tells the château's story every night from May to September.

The little town of Azay-le-Rideau is delightful, too. Look for the decorative Renaissance stone carving on a number of doors and windows in the old streets. The 11th-century **Église de St.-Symphorien,** close to the château, has a double-gabled front with fragments of a sixth-century facade and a row of little statues over the door. ∎

## The Vendée

South of Nantes is the Vendée area of the western Loire, notorious in the late 18th century for counterrevolutionary uprisings and guerrilla warfare. The unrest culminated in the massacre of 1794, in which more than 80,000 royalists died. Memorials and museums detailing the uprising are found in Cholet and Challans.

The Atlantic coast is dotted with small resorts. A bridge links Fromentine to the island of Noirmoutier, a haven of secluded beaches. Inland, canals thread the Marais Poitevin, a marshy landscape that hosts bird sanctuaries.

Near Les Epesses, the Château de Puy de Fou *(tel 02 51 64 11 11, www.puydufou .com/en, check for closings)* is famed for its open-air history pageants starring hundreds of actors.

# Chinon

The best view of Chinon—a small town steeped in history and still dominated by the sprawling ruins of its great fortress—is from the opposite bank of the Vienne River. The formidable fortifications tell their own tale. Always a site of major strategic importance, the château played a key role in Anglo-French skirmishes throughout the Middle Ages.

English king Henry II lived in the most ancient part of the Chinon stronghold—the Fort St. Georges, now demolished, east of the Château du Milieu and the Vieux Logis—and died here in 1189. The French Crown took possession of the castle, and a keep and other fortifications were added in the following century. The best preserved parts date from the 14th century.

Deteriorated as it is, the castle's massive walls, lofty ramparts, and tall towers make it a dramatic place to explore. Portions were recently reconstructed.

On the walls of the Château du Coudray, you can still see the melancholy graffiti carved in 1308 by imprisoned Knights Templar awaiting death by burning.

But Chinon is most famous as the place where Jeanne d'Arc had her fateful interview with the Dauphin, Charles VII, when she recognized him hidden amid a crowd of courtiers and recounted her dream that he would be crowned king. Her memory is evoked at every turn.

The cobbled streets of the old town are charming; the main street, Rue Voltaire, is lined with half-timbered houses, their carved windows and doorways fine examples of Renaissance

Jeanne d'Arc is commemorated at the venerable Château de Chinon, which dates back to the fifth century.

work. Off this street are the Caves Peintes (Painted Cellars), old quarries below the castle, where the local wine confraternity holds meetings. They are also the scene of fictional character Pantagruel's carousings in Rabelais's *Gargantua* and *Pantagruel.*

Rabelais, whose name has entered the language as a synonym for bucolic excess, was born in the late 15th century 3 miles (5 km) southwest of Chinon. His birthplace at La Devinière, a modest manor house in the heart of vineyard country, is now the **Musée Rabelais.** The dwelling has been restored and furnished in 15th-century vernacular style.

Chinon is also known for its well-priced wines. ■

**Chinon**
- 167 D2

**Visitor information**
- place Hofheim
- 02 47 93 17 85
- www.chinon-valdeloire.com

**Château de Chinon**

- route de Tours
- 02 47 93 13 45
- $

**Musée Rabelais**

- La Devinière, D117, Seuilly
- 02 47 95 91 18
- $

# Fontevraud

Allow plenty of time to see Fontevraud, one of the most complete surviving (though heavily restored) collections of medieval monastic buildings anywhere. The church, cloisters, kitchens, refectory, and gardens provide an unrivaled picture of monastic life over 600 years from the 12th century to the 18th.

**Abbaye Royale de Fontevraud**

- 🅰 167 C2
- ✉ place des Plantagenêts
- ☎ 02 41 51 73 52
- 💲 $

**www.abbayede frotevrau.com**

Founded in 1099 by a devout hermit, Robert d'Arbrissel, who embraced the ascetic and silent rule of St. Benedict, Fontevraud consisted of five separate religious establishments. It was unusual in including both monks and nuns in the community, and unique in being governed by a woman. The abbesses were women of considerable influence, often of royal blood, and Fontevraud became a favorite royal sanctuary.

**INSIDER TIP:**

**Fontevraud has become the cultural center of western France, with concerts, theater, and exhibits.**

—ROSEMARY BAILEY
*National Geographic author*

The **Abbaye Royale de Fontevraud** was the retreat chosen by Eleanor of Aquitaine, one-time queen first of France and then of England, and the abbey church became the burial place of the Plantagenets.

The painted 13th-century effigies of Eleanor, her husband Henry II, their son Richard the Lion-Hearted, and their daughter Isabelle of Angoulême are here in the abbey church.

The church is a superb Romanesque building. The simple lines of the nave are superb, and the great columns are topped by intricately and mysteriously carved capitals (binoculars are useful). After the Revolution, parts of the monastery were destroyed, and it was used as a prison from 1804 until 1963. It has been restored, and excavation work continues. Visitors may wander outside the abbey buildings through the medieval gardens, the orangery, and the stables.

The magnificent Renaissance chapter house has fine vaulting, carved doorways, and 16th-century wall paintings. The lovely cloisters also date from the Renaissance, and the vast refectory has Romanesque walls and a Gothic vaulted ceiling. The most intriguing building is the perfectly (some say over-) restored Romanesque kitchen. Octagonal in shape, it has a large central tower and a cluster of chimneys with pepperpot roofs. Inside are no fewer than six hearths, over which meals were once prepared for several hundred members of the community.

Fontevraud is one of Europe's most important centers of medieval archaeology. The recently opened **Musée Ephémère** explores its history. ∎

# Saumur

One of the most charming towns of the Loire Valley, Saumur is renowned for its sparkling wine, its château, and its crack cavalry school. The graceful white turrets of the 14th-century château rise over the town and river today, just as they do in the luminous illustration to the *Très Riches Heures du Duc de Berry*, a book of hours now in one of the châteaus at Chantilly (see p. 118), painted shortly after the château was built.

The terrace of the Château de Saumur commands views of the old town and the Loire.

Once under the control of the kings of England, Saumur became the property of France in the 12th century.

The **Château de Saumur** is undergoing renovation. The museums are closed, but you can visit the courtyard and terrace, with fine views of the town and the river. A survivor of heavy bombing in 1940, the château is surrounded by elegantly restored stone houses. The little winding streets of the town below are lined with half-timbered dwellings, among which Balzac set his novel *Eugène Grandet*. On Place St.-Pierre stands the medieval **Église de St.-Pierre**, containing some fine 16th-century tapestries.

The **École Nationale d'Équitation** (National Riding School), in St.-Hilaire-St.-Florent just west of Saumur, stages riding displays given by the French army's skilled horseback riders. Guided tours of the school's grounds, stables, tack room, and arenas are offered.

Around the village you can sample local sparkling wine in tufa caves near the river. Mushrooms are grown in caves, too; learn more at the **Musée du Champignon** (*St.-Hilaire-St.-Florent, tel 02 41 50 31 55*). ■

**Saumur**
- 🅰 167 C2

**Visitor information**
- ✉ place de la Bilange
- ☎ 02 41 40 20 60

**Château de Saumur**
- ☎ 02 41 40 24 40
- 🕐 Closed Mon. Nov.–March
- 💲 $$

**École Nationale d'Équitation**
- ✉ St.-Hilaire-St.-Florent
- ☎ 02 41 53 50 66
- 🕐 Closed Sun.–Mon.

# Angers

Anjou's ancient capital is the gateway to the western Loire Valley. With an old quarter rich in museums, cafés, and elegant shops, Angers is dominated by the impressive walls and 17 towers of its formidable 13th-century château. Built by Louis IX (St. Louis, R. 1226–1270) within the space of 20 years, this colossus of granite and black schist is approached by a drawbridge across a broad dry moat, now bright with formal plantings of flowers.

**Angers**
🅰 167 C2–C3
Visitor information
✉ place Kennedy
☎ 02 41 23 50 50

www.angersloire
tourisme.com

**Château
d'Angers**
✉ promenade du
Bout-du-Monde
☎ 02 41 86 81 94
💲 $$

The battlements of the Château d'Angers were cut down to hold cannon.

Inside the **Château d'Angers** is the town's premier treasure, the almost surreal 14th-century Apocalypse tapestry. The **Cathédrale St.-Maurice** (4 rue St.-Christophe) has 12th-century stained-glass windows. Nearby is the half-timbered 15th-century **Maison d'Adam**. Two Renaissance palaces in the old quarter house museums: **Hôtel Pincé** (32 bis rue Lenepreu, tel 08 99 23 47 66, closed Mon. except June–Sept.), with classical and Asian art, and the fine-art **Musée des Beaux-Arts** (14 rue du Musée, tel 02 41 05 38 00, closed Mon. except June–Sept.). The 13th-century **Abbaye de Toussaint** (33 bis rue Toussaint, tel 02 41 05 38 90, closed Mon.) displays work by 18th-century sculptor David d'Angers. Across the river, the medieval **Hôpital St.-Jean** (4 boulevard Arago, tel 02 41 24 18 45, closed Mon. Nov.–May) is one of the oldest hospital buildings in France. ■

---

## EXPERIENCE: Go Green

Outside Angers, **Terra Botanica** (route de Cantenay Epinard, tel 02 41 25 00 00, www.terrabotanica.fr., closed Dec.–March) is Europe's first horticultural theme park, devoted entirely to the understanding and discovery of plant life, combining gardens, water features, exotic trees, and greenhouses. Themed adventures will take you on boat trips and treetop rides, searching for nutmeg in Indonesia, battling through the jungle, and investigating the world of medicinal plants.

# Le Loir & Vendôme

To the north of the great Loire is the river Loir, which runs from Illiers-Combray to just above Angers. Vendôme, on a network of islands formed by the Loir, is one of France's most attractive towns. In the Middle Ages, it was famed for its tanneries, mills, and kid gloves. Now the old houses and mills provide second homes for Parisians.

Jean-Baptiste de Rochambeau (1725–1807), who led the French troops during the American Revolution, was born in Vendôme. His statue dominates the Place St.-Martin. The finest sight in town is the **Abbaye de la Trinité**, with a Gothic facade and some of the oldest stained glass in Europe.

Downriver from Vendôme is **Lavardin**, with medieval houses, a Romanesque church, and a fortress. **Trôo** *(www.troovillage.com)* contains troglodyte houses built around an ancient burial mound. Across the river, the church in **St. Jacques-des-Guérets** has Romanesque wall paintings. From Trôo, follow signs to **La Possonnière**,

where the poet Ronsard was born in 1524. Downstream stands the 15th-century **Château du Lude** *(tel 02 43 94 60 09, closed Wed. May–Sept.)*. From here, proceed to the charming town of **La Flèche,** or southwest to **Baugé** and the **Hospice de la Girouardière,** where you can see the Vraie Croix d'Anjou, a cross brought back from the Crusades; during World War II, it was the symbol of the Free French forces. At the annual garden festival at **Château du Lude** *(www.lelude.com),* the first weekend of June, plant collectors and gardeners share their knowledge and enthusiasm with visitors. Workshops on all kinds of gardening subjects are offered. ■

**Vendôme**
- 167 D3

Visitor information
- ✉ Hôtel du Saillant, Parc Ronsard
- ☎ 02 54 77 05 07

**Hospice de la Girouardière**
- 🏠 8 rue de la Girouardière, Baugé
- ☎ 02 41 89 75 49
- 🕐 Open 3–4 p.m. except Tues.

## Unusual Domestic Architecture

The Loire region has the highest concentration of troglodyte dwellings in Europe. For centuries, cave houses were cut out of cliff faces. **Turquant** has several troglodyte dwellings, and the Loire River cliffs are riddled with houses. At **Deneze-sous-Doue** *(tel 02 41 59 15 40)* see an extraordinary cave of mysterious 16th- and 17th-century sculptures. Some houses, such as those in Trôo (see above), were built around ancient burial mounds.

**Rochemenier** has a well-preserved troglodyte village museum, the **Village Troglodyte** *(tel 02 41 59 18 15)*. Its honeycomb of caves includes barns, wine cellars, stables, and dwelling places in use until the 1930s. There is an underground room where the entire village would congregate on long winter evenings spent spinning flax, shelling walnuts, singing, and dancing.

Troglodyte restaurants are cozy spots. Try **Les Caves de Marson** in Rou Marson *(www.cavesdemarson.com)* or **Le Lucifer** in St.-Hilaire-St.-Florent *(tel 02 41 50 00 50)*. Sleep in a cave at the **Hotel Bussy** in Montsoreau *(www.hotel-le-bussy.fr, tel 02 41 38 11 11)* or the **Hotel Demeure de la Vignole** in Turquant *(www.demeure-vignole.com, tel 02 41 53 67 00)*, with a swimming pool dug out of the rock.

# Bourges

In the heart of rural Berry, the region south of the Loire Valley, lies the historic town of Bourges, with its many architectural treasures. Its celebrated Gothic Cathédrale St.-Étienne (made a UNESCO World Heritage site in 1993) is considered one of the most outstanding examples of Gothic architecture in France.

**Bourges**

🅰 167 E2

**Visitor information**

✉ 21 rue Victor-Hugo

☎ 02 48 23 02 60

**www.bourges-tourisme.com**

**Cathédrale St.-Étienne**

☎ 02 48 65 49 44

Built mostly between 1195 and 1260, the cathedral is unusual in having no transepts, so that the interior seems unusually spacious and airy. The facade has five beautifully carved doorways, three towers, and a gorgeous 15th-century rose window. Within, the whole cathedral glows with stained glass; especially notable are the windows telling the story of the Annunciation in the chapel of Jacques Coeur.

You can't go far in Bourges without encountering Jacques Coeur, one of the most powerful men in 15th-century France. Having sailed to the East, trading in silks, spices, and precious metals, he returned to build a superb mansion. His **Palais Jacques Coeur** (rue Jacques Coeur, tel 02 48 24 79 42, guided tours only) incorporates some of the Roman wall of Bourges and was designed in part for defense. But inside, patterned-tile floors, stone fireplaces, and painted ceilings reveal just how elegant Renaissance life could be.

The medieval and Renaissance quarter around the cathedral has other highlights, including a 17th-century garden designed by Le Nôtre, a medieval tithe barn adjoining the cathedral cloister, and many half-timbered, cantilevered houses. Among the grander town houses (hôtels), look for the Hôtel des Échevins and the Hôtel Lallemant, which now houses the **Musée des Arts Décoratifs** (6 rue Bourbonnoux, tel 02 48 57 81 17, closed Sun. a.m. & all day Mon.).

The Hôtel Cujas, built in 1515 for a Florentine merchant, contains the **Musée du Berry** (4 rue des Arènes, tel 02 48 57 81 15, closed Sun. a.m. & all day Tues.) devoted to the history of the Berry region. ∎

Cathédrale St.-Etienne is a Gothic tour de force.

# EXPERIENCE: La Vie en Château

Take a step into history by sampling the traditional luxury of chateau life. The château experience is more and more popular, and all over France there are châteaus, grand and small, luxurious and more modest, offering a variety of facilities and experiences. You can become a guest in a stately manor, a Renaissance château, a medieval castle, or an aristocratic family home for one or more nights; most offer bed and breakfast, and often dinner, and some are available to rent completely for a week. Swimming, golf, or tennis may also be options.

You can dine in grand salons and listen to musical concerts, learn wine appreciation, take cooking classes or dancing lessons, or practice French conversation. A château makes an ideal setting for a romantic wedding.

Small, elegant **Château de la Barre** (Conflans-sur-Anille, www.chateaudelabarre.com, tel 02 43 35 00 17) in the Loir region is surrounded by tranquil parkland. The Count and Countess de Vanssay (he is the 20th-generation count and she is Anglo-American) welcome you into their home, where

Guests at Château de la Barre are treated to live entertainment appropriate to an elegant centuries-old home.

you can spend two or more nights, listening to chamber music in the Grand Salon (surrounded by ancestor portraits), dining on family silver and porcelain in the vast 17th-century dining room, and sleeping in a sumptuous bedroom. More concerts can be heard in the small Romanesque chapels of the Loir.

In the Lorraine region, near Nancy, **Château d'Hattonchâtel** (www.au-chateau.com) dates back in part to the ninth century. After destruction during World War I, it was restored by American Belle Skinner. Indeed, this is a fine base for exploring World War I

sites. You can prepare meals yourself in the château tower or arrange for dinner to be made for you.

**Château Robert** (www.au-chateau.com) in the Landes in Southwest France, is a classic 19th-century château with huge grounds, a saltwater swimming pool, tennis, and trout fishing in the pond. Horseback riding and golf are close by. Weeklong cooking classes are taught, and wine tastings organized.

**Château Juvenal** (www.au-chateau.com), a retreat in the Vaucluse area of Provence, is surrounded by

vineyards and olive groves. Enjoy regional cuisine and the château's own wine. You can join painting and cooking classes; cheese, wine and truffle tastings; and even tango lessons.

Comte and Comtesse des Monstiers Mérinville welcome guests to their Limousin **Château du Fraisse** (www.au-chateau.com), which goes back eight centuries. Approached by a long driveway with a marble columned entrance, it has antiques and offers tennis, French billiards, a dance floor, a bandstand, and even a private chapel.

# More Places to Visit in the Loire Valley

## Lesser Châteaus

**Montreuil-Bellay** (Map 167 C2, visitor information, place de la Concorde, tel 02 41 52 32 39), a river town south of Saumur, has an 11th-century fortress enclosing an elegant and beautifully furnished 15th-century mansion.

The construction of the **Château de Serrant** (Map 167 C2, tel 02 41 39 13 01, closed Tues. Nov.–March) near Angers, surrounded by a moat and attendant swans, took place over two centuries—though you would never guess from the harmony of the design. Inside the opulently decorated château is an enormous library and a bedroom designed for Napoleon.

A drawbridge leads to the small **Château du Plessis-Bourré** (Map 167 C3, tel 02 41 32 06 72), encircled by a moat that reflects its white walls, blue slate roof, and spires. The Renaissance interior is designed for elegance.

---

## EXPERIENCE:
## Le Mans Car Circuit

Drive the famous Le Mans 24-hour car race circuit (tel 02 43 40 24 30, www .lemansdriver.fr). You can do laps in cars and motorbikes on the Bugatti course and the Maison Blanche circuit, or try out the endurance car simulator for the "full experience" of changing drivers and more. Later, the old town of **Le Mans** (Map 167 D3) warrants a spin—on foot.

---

Medieval fortress on the outside—complete with moat, drawbridge, towers, crenellations, and arrow-slit windows—Renaissance palace on the inside, 15th-century **Langeais** (Map 167 D2, tel 02 47 96 72 60) contains fine tapestries.

The **Château de Cheverny** (Map 167 E3, tel 02 54 79 96 29), built between 1620 and 1634, has a classically regular facade and a lavishly painted interior.

The 19th-century novelist George Sand lived in **Nohant** (Map 167 E1, tel 02 54 31 07 37). Here she entertained her many lovers, Chopin among them, and wrote novels. Her house and garden, much as she left them, are open to the public.

## Nantes

The Loire meets the sea just beyond the great estuary city of Nantes, whose wealth was derived from maritime activity. Now one of the most popular places to live in France, Nantes is undergoing a renaissance. The huge 15th-century **Château des Ducs de Bretagne** (www.chateau-nantes.fr) has been extensively renovated, its dramatic granite walls now housing a museum dedicated to the history of the city and its shipbuilding past. The 19th-century neo-Gothic **Palais Dobrée** houses a rich private collection of art, furniture, tapestries, and manuscripts. The 19th-century **Quartier Greslin** is a feast of neoclassical facades, wrought-iron balconies, belle epoque shopping arcades, and art nouveau cafés. Don't miss the celebrated brasserie La Cigale, opposite the theater.

On an entirely different note, for a truly original experience take a ride on a gigantic mechanical elephant. This splendid creation can carry 45 passengers, who control some of its movements. It is the highlight of a gallery tour of the workshops of **Les Machines de l'Île** (www.lesmachines-nantes.fr, $$), a partnership of artist-engineers François Delaroziere and Pierre Orefice, whose workshops occupy former warehouse space on the Île de Nantes.

🅰 166 B2  **Visitor information** ✉ 7 rue du Valmy  ☎ 08 92 46 40 44

## Sancerre

Far up the Loire, Sancerre, a red-roofed town of old streets winding up a hill, is ringed by vineyards and produces fine dry white wine.

🅰 167 F2  **Visitor information** ✉ rue de la Croix de Bois  ☎ 02 48 54 08 21

A variety of grand landscapes: from the Auvergne down to the rich lands around the Rhône and Saône Rivers, and up to the Alps

# Central France
# & the Alps

Pinot Noir grapes drink in the sun.

# Central France & the Alps

This region includes the province of Burgundy, primarily an agricultural region, and the quiet mountains of the Jura in the north. To the south, the Rhône Valley has been an important trade route for millennia. The rugged heights, deep gorges, clear lakes, and open spaces of the Alps in the east attract walkers and skiers, while in the west lie the mountains at the heart of France, the Massif Central.

The Romans left many surviving remains in this area, and Burgundy is rich with religious and architectural sights. The power of the medieval duchy of Burgundy rivaled that of the kingdom of France.

The region's most important river, the Rhône, flows from Lake Geneva in Switzerland. A major producer of silk fabrics for centuries, Lyon, at the confluence of the Rhône and Saône Rivers, is the second largest city in France.

At 15,780 feet (4,810 m), Mont Blanc dominates the French Alps. The mountains of the Jura along the Swiss border are formed of limestone plateaus cut by deep valleys.

At the heart of the Massif Central are the rocks produced by volcanoes—the *puys* that form the highest points of the massif. ■

## NOT TO BE MISSED:

Helping build a medieval castle at Guédelon **194**

Tasting Burgundy vintages along the Côte-d'Or wine route **196–197**

The serene Abbaye de Fontenay **201**

A meal or two in Lyon **212–214**

The marvelous view of Mont Blanc from Chamonix **216**

Hiking to the summit of Puy de Dôme in the Auvergne **224–225**

Driving through the spectacular Gorges du Tarn **226–227**

★Paris

Area of map detail

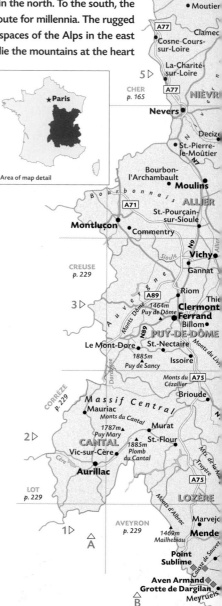

0                    60 kilometers
0          30 miles

AUBE
p. 105

HAUTE-MARNE
p. 105

VOSGES
p. 105

HAUT-RHIN
p. 105

Armançon

Tonnerre          Châtillon-sur-Seine

Chablis
Cravant          Fontenay

Luxeuil-
les-Bains
N19                Lure        Ronchamp
Vesoul                   Belfort

Montbard
Avallon   Semur-en-
Auxois
Vezelay

HAUTE-
SAÔNE

N71
A31            Gray          Ognon          Montbéliard

CÔTE-D'OR                                              TERRITOIRE-
DE-BELFORT

Seine

Pouilly-en-
Auxois          Dijon
Saulieu          A38
Clos de Vougeot          Citeaux
Nuits-
St-Georges
Château-
Chinon    Meursault  Beaune

Pesmes          A36
Besançon          Maîche

Auxonne          DOUBS
Dole
Arc-et-Senans
Seurre

Ouche

Doubs

N57

Chagny
Le Creusot   Chalon-
sur-Saône
Montceau-
les-Mines
Bourbon-
Lancy
N79   Digoin

Autun

SAÔNE
ET-LOIRE

Saône

Salins-les-Bains
Arbois
Poligny
JURA          Champagnole
Cirque de Baume
Lons-le-Saunier
N78   Louhans   Doucier   Cascades du Hérisson

Pontarlier

Ornans

N5

Tournus

SWITZERLAND

Morez

Charolles   Cluny   A6
Paray-
le-Monial

Canal du Centre   Monts du Charolais

Mâcon
A40

St.-Claude
1689m
Mont
Colomby
de Gex

Ain

Lac Léman (Lake Geneva)
Évian-les-Bains
Thonon-
les-Bains
Chablais
Annemasse   Morzine

apalisse   N7

Juliénas
Beaujeu   Fleurie   Bourg-
481m ▲ Mt. Brouilly   en-Bresse
Roanne   Villefranche-
sur-Saône
Oingt

Monts
de la
Madeleine

Bellegarde
St-Julien-
en-Genevois
A40
Rumilly   A41

Oyounax

AIN

HAUTE-SAVOIE
Annecy   Cluses
Megève
Chamonix
4810m ▲ 3842m
Mont Blanc   Aiguille du Midi

Lyonnais   Tarare   A46   Pérouges
LOIRE   Feurs   N89   A42
A72   Montbrison   Monts du Lyonnais
Ambert   Bourgoin-Jallieu
St.-Chamond   Vienne   A48

RHÔNE   LYON

Saône

Rhône

N75

Lac du
Bourget
Aix-les-Bains   Le Châtelard
La-Tour-
du-Pin
A43   Chambéry   A430
Moutiers   La Plagne

Lac d'Annecy

Albertville

3747m
Grande
Sassière
Les Arcs

A47

1634m ▲
Monts du Forez

ST.-ETIENNE   Pélussin
Firminy   N82

HAUTE-
LOIRE   Annonay
Yssingeaux
Le Puy-en-Velay

Loire

Hauterives
A49
ISÈRE
Voiron   St-Pierre-
de-Chartreuse   N6
Valloire
PARC NAT.
RÉGIONAL   Grenoble   Vizille

SAVOIE   Courchevel
Méribel

Arc

A41   A43

Tignes

3676m
Ciamarella

Modane
Tunnel
du Fréjus

ITALY

Lamastre   Isère

Romans-
sur-Isère
Lans-en-Vercors
DU VERCORS
Valence   Vercors
2086m
Mont Aiguille
Die

1753m
Mt. Mezenc
Le Monastier-
sur-Gazeille

Privas

Drôme

Le Bourg-
d'Oisans   3983m
Le Meije   3946m
Massif des Écrins   Mt. Pelvoux
La Mure   Vallouise

Briançon

St.-Véran

HAUTE-
LOIRE

ARDÈCHE
Langogne
Aubenas
Montélimar
Ste.-
Enimie
Largentière
▲1699m
Mt. Lozère   Vallon-
Pont-d'Arc   A7
Florac   Pont d'Arc   Aven de Marzal
Gorges   Gorges de   St.-Martin-
du Tarn   l'Ardèche   d'Ardèche
Aven d'Orgnac

Crest

DRÔME

Serres

Nyons

N75

HAUTES-ALPES
Gap   Embrun
N94

Durance

Guillestre

ALPES-DE-HAUTE-PROVENCE
p. 277

F

E

GARD
p. 277   C

VAUCLUSE
p. 277   D

# Burgundy & the Jura

For much of its history, Burgundy was a powerful independent state, and it retains a strong sense of pride in its regional identity. There is also misty-eyed nostalgia for its glorious past—for tales of Vercingétorix and the last stand of the Gauls. The vanquishing Romans founded several of Burgundy's cities and left remains in places such as Autun.

The small town of Irancy, near Chablis, is known for its vineyards and wine.

Burgundy is one of the richest regions of France, its historic towns and cities the product of many centuries of civilization. The region is best known for producing some of the world's finest wines—a tour of the Côte-d'Or and a visit to the wine town of Beaune are opportunities for any wine lover to savor.

Austere abbeys and superb Romanesque churches testify to the importance of Christianity here throughout the Middle Ages. The Basilique de Ste.-Madeleine in Vézelay was one of the starting points for pilgrimages to Santiago de Compostela (see pp. 264–265).

Between the 10th and 12th centuries, Benedictine rule reached its greatest influence at Cluny. Dissatisfaction with the increasing luxury and slackening discipline amongst the Benedictines led St. Bernard to found a new order in the 12th century, the Cistercians. The Abbaye de Fontenay stands as a tribute to the industry and austerity of Cistercian monastic

life. In Burgundy you can see the architectural development in church building from the Romanesque barrel vault to the Gothic naves of the cathedrals of Sens and Auxerre.

The 13th and 14th centuries saw the rise of the dukes of Burgundy, a golden age evoked in the magnificent palaces, noble mansions, and art collections of Dijon. The châteaus that dot the countryside tell of the wealth of the rulers of Burgundy and their nobles.

Outside its towns and cities, Burgundy is full of wonderful landscapes, from the regional park of the Morvan to the pastures of the Brionnais. To the east, the mountainous region of the Jura is a tranquil land of deep valleys and waterfalls.

Burgundy spans a watershed. The Saône River runs south to the Rhône Valley; the Yonne flows north to join the Seine. In addition, canals link the main towns. A boat ride along Burgundy's waterways makes a truly delightful way to float through history. ■

# Dijon

Bourgeois, comfortable Dijon has for almost 2,000 years been a merchant city on an international trade route. Medieval trade in Eastern spices brought the ingredients for its two most noted gastronomic specialties: mustard and *pain d'épices*. What makes Dijon so pleasurable to visit is its balance of splendid architecture with a serious attitude toward food—and lots of good restaurants.

During the 14th century, Dijon was the capital of the grand dukes of Burgundy, and it is their palace, the **Palais des Ducs,** that dominates the city. The oldest parts remaining are the 14th-century Tour de Bar and 15th-century vaulted ducal kitchens. The Tour Philippe-le-Bon, also 15th century, gives terrific views over the city. In the 17th century, the States General of Burgundy extended the palace as their parliament house. Part of this vast building, a mini-Versailles, now houses the **Musée des Beaux-Arts** (http:// mba.dijon.fr), noted for its Dutch and Flemish masters.

Walk around old Dijon to see its dignified buildings enlivened with statuary and carvings. Rue Verrerie has 15th-century half-timbered houses with stained-glass windows. Rue des Forges, north of the Palais des Ducs, is equally historic: The **Hôtel de Chambellan** (now the tourist office) with its Gothic courtyard and stone spiral staircase dates from the 15th century, while the arcaded facade of the **Hôtel Aubriot** is 13th century. But it was in the 17th and 18th centuries, when Dijon flourished as a strong regional power, that most of its grand mansions were built. The

**Hôtel de Vogüé** has distinctive Burgundian polychrome roof tiles and a pink marble courtyard; the **Maison des Cariatides** has stone caryatids around its windows.

Fine churches include the cathedral and the former **Abbaye St.-Bénigne,** with a beautiful, 11th-century Romanesque crypt beneath it. The superb Gothic **Église de Notre-Dame** has a medieval Jacquemart clock on the facade.

There is a food market every Tuesday, Friday, and Saturday in **Les Halles.** Do try Dijon's famous aperitif, kir (see below), in a café on Place François-Rude. ■

**Dijon**
- 🇦 191 D5

**Visitor information**
- ✉ 34 rue des Forges
- ☎ 08 92 70 05 58

**www.visitdijon.com**

**Palais des Ducs et des États de Bourgogne**
- ✉ place de la Libération
- ☎ 03 80 74 52 09
- 🕐 Closed Tues.
- 💲 $$

**Église de Notre-Dame**
- ✉ place Notre-Dame

---

### Kir, S'il Vous Plaît

Dijon is the place to sample *kir*, a popular drink usually served as an aperitif. It was named after Canon Félix Kir, a longtime mayor of Dijon, who first mixed Bourgogne Aligoté wine with cassis (black currant liqueur).

A pioneer of the town-twinning movement after World War II, Canon Kir offered the drink at receptions. A similar drink had been made with red wine, but according to Kir he had to make it with white because the Germans had imbibed all the red Burgundy.

Kir is now served all over the world in many versons, including *kir royale* (using sparkling wine) and *kir Breton* (using cider).

# EXPERIENCE: Build a Medieval Castle

Deep in the forest of Puisaye in northern Burgundy lies Guédelon, a medieval castle under construction. Using the same methods, tools, and materials of 800 years ago, a dedicated team of 50 people, along with a host of eager volunteers, is building the castle entirely from scratch. Here you can completely immerse yourself in the 13th century—to the sounds of metal on stone, the sawing of wood, the hammer striking the anvil, and horses' hooves pounding on bare earth.

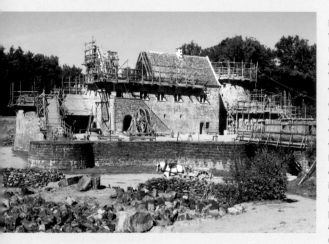

The medieval-style castle of Guédelon is being constructed using only 13th-century tools and techniques.

**Guédelon** *(Chantier Médiéval de Guédelon, Treigny, tel 03 86 45 66 66, $$, participer@ guedelon.fr, www.guedelon .fr)* is the brainchild of Michel Guyot, who began the project in the mid-1990s. Back then, Guyot already had one medieval castle under his belt, neighboring St.-Fargeau, which he had restored from a state of near-dereliction. Eager to understand medieval construction, Guyot decided to build his own castle. Contruction began in 1998.

The plan is a traditional castle of four towers surrounding a courtyard. As of 2011, the Great Hall had been completed.

In the woods around the building site, carpenters, masons, weavers, potters, and blacksmiths all labor away busily. They quarry and hew stones, weave baskets, construct carts, mix mortar, and forge nails just as their forebears did in the 13th century. All transport is by horse and cart, and there is no electricity or modern machinery. The dedicated workers even wear medieval costumes.

Unlike most other building sites, Guédelon is open to the public. In fact, one of the project's main objectives is to explain and demonstrate medieval craftsmanship to as many people as possible. Visitors can sample medieval food and drink at the tavern on-site. Guided tours are available, but be aware that what you see will depend on whatever work happens to be going on at the time. The castle is due for completion in about 20 years, so there is plenty of time for you to pitch in and help. Volunteers are welcome from three days up to one week. The site is located in the middle of the woods, so a car, or at least a bicycle, is essential, as is a grasp of basic French.

For other hands-on projects, **Rempart** *(www.rem part.com/en)* is dedicated to cultural restoration, from medieval gardens to historic trains. **Apare** *(www.apare-gec.org)* organizes volunteer groups in southern France to help rebuild ramparts and restore châteaus. **La Sabranenque** *(www.sab ranenque.com)* runs volunteer programs, such as the restoration of the village of St. Victor la Coste near Avignon, to help maintain the rural Mediterranean habitat and preserve traditional building techniques.

# Beaune

A small town with a big reputation, Beaune is the true nerve center of the wine business in Burgundy. Set among some of the most distinguished vineyards in the world, it is the best place to go if you want to sample a variety of different wines from the region. It is also home to one of Burgundy's most celebrated sights, the Hôtel-Dieu.

To gain an overall view of this handsomely preserved old town, enter it through the 18th-century triumphal arch of **Porte St.-Nicolas** to the north. Walk around the remains of the 11th- to 15th-century ramparts and explore narrow lanes and cobbled courtyards, peering up at the fine Gothic and Renaissance details of the houses. Head for Place Monge, with its 15th-century bell tower and splendid houses such as the 16th-century Hôtel de la Rochepot. North from Place Monge runs Rue de Lorraine, lined with mansions and courtyards richly embellished with Renaissance carving, elaborate ironwork, and stone staircases. The Hôtel de Ville, a former 17th-century convent, houses the **Musée des Beaux-Arts,** featuring Dutch and Flemish paintings and a collection of works by Félix Ziem, born in Beaune in 1821.

The much altered **Église de Notre-Dame** was built in the 12th century in Cluny Romanesque style, with Gothic and Renaissance decorations added later. In its chancel is a beautiful series of five 15th-century tapestries depicting the life of the Virgin Mary.

At the heart of Beaune is **Place de la Halle,** site of the medieval corn market. On Saturdays the market hall and stalls around it are laden with the gastronomic bounty Burgundy produces to complement its wine. The streets all around are lined with wine cellars, many of which offer tastings. If you want to know about the mysteries of wine, make for the **Musée du Vin de Bourgogne.** It is housed in the splendid stone-and-timber 14th- to 16th-century mansion that was once a private residence of the dukes of Burgundy. The entire history of winemaking is recounted, with a fascinating exhibition of old equipment and presses. ∎

**Beaune**
- 191 D5

**Visitor information**
- 6 boulevard Perpreuil
- 03 80 26 21 30
- www.ot-beaune.fr

---

### Hôtel-Dieu

An **extraordinary building with polychrome roof and turret tiles, the Hôtel-Dieu *(rue de l'Hôtel-Dieu, tel 03 80 24 45 00, $$)* was founded as a hospital as the Hundred Years' War ended, in 1443. The last patient left only in 1971. Rooms open to the public include the linen room and pharmacy, but the best is the kitchen, with its great fireplace, spit, and copper utensils. Among the many fine paintings and tapestries, the most famous is the 15th-century altarpiece, the "Last Judgment" by Rogier van der Weyden, its richly painted figures resplendent against a gold background.

---

**Musée des Beaux-Arts**
- rue de l'Hôtel de Ville
- 03 80 22 20 80
- Closed a.m. & Tues. Dec.–March
- $

**Musée du Vin de Bourgogne**
- Hôtel des Ducs de Bourgogne
- 03 80 22 08 19
- $

# Drive Down the Côte-d'Or

The Côte-d'Or, now a UNESCO World Heritage site, is a 30-mile (48 km) strip of land that produces Burgundy's most venerated wines. Often the wine is blended, but a few are so distinguished they are bottled and sold individually; here the winemaker is as important as the *domaine* (similar to the Bordeaux château). Go in late summer, when the weather is still warm but the grapes are ripening, or best of all at harvest time, in early fall.

## Côte de Nuits

Start your tour at **Chenôve ❶**, on the D122, which runs parallel to, and west of, the N74. Here you can see a gargantuan 13th-century wine press in the former press house of the dukes of Burgundy. This is the beginning of the Côte de Nuits region, starring the finest red wines, produced from the tempermental Pinot Noir grape.

Continue to **Gevrey-Chambertin ❷**, with more *grands crus* than any other village in Burgundy. The **Clos de Bèze** is purportedly the oldest vineyard in Burgundy, planted by the Abbey of Bèze in the sixth century.

Continue on the D122 to Chambolle-Musigny. Just south is celebrated **Clos de Vougeot ❸**, founded in the 12th century by the monks of Cîteaux. Today, its 120 acres (50 ha) are divided among 80 owners. The 16th-century **Château du Clos de Vougeot** is the headquarters of the Confrérie des Chevaliers du Tastevin (*www.tastevin-bourgogne.com*), the wine brotherhood founded to promote Burgundy. Visitors are welcome for tastings and to visit its wine museum (*tel 03 80 62 86 09*).

Join the N74 and continue south to **Vosne-Romanée,** which claims six grands crus, including the majestic Romanée-Conti—a little stone cross marks its treasured patch of soil. **Nuits-St.-Georges ❹** (*tel 03 80 62 11 17, www.ot-nuits-st-georges.fr*) has numerous cellars to visit and a 13th-century church; the town gives its name to this section of the Côte d'Or: the Côte de Nuits.

## Côte de Beaune

South of Nuits-St.-Georges on the N74 is the Côte de Beaune, where the soil is lighter and

**NOT TO BE MISSED:**

Château du Clos de Vougeot
• Château Corton-André • Château
de Meursault • View from Orches

chalkier, perfect for the Chardonnay grape. Head first for **Aloxe-Corton ❺** on the D2, home of distinguished red and white wines. Look for signs to the **Château Corton-André,** roofed in shining colored tiles and open to visitors for tastings. Then continue north up the D18 to **Pernand-Vergelesses,** one of the prettiest of the wine villages. Go back down the D18, and continue on the D2 to **Savigny-lès-Beaune.**

After the great wine town of **Beaune ❻** (see p. 195), take the D973 southward. The Côte de Beaune continues with some of the best white wines of Burgundy. A good place to taste them is in **Meursault ❼**, at the **Château de Meursault** (*tel 03 80 26 22 75, www.meursault.com*) with its 14th-century cellars.

**Puligny-Montrachet ❽**, down the D113, is a quiet little village with very distinguished wines. A simple stone gateway leads to the vineyard of Montrachet, regarded by many as the best dry white wine in the world. The D113 continues south to **Santenay.**

Return to Beaune via the Hautes-Côtes, a route that combines vineyards with even more spectacular scenery. Take the D33 up via St.-Aubin to the **Château de la Rochepot ❾** (*tel 03 80 21 71 37, closed Tues. and Nov.–March, www.larochepot.com*), then take the D17 to **Orches,** for views over the Saône to the Jura.

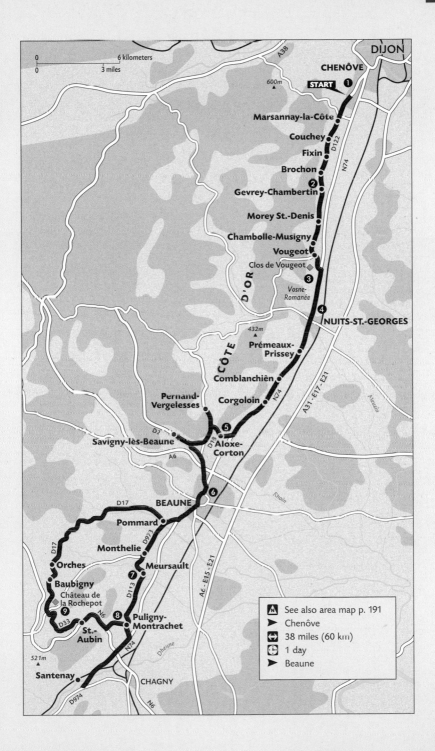

DIJON

CHENÔVE

**START** ❶

600m ▲

Marsannay-la-Côte

Couchey

Fixin

Brochon

Gevrey-Chambertin ❷

Morey St.-Denis

Chambolle-Musigny

Vougeot

Clos de Vougeot ◆

❸

Vosne-Romanée

❹ NUITS-ST.-GEORGES

432m ▲

Prémeaux-Prissey

Comblanchiên

Pernand-Vergelesses

Corgoloin

CÔTE

D'OR

❺

Savigny-lès-Beaune

Aloxe-Corton

❻

BEAUNE

D17

Pommard

Monthelie

Orches

Meursault

Baubigny

❼

Château de la Rochepot ◆

❾

❽

Puligny-Montrachet

St.-Aubin

521m ▲

Santenay

CHAGNY

0    6 kilometers
0    3 miles

A38

D122

N74

A31, E17, E21

N74

A6, E15, E21

D973

D17

D113

N6

D33

N74

D974

N6

A6

D7

D18

🅝 See also area map p. 191
▶ Chenôve
↔ 38 miles (60 km)
🕐 1 day
▶ Beaune

# Sens

If you arrive in Burgundy from the north, the first major town you come to is Sens, always an important crossroads. Its period of greatest influence was the 12th century, when it was an archbishopric with control over most of northern France, including Paris and Chartres.

**Sens**
🅰 190 B6

**Visitor information**
✉ place Jean-Jaurès
☎ 03 86 65 19 49
🕐 Closed Sun. Nov.–Apr.

**Cathédrale St.-Étienne**
✉ place de la République

**Musée de Sens**
✉ place de la Cathédrale
☎ 03 86 83 88 90
🕐 Closed Tues.
💲 $

**Chablis**
🅰 191 C6

**Visitor information**
✉ 1 rue du Maréchal de Lattre de Tassigny
☎ 03 86 42 80 80
www.chablis.fr

The magnificent **Cathédrale St.-Étienne,** one of the first of France's great Gothic cathedrals, shows Sens's medieval importance. Building began in 1130; later additions spanned subsequent developments in the Gothic style. Archbishop Henri le Sanglier, who commissioned the building from William of Sens, was a close friend of St. Bernard of Clairvaux, and the influence of Cistercian austerity is clearly apparent in the simplicity of the structure.

The proportions are mathematically calculated (the width of the nave being twice that of the side aisles), but the overall effect is one of harmonious space. Stained glass fills the tall windows, some of which survive from the 12th century. The west portal is particularly beautiful, despite having lost one of its towers and much of its statuary. In the central doorway, look

for the 12th-century Gothic statue of St. Étienne.

The adjoining archbishop's palace is now the **Musée de Sens,** with one of the richest treasuries in France: a glittering collection of religious art, Byzantine silks, shrouds, altar cloths, reliquaries, and vestments. The museum also has a collection of furniture, ceramics, and Dutch paintings.

A stroll around the cathedral quarter of the town reveals streets of picturesque stone and half-timbered houses dating from the 16th to the 18th centuries. ∎

**INSIDER TIP:**

## Pick up great cheese in Sens at Parret *(1 rue Vieilles Étuves).*

—SHEILA BUCKMASTER
National Geographic Traveler
*magazine editor at large*

## Chablis

Chablis is home to the northernmost of the great Burgundian vineyards, an ancient stone village with one overwhelming interest—the fragrant white wine, pale and dry, to which it has given its name. In spring there is a scent of laburnum and a cool freshness in the air, reminiscent of the wine itself. There are good restaurants and hotels here, and several *domaines* open their cellars for tastings.

To drive around the vineyards (which have been planted with the Chardonnay grape, locally known as "Beaunois"), follow the course of the Serein River on the D91 north toward Maligny. To your right are the *grand cru* vineyards, facing south and southeast. Return on the D131 heading for Milly, from where there is an excellent view of the surprisingly few Chablis vineyards.

# Auxerre

Auxerre is a sleepy little town on the banks of the Yonne River, a perfect starting point for trips on the waterways of Burgundy. From across the river, you can see the steep roofs of the old town and of the churches for which it is famous.

The Abbatiale de St.-Germain, in Auxerre, stands reflected in the Yonne River.

The **Cathédrale St.-Étienne** dominates the town. In 1215, Bishop Guillaume de Seignelay decided to rebuild the existing Romanesque cathedral in the new Gothic style. Two centuries later, the main body of the building was complete, but the cathedral wasn't finished until 1560. The columns and rib vaulting are so subtly arranged they seem to be carrying no weight at all. The airy lightness is increased by the jewel-like colors of the stained glass. The Romanesque crypt stands in complete contrast, its barrel vault and sturdy pillars intact. The apse still has remarkable 12th-century frescoes of Christ on horseback surrounded by angels, vestiges of a scheme that once covered the entire church.

A short walk up Rue Cauchois leads to the **Abbatiale de St.-Germain** (tel 03 86 18 05 50, closed Tues.) and the Musée d'Art et d'Histoire. Hidden beneath the neo-Gothic church is a dim, vaulted Carolingian crypt with ancient stone sarcophagi of long-forgotten bishops and the tomb of St. Germain. The ninth-century frescoes of the stoning of St. Étienne are among the oldest religious wall paintings in France.

The 17th-century town gate, the **Tour de l'Horloge,** has a moondial as well as a sundial in its 15th-century clock face. ■

**Auxerre**
- 190 B5

**Visitor information**
- ✉ 1–2 quai de la République
- ☎ 03 86 52 06 19

www.ot-auxerre.fr

**Cathédrale St.-Étienne**
- ✉ rue Fouriet
- ☎ 03 86 52 23 29
- 💲 Crypt & Treasury: $

# Vézelay

The great Basilique de Ste.-Madeleine in Vézelay rises on a rock from a deep valley. The best way to approach it is to climb the steep main street, following in the steps of the medieval pilgrims who flocked here to worship the (supposed) relics of St. Mary Magdalene.

**Vézelay**

 191 C5

**Visitor information**

✉ rue St.-Étienne

☎ 03 86 33 23 69

**www.vezelaytourisme
.com**

Vézelay's spiritual reputation still draws crowds, and the medieval streets of the town are crammed with bookstores, antique shops, and art galleries. Its ramparts give lovely views of the lush, rolling hills of the surrounding countryside.

Founded in 864, the **Basilique de Ste.-Madeleine** *(place de la Basilique, tel 03 86 33 39 50),* a UNESCO World Heritage site, thrived until 1280, when it emerged that the (supposed) bones of Mary Magdalene were still at St.-Maximin in Provence

and that the relics at Vézelay were fakes. Virtually abandoned, damaged by Protestants in the 16th century, and neglected during the Revolution, the basilica was in a ruinous state when architectural historian Viollet-le-Duc began restoration in the 19th century.

Walk around the outside of the basilica to view the apse with its radiating chapels; the chapter house, which is all that remains from the 12th-century monastery; and the west facade, with its restored 13th-century window and tower.

Then enter the vast narthex, added to accommodate the crowds of pilgrims in the 12th century. The famous tympanum over the inner door is the pièce de résistance of Burgundian Romanesque. With tremendous movement and feeling, it depicts the events of Pentecost: Rays of light streak from the fingers of Christ to the Apostles.

Looking through the door and straight down the aisle, the round Romanesque arches of the nave with alternating light and dark stones lead your eye to the soaring Gothic points of the choir beyond. The carvings of the capitals dwell heavily on the torment awaiting unbelievers. For an insight into the medieval mind-set, go down to the crypt to see the discredited relics. ∎

**Fine Romanesque sculptures decorate the Basilique de
Ste.-Madeleine in Vézelay.**

# Abbaye de Fontenay

The oldest Cistercian monastery still surviving, Fontenay has been superbly restored to give an intriguing picture of monastic life. Beautifully set in a quiet wooded valley, it was founded by St. Bernard of Clairvaux in 1118 and named after the spring there.

Serenity reigns in the Romanesque cloister at the Abbaye de Fontenay.

Aside from the 17th-century abbot's lodging at the western end of the church, all the buildings are original 12th-century structures, albeit restored. Many of the brown Burgundian roof tiles are original, too. The architecture embodies beauty at its most austere, in accordance with St. Bernard's belief that any superfluous decoration distracted from a building's spiritual purpose (see p. 203).

At its heart lies the **cloister,** a square of open galleries arcaded with double columns of golden stone. The **church** abuts the north gallery. Inside, aisles flank the long nave. A subtle glow from the windows enhances the spartan beauty. In the north transept stands a 13th-century statue of the Virgin and Child.

The **chapter house** has exquisite rib vaulting and columns. The monks slept on straw pallets in the **dormitory** above and copied manuscripts in the **scriptorium;** the **warming room** next to it kept the inks (and the monks' hands) from freezing in winter. The **forge,** where the monks worked the iron they dug from the hills, stands near the little river.

Fontenay thrived until the turmoil of the 16th-century religious wars. During the Revolution the abbey was sold and became a paper mill. In 1906, new owners, a branch of the Montgolfier ballooning family, restored it to its original Cistercian form. ■

**Abbaye de Fontenay**
- 191 C5
- Fontenay, Marmagne
- 03 80 92 15 00
- Open year-round. Guided tours in French only, April–Nov.
- $$
- www.abbayede fontenay.com

# Monasteries

The spread of Christianity, and in particular the development of the monasteries, was central to the growth and stability of the kingdom of France in the Middle Ages. Burgundy played a key role in the development of the monasteries in the ninth and tenth centuries. Two of the greatest medieval foundations were at Cluny and Cîteaux.

## Benedictines

The Benedictine order, founded in Italy by St. Benedict in 529, spread rapidly across Europe. "To work is to pray" was their motto. The monks were to do six to eight hours of work daily plus four hours each of prayer and reading. They had no private property other than the habit they wore, a rope and scapular (cloak), a belt, and a knife.

In contrast to the hermetic principles of earlier monasteries, the Benedictines emphasized community—sleeping, praying, reading, and eating together according to a precise daily routine of work and worship. The first monks built their church and dwellings on virgin territory and then supported themselves by farming, planting vineyards, and raising livestock.

Oases of order in a time of chaos, the monasteries quickly became influential throughout Europe. Large (an important monastery might have a thousand or more people attached to it), prosperous, secure, and disciplined, they were often centers of learning and culture.

## Cluny

By the tenth century, the Benedictine abbots were increasingly corrupt, and monks neglected their vows.

Traditional Cistercian Monastery

In response, Cluny (see p. 205) was founded in 910, reforming the order and spreading its influence over much of Europe. Eventually Cluny established some 1,450 daughter houses, and the original monastery grew so large that it required 40 farms, each with its own chapel, to support it.

## Cistercians

But Cluny, too, fell into decadent ways. In reaction, the Cistercian order was founded at Cîteaux, near Dijon, in 1098. Its austerity attracted a young nobleman named Bernard, who established his own monastery at Clairvaux in northern Burgundy. Thousands came to hear him preach, and it was his passionate oratory that launched the Second Crusade from Vézelay. The Cistercian movement grew rapidly, founding hundreds of new monasteries, including Pontigny and Fontenay (see p. 201) in Burgundy.

Bernard revived the Rule of St. Benedict, stressing the importance of manual work, poverty, and simplicity. His veto on superfluous decoration had a profound effect upon Cistercian architecture: For the Cistercians, form followed function, and the austerity of their buildings reflected the asceticism of their lives.

By the time of the Revolution, however, even these great abbeys had become corrupt, exploiting the people and abusing their influence. Deep popular resentment was expressed in brutal dismemberment of the buildings during and after the Revolution. Cluny was destroyed; Cîteaux is still a monastery though most of the buildings are not old. Pontigny and Fontenay, both restored, offer a vision of monastic life as it was intended to be.

Church

Cloisters

Chapter house

# Autun

From a hill just south of the city, there is a glorious view of Autun, one of the most important cities of Roman Gaul. Founded by Emperor Augustus in the first century B.C., Autun is also a gateway to the Morvan, rolling country ideal for walking or horseback riding.

Cathédrale St.-Lazare sits at the heart of medieval Autun.

**Autun**
🅼 191 C4
**Visitor information**
✉ 3 avenue Charles-de-Gaulle
☎ 03 85 86 80 38
www. autun-tourisme.com

**Musée Rolin**
✉ 5 rue des Bancs
☎ 03 85 52 09 76
🕐 Closed Tues.

**Musée Bibracte**
✉ St.-Léger-sous-Beuvray
☎ 03 85 86 52 35
🕐 Closed mid-Nov.–mid.-March
www.bibracte.fr

The substantial legacies of the Roman period include the sanctuary of the **Temple of Janus,** the **Porte d'Arroux** with its sculptured arcades and columns (still the main entrance to the town from the north), and the **Porte St.-André,** designed with separate arches for chariots and pedestrians. The remains of the Roman theater come to life every August with an evocative spectacle of Gallo-Roman life, complete with chariot races.

But this is also a medieval city, still partly cinched by ramparts. Its greatest treasure, the 12th-century Romanesque **Cathédrale St.-Lazare,** is famed for its incomparable sculpture. Gislebertus d'Autun was one of the greatest sculptors of an age that yields the names of few individual artists, and the tympanum over the west portal was his masterpiece. It was saved from destruction during the Revolution because it had been plastered over earlier in the 18th century. His vivid rendering of the Last Judgment, carved between 1130 and 1135, prompted André Malraux to describe him as "a Romanesque Cézanne." The chapter house contains more of his work, including capitals depicting the suicide of Judas and the dream of the three kings.

The **Musée Rolin** is housed in the adjacent 15th-century mansion, built by Nicolas Rolin, who founded the Hôtel-Dieu in Beaune (see p. 195). It contains Gallo-Roman antiquities, as well as Romanesque and Gothic works. The jewel of the collection is again by Gislebertus, a carved fragment taken from the cathedral and discovered built into a wall in 1856. This "Temptation of Eve" depicts Eve with sensuality and subtlety.

On the summit of Mont Beuvray, southwest of Autun, is **Bibracte,** a Gallic *oppidum* (army camp). Here Vercingétorix called a council of war of the Gallic tribes in 52 B.C. in a doomed attempt to defeat the Romans. The **Musée Bibracte** documents this important site. ∎

# Cluny

**Founded in 910, Cluny recently celebrated its 1,100th anniversary. For hundreds of years, the abbey was the most influential power in Christendom, described by Pope Urban II as the "light of the world." But the great abbey buildings, the pinnacle of Romanesque architecture, were torn down after the Revolution, leaving only gutted remains.**

Of the original building, only the south transept and tower still stand. The town of Cluny covers much of the rest, though excavations show the west end of the nave. The church was 600 feet (180 m) long with two towers and double aisles, the interior painted in glowing Byzantine colors. For centuries it resounded to the strains of Gregorian chant, and as if to emphasize the importance of music here, some surviving capitals are carved with scenes of musicians and their instruments. The work of an unknown "master of Cluny," these carvings, on view at the **Musée Ochier** in the 15th-century abbey palace (*Palais Jean de Bourbon, 03 85 59 12 79*) had a major influence on other sculptors, notably at Vézelay and Autun.

To set Cluny in context, visit the Burgundian churches, large and small, that were influenced by it. The architecture of the slightly older abbey church of **Tournus** (*place de l'Abbaye, tel 03 85 27 00 20*), 20 miles (33 km) to the northeast, is powerful and confident, with perfect round arches and attenuated columns. The 11th-century basilica of **Paray-le-Monial** to the west gives an idea of what Cluny actually looked like, on a reduced scale. Soaring to a daring 71 feet (22 m), the nave is crowned by austere, graceful vaulting. Clerestory windows provide the only clue as to how Cluny was lit.

The **Chapelle des Moines**, part of a Cluniac foundation at **Berzé-la-Ville**, southeast of Cluny, hints at how magnificently the abbey was decorated. The apse and walls are covered in frescoes of Christ in Glory surrounded by saints, in rich tones of ocher, blue, gold, and violet.

The **Circuit des Églises Romanes** (*information: Mâcon tourist office, p. 210, or at www.burgundy-tourism.com*) is a self-guided driving tour that takes in ancient churches including the priory of Anzy-le-Duc; Iguerande; and St.-Hilaire at Semur-en-Brionnais, with its octagonal belfry. ∎

## Taizé

**Famous for its meditative chanting and Bible readings in many languages, the village of Taizé (*www.taize.fr*) is a vibrant religious community and place of pilgrimage 4 miles (6.5 km) north of Cluny. Founded in 1940 by a Swiss pastor, Brother Roger, Taizé includes brothers from all denominations and draws thousands of visitors every year to share in simple candlelit worship and the daily life of the community.**

**Cluny**
- 191 C4

**Visitor information**
- 6 rue Mercière
- 03 85 59 05 34
- www.cluny-tourisme.com

**Paray-le-Monial**
- 191 C4

**Visitor information**
- avenue Jean-Paul II
- 03 85 81 10 92

**Berzé-la-Ville**
- 191 C4
- Chapelle des Moines
- 03 85 36 66 52
- Closed Nov.–March

# Food & Drink—Truly Robust Fare

Burgundians and the Lyonnais both lay claim to being the epicenter of French food. Their attitude to eating is summed up in the saying "Better a good meal than fine clothes." It is a robust cuisine, varying from the acme of sophistication to peasant dishes made according to the produce and resources available.

On cold days in the mountains, cheese fondue is a group-pleasing must.

This is a cuisine rich in protein, with quantities of meat and cheese, and sauces of wine and cream. Fine ingredients are plentiful: Bresse is famous for its *appellation contrôlée* chickens, Charollais for its beef. The Burgundian snail must be the plumpest in France, served with a rich emollient of butter and garlic. The Morvan produces one of France's best raw hams. Fish is plentiful, too, and treated in imaginative ways: *Pochouse* is a kind of freshwater bouillabaisse, made with white wine; *quenelles de brochet* are delicate fishballs of pike.

Lyon is celebrated for its many starred restaurants and superstar chefs. Its traditional cuisine is famous for its *charcuterie*, the sausages and other pork products that go so well with Beaujolais Nouveau. Dijon is famous for mustard and for spices that flavor *pain d'épices*, a delicious spice-and-honey cake.

Once you get into the mountains the food becomes more robust, with warming stews, soups, and gratins. *Gratin dauphinois* is a substantial dish of potatoes cooked with eggs, butter, milk, and cheese. Fondue is justly famous, and if you get the opportunity, try

---

## EXPERIENCE:
### Escargots à la Bourguignonne

Burgundy is the place in France to eat snails, fattened on the vine and greatly esteemed. Plump, delicious, and smothered in garlic and butter, **snails** are traditionally served piping hot in a dish with hollows for the shells. You use a thin-tined fork to extract them from their shell. **Chablis** pairs well with snails.

---

lesser known *raclette* and participate in a cozy ritual involving melting pieces of cheese—best on a snowy night. The mountains produce fine butter and cheese: The Jura is the home of Vacherin, the Savoie makes indispensible Gruyère, and the Massif Central produces Cantal, another staple of every French larder, and of course there's the incomparable ewe's milk Roquefort.

The Auvergne volcanic center of the Massif Central also has a strong peasant cuisine, which has been absorbed by the rest of France, often via the small Paris cafés traditionally run by Auvergnats. The key ingredients are potatoes and cabbage; try *potée Auvergnate* (pork with stuffed cabbage). The Auvergne is also noted for its salted hams and dried sausages, and Le Puy is famous for its superior green lentils, now appellation contrôlée.

Cherries, raspberries, plums, and apricots feature on menus. Black currants, with their intense flavor, come deliciously in tarts and preserves, and are distilled into the rich liqueur cassis, a component of local aperitifs (see p. 193).

**Baked snails is just one of Burgundy's many tasty delicacies.**

No visit to this region would be complete without sampling the aristocratic wines of Burgundy: The fragrant whites of Chablis and Meursault, for example and the velvety reds of Gevrey-Chambertin or Nuits-St.-Georges.

**Perfectly aged cheese awaits takers at the Sunday market in Beaune.**

# The Jura

The mountainous region of the Jura, on the Swiss border, covers much of the old region of Franche-Comté, once ruled by the great duchy of Burgundy and part of the nation of France only since the 17th century. The Jura's ancient mountains, which give their name to the Jurassic period, have yielded several important dinosaur remains. Deep valleys with rushing torrents divide the rolling plateaus: The lakes and rivers teem with trout, carp, and pike, and forests of black spruce, pine, and broad-leaved trees cover the slopes.

The church of Arbois glows in the setting sun.

The high rainfall waters peat bogs, which provide a habitat for rare birds, butterflies, and mosses. **Cirque-de-Baumes,** near Lons-le-Saunier, curiously, shelters a pocket of Mediterranean flora and fauna amid its limestone cliffs. Throughout the region, wildflowers carpet the roadsides and meadows in spring and summer.

Dotting the valleys are the Jura's distinctive wooden houses, with enormous chimneys serving as rooms, smokehouses, or even escape hatches when snow buries the house.

The Jura yields some of France's favorite cheeses, such as Morbier and dense, creamy Vacherin. The region also produces its own wine, mostly from a small region around the pretty town of **Arbois,** a favorite haunt of wine lovers. You should try *vin jaune,* a sherrylike wine from Château-Chalon. You may also find the increasingly rare dessert wine known as *vin de paille,* made from grapes left out in the sun on straw mats before they are pressed. Arbois is also famed as the birthplace of Louis Pasteur, the inventor of pasteurization, whose house and laboratory are preserved in the **Maison de Pasteur.**

**Comité Départemental du Jura**

🗺 191 D4–5

**Visitor information**

✉ 8 rue Louis-Rousseau, Lons-le-Saunier

☎ 03 84 87 08 88

**www.jura-tourism .com**

Visitors come to enjoy nature, walking on the lower slopes, canoeing on the rivers, and, in the winter months, skiing. This is also France's wettest region, though there is a dry period in midsummer. Although it is no longer as inaccessible as it used to be, the Jura still is home to plenty of wildlife, including the lynx, otter, and mountain hare.

INSIDER TIP:**

## Worth a visit for wine tasting and garden strolling is medieval Château d'Arlay (www .arlay.com), near Arbois.

—BECCA HENSLEY
National Geographic Traveler
*magazine writer*

## Loue Valley

For a brief visit to the Jura, follow the course of the Loue Valley. Start from **Arc-et-Senans**, with its ambitious 18th-century new town, the **Saline Royale** *(tel 03 81 54 45 45, www.salineroyale.com)*. Built to exploit the local salt mines, Arc-et-Senans now houses two museums featuring exhibitions on art and architecture.

Take the D17 north to Quingey. Now follow the D101 east, changing to the D102 and D103 successively to follow the river upstream to **Ornans**, the most charming town in the valley, with flower-decked balconies overhanging the river. Famous as the birthplace of the great realist painter Gustave Courbet, the town boasts several of his paintings, displayed in his childhood home, now the **Musée Courbet** *(currently under renovation).*

Continue up the valley on the D67, which provides stopping places for admiring the view. Two miles (3 km) past Mouthier, you reach the dramatic source of the Loue, springing in a great torrent from a cavern in the rock, only a short walk from the road. East of Salins-les-Bains, at the source of the Lison Rier, a waterfall plunges into a deep green pool.

To the west is **Lons-le-Saunier** *(place du 11 Novembre, tel 03 84 24 65 01, www.ot-lons-le-saunier .com)*, a pleasant little town handy for many of the region's sights. It was built over a thermal spring first used by the Romans and now supplying both its thermal baths and its swimming pool. ■

### Arbois
🅜 191 D4
**Visitor information**
✉ rue de l'Hôtel de Ville
☎ 03 84 66 55 50

### Arc-et-Senans
🅜 191 D5
**Visitor information**
✉ porche de la Saline Royale
☎ 03 81 57 43 21

### Ornans
🅜 191 E5
**Visitor information**
✉ 7 rue Pierre-Vernier
☎ 03 81 62 21 50

**Musée de la Maison Natale de Gustave Courbet**
✉ Maison Natale de l'Artiste, place Robert-Fernie, Ornans

---

## EXPERIENCE: Cascades du Hérisson

Get a feel for the rugged beauty of the Jura with a walk to explore the spectacular waterfalls of the **Cascades du Hérisson** *(www.cascades-du-herisson .fr)*, the most glorious sight in the Region des Lacs, a magical landscape of villages and waterfalls, mountains and forests.

To reach the waterfalls, walk or drive from the village of Doucier to the **Maison des Cascades** *(tel 03 84 25 77 36)* at the foot of the Cascade d'Eventail, where there is a visitor center. Here you will find information about the history of the valley and the development of the landscape, including the industries dependent on water power.

You can see the dramatic cascades that tumble down the river by following the 4.3-mile (7 km) path along the Hérisson River. The three-hour hike culminates at the top in a magnificent cascade, the Grand Saut, which plunges 200 feet (60 m) to the pool beneath. For the most spectacular views, go after abundant rain, or in winter when the waterfalls are frozen. Wear suitable footgear.

# More Places to Visit in Burgundy & the Jura

## Besançon

The ancient fortress town of Besançon is the capital of Franche-Comté. It now specializes in watchmaking. Appropriately, a 19th-century astronomical clock adorns the 12th-century Gothic **Cathédrale St.-Jean.** The 17th-century citadel houses museums on natural history, Vauban (tel 03 81 87 83 33), and the history of the Resistance (tel 03 81 87 83 12). The **Musée des Beaux-Arts** has works by Courbet, Ingres, and Boucher. www.besancon-tourisme.com ⚠ 191 E5 **Visitor information** ✉ 2 place de la 1ère Armée Française ☎ 03 81 80 92 55

---

### The Swallow Train Line

**La Ligne des Hirondelles** (www.ligne deshirondelles.fr) crosses the Jura from one side to the other, linking Dole to St.-Claude. Originally constructed to transport goods, such as stone, marble, cheese, and crafts, this amazing piece of engineering follows 75 miles (120 km) of track through the wonderful scenery of the Haut Jura regional park, traveling through 36 dramatic tunnels and along 22 viaducts.

---

## Châtillon-sur-Seine

Châtillon-sur-Seine, which is located near the source of the Seine River, is the proud possessor of the Treasure of Vix, shown in the **Musée Archéologique** (7 rue du Bourg, tel 03 80 91 24 97). This Gaulish cache was unearthed in 1953 in Vix, 4 miles (6 km) northwest of Châtillon. A sixth-century B.C. Celtic princess was buried here in a chariot, decked in jewels and gold, and surrounded by artifacts, notably the great Krater of Vix, the largest surviving bronze vessel from antiquity. ⚠ 191 C6 **Visitor information** ✉ place Marmont ☎ 03 80 93 78 40

## Mâcon

Mâcon gives its name to the Mâconnais wine region, which produces red, rosé, and white wines, most notably Pouilly-Fuissé and St.-Véran. Visit the **Maison des Vins** (484 avenue le-Lattre-de-Tassigny, tel 03 85 22 72 20, www.maison-des-vins.com) for information and tastings. The pleasant **Place des Herbes** has an elaborately carved 15th-century timber-framed building. The nearby **Roche de Solutré,** a huge limestone outcrop where the bones of thousands of prehistoric reindeer and horses have been found, has an excellent museum. www.macon-tourism .com ⚠ 191 D4 **Visitor information** ✉ place St.-Pierre ☎ 03 85 21 07 07

## Nevers

Famous for its faience, Nevers has a good collection displayed in the **Musée Municipal** (currently under renovation). You can buy faience from the 17th-century Faïencerie Montagnon (rue de la Porte du Croux, tel 03 86 71 96 90, www.faiencerie-faience-ceramique .faience-montagnon.fr). Architectural highlights include 12th-century ramparts, the 15th-century Palais Ducal, the Romanesque Église St.-Étienne, and the **Cathédrale St.-Cyr,** with the remains of a sixth-century baptistry and a 13th-century Gothic nave. www.nevers tourisme.com ⚠ 190 B4 **Visitor information** ✉ Palais Ducal, rue Sabatier ☎ 03 86 68 46 00

## Ronchamp

The chapel of **Notre-Dame-du-Haut** at Ronchamp, a UNESCO World Heritage site, was built in 1950–54 by Le Corbusier. The most revolutionary work of his sculptural, antirationalist period, it is molded expressively in concrete and creates the perfect atmosphere for prayer and meditation. ⚠ 191 E5 **Visitor information** ✉ place du 14 Juillet ☎ 03 84 20 65 13

# Rhône Valley & the Alps

From the snowfields of the Alps to the olive groves of the Drôme Valley, from the starred restaurants of Lyon to remote mountain refuges, the Rhône-Alpes region embraces a huge variety of landscapes and activities. Wine lovers, skiers, walkers, and culture vultures will all feel at home here.

Climbers head down the Aguille du Midi before venturing on the Mont Blanc.

A critically important trade route, the mighty Rhône River connects north and south. The Alps provide a dramatic backdrop, a skyline of peaks dominated by Mont Blanc, the highest mountain in Europe.

The region's main hub is Lyon, France's second city, an important industrial metropolis with a lively cultural life and a fine arts museum second only to the Louvre in Paris. Justly famed for its cuisine, Lyon also boasts a wealth of exceptional restaurants. The Romans colonized the area in the second century B.C., and substantial Roman remains can be found in Lyon as well as at Vienne and St.-Romain-en-Gal.

The Alps boast some of the world's top-flight ski resorts, such as Chamonix and Courchevel. But the mountains also make a beguiling summer retreat, with limpid blue lakes and gracious spa towns. Several major nature reserves protect the rare wild flora and fauna that abound in the higher reaches.

The peasant life of the mountain farmers and shepherds is not as hard as it once was, but their large timber or stone farmhouses still have the wide balconies essential for winter stores. Imaginative regional museums pay tribute to centuries of traditional life.

To the north lies the rich farmland of the Bresse province. To the south is Nyons, famous for its huge variety of olives. The Beaujolais and Côtes du Rhône vineyards yield good drinking wines as well as coveted appellations like Côte-Rotie and Hermitage. Farther south, the region meets Provence in the gorges of the Ardèche and the lavender fields, olive groves, and sunflower fields of the Drôme Valley. ∎

# Lyon

A few days in Lyon, the second largest city in France, is a treat, not least because it has every right to call itself the gastronomic capital of France. Its key position at the confluence of the Rhône and Saône Rivers has historically made it a major hub on a vital trade route.

**Lyon**
- 🅼 191 D3

**Visitor information**
- ✉ place Bellecour
- ☎ 04 72 77 69 69
- www.lyon-france.com

**Musée Gallo-Romaine**
- ✉ 17 rue Cléberg
- ☎ 04 72 38 49 30
- ⊘ Closed Mon.
- 💲 $

Lyon was founded by the Romans as Lugdunum in 43 B.C., and their great amphitheater on the hill of **Fourvière** is a good place to start a visit. To get there, walk up the winding Chemin du Rosaire, or take the funicular railroad from opposite the cathedral. The view from the top reveals the city on its peninsula (presqu'île) between the two rivers. On a clear day, you can see the Alps.

statues, and coins. Since Roman times, Fourvière has been a site of sanctuaries, the most recent one being the 19th-century **Basilique Notre-Dame-de-Fourvière** (place Fourvière, www.fourviere.org), all turrets, marble, and stained glass.

## Old Lyon

At the bottom of the Fourvière hill, on the west bank of the Saône, lies Old Lyon. One of the largest ensembles of Renaissance buildings in Europe, it is now a UNESCO World Heritage site. In the 15th century, Louis XI granted Lyon the right to hold fairs that attracted merchants from all over Europe. Magnificent hôtels particuliers, or town houses, were built, and since many of the merchants were Italian, there is a distinct Florentine quality to the architecture. Each mansion had a courtyard with a well and often a turret with a spiral staircase. The 16th-century Hôtel Gadagne houses the **Musée Historique de Lyon** and the newly restored **Musée de la Marionnette,** devoted to the puppets of Lyon. At the heart of the old quarter is the **Cathédrale St.-Jean,** a synthesis of Romanesque and Gothic styles, built between 1180 and 1480.

Old Lyon brims with charming places to eat and chat.

**Musée Historique de Lyon & Musée de la Marionnette**
- ✉ Hôtel Gadagne, 1 place du Petit-Collège
- ☎ 04 78 42 03 61
- ⊘ Closed Mon. & Tues.
- 💲 $

Lyon's ruins constitute the earliest Roman site outside Italy. The **Musée Gallo-Romaine**—a modern building cleverly tucked into the hillside, with vast windows overlooking the amphitheater—does a splendid job of evoking everyday Roman life. Its superb collection includes mosaics (notably of a chariot race), inscriptions,

## Modern Lyon

The Presqu'île is the center of modern Lyon, where life

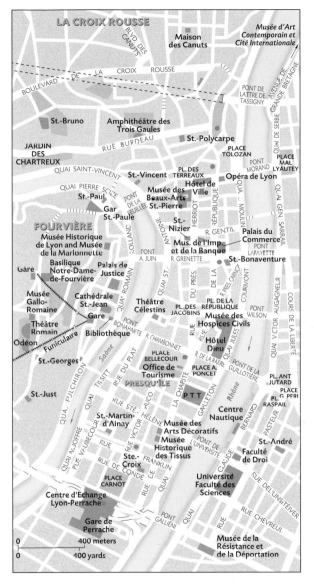

### Centre d'Histoire de la Résistance et de la Déportation

- ✉ 14 avenue Berthelot
- ☎ 01 72 73 99 06
- 🕐 Closed Mon. & Tues.
- 💲 $

www.chrd.lyon.fr

### Musée Historique des Tissus & Musée des Arts Decoratifs

- ✉ 34 rue de la Charité
- ☎ 04 78 38 42 00
- 🕐 Closed Mon.
- 💲 $

www.musee-des-tissus.com

revolves around Place Bellecour. The best shops are here, especially around Rue de la République, Rue Émile-Zola, Rue Gasparin, and Rue du Président Herriot. Silk scarves make good souvenirs.

To the north of the city, the hill of La Croix-Rousse is stacked with the houses of the silk workers (canuts) who made Lyon's fortune in the early 19th century. Their houses had to be tall to accommodate the huge Jacquard

## Musée des Beaux-Arts

✉ 20 place des Terreaux

☎ 04 72 10 17 40

🕐 Closed Tues.

💲 $

www.mba-lyon.fr

## Musée d'Art Contemporain

✉ Cité Internationale, 81 quai Charles-de-Gaulle

☎ 04 72 69 17 17

🕐 Closed Mon.– Tues. & between exhibitions

💲 $

www.mac-lyon.com

looms that transformed the industry from 1804 on. Many of the houses have been converted into fashionable lofts, but the area is still riddled with traboules. These passages played a key part in sheltering members of the Resistance during World War II, and it was here that their leader Jean Moulin was captured by the Nazis. The **Centre d'Histoire de la Résistance et de la Déportation** is housed partly in the cells in which the Gestapo tortured their prisoners.

Set in an 18th-century town house, the **Musée Historique des Tissus** recounts the history of Lyon's silk industry and fabrics in general. Next door is the **Musée des Arts Decoratifs,** full of furniture, tapestries, and porcelain.

The city's artistic life revolves around Place des Terreaux. Here the **Musée des Beaux-Arts,** in a former Benedictine convent, displays works by Veronese, Tintoretto, Rubens, El Greco, and many modern French masters. Jean Nouvel's glass-and-steel dome for the neoclassic opera house towers over the Place des Terreaux, embellished by the modern sculpture of Daniel Buren. The **Musée d'Art Contemporain** is in the Cité Internationale, a modern development on the east bank of the Rhône. ■

## EXPERIENCE: Getting a Taste of Gastronomic Lyon

Long renowned for its food, the city of Lyon is home to some of the most sophisticated restaurants in France. But the city's food story has much humbler origins. In fact, it begins with a group of women known as the *mères Lyonnaises,* or "Lyon mothers."

During the 19th century, after the Revolution, these women left their positions as domestic servants and chefs in the great aristocratic houses of Lyon to set up restaurants. Although their establishments may have been rough, simple places, the food they offered was an innovative combination of bourgeois cuisine and authentic home cooking.

Mère Brazier, one of the most famous of the Lyon mothers, was the first woman to receive three Michelin stars. It was at her restaurant, **Mère Brazier** *(12 rue Royale, tel 04 78 23 17 20, www.lamere brazier.fr),* that the famous chef Paul Bocuse did his apprenticeship.

You can also still sample some of the equally legendary *bouchons* of Lyon, traditional little bistros serving hearty fare like sausages, tripe, *oeufs en meurette* in a rich wine sauce, or black pudding with apples, usually washed down with Beaujolais wine.

To shop for food in Lyon, or simply feast your eyes on the wonderful displays, head for the **Halles de Lyon–Paul Bocuse** *(102 cours Lafayette, closed Mon.),* the traditional covered market halls, now restored and named in honor of the legendary chef who still likes to do his shopping there. You will also discover numerous restaurants and seafood bars. Alternatively, check out the **St.-Antoine Food Market** *(closed Mon.),* on Quai St.-Antoine on the banks of the Saône close to the Place Bellecour, or the **Croix-Rousse Food Market** *(place de la Croix-Rousse, closed Mon.),* in the center of the old silk weavers quarter overlooking the city.

# Beaujolais Country

Beaujolais is one wine region where the landscape doesn't play second fiddle to the vines: Rolling, wooded hills are punctuated by golden-stone châteaus and vignerons' houses with wine cellars on the ground floor, external staircases, and verandas.

The best wine comes from the north, where a day's drive could take in most of the ten Beaujolais *crus*, allowing time for leisurely *dégustations*. **Ville-franche-sur-Saône**, 20 miles (32 km) north of Lyon, is the main town of Beaujolais, a miniature version of Lyon with its Italianate mansions, elegant courtyards, and small cafés serving fresh Beaujolais with *saucissons*. In **Beaujeu,** northeast of Villefranche, the Hospices de Beaujeu have held wine auctions since the 12th century. Taste local wine in the **Place de l'Hôtel de Ville,** which also houses a museum of local traditions.

Quiet winding roads (D26 and D18 northeast from Beaujeu) lead to the **Terrasse de Chiroubles,** where you have wide views of the vineyards. Continuing north on the D26 you come to **Juliénas,** where every building appears to be a wine cellar, even the church. Next stop might be the epony-mous windmill of **Moulin-à-Vent** (to the south of Juliénas on the D266), for wide-ranging views of the Saône Valley and a chance to taste the oldest cru in Beaujolais. **Romanèche-Thorins,** nearby, is home to enthusiast Georges Duboeuf, whose Hameau du Vin offers a wide variety of wines. In **Fleurie,** west on the D32, look

The Chapelle de la Madone overlooks the village of Fleurie.

for the Chapelle de la Madone in the vineyards, and try the local specialty, *andouillettes au Fleurie—*chitterling sausages cooked in Fleurie wine. **Villié-Morgon,** south on the D68, offers wine tastings in the cellar of an 18th-century mansion. Nearby are **Château de Pizay,** with its splendid topiary gardens, and the Renaissance **Château de Corcelles,** painted by Maurice Utrillo. Farther south are the village of **Brouilly** and the **Côte de Brouilly,** vineyards on the slopes of Mont Brouilly, followed by **La Chaise,** a fine 17th-century château with gardens designed by Le Nôtre.

For delightful château accommodations combined with good Beaujolais wine, try the **Château de Bagnols** (*tel 04 74 03 42 77*), southwest of Villefranche. ∎

**Villefranche-sur-Saône**
- 191 C3

Visitor information
- ✉ 96 rue de la Sous-Préfecture
- ☎ 04 74 07 27 40
- www.villefranche.net

**Beaujeu**
- 191 C3

Visitor information
- ✉ place du l'Hôtel de Ville
- ☎ 04 74 69 22 88
- www.aucoeurdu beaujolais.fr

# Mont Blanc & the Mountains

From Lake Geneva almost to the Mediterranean, the majestic snowy peaks of the French Alps offer awe-inspiring mountain landscapes. Most dramatic of all is Mont Blanc, Europe's highest peak at 15,780 feet (4,810 m).

A crisp, clear day offers a clear view of the Alps from the Aguille du Midi near Mont Blanc.

**Chamonix–Mont Blanc**

🅜 191 E3

**Visitor information**

✉ 85 place Triangle-de-l'Amitié

☎ 04 50 53 00 24

**www.chamonix.com**

**Parc National de la Vanoise**

✉ 135 rue du Docteur-Julliand, Chambéry

☎ 04 79 62 30 54

**www.parcnational-vanoise.fr**

At the foot of Mont Blanc sits **Chamonix,** the world capital of mountaineering. Its **Musée Alpin** presents a history of Mont Blanc and its early explorers. Nonclimbers can make the spectacular ascent of neighboring summits by cable car: 12,609 feet (3,842 m) up the **Aiguille du Midi,** or 8,408 feet (2,526 m) up **Le Brevent,** both of which give fabulous views of Mont Blanc. Go early to avoid the crowds and midday mists, and take warm clothes. If you have no head for heights, take the rack railroad up to the glacier of the **Mer de Glace.** Chamonix today is a year-round resort, with swimming, golf, and tennis, as well as winter skiing.

You do not have to be an aficionado of snow to enjoy the Alps. In summer, the air is fresh and clear and the light sharp, the high mountain passes are open, and drifts of alpine flowers cover the pastures. The best way to experience the beauty of the region is by hiking *(see p. 385 for sources of information, or ask at the Chamonix tourist office).*

Never forget, though, that these are major mountains and always take the usual precautions since, even in summer, the weather here can change quickly. Make sure you have warm clothing, good boots, a whistle, food, and a map, and tell someone where you are heading and when you should arrive.

## Ski Resorts

With high altitudes, reliable snow, the very latest in lifts and snowmaking systems, and a wide variety of *pistes* (trails), France offers some of the best skiing in the world for all levels of expertise. Connections between the valleys and pistes are good, enabling you to ski long distances from one valley to the next and really explore the mountains.

Accommodations range from four-star hotels to self-catering chalets. Most of the resorts are within a three-hour drive of the airports at Chambéry, Geneva, or Lyon. **Chamonix, Mégève** *(70 rue Monseigneur Conseil, tel 04 50 21 27 28, www.megeve.com)*, and **Morzine** *(place du Baraty, tel 04 50 74 72 72, www.morzine-avoriaz.com)* are located just one hour from Geneva.

---

The mountain region east of the Rhône formed the independent principality of Savoie until it was ceded to France in 1860. It remained poor and remote until first alpinism and then skiing transformed its economy. Now the mountains and crystalline lakes attract visitors year-round.

**INSIDER TIP:**

You, too, can get water straight from the "source" in Évian. Join the locals and fill your water bottles at the public fountain.

—CAROLINE HICKEY
*National Geographic Traveler Books editor*

### Nature Reserves

The Alps remain a haven for a rich variety of flora and fauna. Savoie contains five major nature reserves, most notably the Vanoise, France's first **national park**. In this superb high mountain habitat lying between Courchevel and **Val-d'Isère**, you might see chamois, ibex, and golden eagles. Remote pastures support countless wildflower species, including crocuses, blue and yellow gentians, numerous lilies and orchids, tulips, and alpine anemones.

### Lakes

Ringed by snowy mountains, the lakes are an unforgettable sight. **Thonon-les-Bains** and **Évian-les-Bains** are both charming spa towns on the banks of Lac Léman (Lake Geneva); from both towns, passenger boats cross the lake to Switzerland. **Aix-les-Bains,** on the banks of Lac du Bourget, is another popular spa town; a boat trip on the lake can include a visit to the Benedictine **Abbaye de Haute-combe.** Rebuilt in 19th-century neo-Gothic, the abbey church contains the tombs of the Savoie kings.

**Annecy,** on the banks of Lac d'Annecy, makes an ideal base for touring the region. It rejoices in a charming old quarter with pastel facades, a château dating from the 12th century, canals and bridges, lakeside cafés, and beaches. ∎

**Val-d'Isère**

 191 E3

✉ Maison de Val-d'Isère

☎ 04 79 32 04 22

**www.valdisere.com**

**Thonon-les-Bains**

191 E4

✉ place du Marché

☎ 04 50 71 55 55

**www.thononlesbains .com**

**Évian-les-Bains**

191 E4

✉ place Pont d'Allinges

☎ 04 50 75 04 26

**www.eviantourism .com**

**Aix-les-Bains**

191 E3

**www.aixlesbains.com**

**Annecy**

191 E3

**Visitor information**

✉ Bonlieu, 1 rue Jean-Jaurès

☎ 04 50 45 00 33

**www.lac-annecy.com**

# Grenoble

**Capital of the old province of Dauphiné, Grenoble, handsomely set at the confluence of the Isère and Drac Rivers, is the only large city in the Alps.**

**Grenoble**
🅰 191 D2
**Visitor information**
✉ 14 rue de la République
☎ 04 76 42 41 41
www.grenoble
-tourisme.com

**Musée
Dauphinois**
✉ 30 rue Maurice-Gignoux
☎ 04 76 87 60 22
🕐 Closed Tues.
💲 $
www.musee
-dauphinois.fr

Grenoble prospered from the 19th-century discovery of hydro-electricity and rapidly developed into a center of chemical and nuclear research. The pace of change accelerated even further after it hosted the Winter Olympics in 1968. The city also has a lively cultural life, animated by its large student population.

Take the cable car to the **Fort de la Bastille,** where orientation tables help interpret the mountain views. Walk down from the fort through the Jardin des Dauphins to the **Musée Dauphinois,** an excellent regional museum in a 17th-century convent building. The **Musée de la Résistance** *(14 rue Hébert, tel 04 76 42 38 53, www.resistance-en-isere.fr)* is nearby.

To see the old quarter, with its 13th-century buildings and church, head for Place St.-André. The cathedral and the bishops' palace are on Place Notre-Dame. Place Grenette and Place Victor-Hugo are both lively squares, good for cafés and shopping. The former Hôtel de Ville houses the **Musée Stendhal** *(1 rue Hector Berlioz, tel 08 99 65 13 83, closed Mon.),* devoted to the Grenoble-born writer. The arts are well supported by the huge complex of the **Musée de Grenoble** *(5 place de Lavalette, tel 04 76 63 44 44, closed Tues., www.museedegrenoble.fr)* and **Maison de la Culture** *(4 rue Paul Claudel, tel 04 76 00 79 79, closed Sun.–Mon., www.mc2grenoble.fr),* for dance, music, and theater. ∎

*"Les bulles"* (the bubbles), a cable car, transports people up to the Fort de la Bastille.

# Chambéry

The historic capital of once-Italian Savoie, Chambéry is another good base for a visit to the Alps. Its dignified old quarter is full of Italianate mansions and little covered passages.

The extraordinary **Fontaine des Éléphants** on the Boulevard de la Colonneis is a monument to the Comte de Boigne, who amassed a fortune in India in the 18th century and left much of it to the municipality. The fountain has become the symbol of the town.

**INSIDER TIP:**

From Renaissance architecture to local pasta specialties on restaurant menus, Chambéry retains a delightful Italian accent.

—SYLVIE BIGAR
National Geographic Traveler
*magazine writer*

Chambéry's icon is the fun, famous Fontaine des Éléphants.

For a hundred years or so in the 15th and 16th centuries, the Holy Shroud was kept here in the Chapelle des Ducs de Savoie, and Chambéry became a pilgrimage town. But in 1578, the shroud was taken to Turin when that city became the administrative capital of the House of Savoie.

Just southeast of Chambéry is **Les Charmettes,** the country retreat of philosopher Jean-Jacques Rousseau, now restored just as he described it in his *Confessions.* ∎

## Lac de Bourguet

Near the elegant spa resort of Aix-les-Bains (see p. 217) and just a few kilometers north of Chambéry, is Lac de Bourguet, its blue water set beautifully in the mountains. All kinds of water sports are available here, including canoeing and kayaking. For sailing, check with **Club Nautique Voile Aix-les Bains** (www.cnva.com), and for water skiing, try **Club Ski Nautique** (www .club-ski-nautique.com). **Bateaux du Lac** (www .compagniedesbateauxdulac. fr) offers cruises across the lake and to the abbey of Hautecombe on the western bank.

**Chambéry**
- 191 C3
Visitor information
- ✉ place de Palais de Justice
- ☎ 04 79 33 42 47
- www.chambery -tourisme.com

**Musée Jean-Jacques Rousseau**
- ✉ 890 chemin des Charmettes
- ☎ 04 79 33 39 44
- 🕐 Closed Tues.
- 💲 $

# Gorges de l'Ardèche

The Gorges de l'Ardèche, in the far south of the Rhône Valley and the Alps region, make a truly stunning tour. For some 20 miles (32 km) between Vallon-Pont-d'Arc and St.-Martin-d'Ardèche, the D290 twists along the rim of the gorge above the river.

The Gorges de l'Ardèche attract kayakers and climbers during the summer months.

**Gorges de l'Ardèche**

🗺 191 C1

**Visitor information**

✉ 1 place de la Gare, Vallon-Pont-d'Arc

☎ 04 75 88 04 01

**www.vallon-pont-darc.com**

Before heading out, take a good look at **Pont d'Arc** itself, a natural limestone bridge hollowed out by the fast-flowing waters of the Ardèche River. Along the route, there are heart-stopping views at every turn, especially on the Haute Corniche, perched dizzyingly high above the river.

Adventurous alternatives to driving include kayaking and white-water rafting: You can rent kayaks in Vallon-Pont-d'Arc and find transportation back at St.-Martin-d'Ardèche (*visitor information at Vallon-Pont-d'Arc*). The Ardèche is one of France's fastest, and potentially most treacherous, rivers; early summer is the safest time for tackling its waters.

The limestone plateau around the gorge is riddled with caves.

The huge **Grotte de la Madeleine,** just off the D290, bristles with stalagmites and stalactites; **Aven d'Orgnac** (*aven* means pothole), just to the west, has spectacular rock formations, colored red by iron oxides and sparkling with crystals. The museum here includes a reconstruction of a Stone Age settlement. The interior of **Aven de Marzal,** a little to the north, also glitters with colored crystals. A museum of speleology includes centuries-old equipment used to explore the cave when it was first discovered.

Pretty villages upstream of the gorge include 12th-century **Balazuc,** on a cliff above the Ardèche River, and **Vogüé,** tucked between cliff and river, with a 12th-century château. ∎

# More Places to Visit in the Rhône Valley & Alps

## Bourg-en-Bresse

The market town of Bourg-en-Bresse is famous for its chickens and for the Flamboyant Gothic **Monastère Royale de Brou,** just outside town. Built between 1505 and 1536 by Margaret of Austria, it has a superbly carved facade, choir stalls, and rood screen. Most gorgeous of all are the tombs, sculpted in exquisite detail from Carrara marble. *www.bourgenbresse.fr* 🅜 191 D3 **Visitor information** ✉ 6 avenue Alsace-Lorraine ☎ 04 74 22 49 40

## Briançon

The highest town in Europe, at 4,300 feet (1,310 m), Briançon was heavily fortified by Vauban, Louis XIV's military architect. He also designed the solid **Église de Notre-Dame** set high on the defensive hill chosen for the citadel. The views over the surrounding mountains in this old part of town are superb. *www.ot-briancon.fr* 🅜 191 E2 **Visitor information** ✉ place du Temple ☎ 04 92 21 08 50

## Hauterives

Located about 15 miles (24 km) north of Romans-sur-Isère on the D538, the bizarre **Palais Idéal** at Hauterives *(Map 191 D2, tel 04 75 68 81 19, www.facteurcheval.com)* was built by local postman Ferdinand Cheval using stones he collected on his route. It blends a variety of Asian architectural styles.

## Nyons

The charming town of Nyons is famous for its olives. The **Musée de l'Olivier** tells the story of olive cultivation. The best time to visit is market day (Thursday), when you can buy a huge variety of olives, olive oil products, and olive-based delicacies. *www.paysdenyons.com* 🅜 191 D1 **Visitor information** ✉ place de la Libération ☎ 04 75 26 10 35

## Parc Naturel Régional du Vercors

Protected here are the pine forests, waterfalls, and gorges of the Vercors massif. This quiet area was a center of the Resistance during World War II, and poignant cemeteries and memorials (in villages such as **Nizier** and **Vassieux**) mark the tragic events that took place here. *http://parc-du-vercours.fr* 🅜 191 D2 **Visitor information** ✉ Maison du Parc, Lans en Vercors ☎ 04 76 94 38 30

INSIDER TIP:

**An archetypal charming medieval French village, Pérouges tips its hat to the present with excellent little shops and cafés.**

—SHEILA BUCKMASTER
National Geographic Traveler *magazine editor at large*

## Pérouges

Some 19 miles (30 km) northeast of Lyon, the ancient town of Pérouges perches atop a hill. You can still see its fortifications, town gates, cobbled streets, timbered balconies, and the marketplace shaded by a linden tree *www.perouges.org* 🅜 191 D3 **Visitor information** ✉ Syndicat d'Initiative, Entrée de la Cité ☎ 04 74 46 70 84

## Vienne

Vienne is home to the **Temple d'Auguste et Livie,** built in 25 B.C.; the remains of the **Théâtre de Cybèle;** and the **Théâtre Antique,** once one of the largest amphitheaters in France. The **Musée des Beaux-Arts et d'Archéologie** has displays about the Roman city. The **Cathédrale St.-Maurice** is the most imposing of Vienne's ancient churches. *www.vienne-tourisme.com* 🅜 191 D3 **Visitor information** ✉ 3 cours Brillier ☎ 04 74 53 80 30

# Massif Central

At the very center of France lies the mountainous region of the Massif Central. Its ancient core is the Auvergne, settled by humans probably longer than anywhere else in France. The influence of the Auvergnats throughout France is considerable, from the many Auvergnat-run Paris cafés to the positions of power occupied by such Auvergnat politicians as Valery Giscard-d'Estaing, Georges Pompidou, and Jacques Chirac.

Of the Massif Central's many faces, the most spectacular are its great volcanoes, their summits offering stellar views of a crater-pitted lunar landscape. The rugged river gorges of the Tarn and the Jonte thrill countless visitors, whether they hike and climb, drive through the canyons, or navigate the rivers by kayak.

South of the Auvergne, the wild uplands of the Cévennes plateau make a haven for wildflowers and rare birds. Such natural beauty and open countryside make this an ideal region for walking, hiking, river rafting, and hang gliding. Those who prefer gentler occupations can choose from a host of scenic drives or indulge in one of the elegant spas.

The history of the Massif Central, which is so ancient that it can be appreciated only on a geological time scale, is explained in a number of museums, including a major new museum of volcanology near Clermont-Ferrand. Regional museums evoke a firmly rooted traditional life, dependent on industries such as silkworm cultivation, knife production, and cheesemaking—the blue sheep's cheese of Roquefort is an undisputed classic.

Distinctive local architecture features granite farms, heavy schist-tiled roofs with dormer windows, and open wooden verandas for drying winter stores. ■

## Cross the Viaduc de Millau

**Millau** (*Office de Tourisme, 1 place du Beffroi, tel 05 65 60 02 42, www.ot-millau.fr*) was long notorious as a traffic bottleneck, as vehicles struggled up and down the steep sides of the Gorges du Tarn. Today, however, a magnificent bridge has reduced the crossing to a matter of minutes.

The **Viaduc de Millau** (*www.leviaducdemillau.com, $*) spans the gorge on a series of delicately soaring concrete pillars, over a distance of 1.5 miles (2.5 km)—a work of art of truly astonishing beauty visible from miles around.

Even before it was finished, the bridge attracted visitors from near and far who came to marvel at the inspired engineering responsible for creating one of the world's highest bridges, the tallest pier is 1,115 feet (340 m)—higher than the Tour Eiffel.

Designed and built by British architect Sir Norman Foster and the French engineering company Eiffage, the bridge can be admired from below or from several viewing points around town. A detailed map of the top views is available from the tourist office. Best of all, head for the motorway parking area, just before the bridge coming from the north, where there is a high-level view, an exhibition space, and a restaurant.

The bridge is a five-minute drive north of Millau on the D911, following signs to Paris. Head toward Albi (junction 45) on the A75, and follow directions to Aire du Viaduc. Foster calls crossing the bridge itself "flying by car."

# Le Puy-en-Velay

Don't rush into the town of Le Puy: Take time to gaze upon its extraordinary setting. The town sits in the middle of a high-rimmed plateau from which erupts a forest of volcanic cones. Perhaps its bizarre surroundings contributed to Le Puy's importance as an early place of worship. For centuries, pilgrims sought it out, and it was the starting point for the first recorded pilgrimage to Santiago de Compostela (see pp. 264–265), led by its bishop in 951.

St.-Michel-d'Aiguilhe sits poised atop one of the volcanic cones that dominate Le Puy-en-Velay.

Start by climbing the **Rocher Corneille** *(tel 04 71 04 11 33, closed mid-Nov.–Jan., $)* for its panoramic view over the old town. Topping this volcanic cone is the massive statue of **Notre-Dame-de-France,** which you can climb up inside.

The old town clusters around the Rocher in a maze of narrow streets. Dominating them is the **Cathédrale Notre-Dame-du-Puy** *(tel 04 71 05 45 52, $, www.cathedraledupuy.org),* built on another volcanic pinnacle with a dramatic approach up the stone steps of Rue des Tables. Currently under restoration, this 12th-century edifice demonstrates

the Muslim influence that filtered along the pilgrim route. Inside, it has lovely 13th-century frescoes and a copy of the Black Madonna, brought back from the Crusades and burned during the Revolution.

Just to the north of the Rocher Corneille, the 11th-century Romanesque chapel of **St.-Michel-d'Aiguilhe** perches on the steepest of the volcanic cones. The graceful curves and diamond patterns of the facade display an Eastern influence.

Lacemaking is a traditional craft in Le Puy, and the **Musée Crozatier** *(Jardin Henri Vinay, tel 04 71 06 62 40, closed Tues. Oct.–April)* has a collection of handmade lace. ■

**Le Puy-en-Velay**
🄰 191 C2
**Visitor information**
✉ place de Clauzel
☎ 04 71 09 38 41
www.ot-lepuyenvelay
.fr

**St.-Michel-d'Aiguilhe**
✉ Aiguilhe
☎ 04 71 09 50 03
🕐 Closed mid-Nov.–mid-Feb. (except for school holidays)
 $
www.rochersaint
michel.fr

# Volcanoes of the Auvergne

An extraordinary lunar landscape of purple cones and craters lies in the middle of France. Most of these *puys* (or peaks) are included in the nature reserve of the Parc Régional des Volcans d'Auvergne, based in the Puy-de-Dôme *département* to the west of Clermont-Ferrand. Today they are all extinct, but three million years ago regular eruptions spewed out the lava that has created this strange and desolate terrain.

Reaching for the sky, the rugged Puy de Sancy is the highest point in the Massif Central.

**Parc Régional des Volcans d'Auvergne Centre d'Information et de Découverte Montlosier**

- ✉ 1.6 miles (2 km) from Pic de La Vache et de Lassolas
- ☎ 04 73 65 64 00

www.parc-volcans -auvergne.com

**Parc Régional Livradois- Forez Centre d'Information**

- ✉ St. Gervais-sous-Meymont
- ☎ 04 73 95 57 57

The volcanoes fall into three groups: The Monts Dôme became extinct only some 4,000 years ago and are still dramatically volcanic in shape. The Monts Dore stopped erupting much longer ago, and their cones have a smoother silhouette. The Cantal volcano, originally huge, has mostly eroded, leaving lava plugs in a system of radiating valleys.

The whole area makes magnificent walking country, but the most spectacular excursion is undoubtedly to the summit of the **Puy de Dôme.** It is the oldest and highest volcano,

at 4,805 feet (1,464 m), of the Monts Dôme chain.

To the Celts, the Puy de Dôme was a royal mountain, on which they worshiped their god of war. The Romans subsequently built a huge temple of lava stones and marble, dedicated to the god Mercury. Not until the mid-18th century was it confirmed that these strange formations were actually volcanoes. Until that time, people believed that the Romans had constructed them. The Auvergne is still reputed to be a place of sorcery and enchantment; some people believe that witches and sorcerers meet at the summit of the Puy de Dôme to perform magic rituals.

You can drive to the summit up a spiraling road *(toll)*, or walk up the original zigzagging Roman track *(park at Ceyssat Pass)*. Before choosing to walk up, bear in mind that this is considered one of the toughest legs on the grueling Tour de France bicycle race. At the top are an information center, observation tables, a restaurant,

**INSIDER TIP:**

**Around the Gothic cathedral in Clermont-Ferrand's old town (see p. 228) are shops with reasonably priced antiques.**

—SYLVIE BIGAR
National Geographic Traveler
*magazine writer*

and a geology museum. The ruins of the Roman temple to Mercury lie just below the summit *(no access for visitors)*.

From the top of the Puy de Dôme, the view encompasses, on a very clear day, almost an eighth of France. Certainly it surveys a chain of more than a hundred volcanic puys—although often their peaks wore down or were blown off long ago. Many of the resulting craters filled with lakes. The view changes by the minute according to the weather and time of day; it's at its most awe inspiring at sunset, starring a stunning palette of colors and dramatic shadows.

## Robert Louis Stevenson in the Cévennes

The most celebrated account of a walk in the Massif Central is Robert Louis Stevenson's *Travels with a Donkey in the Cévennes*. In 1878, Stevenson walked 137 miles (220 km) with his truculent donkey Modestine from le Monastier-sur-Gazeille, south of Le Puy, to Langogne. His journey took him over the granite massif of Mont Lozère to Florac, and then on to St.-Jean-du-Gard and along the Cévennes Corniche. On the way, he slept under the stars or in rudimentary inns. With warmth and humor, he describes his encounters with a colorful variety of characters. Walkers can follow a similar path today, with numerous gites, auberges, refuges, and camping grounds available along the route.

### Vulcania

✉ St. Ours-les-Roches

☎ 08 20 82 78 78

🕐 Open daily mid-March–mid-Oct. Closed Mon.–Tues. Sept.

**www.vulcania.com**

Topping the Monts Dore chain to the south is the **Puy de Sancy,** the highest point in central France at 6,185 feet (1,885 m) and source of the Dordogne River. You can reach the peak by cable car from the town of Le Mont-Dore, followed by a walk.

Recently opened, the **Vulcania** theme park is devoted to vulcanology, with dramatic spectacles and interactive technology. ∎

# Drive Along the Gorges du Tarn

**South of the Massif Central, the Tarn and the Jonte Rivers have cut deep into the limestone plateaus, known as *causses*, creating spectacular canyons and gorges.**

Heading north from **Millau** ❶ (see sidebar p. 222) on the N9-E11, take the D907 northeast along the Tarn River. Near **Les Vignes** ❷, about halfway along the canyon, zigzag up the D995 and then take the D46 to **Point Sublime** ❸ for a terrific view. The most spectacular part of the gorge, Les Détroits, comes between Les Vignes and the little village of **La Malène** ❹ *(tel 04 66 48 50 77, mid-June–mid-Sept., 04 66 48 53 44 out of season)*, a good place from which to take a boat trip downriver. Farther on, the 15th-century **Château de la Caze** *(tel 04 66 48 51 01)* has an excellent restaurant.

Once you arrive at **Ste.-Énimie** ❺, you have a choice of routes. Take the D907 east to just beyond Ispagnac, go right on the N106 to **Florac** ❻, then follow the D907 south into the Parc National des Cévennes. At the junction of the D996 and D983, you can follow the D983, D9, and D260 along the **Corniche des Cévennes** for 31 miles (50 km) to **St.-Jean-du-Gard** ❼ *(tel 04 66 85 32 11)*, which has a good museum of local life, the **Musée des Vallées Cévenoles** *(95 Grande-Rue, tel 04 66 85 10 48)*.

Alternatively, you can head south from Ste.-Énimie on the D986 to Meyrueis across the glorious **Causse Méjean**. From **Meyrueis** ❽ *(tel 04 66 45 60 33)*, the D996 follows the **Gorges de la Jonte** back toward Millau, passing some famous caves on the way: **Aven Armand**, a vast grotto full of colored stalactites, and **Grotte de Dargilan**, where staircases take you down into a series of caves and lakes. Southeast of Meyrueis

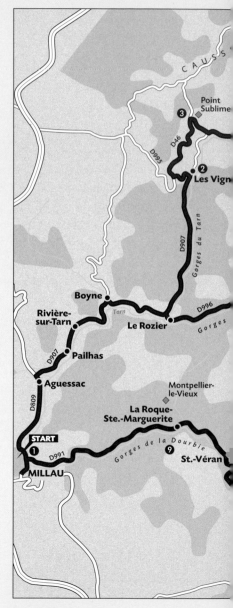

---

## NOT TO BE MISSED:

**Point Sublime • La Malène • Corniche des Cévennes • Grotte de Dargilan**

off the D986 is the **Abîme de Bramabiau,** an abyss with an underground river.

Another drive from Millau takes you along the **Gorges de la Dourbie** ❾ on the D991. To the north is the rock formation

**Montpellier-le-Vieux,** which looks like a ruined town. South of Millau, via the D992 and D23, is **Roquefort-sur-Soulzon,** where you can visit caves in which Roquefort cheese matures.

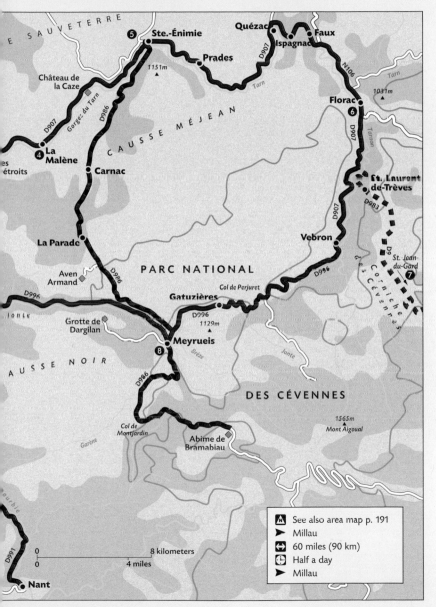

# More Places to Visit in the Massif Central

## Clermont-Ferrand

A bustling commercial town, Clermont-Ferrand was once two towns. Clermont, the older half, has a daily market in Place St.-Pierre and the **Cathédrale Notre-Dame-de-l'Assomption,** with exquisite 12th- to 15th-century stained glass. Farther east is the **Basilique Notre-Dame-du-Port,** a superb example of the Auvergnat Romanesque style. Montferrand, annexed by its neighbor in 1731, is a quieter enclave of restored Renaissance houses. The much-altered old palace was imaginatively modernized around a courtyard, in the style of the Solomon R. Guggenheim Museum in New York, to display the collection of the **Musée des Beaux-Arts.** ⚠ 190 B3 **Visitor information** ✉ place de la Victoire ☎ 04 73 98 65 00

## Thiers

A visit to Thiers is worth it for the views alone. From its perch on the side of the ravine made by the Dorelle River, you can see the volcanic peaks of the Monts Dôme and Monts Dore. The river waters made Thiers's fortune, powering the grinding wheels of the knifemakers and making the town the most important center of cutlerymaking in France. You can investigate the history of cutlery at the **Musée de la Coutellerie,** as well as shop for a huge variety of utensils and knives. ⚠ 190 B3 **Visitor information** ✉ Maison du Pirou ☎ 04 73 80 65 65

## Vichy

Long famous as a spa, Vichy reached its fashionable heyday in the 19th century. You can still stroll around the **Parc des Sources** and take the waters, drink in the Grand Café, see the art nouveau Casino and cast-iron arcades, and seek out the **Source des Célestins** and other springs of Vichy water. Luxury hotels, fine restaurants, and glamorous stores abound, contributing to a seductive fin de siècle charm. Between 1940 and 1944, Vichy found notoriety as the headquarters of the collaborationist French government, close to the border between occupied and unoccupied France. In 1963, Vichy's fortunes changed again when the Allier River was dammed, creating a vast recreational lake. *www.vichy-tourisme.com* ⚠ 190 B3 **Visitor information** ✉ 5 rue du Casino ☎ 04 70 98 71 94

---

## Pulpits in the Desert

Located at Mas Soubeyran in the tiny town of Mialet, not far from St.-Jean-du-Gard, the **Musée du Désert** *(tel 04 66 85 02 72, closed Dec.–Feb., www.museedudesert .com)* is a sombre, inspiring memorial to the oppression of the Huguenots (French Protestants) during the religious wars of the 17th and 18th centuries. The hills of the Cévennes provided sanctuary for the rebellious Camisards ("white shirts"), who held religious services among the caves, rocks, and woods—the wilderness or "desert."

At the remote hamlet of Mas Soubeyran, home of Camisard chief Rolland, you can see the pulpits made from barrels (thus easily disguised), miniature Bibles and other forbidden texts, paintings, and documents that vividly evoke brutal massacres and torture.

From Mas Soubeyran, continue on to the **Grotte de Trabuc** *(guided visits Feb.–Nov.)* and its extraordinary rock formations. Here you can explore the caves where the Huguenots once hid and worshiped.

Combining handsome riverside towns, beautiful countryside
scenery, exquisite fare, and a rich historical and cultural legacy

# Southwest France

Beach chairs await rental in Biarritz.

6 ▷ MAINE-ET-LOIRE *p. 165*
INDRE-ET-LOIRE *p. 165*

Thouars
Loudun
Bressuire
Châtellerault
*N149*
VENDÉE *p. 165*
*Sèvre*
Parthenay
Futuroscope
*N10*
DEUX-SÈVRES
Poitiers

5 ▷ *A10* Chauvigny St.-Savin
INDRE *p. 165*
CHER *p. 165*
*Poitou*
Niort
VIENNE
*N11*
Île de Ré
St.-Martin-de-Ré
La Rochelle
Surgères
Melle
Montmorillon
*Vienne*
*Gartempe*
*Creuse*
Crozant
Boussac
*M a r c h e*
*ALLIER p. 189*
*N147*
*A10*
Fouras
Rochefort
Ruffec
Confolens
Bellac la Souterraine
*A20*
*N145*
Gouzon
Île d'Oléron
St.-Jean-d'Angély
*Angoumois*
HAUTE-VIENNE
CREUSE
Marennes
CHARENTE-MARITIME
Saintes
Cognac
*Charente*
CHARENTE
La Rochefoucauld
Limoges
*Plateaux du Limousin*
St.-Léonard-de-Noblat
Aubusson
*N141*

4 ▷ Royan
Pointe de Grave
Soulac-sur-Mer
Jarnac
Angoulême
*L i m o u s i n*
Plateau de Millevaches
*A89*
Ussel
Barbeterieux-St.-Hilaire
Puyguilhem
CORRÈZE
Bort-les-Orgues
Lesparre-Médoc
Mirambeau
Aubeterre-sur-Dronne
Brantôme
Hautefort
Tulle
*M a s s i f*
Étang d'Hourtin-Carcans
*Médoc*
*Dronne*
Périgueux
*Isle*
Brive-la-Gaillarde
Collonges-la-Rouge
*C e n t r a l*
Pauillac
Blaye
DORDOGNE
*A89*
*N89*
Lascaux
Argentat
Lacanau-Océan
*Gironde*
Grotte de Rouffignac
*Vézère*
Sarlat-la-Canéda
Gouffre de Padirac
CANTAL *p. 189*
Étang de Lacanau
GIRONDE
Libourne
Les Eyzies-de-Tayac
St.-Émilion
Beynac-et-Cazenac
Rocamadour
St.-Céré
*Dordogne*
Gramat
Andernos-les-Bains

3 ▷ *Bassin d'Arcachon*
BORDEAUX
Bergerac
Cadouin
Domme
LOT
Entraygues-sur-Truyère
Arcachon
*A63*
*Garonne*
Castelnaud
Espagnac-Ste.-Eulalie
Figeac
Dune du Pilat
Biron
Grotte de Pech-Merle
Cajarc
Decazeville
Conqu
Étang de Cazaux et de Sanguinet
*Eyre*
La Réole
Monpazier
Cénevières
Larroque-Toirac
Rodez
Étang de Biscarrosse et de Parentis
Langon
Monflanquin
Bonaguil
Cahors
St.-Cirq Lapopie
*Lot*
*Aveyron*
Parentis-en-Born
Casteljaloux
*G u y e n n e*
AVEYR
Mimizan
Marquèze
Villeneuve-sur-Lot
*A20*

2 ▷ *Golfe de Gascogne*
Sabres
Roquefort
Nérac
Agen
TARN-ET-GARONNE
Caussade
Cordes
*N88*
LANDES
*A62*
Moissac
*Viaur*
Castets
Mont-de-Marsan
Condom
Castelsarrasin
Montauban
Carmaux
*Les Landes*
Tartas
Eauze
GERS
*Garonne*
Gaillac
Albi
*N10*
*G a s c o g n e*
*Tarn*
TARN
Hossegor
Dax
Aire-sur-l'Adour
Auch
*A68*
Lavaur
*Monts de Laca*
*N124*
*Adour*
Mirande
Gimone
HAUTE-GARONNE
TOULOUSE
Castres
Biarritz
Bayonne
*A64*
Orthez
*Baïse*
*Save*
Muret
*A64*
Mazamet
St.-Jean-de-Luz
Espelette
Sauveterre-de-Béarn
*Gave de Pau*
Pau
*A64*
*Ariège*
AUDE *p. 277*

1 ▷ St.-Jean-Pied-de-Port
PYRÉNÉES-ATLANTIQUES
Oloron-Ste.-Marie
Tarbes
Lannemezan
St.-Gaudens
*N117*
Grotte du Mas-d'Azil
*N20*
*A66*
Mirepoix
*P a y s B a s q u e*
Grotte de Bétharram
Lourdes
Argelès-Gazost
Laruns
PYRÉNÉES
St.-Lizier
St.-Bertrand-de-Comminges
Roquefixade
Foix
Lescun
Cauterets
St.-Sauveur
*Massif del' Arize*
Montségur
Tarascon-sur-Ariège
*B é a r n*

A
2877m
Pic du Midi d'Ossau
Parc Nat. des Pyrénées
e-Bédeilhac
ARIÈGE
PYRÉNÉES-ORIENTALES *p. 277*

B
3298m
Vignemale
Cirque de Gavarnie
Niaux
Lombrives
3115m
Pic d'Estats
Montaillou

SPAIN
ANDORRA

0 _____ 60 kilometers
0 _____ 30 miles

C
D

INDRE *p. 165*

*Paris*
★
Area of map detail

# Southwest France

Travel through southwest France and you cross some of the country's richest agricultural land before climbing to the high Pyrenees. For centuries, the rivers—the Garonne, fed by the Tarn and Lot flowing down from the Massif Central, and the Dordogne—were the region's main arteries of communication and trade, with goods shipped to and from the port of Bordeaux. Today these great waterways are used more for pleasure than trade.

Until a century ago, the flat, sandy Atlantic coast was wild and inhospitable, and the sands were steadily encroaching inland. To stabilize the land, grasses were sown, followed by the pine trees that now form the great forest of the Landes, the largest pine forest in Europe. The once-threatening sands of the coast provide wide beaches, pounded by rolling Atlantic breakers.

To the south, the great mountain range of the Pyrenees stretches from the Mediterranean to the Atlantic, forming a natural frontier between France and Spain. The southwest's biggest cities are Bordeaux and Toulouse.

Bordeaux was capital of the ancient duchy of Aquitaine, which in the Middle Ages included Gascony, Périgord, Poitou, and Limousin as well as Aquitaine. Toulouse was the seat of the powerful counts of Toulouse and the heart of the glittering troubadour culture. It was the capital of Languedoc, broadly embracing the whole of southern France from Aquitaine to Provence.

By the 12th century, southwest France, ruled autonomously but owing allegiance to the French Crown, was thriving both economically and culturally. But with the dynastic marriages of Eleanor of Aquitaine, and the spread of the Cathar heresy in Languedoc, the stage was set for trouble. Eleanor married the French king, Louis VII, in 1137, but the marriage was annulled, and in 1152, she married Henry Plantagenet, Count of Anjou and Duke of Normandy, who inherited the English Crown.

**NOT TO BE MISSED:**

Unmatched vintages along the Bordeaux wine trail 240–241

Surfing the waves in Biarritz 243

The dramatic Dordogne Valley 248–250

Glimpsing prehistoric paintings in the Lascaux caves 252–253

A pilgrimage to the Abbaye de Ste.-Foy in Conques 258

The stunning Romanesque carvings of Moissac 263

The cirque and waterfall of Gavarnie in the Pyrenees 270

Between them, they ruled most of Britain and western France from Normandy to Aquitaine. Centuries of claims and counter claims ensued, with the territorial ambitions of the rival French and English kingdoms finally erupting into the Hundred Years' War.

In Languedoc, the Albigensian Crusade against the Cathar heresy enabled the power-hungry French Crown to put an end to the autonomy of the counts of Toulouse.

You can still see solid evidence of these conflicts in the fortified *bastide* towns, the castles that pepper the banks of the Dordogne and the Lot, the gaunt Cathar fortresses of the Pyrenean foothills, and the fortified churches of Toulouse and Albi. Paradoxically, these relics of a strife-torn past are now some of the loveliest features of this diverse region. ■

# Aquitaine & the Atlantic Coast

France's southern Atlantic coast is a revelation: one great sweep of beach unfolding from the tip of the Gironde Peninsula to the Spanish border, its dazzling light and pounding white waves earning it the poetic name of the Côte d'Argent, or Silver Coast.

The sands of the Aquitaine coast formed the Dune du Pilat, Europe's highest sand dune.

Beaches, dunes, and huge lakes interspersed with small resorts and fishing ports make this coast perfect for family vacations. For more sophisticated tastes, Biarritz offers classic belle epoque hotels, luxury shops, casinos, and golf clubs. Inland stretches the tremendous wooded expanse of the Landes, Europe's largest pine forest, planted in the 19th century to contain the shifting sands of the coast and now a peaceful green retreat.

In the north of the region lies the quiet city of Poitiers, with a magnificent heritage of Romanesque churches, and now perhaps best known for its 21st-century cinematic theme park, Futuroscope. World famous for its exquisite porcelain and enamels, Limoges to the south has some of the finest museums devoted to the decorative arts to be seen anywhere.

North of the great Gironde estuary lies the irresistibly unspoiled resort of La Rochelle, an ancient port that now contains more yachts than anywhere else on the coast.

Always an important port, the metropolis of Bordeaux offers a gracious 18th-century center, excellent museums and restaurants, and, of course, world-famous wines. No wine lover should miss the chance to visit the surrounding wine country, with its litany of magical names such as Château Mouton-Rothschild, Haut-Brion, St.-Émilion, and Margaux.

Finally, rising into the high Pyrenees in the far south is the French Basque country, a land apart, with its own language, racial identity, cuisine, and customs, which offers an intriguing glimpse into an ancient but still thriving culture with a piquant flavor all its own. ■

# Poitiers

Poised between northern and southern France, Poitiers is an ancient city now reclaiming its heritage after years of decline. Its riches include a great concentration of Romanesque architecture. The city's position on a rocky promontory in a bend of the Clain River is best appreciated from the opposite bank, a view that also shows a cluster of church towers. Battles around this strategic stronghold have changed the course of French history, most famously in 732 when Charles Martel, founder of the Carolingian dynasty, turned the tide on the invading Saracens. In 1356, the Black Prince retained Poitiers and Aquitaine for England with a victory here.

Echoes of this history can still be seen in the city's architectural heritage. The 12th-century **Église de Notre-Dame-la-Grande** (Grande Rue) exemplifies the Poitevin Romanesque style. The west front is a mesmerizing gallery of idiosyncratic medieval sculpture—once brilliantly painted—flanked by a pair of pinecone pinnacles that are the hallmark of this style. The **Palais de Justice** (rue Gambetta) nearby contains magnificent vestiges of the 12th-century palace of the dukes of Aquitaine.

The 11th-century church of **St.-Hilaire-le-Grand** (rue Doyenné) is unique in Europe in having seven aisles, supported by an extraordinary forest of columns, many of them with fascinating carved capitals. The fourth-century **Baptistère de St.-Jean,** said to be the oldest Christian building in France, contains Roman marble columns, frescoes, and a full-immersion baptismal pool. ∎

**INSIDER TIP:**

In summer at dusk, a light display re-creates the colors of the Notre-Dame cathedral during the Middle Ages.

—SHEILA BUCKMASTER
National Geographic Traveler
*magazine editor at large*

**Poitiers**
- 230 C5

Visitor information
- 45 place Charles-de-Gaulle
- 05 49 41 21 24
- www.ot-poitiers.fr

**Baptistère de St.-Jean**
- rue Jean-Jaurès
- Open daily July–Aug. Closed Tues. April, June, & Sept., & Tues. & a.m. Oct.–March
- $

## Parc de Futuroscope

The 21st-century design of Futuroscope (the European Park of the Moving Image) could not be in greater contrast to the stately Romanesque buildings of nearby Poitiers: Half-buried white cubes, white spheres, and mirrored crystalline shapes erupt out of the flat landscape. Every imaginable kind of visual technology is exploited here: screens seven stories high; a "magic carpet" with a screen below as well as in front of you; auditoriums with chairs simulating the movement on screen; 3-D projections; an interactive robot zoo; and the Gyrotour at the top of a rotating tower. Since it opened in 1987, Futuroscope (tel 05 49 49 11 12, $$$–$$$$ depending on length of visit and season, www.futuroscope.com) has become a huge success, attracting several million visitors annually. It is located in Jaunay-Clan, about 4 miles (6 km) north of Poitiers via the N10.

# Food & Drink—Truffles and Tripe

**From Périgord, the region north of the Dordogne River, to the Basque region along the Spanish border, southwest France glories in some of the finest produce and culinary skills that this gastronomically thrilling country has to offer.**

Pigs can be specially trained to seek out truffles in their underground hiding places.

The Aquitaine coast yields fish and seafood in abundance—mussels, scallops, prawns, and most of all oysters—and the Gironde even produces caviar. Périgord is synonymous with foie gras and truffles (see sidebar, p. 247). The traditional cooking medium is goose or duck fat as opposed to butter or olive oil. Try the rich confits (duck or goose preserved in its own fat) and the many other delicious duck and goose dishes prepared in this part of France. Succulent local pork, beef, and lamb are variously enhanced with garlic, herbs, and truffles. *Tripons* (tripe) and *ris de veau* (calf's sweetbreads) are particularly prized.

Wild mushrooms such as chanterelles, morels, and ceps are served simply cooked in butter, as a filling for omelets, or in sauces. Truffles are traditionally savored in slivers, often to perfume an omelet. Walnuts are added to salads and sauces, crushed to make walnut oil, and distilled into eau-de-vie.

Bordeaux enjoys an enviable gastronomic reputation, with sophisticated food to complement its sublime wines. Toulouse and farther south is *cassoulet* country, with numerous contenders for the authentic recipe for this slow-cooked casserole of white beans with sausages and meat, often duck, pork, or mutton, usually topped with a crust of bread crumbs. Farther south still, in the Basque country, the pimiento is king, combined most deliciously with egg in *piperade*. Bayonne ham is justly famous for its aromatic flavor.

Fruit here is superlative, in both quantity and variety. The delicious plums of Agen make the best prunes in France. These are often combined with meat dishes, notably rabbit, or used to make jam.

Among the first-course specialties in southwest France are *chipirons* (squid, often cooked in its own ink), *garbure béarnaise* (thick soup made with cabbage, bacon, and confit of goose or pork), *sobronade* (bean and bacon soup), and *tourain bordelais* (soup of onions, tomatoes, bread, and egg yolks).

Main courses include *boeuf à la sarladaise* (fillet of beef stuffed with pâté de foie gras), *canard aux cèpes* (duck with mushrooms), *cou farci* (stuffed goose neck), *coquilles St.-Jacques à la bordelaise* (scallops sautéed with shallots and parsley), *daube bordelaise* (beef stewed in red wine), *enchaud Périgourdin* (roast pork with garlic), *miques* (little dumplings of bread, boiled in stock), *poulet basquaise* (chicken with tomato, pimento, and Bayonne ham), and *zakiro* (mutton grilled on an open fire—a Basque dish).

Dessert specialties include *kanougas* (chocolate taffy) and *touron* (marzipan—almond paste—loaf with nuts).

*Truffe*, or truffle, is a rare and pricey delicacy found in the southwest and southeast.

## Wines & Spirits

The Bordeaux region, along with Burgundy, produces some of the most exquisite wines in the world. Visit a few of Bordeaux's many châteaus to try the aromatic reds, dry fruity whites, and sublime sweet white wines. Local wines usually represent the best value in restaurants. Aside from the châteaus of Bordeaux, look for the local wines from Bergerac, Buzet, Cahors, Gaillac, and Basque country Irouléguy. The unsurpassed local brandies include Cognac and Armagnac.

## The French Paradox

With a diet rich in saturated fats, butter, cheese, and cream, why do the French have a relatively low rate of heart disease? This is the so-called French Paradox. Initial research suggested that the consumption of red wine might be the key. Subsequent research has challenged the evidence and also suggested that the incidence of heart disease in France has been underestimated. Nevertheless, the correlation between wine and health is striking.

Red wine in particular is a source of resveratrol, which has been linked to longevity and cancer prevention. Another constituent of red wine, procyanidins, is found in greatest concentration in European red wines and correlates with longevity in those regions. Some research suggests that procyanidins may also have an effect on cancer and diabetes. The highest concentration was found in the Tannat grape grown in the Gers area of southwest France. Clinical trials of grape seed extract showed that as little as 200–300 mg per day would lower blood pressure. Two small (4 oz/125 ml) glasses of a procyanidin-rich red wine, such as a Madiran wine made from Tannat, would provide this amount.

Further comparison of the difference between American and French eating habits and health also suggests that the French eat less overall, serve smaller portions, and eat less processed food. Of the fat they do eat, it is largely dairy and vegetable, not trans fats. Also considered significant is the fact that the French eat three meals a day and do not snack. They drink plenty of liquids, including herbal teas; eat mindfully at the table, not in front of the TV; and most of all emphasize freshness and pleasure in food. However, the popularity of *le fast food* and McDonald's is growing in France, and guess what—the French are getting fatter.

# La Rochelle

With its lovely old harbor, splendid towers, and pedestrians-only medieval streets, La Rochelle is one of the prettiest and best preserved ports anywhere on the French Atlantic coast. Now also the biggest yachting center in western France, it is a fashionable and lively place for vacations, buzzing with restaurants and cafés.

**La Rochelle**
🗺 230 B5
**Visitor information**
✉ 2 quai Georges Simenon
☎ 05 46 41 14 68
www.larochelle-tourisme.com

**Musée du Nouveau Monde**
✉ 10 rue Fleuriau
☎ 05 46 41 46 50
🕐 Closed Tues., & a.m. Sat. & Sun.
💲 $

**Muséum d'Histoire Naturelle**
✉ 28 rue Albert 1er
☎ 05 46 41 18 25
🕐 Closed Mon.

Freed of feudal obligations by Eleanor of Aquitaine in the 13th century, this important port later became a hotbed of Protestantism thanks to its trading links with northern Europe. Its most tragic—and heroic—moment came in 1627, when it was besieged by the Catholic forces of Cardinal Richelieu for 15 months. Only 5,000 of the population of 25,000 survived.

The town walls were razed, but the harbor entrance is still guarded by two 14th-century towers, the **Tour de la Chaîne** and the **Tour St.-Nicolas.** A third tower, the **Tour de la Lanterne,** west of the Tour de la Chaîne, was originally a

## Francofolies

For five or six days every July, La Rochelle plays host to Francofolies (www.francofolies.fr), the biggest pop music festival in France. Begun in 1985, Francofolies has become the premier showcase for French and Francophone music, attracting as many as 100,000 spectators every year. Recent star appearances have included Vanessa Paradis, Charlotte Gainsbourg, Emily Loiseau, and Wax Tailor.

lighthouse, with a giant wax candle for its light. You can climb to the top for a good view of the port.

From the old harbor, the Porte de la Grosse Horloge leads into the town, a feast of Renaissance and 18th-century architecture in distinctive Rochelais style, with arcaded shop fronts and roofs hung with fishtail slates.

A grand 18th-century mansion built by wealthy shipowners now houses the **Musée du Nouveau Monde** (Museum of the New World). Exhibitions concentrate on the links between La Rochelle and the Americas, and its influence on Louisiana, Canada, and the West Indies. Recently reopened after major renovation, the **Muséum d'Histoire Naturelle,** located in a mansion with splendid gardens, houses an anthropological collection drawing on the travels of La Rochelle traders since the 17th century.

Just off the coast of La Rochelle, reached by a 2-mile-long (3.2 km) road bridge, is the **Île de Ré.** A peaceful retreat of salt marshes, vineyards, and shallow lagoons, the island attracts all manner of bird life, including curlews, teals, and geese. The capital, **St.-Martin-de-Ré,** is a fishing port of cobbled streets and whitewashed cottages protected by 17th-century ramparts. ∎

# Limoges & Aubusson

For anyone with a passion for the decorative arts—and particularly for porcelain, enamels, and tapestry—Limoges and Aubusson offer rare delights. The discovery of a major deposit of kaolin nearby in 1768 made the name of Limoges synonymous with fine, pure white porcelain. It was to be the foundation of a major industry that produced some of the finest china ever made. Aubusson has been the tapestry capital of the world since the 15th century.

Cathédrale St.-Etienne in Limoges contains a colorful surprise.

## Limoges

The **Musée National Adrien-Dubouché** contains a superb collection of more than 11,000 items of porcelain, chinaware, and metalwork from earliest times to the present.

Centuries before the porcelain industry started, Limoges was already famed throughout Europe for its virtuoso enamels. An unrivaled collection, from the 11th century on, is at the **Musée Municipal de l'Évêché** (closed for renovation). The museum also has paintings, including Renoir's "Portrait of Madame le Coeur," given by the artist to his native city.

Limoges's soaring Gothic **Cathédrale St.-Étienne** has some magnificent stone carving, especially its famous rood screen.

## Aubusson

In the mid-17th century, the tapestry workshops of Aubusson received the royal warrant, but the revocation of the Edict of Nantes in 1685 caused the Huguenot workforce to flee. An 18th-century revival ended with the Revolution. In 1937, designer Jean Lurçat revived the little town's fortunes.

The **Musée Départemental de la Tapisserie** shows work from the 17th, 18th, and 20th centuries. A traditional workshop has been set up in the **Maison du Tapissier** (rue Vieille), a 16th-century weaver's house. At the **Manufacture St.-Jean** (3 rue St.-Jean, tel 05 55 66 10 08, closed Sat.–Sun. Oct.–June), you can watch tapestries and carpets being made. ■

**Limoges**
🅰 230 D4
**Visitor information**
✉ 12 boulevard de Fleurus
☎ 05 55 34 46 87
**www.limoges-tourisme.com**

**Musée National Adrien-Dubouché**
✉ place Winston Churchill
☎ 05 55 33 08 50
🕐 Closed Tues.
💲 $
**www.musee-adrien dubouche.fr**

**Aubusson**
🅰 230 F4
**Visitor information**
✉ rue Vieille
☎ 05 55 66 32 12
**www.ot-aubusson.fr**

**Musée Départemental de la Tapisserie**
✉ avenue des Lissiers
☎ 05 55 83 08 30
🕐 Closed Tues. except p.m. July & Aug.
💲 $

# Bordeaux

Bordeaux enjoys an illustrious reputation as the hub of a large region of vineyards producing some of the finest wines in the world. Although it has been part of the wine trade since Roman times, it is the 18th-century city that you see today, the result of a massive civic rebuilding scheme marked by decades of restoration and cleaning. An urban renewal plan has created new parks, landscaped quays, pedestrian promenades, and a successful new tramway.

**Bordeaux**
🗺 230 B3
**Visitor information**
✉ 12 cours du 30 Juillet
☎ 05 56 00 66 00
**www.bordeaux -tourisme.com**

Start your visit on the waterfront. From the **Pont de Pierre,** a magnificent view takes in the classical facades lining the wharves fronting the St.-Pierre quarter. A stroll along the quays brings you to the stately **Hôtel de la Bourse,** the old maritime exchange, standing on one of the city's most impressive 18th-century squares. Farther along

the waterfront, you reach the vast Esplanade des Quinconces. Towering above it is the **Monument aux Girondins,** erected in memory of local deputies sent to the guillotine by Robespierre.

Inland from the river, the broad tree-lined avenues of Cours de l'Intendance, Cours Georges Clemenceau, and Allées de Tourny, known as the Triangle, enclose the heart of Bordeaux life, full of fashionable shops and traditional cafés. A visit to the **Maison du Vin** (*3 cours du 30 Juillet, tel 05 56 00 22 88*) is an indispensable prelude to any wine tour or tasting. The same street opens out into Place de la Comédie, dominated by the **Grand Théâtre.** Built by Victor Lewis between 1773 and 1780, it boasts a staircase taken by Charles Garnier as his inspiration for the Opéra Garnier in Paris, and a fabulously refurbished auditorium.

To the north lies the old merchants' quarter, now a fashionable bustle of antique shops. Cours Xavier-Arnozan is resplendent with the great houses built by the wine merchants, their classical facades adorned with splendid wrought-iron balconies. Here, too, is the **Musée d'Art Contemporain,** housed in a converted 19th-century spice warehouse.

Pont sur la Garonne, Bordeaux, lit for night

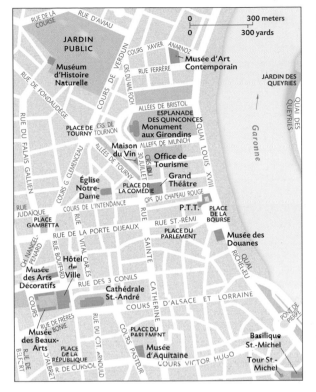

**Grand Théâtre**

- ☒ place de la Comédie
- ⊕ Guided visits by reservation. Information and reservations at the tourist office. Tour: 1 hr.
- ☎ 05 56 00 85 95
- 💲 $$

**Musée d'Art Contemporain**

- ☒ 7 rue Ferrère
- ☎ 05 56 00 81 50
- ⊕ Closed Mon.
- 💲 Free for permanent collection
- www.capc-bordeaux.fr

**Musée d'Aquitaine**

- ☒ 20 cours Pasteur
- ☎ 05 56 01 51 00
- ⊕ Closed Mon.
- 💲 Free for permanent collection

**Musée des Beaux-Arts**

- ☒ 20 cours d'Albret
- ☎ 05 56 10 20 56
- ⊕ Closed Tues.
- 💲 $$

**Musée des Arts Décoratifs**

- ☒ 39 rue Bouffard
- ☎ 05 56 00 72 53
- ⊕ Closed a.m. & all Tues.
- 💲 Free for permanent collection

The most interesting of the city's other museums cluster around the Cathédrale St.-André: The **Musée d'Aquitaine** provides an imaginative overview of local history, both rural and urban. The collection of the **Musée des Beaux-Arts** has Renaissance paintings, two famous Eugène Delacroix canvases, "Greece on the Ruins of Missolonghi" and "The Lion Hunt," and a number of Impressionist works. The **Musée des Arts Décoratifs**, meanwhile, gives a sense of life inside the city's 18th-century mansions, with rooms displaying period furniture, porcelain, glassware, and the wrought iron for which Bordeaux is famous.

The **Cathédrale St.-André** is a vast 11th-century foundation, with later additions including a soaring Flamboyant Gothic choir and transepts. The 13th-century Porte Royale, on the south facade, has a notable tympanum of the Last Judgment. The almost equally immense **Basilique St.-Michel,** off the waterfront to the south of the city, has a freestanding Gothic belfry that at 374 feet (114 m) is the highest tower in southwest France. The terrace halfway up the affords a commanding city view.

To understand the story of this ancient city, visit **Bordeaux Monumental** (28 rue des Argentiers, tel 05 56 48 04 24), an exhibit of its history and buildings. ∎

# Drive Through the Haut-Médoc

In a region that produces the noblest wines in the world, the Médoc—a formerly marshy area northwest of Bordeaux that was drained and planted in the 18th century—boasts the lion's share of the most aristocratic growths.

This day tour of the Haut-Médoc (the upper part of the Médoc) stars some of the most celebrated vineyards in the world. The best time to visit is just before the grapes are harvested in mid-September, when the vine leaves have turned golden and the grapes hang tantalizingly heavy and luscious.

If you prefer to visit another of the Bordeaux wine regions, the **Conseil des Vins du Médoc** *(cours du 30 Juillet, tel 05 56 00 22 66, www.bordeaux.com)* in Bordeaux organizes bus tours and will provide all the information you need. If you wish to travel independently, plan carefully: Try to make an appointment at each vineyard you want to visit (for some, at least two weeks in advance), and remember that you may not be welcome during the grape harvest.

## The Tour

Take the D2 *(Route du Vin)* north out of Bordeaux. Stop first at **Château Siran ❶** *(tel 05 57 88 34 04, www.chateausiran.com)*, splendidly furnished with paintings that include a copy of Caravaggio's "The Young Bacchus." **Château Margaux ❷** *(tel 05 57 88 83 83, closed Sat.–Sun. & Aug., visits by appt. only, www.chateau-margaux.com)*, east of the D2 about 2 miles (3.5 km) farther on, is perhaps the most outstanding of the châteaus, with a grand avenue of trees. Take a detour on the D5 to **Château Maucaillou ❸** and the **Musée des Arts et des Métiers de la Vigne et du Vin** *(tel 05 56 58 01 23, www.chateau-maucaillou.com)*. From Vauban's star-shaped 17th-century **Fort Médoc ❹** *(tel 05 57 88 85 00)* there is a view of the Gironde estuary and, beyond, the vineyards of Blaye.

Back on the D2, you come next to **Château Beychevelle ❺** *(tel 05 56 73 20 70, www.beychevelle.com)*, set in a beautiful 18th-century

**NOT TO BE MISSED:**

Château Siran • Château Margaux • Château Mouton-Rothschild • Château Cos d'Estournel

building. Farther on, **Château Latour ❻** *(tel 05 56 73 19 80, reservation recommended, www .chateau-latour.com)* is named after the tower that stands next to the château. At the river port of **Pauillac,** signs point to some of the most hallowed names in wines. At **Château Mouton-Rothschild ❼** *(tel 05 56 73 20 20, visits by appt. only)*, you may visit the reception rooms and banqueting hall and the display of wine labels commissioned from artists such as Pablo Picasso, Salvador Dali, Jean Cocteau, and Henry Moore. Part of the cellars is now a museum, with paintings, sculpture, tapestries, ceramics, and glass all devoted to wine.

At **Château Lafite-Rothschild ❽**, another fine château in a grand park, there are guided tours *(tel 05 56 59 26 83, by appt. only, www.lafite .com)*. A little farther on the D2, **Château Cos d'Estournel ❾** *(tel 05 56 73 15 50, by appt. only, www.estournel.com)*, a bizarre 18th-century "Oriental" palace with a new modern warehouse designed by Spanish architect Ricardo Bofill, produces one of the five *crus classés* from St.-Estèphe. This little river port has one of the oldest vineyards of the Haut-Médoc.

From here on down the estuary, the land becomes the Médoc rather than the Haut-Médoc and the wines are less well known (but still very distinguished). Retrace your steps, or take the fast route back to Bordeaux on the N215 and D1.

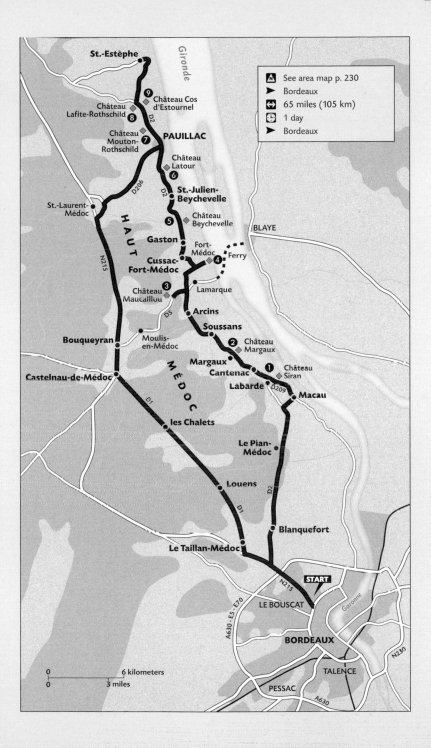

St.-Estèphe

Gironde

⑨ Château Cos
d'Estournel

Château
Lafite-Rothschild ⑧
                    D2

Château      ⑦  PAUILLAC
Mouton-
Rothschild

Château
Latour
        ⑥

St.-Laurent-    D206    D2    St.-Julien-
Médoc                          Beychevelle

HAUT                ⑤    Château
                         Beychevelle

        Gaston    Fort-
                  Médoc
N215    Cussac-        ④  Ferry
        Fort-Médoc

        Château    ③    Lamarque
        Maucaillou
                D5    Arcins

                      Soussans

Bouqueyran    Moulis-        ②  Château
              en-Médoc           Margaux

Castelnau-de-Médoc    Margaux    Château
                      Cantenac  ①  Siran

        MÉDOC         Labarde    D209    Macau

                D1
        les Chalets

                      Le Pian-
                      Médoc

        Louens        D2

                      Blanquefort

Le Taillan-Médoc

                      START

        N215    LE BOUSCAT

                      Garonne

        A630·E5·E70

                      BORDEAUX

        A630·E5·E70              N230

                      TALENCE

        PESSAC    A630

See area map p. 230

▶ Bordeaux

⇄ 65 miles (105 km)

⏱ 1 day

▶ Bordeaux

0        6 kilometers
0    3 miles

# Biarritz

The swankiest and largest resort on the French Atlantic seaboard, Biarritz enjoys a mild climate, invigorated by its perfect position between the Pyrenees and the rugged coast.

Biarritz has drawn a wealth of beach lovers, including Empress Eugénie and Coco Chanel.

## Biarritz

230 B2

**Visitor information**

✉ 1 square d'Ixelles

☎ 05 59 22 37 10

**www.biarritz.fr**

## Musée de la Mer

✉ esplanade de la Rocher de la Vièrge

☎ 05 59 22 75 40

🕐 Closed 2 weeks mid-Jan.

💲 $$

**www.museedelamer .com**

## Musée du Chocolat

✉ 14 avenue Beau Rivage

☎ 05 59 23 27 72

🕐 Closed Sun.

**www.planetemusee duchocolat.com**

The little whaling village of Biarritz first attracted attention in the 19th century, when sea bathing became fashionable. Its fortunes were sealed when Empress Eugénie persuaded her husband, Napoleon III, to build the Villa Eugénie, now the **Hôtel du Palais.** Queen Victoria and so many other royals followed that the resort became known as the beach of kings. Coco Chanel added a note of chic, while the casino, now restored to its art deco magnificence, attracted the world's gamblers.

While these splendors have faded slightly, the coastline is still gorgeous. The **Grande Plage** is the most fashionable stretch of beach. The **Vieux Port** shelters a gentler one, while great waves break on the **Plage de la Côte des Basques,** a place of annual pilgrimage for Basques. It all makes a perfect setting for nonchalant strolling, with cliff walks and promenades lush with tamarisk and purple and blue hydrangeas.

A footbridge from the promontory at the south end of the Grande Plage takes you to the **Rocher de la Vièrge,** with its statue of the Virgin and an exhila-rating view down the coast to Spain. The top of the lighthouse north of the Grande Plage offers an even more thrilling panorama.

On the promontory above the Virgin stands the **Musée de la Mer,** which has displays on local fishing and pools of sharks and seals. The **Musée du Chocolat** offers tours and a tasting, while at Thalmar *(Plage Marbella, tel 05 59 41 75 43, www.biarritz-thalasso.com)* you can take seawater baths and enjoy a massage. ∎

# Bayonne

Now the attractive, elegant capital of the French Basque country, Bayonne was for centuries hotly disputed for its strategic position on the frontier between France and Spain.

Constantly besieged, and controlled by the English for almost 300 years, Bayonne found prosperity in privateering, shipbuilding, and arms manufacture (and gave its name to the bayonet).

The narrow streets around the **Cathédrale Ste.-Marie** are a pleasure to explore. The cathedral, begun in the 13th century, is a monument to changing times and masters. Its soaring Gothic nave, built by the English in the 14th century, is in the northern Gothic style, rare in this region, while French fleur-de-lis decorate the keystones.

Nearby, the excellent **Musée Bonnat** includes works by Rubens, Poussin, and Goya. Located in a beautifully restored 16th-century Basque house, the **Musée Basque** *(quai des Corsaires, tel 05 59 59 08 98, closed Mon., www.musee-basque. com)* offers a comprehensive selection of Basque artifacts.

Bayonne is a good place to buy Basque specialties such as the famous beret, espadrilles, linen, woolen blankets, and aromatic Bayonne chocolate. Try the arcades of Rue Pont-Neuf, between the cathedral and the Hôtel de Ville. ■

**Bayonne**
🅰 230 B2
**Visitor Information**
✉ place des Basques
☎ 08 20 42 64 64
www.bayonne-tourisme.com

**Musée Bonnat**
✉ 5 rue J.-Lafitte
☎ 05 59 59 08 52
🕐 Closed Tues.
www.museebonnat.bayonne.fr

---

## EXPERIENCE: Surfer's Paradise

The great Atlantic waves of Biarritz have made this city the surf capital of Europe. Every April, board riders from all over the globe flock here to participate in the Biarritz Quiksilver surfing competition, which heralds the beginning of the Atlantic surfing season.

Biarritz owes its popularity as a surfing destination to Hollywood. During the 1950s, film stars like Gary Cooper, Bing Crosby, and Rita Hayworth discovered the city's spectacular coast. Then, in 1957, Deborah Kerr and her screenwriting husband, Peter Viertel, arrived in Biarritz to film *The Sun Also Rises*. They began board-surfing and soon inspired the locals to take to the waves. (Occasionally local fishermen had body-surfed in from their boats, but the idea to use boards was brand new.) Plage de la Côte des Basques is now the great surfing beach

where the annual surfing championships take place. Check out **Restaurant Le Surfing** *(9 bd Prince de Galles, tel 05 59 24 78 72, www.lesurfinghiarritz.fr)*, a bar behind the beach, decked out with vintage surfboards.

Learn to surf with qualified instructors at a variety of establishments, including **École de Surf Jo Moraiz** *(2, 3 place Bellevue, tel 05 59 41 22 09, www .jomoraiz.com)* and **École de Surf La Vague Basque** *(3 rue des Landes de Cristobal, tel 05 59 23 61 99, or Plage de la Côte des Basques, tel 06 62 76 17 32, www.vague basque.fr)*. **Biarritz Paradise Surfschool** *(tel 06 14 76 01 18, www.biarritzparadise-surfschool.com)* offers packages to suit all levels, from a single lesson to an entire week of surf camp. Lessons are given on Plage Marbella in July and August, and elsewhere the rest of the year.

# More Places to Visit in Aquitaine & the Atlantic Coast

## Cognac

The port of Cognac on the Charente River is known for one thing: the fine brandy distilled from the wine of the local vineyards. The best producer is **Distillerie Otard** *(tel 05 45 36 88 88)* in its 15th-century château. Look for the black fungus that grows on the warehouses, fed by brandy evaporates, called the "angels' share." To learn more, visit the **Musée des Arts du Cognac** *(place de la Salle Verte, tel 05 45 36 21 10, closed Mon.). www.tourisme-cognac.com* ▲ 230 C4 **Visitor information** ✉ rue du 14 Juillet ☎ 05 45 82 10 71,

## Côte d'Argent

The Aquitaine coast has Europe's highest sand dune, **Dune du Pilat,** and ideal beaches for swimming and surfing in a string of resorts. The main one is **Arcachon** *(visitor information, esplanade Georges-Pompidou, tel 05 57 52 97 97, www.archachon.com),* on the Bassin d'Arcachon, where oysters are cultivated. It is a beguiling 19th-century place with a marina and whimsical vacation villas. Farther south are **Hossegor** *(www.hossegor.fr),* on a saltwater lake, and **Cap-Breton,** with its ancient lighthouse. ▲ 230 B3

## Les Landes

In the 18th century at Les Landes *(Map 230, B2, www.landes-tourisme.info),* coastal dunes were stabilized and marshes drained by the planting of grass and pines. The **Écomusée** *(tel 05 58 08 31 31)* at Marquèze shows the hard nature of traditional life in the Landes.

## St.-Émilion

A medieval walled citadel, St.-Émilion is the very essence of a wine town. The handsome

## Angoulême

The town of Angoulême *(see map on p. 230 C4)* is the world center of comic books, a particular French passion. Every year at the end of January, the festival of **La Bande Dessinée** attracts thousands of enthusiasts. The BDs, as comics are popularly known, are celebrated in a new museum, **La Cité Internationale de la Bande Dessinée et de l'Image** *(121 rue de Bordeaux, tel 05 45 38 65 65, www.citebd.org),* in the old wine warehouses on the banks of the Charente River. The museum's collection of more than 8,000 drawings traces the history of comics over 150 years, including Asterix, Peanuts, Tintin, and Popeye. There is also a browsable library of comic books.

houses of golden limestone make it a picturesque base for visits to nearby wine country. *www.saint-emilion-tourisme.com* ▲ 232 C3 **Visitor information** ✉ place des Creneaux ☎ 05 57 55 28 28

## Saintes

Saintes, in the Charente Valley, contains a rich heritage of Roman and medieval architecture. The **Arc de Germanicus** (now in Place Bassompierre) once stood on a Roman bridge, and there are also the remains of baths and an amphitheater. The 12th-century **Abbaye aux Dames,** a lovely Romanesque building, has beautifully carved portals. About 12.5 miles (20 km) outside Saintes is **Paléosite** *(Sainte Césaire, tel 08 10 13 01 34, www.paleosite.fr),* a new center dedicated to the prehistoric era that was built on the site where a Neandertal woman was found. ▲ 232 B4 **Visitor information** ✉ 62 cours National ☎ 05 46 74 23 82

# The Dordogne & Midi-Pyrénées

The Dordogne touches the hearts and stirs the senses of visitors more than perhaps any other region of France. In the dark days following the outbreak of World War II, its meandering streams, rolling hills, and quiet villages prompted Henry Miller to write in a kind of optimism: "France may one day exist no more, but the Dordogne will live on just as dreams live on and nourish the souls of men."

The Dourdou River, a tributary of the Lot, flows below Conques.

For many foreigners, the name conjures up a large area of elegiac river country. The climate is gentle, the summer sun never as unrelenting as farther south. The Dordogne, Lot, and Tarn Rivers water the land, ensuring a rich variety of crops.

North of the Dordogne River is Périgord, some of France's richest agricultural land. South of the river are treasures of a different kind: underground chasms and grottoes, and some of the finest medieval religious architecture in France. The many castles and *bastides* (fortified towns) are relics of the bitter fighting throughout the Middle Ages.

Market towns such as Sarlat-la-Canéda, Cahors, and Périgueux have historic centers full of shady arcades and ornately carved buildings.

To the south lies the Midi-Pyrénées region. Its capital, Toulouse, is Latin in atmosphere and humming with life. To the east, pink-brick Albi, with its great cathedral and lovely old streets, has an unrivaled collection of works by its famous son, Toulouse-Lautrec. West of Toulouse is the rolling farmland of Gascony, home of Armagnac brandy.

In addition to its impressive religious architecture, the region has some of the most enchanting rural architecture in France. Weathered farms of golden limestone beneath steep slate roofs bristle with dormer windows, little turrets, and elaborate dovecotes. Terra-cotta tiles and vine-shaded verandas herald the deep south. Restored, many of these fine old buildings are now vacation homes. ■

# Around Périgord

The ancient territory of Périgord (largely covered by the present *département* of Dordogne) matches the ideal image of provincial France: lush, gently rural, and dotted with farms and manor houses. The region is united by its rivers, the Dronne, Isle, Vézère, and Dordogne, all of which have provided routes for transporting goods and people since the Gallo-Roman era. Today they make ideal routes for exploring the countryside.

The lovely, picturesque village of Beynac is not far from Périgord.

**Périgueux**

🅐 230 C4

**Visitor information**

✉ 26 place Francheville

☎ 05 53 53 10 63

**www.tourisme-perigueux.fr**

**Brantôme**

🅐 230 C4

**Visitor information**

✉ Pavillon Renaissance, boulevard Charlemagne

☎ 05 53 05 80 63

**www.ville-brantome.fr**

Périgord—so green and tranquil—was the epicenter of the Hundred Years' War and the front line between the kingdom of France and English-held Aquitaine. The fortified towns and châteaus that are such a delight to visit today testify to this belligerence.

Traditionally, this historic region has been divided into Périgord Blanc (so called for the white of its limestone), centered on Périgueux and the Isle River; and Périgord Noir (because of its dense woodland) around Sarlat-la-Canéda in the southeast. More recently, the color scheme has been broadened to include Périgord Vert (the green pastureland of the north) and Périgord Poupre (the vineyards around Bergerac).

## Périgueux

The regional capital, Périgueux, in a loop of the Isle River, makes a good base for touring Périgord. Dominating its skyline are the exotic domes and turrets of the **Cathédrale St.-Front,** the largest cathedral in southwest France. Originally built in the 12th century, the cathedral was restored in the 19th century by architect Paul Abadie, who used it as an inspiration for the Basilique de

Sacré-Coeur in Paris. Its remarkable roof offers a view of the old town at its feet, a tangle of cobbled streets, mullioned windows, and hidden courtyards.

From the **Tour Mataguerre,** part of the medieval ramparts, you can enjoy another splendid view over the rooftops, including the ruins of a Gaulish amphitheater and temple. Be sure to visit the new **Musée Gallo-Roman** *(rue Claude Bernard, tel 05 53 53 00 92, closed Mon. Sept.–June, $),* which reveals the excavated Roman villa of Vesunna and its precious wall paintings.

East of Périgueux, the magnificent 17th-century **Château de Hautefort** stands in wooded parkland embellished with topiary and mosaic parterres.

### Brantôme

North of Périgueux, in the tranquil valley of the Dronne River, lies Brantôme, one of the most charming towns in the whole of Périgord. Stroll along the riverbanks to admire its bridges and riverside garden, its ancient abbey church, and its exceptionally fine 11th-century bell tower.

The first monks here simply carved their monastery out of the cliffs behind the abbey, in caves that are now open to the public: The **Cave of the Last Judgment** has stunning carvings of the Crucifixion and the "Triumph of Death." Pierre de Bourdeille, abbot here in the 16th century, was to earn notoriety with his scurrilous tales of ladies at court, written under the pen name Brantôme.

A few miles northeast of Brantôme, the **Château de Puyguilhem** is a gracious example of French Renaissance architecture ∎

**Château de Hautefort**

🅰 230 D4

☎ 05 53 50 51 23

🕐 Closed Nov.–Mar.

💲 $$

**www.chateau-hautefort.com**

**Château de Puyguilhem**

🅰 230 D4

✉ 05 53 54 82 18

🕐 Closed Jan., & Mon. Oct.–June

💲 $$

"We supped and lay, having amongst other dainties, a dish of truffles, which is a certain earth nut, and found out by a hog trained to it . . . It is in truth an incomparable meat."
*John Evelyn (1644)*

---

## Truffles & Foie Gras: The Inside Story

Truffles and foie gras are the heavenly twins of epicurean indulgence in Périgord, unsurpassed anywhere. Capricious and mysterious, resistant to all attempts at cultivation or scientific analysis, truffles must be sniffed out from their hiding places among the roots of certain oak trees by specially trained pigs or dogs. Their incomparable flavor is not only exquisite but also highly pungent. Sold in specialist markets such as those at Périgueux and Sarlat, truffles fetch as much as $2,000 per pound for white and $600 for black. They may also be bought in cans, carefully graded.

A 19th-century essayist and wit, the Reverend Sydney Smith, defined heaven as "eating pâté de foie gras to the sound of trumpets." Foie gras is made by force-feeding geese or ducks with corn to enlarge their livers, resulting in a rich and deliciously smooth meat. Although many people regard the practice (known as *gavage*) as cruel, it has to be said that the geese flock to be fed. Foie gras comes in many forms, in jars or cans; *foie gras d'oie entier* indicates the best goose liver, presented whole; *bloc de foie gras* describes pieces pressed together to form a block; *mi-cuit* denotes that the liver is cooked enough to keep for about a month. Finest of all is *foie gras truffé,* perfumed with black flowers of truffle.

# Dordogne Valley Drive

One of the most beautiful drives in the Dordogne is upstream along the river valley from Bergerac to Sarlat-la-Canéda, a comfortable two-day excursion of 80 miles (170 km) or so. Here the great river cuts a swath between wooded valleys, fertile farmland, and craggy limestone cliffs topped by picturesque villages and castles at every turn. With its outstanding reputation for fine food and wine, this lovely region provides a perfect combination of the pleasures of the table, the landscape, and history.

Take this drive at a leisurely pace, allowing for frequent stops and exploratory detours, contemplating views, and happily enjoying the moods of the river—brilliant in the sun, silvery in the diffuse light of dusk.

The Dordogne flows wide at **Bergerac ❶** *(visitor information, rue Neuve d'Argenson, tel 05 53 57 03 11, www.bergerac-tourisme.com),* forming a broad alluvial plain that is the main area of tobacco production in France. The old port, once a flourishing center of the wine trade, spans both sides of the river, and the town has winding streets of medieval half-timbered houses. The **Musée du Tabac** *(place du Feu, tel 05 53 63 04 13, closed Sun. a.m.)* in the elegant 17th-century Maison Peyrarède presents a fascinating survey of the evolution of tobacco smoking, with a huge variety of snuffboxes and pipes, including Native American peace

**NOT TO BE MISSED:**

Château de Monbazillac
• Cingle de Trémolat • Abbey of Cadouin • Beynac-et-Cazenac
• La Roque-Gageac

pipes. The **Musée du Vin et de la Batellerie** *(5 rue des Conférences, tel 05 57 57 80 92, closed Sun. & Nov.–March)* celebrates local wines and boat-building. Wines may be tasted at the wine center in the medieval **Cloître des Récollets** *(place du Docteur-Cayla, tel 05 53 63 57 55).*

The most celebrated of the local vintages is the sweet white wine of Monbazillac. The moated 16th-century **Château de Monbazillac** *(tel 05 53 63 65 00, closed Mon. Nov.–March,*

See area map p. 230
► Bergerac
↔ 80 miles (128 km)
🕐 2 days
► Sarlat-la-Canéda

www.chateau-monbazillac.com), on the crest of hills just south of Bergerac on the D13, has an interesting local craft museum and wine tasting.

Return and take the D660 along the north bank of the river from Bergerac. Cross the river at **St.-Capraise-de-Lalinde** ❷ on the D37 to **Château de Lanquais** (tel 05 53 61 24 24, closed Nov.–March & Tues. April–Oct.). Part medieval fortress, part Renaissance palace, the castle occupies a magnificent site above the pretty old village of Lanquais. A reminder of the region's turbulent past can be seen in the damage inflicted by cannonballs during the Wars of Religion. The little town of **Couze-et-St.-Front** ❸, just to the east, is famous for papermaking, once a major industry here; the traditional methods are still used at the **Moulin de Larroque** (tel 05 53 61 01 75, www .moulindelarroque.com, closed Sat.–Sun.). Farther along the south bank, the picturesque village of **St.-Front-de-Colubri** perches on a cliff, offering a superb view of the Dordogne and the Gratusse rapids upriver, the most dangerous stretch to navigate when riverboats traded upstream.

The river now executes one of its extraordinary horseshoe bends, known as cingles, at the **Cingle de Trémolat** ❹. Cross to the north bank of the river at St. Front to go around the cingle and enjoy a panoramic view of the rich pastureland contained in the loop. Trémolat

itself is a charming little village, made famous by director Claude Chabrol as the setting for the film Le Boucher (1969). Between Trémolat and Limeuil, the D31 follows the cliff, overlooking the river.

**Limeuil** lies at the confluence of the Vézère and the Dordogne; here, rocky terraces frame the river, and the little village, with its Renaissance houses and 12th-century church, winds up the hill, providing glorious views. Follow the D51 beside the wide river, flanked by cliffs, then cross it to make a short detour on the D25, through a valley of chestnut woods, to **Cadouin** ❺ (tel 05 53 63 36 28, closed Tues. in winter). This austerely beautiful Cistercian abbey of golden stone has a fine Gothic cloister. From Cadouin, a tiny road loops east to **Urval,** with its vast 12th-century fortified church. From Urval go north to the D25 and then east to **Siorac-en-Périgord** ❻, which has a 17th-century château and a little river beach.

Cross the river back to the north bank and follow the D703E upstream to the market town of **St.-Cyprien** ❼ (visitor information, tel 05 53 30 36 09, www.stcyprien-perigord.com), clustered around its 14th-century church and massive bell tower on a wooded hillside. Continue upstream on the D703; now the valley starts to narrow. Towering above it is the

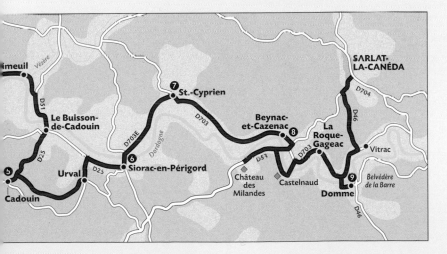

**Free range geese wander the grounds of a farm in the Dordogne.**

formidable château at **Beynac-et-Cazenac** ❽ *(visitor information, tel 05 53 29 43 08)*, sitting like a stone crown on its rock, accessible by a steep footpath or via a detour inland through the pretty little village. Restoration work is gradually bringing this tremendous fortress back to its 13th-century appearance, with drawbridge, portcullis, and medieval kitchen. The vaulted great hall has lovely naive frescoes, and the views from the castle keep are not for the fainthearted.

Beynac was a French bastion during the Hundred Years' War, and glowering opposite it on the south bank is the fortress of **Castelnaud** *(tel 05 53 31 30 00, www.castelnaud.com)*, intermittently an English stronghold. It now houses a museum of siege warfare, including primitive cannons and a reconstructed catapult. Cross the river from the D703 to the D53 under the Château de Castelnaud and make a short detour downstream on this road to visit the 15th-century **Château des Milandes** *(tel 05 53 59 31 21, closed Nov.–March, www.milandes.com)*, once the much-loved home of the remarkable Josephine Baker. Here the American jazz singer and cabaret artist planned to realize her dream of a "world village" with a "rainbow tribe" of 12 children adopted from all over the world. Financial difficulties and frail health forced her to abandon the idea in 1969.

Retrace your steps to Castelnaud, then cross the river and continue east along the D703 to **La Roque-Gageac.** This irresistible place to pause shelters beneath the great craggy cliffside. Relax at a riverside café, stroll around the village with its ocher houses and craft shops, or climb the steep narrow streets to the 12th-century church to admire the view.

Continue along the D703, then cross to the south of the river again on the D46. Just south of the river, take the D50 winding steeply up to **Domme** ❾ *(visitor information, tel 05 53 31 71 00)*, the best preserved and possibly the loveliest of the *bastide* towns (see p. 259). High up on a crag above the river, the narrow, flower-decked streets still shelter within its 12th-century walls. Beneath the 17th-century covered marketplace is a cavern (now reached by an elevator), where it is supposed that the citizens of Domme took refuge during the Hundred Years' War and the Wars of Religion. The **Belvédère de la Barre,** at the end of the Grand-Rue, offers breathtaking panoramas of the river and the surrounding countryside. From Domme, the D50 and D46 take you to **Sarlat-la-Canéda** (see p. 251).

## River Trip by Gabarre

The *gabarres* are the traditional flat-bottomed boats of the Dordogne, once used to transport goods—from wine to salt to wood—between the upper reaches of the river and the sea. Today they make a perfect way to enjoy the slowly meandering river and get fine views of the castles and golden-hued houses of the riverside villages reflected serenely in the water. There are numerous boarding points in Roque-Gageac, Beynac, and Bergerac. For more information, contact **Gabarres de Beynac** *(tel 05 53 28 51 15, www.gabarre-beynac.com)* or inquire directly at the quais or the local tourist office.

# Sarlat-la-Canéda

Nestling in a little wooded valley a few miles north of the Dordogne River, Sarlat is like a living architectural museum, with one of the best ensembles of medieval, Renaissance, and 17th-century buildings in France. Its narrow cobbled streets, surrounded by ramparts, are full of houses rich in carving, their steep roofs sometimes tiled with the traditional limestone slabs. In 1962, Sarlat became one of the first towns in France to be restored and protected as a whole under a national policy of restoration.

Rue de la République (the unfortunate 19th-century boulevard that bisects the town) is lined on both sides with a warren of medieval streets and many handsome buildings. One of the most beautiful, on Place du Peyrou, is the pinnacled 16th-century **Maison de la Boétie,** house of poet Étienne de la Boétie, with graceful arches on the ground floor and delicately carved mullion windows. A relic of the town's powerful 12th-century abbey can still be seen in the **Chapelle des Pénitents Bleus** (*place du Peyrou*). The bizarre conical tower of the **Lanterne des Morts,** in the abbey graveyard, was built to commemorate the sermons and miracles of St. Bernard in Sarlat in 1147.

**Place de la Liberté,** the lovely main square, has lots of cafés and is the focus of Sarlat's famous market on Wednesdays and Saturdays. Then stalls offer truffles, walnuts, and foie gras, as well as everyday items for locals and souvenirs for visitors.

Not surprisingly, Sarlat is a tremendously popular tourist destination, and, if you can, it is best to visit out of season. Take time to wander its fascinating

Sarlat-la-Canéda is a treasure of history—a postcard-pretty home to more than a millennium of architectural notions.

streets, poking into nooks and crannies; best of all, see it by night, when its history and atmosphere are enhanced by a modern system of gas lighting. For a good overall view, drive to the village of **Temniac,** which overlooks Sarlat from the north. ■

**Sarlat-la-Canéda**
🗺 230 D3
**Visitor information**
✉ rue Tourny
☎ 05 53 31 45 45
**www.sarlat
-tourisme.com**

# Lascaux & Prehistoric Cave Paintings

The painted caves at Lascaux have been called the Sistine Chapel of prehistory for the powerful quality of the work. They can now be seen only in replica at Lascaux II. Though a visit there is still an amazing experience, the beautiful Vézère Valley is rich in original marvels, so there are other choices as well.

Prehistoric artists at Lascaux used the cave contours to bring paintings to life.

**Les Eyzies-de-Tayac**

 230 D3

**Visitor information**

✉ 19 avenue de la Préhistoire

☎ 05 53 06 97 05

**www.leseyzies.com**

**Musée National de Préhistoire**

☎ 05 53 06 45 45

🕒 Closed Tues. Sept.–June

💲 $

**www.musee-prehistoire-eyzies.fr**

The area's limestone caves create an underground network of tunnels and caverns protected from the light, with constant temperature and humidity.

Until about 17,000 years ago, people lived in dwellings of skin and turf, under rock overhangs, and sometimes in the cave entrances. Yet the paintings are usually buried deep within the caves' dark interiors, painted or engraved by the light of stone oil lamps or torches. These areas were probably religious sanctuaries devoted to the worship of the animals that sustained Cro-Magnon life. The range of animals depicted includes horses, bison, deer, boars, wolves, foxes, birds, and reptiles, with the occasional mammoth and rhinoceros. Very often the animals are shown pregnant, as if invoking fertility. Human figures appear only rarely.

These early artists used charcoal, ocher, and red and yellow pigments made from oxidized iron, applied with fingers or brushes or blown through tubes. They also scratched and carved with horn, stone, or bone.

Scientific excavations began in the mid-19th century, revealing entire periods of prehistory: The Mousterian, Magdalenian, and other early cultures were named after the finds here. The first skeletons of Cro-Magnon man were discovered in 1868, during excavations for a new railroad line at Cro-Magnon.

## Les Eyzies-de-Tayac

Les Eyzies-de-Tayac is known as the prehistoric capital of the world. Here the **Musée National de Préhistoire** gives an excellent introduction to the subject (though all the information plaques are in French).

A number of caves lie nearby. **Font-de-Gaume,** discovered in 1901, has some of the best art still open to the public, with drawings of deer, horses, and mammoths and a frieze of bison. The **Grotte de Combarelles,** in the Beune Valley east of Les Eyzies de Tayac, discovered in 1910, shelters more than 200 engravings and drawings of animals and magic symbols. Tickets for both sites are subject to daily limits, so arrive early.

The rock shelter of **Cap Blanc,** farther up the Beune Valley, contains a frieze of horses sculptured in relief. At **Rouffignac** almost 5 miles (8 km) of caves and galleries can now be toured by electric train to see drawings of ibex, rhinoceros, mammoths, and fighting stags.

The newly discovered **Grotte-de-Tourtoirac** *(tel 05 53 40 24 77)* boasts spectacular stalactites, explored by descending 82 feet (25 m) by elevator.

## Lascaux

Lascaux itself, close to Montignac farther up the Vézère Valley, lay buried beneath a landslide for thousands of years before being accidentally discovered in 1940 (so the story goes) by children looking for their lost dog. What they found was a prehistoric art gallery of more than 150 paintings and 1,500 engravings, perfectly preserved by a fortuitous glaze of crystals.

Drawings of animals, executed in ocher and red pigments with strong lines of black charcoal, show an astonishingly sophisticated level of artistic skill. Opened to the public in 1948, the caves attracted huge numbers of visitors. In 1963, they were closed after green algae and white calcite were found to be spoiling the paintings.

### Lascaux II

 230 D3

 On the D704E, Montignac

 05 53 05 65 65

 Closed Jan. & Mon. Nov.– Easter

 $$

www.lascaux.culture.fr

---

### Cave Talk

The French word for a cave is *grotte; gouffre* is a chasm with a wide surface opening; *cave,* on the other hand, means cellar or storeroom, often for wine. Signs pointing to a *cave* usually indicate wine for sale and probably tasting.

---

A splendid replica was built nearby at **Lascaux II,** where the paintings were painstakingly copied over 11 years, using the same tools and pigments as the original artists. However, the replica itself is now suffering degradation. Even more worryingly, the original Lascaux caves have developed further problems following the installation of an air-conditioning system. It remains to be seen whether the original paintings can be saved. ∎

# Cahors

The hills to the north and south of Cahors afford panoramic views of the handsome ensemble of towers, ramparts, and bridges that make up the town, almost encircled in a snug loop of the Lot River. Cahors was of significance in the Middle Ages as the capital of Quercy, the limestone area around the river.

Originally built to defend Cahors against invaders, the 14th-century Pont Valentré spans the Lot River.

**Cahors**
🅰 230 D3
**Visitor information**
✉ place François-Mitterrand
☎ 05 65 53 20 65
**www.tourisme-cahors.com**

**Rocamadour**
🅰 230 D3
**Visitor information**
✉ Maison de Tourisme l'Hospitalet
☎ 05 65 33 22 00
**www.rocamadour.com**

**Musée d'Art Sacré**
✉ parvis des Sanctuaires
☎ 05 65 33 23 23

Prosperous and proud of its ancient university, medieval Cahors was an important center of trade, banking, and learning. But in 1360, during the Hundred Years' War, it was handed over to the English. The population fled, and the nearly deserted city never fully recovered.

One outstanding relic of its medieval grandeur survives: the famous 14th-century **Pont Valentré,** now a UNESCO World Heritage site, spanning the river on seven Gothic arches guarded by three fortified towers. According to local legend, the master builder made a pact with the Devil in order to finish the bridge, but by cunning managed to retain his eternal soul.

Lined with plane trees, the main street of Cahors is Boulevard Gambetta, named for the famous 19th-century radical politician Léon Gambetta, a native of the city. The shops here and the nearby covered market supply all manner of local delicacies, including the rich, plummy wine of Cahors known as *vin noir.* To the east of Boulevard Gambetta clusters the old quarter. Alleys crossed by bridges stripe the streets with shadows, and you can follow a marked path through secret gardens.

The light reveals the Renaissance windows, stone carvings, and finely worked wooden corbels of the old quarter's impressive mansions. One of the most entrancing is the **Hôtel Roaldès** *(quai Champollion),* with its south facade of timber and weathered redbrick, Italian-style loggia and tower, and carved north facade.

At the heart of the old town is the Romanesque **Cathédrale St.-Étienne** *(place Aristide-Briand).* The two great domes decorated with 14th-century frescoes give a spacious feel to the interior, and the Flamboyant Gothic cloister has beautiful carvings. But the cathedral's most splendid feature is the 16th-century tympanum over the north door, depicting the Ascension of Christ. ■

# Rocamadour

In a cleft of the great gorge of the Alzou River, Rocamadour is one of the most impressive—and most visited—sites in France. In the 12th century, the village exploded into fame with the discovery of the body of a man, believed to be Zacchaeus, husband of St. Veronica, who was rechristened St. Amadour. Buried beneath an existing chapel dedicated to the Virgin, the remains were soon credited with miracles, and pilgrims came from far and wide.

The grand stairway leads from the village up to the shrine of the Black Virgin and the saint's tomb. The devout climbed the steps on their knees (some still do). Within the **Chapelle de Notre-Dame,** carved into the rock, stands the famous statue of the Black Virgin. Probably a 12th century, the statue is crudely carved, but moving in its simplicity, the wood smoothed and darkened by time. Above it is a ninth-century bell, which is said to ring unaided to foretell a miracle. Down steps to the left of the chapel is the 12th-century crypt with the tomb of St. Amadour. The **Musée d'Art Sacré** displays a tremendous collection of sacred art.

Above the chapel, the climb continues, either past the Stations of the Cross or up to the ramparts of the original fort, built to protect the shrine from the west. ∎

The small village of Rocamadour clings to limestone cliffs in the gorge of the Alzou River.

## Gouffre de Padirac

The **Gouffre de Padirac** (tel 05 65 33 64 56, closed Nov.–March, $$ round-trip, www.gouffre-de-padirac.com), east of Rocamadour on the D673, is a vast limestone chasm, some 330 feet (100 m) wide and 800 feet (246 m) deep. It leads to a series of grottoes that reach at least 9 miles (15 km) underground. In the Middle Ages, it served as a refuge in turbulent times, but only in the late 19th century did speleologists begin to discover its prehistoric significance. Elevators and stairs descend to the bottom of the chasm, and flat-bottomed boats ferry you along the subterranean river and into the illuminated caves. After about 350 yards (315 m), you arrive at the Salle du Grand Dôme, a lofty cavern 295 feet (90 m) high.

# Around the Lot Valley

As it flows toward Cahors, the Lot River cuts through *causses*—limestone plateaus. At one moment, it is overhung by creamy yellow or pink cliffs, with picture-postcard villages and turreted fortresses clinging to their flanks; the next moment, it meanders gently through bucolic meadows and vineyards. To the north, its tributary, the Célé, flows to meet it through a romantic valley studded with prehistoric caves and Renaissance castles.

The small perched village of St.-Cirq-Lapopie draws visitors year-round.

**St.-Cirq-Lapopie**
🗺 230 D3
**Visitor information**
☎ 05 65 31 29 06
**www.saint
-cirqlapopie.com**

**Cajarc**
🗺 230 D3
**Visitor information**
☎ 05 65 40 72 89
**www.cajarc.fr**

*"St.-Cirq has cast a spell on me, the one which lasts for ever. I have no desire to go anywhere else."*

—ANDRÉ BRETON, (1951)

Tourism has come in a gentle way here, with horseback riding, boating, several intriguing small museums, and caves in abundance: Everywhere you will see signs pointing to the *grottes*.

Leave Cahors on the D653, heading east on the D662 to reach **St.-Cirq-Lapopie,** justly designated one of the most beautiful villages in France. The winding cobbled streets, fortified church, and timber-framed houses have all been lovingly restored. Artists have colonized the place since the 1950s, most famously the surrealist writer André Breton (1896–1966). You can follow the artists circuit around the village.

The Lot Valley bristles with castles. At **Cénevières** you can visit the 13th-century château *(tel 05 65 31 27 33, closed Nov.– Easter, www.chateau-cenevieres.com)* overlooking the river and admire its Renaissance additions, including the stone staircase, gallery, and coffered ceilings. You can also enjoy the views, which take in the trogolodyte village carved out of the opposite cliff.

The next major settlement is the pretty riverside resort of **Cajarc,** where the **Maison des Arts Georges Pompidou** (Georges Pompidou, President of France from 1969 to 1974, used to have a house here) stages

**INSIDER TIP:**

**Cross-training sight-seeing: After kayaking the Lot River, climb up to St.-Cirq-Lapopie and admire the med-ieval wooden houses.**

—SYLVIE BIGAR
National Geographic Traveler
*magazine writer*

exhibitions of contemporary European art. Continue up the valley to **Montbrun-les-Bains,** which has another spectacular ruined fortress. At **Larroque-Toirac,** the fairy-tale medieval castle was rebuilt after the English burned it down in the 14th century.

A few miles farther on, the D662 cuts across the *causse* to reach **Figeac,** a beautiful old market town. Tanning was an important industry here, and many of the handsome medieval houses in the old town have octagonal chimneys and open *soleilhos,* drying rooms, on the top floor. The tourist office and local museum are housed in the 13th century **Hôtel de la Monnaie,** the old mint.

Jean-François Champollion, the 19th-century Egyptologist who first deciphered Egyptian hiero-glyphics, was born in Figeac. The newly restored **Musée Champol-lion** is devoted to the writing of the world. The Place des Écritures is floored with an enlarged copy of the Rosetta Stone, created by American Joseph Kosuth.

Leave Figeac on the D13, then turn left on the D41 to follow the lovely valley of the Célé River. Stop to visit the beautiful village of **Espagnac-Ste.-Eulalie** and the atmospheric ruins of the aptly named 13th-century **Prieuré du Val-Paradis.** Continue past peach-colored cliffs and fortified caves to the Benedictine **Abbaye de Marcilhac.** About 3 miles (5 km) farther on, stop at **Sauliac-sur-Célé** for its living museum of 19th-century farm work, the **Musée de Plein Air de Quercy.** Two reconstructed farms illustrate traditional agriculture and crafts.

Beyond Cabrerets and its two commanding castles lie the incomparable treasures of the painted **Grotte de Pech-Merle,** which was discovered in 1922 by two local boys. This remarkable gallery of prehistoric paintings, a staggering 20,000 years old at the most conservative estimate, are still open to public view. You can explore almost a mile of spectacu-lar caves and galleries decorated with glorious paintings of bison and mammoths, silhouettes of horses, female figures, and myste-rious handprints.

## Bérenger's Folly

West of Cahors towers the **Château de Bonaguil,** the ultimate military fantasy. In the late 15th century, Bérenger de Roquefeuil fortified and enlarged the existing 13th-cen-tury keep, determined to build an impregnable castle. Forty years later, he was the proud lord of a masterpiece of military engineering. Sadly, nobody ever attacked him, so Bérenger was never able to prove his point. ◼

**Maison des Arts Georges Pompidou**
- ✉ route de Gréalou
- ☎ 05 65 40 78 19
- www.magp.fr

**Figeac**
- 🄰 231 E3
- Visitor information
- ✉ place Vival
- ☎ 05 65 34 06 25
- www.tourisme-figeac.com

**Musée Champollion**
- ✉ place Champollion
- ☎ 05 65 50 31 08
- 🕐 Closed Mon. Sept.–June
- 💲 $$

**Musée de Plein Air de Quercy**
- ✉ Sauliac-sur-Célé
- ☎ 05 65 31 36 43
- 🕐 Closed Mon.–Tues. & Oct.–March
- 💲 $$

**Grotte de Pech-Merle**
- ✉ Cabrerets
- ☎ 05 65 31 27 05
- 🕐 Closed Nov.–March
- 💲 $$, reservation recommended
- www.pechmerle.com

**Château de Bonaguil**
- ☎ 05 53 71 90 33
- 🕐 Closed Christmas–Jan.
- 💲 $$
- www.bonaguil.org

# Conques

The little village of Conques is tucked away in the steep valley of the Dourdou River. This unlikely setting hides one of the great pilgrimage churches of France, the Abbaye de Ste.-Foy.

Conques is home to one of France's most famous pilgrimage churches, Abbaye de Ste.-Foy.

**Conques**

🅰 231 E3

**Visitor information**

☎ 05 65 72 85 00

**www.tourisme -conques.fr**

**Abbaye de Ste.-Foy**

☎ 08 20 82 08 03

The three great towers of the abbey rise above the village, tiled with the same local slate as the houses. Pilgrims began to come here in the 11th century, when the monks at Conques stole the relics of St. Foy, an early Christian martyr, from Agen. Soon the abbey became a stopping place on the way to Santiago de Compostela (see pp. 264–265) as well as a place of pilgrimage itself.

The 11th-century interior of the church is pure Romanesque, with a soaring nave, beautifully decorated capitals, and three chapels at the rounded east end, built to provide more altars for the pilgrims. The most celebrated feature of the church is the tympanum over the west door,

a masterpiece of 12th-century sculpture depicting the Last Judgment. Unusually, it still has traces of the original color. Note the stained-glass windows created in 1994 by artist Pierre Soulages.

The abbey's Treasury, which survived the Revolution intact, includes enamel work, vestments, and reliquaries, but the star of the collection is the ninth-century reliquary made to hold the bones of St. Foy herself. It is in the form of a statue, made of gold and studded with jewels, cameos, and intaglios, some of which may date from Roman times.

The little village itself is sometimes overwhelmed by visitors to its church, but it has some charming old houses along its steep streets. ■

# Bastide Towns

**Alongside its noble heritage of castles and abbeys, southwest France provides, through its *bastide* towns, insights into life in the war-torn Middle Ages.**

Built in the 13th and 14th centuries, bastides were new towns designed to protect the beleaguered country population during the Hundred Years' War. Those settling the new towns were granted land to support a family, or "to light a fire," and benefited from privileges stated in a town charter, which included freedom from feudal service and the right to hold a market and to elect a council.

The basic design—always with an eye to defense—was a grid of streets around a central arcaded square. Built by both the English and French, they were fortified with massive walls. Since a bastide's inhabitants did not owe allegiance to an overlord, there was no castle for refuge, so churches were fortified as sanctuaries.

**Cordes,** 50 miles (90 km) southeast of Cahors, is one of the earliest of the bastides, founded by the Count of Toulouse in 1222. It is also one of the loveliest, with perfectly preserved ramparts and town gates, and impeccably restored narrow cobbled streets lined with Gothic houses. Beside the vast covered marketplace is the well, bored 375 feet (114 m) deep to provide the town with water during sieges.

**Monpazier,** southeast of Bergerac, is one of the most complete bastide towns. It retains its exquisitely arcaded central square, covered market hall, fortified church, a rectangular pattern of streets, and ancient walls.

**Monflanquin** *(visitor information, place des Arcades, tel 05 53 36 40 19, www.montglanquinetourisme .com),* on a hill southeast of Bergerac, has a warren of tiny medieval streets to explore. Don't miss the arcade-edged square. Above the tourist office is the **Musée des Bastides**, with exhibits that explain the history of these towns.

Other fine examples of bastides include **Domme** (see p. 250), **Toulouse** (see p. 260), **Montauban** (see p. 262), and **Mirepoix** (see p. 276). ■

**Cordes**
 230 D2
**Visitor information**
✉ Maison Fonpeyrouse
☎ 05 63 56 00 52
**www.cordes-sur-ciel .org**

**Monpazier**
🅰 230 D3
**Visitor information**
✉ place des Cornières
☎ 05 53 22 68 59
**www.pays-des -bastides.com**

A pedestrian street in old Toulouse, a bastide town

# Toulouse

A cosmopolitan metropolis, regional capital, and thriving center of technology and aeronautical research, Toulouse—recently voted one of the most desirable places to live in France—still holds at its heart the lovely old *ville rose*, the pink-brick streets making up the old town. History may be powerfully tangible here, but this is still a lively city, with the biggest student population in France outside Paris. Visit the ancient city on foot, then for a change of pace take a trip on the state-of-the-art Métro, with each station credited to a different team of architect and artist.

**Toulouse**
- 🗺 230 D2

**Visitor information**
- ✉ Donjon du Capitole
- ☎ 05 61 11 02 22
- www.ot-toulouse.fr

**Musée des Augustins**
- ✉ 21 rue de Metz
- ☎ 05 61 22 21 82
- www.augustins.org

**Espace d'Art Moderne et Contemporain**
- ✉ Les Abbatoires, 76 Allées Charles-de-Fitte
- ☎ 05 34 51 10 60
- 🕐 Closed a.m. & Mon.
- 💲 $
- www.lesabattoirs.org

**Cité de l'Espace**
- ✉ avenue Jean-Gonord
- ☎ 08 20 37 72 23
- 🕐 Closed Mon. Sept.–Mar. except school vacations
- 💲 $$
- www.cite-espace.com

Start in the **Place du Capitole,** the vast central square. It is dominated by the Capitole itself, the 18th-century **Hôtel de Ville** named after the city's medieval consuls, or *capitouls.* Beginning in the tenth century, Toulouse was the seat of the powerful counts of Toulouse. All this came to a brutal end with the Albigensian Crusade of the 13th century, when Toulouse lost its autonomy. In the 15th century, the city enjoyed another heyday, thanks to the *pastel* or woad plant cultivated here; it yielded a blue dye, to be supplanted by the arrival of indigo from the East in the 16th century. Merchants and capitouls grew rich, building themselves ever more splendid mansions in Italian Renaissance style. Look for the lovely **Hôtel d'Assézat** on Rue de Metz and **Hôtel Bernuy** on Rue Gambetta.

The **Basilique St.-Sernin** *(place St.-Sernin, tel 05 61 21 80 45, closed to visitors Sun. a.m.)* is the largest Romanesque church in Europe (consecrated in 1096, though the nave and tower are from the 13th century) and was the most beautiful of all the pilgrim churches. Follow in the pilgrims' footsteps: through the south portal with its tremendous carvings; down the nave, past glowing frescoes and tapestries, painted capitals, and carved choir stalls; to the 11th-century altar, ambulatory, and rich Treasury below. The Gothic church of **Les Jacobins** *(rue Lakanal)* is also particularly fine.

## INSIDER TIP:

**Test out your moon-walking in an astronaut training session at the popular Cité de l'Espace museum, just outside Toulouse.**

—ROSEMARY BAILEY
*National Geographic author*

Outstanding Romanesque sculptures from the city's churches and cloisters have been gathered together in the **Musée des Augustins.** The redesigned **Muséum de Toulouse** *(35 allée Jules Guesde, tel 05 67 73 84 84, www.museum.toulouse.fr, closed Mon.)* houses the first natural history museum in France. Don't miss the **Espace d'Art Moderne et Contemporain** in the old abbatoirs of St. Cyprien district, one of France's best contemporary art museums. ∎

# Albi

Viewed from the 11th-century Pont Vieux over the Tarn River, Albi presents an unforgettable sight, its pink and ocher houses rising in tiers to the soaring bulk of its cathedral fortress.

Cathédrale Ste.-Cécile overlooks the Tarn River.

**Albi**
 231 E2
Visitor information
✉ Palais de la Berbie, place Ste.-Cécile
☎ 05 63 36 36 00
**www.albi-tourisme .fr**

**Palais de la Berbie: Musée Toulouse-Lautrec**
✉ place Ste.-Cécile
☎ 05 63 49 48 70
🕐 Closed Tues. Oct.–March
💲 $
**www.museetou louselautrec.net**

Like Toulouse, Albi is a *ville rose*, built of the same pink brick. Its single most breathtaking feature is the great **Cathédrale Ste.-Cécile**. The mighty brick walls, buttressed by tremendous piers, are as daunting as they are astonishing. In the spacious nave, built without pillars or transept, is a colorful world of 16th-century Italian wall paintings and ethereally delicate carving. Most remarkable are the filigree rood screen and the fresco of the Last Judgment that covers the west wall.

In the formal gardens of the 13th-century bishop's palace, the **Palais de la Berbie**, the ramparts offer ravishing views of the Tarn. Inside the palace lies an extensive collection of works by Henri de Toulouse-Lautrec, who was born in Albi (see sidebar).

In the old town, you will find the **Maison Enjalbert** and

**Hôtel de Reynes**, both built in the 16th century, as well as the Romanesque **Église de St.-Salvy** *(rue Mariès)*, with a lovely 13th-century cloister. ∎

## Toulouse-Lautrec

Born in Albi in 1864, Henri de Toulouse-Lautrec was descended from the counts of Toulouse. Crippled and stunted in his youth by what may have been brittle bone disease, he sought solace in painting and freedom in the bohemian world of the Montmartre quarter of Paris. A superb draftsman with a wide technical range, he used just a few expressive strokes to convey the scenes that caught his eye. The newly renovated **Musée Toulouse-Lautrec**, in the Palais de la Berbie, has a collection of more than 600 of his works, ranging from early landscapes and portraits to sketches and book illustrations, drawings and paintings, lithographs and posters.

# Montauban

Another historic pink-brick town on the Tarn River, Montauban was founded in the 12th century by the Count of Toulouse. In the 16th century, the town became an important center of Protestantism and even resisted a siege by Louis XIII—despite the fact that the king had arranged a special lunch to view the assault.

An arcaded central square lies at the heart of Montauban, founded in the 12th century.

**Montauban**
- 230 D2

**Visitor information**
- 4 rue du Collège
- 05 63 63 60 60

www.montauban
-tourisme.com

**Musée Ingres**
- Palais Épiscopal, 19 rue de l'Hôtel de Ville
- Closed Mon. except July–Aug. & Sun. a.m. Nov.–Mar.
- $

The focus of the town is the **Place Nationale,** which owes its satisfying unity to the fact that it was rebuilt in the 17th century following a fire. Its brick buildings are handsome, and the square's shady arcades (site of a regular market) make it a fine place to shop or sit in a café.

The fortified **Église de St.-Jacques,** largely dating back to the 13th century, stands near the Pont Vieux, which is similar in style to the bridge at Albi and has a fine view of the river. At the end of the bridge stands the former bishop's palace, now the **Musée Ingres.** On his death,

**INSIDER TIP:**

**Stop at Guymare (939 avenue de l'Europe), for a scoop or two of artisinal ice cream.**

—SHEILA BUCKMASTER
National Geographic Traveler
*magazine editor at large*

Jean-Auguste-Dominique Ingres left his studio contents (including Greek vases and Roman sculpture), his violin, his paintbox, and many of his drawings to his native town. Also here are sculptures by another native of Montauban, Emile-Antoine Bourdelle. ∎

# Moissac

The small town of Moissac on the north bank of the Tarn River is famed for the carvings on its abbey church, once one of the great abbeys of France. Wander around the peaceful cloisters and admire the celebrated Romanesque sculpture.

In the 11th century, the **Abbaye de St.-Pierre** at Moissac became a daughter foundation of the abbey of Cluny (see p. 205). The church—part Romanesque and part Gothic—is certainly impressive, but the 12th-century carvings on its south portal will stop you in your tracks. A scalloped decoration frames the doorway, and a central column entwined with lions supports the tympanum. In minute and still perfect detail (even the revolutionaries stayed their hammers), it depicts St. John's vision of the Apocalypse from the Book of Revelation. In the middle sits Christ in Majesty surrounded by the Evangelists, angels, and symbolic beasts. The flowing figure of Jeremiah on the western door jamb has a melancholy beauty. On the east side, Avarice and Unchastity writhe in torment. In the arcaded cloisters, the 76 slender columns support graceful arcades, their capitals carved with infinite delicacy, depicting a cornucopia of plants, animals, and biblical characters. ∎

**Moissac**
- 📍 230 D2

**Visitor information**
- ✉ 6 place Durand-de-Bredon
- ☎ 05 63 04 01 85
- **www.moissac.fr**

**Abbaye de St.-Pierre**
- ✉ place St.-Pierre
- 💲 $

---

## Romanesque Sculpture

You may not realize it, but when you look closely at the beautiful Romanesque sculpture that adorns so many of the chapels and churches throughout France, you are really peering directly into the medieval mind. In fact, the figures and stories portrayed in these wonderfully vigorous decorations offer us a picture of a period and its people of which we have very little record otherwise.

Figurative sculpture became very popular during the 11th and 12th centuries, when craftsmen and artisans adorned column capitals, doorways, and tympana with glorious carvings that told a wealth of stories. The carvings are full of detail—some of it endearing, though very often quite frightening. The narratives are usually biblical, from the familiar story of the Nativity to the Last Judgment, with the hanging of Judas a particular favorite. Fearsome demons and dragons abound. All were motifs designed to instruct the faithful on the realities of hell and the promise of paradise.

The sculptors themselves were usually anonymous, and they often used local characters as their models. The average medieval churchgoer would have recognized and possibly even chuckled at the portraits of their friends and neighbors, depicted jokingly as people with toothaches, boils, and squints.

Romanesque sculpture also marks an important break away from classical portraiture to something more modern, expressive, and realistic.

# The Road to Compostela

**The symbol of the scallop shell marks stages on the pilgrim route to Santiago de Compostela in northwest Spain, one of the greatest shrines of medieval Christendom. Four main routes threaded across France: from Paris; from Vézelay in Burgundy; from Le Puy-en-Velay in the Auvergne; and from St.-Gilles, near Arles in Provence. All converged in the southwest to cross the Pyrenees and continue through Navarre on a single path.**

Believers pray at the old town church in St.-Jean-Pied-de-Port.

Thousands of pilgrims and travelers still follow the routes today, passing through the same towns and villages as the original pilgrims. They, too, worship in the great churches of Conques or Toulouse, wonder at the finely carved cloisters and tympanum of Moissac, pause to pray at wayside shrines and crosses, or seek shelter in tiny frescoed chapels. They may have different reasons for making this pilgrimage: Some may still walk the route for religious reasons, some to better understand their forebears, some just to enjoy the scenery along the way. But, like the medieval pilgrims, they find satisfaction in the journey.

The object of the pilgrims' travels is the shrine of St. James (Santiago), the disciple who is believed to have brought Christianity to Spain, then part of the Roman Empire. On his return to Judea, he was executed by Herod, and his followers returned with his martyred body to Galicia in Spain. As they approached the shore, they saw a vision of a man covered in scallop shells rise out of the waves on horseback; the scallop shell then became the pilgrimage emblem. The body of St. James was buried, and subsequently most of Spain fell to the Moors. Then, in 814, a vision of stars (compostela means field of stars) showed the way to the saint's tomb, and on July 25 (now the feast of Santiago) the body was discovered. Soon a church was built on the spot: The present building at Compostela is a vast Romanesque church with an elaborate baroque facade added later.

Pilgrims were lured with the promise of indulgences—forgiveness of their sins and remission of time in purgatory—and pilgrimages became enormously popular. The first recorded pilgrimage to Compostela was carried out by the bishop of Le Puy in 951.

Vital encouragement for the pilgrimage route was provided by the formidably powerful Benedictine abbey of Cluny in Burgundy (see p. 205), which established daughter houses, churches, and shrines along the way and donated relics to enhance their prestige and

**Details highlighting pilgrims and the ancient route can be found all along the way.**

## INSIDER TIP:

**Along the old pilgrim route, spend the night in the tiny, charming town of St.-Bertand-de-Comminges, at the inexpensive Hôtel du Comminges. It's right near the cathedral and the Roman excavations.**

—GILLES MINGASSON
*National Geographic photographer*

power. No shrine or place of pilgrimage was complete without a relic preserved in reliquaries of gold and silver embellished with jewels. Bones of saints were treasured, and pieces of the True Cross were considered especially valuable. Santiago de Compostela boasted the body of St. James, and many pilgrims would, en route, have prayed at shrines containing parts of no fewer than five Apostles and, at the Basilique St.-Sernin in Toulouse (see p. 260),

a sliver of the True Cross. It was many centuries before the authenticity of these relics was called into question. Intense and sometimes unseemly competition raged for the most potent relics. A monk from the abbey at Conques, for example, stole the relics of St. Foy from Agen. Vézelay was equally unscrupulous in refusing to return the remains of Mary Magdalene, sent to the city (somewhat ironically) for protection.

Often pilgrims doggedly tramped the sacred path for years, suffering hardship and danger. Moved by their plight, at the end of the 12th century a monk from Poitou by the name of Amery Picaud penned the *Liber Sancti Jacobi*. This early guidebook gave details of the best places for sustenance, the most reliable sources of water, and the most rewarding chapels or monasteries to visit on the way.

Pilgrims wore the sign of the scallop shell to denote their calling. Even today it still works its magic. In 1987, the European Community officially recognized a system of signposting that had been devised using the scallop shell. It described the pilgrim route to Compostela as "one of the oldest signs of European cooperation and enterprise . . . a key part of our European heritage."

# More Places to Visit in the Dordogne & Midi-Pyrénées

### Château de Biron

Just south of the *bastide* town of Monpazier (see p. 259), the gargantuan Château de Biron dominates a great swath of countryside as it has since its 12th-century beginnings. The original keep was added to by generation after generation of the Gontaut family, until it was taken over by the local *département* authorities in 1978. Restoration is still in progress, and the château serves as an arts center during the summer. The feudal core of the buildings was enlarged with graceful Renaissance additions in the 16th century, including the beautiful double chapel—to house the family tombs above, with space for villagers to worship below.
230 D3 ☎ 05 53 63 13 39 ⏰ Open daily July–Aug. Closed Jan. & Mon. & Fri.– Sat. Nov.–March

### Collonges-la-Rouge

The lords of Turenne built this red village, its delightful mansions, towers, turrets, market hall, and château forming an almost bizarre homogeneity. The white limestone tympanum of the otherwise red church (constructed in the 11th–12th centuries) comes almost as a relief. Stroll along Rue Noire in the oldest quarter to gain a good sense of the whole.
230 D3

### St.-Céré

St.-Céré is a charming little market town, well situated for excursions to the Lot Valley. The Bave River ripples past its handsome streets, market square, and 15th-century balconied mansions. Above it to the north loom the two keeps (12th and 15th centuries) of the castle of **St.-Laurent-les-Tours,** home of the artist Jean Lurçat from 1945 to his death in 1966. Now it houses a museum of his work, and galleries in the town sell both original works and prints.
230 D3 **Visitor Information** ✉ 13 avenue François de Maynard ☎ 05 65 38 11 85

Collonges-la-Rouge gets its name from its wealth of red buildings.

# The Pyrenees

Visible from the flat Plain of Aquitaine and—on a clear day—from the fringes of the Massif Central, the Pyrenees fill the horizon with unsurpassed grandeur. Here you will find majesty and solitude, combined with lush, green valleys, rushing waterfalls, and rare flora and fauna. In spring and summer, the alpine meadows are embroidered with flowers, while in winter the mountains offer a variety of ski slopes. But perhaps the best time of all is the *arrière-saison*, the golden days of autumn when wisps of woodsmoke scent the air.

Fabulous views of the Pyrenees from Col du Somport, a pass between France and Spain, abound.

Spanning the frontier between Spain and France, the Pyrenees really belong to neither. For centuries, the main part of the Pyrenees consisted of a patchwork of tiny republics. The region still retains a sense of independent little states, each proud of its history and traditions.

There are few better ways of experiencing the mountains at close hand than by walking (see sidebar). Public transportation is erratic, with the delightful exception of some mountain trains and cable cars, so a car is almost essential. The roads are usually good and well signposted, though gas stations are few and far between and snow closes many higher roads from October to May. Remember your passport if you plan to cross to Spain. ■

## Walking in the Pyrenees

The Pyrenees mountains are a paradise for walkers, with the GR10, one of France's most famous long-distance footpaths, crossing the entire range from the Mediterranean to the Atlantic. Any serious walk in the mountains takes time, so consider camping out or staying overnight in refuges, undoubtedly the best way to experience the Pyrenees. Remember that these are serious mountains with attendant dangers. Always check the weather forecast before setting out and go properly equipped with good boots, water, and maps.

# Parc National des Pyrénées Occidentales

Established in 1967 and covering 113,000 acres (45,700 ha), the Western Pyrenees National Park encompasses some of the most spectacular scenery in the Pyrenees, including the breathtaking Cirque de Gavarnie. It is home to a number of rare and endangered species, including golden eagles, griffon vultures, lynx, ibex, and a few Pyrenean brown bears. Hunting and flower picking are strictly prohibited, and camping in the wild is permitted only at distances equivalent to more than an hour's trek from the road (and you must be off by sunrise).

Clouds shroud the mountain near a hiking trail in the Cirque de Gavernie.

**La Vallée d'Aspe**

**Visitor information**

✉ place François Saraille, Bedous

☎ 05 59 34 57 57

**www.tourisme-aspe .com**

A number of magnificent valley roads climb up into the park, following the courses of the many rivers flowing from the mountains. The surrounding towns and villages are well equipped with hotels, restaurants, campsites, and mountain guides. Maisons du Parc are official information centers advising about walks, weather, wildlife, and the rich flora of the region.

## La Vallée d'Aspe

To the west of the park, the N134 follows a Roman road along the valley of the Aspe

from Oloron-Ste.-Marie, climbing to 5,354 feet (1,632 m) to enter Spain at the **Col du Somport.** This was the crossing place of the Saracen army on its way to defeat by Charles Martel in 732 and was trodden for centuries by pilgrims on their journey to Compostela (see pp. 264–265). In 2003, a controversial 5-mile (8 km) road tunnel was finally pierced through the col. This should relieve the traffic bottlenecks of the coastal routes, but it threatens the peace of the valley and the last habitat of the Pyrenean brown bear. The village of **Lescun,** about halfway up the valley, offers views of the rock amphitheater and pinnacles of the Cirque de Lescun.

## Vallée d'Ossau

Just to the east, the D934 heads up the valley of the Ossau, leaving Pau behind to climb through spa towns perched between river and mountainside. Look for the golden eagles, goshawks, peregrines, and vultures for which this valley is famous.

Continue through Laruns and Gabas, then turn southwest on the D231 to reach the artificial **Lac de Bious-Artigues,** part of the great Pyrenean hydroelectric network. From here, a marked footpath takes you on a spectacular four-hour walk around the **Lacs d'Ayous.** The path passes through forests and mountain pastures covered with spring wildflowers. Above you towers the extinct volcano of the **Pic du Midi d'Ossau** (see below). Herds of *isars,* a wild goat, graze its slopes. A cable car runs from Gabas to Pic de la Sagette, at 7,550 feet (2,134 m), giving marvelous views.

Retrace your steps to Laruns to head east on the D198, a superb drive that swoops over two dramatic *cols* (passes) to reach Argelès-Gazost. Heading south on the D921 to Gavarnie, you pass the tiny village of **St.-Savin,** the

**Maison de la Vallée d'Ossau**
✉ Laruns
☎ 05 59 05 31 41

---

# EXPERIENCE: Spend the Night on Pic du Midi

At 9,439 feet (2,877 m), the Pic du Midi was one of the great challenges for 19th-century tourists to the Pyrenees. Today it is the most accessible of the high peaks, with two cable cars making the 15-minute trip to the summit, weather permitting. At the top, you will enjoy one of the most sublime views in the Pyrenees: On a clear day, it is possible to see as far as the Atlantic Ocean, a distance of nearly 100 miles (160 km).

At the summit you will also find an observatory and a star museum. The observatory was built in 1880, a staggering achievement because most of the building material had to be brought up on the backs of porters and mules. For a long time, it was the highest observatory in Europe, and even now it is exceeded only by three others, one in Spain and the others in the Canary Islands.

Threatened with closure in 1983, the observatory nearly fell victim to scientific developments and budget restrictions. Instead, it was relaunched with a new role. It still operates as a meteorological station, supplying Météo-France with data, and as a stellar observatory, but now it also offers a museum devoted to the stars. Furthermore it allows all visitors to enjoy an unrivaled experience of a high-mountain summit without requiring a demanding climb. Accommodations (tel 08 25 00 28 77, www.picdumidi.com) once reserved for observatory staff are now open to the public, so anyone can stay overnight at the summit to stargaze and then see the sun rise the next morning.

The observatory is open year-round but is closed Tuesdays in the off-season. To get there, drive to La Mongie or take the shuttle bus from Argelès-Gazost, Lourdes, or Bagnères-de-Bigorre. Cable cars depart for the summit every 15 minutes. Check the weather before leaving, and take warm clothing, sunglasses, and sunscreen.

## Pyrenean Wildlife

The Pyrenees are home to more than 400 species of flowers, 160 of which are found nowhere else in the world—including Pyrenean ramonda and saxifrage, separate species of columbines and lilies, tiny purple crocuses, and pink androsace. This diverse and rich flora supports a number of unique butterflies, such as the Gavarnie blue and the Gavarnie ringlet.

On the upper mountain slopes, large raptors breed relatively undisturbed. The magnificent birds circling high in the sky are the griffon vulture, lammergeyer (or bearded vulture), and Egyptian vulture.

Mammals that call these mountains home include the isard, or Pyrenean antelope. The symbol of the park, the isard has horns that curve distinctively back at the tip. Its numbers are now increasing; it can be spotted on rocky outcrops high in the mountains. Other rare mammal species include the snow partridge, the marmot, and the Pyrenean desman, a tiny aquatic mammal.

A handful of brown bears also live in the Pyrenees, but these are threatened with extinction as they are driven farther away from their natural habitat in the lower stretches of the park and into the high reaches of the mountains. Efforts to reintroduce bears have met with bitter opposition from farmers.

---

**Cauterets**

🅜 230 C1

**Visitor information**

✉ place du Maréchal Foch

☎ 05 62 92 50 50

www.cauterets.com

**Cirque de Gavarnie**

🅜 230 C1

www.gavarnie.com

**Gavarnie**

**Visitor information**

☎ 05 62 92 49 10

site of an 11th-century abbey that once controlled the entire valley; the 12th-century church and chapter house survive. Opposite rise the ruins of the Château de Beaucens, now a bird sanctuary.

### Cauterets & Gavarnie

From Pierrefitte-Nestalas, you have the choice of two remarkable valleys. The D920 runs along the narrow gorge to the grand old spa town of **Cauterets.** From here, a fine walk leads you past waterfalls to the **Pont d'Espagne,** where three cataracts converge. Farther up lies the **Lac de Gaube** at 5,660 feet (1,725 m), dominated by the snowy peak of Vignemale, at 10,814 feet (3,298 m), the highest of the frontier summits.

The D921, the other route from Pierrefitte-Nestalas, runs up the Gorge de Luz to **St.-Sauveur,** once an important frontier post and a fashionable 19th-century spa. The gorge allows a glimpse of the Pyrenees' most famous sight: the **Cirque de Gavarnie.**

From Gavarnie village you must walk or ride by donkey or horse to the cirque itself, a breathtaking rocky amphitheater rimmed by peaks up to 10,000 feet (3,048 m) high. Waterfalls cascade down the cirque, the most spectacular of all being the **Grande Cascade de Gavarnie.** Plunging 1,385 feet (422 m), it is Europe's highest waterfall and a UNESCO World Heritage site. To the right is the Brèche de Roland, where, in the medieval epic poem *La Chanson de Roland,* the hero tried to break his enchanted sword rather than relinquish it to the infidel, and instead hacked a crevasse 400 feet (120 m) deep.

From Luz-St.-Sauveur follow the D918 via Barèges to the **Col de Tourmalet.** This pass, at 6,941 feet (2,115 m), is the highest in the mountains accessible by car. ∎

# Pau

**Pau is a fine place to start a visit to the Pyrenees.** The Boulevard des Pyrénées, below the château, offers a glorious panorama of the mountains encompassing no fewer than 83 peaks on a clear day. The city owes much of its elegance, curiously, to the British. The original British residents were retired officers of Wellington's army who decided to stay on after the Peninsula Campaign (1807–1814). They were joined later by compatriots attracted by the healthy air.

Elegant and relaxed, Pau invites you to saunter down its leafy boulevards, past elegant mansions and art nouveau villas, and along the narrow cobbled streets lined with half-timbered houses. At the western end of the Boulevard des Pyrénées, overlooking the Gave de Pau River, rises the **Château Pau.** Originally a hunting lodge built by the counts of Foix, it has a great redbrick keep that was added in the 14th century by Gaston Fébus, defender of the duchy of Foix from all comers.

In the 16th century, Margaret of Angoulême transformed the château into a Renaissance palace, with finely carved doorways, windows, and archways. This was the birthplace of her grandson, Henri of Navarre, who ascended to the throne of France in 1859 as Henri IV. A tour of the château includes the fine Gobelins tapestries in the state rooms, the magnificent Second Empire apartments of Empress Eugénie, the 16th-century kitchens, and a giant tortoise shell that reputedly served as the infant Henri's cradle.

The impressive **Musée des Beaux-Arts** (*rue Mathieu-Lalanne, tel 05 59 27 33 02, closed Tues., $*), northeast of the château, includes works by El Greco, Rubens,

A bouquet of French flags graces Château de Pau.

and Degas, plus painters of the Pyrenees. Pau's role in the early days of aviation and the school founded by the Wright brothers is celebrated in a new museum, **Pau Wright Aviation** (*Palais Beaumont, tel 06 75 29 47 33*).

**Jurançon** lies just across the Gave de Pau River. A wine route is signposted to guide you through the vineyards. Ask at the Pau tourist office for information on the route and about vineyards that welcome visitors. ∎

**Pau**
- 230 C2

**Visitor information**
- place Royale
- 05 59 27 27 08
- www.pau.fr

**Musée National du Château de Pau**
- rue du Château
- 05 59 82 38 00
- $. Guided visits only

www.musee-chateau-pau.fr

# Lourdes

The most popular Christian shrine in the world, Lourdes is also the gateway to the valleys of the Arrens, Cauterets, Ossau, and Gavarnie Rivers. Five million pilgrims flock to Lourdes annually, and the town has more hotels than anywhere else in France outside Paris. The faithful come in search of miracle cures for sickness and disability, many making the trip of a lifetime. Despite its formidable commercial trappings, Lourdes does not disappoint them.

The shrine of St. Bernadette in Lourdes remains the most popular Christian shrine in the world.

**Lourdes**

📍 230 C1

**Visitor information**

✉ place Peyramale

☎ 05 62 42 77 40

**www.lourdes-infotourisme.com**

**Musée Pyrénéen d'Art et de Traditions Populaires**

✉ Le Château Fort

☎ 05 62 42 37 37

💲 $

It all began in January 1858, when a 14-year-old girl called Bernadette Soubirous claimed to have seen visions of the Virgin Mary. Divine directions led her to the spring in the Grotte de Massabielle, and ever since her last vision in 1862, pilgrims have come to the tiny cave to fill their bottles with miraculous waters and abandon their crutches. Some visit the humble little house on Rue des Petits-Fossés where she lived with her family.

A church was built over the miraculous grotto, where a statue of the Virgin stands in the apparition niche. In addition to the **Basilique du Rosaire,** built in honor of Bernadette in 1889, a vast underground church, the **Basilique St.-Pie X,** was consecrated in 1958, the centenary of the visions. It can hold nearly 30,000 people.

The range of entertainment offered in the town includes a waxworks museum depicting the life of Christ and the life of Bernadette, and a miniature stone model of Lourdes as it was in the time of Bernadette.

The older part of Lourdes, by the castle on the other side of the Gave de Pau River, contains the **Musée Pyrénéen d'Art et de Traditions Populaires.** Devoted in part to the *pyrénéistes,* pioneer climbers in these mountains, the museum displays early equipment, maps, and drawings alongside exhibits devoted to local crafts and costumes, and Pyrenean wildlife. A funicular railway will take you to the top of the nearby Pic du Jer for some fine views.

Some 9 miles (15 km) southwest of Lourdes are the spectacular **Bétharram caves** *(tel 05 62 41 80 04, closed Nov.–Dec. & a.m. Feb.–March).* There, a miniature railroad and barges ferry visitors on an underground river through a landscape of fantastic limestone formations. ∎

# St.-Bertrand-de-Comminges

Once an important Roman town, St.-Bertrand-de-Comminges still contains vestiges of this former glory. These include traces of thermal baths, a theater, and a temple, together with the ruins of a broad arcaded market square and a Christian basilica added in the fifth century. Barbarian invasions from the north and the plague combined to destroy the town, which lay in ruins until the 11th century. It was at this point that a local count, later to be canonized as St. Bertrand, embarked on the building of a cathedral.

Dubbed the Mont-St.-Michel of the Pyrenees, the **Cathédrale Ste.-Marie** completely overwhelms the tiny 15th- and 16th-century village that clusters beneath it. The beauty of its setting, the grandeur of its architecture, and the artistic

**INSIDER TIP:**

**Local historic sites are the venues for the annual summer Festival du Comminges (www.festival-du-com minges.com), primarily classical music.**

—AMY ALIPIO
National Geographic Traveler
*magazine associate editor*

treasures it contains make this one of the most outstanding buildings in the Pyrenees.

The church is Romanesque with later Gothic additions, notably in the exquisite cloister. The superb carvings of its capitals frame sublime views of the mountains beyond.

Within, the cathedral contains a virtuoso feast of 16th-century woodcarving in its organ loft,

and most particularly in its choir stalls and misericords. Here the medieval craftsmen depicted in riotously entertaining detail a gallery of devout, humorous, and even satirical figures and scenes, no doubt based on local characters known to them all.

In the shadow of this magnificent monument are the streets of the little village, its stone and timber-framed houses painstakingly restored. A couple of miles down the valley, the lovely 12th century Romanesque **Église de St.-Just-de-Valcabrère** incorporates a patchwork of Roman masonry, from capitals to marble sarcophagi, that has been recycled from the ruins of the Roman city. ■

**St.-Bertrand-de-Comminges**

🅰 230 C1

**Visitor Information**

✉ Les Olivetains, parvis de la Cathédrale

☎ 05 61 89 04 91

🕒 Closed Jan. & Mon. Nov.–March

💲 $

---

## Beware of Hunters

French country folk love hunting with shotguns, and they go after everything from deer and wild boar to small birds. So beware if you are walking in the country, especially during hunting season (Aug.–Nov.) and on Sundays. Wear bright colors, keep an ear out for the barking of hunting dogs, and avoid anywhere sign-posted for *la chasse*.

Look for the resulting produce in the restaurants and markets: partridge, quail, wild boar sausage, and venison.

# Around the Ariège Valley

Rich with interest—from Cathar castles to painted prehistoric caves—and easily accessible (about an hour's drive) from Toulouse, the Ariège Valley is one of the best areas of the Pyrenees for a short visit. It has been designated a regional park to protect and revitalize the region.

Like something from a storybook, Foix's 11th-century castle looms over Ariège's capital.

**St.-Lizier**

230 D1

**Visitor information**

✉ place de l'Église

☎ 05 61 96 77 77

www.st-lizier.fr

**Foix**

230 D1

**Visitor information**

✉ 29 rue Delcassé

☎ 05 61 65 12 12

www.tourisme-foix-varilhes.fr

From Toulouse, approach the Ariège along the beautiful valley of the Lèze River. Though the wild mountain scenery is dramatic, the driving is not too hairraising. At Pailhès, make a pretty detour west along the D119 to **Grotte du Mas d'Azil,** a spectacular cave with a vast tunnel. Leading off the main cave are smaller ones inhabited by prehistoric people for some 20,000 years. A guided tour takes in some of the prehistoric artifacts discovered here. More recently, the caves have served as sanctuary for Protestants, Cathars, and even earlier religious refugees: A little chapel found here dates back to the third century.

## St.-Lizier

Proceed along the D119 and turn right onto the D117 to reach St.-Lizier, a fortified medieval hilltop village distinguished by two cathedrals. The **Cathédrale St.-Lizier,** in the lower town, has Romanesque frescoes and a delightful two-story cloister. Its exquisite pink-brick Gothic bell tower, modeled on St.-Sernin in Toulouse (see p. 260), makes a stunning sight against the distant peaks. The **Cathédrale de la Sède** dates from the 12th century.

## Foix

Farther east, Foix, capital of the Ariège, was the power base of the turbulent counts of Foix in the Middle Ages. Four times Simon de Montfort besieged the castle before finally capturing this bastion of the Cathar faith in 1211. Nowadays it is a pleasant town of winding old streets, dominated by the three keeps of its castle, the earliest dating from the 11th century and worth climbing for its commanding views over the town and foothills of the Pyrenees.

## Prehistoric Caves

A little way to the south on the N20, **Tarascon-sur-Ariège** is in the middle of a number of prehistoric caves. **Bédeilhac** *(Map 230 D1, tel 05 61 05 95 06)*, northwest of Tarascon-sur-Ariège, is a gigantic cave bristling with stalagmites, its walls covered with paleolithic images of animals painted some 15,000 years ago. **Lombrives** *(Map 230 D1, tel 05 61 05 98 40)*, to the southeast, has a vast 380-foot-high (117 m) cavern known as La Cathédrale, where a little train takes you right through the caves. Most impressive of all the caves, however, are those at **Niaux** (see sidebar).

The village of Niaux has the **Musée Pyrénéen** *(tel 05 61 05 88 36)*, which is devoted to crafts, costumes, and traditional life in the Ariège. For a taste of prehistory, visit the **Parc de la Préhistoire** in Tarascon.

## Montségur

Heading back northward on the N20, turn right just before Foix onto the twisting D9. The road passes under the walls of two Cathar fortresses, Montgaillard and Roquefixade, before reaching **Montségur**, the tragic last bastion of Catharism.

After the Treaty of Meaux gave legal backing to the Albigensian Crusade (see pp. 320–321), this region became the center of Cathar resistance. As fortress after fortress fell, the lord of Montségur turned this bleak, comfortless castle into a refuge for all Cathar heretics. In 1244, however, after a ten-month siege and despairing of relief, the Cathars surrendered. Under the terms of the truce, those who recanted their faith would go free. Two weeks later, more than 200 Cathars—men, women, and children—who refused to recant were burned alive on a vast pyre. A monument in their memory stands at the foot of the château. ■

PREHISTORIC CAVES
The caves described in the text open at varying times throughout the year, and some may be seen only by appointment, as numbers are limited. Before visiting, check times with the tourist office in Foix, or phone the site directly for information.

**Parc de la Préhistoire**
☏ 05 61 05 10 10
🕐 Closed Mon. Sept.–Oct.
💲 $$

**Château de Montségur**
☏ 05 61 01 06 94
🕐 Closed Jan.
💲 $
www.montsegur.fr

### Niaux Caves

Located south of Tarascon-sur-Ariège, the caves at Niaux boast some of the finest prehistoric cave paintings in Europe: vigorous drawings of bison, horses, and deer, with delicately rendered details. Unlike the caves at Lascaux in the Dordogne (see pp. 252–253), the Niaux caves *(tel 05 61 05 88 37 or 05 61 05 10 10, closed Mon., English tour at 1 p.m., www.ariege.com/niaux)* are still open to the public. So far no deterioration has been detected, but entrance is strictly controlled. It is essential that you book ahead, either by phone or in person at the caves. Ensure you have sturdy footwear, because the cave floor can be uneven and slippery, and light is kept to a minimum. Claustrophobics beware.

# More Places to Visit in the Pyrenees

The ancient bridge of St.-Jean-Pied-de-Port leads to the whitewashed facades of the old town.

## Mirepoix

The 13th-century *bastide* town of Mirepoix, northeast of Foix, is celebrated for the beautiful half-timbered arcading of its main square and for the enormous Gothic nave and graceful spire of its cathedral. The liveliest time to visit is market day (Thurs. or Sat.) or during the twice-monthly cattle market. *www.tourisme-mirepoix.com* 230 D1 **Visitor information** ✉ place du Maréchal Leclerc ☎ 05 61 68 83 76

## Oloron-Ste.-Marie

This little market town, on the N134 at the junction of the Ossau and Aspe Valleys, is distinguished by the **Cathédrale Ste.-Marie,** with its Romanesque doorway of carved marble, and the **Église Ste.-Croix,** with its 13th-century Spanish stonework. *www .tourisme-oloron.com* 230 B1 **Visitor Information** ✉ allée du Comte de Tréville ☎ 05 59 39 98 00

## St.-Jean-Pied-de-Port

On the D933 at the foot of the Roncesvalles Pass, St.-Jean-Pied-de-Port was on one of the pilgrim roads to Santiago de Compostela. It is also the site where Roland was defeated by the Basques, immortalized in the medieval poem *La Chanson de Roland.* The cobbled old town and the new town on the opposite bank of the Nive River are both enclosed by 15th- to 17th-century fortifications.
230 B1 **Visitor Information** ✉ place Charles de Gaulle ☎ 05 59 37 03 57

## Sauveterre-de-Béarn

A lovely town on the N124 with fine river views, a 13th-century church, castle ruins, and the remains of a fortified bridge, Sauveterre is best known today as the venue for the annual world salmon-fishing championships in July.
230 B2 **Visitor Information** ✉ place Royale ☎ 05 59 38 58 65

## Tarbes

Tarbes stands on the west bank of the Adour River east of Pau and just off the east–west motorway, La Pyrénéenne. In the center of town lies the **Musée Massey,** devoted mainly to the Hussars. The birthplace of World War I commander Maréchal Foch now houses a museum. The stud farm **Le Haras** stages displays of horsemanship. *www.tarbes.com* 230 C1 **Visitor Information** ✉ 3 cours Gambetta ☎ 05 62 51 30 31

Roman monuments, medieval villages, sandy beaches, and endless lavender against a backdrop of sweet sunshine

# South of France

The lavender festival in Sault is an exquisitely aromatic affair.

# South of France

The South of France is a hugely popular vacation region and a highly desirable place to live. It remains warm for much of the year, with pockets of the Côte d'Azur, sheltered by mountains, being particularly mild. Summers are very hot and dry. The only blight is the cold wind of the Mistral, which howls down from the north in winter. Millions come to the South of France: to the Côte d'Azur, the villages of Provence, and the vacation lands of Languedoc-Roussillon.

The Massif Central and the Alps divide the Mediterranean coast geographically from the rest of France. This coast's main connection with the north is the great Rhône River. To the east, the mountains drop almost to the sea, and much of the Côte d'Azur is rocky. Beyond the Rhône delta to the west, the coast sweeps in a great arc, fringed with beach resorts and washed by clear waters.

The plain of Languedoc-Roussillon is intensively cultivated, producing a wide range of fruit and particularly wine, which is rapidly improving in quality. Shellfish are cultivated in the lagoons that edge the coast. To the north are the foothills of the Cévennes, and farther south, the Pyrenees form a frontier with Spain.

Marseille is the biggest city in the south, and France's largest port. Sète, to the east, is another important port. Nîmes and Montpellier are both highly attractive cities, centers of high-tech industry and key links in the developing Mediterranean sunbelt.

Historically, the Romans played a key role throughout the region. The whole of the south coast was their Provincia, with Narbonne as its capital. Many of their buildings survive, notably the Pont du Gard, the amphitheaters of Arles and Nîmes, and the theater at Orange.

Throughout the Middle Ages, Provence and Languedoc were famous for the "courts of love" and the poetry of the troubadours, and in the 19th century local enthusiasts made efforts to revive the Provençal language and identity. Like much of the rest of France, the region suffered during the 16th-century Wars of Religion, when towns

## NOT TO BE MISSED:

and cities were seriously damaged. In the 18th and 19th centuries, the English came to the South of France for health cures and winter holidays. By the 1920s, sunbathing had become fashionable and the Côte d'Azur the land of summer vacations. In the 1960s, the Languedoc-Roussillon coast was developed as a vacation playgrounds with some areas set aside as nature reserves and animal parks.

The light and color that are so characteristic of the South of France have always attracted artists and have given rise to such important artistic movements as cubism and fauvism. The legacy of the creative spirit is clearly evident in the many fine art museums that dot the region.

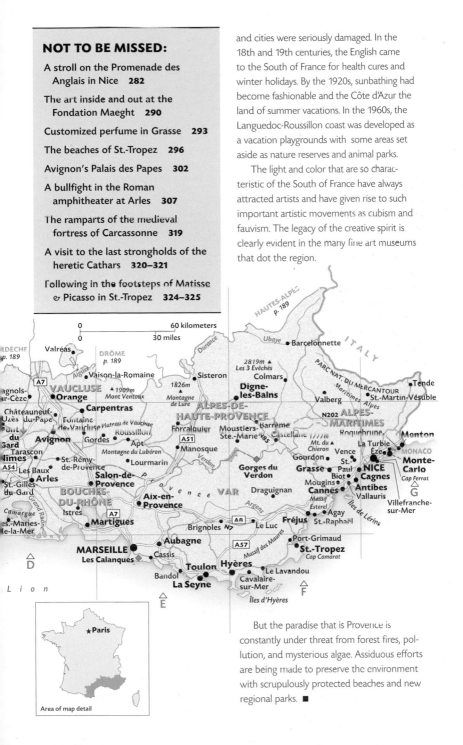

But the paradise that is Provence is constantly under threat from forest fires, pollution, and mysterious algae. Assiduous efforts are being made to preserve the environment with scrupulously protected beaches and new regional parks. ∎

# Côte d'Azur

Breathtaking beauty, clear blue waters, and a superb climate have earned the French Riviera, or Azure Coast, a premier position among the world's stylish vacation playgrounds. Despite the crowds, the coast retains its glamour and its place in the social calendars of the world's elite. The harbors are full of megayachts; superb restaurants, nightclubs, and casinos cater to serious eating, partying, and playing; and the exclusive beaches gleam with oiled bodies.

On the waterfront: Exclusivity in Monaco's Monte Carlo doesn't necessarily mean "singularly unique," as these docked yachts would suggest.

The Romans built spas and villas designed to catch the sea breezes along the coast, but only in the 19th century, with the arrival of the English aristocracy in search of health cures and botanical specimens, was the Côte d'Azur as we know it invented. Wealthy visitors from America and Europe followed, building villas and playing the tables at Monte Carlo's casino.

In the 1920s, Coco Chanel popularized sunbathing and F. Scott Fitzgerald wrote the jazz age into existence. After World War II, Brigitte Bardot launched St.-Tropez as a symbol of the new Côte d'Azur.

But the coast offers more. Its museums are filled with modern art (much of it created here), and world-class jazz musicians play in Roman amphitheaters on starry nights. The simplest delights are perhaps the most potent and enduring: the brilliant blue sea, pine-shaded beaches, and cliff-top views; the scent of herbs and lavender, mimosa and pine; and terra-cotta villages perched among spectacular rocky landscapes a few miles inland. ■

# Gardens of the Côte d'Azur

Sheltered to the north by mountains, untouched by frost throughout the winter, and blessed with an early, balmy spring, the Côte d'Azur is a paradise for gardeners and garden lovers.

The opulent villas that sprang up along the coast in the 19th and early 20th centuries were surrounded by equally sumptuous gardens. Glamorous and eclectic, the gardens revel in exotic plants, while at the same time retaining characteristic French restraint.

## Menton

Cosseted Menton boasts a particularly impressive clutch of these subtropical paradises, in which fountains and shady terraces, creative topiaries, and distant vistas combine irresistibly. For sheer variety of palms and subtropical species, the **Jardin Botanique du Val Rameh** is hard to equal.

English landscape designer Lawrence Johnston made his only French garden at **Jardin de la Serre de la Madone** *(Val de Gorbio, tel 04 93 57 73 90, www .serredelamadone)*, outside Menton. Here he grew the plants that he had collected from China, South Africa, and elsewhere.

## Cap Ferrat & Hyères

At Cap Ferrat, visit the **Jardin & Musée Ephrussi-de-Rothschild.** Gardens of every inspiration— from Italian to Japanese, by way of grottoes, a temple of Diana, and a cactus collection—cluster in the shade of umbrella pines against a backdrop of aquamarine sea. In Hyères, **Parc St.-Bernard** *(follow signs from Cours de Strasbourg)* is a cornucopia of Mediterranean flora. And **Parc Ste.-Claire** *(boulevard Victor Basch)* contains ravishing terraced gardens established by American writer Edith Wharton. ■

### Menton
🅰 279 G3
**Visitor information**
✉ 8 avenue Boyer
☎ 04 92 41 76 76
**www.menton.fr**

### Jardin Botanique du Val Rameh
✉ avenue St.-Jacques, Menton
☎ 04 93 35 86 72
💲 $

### Jardin & Musée Ephrussi-de-Rothschild
✉ Cap Ferrat
☎ 04 93 01 33 09
🕐 Closed Mon.– Fri. a.m. Nov.– mid-Feb.
**www.villa-ephrussi .com**

## Domaine du Rayol

The splendid botanical gardens of Domaine du Rayol *(Avenue des Belges, Rayol-Canadel-sur-Mer, tel 04 98 04 44 00, www.domainedurayol.org)* are in the Var, on the Corniches des Maures above Rayol-Canadel-sur-Mer. Designed as a botanical index of all the regions of the world with a Mediterranean climate, the 50-acre (20 ha) site features different areas dedicated to the plants of South Africa, California, Chile, the Canary Islands, and Australia.

Established by a Parisian banker in 1910, the belle epoque villa and exotic garden were threatened by property speculators in 1989. The Conservatoire du Littoral, an organization dedicated to conserving the coast, stepped in and saved the site.

Guided and themed walks of the gardens are offered with commentaries in French, English, and German. Learn about aromatic plants and exotic winter flowers, or walk the mimosa trail. The gardens, open year-round, are at their best in springtime. There is a library, café, workshops, musical evenings in summer, and even a guided underwater tour.

# Nice

Combining a Provençal heart with a welcoming joie de vivre, and a wealth of museums with a profusion of gardens, fountains, and palm trees, the wonderful city of Nice raises life alfresco to an art form.

Lined with grand hotels, Nice's Promenade des Anglais is the last word in overbuilt elegance.

**Nice**
🅰 279 G3
**Visitor information**
✉ 5 promenade des Anglais
☎ 08 92 70 74 07
**www.nicetourisme .com**

**Musée d'Art Moderne et d'Art Contemporain**
✉ promenade des Arts
☎ 04 97 13 42 01
🕐 Closed Mon.
💲 $. Free 1st & 3rd Sun. of month
**www.mamac-nice.org**

## Old Nice

Once deliciously dangerous and seedy, old Nice is now a fashionable enclave of bistros, nightclubs, and galleries. But the authentic aroma of dried fish and garlic still hangs in the air, and its little shops remain the best place to buy virgin olive oil. The outdoor market on Cours Saleya is famous for its flowers and local produce. Lunch on delicious, inexpensive Niçois specialties in one of the cafés.

The tiny squares and lovely chapels of the old town are dominated by the huge dim cathedral with its dome of glazed tiles. Of the palaces and *hôtels particuliers* (mansions), the grandest is the 17th-century **Palais Lascaris** (*15 rue Droite, tel 04 93 62 05 54, closed Tues.*), with frescoed ceilings and

rococo silver inlaid doors. Take the elevator up to the park to enjoy the waterfall, café, and views.

Old Nice ends at the Paillon River, now the site of spacious gardens, squares, and fountains, as well as the striking glass-and-marble **Musée d'Art Moderne et d'Art Contemporain (MAMAC).** The collections focus on French and American avant garde art.

## City Center

To the west of the old town stretches the **Promenade des Anglais.** It is lined with grand hotels, including the magnificent Negresco (see p.372), with its huge Baccarat chandelier. The newly restored Palais Masséna, a spendid belle epoque villa, houses the **Musée d'Art et d'Histoire** (*65 rue de France, tel 04 93 91 19 19, closed Tues.*).

Beyond the river lies 19th-century Nice: dignified arcaded squares, Italianate apartment buildings, fashionable shops, and an array of art galleries. The **Musée International d'Art Naïf** (*Château Sainte-Hélène, avenue de Fabron, tel 04 93 71 78 33, closed Tues., www.midan.org*) is in a pink château; and the **Musée des Beaux-Arts** has works by Monet, Degas, and Sisley. Frescoes and icons are displayed in the ornate Russian Orthodox cathedral, **Cathédrale-St.-Nicolas,** on Boulevard Tzaréwitch.

## EXPERIENCE: Up into the Mountains by Rail

Two small tourist trains provide a splendid way to explore the hinterland of the Côte d'Azur without a car. Departing from Nice daily at 9 a.m., the **Train des Merveilles** *(tel 08 91 70 30 00, www .beyond.fr/travel/railcuneo.html)* will take you to Peillon, the Roya-Bévéra Valley, and the Mercantour Park and Vallée des Merveilles. It has an *espace rotonde* with panoramic windows. The **Train des Pignes** *(tel 04 97 03 80 80; www .trainprovence.com)*, now a protected historic monument, offering a tour of the villages that sit perched between Nice and Digne. It climbs to more than 3,300 feet (1,000 m) through 50 tunnels, bridges, and viaducts. This steam train makes four round-trips daily from Nice.

### Cimiez

Art treasures dot the wealthy suburb of Cimiez, a cradle of hills to the north where you can see the remains of the original Roman settlement. Among the fabulous collection at the **Musée National Marc Chagall** *(avenue du Dr. Ménard, tel 04 93 53 87 20, closed Tues., www .musee-chagall.fr)* are Chagall's "Biblical Message" canvases.

Farther up the hill, a 17th-century villa houses the **Musée Matisse** *(164 avenue des Arènes de Cimiez, tel 04 93 81 08 08, closed Tues., $)*, with Matisse's personal collection, including still lifes and sketches of Chapelle de la Rosaire, as well as the "Tempête à Nice." Vence. ∎

**Musée des Beaux-Arts**

✉ 33 avenue des Baumettes

☎ 04 92 15 28 28

🕐 Closed Mon.

💲 $

**www.musee-beaux-arts-nice.org**

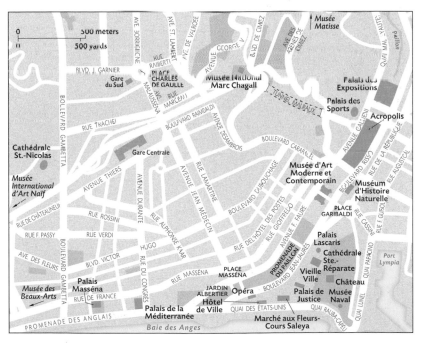

# The Corniches

In a region with such a wealth of spectacular beauty, the stretch of coast between Menton and Nice is particularly outstanding. The best way to drink in the glorious views of cliffs, sea, and extravagant villas set among palm trees is to take the corniche roads. Of the three, the Grande and Moyenne Corniches offer the most sweeping panoramas, while the Corniche Inférieure, closest to the sea, has the worst traffic and the best views of luxurious resorts. This round-trip takes two lower roads from Nice to Menton, returning mainly on the Grand Corniche.

The sixth-century Trophée des Alpes dominates the town of La Turbie.

**Villefranche-sur-Mer**

   279 G3

**Visitor information**

✉   square François-Binon

☎   04 93 01 73 68

www.villefranche-sur-mer.fr

## Corniche Inférieure

From Nice, the N98 circles the Cap de Nice and passes through the port to reach **Villefranche-sur-Mer.** Here, narrow streets rush steeply down to the deep natural harbor that has turned this small fishing village into an important naval port, lending it a more raffish flavor than most of this coast. Pretty, pastel-colored houses and lively cafés line the tiny harbor, overlooked by the **Chapelle St.-Pierre,** a beguiling little church decorated by Jean Cocteau in 1957.

Jutting out into the sea just beyond Villefranche, the peninsula of **Cap Ferrat,** together with those of Cap d'Ail and Cap Martin farther along the coast, is famously the preserve of the seriously rich, its natural beauty embedded with fabulous villas and luxuriant gardens. Do not miss the **Musée Ephrussi-de-Rothschild,** a pink-and-white villa with marble floors and Tiepolo ceilings, housing a superb decorative arts collection and surrounded by magnificent gardens (see p. 281). At the end of the *cap,* the rocky end of the peninsula, is the **Grand Hôtel du Cap-Ferrat** (see p. 372), featuring among other luxuries a funicular railroad to the beach. The little fishing and yachting village of **St.-Jean-Cap-Ferrat** makes a picturesque place for lunch; relatively quiet **Plage des Fossés** leads to a path around the peninsula with fantastic views.

A couple of miles farther east of Villefranche on the N98, sheltered **Beaulieu-sur-Mer** has some extremely grand hotels. Its most bizarre and delightful offering is the remarkable **Villa Kérylos,** an authentic reproduction of an ancient Greek villa, in which the eccentric archaeologist Théodore Reinach lived in the manner of an Athenian citizen. One of his few concessions to the 20th century was glass in the windows.

## Moyenne Corniche

Continuing around the coast, the road threads past rocky bays and caps. As it nears **Monaco** (see pp. 288–289), avoid the traffic by diverting onto the Moyenne Corniche (N7) as far as Menton.

**Menton** (see p. 281), only a mile (1.5 km) from the Italian border, remains the grande dame of the littoral: genteel, cradled by mountains, with tropical gardens. The steep streets of old Menton drop down to the **Promenade du Soleil,** lined with cafés, restaurants, and palm trees.

This is Cocteau's town: See the **Musée Jean-Cocteau,** housed in a 17th-century fort, to enjoy a collection of his drawings, mosaics, and ceramics. Best of all, visit the **Hôtel de Ville,** where he

decorated the Salle des Mariages in his own inimitable fashion. The 17th-century **Église de St.-Michel** is the setting for a chamber music festival in August. From Menton, head back on the N7 to Roquebrune-Cap-Martin.

## Grande Corniche

Turn inland onto the Grande Corniche (the D2564) to **Roquebrune,** a medieval village of steep streets and vaulted alleys, opening to magnificent sea views. Follow this spectacular road westward for about 4 miles (6 km) to **La Turbie** and the Trophée des Alpes. A little garden on the cliff edge offers fine views out to sea and a superb panorama of Monaco.

At Col d'Èze, 4 miles (6 km) farther, the D45 leads to the tiny village of **Èze,** perched dizzyingly over the Mediterranean. Visitors now throng its exquisitely restored streets, covered alleyways, and steep, twisting stairways.

Return to the winding Moyenne Corniche (N7) from Èze to Nice, stopping at the pull-offs provided to savor the ravishing views. ∎

# Food & Drink—Sun-kissed Fare

*Cuisine du soleil,* cuisine of the sun, is the name given to the food of this blessed region. It is a Mediterranean cuisine—luscious, aromatic, and, as it happens, healthy. Market stalls are laden with seasonal local produce like peppers, tomatoes, figs, melons, cherries, peaches, and especially olives. It is the olive that is most central to southern cooking, its oil used almost exclusively instead of animal fat. More than 15 different olive varieties are grown in Provence, destined for olive oil or the table. Garlic is the other keynote, along with herbs like rosemary, thyme, and marjoram, which grow wild in the countryside.

Olives galore for sale at the St.-Rémy-de-Provence farmers' market

To the east the cuisine of the South of France has an Italian accent, and local specialties include *socca* (chickpea flour) pancakes; *pissaladière,* a pizza with onions, anchovies, and black olives; *pistou,* vegetable soup with basil; stuffed zucchini flowers; and the ubiquitous *pan bagnat,* a large roll stuffed with *salade Niçoise.*

Farther west the influence is Spanish. In Roussillon, look for *cargolade,* a grill of snails and sausages served with *aïoli,* a rich golden mayonnaise made from olive oil, garlic, and egg yolk, served with raw vegetables, fish, or soup. Anchovies are another specialty, good with grilled red peppers.

All along the Mediterranean coast there is excellent fish and seafood. In Languedoc–Roussillon, the saltwater lagoons produce mussels, oysters, and more obscure marine delicacies such as sea urchins and crayfish. Bouillabaisse fish stew is a key specialty (see sidebar opposite). A simple *soupe de poisson* is also delicious, served with croutons and *rouille,* a hot red pepper mayonnaise. *Bourride* is another fish stew, with aïoli added at the last moment. Simple fish dishes like grilled sardines or red mullet are always good, as is *brandade,* a puree of salt cod and olive oil.

The south is certainly the best place in France to be a vegetarian, but there are plenty

of good meat dishes, too. Lamb from the Sisteron area, grazed on fragrant herb-rich vegetation, is a great delicacy. Rich, slow-cooked *daubes* are serious affairs. Usually beef stewed in red wine (often with olives and tomatoes), they are also made with other ingredients, including calamari. In the Camargue, you should try *gardiane de taureau*, bull's meat stew, usually served with the delicious nutty rice grown locally.

Among the light menu items of note, for enjoying with a cocktail, starting a meal, or for a snack, there is *anchoade* (anchovy dip), salade Niçoise (tomatoes, anchovies, hard-boiled eggs, olives, and sometimes tuna and beans), and t*apenade* (a puree of olives and anchovies). Main course options include *aubergines farcies à la Provençale* (eggplant stuffed with meat, onions, and herbs, served with tomato sauce), *perdrix à la Catalane* (partridge with orange and pepper sauce), and *stockfish à la Niçoise* (dried cod stewed with onions, tomatoes, garlic, and herbs). Regional vegetarian courses include *artichauts à la barigoule* (small artichokes stewed in oil and white wine), *fleurs de courges farcies* (stuffed zucchini flowers), and *ratatouille* (a stew of eggplant, zucchini, peppers, and tomatoes).

What to drink with your meal is never a problem. Languedoc-Roussillon produces most of France's table wine, and its wines are becoming increasingly respected. Drink

**The traditional Provençal fish stew, bouillabaisse, originated in the port city of Marseille.**

the local *vin de pays* or sample slightly more expensive local wines from Corbières, Nîmes, Minervois, Fitou, and the Côtes de Roussillon. In Provence, look for Châteauneuf-du-Pape or Gigondas. Along the coast, the local selection of wines is more limited; try the Côtes de Provence rosé or Bandol.

Aniseed-flavored pastis is a popular aperitif, and sweet dessert wines include Banyuls and various Muscats, especially from Beaumes-de-Venise and Rivesaltes

Even after a full dinner there is always room for *calissons d'Aix* (almond cookies) or *crème Catalane* (caramelized egg custard).

---

## EXPERIENCE: Cooking Bouillabaisse in Marseille

Fierce argument continues to rage over the exact recipe for this magnificent fish stew, a specialty of the Mediterranean that the city of Marseille claims as its own. **Restaurant Miramar** *(12 quai du Port, Marseille, tel 04 91 91 10 40, www .bouillabaisse.com)* has the reputation of serving one of the best versions in town, prepared by chef Christian Buffa. Here you can also learn how to make the famous dish yourself.

The lesson begins on Saturday morning with a trip to the fish market in the Vieux Port to select the right fish (monkfish, eel, and red mullet are considered essential). Then you head back to the kitchen, where you will spend four hours preparing and cooking the dish. Finally, you will have a chance to savor the result. Traditionally the fish broth is served first and then the fish itself, accompanied by *rouille*, a peppery mayonnaise.

# Monaco

Smaller than New York's Central Park, the tiny independent state and tax haven of Monaco is a magnet for those in search of glamour. Visitors flock to Monaco for its glittering night-life, luxurious hotels, and expensive restaurants. After his accession in 1949, Prince Rainier III transformed the principality, extending it vertically and horizontally with skyscrapers and landfill, and earning it the epithets "Hong Kong on the Mediterranean" and "Las Vegas *plage*."

The fairy-tale principality of Monaco is sometimes called the Hong Kong on the Mediterranean.

**Monaco**
🅰 279 G3
**Visitor information**
✉ 2A boulevard des Moulins, Monte Carlo
☎ 377 92 16 61 16
www.visitmonaco.com

**Palais Princier**
✉ place du Palais
☎ 377 93 25 18 31
🕓 Closed Nov.–March
💲 $

The old town of Monaco, out on the jagged promontory of the Rocher, is an immaculate affair of elegant mansions, charming little squares and foun-tains, and, of course, souvenir stores. The **Palais Princier,** seat of the Grimaldi family (see sidebar opposite), has sections dating from every century since 1000. Packed with gorgeous fur-niture, paintings, and frescoes, it is open to visitors only when the prince is away. But the changing of the palace guard outside is a

daily spectacle. The great white 19th-century neo-Romanesque cathedral nearby contains the tomb of Princess Grace, perpetually strewn with roses. On the cliff is the world-class **Musée Océanographique.**

South of the Rocher lie the new marina of **Fontvieille,** the **Princess Grace Rose Garden** *(Roseraie Princesse Grace Avenue des Guelfes),* and the port of **La Con-damine,** a vast marina with prom-enades for yacht-ogling. On the cliffs behind rise the magnificently

**INSIDER TIP:**

Colorful clownfish and prehistoric chambered nautiluses reside at Monaco's oceanographic museum, one of the world's oldest.

—KRISTEN GUNDERSON
*National Geographic researcher*

situated **Jardin Exotique,** sheltering a huge range of exotic plants, as well as prehistoric caves and an anthropological museum. Located in two restored villas, the **Nouveau Musée National de Monaco** is dedicated to art and performance.

Monaco hosts a constant round of festivals, fireworks, and rallies, culminating in the Grand Prix every May, when the roads are closed to traffic and the entire port becomes a racetrack.

## Monte Carlo

Beyond the port is Monte Carlo, with its fabled casino and opera, which should not be missed. To make sure visitors look the part, there's a dress code. Designed by Charles Garnier, who was also responsible for the Opéra Garnier in Paris, the interiors retain their extravagant belle epoque glamour.

The palm tree gardens around the casino and the wonderful terrace surrounding them afford beautiful views over the Mediterranean. More ostentatious opulence is provided by a string of Monte Carlo's sumptuous hotels, most notably the **Hôtel de Paris** (*www.hoteldeparismonte carlo.com*) and the **Hôtel Hermitage** (*www.hotelhermitagemontecarlo .com*), with its famous, elegant winter-garden foyer luxuriating under a glass roof designed by Gustave Eiffel. ∎

**Musée Océanographique**

✉ avenue St.-Martin
☎ 377 93 15 36 00
💲 $$
**www.oceano.org**

**Jardin Exotique**
✉ boulevard du Jardin Exotique Moneghetti
☎ 377 93 15 29 80
💲 $$

**Nouveau Musée National de Monaco**
✉ 8 rue Honoré Labande
☎ 377 98 98 19 62
**www.nmnm.mc**

**Monte Carlo**
🗺 279 G3
**www.visitmonaco .com**

---

## The Grimaldis

The Grimaldi family has ruled the independent principality of Monaco since the 14th century, making it the longest reigning dynasty in Europe. In its heyday, Monaco stretched from Menton to Antibes, living off taxes levied on the lemons and olives of Menton. When Menton was ceded to France in 1860, financial disaster loomed, but the reigning prince, Charles III, had the inspired idea of opening a casino (gaming rooms were banned in France at this time) on the hill, named Monte Carlo in his honor. New railroad connections along the coast helped attract a dazzling clientele, and the venture proved so lucrative that Charles was able to waive taxation for his subjects.

Thus has Monaco prospered and, along with it, the Grimaldi family. The right touch of glamour was added in 1956, when Prince Rainier III married American actress Grace Kelly. For years they were a fairy-tale couple, but since her death in a car accident in 1982, the family has been beset by problems: Princess Caroline's first husband was killed in a boat race, while Princess Stephanie was a source of scandal, leaving behind a trail of broken romances and abandoned careers. Prince Albert succeeded Rainier upon his death in 2005, with the apparent intention of making Monaco more democratic and financially accountable.

# Around St.-Paul de Vence

Set in the hills behind the Baie des Anges, St.-Paul de Vence is a perfectly preserved hill village, encircled by 16th-century ramparts, overlooking terra-cotta roofs, cypresses, and azure swimming pools. Though tiny, St.-Paul de Vence has gained an international reputation, thanks in large measure to the illustrious catalog of artists and writers who have lived and worked here. Today its galleries and restaurants attract thousands of visitors.

The cobbled streets and fountains of St.-Paul-de-Vence survive from medieval times.

**St.-Paul de Vence**
🅜 279 F3
**Visitor Information**
✉ Maison de la Tour, 2 rue Grande
☎ 04 93 32 86 95
**www.saint-paulde vence.com**

**Fondation Maeght**
✉ Montée des Trious
☎ 04 93 32 81 63
💲 $$
**www.fondation-maeght.com**

## St.-Paul de Vence

Entering the chic little village through the 13th-century gate, you follow Rue Grande past the fountain to the 12th-century Gothic church and the local history museum. The museum features photos of the celebrities who have visited St.-Paul: Simone de Beauvoir, Catherine Deneuve, F. Scott Fitzgerald, and many more.

But the village is famed for the **Fondation Maeght,** one of the world's most distinguished modern art museums, surrounded by a labyrinth of witty, colorful modern sculpture and tinkling fountains by Miró, Calder, and others. Attenuated Giacometti figures stroll across the courtyard, and the chapel is decorated by Braque. The founders, Aimé and Marguerite Maeght, commissioned the Spanish architect José-Luis Sert to design a building conceived in harmony with the works within, and the result is extremely impressive.

At the famous **Colombe d'Or** (see p. 373) hotel-restaurant, you can dine on the terrace surrounded by a priceless collection of art, including works by Picasso, Dufy, Modigliani, and a great many others, all donated by impecunious artists in exchange for their keep.

## Cagnes

The best part of nearby Cagnes is the original village of **Haut-de-Cagnes,** with its narrow medieval village streets and steep stairways, crowned by the 14th-century **Château Grimaldi** *(tel 04 92 02 47 30, closed Tues.).* Within its fortress walls is a spectacular Renaissance interior that now houses a museum devoted to the olive; a collection of modern Mediterranean

**INSIDER TIP:**

**A market town for centuries, Vence is the place to get picnic provisions. Do your shopping on Rue du Marché, a skinny street in the medieval part of town.**

—SHEILA BUCKMASTER
National Geographic Traveler
*magazine editor at large*

art with works by Matisse, Chagall, and more; and the Suzy Solidor collection: 40 portraits of the 1930s nightclub singer by artists including Cocteau, Dufy, and Tamara de Lempicka.

Renoir spent the last 20 years of his life in Cagnes, at the Maison Les Collettes, where the heat helped to ease the pain of his arthritis. The fine old house, set among the ancient olive trees

### A Haven for the Creative

**In a satisfying circular movement, the works of artists and writers that this region inspired now inform our image of it. Picasso's nymphs and sea urchins, Matisse's views of the sea, and Renoir's golden light and olive trees are constant presences. It was the intensity of the light that attracted the Impressionists. Now we see the luminous skies and seas through their eyes in galleries and museums amid the settings that inspired them.**

**Writers, too, have flocked here. Colette penned evocative portraits of Provençal life. Ford Madox Ford and Aldous Huxley worked here; and Katherine Mansfield and D. H. Lawrence died here. F. Scott Fitzgerald portrayed the beautiful people who partied here.**

that fascinated him, is now the **Musée Renoir,** with one studio preserved just as he left it, complete with palette and easel (at which he painted with the brush strapped to his hand when his fingers were too painful).

### Vence

The town of Vence perches high, surrounded by rose farms. Just outside is the remarkable **Chapelle du Rosaire** *(avenue Henri-Matisse, tel 04 93 58 03 26, closed Nov.),* decorated by Matisse at the end of his life when he, too, was afflicted by arthritis. In an otherwise all white interior, the pared-down monochrome drawings of the Stations of the Cross and the aqueous greens, blues, and yellows of the stained glass are a tribute to the artist's dedication. ■

**Cagnes**

⚠ 279 F3

**Visitor information**

✉ boulevard Maréchal Juin

☏ 04 93 20 61 64

**www.cagnes-tourisme.com**

**Musée Renoir (Maison Les Collettes)**

✉ 19 chemin des Collettes

☏ 04 93 20 61 07

🕐 Closed Tues.

💲 $

**Vence**

⚠ 279 F3

**Visitor information**

✉ place du Grand-Jardin

☏ 04 93 58 06 38

**www.ville-vence.fr**

# In & Around Grasse

Nestling in a cradle of hills behind Cannes lies the perfume capital of the world: charming, sleepy Grasse. The surrounding landscape is a fragrant sea of flowers: Golden mimosa clothes the hillsides in January and February, followed by summer roses and lavender and autumn jasmine, all heady with scent. The town itself is an intriguing warren of steep, arcaded streets, with Renaissance details betraying the influence of Italian merchants.

**Grasse**

🅰 279 F3

**Visitor information**

✉ 22 place du Cours Honoré-Cresp

☎ 04 93 36 66 66

www.grasse.fr

**Villa-Musée Fragonard**

✉ 23 boulevard Fragonard

☎ 04 93 36 01 61

🕐 Closed Tues. Oct.–May & all Nov.

💲 $

## Grasse

In the Middle Ages, tanning was the main industry here, but the 16th-century vogue for scented gloves sparked the perfume industry. By the 18th century, Grasse had become the world center of scent. Today every shop in Grasse seems to sell perfume and flower waters. The market in Place aux Aires sells dried flowers and herbs.

The Molinard and Fragonard perfume companies have museums and provide tours. The **Musée International de la Parfumerie** *(8 place du Cours, tel 04 97 05 58 00, $)* provides a splendid introduction to the art of perfumery, with a beautiful collection of bottles from all over the world and its own rooftop garden of fragrant plants.

The artist and engraver Jean-Honoré Fragonard (1732–1806) was born in Grasse. The **Villa-Musée Fragonard,** where he lived, contains some of his drawings and copies of wall panels. A rare religious work by him hangs in the **Cathédrale Notre-Dame-du-Puy** *(place du Petit-Puy),* started in the 12th century, as well as three works by Rubens and a 16th-century triptych by Bréa.

## Gourdon

To the north of Grasse, a wonderful drive past the rocky ravines and rushing waterfalls of the **Gorges du Loup** takes you up to Gourdon, one of the most spectacular *villages perchés* (hill villages) in the region. From the approach road, you can see the precipitous drop of several hundred feet below Gourdon's castle walls, and the view from the top is just as dramatic. The castle is perched right on the cliff edge with vertiginous views of the Loup valley. There are stunning gardens *(tel 04 93 09 68 02, April-Sept., www.chateau-gourdon .com).* The main terrace, la Terrasse d'Honneur, has 17th-century

Fragrant jasmine grows in abundance around Grasse.

## EXPERIENCE: The Perfumes of Provence

Can't get enough of the heady scents of Provence? Learn to make your own customized fragrance at the **Musée International de la Parfumerie** (see p. 292). Find out all about the music of perfume—the top note, the volatile smell you first notice that stays on the skin for 5 to 15 minutes; the flower-based "heart note" that stays for up to seven hours; and the base note, the strong heady smell of ambers, musks, patchoulis, and vanillas that remains for a few days.

A wonderful time to visit the region is during the local **flower harvests.** The jasmine festival in Grasse takes place in August, or head for the lavender festival in Dignes-les-Bains in July. In winter follow the **Mimosa Route,** from Bormes-les-Mimosas to Grasse, to enjoy the symbol of the Riviera in winter, golden flowers with a scent that seems impossibly exotic. It is recommended that you attempt the 81-mile (130 km) journey from January to March.

formal gardens designed by André Le Nôtre, with an herb garden around an ancient sundial, Italianate designs, and a rock garden of alpine plants.

### The Coast

The coast south of Grasse is first and foremost Picasso country. The artist spent much of his life in Juan-les-Pins, Antibes, and Cannes. He died in **Mougins,** now a chic hilltop village with splendid views and numerous art galleries. The **Musée de la Photographie** (67 rue de l'Église, tel 04 93 75 85 67) has a collection of photos of Picasso by Lartigue, Doisneau, and Villiers. Mougins is also a place for serious eating. Most serious of all is the **Moulin de Mougins** (see p. 371), a mill that has been transformed into a paradise of French gastronomy.

**Vallauris,** in the hinterland of Cannes, owes its fame to Picasso, who revived its fortunes as a pottery center by working in a ceramic studio there. The main street, Avenue Georges-Clemenceau, is packed with shops selling pottery. The Galerie Madoura (www.madoura.com), where Picasso worked, is still the place for high-quality pots at a price. In 1952, the artist painted the Romanesque chapel of the 16th-century Renaissance château with his tremendous "War and Peace" composition, and in the same year he gave the town his life-size bronze, "Man with Sheep," which stands in Place Paul-Isnard.

Just up the coast, the ancient village of **Biot** has a charming medieval quarter and a famous glass factory. The **Musée National Fernand-Léger** (chemin du Val-de-Pome, tel 04 92 91 50 20, closed Tues., www.musee-fernandleger.fr), just outside the village, houses Fernand-Léger's own collection in a custom-built museum, its exterior adorned with brilliant ceramic panels and mosaics. Kids will enjoy **Marineland** (Antibes, tel 04 93 33 49 49, $; www.marineland.fr), a huge watery theme park full of whales and dolphins. ∎

**Gourdon**
🅰 279 F3
**Visitor information**
✉ 24 rue de Majou
☎ 05 65 27 52 50
www.tourisme
-gourdon.com

**Mougins**
🅰 279 F3
**Visitor information**
✉ avenue Charles-Mallet
☎ 04 93 75 87 67

**Vallauris**
🅰 279 F3
**Visitor information**
✉ square du 8 mai 1945
☎ 04 93 63 82 58

**Biot**
🅰 279 F3
**Visitor information**
✉ 46 rue St.-Sebastian
☎ 04 93 65 78 00
www.biot.fr

# Antibes

Cap d'Antibes remains one of the truly exclusive hideaways of the Côte d'Azur, its exotic belle-epoque and modernist villas and fabulous hotels discreetly veiled by dense vegetation, through which paths lead to private beaches. But the public beaches here, though mostly rocky, are unspoiled; try Plage de la Sales, on the eastern shore, or tiny Plage de la Garoupe. Antibes itself is an ancient town facing Nice across the Baie des Anges.

The city of Antibes graces the French Riviera.

the works are beautifully displayed in the lustrous sea light pouring in through the windows. Paintings by Nicolas de Staël are also on show, along with works by artists of the school of Nice. The terrace garden provides the perfect setting for sculptures silhouetted against the sea.

The **Musée d'Histoire et d'Archéologie,** farther along the ramparts, presents Greek, Roman, and other finds in two huge barrel-vaulted chambers.

**Antibes**
- 🅰 279 F3

**Visitor information**
- ✉ 11 place du Général de Gaulle
- ☎ 04 97 23 11 11

**www.antibes-juan lespins.com**

**Musée Picasso/ Château Grimaldi**
- ✉ place Mariejol
- ☎ 04 92 90 54 20
- 🕐 Closed Mon.
- 💲 $$

**Musée d'Histoire et d'Archéologie**
- ✉ Bastion St-André, avenue Adm. de Grasse
- ☎ 04 92 90 54 35
- 🕐 Closed Mon. & Nov.
- 💲 $

A Greek settlement (Antipolis) that later became a frontier town (neighboring Nice was in Savoie), Antibes had its fortress and port reconstructed by Vauban in the 17th century. Above the harbor is the old town, a maze of narrow streets with one of the region's best markets every morning (and a great flea market twice a week).

On the ramparts, overlooking the sea, looms the 16th-century **Château Grimaldi.** Here, Picasso was given a studio after World War II, and in gratitude he gave the town paintings, drawings, and ceramics of the period, including "La Joie de Vivre," "Night Fishing at Antibes," and the "Antipolis Suite." The château is now the revamped **Musée Picasso,** and

**INSIDER TIP:**

**Head to La Garoupe beach, a small enclave outside Antibes where the likes of Picasso and F. Scott Fitzgerald frolicked in the 1920s.**

—SYLVIE BIGAR
*National Geographic Traveler*
magazine writer

By day, **Juan-les-Pins** (*visitor information, tel 04 97 23 11 10*), west of Antibes, seems much like other resorts along the coast, but by night it comes alive, and the July jazz festival under the eponymous pines is hard to beat. ■

# Cannes

A perfect Riviera base and one of southern France's most glamorous cities, Cannes is big enough to have all the grand hotels, restaurants, beaches, and shopping you could ever want, and small enough to walk around. It also offers easy access to inland beauty spots such as Grasse and Mougins.

In 1834, when Cannes was just a fishing village, the former British lord chancellor, Lord Brougham, was on his way to Nice when he was held up here by a cholera scare. Falling in love with the place, he built a summer villa; other foreigners soon followed, and Cannes blossomed.

Now Cannes is best known for the International Film Festival held every May. The action centers on **La Croisette,** lined with palm trees, grand boutiques, and world-famous hotels such as the Carlton (see p. 370). The Carlton terrace is the place favored by movie moguls for cocktails during the film festival.

The beach is wide, sandy, and mostly private: Cannes is chic and expensive and determined to stay that way. To the west of the new **Palais des Festivals,** the main venue for the film festival, lies the yacht-filled harbor of the old port, also the scene of the morning flower market. The covered **Marché de Forville,** two blocks inland, offers a mouthwatering array of all the local delicacies.

From the market, little lanes lead up to the old town of **Le Suquet,** a charming alternative to the ostentatious pleasures of the seafront, with lots of restaurants to choose from. If you climb as far as the 11th-century **Tour du Mont Chevalier,** you will be rewarded by a splendid view along the coast. Above Cannes the immodestly named and exclusive **Corniche du Paradis Terrestre** also offers spectacular views, particularly of the Bastille Day (July 14) fireworks.

## Cannes

🗺 279 F3

**Visitor information**

✉ Palais des Festivals

☎ 04 92 99 84 22

**www.cannes.fr**

---

### EXPERIENCE:
## Grape Harvesting

While in southern France, consider taking part in the grape harvest at **Château de Berne** (tel 04 94 60 48 88, www.chateau berne.com), a 1,360-acre (550 ha) estate west of Cannes. The 18th-century château has a tour-star hotel, as well as a food and wine school. Help pick grapes and learn about cultivating vines and making wine.

---

From Cannes you can take a boat (tel 04 93 38 66 33 or 04 92 98 71 36, $$$$$) to the peaceful **Îles de Lérins,** visible across the bay. The monastery on St.-Honorat once controlled much of the coast; now the monks cultivate lavender and grapes, and the simplicity of their lives is in startling contrast with that on the worldly shores opposite. The island of Ste.-Marguerite is still forested. In the 17th century, the prison here held the Man in the Iron Mask. ∎

# St.-Tropez

Until fairly recent times just a tiny fishing village more easily reached by sea than land, St.-Tropez has become one of the hot spots for which the Côte d'Azur is famous.

**St.-Tropez**
🅐 279 F2
**Visitor information**
✉ quai Jean-Jaurès, avenue Général de Gaulle
☎ 04 94 97 45 21
**www.ot-saint-tropez.com**

**Musée de l'Annonciade**
✉ quai St.-Raphael
☎ 04 94 17 84 10
🕐 Closed Tues.
💲 $

Guy de Maupassant moved here in the 1880s, followed soon after by painter Paul Signac, whose villa became a haven for artists. Another bohemian influx came in the 1930s, led by Jean Cocteau and Colette. And, in the 1950s, Brigitte Bardot (see sidebar below) arrived as the ultimate crowd puller. Now celebrities moor their yachts or have villas here, attracting hordes of visitors. Rich bohemians rent restored village houses on the surrounding hills and spend their days on **Plage de Pampelonne** (the hippest by far) and other inviting beaches.

And yet the little town remains charming: Visit the market on Place des Lices in the morning, and in the evening head for the cafés around the harbor. The 16th-century citadel offers evocative views. The same panoramas translated into paint are on view in the **Musée de l'Annonciade.** The old chapel of the Annunciation now

**INSIDER TIP:**

**Summer remains the peak season for celebrity-spotting on St.-Tropez's ever trendy Pampelonne beach.**

—KRISTEN GUNDERSON
*National Geographic researcher*

houses the art collection given to St.-Tropez by Georges Grammont. Excellent examples of Postimpressionism include works by Derain, Signac, Seurat, Dufy, and Braque, many of whom were pilgrims to the quiet of old St.-Tropez.

At the eastern end of town, above the harbor, the **citadel** *(rue de la Citadelle)* guarded the town. The hexagonal keep, built in the 16th century, has three towers and ramparts giving views out to sea. Inside is a maritime museum, a branch of that in the Palais de Chaillot in Paris (see p. 94). ∎

## Brigitte Bardot

In 1956, movie director Roger Vadim and a film crew burst into St.-Tropez to make a film starring his little-known actress wife. The film was *Et Dieu Créa la Femme (And God Created Woman)*, the actress was Brigitte Bardot, and St.-Tropez never looked back.

The daughter of bourgeois Parisian parents, Bardot had been working as a model when she met Vadim at the age of 15. The nudity and love scenes in *And*

*God Created Woman* caused a scandal, and the film was a huge success. B.B. shot to stardom, and her sun-kissed, barefoot, *femme-enfant* brand of sexuality made her an icon for a whole generation.

Bardot still lives in her villa outside St.-Tropez. But after three marriages and many love affairs, she has turned her attention to animals and devotes herself to animal rights causes.

# Hyères & Îles d'Hyères

The most venerable and southerly of the Côte d'Azur's resorts is dignified and old-fashioned Hyères. In the 19th century, it was a favorite wintering place for Empress Eugénie, Queen Victoria, Robert Louis Stevenson, Edith Wharton, and members of the British aristocracy in search of health cures. But it never attracted the crowds that flocked to Nice and Cannes.

## Hyères

Despite wholesale development of its coastal suburbs, Hyères, with miles of sandy beach, has kept its slightly faded charm and is much in demand as a film set for belle epoque dramas.

Palm trees and Moorish architecture impart an exotic quality on the broad 19th-century boulevards. Through a medieval gatehouse is the old town, with streets climbing the slopes of Casteau hill, lovely gardens, and sea views. The 12th-century **Tour St.-Blaise** and **Église de St.-Paul** hint at Hyères's former status.

**INSIDER TIP:**

**Rent a bicycle on the island of Porquerolles and pedal to the north coast for magnificent views of the Mediterranean Sea.**

—ASHLEY THOMPSON
*Former National Geographic researcher*

## Îles d'Hyères

The three exotically beautiful Îles d'Hyères, former haunt of pirates and now partly given over to the French armed forces, are remarkable, unspoiled, protected environments. Cars

The picturesque port of Île de Port-Cros is dotted with palms.

are restricted, so the islands are ideal for bathing and gentle walks among the scented *maquis*.

On **Porquerolles,** the largest island, you can explore the rocky creeks of the north coast (not safe for swimming) and the sandy coves of the south. Watered with natural springs and rich in flora and fauna, **Port-Cros,** a national park since 1963, is strictly protected. Offshore is a marine nature reserve: From the beach at La Palud, you can dive along an underwater trail to see a fantastic range of sea creatures, including sponges, sea urchins, octopuses, and moray eels. And for real nature lovers, the **Île du Levant** contains the world's oldest nudist colony, Héliopolis. ∎

### Hyères
▲ 279 F2
**Visitor information**
✉ avenue de Belgique
☎ 04 94 01 84 50
**www.hyeres-tourisme.com**

**FERRIES**
Ferries to the Îles d'Hyères run from Hyères harbor (90 minutes, tel 04 94 58 21 81); from Le Lavandou (35 minutes, Gare Maritime, tel 04 94 71 01 02); and from Cavalaire-sur-Mer (45 minutes, tel 04 94 64 08 04). Round-trip fare: $$$$

# Marseille

France's oldest and largest port is tough, raffish, cosmopolitan, and now undergoing a cultural renaissance. Founded by the Greeks in the seventh century B.C, it remained independent of France until the 15th century, after which it made a specialty of its own Mediterranean brand of turbulence. The revolutionary hymn "The Marseillaise" owes its name to the fervor of the Marseillais rebels.

After centuries of grittiness, Marseille's Vieux Port (Old Port) sparkles with economic renewal.

La Vieille Charité, which now houses the **Musée d'Archéologie Méditerranéenne.** Nearby, the 19th-century **Cathédrale de la Major** *(esplanade de la Tourette)* dwarfs the 12th-century **Ancienne Major,** the original cathedral that was partially destroyed to make space for the new one. The **Musée des Docks Romains** displays Roman finds.

**INSIDER TIP:**

**Between Marseille and Cassis lie the *calanques*, a nature preserve of fjordlike inlets and azure waters loved by the locals. Everyone, it seems, has a favorite calanque.**

—TOM MUELLER
National Geographic Traveler
*magazine writer*

**Marseille**
⚠ 279 E2
**Visitor information**
✉ 4 La Canebière
☎ 04 91 13 89 00
www.marseille-tourisme.com

**Musée d'Archéologie Méditerranéenne**
✉ 2 rue de la Charité
☎ 04 91 14 58 58
⊕ Closed Mon.

**Musée des Docks Romains**
✉ place Vivaux
☎ 04 91 91 24 62
⊕ Closed Mon.
💲 $

France's gateway to the Middle East and North Africa, Marseille has always ben a cultural melting pot. While their ships moored in the harbor, Western magnates and Eastern potentates once met along **La Canebière,** a bustling, slightly run-down thoroughfare.The **Vieux Port** remains the city's focus, its old forts now overlooking a fish market and some superb seafood restaurants.

To the north of the port, the old quarter of Le Panier was largely dynamited by the Germans during World War II. A few historic buildings remain, including the 17th-century hospice of

East of the port, the 19th-century Palais de Longchamp now houses the **Musée des Beaux-Arts** *(blvd. Longchamp, currently closed for renovations).* To the south stands the fifth-century foundation of the **Basilique St.-Victor** *(quai de Rive Neuve).* Nearby is

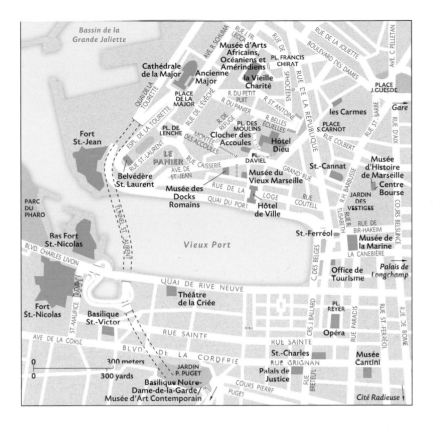

the dominating 19th-century **Basilique Notre-Dame-de-la-Garde** (parvis de la Basilique de Notre-Dame de la Garde).

The city's commitment to modern architecture is evident in Will Alsop's **Hôtel du Département** and in Le Corbusier's **Cité Radieuse** near the **Musée Cantini,** a modern art gallery. The **Musée d'Art Contemporain,** in a 17th-century mansion, has a good collection of modern art.

Marseille's corniche, Boulevard J. F. Kennedy, offers views to the island prison of **Château d'If** and paths to the Malmousque

promontory. At the end is the city's main beach, **Plage du Prado**

Eastward toward **Cassis,** inlets in white cliffs, called calanques, are now protected Their beaches are accessible only by scrambling down the cliffs. Cassis has good fish restaurants around its harbor. To the west, lie the calanques and villages of the **Côte Bleue.**

Named European Capital of Culture for 2013, Marseille has set its sights on comprehensive urban revitalization. The EuroMéditerranée (www.euromediterranee.fr) urban renewal and development project is already transforming a large area along the coast. ∎

**Musée Cantini**
- ✉ 19 rue Grignan
- ☎ 04 91 54 77 75
- 🕒 Closed Mon.

**Musée d'Art Contemporain**
- ✉ 69 avenue d'Haifa
- ☎ 04 91 25 01 07
- 🕒 Closed Mon.

**Cassis**
- 🅰 279 E2
- **Visitor information**
- ✉ quai des Moulins
- ☎ 08 92 25 98 92
- **www.ot-cassis.com**

# More Places to Visit in the Côte d'Azur

## Esterel Massif

The Esterel Massif boasts a rare stretch of unspoiled coastline in the Côte d'Azur, a landscape of jagged cliffs and forested ravines. A spectacular corniche winds through pine forests, past porphyry cliffs and aquamarine *calanques*. Stop at **Pointe de l'Esquillon** for a grand view of the Mediterranean, the Esterel Massif, and the cliffs of Cap Roux. From **Agay** *(visitor information, place Gianetti, tel 04 94 82 01 85; www.agay.fr)*, in its beautiful bay, you can walk across the Cap du Dramont to Le Dramont, where American troops established a beachhead in 1944.
🅰 279 F3

## Fréjus

A Roman port (Forum Julii) founded by Julius Caesar, Fréjus is particularly rich in Roman and medieval remains. Though the port has silted up, a sizable amphitheater remains, along with parts of an aqueduct, a gateway, and a theater. Highlights of the medieval **Cité Épiscopale** include the Gothic and Renaissance cathedral with its elegant cloister, the 14th-century bishops' palace, and one of the oldest baptisteries in France, probably fifth century—an octagon of Corinthian columns pilfered from the forum.
*www.frejus.fr* 🅰 279 F3  **Visitor Information** ✉ 325 rue de Jean-Jaurès ☎ 04 94 51 83 83

## Port-Grimaud

Port-Grimaud *(www.grimaud-provence .com)*, across the bay from St.-Tropez, is an intriguing 1960s precursor of the return of vernacular architecture—a clever pastiche of a Provençal fishing village, built by architect François Spoerry in 1968. The Venetian-style lagoon village has matured well to resemble a genuine ancient village.
🅰 279 F2

## Toulon

The great naval port of Toulon lies on a deep natural harbor. The harborside **Quai de Stalingrad,** rebuilt after the war, is now lined with shops and cafés. To the north is the old town, a picturesque jumble of buildings, including the 11th-century **Cathédrale Ste.-Marie-Majeure,** remodeled in the 17th century. The **Musée National de la Marine** *(place Monsenergue, tel 04 94 02 02 01; www .musee-marine.fr)* presents the city's long and eventful maritime history. *www.toulontour isme.com* 🅰 279 E2  **Visitor information** ✉ 334 avenue de la République ☎ 04 94 18 53 00

## Protecting the Mediterranean

According to the first census of marine life published in 2010, the Mediterranean is the "world's most threatened sea," seriously at risk from over-fishing, as well as the pressure of increasing human population and pollution. Great efforts are being made to protect the Mediterranean, including the establishment of marine protected areas. The French Mediterranean coast now has several protected marine parks: **Parc National de Port-Cros** (*www.portcrosparcnational .fr*), along the coast of Hyères and the Île de Porquerolles; the **Banyuls marine reserve;** the *calanques* near Marseille; and the **Réserve Naturelle de Scandola** in Corsica. The Blue Flag classification of beaches, a measure of environmental quality, was originally conceived in France as le Pavillon Bleu. According to the most recent assessment, the Mediterranean coast has 178 Blue Flag beaches.

# Provence

Land of lavender fields and olive groves, scented hillsides and fertile valleys, dazzling colors and limpid light, Provence is lauded for all its ravishing natural gifts. Only the maddening winter Mistral wind blights this garden of Eden: To withstand it, the traditional blue-shuttered farmhouses (mas) are built without windows in their north-facing walls.

Sunshine filled Provence's tiny patches of farmland are a Roman legacy.

Provence was colonized by the Greeks before the Romans called it Provincia and left behind great amphitheaters and monuments at Arles and Orange, among the finest in France. Medieval popes based themselves in Avignon, where the Palais des Papes remains, a testament to their power. Great Cistercian abbeys bear witness to the less worldly side of medieval Christianity. The strong regional identity is evident in the cosmopolitan city of Aix-en-Provence, with its long literary and cultural history, and in Arles, home to proud Provençal folklore.

The region's natural wonders range from the Gorges du Verdon to the mysterious Fontaine de Vaucluse. Mont Ventoux is the highest point of the region; its most distinctive part is the wide expanse of the Camargue.

Perhaps most delightful of all are the simple pleasures: a quiet pastis on a café terrace, a game of boules in a village square, produce-laden market stalls, local lavender and honey, and traditional Provençal fabrics. And no aspect of Provence is more evocative than the unspoiled villages perchés (hill villages) of areas such as the Lubéron. For a perfect day, you can explore one of these ancient terra-cotta-roofed villages, visit an art gallery, and stroll past fields of wildflowers or aromatic herbs.

In this land of sensual delights, fine restaurants abound. But a picnic is a perfect way to savor the fragrant melons, peaches, and cherries, the goat's cheeses, and the tomatoes and olives that are found here. Or simply take a nap in the shade of an olive tree and enjoy la vie en plein air. You will want to stay forever. ■

# Avignon

Secure within its great walls, Avignon retains the grand self-assurance of its 14th-century heyday, when a series of popes lived here. Then the narrow streets teemed with the comings and goings of the papal court. These days the city is a thriving cultural center, animated every summer by its music and drama festival, when palace courtyards and grand mansions serve as backdrops for the events. The focus at festival time is the Place de l'Horloge, with its Gothic clock tower and lively cafés.

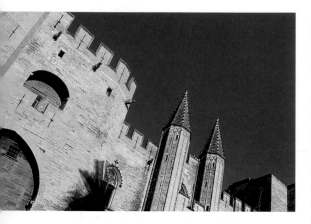

The Palais des Papes in Avignon, early papal center of power

**Avignon**

🅰 279 D3

**Visitor Information**

✉ 41 cours Jean-Jaurès

☎ 04 32 74 32 74

www.avignon
-tourisme.com

**Palais des Papes**

✉ place du Palais

☎ 04 90 27 50 00

www.palais-des-papes.
com

**Musée Calvet**

✉ 65 rue Joseph-Vernant

☎ 04 90 86 33 84

🕐 Closed Tues.

www.musee-calvet.org

The coldly magnificent **Palais des Papes** dominates the historic city. Actually two palaces, begun in 1334, most of the interior of this great white edifice is empty after the depredations of the Revolution, but six magnificent Gobelins tapestries and remarkable frescoes by Matteo Giovanetti reflect its former glory. The Chambre du Cerf, study of Clement VI, has beautiful ceramic tiles and frescoes.

The lovely 14th-century **Petit Palais** *(tel 04 90 86 44 58, closed Tues.)* opposite contains distinguished medieval painting and sculpture—an impressive introduction to the International Gothic style pioneered in Avignon

by 14th-century Italian artists. Treats here include works by Simone Martine and a Botticelli "Madonna and Child."

Next to the palace stands the **Cathédrale Notre-Dame-des-Doms** and, behind it, the lovely park of the **Rocher des Doms.** Below are the Rhône River and the celebrated remains of the Pont St.-Bénézet, usually known as the **Pont d'Avignon.** Sadly truncated, the 12th-century bridge was partly swept away by the Rhône in the 17th century. Only four spans of the original 22 remain.

To the south are the narrow streets of the old town, one of the prettiest of which is **Rue des Teinturiers,** beside the Sorgue River. Here, until the 19th century, dyers produced the Provençal patterned cottons known as Indiennes, inspired by Indian calicos brought back from the Crusades. Museums here include the eclectic **Musée Calvet;** the **Fondation Angladon-Dubruje-aud** *(rue Laboureur, tel 04 90 82 29 03),* with the only van Gogh painting still in Provence, "Les Wagons de Chemin de Fer"; and the contemporary art of the **Collection Lambert** *(rue Violette, tel 04 90 16 56 21; www.collectionlambert.com).* ∎

# In & Around Orange

Visit Orange for its magnificent Roman heritage: Its triumphal arch and theater are among the best Roman remains in the world. Lying in the Rhône Valley on the Roman Via Agrippa, Orange was (and still is) the gateway between north and south. Under the emperor Augustus it was a thriving city, some three times its present size, with temples, baths, and a stadium, as well as other grand buildings. In the 16th century, Orange was inherited by William, Prince of Nassau, ancestor of the Dutch royal family.

## Orange

Visitors to Orange still enter the city from the north through the Roman-era **triumphal arch,** now beautifully restored. Built about 20 B.C. to commemorate Julius Caesar's victory over the Greeks at Massina (Marseille), this monumental masterpiece is encrusted with intricately carved battle scenes.

**INSIDER TIP:**

**Don't miss the small Musée d'Art et d'Histoire d'Orange, across the street from the ancient Roman theater, with artifacts tracing Roman culture.**

—BARBARA NOE
*National Geographic Books editor*

The arch is dwarfed by the **Théâtre Antique.** The most complete surviving example of a Roman theater anywhere, the Théâtre Antique still has most of its original seating (for 8,000), some of its columns and arches, and its tremendous stage wall, dwarfing a huge statue of

Emperor Augustus. The acoustics here are perfect, and the theater provides a superb setting for a music festival each July, with concerts and opera on offer. It now has a new discreet glass-and-steel roof.

To the south is **Châteauneuf-du-Pape,** planted by the popes and the most distinguished of the Côtes du Rhône vineyards.

### Vaison-la-Romaine

Northeast of Orange is Vaison-la-Romaine, an attractive town with a venerable history. Excavations revealed sections of a Roman city *(Fouilles de Puymin, place du Chanoine-Sautel, tel 04 90 36 50 48, closed Jan.–Feb.),* complete with a basilica, baths, and a theater, now the venue for a music festival each July. The excellent **archaeological museum** on the site has a number of finds, notably an exquisite peacock mosaic.

Over the river, across a Roman bridge, is the **Haute Ville;** little cobbled streets twist through a clutch of restored 14th-century houses before rising up to the ruins of the town's château. The Romanesque cathedral has a 6th-century apse and marble altar, and a 12th-century cloister with wonderful carvings. ∎

**Orange**
 279 D4
**Visitor information**
✉ 5 cours Aristide-Briand
☎ 04 90 34 70 88
www.otorange.fr

**Théâtre Antique**
✉ place des Frères-Mounet
☎ 04 90 51 17 60
💲 $

**Châteauneuf-du-Pape**
279 D3
**Visitor information**
✉ place du Portail
☎ 04 90 83 71 08

**Vaison-la-Romaine**
279 D4
**Visitor information**
✉ place du Chanoine-Sautel
☎ 04 90 36 02 11
🕐 Closed Sun.

*"As if in answer to the insistent call of far-off Roman trumpets, I set out one early Autumn for Provence."*

—Augustus John
(1878–1961)

# Around the Lubéron

The ridge of hills from Manosque to Cavaillon, and the valleys on either side, form the Lubéron. A tour of this haven of lavender fields, vineyards, and orchards might offer any number of *villages perchés,* majestic mountain views, and fine walking.

Gordes might well be the most beautiful town in Provence.

**Apt**

🏔 279 E3

**Visitor information**

✉ 20 avenue Philippe-de-Girard

☎ 04 90 74 03 18

**Maison du Parc Naturel Régional de Lubéron, Apt**

☎ 04 90 04 42 00

**Roussillon**

🏔 279 E3

**Visitor information**

✉ place de la Poste

☎ 04 90 05 60 25

**Gordes**

🏔 279 E3

**Visitor information**

✉ place du Château

☎ 04 90 72 02 75

In the north of the region, steep ravines split the hills of the Lubéron massif, most of which lies in the Vaucluse *département,* and oaks grow down into the valleys. To the south, more fertile land slopes to the Durance River. The Grand Lubéron in the east has been designated a *parc naturel régional,* its headquarters in the little town of **Apt.**

The **Maison du Parc** in Apt has videos and information about local walks, wildlife, and vegetation. The town's main square offers *boules* and fountains in the shade of linden trees. The 11th-century **Cathédrale Ste.-Anne** *(rue Ste.Anne, 04 90 04 61 71)* shelters the saint's shroud, and a small archaeological museum documents the town's Roman past. Apt's Saturday market is a lively affair with specialties of local crystallized fruits, lavender oil, and handsome pottery.

Southeast of Apt, a strenuous walk from Auribeau leads up to the **Mourre Nègre,** the highest peak of the Montagne du Lubéron, with fine views available in all directions.

Before the days of synthetic dyes, ocher quarrying was a major industry in the Lubéron. North of the Mourre Nègre are the abandoned quarries of the **Colorado de Rustrel,** a towering landscape in every shade of red and orange.

The walls and archways of the pretty village of **Roussillon,** just northwest of Apt, range from brick red through rose to crimson. The **Falaises du Sang** (Cliffs of Blood) outside the village are spectacular in the setting sun.

Beyond the Vaucluse plateau to the north looms the great summit of **Mont Ventoux,** more than 6,000 feet (1,900 m) high. The walk to the top (from Brantes, Malaucène, or Bédoin) is a breezy but fabulous climb; it is also possible to drive, or even cycle (the Tour de France has included the peak on its route).

The western Lubéron—the Petit Lubéron—is studded with delightful villages. Tiny **Bonnieux** *(visitor information, place Carnot, tel 04 90 75 91 90)* clings to a hilltop, offering a glorious view of the valley, and the **Musée de la Boulangerie,** a bread museum *(tel 04 90 75 88 34, closed Tues. & Nov.–March).* **Oppède-le-Vieux** has a ruined castle, and **Ménerbes** starred in British writer Peter Mayle's *A Year in Provence*. The picturesque village of **Gordes** clusters below its splendid 16th-century château, which displays contemporary art. The nearby **Village des Bories** is a collection of ancient dwellings, some of which were inhabited into the 20th century. Just north of Gordes is the Cistercian **Abbaye de Sénanque,** the pale stones of its chapel and cloister contrasting beautifully with the surrounding lavender.

    **Fontaine-de-Vaucluse** sits along a gorge, at the foot of which lies the Sorgue River's source. In winter and spring, an underground torrent erupts into a deep, dark green pool. It was here that Petrarch composed many of his sonnets to Laura. The **Musée Pétrarque** displays editions of his poems illustrated by Picasso, Miró, and others. The **Moulin à Papier Vallis Clausa** *(04 90 20 34 14)* has made paper here since the 16th century. ■

### Abbaye de Sénanque

☎ 04 90 72 05 72

🕑 Guided visits only; reservations recommended

💲 $

### Fontaine-de-Vaucluse

🗺 279 D3

**Visitor information**

✉ chemin de la Fontaine

☎ 04 90 20 32 22

### Musée Pétrarque

✉ rive gauche de la Sorguem, Fontaine-de-Vaucluse

☎ 04 90 20 37 20

🕑 Closed Tues.

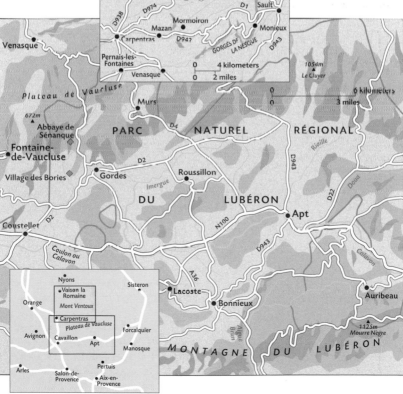

# Arles

Climb to the top tier of the Roman arena for the best view of Arles, south of the Lubéron, looking across the terra-cotta roofs and ocher walls to the Rhône River.

The Roman arena in Arles illuminated at night spotlights ancient majesty.

**Arles**

🗺 279 D3

**Visitor information**

✉ boulevard des Lices

☎ 04 90 18 41 20

**www.arlestourisme .com**

**Arènes Romaines**

✉ Rond-point des Arènes

☎ 04 90 49 78 66

💲 $

**Musée de l'Arles Antique**

✉ Presqu'île du cirque Romain

☎ 04 90 18 88 88

🕓 Closed Tues.

💲 $

**www.arles-antique .cg13.fr**

Enough remains of this great Roman city to convey a powerful sense of history. Now used for bullfights and festival pageants, the vast first-century **Arènes Romaines** was once the scene of gladiatorial combat. Measuring 446 feet by 351 feet (136 m by 107 m) with two stories each made up of 60 arches, it could seat 25,000 spectators. As you walk around the lower arcade of the arena, look for the tunnels through which wild beasts charged into the arena.

Nearby is the slightly earlier Roman theater. The two great columns of the stage wall (formerly used to hang prisoners) today provide a backdrop for performances during the Arles Festival in late June and early July.

The town's Roman remains are rivaled by its medieval buildings, notably the **Église St.-Trophime** (*place de la République*). A masterpiece of Provençal Romanesque, this cathedral is famed for its glorious cloister and an elaborately carved 12th-century portal.

Not content with being, in Chateaubriand's words, a great "open-air museum," Arles has a number of exceptional indoor museums. The mpressive **Musée de l'Arles Antique** on the riverbank covers the city's Roman history. The **Museon Arlaten** is devoted to Provençal folklore, crafts, and costumes, while the excellent **Musée Réattu** includes 57 Picasso drawings donated by the artist, who reveled in

**INSIDER TIP:**

Fans of van Gogh: Follow the art trail around town with panels of his most famous artworks set up on the precise spots where he painted them.

—BARBARA NOE
*National Geographic Books editor*

the bullfights staged in Arles.

But the artist most closely associated with Arles is without doubt Vincent van Gogh. It was in Arles that he fell in love with the south and its brilliant colors; here in 1888 that he painted some of his best known works, including "Sunflowers" and "Chair"; and here that shortly afterward he sliced off his ear in a fit of dementia. The **Fondation Vincent van Gogh** makes up for its lack of original van Gogh works with paintings inspired by him. The **Espace van Gogh** *(place Docteur Felix Rey),* once the hospital where the artist was committed, is now an exhibition space and library with a garden planted to look like a van Gogh painting.

Arles today comes alive with a variety of festivals, including the Fête St.-Jean on June 24 and the Easter bullfights, when Arlésiens emerge wearing full costume, the men in cowboy outfits, the women in intricate lace headdresses and gorgeous embroidered shawls. Arles also hosts an important annual photography festival, Les Rencontre des Arles.

Just outside Arles, the ancient burial ground of **Les Alyscamps** *(tel 04 90 49 36 74),* painted by van Gogh, is a serene avenue of tombs and sarcophagi. ■

**Museon Arlaten**
- ⊠ 29 rue de la République
- ☎ 04 90 96 08 23
- ⊕ Closed for renovation until 2013
- 💲 $
- www.museonarlaten.fr

**Musée Réattu**
- ⊠ 10 rue du Grand Prieuré
- ☎ 04 90 49 37 58
- 💲 $
- www.museereattu.arles.fr

**Fondation Vincent van Gogh**
- ⊠ 24 rond-point des Arènes
- ☎ 04 90 49 94 04

---

# EXPERIENCE: Bullfighting—Choose Your Style

Although bullfighting is held in high regard in southern France, its pros and cons are passionately debated. Animal rights activists are pitted against aficionados who consider bullfighting a noble art form. In fact, there are two styles of bullfight.

In the Spanish *corrida,* which you can seen at the Roman arena in Nîmes *(www.aenesdeimes.com, see sidebar p.317)* the bull is killed after much fanfare. Best time to be there is in May, for the Feria festival.

More preferable perhaps is the Course Camarguaise, which you can see in Arles *(www.arenes-arles.com).* Go in July for the Cocade d'Or festival. This style of bullfighting is more sport than ritual, and the bull is more equally matched with his human opponents. Here the bull is not killed but spends only 15 minutes in the arena, where it is chased by the *raseteurs,* who gesture and run across the arena to attract the bull. Using a *crochet,* or metal comb, they try to snatch the *cocarde* and *ficelles* (rosette and tassels) attached to the bull's head. The bull chases the raseteur, who escapes behind the barrier, often just in the nick of time. The raseteurs are awarded points for their skill and courage; the bulls are applauded as they leave the ring and honored with statues in their memory.

# The Camargue

Eerily beautiful, this vast wetland area formed by the Rhône delta is a world of infinite horizons, swaying grasses, and blue lagoons, all suffused with an extraordinary light.

The *roussataio*—the releasing of horses and mares into the city streets—is a Camargue tradition.

The Camargue's unique ecology includes abundant wildlife, most notably flamboyant flocks of flamingos. The glittering salt flats yield vast amounts of salt, and a tasty variety of rice grows here. The pastures are grazed by native white horses, ridden by the Camarguais herdsmen known as *gardians*. These hardy people cling passionately to their traditional way of life, herding their small black bulls destined for the arenas of Nîmes or Arles. The gardians still live in the low white cabins integral to the Camargue landscape.

The history and traditions of this extraordinary wilderness, now protected as a *parc régional,* are traced at the **Musée Camarguais** *(Mas du Pont de Rousty, tel 04 90 97 10 82, closed Tues. & Oct.–March),* the park's main center. Located southwest of Arles on the D570, the museum explores different aspects of local life: agriculture, fishing, breeding stock, and domestic activities. It also has information on walking and riding, and on ranches converted into hotels and restaurants.

## Stes.-Maries-de-la-Mer

Stes.-Maries-de-la-Mer nestles cozily around its vast fortified church (climb up to the roof for excellent views) and is now surrounded by stores bursting with all things Provençal. The

**INSIDER TIP:**

The local *fleur de sel de Camargue*—gourmet sea salt with just a hint of violets—makes an excellent gift for friends back home.

—BARBARA NOE
*National Geographic Books editor*

**Musée Baroncelli** *(rue Victor-Hugo, tel 04 90 97 87 60, closed Tues.)*, housed in the old town hall, has fascinating displays on Camargue traditions.

In a tradition dating back to the 16th century, every year on May 24 and 25, gypsy pilgrims flock to the town to take part in a procession carrying the statue of St. Sarah, patron saint of gypsies, to the sea to be blessed. During the festival, the streets throb with flamenco, horse races, and a kaleidoscope of costumes. Carmaguais

dishes available in the restaurants here include *boeuf gardian*, a rich stew of bull's meat, best enjoyed with nutty Camargue rice.

## St.-Gilles-du-Gard

To the north lies St.-Gilles-du-Gard, dubbed the "Gateway to the Camargue," a tiny village dominated by a church. Statues of the saints crowd around the three beautifully carved 12th-century portals, and a spiral staircase winds up its bell tower.

## Aigues-Mortes

The far western edge of the Camargue is guarded by the haunting medieval walled town of Aigues-Mortes (Place of the Dead Waters). Once an important port, it is now silted up and marooned 3 miles (5 km) from the sea. The town walls, accessed via the **Musée Archéologique** *(tel 04 66 53 61 55)*, offer the best views. ■

**Stes.-Maries-de-la-Mer**
🅰 279 D3
**Visitor information**
✉ 5 avenue Van Gogh
☎ 04 90 97 82 55
www.saintesmaries
.com

**St.-Gilles-du-Gard**
🅰 279 D3
**Visitor information**
✉ place Mistral
☎ 04 66 87 33 75
http://ot-saint
-gilles.pagesper
so-orange.fr

**Aigues-Mortes**
🅰 279 D3
**Visitor information**
✉ place St.-Louis
☎ 04 66 53 73 00
www.ot-aigues
mortes.fr

## Nature Reserve

One of Europe's major wetlands, the Camargue is an important haven for a wide variety of animals, grasses, and flowers, which thrive in its huge flat marshlands dotted with shallow saltwater lagoons *(étangs)*. The great central **Étang de Vaccarès**, covering 16,000 acres (6,500 ha), has been designated a zoological and botanical reserve. Access is severely restricted (this is, for example, the only breeding site in France for the slender-billed gull and the red-crested pochard). A walk along the **Digue de la Mer** from Stes.-Maries-de-la-Mer provides good views of the reserve, and various points on the D37 and C134

may offer sightings of herring gulls and black-headed gulls, herons, avocets, egrets, and—most memorable of all—the famous flamingos (their distinctive pink color comes from the tiny crustaceans on which they feed). The visitor center at **La Capelière** *(closed Sun.)*, on the east side of the Étang de Vaccarès, provides information on the reserve, along with an exhibition following the Camargue through the seasons. The **Parc Ornithologique** *(tel 04 90 97 82 62, www.parcornithologique.com)* at Pont-de-Gau north of Stes.-Maries-de-la-Mer displays a variety of birds including, Egyptian vultures, black kites, and eagle owls.

# Les Baux-de-Provence

Rising above the white limestone crags of Les Alpilles, the ruins of the feudal citadel of Les Baux (as it's usually known) meld into the rocky outcrop on which they stand.

**Les Baux**
🗺 279 D3
**Visitor information**
✉ rue Porte Mage
☎ 04 90 54 34 39
www.lesbauxde
provence.com

**Musée de l'Histoire de la Citadelle**
✉ Château des Baux de Provence
☎ 04 90 54 55 56
💲 $

**Cathédrale d'Images**
✉ route Val d'Enfer
☎ 04 90 54 22 34
www.cathedrale-images.com

This was once the stronghold of the powerful, proud, and blood-thirsty lords of Baux. With their ancestry dating back to the Magi king Balthazar, the lords placed the Star of Bethlehem on their coat of arms and terrorized the region for much of the Middle Ages. Most infamous of all was the psychopathically violent Raymond de Turenne, known as the "scourge of Provence." In the 14th century, he amused himself by forcing his prisoners to leap to their deaths from the castle walls.

**INSIDER TIP:**

**Christmas Eve in Les Baux is an experience of a lifetime with a candlelight procession that winds up at tiny St.-Vincent church for the Shepherds Mass.**

—SHEILA BUCKMASTER
*National Geographic Traveler magazine editor at large*

In the 13th century, by contrast, Les Baux was the embodiment of romance, the most famous of the Provençal courts of love that lured troubadours from afar to serenade noble ladies. But the great citadel was to come to an ignominious end in 1632, when Cardinal Richelieu, finally tiring of the rebellious

lords and inhabitants of Les Baux, ordered the entire edifice to be demolished. The result is the magnificent ruin visible today, strung out along a narrow and vertiginous spit.

Enter the **Ville Morte** (Dead City) through the 14th-century **Tour du Brau,** which houses the castle's museum. From here, you can climb over the ruins of the castle and early village, discovering remnants of towers and walls. The edge of the escarpment offers tremendous views across the contorted rocks of the **Val d'Enfer,** the legendary haunt of witches and reputedly the inspiration for the setting of Dante's *Inferno*.

The village below the citadel dates mainly from the 16th and 17th centuries, with a number of Renaissance chapels and mansions now containing museums. The **Fondation Louis Jou** in the Hôtel Jean de Brion displays the paraphernalia of a master typographer; the **Musée des Santons** in the Ancien Hôtel de Ville *(rue Porte Mage)* is devoted to the clay figures that decorate Provençal Christmas cribs.

Just outside Les Baux is the **Cathédrale d'Images,** an empty quarry with cavernous spaces illuminated by extraordinary visual projections and used as a film set by Jean Cocteau and other directors. ∎

# Aix-en-Provence

"The most beautiful town in France after Paris," according to an 18th-century traveler, Aix is a chic and elegant city, with graceful boulevards, shady squares, and hundreds of beautifully carved stone fountains. Water is the raison d'être of the city, founded by the Roman consul Sextius, who was attracted by the hot springs that are still in use today.

Rotonde at the Place General-de-Gaulle at the entrance to the Cours Mirabeau, Aix-en-Provence

## Cours Mirabeau

At the heart of Aix lies the majestic Cours Mirabeau, the famous tree-shaded boulevard laid out on the site of the old ramparts, flanked by elegant 17th- and 18th-century houses and punctuated by beautiful fountains. Take time to watch the world go by from the terrace of one of the cafés here, such as Les Deux Garçons, a favorite haunt of artists and intellectuals since 1792.

## Old Town

To the north, the old town extends through a maze of squares. On Saturdays, when it is taken over by a market, this area is even more irresistible. Distinguished buildings include the 17th-century **Hôtel de Ville** and the old bishops' palace, or Ancien Achevêché, which now houses the **Musée des Tapisseries.** Next door is the lovely Gothic **Cathédrale St.-Sauveur,** unmistakable

## Aix-en-Provence

279 E3

**Visitor information**

✉ 2 place Général-de-Gaulle

☎ 04 42 16 11 61

**www.aixenprovence tourism.com**

**Musée des Tapisseries**

✉ place de l'Ancien-Archevêché

☎ 04 42 23 09 91

🕐 Closed Tues.

💲 $

**Cathédrale St.-Sauveur**

✉ place de l'Université

**Musée Granet**

✉ place St.-Jean-de-Malte

☎ 04 42 52 88 32

www.museegranet-aixenprovence.fr

**Atelier Paul Cézanne**

✉ 9 avenue Paul Cézanne

☎ 04 42 21 06 53

www.atelier-cezanne.com

**Fondation Vasarely**

✉ 1 avenue Marcel Panol

☎ 04 42 20 01 09

www.fondation vasarely.fr

for its 16th-century carved doors, the cool columns of its 5th-century Merovingian baptistry, and its Romanesque cloisters. Among its treasures is Nicolas Froment's 15th-century triptych, "Burning Bush."

## Cézanne's City

South of Cours Mirabeau is the elegant Quartier Mazarin. The **Musée Granet** has eight works by Paul Cézanne, Aix's most famous son (see sidebar below). A Cézanne circuit leads you around town. Visit the **Atelier Paul Cézanne,**

where the artist worked from 1897 until he died in 1906. It has been re-created just as he might have left it.

West of the city center, is the **Fondation Vasarely,** an extraordinary museum designed by the artist himself, with exterior walls that look like his paintings.

**INSIDER TIP:**

**To really connect with the spirit of the place, find a small rural church and spend some time strolling through its cemetery, preferably in the spring.**

—DIANA PARSELL
*National Geographic Books
contributor*

## Outside of Town

Just under 2 miles (3 km) north of the city is the **Oppidum d'Entremont** *(www.entremont .culture.gouv.fr, closed Tues.),* site of the original Gallic settlement of Aix. Excavations have revealed fortifications and commercial and residential buildings.

West of the city is the **Site Memorial Les Milles** *(www .campdesmilles.org),* a brick factory used as a concentration camp during World War II. Artists and intellectuals considered "undesirables" were imprisoned here, among them Max Ernst. Documents and photos tell the story; in the refectory are restored fragments of caricatures and murals done by the prisoners. ∎

### In the Footsteps of Cézanne

Want to see Aix-en-Provence the way Cézanne did? Every Thursday in July, the **Atelier Paul Cézanne** offers artistic exchanges and a country picnic in the gardens of the artist's studio. Events begin at 7 p.m. Or consider taking a sketching trip to discover some of the beautiful spots around the city. If you would like to improve your artistic skills, the **Académie Libre** *(www.academielibre.com)* has courses available for artists of all levels, from beginners to experienced. The **Aix City Pass,** which is available at the tourist office, includes a guided tour of the city, a tour of Cézanne's studio, and a visit to Fondation Vasarely, the Cézanne family estate.

# Gorges du Verdon

The deepest, widest gorge in Europe, this natural wonder and precious refuge is a *parc naturel régional* sheltering unusual flora and fauna. For a circular tour starting from Castellane, an ancient town of ruined ramparts and now a busy tourist center, you need to allow a day and plenty of gas. The route affords breathtaking views, but beware hairpin turns and precipices.

With plunging limestone walls and vertiginous views, the Gorges du Verdon does not disappoint.

Leave Castellane westward on the D952. At **Point Sublime,** on the north bank, hikers can walk down 590 feet (180 m) to the bottom of the gorge. The D23 then loops off to the south, providing spectacular views before rejoining the main D952 at **La Palad-sur-Verdon** to skirt the canyon.

Set in a deep ravine above the western end of the canyon is **Moustiers-Ste.-Marie,** a 15th-century settlement known for its pottery; see some at the **Musée de la Faience** (*tel 04 92 74 61 64*). From here head south on the D957 past the **Lac de Sainte-Croix,** an artificial lake of

cobalt blue waters, then turn left along the south side of the canyon on the Corniche Sublime, the D71. Views abound, particularly at **Pont de l'Artuby,** spanning the gorge of the Artuby River, and at the **Balcons de la Mescla.** These "balconies" drop almost vertically to the churning waters far below.

To return to Castellane, follow the D71 east, turn north on the D90 (a steep, narrow road), and north again on the D955 to rejoin the D952. For an easier route, take the D71 east to the D21 at Comps-sur-Artuby. Turn east on this road, and almost immediately turn left on the D955 and proceed north to the D952. ∎

## Castellane
🗺 279 F3
**Visitor information**
✉ rue Nationale
☎ 04 92 83 61 14
**www.castellane.org**

## Moustiers-Ste.-Marie
🗺 279 F3
**Visitor information**
✉ place de l'Église
☎ 04 92 74 67 84;
04 92 72 56 60
(sailing club)
🕐 Closed a.m.
Oct.–May
**www.moustiers.eu**

# More Places to Visit in Provence

## Haute-Provence

Located in Provence's northeast corner, the Haute-Provence is a mountainous region of remote villages, river gorges, pine forests, and sheep pastures. Discover the area by narrow-gauge railroad, the **Chemins de Fer de Provence** (www.trainprovence.com), which runs from Nice to the spa town of **Digne-les-Bains** (visitor information, place du Tampinet, tel 04 92 36 62 62; www.ot-dignelesbains.fr), the regional capital as well as the processing center for the lavender crop. Near the Italian

> **INSIDER TIP:**
>
> **In St.-Rémy-de-Provence, great affordable, fragrant souvenirs are the blocks of pastel colored soaps (some of them infused with olive oil) and the pretty wands made of small lavender bouquets.**
>
> —RAPHAEL KADUSHIN
> National Geographic Traveler *magazine writer*

---

## EXPERIENCE:
## Art Refuges

In the Hautes Alpes of Provence, acclaimed British land artist Andy Goldsworthy has decorated a series of mountain refuges in his inimitable style, reflecting and appreciating the many varied forms of nature. You can follow the entire 93-mile (150 km) route, staying in some of the refuges, or visit them individually. Start from the **Gassendi Museum** (tel 04 92 31 45 29; www.musee-gassendi.org) in Digne, where there is an introductory exhibition. Inquire at the museum for a key to the refuges or to arrange a guide.

---

border, the **Parc National du Mercantour** (contact Bureau des Guides de Mercantour, tel 04 93 03 26 60, www.mercantour.eu) shelters ibex and chamois. At the **Musée des Merveilles** (avenue 16 Septembre, tel 04 93 04 32 50, www.museedesmerveilles.com) in Tende, you'll find amazing carvings and interactive exhibits relating to the park's prehistory.

## St.-Rémy-de-Provence

On the fertile plain north of the Chaîne des Alpilles, you'll find this charming market

town. In 1889, Vincent van Gogh became a patient at the hospital of **St.-Paul-de-Mausole.** You can visit its 12th-century cloister and also the **Centre d'Art Présence van Gogh** in the 18th-century Hôtel Estrine. The **Musée des Arômes et des Parfums** is dedicated to the tradition of herb growing. St.-Rémy is most celebrated for the ruins of a Greco-Roman town at nearby **Glanum,** which has baths, a forum, a theater, wonderful sculptures, and a sacred spring. www.saintremy-de-provence.com 🗺 279 D3 **Visitor information** ✉ place Jean-Jaurès ☎ 04 90 92 05 22

## Tarascon

Perched beside the Rhône, Tarascon is dominated by its 15th-century Gothic château, once a lively center of medieval culture. The 12th-century **Église de Ste.-Marthe,** opposite, is dedicated to the saint who reputedly saved the town from an amphibious monster, the Tarasque, a victory still celebrated on the last weekend in June. The **Musée Souleïado** (www.souleiado-lemusee.com) displays antique and contemporary Provençal fabrics, with workshops and a shop. www.tarascon.org 🗺 279 D3 **Visitor information** ✉ rue des Halles ☎ 04 90 91 03 52

# Languedoc-Roussillon

The "other" South of France, Languedoc-Roussillon, is every bit as dazzling as Provence and the Côte d'Azur, but flaunts itself less. Its two provinces extend from the Rhône to the Pyrenees, and from the coast to the highlands of the Cévennes, Corbières, and Minervois. Languedoc owes its name to the medieval language of the troubadours, *la langue d'oc*. In Spanish-flavored Roussillon, the Catalan language is still common, and on village squares you may well see the national dance, the *sardaña*.

The busy port of Sète boasts a network of canals and bridges surrounded by old buildings.

No other region of France encompasses such a variety of landscape. The wine villages of the coastal plain, surrounded by vineyards and thyme-scented *garrigue*, epitomize the sunbaked Midi; beneath the snowcapped Pyrenees, orchards of peach and plum, almond and cherry flourish among pastures rich with wildflowers in spring and threaded by paths. Walkers will relish the lonely Corbières hills and the uplands of the Haut-Languedoc. The fishing villages and saltwater lagoons are a paradise not only for wildlife but also for artists.

There is a rich legacy of Roman *(romain)* and Romanesque *(roman)* architecture, from the Roman monuments of Nîmes and the Pont du Gard to the Moorish-influenced Romanesque abbeys of Roussillon.

A romance language derived from Latin, the langue d'oc takes it name ultimately from the Latin formula for "yes," *hoc ille*. In the south of France this became *oc*, in the north *il*. Thus the language of the south became known as *langue d'oc* and that of the north as *langue d'oïl*—modern French.

The language of the troubadours and their lyric poetry, the langue d'oc survived determined efforts by the French to eradicate it. You can still hear it in the patois spoken by older people in markets and cafés, and in the Occitan (Provençal) language now taught in schools and universities. ■

# Montpellier

Founded in the tenth century, Montpellier is now one of the liveliest and fastest growing cities in the South of France. Its ancient medical school and university still attract many students.

At the center of Montpellier, a lively university town founded in the tenth century, is the Place de la Comédie.

**Montpellier**
🄼 278 C3

**Visitor information**
✉ allée Jean-de-Lattre de Tassigny
☎ 04 67 60 60 60

**www.ot-montpellier .fr**

Life in Montpellier revolves around **Place de la Comédie,** a square that bustles with cafés. At one end stand the 19th-century opera house that gives the *place* its name and a fountain topped by Étienne d'Antoine's statue of the three Graces. North and west of the place lie the car-free, winding medieval streets lined with stately 17th- and 18th-century mansions.

In the 16th and 17th centuries, Montpellier became a stronghold of Protestantism. Louis XIII subjected the city to a devastating eight-month siege in 1622, leaving little of its medieval fabric intact. But the city turned this to its advantage, building great mansions arranged around courtyards with stone staircases. Ones open to visitors include the **Hôtel de**

Manse on Rue Embouque-d'Or and the **Hôtel des Trésoriers de la Bourse** on Rue Ancien-Courrier. The Hôtel Lunaret on Rue des Trésoriers-de-France, a masterpiece built by Jacques Coeur, Charles VII's treasurer, houses the **Musée Languedocien** *(entrance at 7 rue Jacques Coeur, tel 04 67 52 93 03, closed Sun.; www.musee -languedocien.com).*

The 17th-century former bishops' palace beside the cathedral, now the medical school, contains the French and Italian drawings of the **Musée Atger.** The superb **Musée Fabre** *(39 blvd. Bonne Nouvelle, tel 04 67 14 83 00; http://museefabre .montpellier-agglo.com)* has works by Veronese, Courbet, Poussin, Delaunay, and many others.

To savor Montpellier's setting between the Cévennes and the sea, stroll along the **Promenade du Peyrou,** formal 18th-century gardens dominated by a neoclassic *château d'eau,* an elaborate fountain, and the aqueduct that used to bring water to the city. North of the promenade is the **Jardin des Plantes,** one of the oldest botanical gardens in Europe.

Like its neighbor and rival, Nîmes, Montpellier prides itself on its modern architecture, including Ricardo Bofill's postmodern Antigone quarter (east of the Esplanade Charles-de-Gaulle) and squares based on a reinterpretation of classical architecture. ■

# Nîmes

**Nîmes combines ancient history and modern life with tremendous brio and zest, at its most colorful during the Féria du Pentecôte, the annual bullfighting and folklore festival in May.**

Nîmes owes its chief glories to the Romans, who settled around the spring of Nemausus and built a range of fortifications and public buildings. Emperor Augustus gave the city its walls and gates, as recorded on the **Porte d'Auguste.** Most impressive is **Les Arènes** *(tel 04 66 21 82 56),* a perfect oval arena two

**INSIDER TIP:**

**A must-taste treat is the locally made** *croquant villaret,* **an almond cookie that is great with coffee.**

—SHEILA BUCKMASTER
National Geographic Traveler
*magazine editor at large*

stories high, skillfully engineered and constructed in the first century A.D. The seating (for 24,000) was segregated according to rank and gender.

The city's other Roman glory, the 2,000-year-old temple known as the **Maison Carrée,** is now an exhibition space for current archaeological research. Opposite stands the **Carrée d'Art,** a vast art gallery and library designed by British architect Norman Foster as a glass-and-aluminum tribute to the ancient temple.

The old town is a charming jumble of narrow streets, shady squares, and fountains. Many

of the 16th- and 17th-century houses are a legacy of the textile industry (this is the birthplace of the fabric called "de Nîmes"—denim), founded by a number of enterprising Protestants who, barred from public office, threw themselves into trade.

For a quiet retreat, head to the **Jardin de la Fontaine** *(quai de la Fontaine),* which contains the springs and ruins of a Roman nymphaeum. The **Tour Magne** above, part of Augustus's city walls, offers good views of the city and the surrounding countryside. ■

**Nîmes**
 279 D3
**Visitor information**
✉ 6 rue Auguste
☎ 04 66 58 38 00
**www.ot-nimes.fr**

**Maison Carrée**
✉ place de la Maison Carrée
☎ 04 66 21 82 56

**Carrée d'Art**
✉ place de la Maison Carrée
☎ 04 66 76 35 70
🕐 Closed Mon.
💲 $

## Good Seats

**Built around 70 A.D. to hold some 20,000 people, the Roman amphitheater *(www.arenes-nimes.com)* in Nîmes is one of the largest and best preserved in France. The original fighting spectacles featured animals and gladiators. Spectators, positioned according to social status, were shaded from the sun by a canopy supported by ropes attached to poles. Now you can see the Roman games staged as a historic pageant with several hundred participants in gladiatorial combat. You can also attend bullfights (see sidebar p. 307).**

# Pont du Gard

As beautiful as it is functional, the Pont du Gard is an indication of the heroic scale on which the Romans built and thought. The problem was simple enough: The spring at Nîmes was not sufficient to supply the growing city with water. The solution was radical: Fresh water would be piped from springs at Uzès, some 30 miles (48 km) away, along a system of aqueducts, trenches, and tunnels carved out of the solid rock. The total drop was a mere 56 feet (17 m), and the engineering skills involved were immense.

Having survived many floods, the Pont du Gard is a tribute to Roman engineering skills.

**Pont du Gard**

🅰 279 D3

**Visitor information**

✉ place des Grands Jours, Remoulins

☎ 08 20 90 33 30

**www.pontdugard.fr**

Two millennia later, the aqueduct spans the Gardon River virtually unchanged, despite the depredations of time. Even the marks of the Roman builders can still be seen on some of the stones (the largest of which weighs six tons), along with graffiti left by young French *compagnons* or journeymen masons, for whom this used to be a place of pilgrimage.

You may wonder why it was necessary to build on such a monumental scale. In winter, the river may swell to become a rushing torrent, capable of destroying modern bridges. The

Roman engineers designed the aqueduct with a slight curve that enabled it to withstand a great pressure of water; it was tested again in recent years, when floods devastated Nîmes. Other technical refinements are the almost imperceptible fall that carried the water along and the waterproof rendering that sealed the inside of the channel along the top.

The Pont du Gard is just outside the village of Remoulins. You can see it from the visitor centers on both banks of the Gardon River. For the right bank, turn off from the D981; for the left bank, take the D19. ■

# Carcassonne

**The turreted and machicolated double walls of Carcassonne crystallize our notions of the perfect medieval citadel. Sieges heroically resisted, knights in armor jousting in the lists, and troubadour romance spring to mind in this evocative setting.**

The largest and most impressive medieval citadel in Europe, Carcassonne was known to the Celts and fortified by the Romans. Commanding the communication route between Toulouse and the Mediterranean, it was coveted by Visigoths, Saracens, and Charlemagne. In the 13th century, Simon de Montfort's army arrived at Carcassonne, by then a Cathar stronghold, and—fresh from their massacre of the Cathars of Béziers—besieged and captured it.

De Montfort made the citadel the headquarters for his murderous raids. The inhabitants rebelled, but Louis IX moved them to the new *bastide* he built below the city. Thus the twin sites of Carcassonne evolved. In the late 13th century, Philip the Bold massively strengthened the citadel's defenses, creating a bulwark against Spain.

But when the French annexed Roussillon in 1659, the Spanish border shifted southward, and the citadel became redundant. The *ville basse* prospered and the *cité* declined so far that in the mid-19th century it was decided to demolish the remaining fortifications. Mercifully, the architect and medievalist Viollet-le-Duc stepped in to save this jewel. Thanks to him, we can now see a complete medieval city. Wander between the two sets of ramparts, then penetrate the twin sandstone towers of the **Narbonne Gate,** with its portcullis and drawbridge. Inside is a warren of meticulously restored medieval houses (not to mention hotels, restaurants, and souvenir stores).

The core of the city is the 12th-century **Château Comtal.** You can walk around the ramparts past medieval defenses: watchtowers, posterns, and machicolations for hurling boiling oil and stones on attackers. The Romanesque and Gothic **Cathédrale St.-Nazaire** boasts superb stained glass and the 13th-century "siege stone," perhaps depicting the siege of Carcassonne in 1209. ◼

**Carcassonne**
🅜 278 B2
**Visitor information**
✉ 28 rue de Verdun
☎ 04 68 10 24 30
**www.carcassonne -tourisme.com**

**Cité Medieval et Château Comtal**
☎ 04 68 11 70 72
💲 $; guided tour obligatory

**THE CITY ABLAZE**
The annual Festival de la Cité begins July 8 and culminates in the "Burning of the City" (L'embrasement de la Cité) on July 14—Bastille Day, the great French national holiday.

**The medieval fortress of Carcassonne, overlooking southern France countryside, has seen its fair share of history.**

# Drive the Cathar Trail

Follow this trail to the last strongholds of the Cathars, where they took refuge in perilously inaccessible castles and fortified hilltop villages, in the wild and inhospitable foothills of the Pyrenees. Though the route is mountainous, the driving isn't difficult.

Montségur gives new dramatic meaning to the concept of "perched."

The golden era of the Languedoc was cut short in the 13th century with the ferocious crusade against the Cathar heretics. The Cathars (also known as Albigensians

**NOT TO BE MISSED:**

Villerouge-Termenès • Château de Peyrepertuse • Château de Quéribus • Musée de Quercorb • Montségur

after the town of Albi) pursued a faith of high moral principles ("Cathar" is derived from the Greek *katharos*, meaning "pure") and were critical of the corruption of the Church. The key to their heresy lay in their Manichean belief in the dual powers of good and evil, and the resulting conviction that only the world of the spirit was good, while the material world was irredeemably evil. Their leaders, known as *perfecti*, traveled the countryside preaching and teaching in *langue d'oc*.

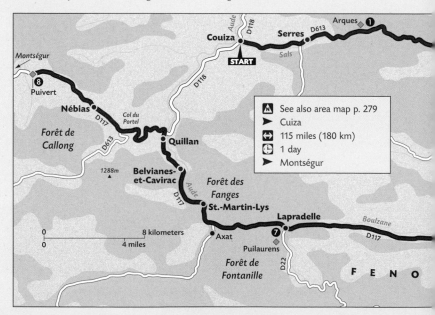

See also area map p. 279
► Cuiza
⟷ 115 miles (180 km)
🕐 1 day
► Montségur

In 1209, the pope and the French king launched a crusade led by the ruthless Simon de Montfort. The heretics sought refuge in the isolated castles of the Corbières, whose names are forever linked with the memory of the doomed Cathars they sheltered.

A mountain drive takes you to a number of Cathar castles. Start from **Couiza** on the D118, 25 miles (40 km) south of Carcassonne, and take the D613 east to **Arques ❶** *(tel 04 68 69 82 87)*, with its preserved 13th-century keep. Turn north on the D40 for a difficult climb to the ruins of **Termes ❷** *(tel 04 68 70 09 20)* and the **Château de Durfort ❸**, dramatically perched over a ravine. Montfort's capture of the apparently unassailable Termes in 1210 sent shudders of foreboding through all the other Cathar fortresses.

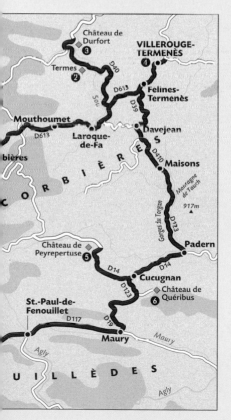

Return to the D613 and go east to the village of **Villerouge-Termenès ❹**, which has grown up around the great stone towers of its castle *(tel 04 68 70 09 11)*. This was the refuge of the last Cathar "perfect," who was finally burned at the stake in 1321. A banquet is held in the courtyard each year in his honor.

Double back on the D613 for 2 miles (3 km) to just beyond Félines-Termenès, then head south to Padern, through the rocky gorge of the Torgan River. Go west on the D14 to some mighty spectacular castles.

**Château de Peyrepertuse ❺** *(tel 06 71 58 63 36)* is reached by a 30-minute drive up a long, winding road. The castle stretches out to fit its dizzy perch, in places only a few yards wide, with one narrow entrance. Inside is a simple Romanesque chapel, and beyond it another flight of exposed steps leads up to the final refuge. The wind takes your breath away, as does the view.

Visible from Peyrepertuse is the **Château de Quéribus ❻** *(tel 04 68 45 03 69)*, its keep and remarkable chapel dominating the Roussillon plain. Backtrack on the D14 for 5 miles (8 km) and take the D123 to reach this last stronghold of the Cathars. It proved impregnable, finally surrendering peacefully in 1255. A single stairway is still the only access.

Proceed southwest on the D19 and D117 to the more accessible **Puilaurens ❼** *(tel 04 68 20 65 26)*, bristling with machicolations, arrow-slit windows, and ramparts. The single stone stairway, zigzagging precariously to the top, ensured that no assailant went unnoticed.

Take the D117 to Quillan, south of Couiza, and head west, still on the D117, to **Puivert ❽** *(tel 04 68 20 80 98)*, more palace than castle, despite its sturdy defenses. You can also visit the **Musée de Quercorb** *(16 rue Bairy du Lion, tel 04 68 20 80 98, closed Nov.– March)*, for exhibitions on local traditions and medieval music. Farther west (on the D117 and D9) rises the great rock of **Montségur,** the Cathar headquarters and site of a terrible massacre (see p. 275).

# Romanesque Abbeys

Among the chief glories of Languedoc-Roussillon are its Romanesque abbeys. These lovely buildings, dating from the 10th to 12th centuries, combine simple, austere spaces with exquisitely carved stone capitals and panels. Some are set in remote places and preserve the peaceful monastic atmosphere. These abbeys have been beautifully restored, and you can see several in a tour of the Roussillon *département* around Perpignan.

The picturesque village of St.-Guilhem-le-Désert is anchored by its austere abbey.

**St.-Michel-de-Cuxa**

🗺 278 B1

**Visitor information**

✉ Codalet

☎ 04 68 96 15 35

🕐 Closed a.m. Sun. & religious holidays

💲 $

**St.-Martin-du-Canigou**

☎ 04 68 05 50 03

http://stmartindu canigou.org

## St.-Michel-de-Cuxa

Founded by the Benedictines in 878, the lovely monastery of St.-Michel-de-Cuxa outside Prades is actually pre-Romanesque. Its unusual keyhole-shaped arches are in the Mozarabic style, a legacy of the Moorish occupation of the region. The abbey's surviving great square tower, in bleached ocher-colored stone, is beautifully silhouetted against the dark massif of Mont Canigou. The finest of the capitals from the 12th-century pink marble cloister, looted after the Revolution, was found in

Prades in 1909 and sold to the Metropolitan Museum of Art in New York City.

## St.-Martin-du-Canigou

On a crag set high up on the slopes of Mont Canigou, the silent, ascetic retreat of St.-Martin-du-Canigou is accessible only by jeep or a 40-minute climb on foot. But its beauty and setting more than repay the effort. A guided tour showcases the cloister, Romanesque chapel, and tombs of Guifred, Count of Cerdagne (who founded the monastery in the 11th century in penance for killing his wife and his son) and his second wife.

## Serrabone

The Augustinian priory of Ser rabone also clings to the side of Mont Canigou, commanding a spectacular view of the surrounding peaks. It is set in a lovely garden of vines, shrubs, and fragrant herbs (where you may picnic). The beautifully simple 11th century church houses a splendid tribune of pink marble columns and arches, carved with an astonishing array of mythical beasts, flowers, and human figures. The marble cloister arches frame the mountain views.

## Elne

Among the orchards and vines south of Perpignan is the ancient town of Elne, which every year hosts a music festival in its 11th-century cathedral. Elne's incomparable treasure is its cloister, where the marble capitals were vigorously carved; several feature monks peeking

around doors. The oldest (12th century) and finest tell the Creation story: The panel of Adam and Eve is a masterpiece.

## St.-Guilhem-le-Désert

Half hidden in the Hérault gorge, north of Montpellier, are the picturesque village and austere abbey of St.-Guilhem-le-Désert. Guilhem of Aquitaine, a lieutenant of Charlemagne, founded the abbey in the ninth century. His piety, coupled with a relic of the True Cross awarded him by Charlemagne, assured him a following even in this remote spot.

You climb up to the abbey through the charming village below. The abbey church is a perfect example of the simplicity and strength of Romanesque building, with a great barrel vaulted nave, massive pillars, and sturdy arches.

Two galleries of the cloister are still here, but to see the rest you must go to the Cloisters, part of the Metropolitan Museum of Art in New York, where they join those from St.-Michel-de-Cuxa. ■

**Serrabone**
278 B1
**Visitor information**
Prieuré de Serrabone et Jardin Mediterranéen, Boule d'Amont
04 68 84 09 30
$

**Elne**
278 B1
**Visitor information**
place Sant Jordi
04 68 22 05 07
www.ot-elne.fr

**St.-Guilhem-le-Désert**
278 C3
**Visitor information**
St.-Guilhem-le-Désert
04 67 57 44 33
www.saint-guilhem-le-desert.com

## Pablo Casals Festival: Celebrating a Local Star

As the Spanish Civil War drew to a close, the great Catalan cellist Pablo Casals took refuge in the little Pyrenean town of **Prades,** escaping from Franco. At the end of World War II, bitterly disappointed at the reluctance of the West to liberate Spain from the fascists, he protested by refusing to play in public, calling this "the greatest sacrifice of my life."

Attempts were made to persuade him to perform in the U.S. for large sums of money, but he always refused. Eventually the Americans decided to come to him and suggested a musical festival in Prades. This became the Prades Bach festival (tel 04 68 96 33 07, www.prades-festival-casals.com, late July–early Aug.), now a key date on the European music calendar. St.-Michel-de-Cuxa is the primary performing space, its high Romanesque vault providing sublime acoustics, with many other concerts in small area churches.

# Collioure & the Côte Vermeille

The Côte Vermeille, where the Pyrenees tumble into the cerulean blue Mediterranean, is by far the most beautiful section of the Languedoc coast. The jewel of the coast is the little port of Collioure. In the early 20th century, its brilliant light, gaily painted fishing boats, and colorful stuccoed houses inspired Matisse and other artists to experiment with the violent eruptions of pure color that earned them the soubriquet *fauvist* (literally "wild beast").

**Collioure**

🗺 278 C1

**Visitor information**

✉ place du 18 Juin

☎ 04 68 82 15 47

**www.collioure.com**

**Banyuls-sur-Mer**

🗺 278 C1

**Visitor information**

✉ avenue République

☎ 04 68 88 31 58

**www.banyuls-sur-mer.com**

Collioure's harbor is flanked by the **Château Royal** *(tel 04 68 82 06 43)*, built by the Knights Templar in the 13th century and later reinforced by Vauban. It is now used for art exhibitions. The 14th-century **Église de Notre-Dame-des-Anges** has borrowed the former lighthouse as its bell tower. Three small sheltered beaches extend beneath harborside restaurants with sunny terraces, where you can indulge in locally caught fish and Collioure wine.

South of Collioure, the road runs past the steeply terraced vineyards of **Banyuls-sur-Mer.** Stop at **Cap Béar** for a dazzling panorama of mountains and sea. Banyuls itself is as sweet as its wine, with palm-shaded cafés, a little beach, and wine *caves* along the ancient narrow streets. On the southern side of the town is an oceanographic research institute with an aquarium of local sea life *(tel 04 68 88 73 39)*. At the most southerly point of the French coast, **Cerbère** flies the red-and-gold Catalan flag. ■

## Dynamite Beach

To appreciate the efforts made to conserve the beaches along the Mediterranean, visit **Paulilles** on the Côte Vermeille. A fine sandy beach, fringed by pines, sheltered by hills and vineyards, with good safe swimming, Paulilles is close to the marine reserve of Banyuls. Until 1984, the beach was also the site of a dynamite factory.

Dynamite inventor (and Nobel prize endower) Alfred Nobel founded the factory in 1870. He chose the site because it was far from the eastern front with Germany and close to Port Vendres, which enabled easy shipping to French colonies. Futhermore, its location close to the sea

provided a kind of safety measure in the case of explosion.

After the site closed, it fell victim to neglect. It was also the subject of more than one squabble, as organizations vied to pursue projects as varied as a nuclear power station and a pharaonic marina.

Finally the Conservatoire de Littoral intervened, and now the site, opened in September 2008, is a triumph. Preserving its heritage and beauty for public use, Paulilles includes a museum and preserved industrial buildings, a fine park of exotic trees and plants, and a gorgeous public beach. The marine area around the beach is also a protected zone.

# Céret & the Tech Valley

A 14th-century single-span bridge across the Tech River, the Pont du Diable leads into the winding streets and shady squares of Spanish-style Céret, capital of the Vallespir (the Tech Valley). Catalan Céret is a lively center, with colorful Easter celebrations, an international festival in August, and bullfights in its arena.

## Céret

Céret's charms once attracted artists like Picasso and Braque. Here, they painted works such as "Landscape at Céret" (Picasso, 1911) and "Rooftops, Céret" (Braque, 1911). Their evenings at the **Grand Café** *(boulevard Maréchal-Joffre, tel 04 68 87 02 85)* left tangible evidence: several Picasso drawings on café notepaper.

Céret has an excellent **Musée d'Art Moderne** *(8 boulevard Maréchal-Joffre, tel 04 68 87 27 76,*

Pont du Diable, set in stone, spans more than six centuries.

*closed Tues. Oct.–April).* A modern building of ocher terraces and shady patios, the museum houses works by Catalan artists Capdeville and Tapiès, as well as canvases by Dufy and Chagall; a series of ceramic bowls from Vallauris by Picasso, depicting bullfighting and

donated by the artist; and a fine early Picasso, "Portrait of Corina Père Romeu" (1902).

## Tech Valley

The valley stretches westward from Céret to the Roman spa town of **Amélie-les-Bains.** A few miles farther on the D115 is **Arles-sur-Tech** *(www.ville-arles -sur-tech.fr),* where a Benedictine abbey was founded in 900. The Romanesque church was rebuilt in the 12th century.

Farther up the remote valley is the **Gorges de la Fou,** allegedly the world's narrowest gorge. An iron walkway winds through the cliffs, accessible only on foot and with mandatory protective headgear. ■

**Céret**
🅐 278 B1
**Visitor information**
✉ 1 avenue Georges-Clemenceau
☎ 04 68 87 00 53
**www.ot-ceret.fr**

**Amélie-les-Bains**
🅐 278 B1
**Visitor information**
✉ quai 8 Mai
☎ 04 68 39 01 98
**www.amelie-les -bains.com**

# Perpignan & French Catalonia

With its historical roots in the county of Barcelona and the kingdoms of Aragon and Majorca, it is not surprising that Roussillon often feels more Spanish than French. It is proudly conscious of its distinct identity as French Catalonia: The red-and-yellow Catalan flag flutters everywhere, the national dance, the *sardaña,* is danced solemnly in village squares, and many people speak Catalan, sometimes still as a first language.

Winding streets and colorful facades make up the old quarter of Perpignan, the capital of French Catalonia.

The sunny southern city of **Perpignan** is the capital of French Catalonia, with a strong Spanish influence underscored by the large population of émigrés from Franco's Spain.

The **Palais des Rois de Majorque** takes up virtually a quarter of the old town—in the 13th century, the city was the capital of the kings of Majorca. Within its 17th-century ramparts, the vast two-story palace and its arcaded courtyard, its beautifully frescoed and tiled royal chapels, and its great Gothic hall show unmistakable Spanish-Moorish influence.

The focus of the old town lies to the north, in **Place de la Loge.** Here, among pink marble-paved streets and narrow alleys, stands the **Loge de Mer.** Built in exquisite 14th-century Gothic style as the city's stock exchange and maritime court, it boasts carved wooden ceilings and sculpted windows. The ground floor houses a restaurant where you can inspect the glories up close. Its gargoyles and filigree balustrades, meanwhile, may be contemplated from one of the cafés on the square. Beside it stands the 14th-century **Hôtel de Ville,** with its superb 17th-century gates, and the 15th-century Roussillon parliament building, the **Palais de la Députation.**

## Good Friday in Perpignan

The most dramatic time to be in Perpignan is Good Friday for La Sanch procession to the cathedral. The procession has taken place since the Middle Ages, when the Red Penitents Brotherhood accompanied condemned prisoners to the gallows. Today the penitents wind slowly through the medieval streets of the old town, tolling bells, garbed in sinister pointed black hoods and red robes, some barefoot, carrying crucifixes and reliquaries. Young and old participate, and locals and visitors cram the streets to watch.

Le Castillet, a 14th-century gateway, houses the **Musée Casa Païral**, a museum of Catalan traditions and crafts. **Musée Rigaud** shows work by Perpignan-born Hyacinthe Rigaud, along with paintings by Dufy and Picasso and works by sculptor Aristide Maillol.

The 14th-century **Cathédrale de St.-Jean** dominates Place de Gambetta, a former parade ground lined with 16th-century houses. Built by the kings of Majorca, the cathedral is in the Roussillon style of red brick and pebbles and has a typical southern Gothic wrought-iron bell tower. Inside, candlelight illuminates frescoed walls, stained glass, and a glowing gilt altar. In a chapel on the south side hangs the harrowing 14th-century wooden statue of the Devôt Christ, which is carried through the streets on Good Friday by a brotherhood of penitents (see sidebar this page). Beside the chapel is the huge **Campo Santo,** one of France's oldest cloistered cemeteries, which has been restored and is now used for atmospheric summer concerts.

## Around Perpignan

The beaches of **St.-Cyprien-Plage** and **Canet-Plage,** both within convenient reach of Perpignan, are popular but otherwise unremarkable. The remains of Europe's oldest human being, dating back to about 450,000 B.C., were discovered in 1971 at **Tautavel.** The **Musée de la Préhistoire** tells the story and displays a reconstruction of the famous skull.

**INSIDER TIP:**

**Salvador Dalí called Perpignan's train station the "center of the universe," but the city's Catalan influence on food and festivities is the bigger draw.**

—DAVE YODER
*National Geographic photographer*

Dominating Perpignan is the snowy peak of **Mont Canigou** (9,138 feet/2,785 m), sacred and mystical mountain of the Catalans, with a great iron cross perched on its summit. The climb to the top from Vernet-les-Bains to Cortalets is a magnificent experience. ∎

**Perpignan**
🅰 278 B2
**Visitor information**
✉ place Armand Lanoux
☎ 04 68 66 30 30
**www.perpignan**
**.tourisme.com**

**Palais des Rois de Majorque**
✉ 4 rue des Archers
☎ 04 68 34 48 29
💲 $

**Musée Casa Païral—Le Castillet**
✉ place Verdun
☎ 04 68 66 30 30
🕐 Closed Tues.
💲 $

**Musée Rigaud**
✉ 16 rue de l'Ange
☎ 04 68 35 43 40
🕐 Closed Tues.
💲 $

**Tautavel**
🅰 278 B2

**Musée de La Préhistoire**
✉ avenue Leon-Jean-Gregory
☎ 04 68 29 07 76
**www.tautavel.com**
💲 $$

# More Places to Visit in Languedoc-Roussillon

## Béziers

This lively city climbs steeply up the left bank of the Orb River to the vast 14th-century **Cathédrale St.-Nazaire.** Southwest of Béziers stands **Oppidum d'Ensérune,** one of France's most important pre-Roman sites. *www.beziers-tourisme.fr* 🅰 278 C2 **Visitor Information** ✉ 29 avenue Saint-Saens ☎ 04 67 76 84 00

## Canal du Midi

Stretching 150 miles (241 km) from Toulouse to the Mediterranean at Sète or Agde, the Canal du Midi is a feat of engineering and an architectural masterpiece. 🅰 278 A2–C2

## Narbonne

Capital of the largest Roman province in Gaul and a great port until the Middle Ages, Narbonne is prosperous again thanks to the surrounding wine region. In the historic heart looms the fortified **Palais des Archevêques,** the archbishops' palace, built in the 13th and 14th centuries. Beside it, the unfinished Gothic cathedral displays a fine cloister, 14th-century stained glass, and beautiful tapestries. Behind lies a vestige of Roman Narbo, underground warehouses known as the **Horreum.** *www.mairie -narbonne.fr* 🅰 278 B2 **Visitor information** ✉ place R. Salengro ☎ 04 68 65 15 60

## Sète

Stroll along the **Grand Canal** in busy Sète to discover a string of excellent seafood restaurants. Sète is liveliest in August during the water jousting tournaments. *www.ot-sete.fr* 🅰 278 C3 **Visitor information** ✉ 60 Grand' Rue Mario-Roustan ☎ 04 67 74 71 71

## Villefranche-de-Conflent

Founded in the 12th century, Villefranche has a perfectly preserved medieval garrison. Its only alterations date from the 17th century, when Vauban added massive ramparts, gates, and **Fort Libéria.** The fort is accessible by footpath or underground passage. *www.villefranchedeconflent.fr* 🅰 278 B1 **Visitor information** ✉ place de l'Église ☎ 04 68 96 22 96,

---

## EXPERIENCE: The Little Yellow Train

The **Petit Train Jaune** (Little Yellow Train; *www.voyages-sncf.com, www .trainstouristiques-ter.com/train_jaune*) is a narrow-gauge railway that makes a dramatic journey through the Pyrenees, traveling over vertiginous gorges and viaducts via the highest station in France. It was an extraordinary achievement when it was built in 1927, the highest line in France crossing the Têt Valley at a height of 262 feet (80 m), with a particularly spectacular granite viaduct of 16 arches, 213 feet (65 m) in height.
    The train starts from Villefranche-de-Conflent and ends at Latour de Carol, traveling via Font-Romeu and Bolquère-Eyne, the highest rail station in France at 5,226 feet (1,593 m).
    Although very popular with travelers (for a seat in the open-air carriages, it is advisable to arrive early in summer), the train—sometimes called the "Métro of the Pyrenees"—also fulfills an important local function by linking the small villages of the Cerdagne with the plain.
    The train was recently threatened with closure, but there was considerable protest, and its future has now been secured. The train has even been awarded UNESCO World Heritage status.

An island in the Mediterranean 140 miles (225 km) from Nice and 90 miles (145 km) from Italy; part of France now but Italian for centuries

# Corsica

A tribute to famed native son Napoleon Bonaparte

# Corsica

Perhaps the best way to soak up the flavor of Corsica is to sip an aperitif on a café terrace in the early evening and observe the *passagiata*–locals on their nightly stroll. Like the local language, this custom is more Italian than French, but Corsica is far too independent to be described in terms of either. It has been a French province since 1769, after several centuries of Italian rule. In the 18th century, it enjoyed a brief (and nostalgically evoked) period of autonomy.

Bonifacio's fortified upper town blends into the limestone cliffs on which it sits.

The third largest island in the Mediterranean, Corsica is a wild and beautiful place, aptly described as a mountain in the sea. The coastline is glorious, with rugged cliffs

## NOT TO BE MISSED:

The *passagiata*–evening stroll–in the old town of Bastia **330**

Swimming in the sparkling clear water off Cap Corse **331**

A boat trip around the Golfe de Porto **332**

The curious ancient menhirs of Filitosa **333**

Walking along the GR20 across the mountains **334**

and wonderful beaches.. Parts are now fully developed resorts with huge marinas, water sports of all kinds, and frenetic nightlife. Coastal ports such as Ajaccio, Bastia, and Bonifacio are as colorful and lively as anywhere in the Mediterranean. But there are still plenty of remote coves and deserted beaches to discover, and the mountains are a paradise for nature lovers. Corsica also has a legacy of fine Romanesque churches and several important megalithic monuments, most notably the stone warriors of Filitosa.

The real Corsica lives on behind the coastal facade: Shepherds still move their flocks between lowlands and higher pastures every year, and religious festivals are celebrated with medieval passion. In the mountains and fortified citadels, Corsica's stormy past of bandits and vendettas never seems very far away. ■

# Around the Island

The most romantic way to get to Corsica is by sea—by ferry either into Bastia in the north or Bonifacio or Ajaccio in the south. As you disembark, the fragrance of the herb-scented *maquis*, for which the island is famous, greets you.

Bustling, colorful **Bastia** *(Map C4),* a good starting point, is dominated by a great 16th-century Genoese citadel above the old harbor. Life revolves around **Place St. Nicolas** (the tourist office is here, *tel 04 95 54 20 40, www.bastia-tourisme.com),* with its warren of Italianate streets. The extensively renovated 14th-century **Palais des Gouvernours** *(tel 04 95 31 09 12, www.musee-bastia.com, closed Mon., $)* houses the Musée d'Ethnographie, explaining the history of the island. The port itself has a lively waterfront with plenty of cafés and restaurants flanking the 17th-century **Église de St.-Jean-Baptiste.**

North of Bastia stretches the peninsula of **Cap Corse.** You can drive around it in a day, stopping at beaches and fishing ports.

Along the eastern shore is **Erbalunga,** a fishing harbor favored by artists. A rewarding detour might take in the villages of **Macinaggio, Rogliano,** and the castle of **San Colombano.** Down the west coast, the road is often precipitous, but the views are ample compensation. **Canari** has a superb 12th-century Pisan-Romanesque church, with a fine view out to sea. The Genoese watchtower at **Nonza** also gives a magnificent view over the **Golfe de St.-Florent** to the south.

**Calvi**

331 B4

**Visitor information**

✉ Port de Plaisance

☎ 04 95 65 16 67

**Porto**

331 A3

**Visitor information**

✉ place de la Marine

☎ 04 95 26 10 55

**Palais Fesch**

✉ 50 rue Fesch

☎ 04 95 21 48 17

🕓 Closed Sun & Mon.

💲 $$

## Nebbio Valley & Monte Grosso

**St.-Florent** *(Map 331 C4, visitor information, tel 04 95 37 06 04)* in the Nebbio Valley basin is positively chic, with a marina full of yachts. The **Île Rousse,** a major resort named for its red cliffs, is best avoided in high summer. Charming **Calvi,** enclosed on its promontory and dominated by a baroque church, can also get very crowded.

A splendid drive leads inland from the L'Île-Rousse to **Belgodère** and **Muro,** villages with superb sea views. **Calenzana** *(Map 331 B4)* is a starting point for long-distance hiking trails and for the route up Monte Grosso.

The **Golfe de Porto** is so beautiful that it is protected in its entirety; wonderful drives and boat trips go around the coast. The red cliffs at **Calanche,** dipping straight into the sea, are best seen

by boat *(ask at the information office in Porto).* **Porto** is a pretty little harbor but very popular; a better bet is **Piana.**

## Ajaccio & Prehistoric Corsica

The capital of southern Corsica is **Ajaccio** *(Map 331 A2–A3, visitor information, boulevard du Roi Jerome, tel 04 95 51 53 03).* Cradled by mountains, this bustling town basks in Corsica's mildest climate. There is a distinctly Arab flavor to its white stucco houses, fountains, and palm trees. Napoleon Bonaparte was born here, and the evidence is everywhere. The **Maison Bonaparte** *(rue St.-Charles),* where he grew up, has family portraits and memorabilia. The **Palais Fesch,** built by Napoleon's uncle, houses a magnificent collection of Italian art plundered during Napoleon's

Sailboats and fishing craft anchor in pretty Macinaggio, a small port town north of Bastia.

Italian campaign. The **Chapelle Impériale** next door was built by Napoleon III as a Bonaparte family mausoleum. There is a splendid view of the town and the bay from the **Jetée de la Citadelle.** Ajaccio is as close as you can get to the Côte d'Azur in Corsica, with good restaurants, cafés, a marina crowded with yachts, and a casino. At the bay's northern tip rise the **Îles Sanguinaires,** rocky islets so named because they glow blood red at sunset.

## INSIDER TIP:

**Porto-Vecchio's white sand beaches and impossibly clear turquoise water feel more Caribbean than European.**

—SYLVIE BIGAR
National Geographic Traveler
*magazine writer*

To the south is **Filitosa** *(Map 331 B2)* with 3,000-year-old menhirs carved to resemble armed warriors. Some of the best are displayed in the Musée de Préhistoire Corse in Sartène (see below).

At the extreme south of Corsica is the port of **Bonifacio,** its upper town set on craggy limestone cliffs hollowed into caves by the sea. From here the views in clear weather stretch as far as Sardinia. The 12th-century citadel was once the headquarters of the French Foreign Legion.

## Porto-Vecchio & Inland

The **Golfe de Porto-Vecchio** *(Map 331 C2)* offers splendid beaches. This is the beginning of the Côte des Nacres (Mother-of-Pearl Coast), with marinas, bars, and discos. Inland is **Solenzara** *(Map 331 C2);* winding roads lead to the pass at Col de Bavella, dominated by the statue of Notre-Dame de Bavella.

## Sartène

An inland mountain town of granite walls and cobbled lanes above the Rizzanese Valle, Sartène has an old Genoese palace that is now a wine center with tastings of the local Sartènais wine. The **Église de Ste.-Marie** houses the wooden cross and iron chain used for the local religious procession of U Catenacciu (The Chained One). On Good Friday, a citizen, disguised in red robes and hood, reenacts Christ's struggle to carry the cross to Calvary. A candlelit procession follows. The newly renovated **Musée de Préhistoire Corse** *(rue Croce, tel 04 95 77 01 09)* in Sartène's old prison has archaeological finds from all over the island.

## Corte

Corte is the main university town. From 1755 to 1769, it was the capital of a briefly independent Corsica. The old town's steep streets and the citadel—housing the **Musée de la Corse** *(tel 04 95 45 25 45)*—sit on a rocky promontory. A good way to reach Corte is by the narrow-gauge railroad that runs between Bastia and Ajaccio. ∎

**Site Préhistorique de Filitosa**
☏ 04 95 74 00 91

**Bonifacio**
🅰 331 B1
Visitor information
✉ 2 rue Fred. Scamaioni
☏ 04 95 73 11 88
🕐 Closed Nov.– Easter

**Sartène**
🅰 331 B2
Visitor information
✉ 14 cours Soeur Amelie
☏ 04 95 77 15 40

**Corte**
🅰 331 B3
Visitor information
✉ La Citadelle
☏ 04 95 46 26 70
**www.corte-tourisme .com**

# Walking in Corsica

Experiencing Corsica by foot involves rugged landscapes and grand flora. A long-distance trail (GR20) crosses the mountainous center of the island from north to south through the Parc Naturel Régional de la Corse, a vast conservation area of mountains and coastline.

**Corte**
🏔 331 B3
**Visitor information**
✉ La Citadelle
☎ 04 95 46 26 70
**www.corte-tourisme .com**

A 15-minute drive from bustling Calvi is the perched village of Montemaggiore, a quiet place that's a magnet for hikers.

Starting from Calenzana, just inland from Calvi, and ending at Conca on the Golfe de Porto-Vecchio, the GR20 is about 130 miles (210 km) long and can take up to 15 days to walk. Basic mountain refuges are set along the way (bring your own food). The first section between Calenzana and Vizzavona is the most difficult: Experience of mountain walking is essential, but the rewards great.

An easier alternative is the **Mare e Monti Trail** between Calenzana and Cargese. You can take the train to Corte or Vizzavona from Ajaccio or Bastia. **Corte** makes a good base for walking; suggestions are the **Gorges de la Restonica, Lac de Melo,** and the **Forêt de Vizzavona,** where several hiking trails are marked. ■

## Wildflowers

Corsica is famous for its *maquis*, the aromatic undergrowth of shrubs and herbs that covers most of the island. Once, the island was forested, mainly by oaks, like those at Porto-Vecchio. When the trees were felled, the vegetation became maquis, a spiny thicket of lentisk, Spanish broom and juniper, wild olive, rock rose, thyme, rosemary, and lavender. (In World War II, partisans hid in the maquis of southern France, giving the Resistance its other name, the Maquis.) In Corsica, spring is the best time to see the maquis in flower, with unique species such as the Corsican crocus and Corsican hellebore.

# Travelwise

The Paris subway's pretty art nouveau signs bespeak a strong sense of place.

# TRAVELWISE

## PLANNING YOUR TRIP

### When to Go

Choosing when to go depends on what type of vacation you are looking for. The French Government Tourist Office (F.G.T.O.) has a number of offices outside France to advise you (see p. 342). Air France offices abroad also offer many vacation services beyond booking flights (see p. 337). Once you have decided which areas you want to visit, you can contact the region's Comité Departmental de Tourisme (C.D.T.) or the local visitor information office for more information. Most big towns have either a Syndicat d'Initiative or an Office de Tourisme, while in smaller villages, the town hall (mairie) provides details.

www.tourisme.fr
www.culture.fr

There are several excellent English- language websites which are a mine of information:

www.franceguide.com
www.holidayfrance.org.uk
www.francetourism.com
www.paris.org
www.info-france-usa.org
www.visitmonaco.com
www.anglophone-direct.com
www.france.angloinfo.com
www.frenchentree.com
www.informationfrance.com
www.francethisway.com

## Climate

Partly in both northern and southern Europe, France has three different climates: Atlantic, Mediterranean, and continental. Winter temperatures throughout France may drop below freezing, with winds and storms lashing the Atlantic coastal regions. Southern Atlantic and Mediterranean France, though much warmer, nevertheless has a chilly winter. Snow is not unknown in the south. The continental climate of eastern France is generally cooler in both winter and summer, but is subject to the greatest extremes, with cold winters followed by hot and sometimes stormy summers.

Overall, winter temperatures in France vary from around 15° to 50°F (-10° to 10°C), and summer temperatures from around 65° to 85°F (18° to 30°C) in the hottest areas.

## Main Events

Throughout the year, France is alive with festivals, ranging from the major traditional fêtes, such as the flower festival in Nice to tiny village celebrations of the local harvest of, say, garlic or chestnuts. Others, such as the famous pardon processions in Brittany, celebrate individual saints' days.

More and more French towns and cities stage cultural events such as jazz, opera, and theater festivals, and these often take place in historic buildings, from Romanesque abbeys to Roman amphitheaters. Depending on the event, most tickets can be bought at the door, but for blockbuster concerts summer months, reserve in advance online, over the phone, or at the FNAC chains or Virgin Megastores in major towns.

Although most of the major festivals take place during the summer months, others are seasonal; wine festivals, for example, take place in October, after the vendange (grape harvest). Religious festivals are often celebrated with great ceremony, and Easter and Christmas both offer opportunities to see and participate in traditional local events.

**January** Paris fashion shows; Limoux Carnival.

**February** Menton Lemon Festival; Nice Carnival.

**March** Monte-Carlo festival of contemporary film music.

**April** Lourdes Sacred Music Festival; Easter celebrations; Paris marathon; Le Mans motorcycle race.

**May** Cannes Film Festival; Grasse international rose show; Mâcon wine fair; Stes.-Marie-de-la-Mer gypsy pilgrimage; Monaco Grand Prix; Nîmes feria.

**June** Strasbourg Music Festival; Les Imaginaires at Mont-St.-Michel; Chartres International Organ Festival; Noirlac Music Festival; Le Mans 24-hour car race; Chantilly Prix de Diane Hermès horse race.

**July** Tour de France; Aix-en-Provence Festival; Antibes Jazz Festival; Avignon Festival; Bastille Day, celebrated throughout France on the 14th; Nice Jazz Festival; Quimper Fêtes de Cornouailles.

**August** Antibes International fireworks festival; Lorient Celtic Festival; Marciac Jazz Festival; Menton International Chamber Music Festival; Dijon grape harvest and folk fair; Bagnères de Luchon flower festival.

**October** Dijon International Gastronomy Fair; Paris Motor Show; Paris Jazz Festival.

**November** Beaujolais Nouveau celebrations; Beaune wine auction; Dijon Gastronomic Fair.

**December** Paris Boat Show; Strasbourg Christmas market.

## What to Take

You can buy anything you need in France. Pharmacies offer a wide range of drugs and medical supplies, along with expert advice, but you should bring any prescription drugs you might need. If you wear them, a second pair of glasses or contact lenses are a legal requirement if you plan to drive. Sunscreen and anti-mosquito products are advisable in summer. Clothing will depend on your destination and when you travel. You will only need to really dress up for big-city restaurants or casinos; don't be too casual, however. Sports equipment can be rented, but bring personal equipment like walking boots with you. In France, electricity is 220 volts, 50 Hz, and most plugs have two round pins. If you bring electrical equipment, you will need an adapter, and, for U.S. appliances, a transformer.

Last, don't forget the essentials: passport, driver's license, ATM card, and insurance documentation.

## Insurance
Make sure you have adequate coverage for medical treatment and expenses, including repatriation and baggage and money loss.

## HOW TO GET TO FRANCE
### Passports
U.S. and Canadian citizens need only a passport to enter France for up to 90 days' stay. No visa is required.

### Airlines
All the major airlines have flights to France, and many arrange package tours and budget-price flights. Nonstop flights from North America all go to Paris (Delta also flies nonstop to Nice and Lyon). You will arrive in Paris from abroad either at Roissy–Charles de Gaulle or Orly Sud airport. Package tours may fly into other airports.

### Useful numbers in France
**Air France,** tel 08 20 82 08 20, www.airfrance.com
**American Airlines,** tel 08 10 87 28 72, www.aa.com
**Continental,** tel 01 71 23 03 35, www.continental.com
**Delta,** tel 08 11 64 00 05 www.delta.com
**United,** tel 08 10 72 72 72, www.united.com
**Ryanair,** tel 08 92 23 23 75, www.ryanair.com
**Easyjet,** tel 08 26 10 26 11, www.easyjet.com

## Budget Airlines
The growth of budget airlines has created options for less expensive flights from Britain to regional airports in France. It is a volatile market, however, with frequent changes.

## Airports
### Roissy-Charles de Gaulle (CDG)
Tel 01 48 62 22 80
Roissy-Charles de Gaulle is 15 miles (26 km) north of Paris near the A1 autoroute. From here you can get on the Paris périphérique (beltway). The airport bus from Roissy-C.D.G. (lines 1 and 2) will take you as far as Rue Scribe; it runs every day between 5:45 a.m. and 11 p.m. An airport bus goes to the Gare de l'Est main-line railroad station. There is also a rail service (RER B every 15 minutes) with stops at Gare du Nord, Châtelet, St.-Michel, Notre-Dame, Luxembourg, Port Royal, Denfert-Rochereau, and Cité Universitaire. Taxis are very expensive.

### Orly Sud
Tel 01 49 75 15 15
Orly is 10 miles (15 km) south of Paris. A shuttle bus links Orly Sud (international flights) to Orly Ouest (national flights) every 15 minutes between 6 a.m. and 11:30 p.m. The jetbus from the

Orly airports runs to Denfert-Rochereau Métro station from 6 a.m. to 10:30 p.m. The railroad service from Orly to central Paris (RER C every 15 minutes) takes approximately 40 minutes. Tickets for rail services can be bought inside the airport terminals from a computerized ticket machine.

Buses to connect with rail services are within easy access. Besides renting a car, the rail links are the easiest way to get into the city, and most railroad stations are close to a Métro station, or linked to one. An airport bus runs between Orly and Roissy-C.D.G. every 20 minutes. The Orlyval bus links up with the RER B rail line, which goes out to Roissy-C.D.G.

## From the United Kingdom
Eurotunnel (or the Channel Tunnel) offers a fast, frequent rail service (**Eurostar,** www.eurostar.com) between London, Lille, and Paris. The SNCF central reservation office is in Paris (tel 08 36 35 35 35, www.sncf.com). **Le Shuttle** (www.eurotunnel.com) transports cars and passengers between Folkestone and Calais. The journey through the tunnel lasts about 35 minutes. Le Shuttle runs 24 hours a day year-round.

Several ferry and hovercraft services operate from the U.K. to the northern French ports. For information, contact **Brittany Ferries** (Portsmouth and Plymouth to St. Malo, Caen, and Roscoff), Wharf Road, Portsmouth PO2 8RU, Tel 08 70 53 60 360, www.brittany-ferries.com. **Norfolkline** (Dover to Dunkerque), tel 08 70 16 42 114, www.norfolkline.com. **P&O** (Dover to Calais and Portsmouth to Le Havre, Cherbourg, and St. Malo), Channel View Road, Dover CT17 9TJ, tel 08 70 59 80 333, www.poferries.com.

# GETTING AROUND
## By Airplane
Air France is the main domestic airline in France (tel 08 20 82 08 20, www.airfrance.com)

## By Train
The French national railroad, the **SNCF** (Société Nationale des Chemins de Fer), links Paris and all major cities. You can buy train tickets in advance from your travel agent or an SNCF office (tel 008 91 36 35, www.sncf.fr), or at a station or travel agency (agence de voyage) in France.

Some services require a seat reservation as well as a ticket, and stations often have separate ticket and reservation desks. You can travel to all major cities from Paris by TGV (Train à Grande Vitesse), or by regular train. The Motorail service transports passengers together with their cars or motorbikes. Both the TGV and the Motorail service require reservations.

For long-distance journeys, you can travel overnight by couchette (shared sleeping car) or voiture-lit (private sleeping car). Both of these services must be reserved in advance.

If you buy your train ticket in France, you must punch it at the time-stamping machine (composteur) by the platform entrance before boarding. Once stamped, a ticket is valid for 24 hours.

Foreign visitors to France can buy a special vacation rail pass valid for up to one month. The pass costs less than individual tickets and often offers reduced rates on other transportation. Ask for details of La Carte "France Vacances Pass." North Americans have a wide choice of passes, including Eurailpass, Flexipass, and Saver Pass, which can only be purchased in the U.S. (1-877-257-2887, www.raileurope.com). The France Rail 'n' Drive pass offers a flexible rail and car rental package, while the Fly, Rail, and Drive pass combines internal flights with train travel and car rental. Discounts are available for students and senior citizens.

## By Car
France has a good network of roads, from small and often picturesque C and D roads to autoroutes, often called péages, because a toll (péage) must be paid. Occasionally you pay a fixed fee upon entering a section of autoroute; more often you are given a ticket as you enter, and you pay as you leave according to the distance traveled. Credit cards are accepted in the pay booths. There are gas stations with 24-hour service approximately every 15 miles (20 km), but there are also, more frequently, parking and picnic places (called Aires). The main routes nationales between towns and cities (N on maps) are generally in excellent condition.

### Renting a Car
Arrange a car rental with your local travel agent before leaving home—it can be much cheaper. Otherwise there are desks in airports and major railroad stations in France. There are fly-drive options with most flights, and the SNCF offers a train/car rental package.

Central offices:
**ADA,** www.ada.fr
**Avis,** tel 08 20 05 05 05, www.avis.fr
**Budget,** tel 08 25 00 35 64, www.budget.com
**Europcar,** tel 08 25 35 83 58, www.europcar.com
**Hertz,** tel 01 41 91 95 25, www.hertz.com

To rent a car, you must have a current driver's license (held for at least three years) and be at least 21 years old. Some companies will not rent to people under 26 or over 60.

### Age Limits & Licenses
The minimum age limit for driving in France is 18 years. Visitors from North America and the U.K. need only their home driver's license. Drivers who wear glasses or contacts must have a pair with them while driving.

### Breakdown Assistance
Autoroutes and routes nationales have emergency telephones every mile (2 km). Police stations (gendarmeries) have information about breakdown services or garages—call them at (17). For accidents, see p. 343.

### Busy Periods
Roads will be busy from the beginning of July and especially around August 15, a major national holiday. In summer, watch for the small green BIS (Bison Futé) signs which indicate alternative routes. A brochure in English on the Bison Futé routes is available from French government tourist offices.

### Children
Children under ten must travel in the rear seat.

### Drunk Driving
The French drunk-driving limit is 50 mg of alcohol per 100 ml of blood (.05%). This can mean that as little as one glass of beer can take you up to the limit.

### Gas
Fuel is sold by the liter (3.75 liters equals an American gallon). Most gas stations accept credit cards. Be aware that 24-hour self-service machines will take only Cartes Bancaires (French bank cards) and no other credit cards.

## Headlights

Motorcycles must have headlights on when moving, and cars must use headlights in poor visibility. All vehicles must carry a spare set of lightbulbs.

## On-the-spot Fines

On-the-spot fines may be levied by police for several offenses, including speeding, not wearing seat belts, and not having the car's documentation with you. Speedcheck cameras are very common.

## Parking

Some French towns and cities have blue zones where parking is free for up to an hour. You need to display a parking disk (disque de stationnement), which you obtain from garages, tabacs, and tourist offices. Otherwise, most towns have on-street parking machines (horodateurs). Coins required vary from 20 cents to 2 euros. Multistory parking garages are common. Some close overnight and may shut by 8 p.m.

## Priorité à Droite

Traditionally, priority on French roads was given to vehicles approaching from the right, except where otherwise indicated. Nowadays, on main roads, the major road will normally have priority, with traffic being halted on minor approach roads with one of the following signs:
• Cedez le passage: yield
• Vous n'avez pas la priorité: you do not have right of way
• Passage protégé: no right of way
A yellow diamond sign indicates that you have priority; a diamond sign with a diagonal black line indicates that you do not.

Take care in small towns and rural areas without road markings, where you may be expected to yield to traffic coming from the right. If oncoming drivers flash their headlights, it is to indicate that they have priority, not the other way around. Priority is always given to emergency and public utility vehicles.

## Road Conditions

For current road conditions, telephone the Inter Service Route line or tune into the local radio frequency (often indicated on signs beside roads). Autoroute information, tel 08 26 02 20 22, www.autoroutes.fr.

## Road Signs

• Access interdit: no entry
• Allumez vos feux: switch on lights
• Interdiction de stationner: no parking
• Passage pour piétons: pedestrian crossing
• Sens unique: one-way traffic
• Virages sur...km: curves for...km
• Zone bleue: parking disk required

## Seat Belts

The wearing of seat belts is mandatory in both the front and rear seats.

## Speed Limits

There are different speed limits for normal weather and times of poor visibility (heavy rain or fog). Autoroutes have limits of 75–85 mph (110–130 kph; slower limit applies in poor visibility); two-lane roads 60–75 mph (90–110 kph); other open roads 50–55 mph (80–90 kph); and towns 30 mph (50 kph).

## Traffic Circles

Vehicles already on a traffic circle have priority, except very occasionally in small towns where priorité à droite still applies.

## Traffic Lights

Signals are sometimes suspended high over the road and can easily be missed.

## Green Travel

Travel by train and local public transport is the most eco-friendly way to go. Or put your car on the train and only drive when you get there. For information on carbon offsetting go to:
www.carbonfund.org
www.ecotourism.org
www.theinternationalcentrefor
responsibletourism.org
www.climatecare.org

## Transportation in Paris

### Taxis

Taxis can be found outside every main-line train station and airport, and at taxi ranks throughout the city. You can also call a taxi (01 45 30 30 30).
Taxi drivers in Paris operate on three tariffs:
• Tariff A, 7 a.m. to 7 p.m.
• Tariff B, 7 p.m. to 7 a.m.
• Tariff C, at night in the suburbs and during the day in the outlying districts of Hauts-de-Seine, Seine St. Denis, and Val-de-Marne, when the taxi has no client for the return journey.

Extra charges are added for pickups at train stations, luggage weighing over 12 lbs/5kg, a fourth passenger (the driver can refuse to take more than three passengers), and an animal (except for a seeing-eye dog). A 10 percent tip to taxi drivers is usual.

### Public Transportation

There are three kinds of public transportation in Paris: Métropolitan (Métro), Réseau Express Régional (RER)—high speed suburban rail lines—and Autocar (the bus, sometimes called "car"). A Carte Orange is good for unlimited trips on Métro, RER, and buses for one week, or for a month. You will need a passport-size photograph for a Carte Orange. A Paris Visite card is available at Métro stations and is good for one, two, three, or five days and entitles you to unlimited use of public transportation and discounts at some sights. The Formule 1 card, also available at the Métro ticket booths, is good for all transportation for one day only. If you need advice on bus, Métro, or rail travel, ask at a tourist office.

## Using the Métro

Maps are posted in every Métro station, or ask for a free *Plan du Métro* when you buy a ticket. Each line has a number and is identified by the station at the end of the line. A *carnet* (book) of ten tickets is a useful savings if you plan to use the Métro frequently. A Carte Orange is good for unlimited trips on Métro, RER, and buses for one week, or for a month. You will need a passport-size photograph for a Carte Orange. A Paris Visite card is available at Métro stations and is good for one, two, three, or five days and entitles you to unlimited use of public transportation and discounts at some sights. The Formule 1 card, also available at the Métro ticket booths, is good for all transportation for one day only. If you need advice on bus, Métro, or rail travel, ask at a tourist office.

## Vélib' Bikes

This is self-service bike-hire system in Paris and several other cities, including Nice and Perpignan. You will need a credit card to for deposit. (www.velib.paris.fr)

## PRACTICAL ADVICE
## Communications
### Post Offices

The PTT (pronounced *pay-tay-tay*) controls both the mail and telecommunication services. Offices are open from 9 a.m. to 5 p.m. on weekdays and from 9 a.m. to noon on Saturdays (in smaller towns, offices will close for lunch and in villages, they may only be open for two or three hours on weekday mornings). Mail can be delivered to you at a post office if it is marked "Poste Restante" with the postal code of the Bureau de Poste at which you collect it; you will have to pay a fee for each item of mail (www.laposte.fr).

### Mailboxes

Yellow *boîtes postales* (mailboxes) are located outside every PTT and on walls in larger towns. They may have separate compartments for local mail, *départemental* (mail within the département), and *autres départements/destinations* (elsewhere in France and foreign).

### Telephones

French telephone numbers have ten digits usually written divided into pairs, for example, 01 23 45 67 89. Numbers in Paris begin with 01, numbers in the northwest of the country begin with 02, in the northeast with 03, southeast with 04, and southwest with 05. Reach an operator by dialing 12.

To call a French number (for example, 01 23 45 67 89) from abroad, dial the international code (011 from United States and Canada, 00 from the U.K.), then the code for France (33), followed by the number, omitting the first 0: 011 33 1 23 45 67 89. Numbers beginning in 08 are accessible only in France. French mobile numbers begin with 06.

### Phone Booths

*Cabines téléphoniques* stand outside larger post offices, in railroad stations and airports, or near roads or parking garages in towns and villages. They take either phone cards or credit cards. Post offices contain telephones where you can make your call first and pay at the counter afterward. Phones in bars and cafés may still take cash, and proprietors will usually permit use of the phone in an emergency. Phone cards *(télécartes)* can be bought at post offices, newsagents, and any tobacconist *(bureau de tabac)*.

### International Calls

To make an international call from France, dial 00 followed by the country's international code. These can be found in the front of the Pages Jaunes section of the *annuaire* or posted in a telephone booth. Some useful ones are: Australia 61; Canada 1; Ireland 353; United Kingdom 44; United States 1.

For international directory assistance, dial 32 12, followed by the country code. Additional information can be found at www.pagesjaunes.fr.

To dial toll-free numbers *(numéros verts)*, insert a card or money to make the connection (coins will be returned after the call, units will not be registered against cards). Reduced-rate calls in France and Europe are 7 p.m.–8 a.m. weekdays, noon Sat–8 a.m. Mon.; for U.S. and Canada, 7 p.m.–1 p.m., Mon.–Fri., and all day Sat. & Sun. Reduced rates also apply on public holidays.

### Mobile Phones

Many mobiles can be used in France, so long as there is network coverage. Don't rely on it in rural or mountainous regions. Making or receiving international calls can be very expensive. Of the U.S.-based mobiles, only those that are "tri-band" will work in France. Consult your provider before you travel to see if they have arrangements for making international calls.

If you need to make a lot of local calls, it may be worth buying a French SIM card and charge cards from French operators (Orange, SFR, and Boygues), which have public shops. There are also many Web-based services, such as Skype and VOIP ('Voice Over Internet Protocol') that will allow you to make free calls via your computer to other Skype users or cheaper calls to mobiles or land-lines.

## Internet
Wi-Fi is widely available in hotels, cafés, and bars. Broadband (ADSL) is also widely available. Libraries and tourist offices may provide access.

## Départements
France is divided into 96 administrative *départements*, each named after a principal river and identified by a number. When making any inquiries about a region, it is helpful to know the *département* names and numbers: for example 09 *(zero-neuf)* Ariège.

## Conversions
1 kilo = 2.2 lbs
1 litre = 0.26 U.S. gallons
1 mile = 1.6 km

## Etiquette & Local Customs
Etiquette is very important in France. Always be ready to shake hands when you are introduced, and when you meet friends and acquaintances. Kissing on both cheeks is also very common. When entering any establishment, it is polite to offer a general *"Bonjour, messieurs/dames."* Young women are addressed as *"Mademoiselle"*, a woman in her 20s or older as *"Madame."* Address a waiter as *"Monsieur"*–*"Garçon"* (boy) is not acceptable—and call a waitress either *"Madame"* or *"Mademoiselle."*

When visiting churches and cathedrals, dress appropriately and respect the sensitivities of those who are there for devotional purposes. Visitors are requested not to walk around religious buildings during services. Even though in most cases no fee is charged to visit a church or cathedral, it is polite to contribute to one of the donation boxes.

## Holidays
All banks, post offices, and many museums, galleries, and stores close on these national holidays:
January 1 *(Jour de l'An)*
Easter Sunday *(Pâques)* and Monday
May 1 *(Fête du Travail)*
May 8 *(Victoire 1945)*
Ascension *(Ascension)*
Pentecost *(Pentecôte)*
July 14 *(Fête Nationale)*
August 15 *(Assomption)*
November 1 *(Toussaint)*
November 11 *(Armistice 1918)*
December 25 *(Noël)*

## Media
### American & British newspapers
Newspapers and magazines are sold in Maisons de la Presse, many of which stock American or British newspapers (often the previous day's edition). International newspapers are available in airports, major railroad stations, and most large hotels.

Regional newspapers contain national and international as well as local news, and are often read more than the national press. The main national dailies are Le Monde, conservative Le Figaro, and left-wing Libération and L'Humanité. American and British dailies—the International Herald Tribune, Times, and Daily Telegraph—are widely available in major towns and cities.

### TV Channels
French television offers six TV channels: TF1, France 2, France 3, 5, and La Cinquième, which in the evening, becomes Arte, a combined Franco-German transmission), and M6. TF1 occasionally shows undubbed American films with French subtitles; Arte more frequently shows subtitled international films and art programs. The main television news programs are at 1 p.m. and 8 p.m. You can also see cable and satellite channels such as CNN, MTV, and BBC World.

### Radio
The national radio station, France Inter (1892m long wave), broadcasts English-language news twice a day in summer (generally at 9 a.m. and 4 p.m.). During the peak holiday period, other local stations may have English broadcasts. On the Mediterranean, Riviera Radio (106.3 and 106.5 kHz) broadcasts 24 hours a day in English.

## Money Matters
The euro is available in 500, 200, 100, 50, 20, 10, and 5 euro notes, 2 and 1 euro coins, and 50, 20, 10, 5, and 1 cent coins.

Most major banks have ATMs for bank (debit) cards and international credit cards with instructions in a choice of languages. You can withdraw money from your own account in euros, but you may be charged a fee. You will need a four-digit PIN: Arrange this with your bank before leaving home. Currency can be exchanged in banks and bureaux de change in train stations and airports.

Credit cards are widely accepted. Visa is by far the most common. Mastercard (Access/Eurocard) and Diners Club are also widely accepted, while American Express is less popular. Carte Bancaire (CB) is a French card encompassing both Visa and Mastercard.

## Opening Times

Nearly all stores and offices close for lunch from noon to 2 p.m., often to 3 p.m. or 4 p.m. in summer in the south. Many stores close for the morning or all day Mon. or Wed.

**Banks** 9 a.m.–5 p.m. Mon.–Sat., closing for lunch

**Post offices** 9 a.m.–6 p.m. weekdays, closing for lunch; 9 a.m. to noon Sat.

**Stores** 9 a.m.–7 p.m. Mon.– Sat., closing for lunch; some food stores also open on Sun a.m.

**Grocery stores** 9 a.m.–7 p.m. Mon.–Sat., some closing for lunch except Sat. and sometimes Fri.

**Bureaux de Tabac** and **Maisons de la Presse** 8 a.m.–7 p.m. Mon. –Sat., 8 a.m.–noon Sun.

**Gas stations** usually close at 9 p.m. except on autoroutes.

**Museums** close for lunch from noon to 2 p.m, except perhaps during the months of July and/ or August. Municipal museums usually close on Mon., national museums on Tues.

## Pets

Animals under 3 months old are not allowed into France; older pets must have a certificate attesting that they have had a rabies vaccination within the last year, or an official declaration that they have been brought from a rabies-free area.

## Time Differences

France runs on CET (Central European Time), one hour ahead of Greenwich Mean Time, six hours ahead of Eastern Standard Time. France uses the 24-hour clock.

## Tipping

Most restaurant bills include a service charge, generally indicated at the bottom of the menu. If in doubt, ask: *Est-ce que le service est compris?* It is usual to leave a small additional tip for the waiter if the service has been good. It is customary to tip taxi drivers 10 percent, though this is not obligatory. Give porters, doormen, tour guides, and hairdressers a tip of 1–2 euros; usherettes and cloakroom attendants 5 euros. There is no need to leave a tip for hotel maids unless you have required out-of-the-ordinary service.

## Toilets

Self-cleaning toilet cabins can be found on the street (not wheelchair accessible). You can use the toilet in a bar or café, signposted *les toilettes* or *les WC* (pronounced *lay vay-say*). Public toilets vary; some, particularly in the south, are old-fashioned squat toilets. If there is an attendant; tip with small change.

## Tourist Offices

### U.S.A.

**East Coast**

Maison de la France
825 Third Ave.
New York, NY 10022
Tel 212/838-7800
Fax 212/838-7855

**West Coast**

9454 Wilshire Blvd., Suite 715
Beverly Hills, CA 90212
Tel 310/271-6665
Fax 310/276-2835

**Midwest**

676 North Michigan Ave.
Chicago, IL 60611
Fax 312/337-6339

### CANADA

**Montréal**

1981 Ave. McGill College, #490
Montréal, Quebec H3A 2W9
Tel 514/876-9881
Fax 514/845-4868

### FRANCE

Maison de la France
23 Place de Catalogne
75014 Paris
Tel 01 42 96 70 00
www.franceguide.com

## TRAVELERS WITH DISABILITIES

France can be difficult for disabled travelers, especially on the steep winding streets of old towns and villages. Parking spaces are provided (bring your international orange disc with you), and wheelchairs can be rented through pharmacies. Wheelchair access is often limited, though newer museums will offer facilities, and beaches try to provide access. SNCF has train carriages designed to accommodate wheelchairs, and taxi drivers are obliged to take disabled people and guide dogs. More and more hotels have specially adapted rooms. For more information contact:

**Association des Paralysés de France,** tel 01 40 78 69 00, www.apf.asso.fr

**Access in Paris,** www.access inparis.org

**Federation Francaise Handisport,** tel 01 40 31 45 00, www .handisport.org; information on sports and leisure facilities

**Le Guide Accessible Accommodation,** www.guide-accessible .com; restaurants, etc.

**Mobility International USA,** 132 E. Broadway, Ste. 343, Eugene, OR USA 97401, tel 541/343-1284, www.miusa.org; information for disabled travelers

## EMERGENCIES

### Embassies in France

**U.S. Embassy** 2 avenue Gabriel, Paris 75008, tel 01 43 12 22 22; **Visas** 4 avenue Gabriel, Paris 75008, tel 08 10 26 46 26; **Consulate** Place Varian Fry, 13286 Marseille Cedaz 6, tel 04 91 54 92 00.

**Canadian Embassy** 35 avenue Montaigne, Paris 75008, tel 01 44 43 29 00; **Consulate** 37 avenue Montaigne, Paris 75008, tel 01 44 43 29 02

British Embassy 35 rue du Faubourg St.-Honore, Paris 75008, tel 01 44 51 31 00.

## Emergency Phone Numbers

**15 SAMU** (Service d'Aide Medicale d'Urgence) Ambulance
**17 Police secours** (police rescue)
**18 Pompiers** (fire rescue)
Both police and fire rescue have medical backup and work in close contact with SAMU. For legal assistance in an emergency, contact your embassy or consulate for English-speaking lawyers.

## What to Do in the Event of a Car Accident

There is no need to involve the police if you have an accident in which no one has been hurt. The official procedure is for each driver to fill out a *constat à l'amiable*, each signing the other's copy. Phone the rental company and explain what has happened.

If you are involved in a serious road accident, phone the police (17) or fire rescue (18). These numbers are free, but in a phone booth you need to insert a coin or card to make a connection (it is returned to you after the call). A number and address in the telephone booth will say where you are. Alternatively, you may find the local *police secours* number posted in the phone booth.

## Lost Property

If you lose something on a bus or the Métro, first try the terminal to see if it has been handed in. In Paris, after 48 hours, you can go to the Bureau des Objets Trouvés, 36 rue des Morillons, 75015 Paris, tel 08 21 00 25 25, where you have to pay 4 percent of the value of any item reclaimed. To report a theft or loss, go to a *gendarmerie* or *commissariat de police*. Their telephone numbers are in the front of local directories.

If you lose your passport, report first to the police, then to the nearest embassy or consulate (see above). If you are detained by the police for any reason, you are entitled to call the nearest consulate for a member of the staff to come to your assistance.

## Lost credit cards

**American Express:** tel 01 47 77 72 00, www.americanexpress.com
**Diners Club:** tel 08 20 82 05 36
**Mastercard:** tel 08 00 90 13 87, www.mastercard.com
**Visa:** tel 08 00 90 11 79, www.visaeurope.com

## Health

Check that your health insurance covers visits to France. Pharmacies—recognizable by a green cross sign—are staffed by pharmacists who can recommend treatment and tell you if you need to see a doctor and where to find one. The fee to see a doctor is 23 euros; for a doctor to come out to see you is at least 30 euros. For serious injury, go to a hospital emergency room (*urgences*).

To renew a prescription, take your medicine in its package to a pharmacy. If they do not have that product, they will try to find its equivalent. If they can only sell it to you with a prescription, they will direct you to the nearest doctor.

## International Association for Medical Assistance to Travelers

IAMAT is a nonprofit organization that anyone can join free of charge. Members receive a directory of English-speaking IAMAT doctors on call 24 hours a day and are entitled to services at set rates.
**U.S.:** 1623 Military Rd., #279, Niagara Falls, NY 14304, tel 716/754-4883
**Canada:** 67 Mowat Ave., Toronto, M6K 3ER, tel 416/652-0137

## Medical Emergencies

For an ambulance, dial 15, Service d'Aide Médicale d'Urgence. French medical treatment is of a high standard, and facilities are generally excellent. In rural areas, the *pompiers* (fire brigades) are also trained paramedics and can be called in an emergency (call 15). In major cities, a 24-hour doctor service (*médécin de garde*) is available. Emergency heart defibrillator kits are now available –usually outside the *mairie* (town hall) in many small villages emergency services may take some time to get there. In Paris, the American Hospital is at 63 boulevard Victor-Hugo, Neuilly 92292, tel 01 46 41 25 25.

## FURTHER READING

*Paris to the Moon,* Adam Gopnik (Random House, 2001)
*On the Brink,* Jonathan Fenby. (Abacus, 2002)
*Footsteps,* Richard Holmes (Flamingo, 2004)
*Celestine: Voices from a French Village,* Gillian Tindall (Minerva, 1996)
*Paris: The Secret History,* Andrew Hussey (Penguin, 2006)
*The Cathedral Builders,* Jean Gimpel (Harper & Row, 1984)
*The Food Lovers Guide to France,* Patricia Wells (Workman Publishing, 1999)
*Fragile Glory: A Portrait of France and the French,* Richard Bernstein (Plume, 1991)
*The French,* Theodore Zeldin (Kodansha, 1996)
*A Little Tour in France,* Henry James (Farrar, Straus and Giroux, 1983)
*Montaillou,* Emmanuel Le Roy Ladurie (Gallimard, 1978)
*A Moveable Feast,* Ernest Hemingway (Scribner, 1964)
*Two Towns in Provence,* M.F.K. Fisher (Vintage Books, 1983)

# Hotels & Restaurants

Excellent and varied accommodation is available all over France, ranging from grand hotels to cozy farmhouses. You can splurge on some of the finest hotels in the world or stay at cheap motel-style chains such as Formule 1 or Balladins, which will accommodate a family of four for less than 25 euros per night. You can stay in grand châteaus, or seek out small farmhouses *(chambres d'hôte)* for bed and breakfast and meals of homegrown produce. Obviously, facilities will be reflected in the price, and in cheaper hotels you may not have private baths.

## Hotels

Many hotels offer *pension* or *demi pension* accommodations. *Demi-pension* includes breakfast and dinner, while full *pension* includes lunch, as well.

## Grading System

French hotels are officially graded according to a star system, from four to one stars, indicating the minimum level of facilities. A top-tier five stars has just been awarded. The requirements of the lesser grades are assumed in the higher ones. A few hotels in this selection, either restaurants with rooms or château hotels, are not star-rated.

❁❁❁❁ Four stars indicate a hotel with a restaurant and all rooms with private bath/shower rooms.

❁❁❁ Three-star hotels have at least 80 percent of the rooms with bath/shower and offer breakfast in the room.

❁❁ Two-star establishments must have 40 percent of the rooms with bath/shower and a telephone in each room.

❁ One-star hotels offer plain but adequate accommodation.

## Organization

The following is a selection of good quality hotels throughout the country (listed by location and price, then in alphabetical order). Wherever possible, we have chosen hotels that are both individual and typical, perhaps with notable local or historic associations.

Please note that, **unless otherwise stated:**

1. Breakfast is not included in the price.
2. The hotel has a restaurant. If it is outstanding, the restaurant symbol is also given or reference is made to a separate entry for the restaurant.
3. All rooms have a telephone and television.

Room price categories are given only as guidance and do not take into account seasonal variations. Further taxes may be added to the price. Prices are per (double) room. In high season, always try to book in advance, if possible confirming by fax. You may be asked for a deposit or credit card number.

### Credit & Debit Cards

Many hotels accept all major cards. Smaller ones may only accept some, as shown in their entry. Abbreviations used are: AE (American Express), CB (Carte Bancaire), DC (Diners Club), MC (Mastercard), V (Visa).

### Hotel Chains & Groups
**U.S. contact numbers**
**Concorde Hotels,** tel 800/888-4747, www.concorde-hotels.com
**Hilton,** tel 800/445-8667, www.hilton.com
**Leading Hotels of the World,** 800/223-6800,www.lhw.com
**Relais & Châteaux,** tel 800/735-2478, www.relaischateaux.com

**French contact numbers:**
**Maisons des Gîtes de France,** tel 01 49 70 75 85

**Châteaux and Hotels Collection,** tel 01 72 72 92 02, www.chateaux hotels.com
Many départements have a Loisirs Acceuil booking service to reserve hotels, gîtes, and campsites; ask the French Tourist Office, or the local tourist office for a list

### Restaurants
Wherever you go, you will find a wide variety of restaurants, from humble auberges to the great classics. Many hotels have their own restaurants, and some restaurants also rent rooms.

Our selection (listed by location, price, then in alphabetical order) suggests good regional restaurants offering typical local dishes, as well as including some of the great stars of French cuisine. In the regions, it is always worth seeking out typical local restaurants and sampling the specialties of the area. See each regional food section for a guide to local cuisine and dishes, and the menu reader on p. 388.
L = lunch      D = dinner

### Dining Hours in France
Lunch usually starts around midday and continues until 2 p.m. Dinner is eaten around 8 p.m. but may start about 7 p.m.; in smaller places or in the countryside, you may be too late after 9 p.m. Dinner tends to be earlier in the north of the country, later as you go south.

At the height of the season, or if you have a particular place in mind, make a reservation.

🏨 Hotel  🍴 Restaurant  🛏 No. of Guest Rooms  🅿 Parking  Ⓜ Métro  🕐 Closed  🛗 Elevator

## PRICES

**HOTELS**
An indication of the cost of a double room in the high season is given by **$** signs.

| | |
|---|---|
| **$$$$$** | Over $400 |
| **$$$$** | $300–$400 |
| **$$$** | $200–$300 |
| **$$** | $100–$200 |
| **$** | Under $100 |

**RESTAURANTS**
An indication of the cost of a three-course meal without drinks is given by **$** signs.

| | |
|---|---|
| **$$$$$** | Over $150 |
| **$$$$** | $100–$150 |
| **$$$** | $80–$100 |
| **$$** | $60–$80 |
| **$** | Under $60 |

Restaurants often have outdoor tables for good weather, and even in towns and cities you may find yourself sitting on the sidewalk or in a courtyard. Facilities for outside dining are mentioned here only where the view, or perhaps the garden, is of particular note.

Menus must by law be displayed outside any establishment serving food, and studying and comparing these before making your choice is part of the pleasure. Most restaurants offer one or more *prix-fixe* menus—set meals at a fixed price, sometimes including wine. Otherwise (and usually more expensively), you order individual items *à la carte*—from the menu.

The French usually eat a salad after the main course and sometimes with the cheese course, which comes before dessert. Bread and water are supplied free. (French tap water is safe to drink.)

Wine lists in the regions are often dominated by local wines, and all restaurants offer a *vin de pays* by the carafe or demi-carafe. Although smoking is now forbidden by law in all public places in France, some hotels and restaurants have smoking terraces.

### Cafés
Cafés remain a French institution, good for morning coffee, leisurely drinks, or modest meals. In small towns and villages, they are very much the center of local life. Note that drinking at the bar is cheaper than sitting at a table.

### Tipping
A service charge is usually included in the bill. Only add more if the service has been particularly good.

## ■ PARIS

### ÎLE DE LA CITÉ

#### ⊞ DU JEU DE PAUME
**$$$ ◔◔◔◔**
54 RUE ST.-LOUIS-EN-L'ÎLE
TEL 01 43 26 14 18
FAX 01 40 46 02 76
www.jeudepaumehotel.com
In the 17th century, Court (Royal) tennis was played in this building, now creatively converted into an attractive hotel. Rooms are chic and modern. Garden.
① 30 🚇 Pont-Marie ⊟ 🄲
🄲 All major cards

#### ⊞ DE LUTÈCE
**$$$ ◔◔◔**
65 RUE ST.-LOUIS-EN-L'ÎLE, 75004
TEL 01 43 26 23 52
FAX 01 43 29 60 25
www.paris-hotel-lutece.com
A fire burns in the lobby's fireplace, and each modest room has an interesting detail, like exposed beams or a pretty mirror.

① 23 🄲 🚇 Pont Marie
⊟ AE, MC, V

#### ▯ LA TOUR D'ARGENT
**$$$$$**
15 QUAI DE LA TOURNELLE
TEL 01 43 54 23 31
FAX 01 44 07 12 04
www.latourdargent.com
On a quay just across the Seine from the Île. Perhaps no longer the peak of excellence it once was, but it still has one Michelin star and is a favorite with visitors for its duckling, and its view of the Seine River and Notre-Dame.
🚇 Pont Marie 🕒 Closed Sun.
& Mon. & all of Aug.
⊟ 🄲 🄲 All major cards

### LEFT BANK

#### ⊞ RELAIS CHRISTINE
**$$$$$ ◔◔◔◔**
3 RUE CHRISTINE
TEL 01 40 51 60 80
FAX 01 40 51 60 81
www.relais-christine.com
Discreet luxury in a former convent. No restaurant, but breakfast served in the vaulted, 13th-century kitchens. Garden.
① 35 rooms + 16 duplex 🅿
🚇 Odéon ⊟ 🄲 🄲 All major cards

#### ⊞ DUC DE SAINT-SIMON
**$$$$ ◔◔◔**
14 RUE ST.-SIMON
TEL 01 44 39 20 20
FAX 01 45 48 68 25
www.hotelducdesaintsimon
.com
A luxurious haven, with exquisite antique furnishings. There is a charming basement breakfast room and courtyard garden, but no restaurant.
① 29 + 5 suites 🚇 Rue du Bac
⊟ 🄲 AE, DC, MC, V

#### ⊞ L'HÔTEL
**$$$$**
13 RUE DES BEAUX-ARTS
TEL 01 44 41 99 00

FAX 01 43 25 64 81
www.l-hotel.com
Beautifully renovated hotel
with magnificent staircase
and swimming pool. Famous
for the room where Oscar
Wilde died—now with its own
terrace.
🚇 St.-Germain-des-Prés
🛏 🏨 All major cards

## 🏨 LUTÉTIA
**$$$$ ✪✪✪✪**
45 BOULEVARD RASPAIL
TEL 01 49 54 46 46
FAX 01 49 54 46 00
www.lutetia-paris.com
Behind the striking facade of
this enormous art deco pile,
the interior has been elegantly
restyled by designer Sonia
Rykiel. Its restaurant "Paris"
has a Michelin star, and there's
a brasserie, too.
ⓘ 220 + 30 suites 🚇 Sèvres-
Babylone 🛗 🌀 🌀 🍷
🏨 All major cards

## 🏨 DE VIEUX PARIS
**$$$ ✪✪✪✪**
9 RUE GIT LE COEUR
TEL 01 44 32 15 90
FAX 01 43 26 00 15
www.vieuxparis.com
The famous Beat hotel that
in the 1950s and 1960s accom-
modated writers William
Burroughs and Allen Ginsberg.
The 15th-century building has
been refurbished, but rooms
are small.
ⓘ 13 + 7 suites 🚇 St.-Michel
🏨 All major cards

## 🏨 ST.-BEUVE
**$$$ ✪✪✪**
9 RUE STE.-BEUVE
TEL 01 45 48 20 07
FAX 01 45 48 67 52
www.parishotelcharme.com
A pleasing and friendly
hotel that combines antique
furniture and contemporary
artworks. No restaurant.
ⓘ 22 🛗 🌀 🏨 All major cards

## 🍴 LE JULES VERNE
**$$$$$**
TOUR EIFFEL, 2ND FLOOR
TEL 01 45 55 61 44
www.lejulesverne-paris.com
Dinner with a view, *bien sûr*,
at this Michelin one-star
restaurant in one of Paris's
most famous monuments. Not
surprisingly, it is essential to
book—and weeks ahead.
🚇 Trocadéro 🌀 🏨 All major
cards

## 🍴 CLOSERIE DES LILAS
**$$$$**
171 BLVD. MONTPARNASSE
TEL 01 40 51 34 50
www.closeriedeslilas.fr
This bar/brasserie/restaurant,
once a hangout of Picasso,
Hemingway, Apollinaire, Lenin,
and others, is a good place to
eat and drink amid the literary
crowd.
🚇 Vavin 🏨 All major cards

## 🍴 VIOLON D'INGRES
**$$$$**
135 RUE ST.-DOMINIQUE
TEL 01 45 55 15 05
www.leviolondingres.com
Christian Constant, the former
chef at Les Ambassadeurs in
Hôtel de Crillon, provides the
same high-quality cuisine at
lower prices at this Michelin
one-star restaurant.
🚇 Pont de l'Alma 🕐 Closed
Sun., Mon., & all of Aug.
🌀 🏨 AE, CB, MC, V

## 🍴 LE DÔME
**$$$**
108 BLVD. MONTPARNASSE
TEL 01 43 35 25 81
A famous Montparnasse
brasserie. Fish and seafood
in a lively ambience.
🚇 Montparnasse 🕐 Closed
Sun.–Mon. in July and Aug.
🌀 🏨 All major cards

## 🍴 SPOON
**$$$**
14 RUE DE MARIGNAN
TEL 01 40 76 34 44

www.spoon.tm.fr
Popular spot where you can
create your own personal menu
from any of the dishes offered.
Speedy Spoon is good for a
quick lunch.
🚇 Franklin D. Roosevelt
🕐 Closed Sat.–Sun. & most
of Aug. 🌀 🏨 AE, DC,
MC, V

## 🍴 LA BASTIDE ODÉON
**$$**
7 RUE CORNEILLE, 75006
TEL 01 43 26 03 65
www.bastide-odeon.com
Provençal cooking with a
modern twist in a pretty set-
ting. Fixed-price lunch menus
available.
🚇 Odéon 🕐 Closed Sun.– Mon.
& Aug. 🏨 AE, MC, V

## 🍴 BRASSERIE LIPP
**$$**
151 BOULEVARD ST.-GERMAIN
TEL 01 45 48 53 91
www.ila-chateau.com/lipp
Perhaps more noted for its historical and literary connections,
and wonderful turn-of-the-cen-
tury decor, than for the food.
🚇 St.-Germain-des-Prés
🌀 🏨 AE, MC, V

## 🍴 LA COUPOLE
**$$**
102 BLVD. MONTPARNASSE
TEL 01 43 20 14 20
www.lacoupoleparis.com
A legendary art deco bras-
serie—everyone who was
anyone (including, of course,
Hemingway) came here in the
1920s. Good food, and great
service, too.
🚇 Montparnasse 🌀 🏨 All
major cards

## 🍴 L'OS À MOELLE
**$$**
3 RUE VASCO DE GAMA, 75015
TEL 01 45 57 27 27
Trained by Christian Constant,
the young chef makes a serious
effort to provide refined cuisine
at low prices. Fixed-price menus.

---

🏨 Hotel   🍴 Restaurant   ⓘ No. of Guest Rooms   🅿 Parking   🚇 Métro   🕐 Closed   🛗 Elevator

🔲 Lourmel 🕒 Closed Sun.–
Mon., & Aug. 🔲 All major
cards

### 🔲 LE PROCOPE
**$$**
13 RUE DE L'ANCIENNE COMÉDIE
TEL 01 40 46 79 00
www.procope.com
Restored to its 17th-century
splendor, Le Procope (see
p. 70) serves popular brasserie
dishes. Sorbets and ice creams
are a specialty.
🔲 Odéon 🔲 🔲 AE, MC

## RIGHT BANK

### 🔲 BALZAC
### 🔲 $$$$$ ✪✪✪✪
6 RUE BALZAC
TEL 01 44 35 18 00
FAX 01 44 35 18 05
www.hotelbalzac.com
The belle epoque building has
huge rooms, newly renovated
with sumptuous furnishings
and hi-tech equipment.
🔲 56 + 14 suites 🔲 George V
🔲 🔲 🔲 All major cards

### 🔲 BRISTOL
### $$$$$ ✪✪✪✪
112 RUE DU FAUBOURG
ST.-HONORÉ
TEL 01 53 43 43 00
FAX 01 53 43 43 01
www.lebristolparis.com
Luxury and discretion for the
rich and/or famous, with fine
works of art, tapestries, and
Persian carpets. Garden.
🔲 195 + suites 🔲 St.-Philippe-
du-Roule 🔲 🔲 🔲 🔲 🔲 All
major cards

### 🔲 DE CRILLON
### 🔲 $$$$$ ✪✪✪✪
10 PLACE DE LA CONCORDE
TEL 01 44 71 15 00
FAX 01 44 71 15 02
www.crillon.com
One of the great palace hotels,
with views over the Place de
la Concorde. Two restaurants.
Winter garden.

🔲 163 + suites 🔲 Concorde
🔲 🔲 🔲 All major cards

### 🔲 FOUR SEASONS
### GEORGE V
### $$$$$ ✪✪✪✪✪
31 AVENUE GEORGE V
TEL 01 49 52 70 00
FAX 01 49 52 70 10
www.fourseasons.com
Recent refurbishment has
brought this venerable palace
hotel luxuriously up-to-date.
Courtyard garden.
🔲 260 🔲 George V 🔲 🔲 🔲
🔲 🔲 All major cards

### 🔲 MARIGNAN–CHAMPS-
### ÉLYSÉES
### $$$$$ ✪✪✪✪
12 RUE MARIGNAN
TEL 01 40 76 34 56
FAX 01 40 76 34 34
www.hotelmarignan.fr
A Beauvais tapestry in the
salon, antique furnishings, and
comfortable rooms.
🔲 73 rooms 🔲 Franklin D.
Roosevelt 🔲 🔲 🔲 All major
cards

### 🔲 PAVILLON
### DE LA REINE
### $$$$$ ✪✪✪✪
28 PLACE DES VOSGES
TEL 01 40 29 19 19
FAX 01 40 29 19 20
www.pavillon-de-la-reine.com
Elegant, antique-furnished
rooms, some with four-poster
beds. Pretty courtyard.
🔲 31 + 14 suites + 10 duplex
🔲 St.-Paul 🔲 🔲 🔲 All major
cards

### 🔲 VERNET
### 🔲 $$$$$ ✪✪✪✪
25 RUE VERNET
TEL 01 44 31 98 00
FAX 01 44 31 85 69
www.hotelvernet.com
Fireplace and piano in the lobby,
jacuzzis in rooms. Belle epoque
restaurant.
🔲 42 + 9 suites 🔲 George V
🔲 🔲 🔲 All major cards

### 🔲 PERGOLÈSE
### $$$$ ✪✪✪✪
3 RUE PERGOLÈSE
TEL 01 53 64 04 04
FAX 01 53 64 04 40
www.parishotelpergolese.com
Modern designer decor and
marble bathrooms. Near the
Arc de Triomphe.
🔲 40 🔲 Argentine 🔲 🔲 All
major cards

### 🔲 LE RELAIS DU LOUVRE
### $$$ ✪✪✪
19 RUE DES PRÊTRES–
ST.-GERMAIN-L'AUXERROIS
TEL 01 40 41 96 42
FAX 01 40 41 96 44
www.relaisdulouvre.com
A cozy little hotel with a gar-
den, between the Louvre and
St.-Germain-l'Auxerrois.
🔲 20 🔲 Louvre or Pont-Neuf
🔲 🔲 All major cards

### 🔲 ALAIN DUCASSE AU
### PLAZA ATHÉNÉE
### $$$$$
HOTEL PLAZA ATHÉNÉE,
25 AVENUE MONTAIGNE
TEL 01 53 67 65 00
www.alain-ducasse.com
Three Michelin stars for
this fabulous Ducasse establishment, with luxurious food
and impeccable service.
🔲 Alma Marceau 🕒 Open
Wed.–Fri. for D, Thurs. & Fri. for
L; Closed mid-July–mid-Aug.
& last 2 weeks of Dec. 🔲 🔲 All
major cards

### 🔲 L'AMBROISIE
### $$$$$
9 PLACE DES VOSGES
TEL 01 42 78 51 45
www.ambroisie-placedes
vosges.com
Classic French food (too classic
for some) and three Michelin
stars in an exquisite setting on
the lovely Place des Vosges.
Reservations essential.
🔲 St.-Paul 🕒 Closed Sun.,
Mon., and Aug. & Feb. school
vacation 🔲 🔲 AE, MC, V

---

🔲 Nonsmoking   🔲 Air-conditioning   🔲 Indoor Pool   🔲 Outdoor Pool   🔲 Health Club   🔲 Credit Cards

## 🍴 CARRÉ DES FEUILLANTS
**$$$$$**
14 RUE CASTIGLIONE
TEL 01 42 86 82 82
www.carredesfeuillants.fr
Chef Alain Dutournier offers traditional southwestern cuisine: variations on foie gras, truffles. Two Michelin stars.
🚇 Concorde or Tuileries
🕐 Closed Sat. –Sun. & Aug.
⬢ All major cards

## 🍴 PIERRE GAGNAIRE
**$$$$$**
6 RUE BALZAC
TEL 01 58 36 12 50
www.pierre-gagnaire.com
One of France's most innovative chefs. Three Michelin stars. Don't miss the "grand dessert." Small; book far ahead.
🚇 George-V 🕐 Closed Sat. & Sun. L, also Feb. school vacation, & July–mid-Aug. 🔲 ⬢ All major cards

## 🍴 SENDERENS
**$$$$$**
9 PLACE DE LA MADELEINE
TEL 01 42 65 22 90
www.senderens.fr
Chef Alain Senderens has reinvented his famed haute-cuisine restaurant (two Michelin stars)with a modern interior and eclectic original dishes.
🚇 Madeleine 🕐 Closed first 3 weeks of Aug. 🔲 ⬢ All major cards

## 🍴 TAILLEVENT
**$$$$$**
15 RUE LAMENNAIS
TEL 01 44 95 15 01
www.taillevent.com
A long-standing leader in haute cuisine with two Michelin stars, Taillevent has lovely dining rooms, perfect service, and a renowned wine cellar. Reservations essential.
🚇 George V 🕐 Closed Sat., Sun., public holidays & Aug.
🔲 ⬢ All major cards

## 🍴 LA MAISON BLANCHE
**$$$$**
15 AVENUE MONTAIGNE
TEL 01 47 23 55 99
www.maison-blanche.fr
A fashionable crowd, modern decor, and views over the Seine.
🚇 Alma-Marceau 🕐 Closed Sat. L, Sun., & Aug. 🔲 ⬢ AE, CB, MC, V

## 🍴 LA MASCOTTE
**$$$**
52 RUE DES ABBESSES, 75018
TEL 01 46 06 28 15
www.la-mascotte-mont martre.com
Old-time Paris the way we like it in this lively brasserie, where the waiters still wear the traditional vest and long apron and like to joke with the customers while they sample their seafood and steaks.
🚇 Abbesses ⬢ V

## 🍴 LE TRAIN BLEU
**$$$**
GARE DE LYON, 20 BOULEVARD DIDEROT
TEL 01 43 43 09 06
www.le-train-bleu.com
Breathtaking belle epoque decoration in this railroad-station restaurant. Typical brasserie food.
🚇 Gare de Lyon 🕐 Closed Sun. 🔲 ⬢ All major cards

## 🍴 ANGÉLINA
**$$**
226 RUE DE RIVOLI
TEL 01 42 60 82 00
Join the fashion crowd for hot chocolate in this elegant tea-room. You may have to wait in line on the weekends.
🚇 Tuileries 🕐 Closed D & Tues. in Aug. 🔲 ⬢ AE, V

## 🍴 AU PIED DE COCHON
**$$**
6 RUE COQUILLIÈRE
TEL 01 40 13 77 00
www.pieddecochon.com
Lively all-night restaurant serv-

ing brasserie dishes; specialties include pig's feet and shellfish platters.
🚇 Louvre or Les Halles ⬢ All major cards

## 🍴 BOFINGER
**$$**
5 & 7 RUE DE LA BASTILLE
TEL 01 42 72 87 82
www.bofingerparis.com
Huge mirrors at this classic 19th-century brasserie. Try the *choucroute*.
🚇 Bastille 🔲 ⬢ All major cards

## 🍴 HARRY'S NEW YORK BAR
**$**
5 RUE DAUNOU
TEL 01 42 61 71 14
www.harrys-bar.fr
New York–style piano bar once popular with Hemingway and F. Scott Fitzgerald. Recommended: the Bloody Marys.
🚇 Opéra ⬢ AE, CB, DC, V

---

### PRICES

**HOTELS**
An indication of the cost of a double room in the high season is given by **$** signs.

| | |
|---|---|
| **$$$$$** | Over $400 |
| **$$$$** | $300–$400 |
| **$$$** | $200–$300 |
| **$$** | $100–$200 |
| **$** | Under $100 |

**RESTAURANTS**
An indication of the cost of a three-course meal without drinks is given by **$** signs.

| | |
|---|---|
| **$$$$$** | Over $150 |
| **$$$$** | $100–$150 |
| **$$$** | $80–$100 |
| **$$** | $60–$80 |
| **$** | Under $60 |

---

🏨 Hotel  🍴 Restaurant  🛏 No. of Guest Rooms  🅿 Parking  🚇 Métro  🕐 Closed  ⬢ Elevator

## OUTER PARIS

### LE PRÉ CATELAN
$$$$
ROUTE DE SURESNES
TEL 01 44 14 41 14
www.precatelanparis.com
Talented chef Frédéric Anton has livened up the cuisine of this lovely restaurant. Now has three Michelin stars.
Porte-Maillot, then Bus 144 (until 8 p.m.) Closed Mon. & Sun., all of Aug. All major cards

### BRASSERIE FLO
$$
7 COUR DES PETITES-ÉCURIES
TEL 01 47 70 13 59
www.flobrasseries.com
A sparkling, 19th-century brasserie where the menu has typical brasserie dishes. Friendly service.
Château-d'Eau All major cards

### CHÉRI BIBI
$$
15 RUE ANDRÉ-DEL-SARTE, 75018
TEL 01 42 54 88 96
A trendy young crowd frequents this lively place furnished with flea market furniture to dine on traditional French dishes made with quality ingredients. Dinner only.
Château Rouge Closed Sun. & 3 weeks in Aug. DC, MC, V

## NORTHERN FRANCE

### NORD & PICARDIE

### AIRE-SUR-LA-LYS

### HOSTELLERIE DES TROIS MOUSQUETAIRES
$/$$ 0000
CHÂTEAU DU FORT DE LA REDOUTE
TEL 03 21 39 01 11

FAX 03 21 39 50 10
www.hostelleriedes3mous
quetaires.com
A family-run hotel in a large wooded garden. The interior is in grand, traditional style; older, larger guest rooms are very elegant. Golf course.
33 Closed mid-Dec.– mid-Jan. AE, MC, V

## AMIENS

### MARISSONS
$/$$$
PONT DODANE
TEL 03 22 92 96 66
www.les-marissons.fr
Converted 15th-century boathouse in Amiens's old quarter. Imaginative cooking and Amiens specialties such as canard en croûte de foie gras.
Closed Wed. & Sat. L, & Sun. D All major cards

## BOULOGNE-SUR-MER

### MÉTROPOLE
$ 000
51–53 RUE THIERS
TEL 03 21 31 54 30
FAX 03 21 30 45 72
www.hotel-metropole
-boulogne.com
Between the ramparts and the sea, this quiet hotel has a delightful garden. No restaurant.
25 Closed late Dec.– early Jan. AE, MC, V

## CALAIS

### MEURICE
$/$$$ 000
5 RUE EDMOND-ROCHE
TEL 03 21 34 57 03
FAX 03 21 96 28 12
www.hotel-meurice.fr
Until World War II, the Meurice was one of France's luxury hotels. It was restored in 1953, and today offers comfortable hospitality to travelers. Restaurant La Diligence serves good standard French cuisine.

41 Restaurant closed Sat. L All major cards

## HESDIN-L'ABBÉ

### CLÉRY
$/$$$ 000
TEL 03 21 83 19 83
FAX 03 21 87 52 59
www.hotelclery-hesdin-labbe
.com
A dignified 18th-century house surrounded by parkland. Sitting room with log fire; contemporary decor. Tennis.
27 Restaurant closed all Sat. & Sun. D All major cards

## LILLE

## SOMETHING SPECIAL

### GRAND HÔTEL BELLEVUE
Mozart once stayed in this 18th-century Bourbon hotel close to the Opéra, the Palais de la Musique, and the Palais de Congrès. The building is a fine example of Lille architecture with classic decor. No restaurant.
$$$ 000
5 RUE JEAN-ROISIN
TEL 03 20 57 45 64
FAX 03 20 40 07 93
www.grandhotelbellevue.com
61 All major cards

### L'HUÎTRIÈRE
$$$$/$$$$$
3 RUE DES CHATS-BOSSUS
TEL 03 20 55 43 41
www.huitriere.fr
A very fashionable establishment, with one Michelin star, in the old town. An art deco, blue-and-gold tiled entrance leads to a richly furnished dining room. Excellent seafood and regional cuisine.
Closed Sun. D, public holidays. D, & Aug. All major cards

### 🍴 BRASSERIE DE LA PAIX
**$$**
25 PLACE RIHOUR
TEL 03 20 54 70 41
www.paix.restaurantsdelille
.com
Typical northern brasserie with
art deco furnishings and cozy
banquettes serving classic fare.
🕐 Closed Sun. 🕲 AE, MC, V

## MONTREUIL-SUR-MER

### 🏨 CHÂTEAU DE
### 🍴 MONTREUIL
**$$$$ 0000**
4 CHAUSSÉE DE CAPUCINS
TEL 03 21 81 53 04
FAX 03 21 81 36 43
www.chateaudemontreuil
.com
Tastefully decorated bed-
rooms look out over the gar-
dens of this secluded château
on the edge of town. The
one-star Michelin restaurant
specializes in seafood.
🛏 13 🅿 🕐 Closed mid-Dec.–
Feb. & Mon. except July & Aug.
🕲 All major cards

### 🍴 AUBERGE DE LA
### GRENOUILLÈRE
**$$$/$$$$**
LA MADELEINE-SOUS-
MONTREUIL
TEL 03 21 06 07 22
www.lagrenouillere.fr
A charming Picardie farm-
house, particularly popular for
lunch on the terrace. Try dishes
like pré-salé agneau de la baie de
Somme, or the house specialty,
frogs legs with garlic and fried
parsley.
🕐 Closed Tues. & Wed.
(except July & Aug.) & Dec.–
Jan. 🕲 🕲 All major cards

## CHAMPAGNE

## REIMS

### 🏨 LES CRAYÈRES
### 🍴 $$$$$ 00000
64 BOULEVARD

HENRY-VASNIER
TEL 03 26 24 90 00
www.lescrayeres.com
A beautiful turn-of-the-
20th-century family château,
home to master chef Gérard
Boyer and the epitome of
French refinement and luxury.
Restaurant offers dishes that
include lamb with truffles
en croûte and pig's trotters
stuffed with foie gras. Huge
wine list and, of course, lots
of Champagne. Reservations
essential.
🛏 16 + 3 suites 🕐 Closed
Jan.; restaurant closed Mon. &
Tues. 🕲 🕲 🕲 All major cards

### 🏨 DE LA PAIX
**$/$$ 000**
9 RUE BUIRETTE
TEL 03 26 40 04 08
FAX 03 26 47 75 04
www.hotel-lapaix.fr
In the heart of the car-free
center, this is a peaceful
old hotel with a garden.
Rich, warm interior decor
and guest rooms that are
modern and comfortably
furnished.
🛏 168 🅿 🕲 🕲 🏊 🕲 All
major cards

### 🍴 FLO
**$$$**
96 PLACE DE DROUET D'ERLON
TEL 03 26 91 40 50
FAX 03 26 91 40 54
www.floreims.com
Art deco, mosaics, and
chandeliers in this large bras-
serie with a popular terrace,
the place for oysters and
Champagne.
🕲 All major cards

## ALSACE & LORRAINE

## COLMAR

### 🏨 HOSTELLERIE LE
### 🍴 MARÉCHAL
**$$$ 000**
4 PLACE SIX MONTAGNES
NOIRES

TEL 03 89 41 60 32
FAX 03 89 24 59 40
www.le-marechal.com
A 16th-century half-timbered
hotel and restaurant, beautifully situated canalside in
Colmar's "Little Venice."
Specialties include terrine
de foie de canard à la gelée au
muscat d'Alsace and lobster and
monkfish salad with truffle
vinaigrette.
🛏 30 🕲 🕲 🕲 All major
cards

### 🏨 GRAND HÔTEL
### 🍴 BRISTOL
**$/$$ 000**
7 PLACE DE LA GARE
TEL 03 89 23 59 59
REST. 03 89 23 15 86
FAX 03 89 23 92 26
www.grand-hotel-bristol.com
A beautifully decorated,
central hotel with turn-of-
the-20th-century elegance.
Two good restaurants: the
Michelin one-star Rendezvous
de Chasse and the more
informal l'Auberge.
🛏 70 🕲 🕲 All major cards

## KAYSERSBERG

### 🏨 CHAMBARD
### 🍴 MARÉCHAL
**$$$$ 0000**
9 RUE DU GÉNÉRAL-DE-GAULLE
TEL 03 89 47 10 17
FAX 03 89 47 35 03
www.lechambard.fr
Stylish hotel with modern
rooms, spa, and a restaurant
renowned for Alsace wine
and regional cuisine; try the
foie gras with choucroute,
or the celebrated platter of
three meats—pork, lamb
and beef.
🛏 32 + 5 suites + 6 deluxe
suites 🕐 Closed mid-Nov.–Feb.;
restaurant closed Mon., Tues. L
& Wed. L 🕲 🕲 AE, MC, V

---

🏨 Hotel  🍴 Restaurant  🛏 No. of Guest Rooms  🅿 Parking  🚇 Métro  🕐 Closed  🛗 Elevator

## MARLENHEIM

### 🏨 LE CERF
### 🍴 $$/$$$
30 RUE DU GÉNÉRAL-DE-GAULLE
TEL 03 88 87 73 73
FAX 03 88 87 68 08
www.lecerf.com
This picturesque inn with a flowery courtyard, located in a village on the N4 21 miles (30 km) west of Strasbourg, contains a Michelin one-star restaurant specializing in Alsatian dishes such as *tête de veau* or sauerkraut with pork and foie gras.
🛏 18 🅿 ➕ Restaurant closed Tues.–Wed. 🆒 🆔 All major cards

## NANCY

### 🏨 GRAND HÔTEL DE
### 🍴 LA REINE
### $$$$ ◐◐◐
2 PLACE STANISLAS
TEL 03 83 35 03 01
FAX 03 83 32 86 04
www.hoteldelareine.com
This exquisite 18th-century palace, one of the historic buildings in the heart of Nancy, was once the home of Marie-Antoinette. Luxurious guest rooms are furnished in Louis XV style. The hotel's restaurant is called Stanislas, after the dethroned Polish king.
🛏 48 🆒 🆔 ♿ 🆔 All major cards

## STRASBOURG

### 🏨 MONOPOLE
### MÉTROPOLE
### $/$$$ ◐◐◐
16 RUE KUHN
TEL 03 88 14 39 14
FAX 03 88 32 82 55
www.bw-monopole.com
Close to the historic Petite France district, this peaceful, grand hotel offers rooms either in contemporary

mode or in traditional Alsatian style.
🛏 90 🅿 🆒 🆔 🆔 All major cards

### 🍴 AU CROCODILE
### $$$$/$$$$$
10 RUE DE L'OUTRE
TEL 03 88 32 13 02
www.au-crocodile.com
With luxurious surroundings, impeccable service, and one Michelin star, the Crocodile is the most stylish restaurant in Strasbourg. Favorite dishes here include roast monkfish with fennel confit and saffron tomatoes.
➕ Closed Sun.–Mon. & 3 weeks July–Aug. 🆒 🆔 All major cards

### 🍴 BUEREHIESEL
### $$$$/$$$$$
4 PARC ORANGERIE
TEL 03 88 45 56 65
www.buerehiesel.com
A reconstructed Alsatian farmhouse is now a Michelin one-star restaurant. Chef Eric Westermann offers seasonal delicacies such as Bresse chicken with potatoes and artichokes. Inventive desserts include brioche with pear and beer flavored ice cream.
🅿 ➕ Closed Sun. & Mon. 🆒 🆔 All major cards

## VERDUN

### 🏨 LE COQ HARDI
### 🍴 $$/$$$ ◐◐◐
8 AVENUE DE LA VICTOIRE
TEL 03 29 86 36 36
www.coq-hardi.com
A delightful hotel with a typical Lorraine facade of flowery window boxes and an interior of polished oak. Excellent restaurant.
🛏 34 + 3 suites ➕ Restaurant closed Fri., Sat. L, Sun. D, except public holidays 🆒 ♿ 🆔 All major cards

## ■ NORMANDY & BRITTANY

## NORMANDY

## AUDRIEU

### 🏨 CHÂTEAU D'AUDRIEU
### 🍴 $$$/$$$$$
TEL 02 31 80 21 52
FAX 02 31 80 24 73
www.chateaudaudrieu.com
Between Bayeux and Caen, this 18th-century château surrounded by parkland has period decoration and an elegant one-star Michelin restaurant.
🛏 23 + 6 suites ➕ Restaurant closed Mon., L except Sat. & Sun., & mid-Dec.–Jan. 🆔 🆔 All major cards

## BAYEUX

### 🏨 D'ARGOUGES
### $ ◐◐
21 RUE ST.-PATRICE
TEL 02 31 92 88 86
FAX 02 31 92 69 16
www.hotel-dargouges.com
Set in a peaceful garden, this old family mansion is within walking distance of the town's center. No restaurant.
🛏 28 🅿 🆒 🆔 All major cards

### 🏨 LION D'OR
### 🍴 $ ◐◐◐
71 RUE ST.-JEAN
TEL 02 31 92 06 90
FAX 02 31 22 15 64
www.liondor-bayeux.fr
An attractive 17th-century post house around a central courtyard boasts a good-value restaurant serving dishes such as duck foie gras with honey and succulent sausages.
🛏 25 🅿 ➕ Restaurant closed Sun. D, Mon. D; Nov.–March, Mon.–Tues. L, & Sat. L 🆔 All major cards

## BEUVRON-EN-AUGE

### 🍴 LE PAVÉ D'AUGE
$$$
TEL 02 31 79 26 71
www.pavedauge.com
Michelin one-star restaurant in the covered market hall, serving simply cooked, local ingredients. Try lobster with herb butter, and local cheeses and Calvados.
🕐 Closed Mon. late Nov.–end Dec., Feb. school holidays, & Tues. Sept.–April 🚇 MC, V

## CABOURG

## SOMETHING SPECIAL

### 🏨 GRAND HÔTEL
Cabourg's Grand Hôtel stylishly dominates the seafront just as it did in Marcel Proust's novel *Remembrance of Things Past*. Proust often stayed here, and the hotel restaurant still serves the memorable madeleine cakes.
$$/$$$$ ✪✪✪✪
PROMENADE MARCEL-PROUST
TEL 02 31 91 01 79
FAX 02 31 24 03 20
www.mgallery.com
ⓘ 70 🅿 🕐 Restaurant closed Jan. & Mon.–Tues. Sept.–June 🚇 All major cards

## CAEN

### 🍴 LE CARLOTTA
$$
15 QUAI VENDEUVE
TEL 02 31 86 68 99
www.lecarlotta.fr
Art deco–style brasserie with a veranda overlooking the port. Fish is a specialty.
🕐 Closed Sun. & Sat. L
🚇 AE, MC, V

## DEAUVILLE

### 🏨 NORMANDY-BARRIERE
### 🍴 $$$$$
TEL 02 31 98 66 22

FAX 02 31 98 66 23
38 RUE J. MERMOZ
www.lucienbarriere.com
Classic belle epoque mansion where the stars like to stay (Anouk Aimée likes a sea-facing window). Courtyard restaurant for summer dining.
ⓘ 290 + 28 suites + 8 apts.
🚇 🚇 🚇 All major cards

### 🍴 LE SPINNAKER
$$/$$$
52 RUE MIRABEAU
TEL 02 31 88 24 40
www.spinnakerdeauville.com
A highly regarded seafood restaurant on the promenade, serving traditional Norman cuisine with plenty of cider and Calvados. The baked lobster in cider vinegar is a special treat.
🕐 Closed Mon. & Tues (except July–mid-Sept.) & part of Jan., June, & Nov. 🚇 All major cards

## DIEPPE

### 🍴 LA MARMITE DIEPPOISE
$$$
8 RUE ST.-JEAN
TEL 02 35 84 24 26
A popular restaurant located close to the harbor named after its most famous local dish: fish and shellfish in a cream sauce.
🕐 Closed Sun. D & Mon.
🚇 MC, V

## DINARD

### 🏨 LE GRAND HÔTEL DE
### 🍴 DINARD
$$$/$$$$ ✪✪✪✪
46 AVENUE GEORGE V
www.lucienbarriere.com
TEL 02 99 88 26 26
FAX 02 99 88 26 27
Dinard's classic grand hotel on the promenade. The estaurant and café are popular during the film festival.
ⓘ 90 🅿 🕐 Closed Dec.–March 🚇 🚇 🚇 🚇 All major cards

## HONFLEUR

### 🏨 LA FERME SAINT-
### 🍴 SIMÉON
$$$/$$$$$ ✪✪✪✪
RUE ADOLPHE-MARAIS
TEL 02 31 81 78 00
FAX 02 31 89 48 48
www.fermesaintsimeon.fr
This peaceful 17th-century farmhouse was a favorite with the Impressionists. The restaurant serves specialties such as stuffed *pré-salé* lamb. Sauna, solarium, and hydrotherapy complex.
ⓘ 31 + 3 suites 🚇 🚇 🚇 AE, MC, V

### 🏨 L'ABSINTHE
$$$
1 RUE DE LA VILLE
TEL 02 31 89 23 23
FAX 02 31 89 53 60
www.absinthe.fr
A charming small hotel in a 16th-century presbytery by the harbor. No restaurant.

---

🕒 Closed mid-Nov.–mid-Dec.
♿ 🚭 All major cards

## 🍽 SA.QUA.NA
**$$$$**
22 PLACE HAMELIN
TEL 02 31 89 40 80
www.alexandre-bourdas.com
Sa.Qua.Na stands for Saveurs,
Quality, Nature–or "fish"
(sakana) in Japanese. Chef
Alexandre Bourdas, with one
Michelin star, adds a touch of
zen to local food–such as lobster with lime and coconut.
🕒 Closed Mon.–Wed. ❄
🚭 AE, MC, V

## LA BOUILLE

### 🏨 BELLEVUE
## 🍽 $$ ✪✪
13 QUAI H MALOT
TEL 02 35 18 05 05
FAX 02 35 18 00 92
A good-value small hotel on
the banks of the Seine River
with a rustically wood-beamed
restaurant.
🕒 Closed mid July–mid-Aug.
🚭 AE, MC, V

## LE BEC-HELLOUIN

### 🏨 L'AUBERGE DE L'ABBAYE
**$ ✪✪✪**
12 PLACE GUILLAUME LE
CONQUEROR
TEL 02 32 44 86 02
FAX 02 32 46 32 23
www.auberge-abbaye-bec-
hellouin.com
An 18th-century inn with a
terrace near Bec-Hellouin
monastery. The restaurant
serves regional specialties
based on cider and apples.
🚪 11 🅿 🕒 Hotel closed mid-
Nov. to mid Feb.; restaurant
closed Mon. & Tues. Nov.–
Easter 🚭 AE, MC, V

## LES ANDELYS

### 🏨 LA CHAÎNE D'OR
**$/$$$ ✪✪✪**
27 RUE GRANDE
TEL 02 32 54 00 31
FAX 02 32 54 05 68
www.hotel-lachainedor.com
Overlooked by the ruins of the
Château Gaillard, this 18th-
century auberge stands beside
the Seine. Picturesque views
from most rooms and from
the restaurant. Terrace.
🚪 10 🅿 🕒 Closed Sun.
D, Mon–Tues. Nov.–March,
& Mon. April–Oct. 🚭 AE,
MC, V

## MONT ST.-MICHEL

## SOMETHING SPECIAL

### 🍽 LA MÈRE POULARD
Visitors from Ernest Heming-
way to Margaret Thatcher
have sampled the famous
Omelette Mère Poulard, made
from a secret recipe over an
open fire, and still as popular
as ever at this long-established
restaurant. Other specialties
include grilled pink lobster and
rack of lamb. Rooms available.
**$$$ ✪✪✪**
GRANDE RUE
TEL 02 33 89 68 68
www.mere-poulard.fr
🚪 27 🚭 All major cards

## PONT-AUDEMER

### 🏨 BELLE ISLE SUR RISLE
**$$$/$$$$ ✪✪✪✪**
112 ROUTE DE ROUEN
TEL 02 32 56 96 22
FAX 02 32 42 88 96
www.bellile.com
Beautiful grounds with ancient
trees surround this handsome
mansion on an island in the
Risle River. Elegantly furnished
guest rooms . Sauna, tennis.
🚪 24 🅿 🕒 Closed Jan.–mid-
March; restaurant closed L
Mon.–Wed. ❄ 🌊 💪 🚭 All
major cards

## PORT-EN-BESSIN

### 🏨 LA CHENEVIÈRE
## 🍽 $$$/$$$$ ✪✪✪✪
ESCURES-COMMES
(NW OF BAYEUX)
www.lacheneviere.com
TEL 02 31 51 25 25
FAX 02 31 51 25 20
A noble Normandy mansion
dating from the 1800s, with
an excellent restaurant, set in a
tree-lined park a short distance
from the sea and Omaha
Beach golf course. Each room
has its own little secret garden.
🚪 18 + 3 suites 🅿 🕒 Closed
Dec.–Feb. ❄ 🌊 🚭 All major
cards

## ROUEN

### 🏨 CATHÉDRALE
**$ ✪✪**
12 RUE ST.-ROMAIN
TEL 02 35 71 57 95
FAX 02 35 70 15 54
www.hotel-de-la-cathedrale.fr
This old, half-timbered town
hotel has a flowery courtyard
and a salon du thé. No
restaurant.
🚪 24 🚭 AE, MC, V

### 🍽 GILL
**$$$$**
9 QUAI DE LA BOURSE
TEL 02 35 71 16 14
www.gill.fr
Modern and elegant, one of
Rouen's top restaurants with
two Michelin stars. Fresh food
is cooked with great style here.
Sample such delicacies as lan-
goustine ravioli and the Rouen
specialty, pigeon stuffed with
liver and cooked in a sauce of
its own blood.
🕒 Closed Mon. & Tues. and
most of April & Aug.
🚭 ❄ 🚭 All major cards

## TROUVILLE-SUR-MER

### 🍽 LES VAPEURS
**$$**
160 BOULEVARD FERNAND-

MOREAUX
TEL 02 31 88 15 24
www.lesvapeurs.fr
A popular art deco brasserie close to the fish market, with fresh dishes to suit late-nighters and early risers. The shrimp and the *moules frites* (mussels with french fries) are especially recommended.
🐾 AE, MC, V

## BRITTANY

## BREST

🏨 **CORNICHE**
$ 🔴🔴🔴
1 RUE AMIRAL NICOL
TEL 02 98 45 12 42
FAX 02 98 49 01 53
www.hotel-la-corniche.com
A modern hotel built in the old Breton style. On the coast road west of the town. Tennis.
🛏 16 🐾 AE, MC, V

## CONCARNEAU

🍴 **COQUILLE**
$$$
QUAI MOROS
TEL 02 98 97 08 52
www.lacoquille-concarneau.com
An attractive Breton-style restaurant in the old port serving a variety of fresh fish and seafood.
🕐 Closed Sun. D & Mon.
🔲 🐾 AE, MC, V

🍴 **CRÊPERIE DES REMPARTS**
$
31 RUE THÉOPHILE-LOUARN
TEL 02 98 50 65 66
Situated in the Ville Close (walled town), this is a good place to sample excellent *crêpes* and *galettes*.
🕐 Closed Mon. except July–Aug. 🐾 MC, V

## DINAN

🍴 **MÈRE POURCEL**
$$/$$$$
3 PLACE DES MERCIERS
TEL 02 96 39 03 80
www.chezlamerepourcel.com
Restaurant in a historic 15th-century Breton building. Menu changes seasonally, and the wine list is excellent.
🕐 Closed Sun. D, Wed. & Tues. D Oct.–April 🐾 All major cards

## LA GOUESNIÈRE

🏨 **CHÂTEAU DE BONABON**
🍴
$$$/$$$$ 🔴🔴🔴🔴
1 RUE ALFRED DE FOLLINY
TEL 02 99 58 24 50
FAX 02 99 58 28 41
www.hotel-chateau-bonaban.com
Elegant 17th-century riverside chateau, with original furnishings, surrounded by parkland, with its own chapel and gourmet restaurant.
🅿 🕐 Restaurant closed weekday L 🐾 AE, MC, V

## LORIENT

🍴 **L'AMPHITRYON**
$$/$$$$
127 RUE DU COLONEL MULLER
TEL 02 97 83 34 04
www.amphitryon-abadie.com
Friendly, local restaurant with two Michelin stars serving fresh seafood.
🕐 Closed Sun.–Mon. 🔲
🐾 AE, MC, V

## PONT-AVEN

🍴 **MOULIN DE ROSMADEC**
$$/$$$
TEL 02 98 06 00 22
www.moulinderosmadec.com
A Michelin one-star restaurant in an old millhouse near the bridge in the town center. Traditional Breton decor. Specialties include grilled Breton lobster, *sauté de langoustines*, and beautifully prepared artichokes. Reservations essential.
🛏 4 🕐 Closed Mon. L Oct.–May, Sun. D, & Thurs. 🐾 AE, MC, V

## QUIMPER

🏨 **CHÂTEAU DE GUILGUIFFIN**
$$$
LANDULEC (ON THE D874 SOUTH OF QUIMPER)
TEL 02 98 91 52 11
FAX 02 98 91 52 52
www.chateau-guilguiffin.com
Large château surrounded by wild and magnificent parkland. No restaurant, but brunch and/or buffet supper served by arrangement. Price includes breakfast.
🛏 3 + 2 suites 🕐 By reservation only in winter 🐾 All major cards

🍴 **L'AMBROISIE**
$$$
49 RUE ELIE-FRÉRON
TEL 02 98 95 00 02
www.ambroisie-quimper.com
Conveniently situated close to the cathedral and well known for its excellent fish and imaginative desserts.
🕐 Closed Sun. D & Mon.
🐾 MC, V

## QUIMPERLÉ

🏨 **CHÂTEAU DE KERLAREC**
$$
ARZANO (ON THE D22 NE OF QUIMPERLÉ)
TEL 02 98 71 75 06
FAX 02 98 71 74 55
www.chateau-de-kerlarec.com
Château on wooded grounds, built around 1860 and still retaining its period character. Fish, seafood, and Breton specialties prepared if requested beforehand. Tennis. Price includes breakfast.
🛏 5 🅿 🚾 🔲 🐾 No credit cards

## RENNES

### 🍽 AUBERGE ST.-SAUVEUR
$$
6 RUE ST.-SAVEUR
TEL 02 99 79 32 56
A handsome half-timbered building that survived the great fire of 1750. Inside, it retains the traditional atmosphere. Specialties include Breton lobster and other shellfish and fish dishes.
🕐 Closed Sat. L, Sun., Mon. D, & 3 weeks in Aug. 💳 AE, MC, V

## RIEC-SUR-BELON

### 🍽 CHEZ JACKY
$$$
PORT DE BELON
TEL 02 98 06 90 32
www.chez-jacky.com
The place to eat Belon oysters—a basic, authentic restaurant on the Belon River with oyster beds right next to the restaurant. The *plateau de fruits de mer* is a treat. Reservations essential.
🕐 Closed Mon.–Sun. D & Oct.–Easter 💳 MC, V

## ROSCOFF

### 🏨🍽 BRITTANY
$$/$$$ ⚫⚫⚫
BOULEVARD STE.-BARBE
TEL 02 98 69 70 78
FAX 02 98 61 13 29
www.hotel-brittany.com
Stone manor house facing the old port of Roscoff and l'Île de Batz, with a renowned restaurant, the Yachtman.
🛏 25 🅿 🕐 Closed Nov.–March; restaurant closed Mon. 💳 AE, MC, V

### 🏨 LE TEMPS DE VIVRE
$$$
PLACE EGLISE
TEL 02 98 19 27 28
FAX 02 98 19 33 00
www.tycoz.com/letemps devivre

Granite Breton house with stylish interior, on the shore with wonderful views of the ocean. The Michelin one-star restaurant next door offers imaginative local specialties.
🛏 15 🕐 Closed Sun. & Mon. in winter 💳 All major cards

## STE.-ANNE-LA-PALUD

### 🏨🍽 DE LA PLAGE
$$$$ ⚫⚫⚫⚫
TEL 02 98 92 50 12
FAX 02 98 92 56 54
www.plage.com
A classic seaside hotel right on a tiny remote beach. Sea views and sunsets from the excellent restaurant. Great local crab and the Breton speciality, a *pot au feu* of lobster and vegetables.
🛏 26 + 4 suites 🅿 🕐 Restaurant closed Nov.–March; L Thurs., Sat,. & Sun. only 🏊 💳 All major cards

## ST.-MALO

### 🏨 GRAND HÔTEL DES THERMES
$$$/$$$$$ ⚫⚫⚫⚫
100 BOULEVARD HÉBERT, COURTOISVILLE
TEL 02 99 40 75 75
FAX 02 99 40 76 00
www.thalassotherapie.com
A hotel on the seafront with a garden, a sea-therapy center, six pools, and two restaurants.
🛏 168 + 7 suites 🅿 🕐 Closed 2 weeks in Jan. 🏊🏊 💳 All major cards

### 🏨 LA KORRIGANE
$$/$$$ ⚫⚫⚫
39 RUE LE POMELLEC, ST.-SERVAN
TEL 02 99 81 65 85
FAX 02 99 82 23 89
www.st-malo-hotel-korrigane.com
An elegantly furnished turn-of-the-20th-century mansion near the harbor. Beautiful guest rooms, two sitting rooms, and a pretty garden.
🛏 12 🅿 💳 AE, MC, V

### 🍽 LA DUCHESSE ANNE
$$$
5 PLACE GUY-LA-CHAMBRE
TEL 02 99 40 85 33
www.chateauxhotels.co.uk/a-la-duchesse-anne-359
A veritable institution with elegant decor and impeccable cuisine. Specialties include *foie gras de canard* and local grilled lobster.
🕐 Closed Mon. L & Wed., Sun. D in winter, & Dec.–Jan. 💳 MC, V

### 🍽 L'UNIVERS
$$
PLACE CHATEAUBRIAND
TEL 02 99 40 89 52
www.hotel-univers-saintmalo.com
This popular restaurant within the walls of the old town offers excellent seafood.
💳 All major cards

## ST.-THÉGONNEC

### 🍽 AUBERGE ST.-THÉGONNEC
$/$$$
6 PLACE MARIE
TEL 02 98 79 61 18
www.aubergesaintthegonec.com
A traditional auberge in a village known for its parish close. Good simple Breton cooking. Rooms also available.
🛏 19 🕐 Closed Sun., Sept.–March 💳 MC, V

## TRÉBEURDEN

### 🏨 TI AL-LANNEC
$/$$$ ⚫⚫⚫
14 ALLÉE DE MEZO-GUEN
TEL 02 96 15 01 01
FAX 02 96 23 62 14
www.tiallannec.com
On wooded grounds overlooking the Bay of Lannion, with a path to the sea. Some rooms have terraces or verandas. Tennis, sauna.
🛏 29 🕐 Closed Nov.–Feb. 💳 CB, DC, MC, V

## VANNES

### 🏨 LA MARÉBAUDIÈRE
**$ ☉☉☉**
4 RUE ARISTIDE-BRIAND
TEL 02 97 47 34 29
FAX 02 97 54 14 11
www.marebaudiere.com
A quiet, stylishly decorated
hotel with a garden, near the
old town. No restaurant.
ⓘ 41 🅿 Ⓢ 🅐 All major cards

## ■ LOIRE VALLEY

### AMBOISE

### 🏨 LE CHOISEUL
🍽 **$$/$$$$ ☉☉☉☉**
36 QUAI CHARLES-GUINOT
TEL 02 47 30 45 45
FAX 02 47 30 46 10
www.le-choiseul.com
An elegant, 18th-century
mansion, close to the château,
facing the Loire River, with a
flower garden and restaurant.
ⓘ 29 + 3 suites 🅿 Ⓢ Ⓢ 🏊
🅐 All major cards

### 🏨 LE LION D'OR
**$ ☉☉**
17 QUAI CHARLES-GUINOT
TEL 02 47 57 00 23
FAX 02 47 23 22 49
A traditionally run hotel, close
to the château beside the Loire.
ⓘ 21 🅿 🕒 Closed Dec. 1–15
& Jan. 🅐 V

### ANGERS

### 🏨 ANJOU
🍽 **$/$$$ ☉☉☉☉**
1 BOULEVARD MARÉCHAL FOCH
TEL 02 41 21 12 11
FAX 02 41 87 22 21
www.hoteldanjou.fr
Large 19th-century hotel,
beautifully renovated, close to
the old town. The restaurant,
Salamandre, has Renaissance
decor as a backdrop to very
good value food; try the ravioli
stuffed with lobster or the

excellent fish soups.
ⓘ 53 🅿 🕒 Restaurant closed
Sun. Ⓒ 🅐 All major cards

### 🏨 FRANCE
**$ ☉☉☉**
8 PLACE DE LA GARE
TEL 02 41 88 49 42
FAX 02 41 87 19 50
www.hoteldefrance-angers
.com
A classic hotel conveniently
situated near the railroad
station and major sights, with
Plantagenêts restaurant.
ⓘ 56 🕒 Restaurant closed
Sat. L, Sun. D, & all of Aug.
Ⓢ Ⓒ 🅐 All major cards

### 🍽 LES TROIS RIVIÈRES
**$$$**
62 PROMENADE DE RECULÉE
TEL 02 41 73 31 88
www.lestroisrivieres.fr
A popular restaurant beside
the river with fine views. Spe-
cializes in fish. Open daily.
🅿 🅐 MC, V

## AZAY-LE-RIDEAU

### 🍽 GRAND MONARQUE
**$$/$$$**
PLACE DE LA RÉPUBLIQUE
TEL 02 47 45 40 08
www.legrandmonarque.com
A friendly hotel-restaurant
with a shady terrace. Delicious
local fare; river salmon, and
goat's cheese, for example,
complemented by Azay-le-
Rideau's wine.
ⓘ 24 🕒 Closed Dec.–mid-Feb.
🅐 AE, MC, V

## BLOIS

### 🏨 LE MÉDICIS
**$/$$ ☉☉☉**
2 ALLÉE FRANÇOIS 1ER
TEL 02 54 43 94 04
FAX 02 54 42 04 05
www.le-medicis.com
An elegant 19th-century hotel
within walking distance of
the château and close to the

### PRICES

**HOTELS**
An indication of the cost of
a double room in the high
season is given by $ signs.

| | |
|---|---|
| **$$$$$** | Over $400 |
| **$$$$** | $300–$400 |
| **$$$** | $200–$300 |
| **$$** | $100–$200 |
| **$** | Under $100 |

**RESTAURANTS**
An indication of the cost of
a three-course meal without
drinks is given by $ signs.

| | |
|---|---|
| **$$$$$** | Over $150 |
| **$$$$** | $100–$150 |
| **$$$** | $80–$100 |
| **$$** | $60–$80 |
| **$** | Under $60 |

railroad station. Restaurant
with classic cuisine.
ⓘ 12 🕒 Closed Sun. 🕒 Oct.–
Easter & Jan. Ⓒ 🅐 All
major cards

### 🏨 ANNE DE BRETAGNE
**$ ☉☉**
31 AVENUE JEAN-LAIGRET
TEL 02 54 78 05 38
FAX 02 54 74 37 79
www.annedebretagne.free.fr
Situated on a small square
close to the château, this modest hotel is quiet and friendly.
ⓘ 28 🅐 MC, V

### 🍽 AU RENDEZVOUS DES
**PÊCHEURS**
**$$$**
27 RUE FOIX
TEL 02 54 74 67 48
www.rendezvousdespecheurs
.com
A simple little bistro serving
excellent fish dishes; try the
asparagus and langoustine.
Reservations suggested.

---

🏨 Hotel 🍽 Restaurant ⓘ No. of Guest Rooms 🅿 Parking 🚇 Métro 🕒 Closed ⊟ Elevator

⊕ Closed Sun. & Mon. L, & first 3 weeks in Aug. ⬛ ⬛ MC, V

## SOMETHING SPECIAL

### 🍴 L'ORANGERIE DU CHÂTEAU

A lovely terrace restaurant in the château orangery. Specialties include perch with asparagus (in season), *filet de pigeonneau à la Vendômoise,* and *panier de poudre d'ail.*
**$$/$$$$**
1 AVENUE JEAN LAIGRET
TEL 02 54 78 05 36
www.orangerie-du-chateau.fr
⊕ Closed Sun. D, Wed., 1 week in Aug., Feb. school holidays, & Tues. D Nov. –Easter ⬛ AE, MC, V

## BOURGES

### 🍴 LE D'ANTAN SANCERROIS
**$$**
50 RUE BOURBONNOUX
TEL 02 48 65 96 26
www.dantansancerrois.fr
A popular restaurant in a venerable building, with excellent local cooking and one Michelin star.
⊕ Closed Sun. & Mon.
⬛ AE, MC, V

## CHAMBORD

### 🏨 LE GRAND SAINT-MICHEL
**$ ○○○**
TEL 02 54 20 31 31
FAX 02 54 20 36 40
www.saintmichel-chambord.com
Quiet hotel close to the château and on the edge of the forest. Reservations required. The restaurant serves good traditional and regional cuisine on the terrace. Tennis.
ⓘ 38 🅿 ⬛ MC, V

## CHAMPIGNÉ

### 🏨🍴 CHÂTEAU DES BRIOTTIÈRES
**$$$**
ROUTE DE MARIGNE
TEL 02 41 42 00 02
FAX 02 41 42 01 55
www.briottieres.com
An intimate 18th-century family-owned château, full of antiques, with lovely gardens. Dine on traditional Anjou cuisine in the elegant dining room.
🅿 ⬛ AE, MC, V

## CHENONCEAUX

### 🏨🍴 BON LABOUREUR ET CHÂTEAU
**$$$ ○○○**
6 RUE DU DR. BRETONNEAU
TEL 02 47 23 90 02
FAX 02 47 23 82 01
www.bonlaboureur.com
This village-center hotel has been family run for generations. Chintz-bedecked living rooms and pleasant bedrooms overlook a courtyard. Michelin one-star restaurant serves nouvelle cuisine.
ⓘ 22 + 5 suites 🅿 ⊕ Closed Tues. L & Jan. ⬛ ⬛ ⬛ AE, MC, V

### 🏨 LA ROSERAIE
**$$ ○○○**
7 RUE DU DR. BRETONNEAU
TEL 02 47 23 90 09
FAX 02 47 23 91 59
www.hotel-chenonceau.com
A charming hotel with a garden, tastefully decorated rooms, and beamed dining room. Terrace for dining.
ⓘ 17 🅿 ⊕ Closed mid-Nov.– mid- Feb. ⬛ ⬛ ⬛ MC, V

## CHINON

### 🏨🍴 CHÂTEAU DE MARÇAY
**$$/$$$$ ○○○○**
MARÇAY (4 MILES/6 KM S OF CHINON VIA D749 & D116)

TEL 02 47 93 03 47
FAX 02 47 93 45 33
www.chateaudemarcay.com
A medieval turreted château in its own parkland with a Michelin one-star restaurant. Tennis.
ⓘ 30 + 4 suites 🅿 ⊕ Closed mid-Jan.–mid-March ⬛ ⬛ All major cards

### 🏨 DIDEROT
**$ ○○**
4 RUE BUFFON
TEL 02 47 93 18 87
FAX 02 47 93 37 10
A pretty, creeper-covered town house in a quiet courtyard. Breakfast served on the terrace or in the rustic dining room. No TV in rooms.
ⓘ 28 🅿 ⬛ Rooms ⬛ All major cards

### 🍴 HOSTELLERIE GARGANTUA
**$$**
73 RUE VOLTAIRE
TEL 02 47 93 04 71
www.hotel-gargantua.com
Popular restaurant in a Renaissance palace overlooking the river. Eight rooms available.
⊕ Closed Wed. ⬛ MC, V

## FONTEVRAUD

### 🏨 LA CROIX BLANCHE
**$ ○○**
7 PLACE DES PLANTAGENÊTS
TEL 02 41 51 71 11
FAX 02 41 38 15 38
www.fontevraud.net
A simple but agreeable hotel close to the abbey with rooms overlooking the garden and restaurant.
ⓘ 21 🅿 ⬛ AE, MC, V

### 🍴 LA LICORNE
**$$$$**
ALLÉE STE.-CATHERINE
TEL 02 41 51 72 49
A restaurant in an 18th-century building. Try the langoustine ravioli and roasted Loire salmon with vanilla butter and Loire wines.

---

Reservations required.
🕘 Closed Sun. D, Mon., and
Wed. D 🦑 AE, MC, V

### 🍴 LA ROUTE D'OR
**$$**
PLACE DE L'ÉGLISE,
CANDES-ST.-MARTIN
TEL 02 47 95 81 10
A tiny restaurant in the
village of Candes-St.-Martin
east of Fontevraud. Tables in
a cellar dining room or on
the cobbled square. Try perch
in foie gras or baby eels
flavored with Roquefort.
🕘 Closed Tues. & Wed. Nov.–
March 🦑 MC, V

## JOUÉ-LÈS-TOURS

### 🏨 CHÂTEAU DE BEAULIEU
**$$/$$$ ❊❊❊**
67 RUE DE BEAULIEU
TEL 02 47 53 20 26
FAX 02 47 53 84 20
www.chateaudebeaulieu.fr
A 17th-century manor house
hotel in quiet surroundings
with a garden and beautiful
rooms.
🛈 19 🅿 🔇 🦑 AE, MC, V

## SOMETHING SPECIAL

### 🏨 HOSTELLERIE PRIEURÉ ST.-LAZARE
This well-modernized hotel
is in the old St.-Lazare priory,
within the abbey. The 19th-
century wing contains the
guest rooms , and in summer
the restaurant tables spread
out into the cloisters.
**$ ❊❊❊**
RUE ST. JEAN DE L'HABIT
TEL 02 41 51 73 16
FAX 02 41 51 75 50
www.hotelfp-fontevraud.com
🛈 52 🅿 🕘 Closed early
Aug. & Nov.–March 🔇 🦑 AE,
MC, V

## LA FLÈCHE

### 🏨 LE RELAIS CICERO
**$/$$ ❊❊❊**
18 BOULEVARD D'ALGER
TEL 02 43 94 14 14
FAX 02 43 45 98 96
www.cicero.fr
A stately, 17th-century mansion, with the peaceful ambience of the convent it once
was. No restaurant.
🛈 21 🕘 Closed early Aug. & late
Dec.–early Jan. 🦑 AE, MC, V

## LAMOTTE-BEUVRON

### 🍴 TATIN
**$$/$$$**
5 AVENUE DE VIERZON
TEL 02 54 88 00 03
www.hotel-tatin.fr
A small hotel-restaurant
serving simple local cuisine
with excellent game and fish.
It claims to be the originator
of *tarte Tatin,* the upside-down
caramelized apple tart; it is
always available here.
🅿 🕘 Closed Sun. D, all Mon.
🔇 🦑 All major cards

## LE MANS

### 🏨 CHANTECLER
**$ ❊❊❊**
50 RUE DE LA PELOUSE
TEL 02 43 14 40 00
FAX 02 43 77 16 28
www.hotelchantecler.fr
A modern hotel close to the
old town. No restaurant.
🛈 32 + 3 suites 🅿 🦑 All
major cards

## LOCHES

### 🏨 LE GEORGE SAND
**$/$$ ❊❊**
39 RUE QUINTEFOL
TEL 02 47 59 39 74
FAX 02 47 91 55 75
www.hotelrestaurant-george
sand.com
Former 17th-century coach inn
beneath the castle ramparts
with stone staircases and a

medieval watchtower. Rooms
overlook the castle or the river,
and meals are served on the
terrace in fine weather.
🛈 20 🦑 AE, MC, V

## MONTBAZON

### 🏨 CHÂTEAU D'ARTIGNY
### 🍴 **$$$/$$$$$ ❊❊❊❊**
TEL 02 47 34 30 30
FAX 02 47 34 30 39
www.artigny.com
Beautiful white-stone château
in its own wooded parkland,
overlooking the Indre Valley.
Built for the *parfumier* Coty,
its sumptuous interior is
sometimes a venue for musical
evenings. Rooms in the château and the lodge by the river.
Excellent cuisine, impressive
wine cellar. Sauna, tennis, small
golf course.
🛈 65 + 4 duplex 🅿 🔇 🏊 💈
🦑 All major cards

## MONTLOUIS-SUR-LOIRE

### 🏨 CHÂTEAU DE LA BOURDAISIÈRE
**$$$/$$$$**
25 RUE DE LA BOURDAISIÈRE
TEL 02 47 45 16 31
FAX 02 47 45 09 11
www.chateaulabourdaisiere
.com
Charming château in parkland,
built for Marie Gaudin, the
mistress of François I. The
beautifully furnished rooms
have period pieces. Tennis,
horseback riding. Reserva-
tions only. No restaurant.
🛈 10 🅿 🕘 Closed Nov.–March
🏊 🦑 MC, V

## NANTES

### 🏨 LA PÉROUSE
**$ ❊❊❊**
3 ALLÉE DUQUESNE
TEL 02 40 89 75 00
FAX 02 40 89 76 00
www.hotel-laperouse.fr
Situated in the Cours des
Cinquante Otages, this mod-

ern building has won awards for its minimalist design.

(i) 47 🚭 🚭 🖾 All major cards

## SOMETHING SPECIAL

### 🍴 LA CIGALE
Famous belle epoque café/brasserie in the center of Nantes serving superb fish and seafood.
$$
4 PLACE GRASLIN
TEL 02 51 84 94 94
www.lacigale.com
🖾 MC, V

## ORLÉANS

### 🏨 DES CÈDRES
$ ✪✪✪
17 RUE MARÉCHAL FOCH
TEL 02 38 62 22 92
FAX 02 38 81 76 46
www.hoteldescedres.com
A modern, well-run hotel on a quiet street, just outside the town center. Large rooms and a garden. No restaurant.
(i) 34 ⊕ Closed Dec. 24–Jan. 2 🚭 Rooms 🖾 AE, MC, V

### 🏨 LE RIVAGE
$ ✪✪
635 RUE REINE BLANCHE, OLIVET
TEL 02 38 66 02 93
FAX 02 38 56 31 11
Situated 3 miles (5 km) south of Orléans beside the Loire, this modern hotel offers meals on the terrace overlooking the river. Tennis.
(i) 17 🅿 ⊕ Closed late Dec.–late Jan.; restaurant closed D Sat. & Sun. Nov.–March 🖾 All major cards

## ROMORANTIN-LANTHENAY

### 🏨 GRAND HÔTEL DU 🍴 LION D'OR
$$/$$$$
69 RUE CLEMENCEAU
TEL 02 54 94 15 15
FAX 02 54 88 24 87

www.hotel-liondor.fr
Luxurious château with a beautiful garden and Michelin one-star restaurant, thought by some to be the best cooking in the Loire Valley. Wonderful local produce such as white asparagus and wild mushrooms in season; the frog's legs and the caramelized brioche with angelica sorbet are especially recommended.
(i) 13 + 3 suites ⊕ Closed mid-Feb.–mid-March; restaurant closed Tues. L 🚭 🖾 All major cards

## SACHE

### 🍴 AUBERGE DU XIIÈME SIÈCLE
$$/$$$
RUE PRINCIPALE
TEL 02 47 26 88 77
Half-timbered inn with a medieval interior, opposite the manor house where Balzac used to write. Good-value traditional cooking.
⊕ Closed Sun. D, Mon. & Tues. L 🖾 MC, V

## SAUMUR

### 🏨 ANNE D'ANJOU
$$ ✪✪✪
32 QUAI MAYAUD
TEL 02 41 67 30 30
FAX 02 41 67 51 00
www.hotel-anneanjou.com
An 18th-century building overlooking the Loire. There is a good affiliated restaurant in the hotel gardens called Les Ménestrels (11 rue Raspail, tel 02 41 67 71 10).
(i) 50 🅿 🖾 All major cards

## TOURS

## SOMETHING SPECIAL

### 🏨 LES HAUTES ROCHES
Four miles (6.5 km) upstream from Tours, this elegant troglodyte hotel on the north bank of the river has rooms carved out of the rock.

The restaurant offers classic Michelin one-star cooking; meals are served on a delightful terrace overlooking the river. Try the rabbit and foie gras terrine, and the Grand Marnier soufflé.
$$$/$$$$ ✪✪✪
86 QUAI DE LA LOIRE
ROCHECORBON
TEL 02 47 52 88 88
FAX 02 47 52 81 30
www.leshautesroches.com
(i) 14 ⊕ Hotel closed Feb.–March; restaurant closed Sun. & Mon. D 🖾 All major cards

### 🏨 L'UNIVERS 🍴 $$$ ✪✪✪
5 BOULEVARD HEURTELOUP
TEL 02 47 05 37 12
FAX 02 47 61 51 80
www.oceaniahotels.com
Situated in the town center, this grand hotel in the classic style once hosted Henry James. (He remarked on the overwhelming politeness of the staff.) Frescoes of famous visitors from 1846 to the present day decorate the walls. Highly rated affiliated restaurant, La Touraine.
(i) 85 + 8 suites 🅿 ⊕ Restaurant closed Sat. & Sun. except D July–Aug. 🚭 Rooms 🚭 🖾 All major cards

### 🏨 CODU MANOIR
$ ✪✪
2 RUE TRAVERSIÈRE
TEL 02 47 05 37 37
FAX 02 47 05 16 00
www.hotel.manoir.tours.voila.net
A small and charming hotel in a 19th-century building close to the railroad station and the old town. Prettily decorated rooms. No restaurant.
(i) 20 🅿 🖾 All major cards

### 🍴 OLIVIER ARLOT
$
33 RUE COLBERT
TEL 02 47 66 33 08

Contemporary bistro style with fixed menus, seasonal food, and selection of local wine available by the glass.
🕐 Closed Sat., Sun., & Aug.
🏊 🕭 AE, MC, V

## SOMETHING SPECIAL

### 🍴 LES CAVES DE MARSON
A delightful troglodyte restaurant near Saumur with candlelit dining rooms quarried out of the *tufa* caves. Try the *fouaces*, stuffed wheat pancakes cooked in a traditional wood-fired oven.
$
1 RUE HENRI FRICOTELLE
TEL 02 41 50 50 05
FAX 02 41 50 94 01
www.cavesdemarson.com
🕭 AE, MC, V

---

# ■ CENTRAL FRANCE

## BURGUNDY & THE JURA

## AUXERRE

### 🏨 PARC DES MARÉCHAUX
$/$$ ❍❍❍
6 AVENUE FOCH
TEL 03 86 51 43 77
FAX 03 86 51 31 72
www.hotel-parcmarechaux.com
A large 19th-century house close to the town center, with traditionally decorated rooms, some looking out onto the park. No restaurant.
🛈 25 🅿 🏊 🕭 All major cards

## AVALLON

### 🏨 CHÂTEAU DE VAULT-DE-LUGNY
$$$/$$$$$ ❍❍❍❍
TEL 03 86 34 07 86
FAX 03 86 34 16 36
www.lugny.fr
A beautifully restored, 16th-century country mansion standing on its own grounds. Some guest rooms have four-

poster or canopy beds. The restaurant serves traditional cuisine and is open only to hotel guests. Tennis, fishing.
🛈 12 🅿 🕐 Closed mid-Nov.– late- March 🕭 All major cards

## BEAUNE

### 🏨 LE CEP
$$$ ❍❍❍❍
27 RUE MAUFOUX
TEL 03 80 22 35 48
FAX 03 80 22 76 80
www.hotel-cep-beaune.com
A 16th-century hotel decorated in Renaissance style close to the Hôtel-Dieu.
🛈 56 🅿 🛗 🕭 All major cards

### 🍴 JARDIN DES REMPARTS
$$$$
10 RUE HÔTEL-DIEU
TEL 03 80 24 79 41
www.le-jardin-des-remparts.com
Dine on the garden terrace of this popular restaurant known for its wines as well as for its excellent cuisine; try the warm chocolate gâteau.
🕐 Closed Sun., Mon. (except public holidays), & Dec.
🕭 MC, V

### 🍴 LA BOUZEROTTE
$/$$$
BOUZE-LÈS-BEAUNE
TEL 03 80 26 01 37
www.labouzerotte.com
A village restaurant with simple country-style food, including rich omelets with bacon and potatoes, delicious salads picked from the garden, and fruit tarts. Sunny terrace for outside dining or open fire indoors.
🕐 Closed Mon. & Tues. 🕭 AE, MC, V

## CHABLIS

### 🏨 HOSTELLERIE DES CLOS
### 🍴 $$ ❍❍❍
18 RUE JULES RATHIER
TEL 03 86 42 10 63

FAX 03 86 42 17 11
www.hostellerie-des-clos.fr
This stylishly comfortable hotel in a medieval hospice has individually furnished guest rooms. The Michelin one-star restaurant serves dishes such as a *fricassée* of Burgundy snails and veal kidneys. A wide variety of local Chablis wines includes many by the glass.
🛈 26 🅿 🕐 Closed late Dec.– mid-Jan.; restaurant closed Mon.–Thurs. L. 🕭 AE, MC, V

## CHAGNY

### 🏨 LAMELOISE
### 🍴 $$$$/$$$$$
PLACE D'ARMES
TEL 03 85 87 65 65
FAX 03 85 87 03 57
www.lameloise.fr
A 15th-century hotel with traditional wood-beamed Burgundian decor contains one of Burgundy's great restaurants—a Michelin three-star establishment, friendly and family

---

run. Excellent local cheeses. Reservations essential. **(I)** 16 **(⊡)** Closed Tues. & Wed., & late Dec.–late Jan. **(⊗)** All major cards

## CLUNY

### 🏨 DE BOURGOGNE
**$/$$** ✪✪✪
PLACE DE L'ABBAYE
TEL 03 85 59 00 58
FAX 03 85 59 03 73
www.hotel-cluny.com
A 19th-century mansion built over part of the remains of Cluny abbey. Stone walls, period furniture, and objets d'art. The well-regarded restaurant serves Burgundian cuisine.
**(I)** 14 + 3 suites **P** **(⊡)** Closed Dec.–Jan. & Tues.–Wed., restaurant closed Tues. & Wed. **(⊗)** **(⊗)** AE, MC, V

## DIJON

### 🏨🍴 HOSTELLERIE CHAPEAU ROUGE
**$$/$$$** ✪✪✪✪
5 RUE MICHELET
TEL 03 80 50 88 88
FAX 03 80 50 88 89
www.chapeau-rouge.fr
This elegant historic hotel in the center of Dijon is a local landmark, with a Michelin one-star restaurant offering Burgundian classics.
**(I)** 30 **(⊗)** **(⊗)** All major cards

### 🏨🍴 LES OENOPHILES
**$$$**
HÔTEL PHILIPPE LE BON
18 RUE STE. ANNE
TEL 03 80 30 73 52
www.hotelphilippelebon.com
The restaurant in this grand 15th-century mansion serves magnificent traditional dishes like coq au vin, snails in Meursault sauce, and the Dijon specialty saddle of hare marinated in *marc de Bourgogne*. It is also home to the Compagnie Bourguignonne

des Oenophiles (Burgundian wine lovers) so you can expect a superb selection of the region's wines.
**(I)** 32 **P** **(⊡)** Closed Sun., and L. mid-Aug. **(⊗)** **(⊗)** All major cards

### 🍴 STÉPHANE DERBORD
**$$/$$$$**
10 PLACE DE PRÉSIDENT WILSON
TEL 03 80 67 74 64
www.restaurantstephane derbord.fr
Celebrated for his modern way with traditional cuisine Stephane Derbord, is one of Dijon's star chefs. Try his escargots de Bourgogne or the local specialty of freshwater fish in white wine. One Michelin star.
**(⊡)** Closed Sun. & Mon. **(⊗)** **(⊗)** All major cards

## GEVREY-CHAMBERTIN

### 🏨 LES GRANDS CRUS
**$** ✪✪✪
ROUTE DE LAVAUX
TEL 03 80 34 34 15
FAX 03 80 51 89 07
www.hoteldesgrandscrus.com
A modern hotel in the village center, but in traditional Burgundian style giving superb views over the vineyards. Break fast in the little flowery garden. No restaurant.
**(I)** 24 **P** **(⊡)** Closed early Dec.–late Feb. **(⊗)** AE, MC, V

## GEX

### 🏨 AUBERGE DES CHASSEURS
**$/$$** ✪✪✪
NAZ-DESSUS, ECHENEVEX
TEL 04 50 41 54 07
FAX 04 50 41 90 61
www.aubergedeschasseurs .com
Just south of Gex in the Jura Mountains, this delightful farmhouse has a well-tended garden and wonderful views.
**(I)** 15 **P** **(⊡)** Closed Nov.–Feb.; restaurant closed Sun. D, Mon., Tues. & Wed. L **(⊗)** **(⊗)** AE, MC, V

## LA BUSSIÈRE-SUR-OUCHE

### 🏨 ABBAYE DE LA BUSSIÈRE, COTE D'OR
**$$$**
TEL 03 80 49 02 20
FAX 03 80 49 05 23
www.abbayedelabussiere.fr
Lovingly restored old abbey with ancient frescoes, surrounded by its own parkland. Restaurant offers local specialties like Charolais beef served with fine Burgundy wines.
**(I)** 16 **P** **(⊡)** Closed Mon.; restaurant closed Mon., Tues., and L except Sun. **(⊗)** AE, MC, V

## SAULIEU

### 🍴 LE RELAIS BERNARD LOISEAU
**$$$$$**
2 RUE ARGENTINE
TEL 03 80 90 53 53
FAX 03 80 64 08 92
www.bernard-loiseau.com
Famed restaurant and hotel of the late lamented chef Bernard Loiseau, now run by his wife. Still the same imaginative *cuisine légère*, with three Michelin stars in a delightful setting with a garden.
**(I)** 23 + 7 suites + 3 duplex **(⊡)** Restaurant closed Tues. & Wed. in winter **(⊗)** **(⊗)** **(⊗)** **(⊗)** All major cards

## VÉZELAY

### 🏨🍴 L'ESPÉRANCE
**$$$$$** ✪✪✪✪
ST.-PÈRE DE VEZELAY
TEL 03 86 33 39 10
FAX 03 86 33 26 15
www.marc-meneau -esperance.com
In a village just south of Vézelay, this charming country hotel has an intimate restaurant in the hotel conservatory, the setting for the Michelin two-star cooking of chef Marc Meneau, who treats local ingredients with great imagination. Try potato pancakes with caviar, or turbot in a crust of salt with

lobster butter, served with the wines of Vézelay and Chablis. Some rooms in a restored watermill.

ⓘ 19 + 5 suites ⊞ Restaurant closed Tues. & Jan.–mid-March ⬩ Restaurant ⬩ All major cards

## RHÔNE VALLEY & THE ALPS

### BAGNOLS

### ⬚ CHÂTEAU DE
### ⓘⓘ BAGNOLS
### $$$$ ✪✪✪✪

TEL 04 74 71 40 00
FAX 04 74 71 40 49
www.chateaudebagnols.fr
A beautifully restored moated castle of golden stone with exquisitely landscaped gardens. Antiques and silk draperies enhance the elegant interior. The Michelin one-star restaurant excels in regional dishes such as fillet of beef with *girolles* and a ravioli of fresh peas.

ⓘ 16 + 4 suites ⓟ ⊞ Closed early Jan.–March & Nov.–late Dec. ⬩ ⬩ Rooms ⬩ ⬩ All major cards

## CHAMONIX-MONT-BLANC

### ⬚ GRAND HOTEL DES
### ALPES
### $$$

75 RUE DU DR. PACCARD
TEL 04 50 55 37 80
FAX 04 50 55 88 50
www.grandhoteldesalpes.com
A legendary grand hotel of 19th century, now superbly restored to its original atmosphere with cozy bars and elegant salons.

ⓘ 30 ⊞ Closed Oct.–Nov. & May ⬩ All major cards

## COURCHEVEL

### ⬚ LA SIVOLIÈRE
### $$$/$$$$ ✪✪✪✪✪

QUARTIER DES CHENUS
TEL 04 79 08 08 33
FAX 04 79 08 15 73
www.hotel-la-sivoliere.com
A charming, tasteful chalet hotel at the foot of the Courchevel ski runs. Very comfortable and exquisitely decorated. Restaurant.

ⓘ 32 ⓟ ⊞ Closed May–Dec. ⬩ ⬩ ⬩ MC, V

### ⓘⓘ LE BATEAU IVRE
### $$$$/$$$$$

HÔTEL POMME DE PIN
TEL 04 79 00 11 71
www.bateauivre-courchevel .com
A Michelin two-star restaurant with glorious panoramic mountain views serving hearty fare such as roast scallops and stuffed pig's trotters.

⊞ Closed mid-April–mid-Dec. ⬩ All major cards

## GRENOBLE

### ⬚ CHÂTEAU DE LA
### COMMANDERIE
### $/$$ ✪✪✪

17 AVENUE D'ÉCHIROLLES
TEL 04 76 25 34 58
FAX 04 76 24 07 31
www.commanderie.fr
Just outside Grenoble and close to the ski slopes, this historic château has a walled garden, tapestry-hung rooms, and beautiful guest rooms .

ⓘ 25 ⓟ ⊞ Closed Sat. L, Sun.–Mon., & late Dec.–early Jan. ⬩ ⬩ All major cards

## JULIÉNAS

### ⓘⓘ LA COQ À JULIÉNAS
### $$

PLACE DU MARCHÉ
TEL 04 74 04 41 98
www.coq-julienas.com
A Beaujolais bistro in the wine village famous for its special recipe for coq au vin and other traditional favorites.

⊞ Closed Tues. & Wed., & late Dec.–early March ⬩ All major cards

## LA MALÈNE

### ⬚ CHÂTEAU DE LA CAZE
### $$/$$$$ ✪✪✪✪

TEL 04 66 48 51 01
FAX 04 66 48 55 75
www.chateaudelacaze.com
A wonderfully romantic, 15th-century château on the banks of the Tarn, perfect for a meal or a stay while touring the Tarn Gorges.

ⓘ 13 ⊞ Closed Wed. & Nov.–March ⬩ All major cards

## LYON

### ⬚ VILLA FLORENTINE
### ⓘⓘ $$$$/$$$$$ ✪✪✪✪

25 MONTÉE ST.-BARTHÉLEMY
TEL 04 72 56 56 56
FAX 04 72 40 90 56
www.villaflorentine.com
A romantic hotel with a wonderful view over the red roofs of old Lyon, a favorite with visiting heads of state. Michelin one-star restaurant, Les Terrasses de Lyon; try the lamb cooked in milk with anchovies.

ⓘ 16 + 3 suites ⓟ ⊞ Restaurant closed Sun. & Mon. ⬩ ⬩ ⬩ All major cards

### ⬚ COUR DES LOGES
### ⓘⓘ $$$$ ✪✪✪✪

6 RUE BOEUF
TEL 04 72 77 44 44
FAX 04 72 40 93 61
www.courdesloges.com
A gorgeous hotel in the old town, with a contemporary interior created around 15th-century courtyard and galleries. Stylish restaurant.

ⓘ 52 ⊞ Restaurant closed July, Sun. & Mon. in Aug. ⬩ All major cards

### ⓘⓘ LÉON DE LYON
### $$$$$

1 RUE PLENEY
TEL 04 72 10 11 12
One of Lyon's great brasseries, long established on a narrow street off Quai St.-Antoine.

The menu includes traditional Lyon favorites such as sausages, lentils, and rich potato gratin, along with more modern lightweight fare. Superb cheese board and wine list.
**P** 🚭 ❄ 🔇 AE, MC, V

## 🍴 PAUL BOCUSE
**$$$$$**
40 RUE DE LA PLAGE
TEL 04 72 42 90 90
www.bocuse.com
Paul Bocuse's restaurant is 9 miles (16 km) north of Lyon, but it is worth the pilgrimage, and plenty of people make it to this Michelin three-star restaurant. They find simple, perfect food—exquisite roast chicken, creamy potato gratin, and luxuries like truffle soup, grandly served. There's even a *jeunes gourmands* menu for children.
**P** 🚭 🔇 All major cards

## 🍴 LA MÈRE BRAZIER
**$$$**
12 RUE ROYALE 69001
TEL 04 78 23 17 20
www.lamerebrazier.fr
A Lyon legend (Mère Brazier inspired generations of chefs) remains a fine restaurant, with two Michelin stars. Try the specialties of spider crabs and Bresse chicken.
🕐 Closed Sat. & Sun., 3 weeks in Aug. 🔇 AE, MC, V

## MÉGÈVE

## 🏨 CHALET DU MONTE 🍴 D'ARBOIS
**$$$/$$$$$** ✪✪✪✪
ROUTE MONT D'ARBOIS
TEL/FAX 04 50 21 25 03
www.domainedumont
darbois.com
This magnificent hotel in a peaceful setting was once home to the Rothschild family. The restaurant serves choice meals accompanied by an excellent wine list.
🛏 23 + 6 suites 🕐 Closed

mid-April–mid-June & mid-Sept.–mid-Dec. 🏊 🎾
🔇 All major cards

## MÉRIBEL

## 🏨 LE GRAND COEUR
**$$$$/$$$$$** ✪✪✪✪
TEL 04 79 08 60 03
FAX 04 79 08 58 38
www.legrandcoeur.com
One of Méribel's grand hotels, a luxury establishment with every comfort, located in the town center. Spa and restaurant.
🛏 41 **P** 🕐 Closed mid-April–mid- Dec. 🏊 🎾 🔇 All major cards

## PÉROUGES

## 🏨 L'HOSTELLERIE DE PÉROUGES
**$$$/$$$$** ✪✪✪/✪✪✪✪
PLACE DU TILLEUL
TEL 04 74 61 00 88
FAX 04 74 34 77 90
www.hostelleriedeperouges
.com
An old Bresse inn in this restored medieval town. Guest rooms in the 14th-century parts of the building are decorated in the style of the original sleeping quarters.
🛏 15 **P** 🔇 AE, MC, V

## MASSIF CENTRAL

## LAGUIOLE

## 🏨 HOTEL RESTAURANT 🍴 MICHEL BRAS
**$$$$$**
ROUTE DE L'AUBRAC
TEL 05 65 51 18 20
FAX 05 65 48 47 02
www.michel-bras.com
On the remote plateau of Aubrac is a modern hotel and restaurant where Michelin three-star chef Michael Bras brings a touch of genius to local cuisine and ingredients; like "gargouillou," a mix of

herbs, vegetables and salads. Reservations essential.
**P** 🕐 Closed Mon. except July & Aug. ❄ 🏊 🔇 All major cards

## SALERS

## 🏨 LES REMPARTS
**$** ✪✪
ESPLANADE BARROUZE
TEL 04 71 40 70 33
FAX 04 71 40 75 32
www.salers-hotel-remparts
.com
Perched on the edge of the ancient fortifications of medieval Salers, this hotel has spectacular views and delicious local cooking.
🛏 18 🕐 Closed mid-Oct.–mid-Dec. 🔇 MC, V

## VICHY

## 🏨 PAVILLON D'ENGHIEN 🍴
**$** ✪✪✪
32 RUE CALLOU
TEL 04 70 98 33 30
FAX 04 70 31 67 82
www.pavillondenghien.com
A small, old-fashioned hotel near the Enghien gardens and Callou baths, with a restaurant, Jardins d'Enghien.
🛏 22 🕐 Closed late Dec.–early Feb.; restaurant closed Sun. D and Mon. (except public hols.) 🏊 🔇 All major cards

## 🍴 L'ALAMBIC
**$$/$$$**
8 RUE NICOLAS-LARBAUD
TEL 04 70 59 12 71
A popular little restaurant with a welcoming atmosphere and beautifully presented cuisine. Try the mesclun salad with langoustine tails or chicken tournedos stuffed with snails. Superb wine list. Reservations advised.
🕐 Closed Sun. D, Mon. &Tues. & 3 weeks in Aug. 🚭
🔇 MC, V

# ■ SOUTHWEST FRANCE

## AQUITAINE & THE ATLANTIC COAST

### AINHOA

**▥ ITHURRIA**
**▯ $$/$$$**
PLACE DU FRONTON
TEL 05 59 29 92 11
FAX 05 59 29 81 28
www.ithurria.com
A charming hotel and Michelin one-star restaurant with garden. Typical dishes include *foie gras des Landes*, roast pigeon with garlic, and Basque cassoulet with red beans.
🛈 28 ⊕ Open April–Nov.; restaurant closed Wed. & Thurs. L except July–Aug. 🗚 🗟 All major cards

### ARCACHON

**▯ CHEZ YVETTE**
**$/$$**
59 BOULEVARD DU GÉNÉRAL LECLERC
TEL 05 56 83 05 11
A real seasonal table with produce fresh from the market or the garden. Try the *fricassée* of octopus with Espelette peppers or *soupe de poisson d'Arcachon*.
🗚 🗟 All major cards

### BIARRITZ

**▥ HOTEL DE PALAIS**
**▯ $$$$**
1 AVE DE L'IMPERATRICE
TEL 05 59 41 64 00
FAX 05 59 41 67 99
www.hotel-du-palais.com
Truly a palace, with chandeliers and marble pillars, rotunda restaurant overlooking the sea (best at sunset), two pools, fabulous luxury spa, and Michelin star restaurant.
🛈 122 🅿 ⊕ Restaurant closed Feb. 🗚 🗟 🗟 All major cards

**▥ CHÂTEAU DU CLAIR DE LUNE**
**$$ ○○○**
48 AVENUE ALAN-SEEGER
TEL 05 59 41 53 20
FAX 05 59 41 53 29
www.hotelclairlune.com
An elegant fin-de-siècle family house set in a quiet park south of Biarritz. Breakfast around one large table. No restaurant.
🛈 15 🅿 🗟 MC, V

**▯ CAFÉ DE LA GRANDE PLAGE**
**$$/$$$**
1 AVENUE EDOUARD VII
TEL 05 59 22 77 88
The terrace of this classic art deco café, serving drinks and excellent food based on Basque cuisine, offers glorious views over the ocean.
🗟 All major cards

**▯ CAMPAGNE ET GOURMANDISE**
**$$**
52 AVENUE ALAN-SEEGER
TEL 05 59 41 10 11
www.campagneetgourman dise.com
This restaurant south of Biarritz has panoramic views of the Pyrenees. Typical dishes include *fricassée de champignons en cappuccino d'herbes* and oxtail with foie gras.
⊕ Closed Sun. D, Mon. L, & Wed. 🗟 All major cards

### BIDARRAY

**▯ OSTAPE**
**$$$$**
CHAHATOA
TEL 05 59 37 91 91
FAX 05 59 37 91 92
www.ostape.com
An estate of Basque villas surrounded by gardens and mountains, where you can sample stylish regional cuisine from a 17th-century farmhouse. Lovely outdoor pool with panoramic views.

### BORDEAUX

**▥ REGENT GRAND HOTEL**
**$$$$$**
2 PLACE DE LA COMÉDIE
TEL 05 57 30 44 44
FAX 05 57 30 44 45
www.theregentbordeaux.com
An 18th-century building opposite the Grand Théâtre, completely refurbished in last-word luxury, glass domes, velvet drapes, and terrace. Michelin one-star restaurant.
🛈 150 ⊕ Restaurant closed Sun., Mon., & most of Aug.
🗚 🗟 All major cards

**▥ BURDIGALA**
**$$$$ ○○○○○**
115 RUE GEORGES-BONNAC
TEL 05 56 90 16 16
FAX 05 56 93 15 06
www.burdigala.com
A beautifully decorated hotel

---
▥ Hotel  ▯ Restaurant  🛈 No. of Guest Rooms  🅿 Parking  🚇 Métro  ⊕ Closed  🛗 Elevator

with every comfort, just outside the city center.
**(i)** 68 + 15 suites **P** 🛎 Rooms 🌊 🐎 🐾 All major cards

### 🏨 NORMANDIE
**$$ ✪✪✪**
7 COURS 30-JUILLET
TEL 05 56 52 16 80
FAX 05 56 51 68 91
www.hotel-de-normandie-bordeaux.com
Opposite the Maison du Vin, this central hotel is comfortable and welcoming. Some rooms have balconies.
**(i)** 100 🐎 🐾 All major cards

### 🍴 LA TUPINA
**$$$**
6 RUE PORTE DE LA MONNAIE
TEL 05 56 91 56 37
www.latupina.com
Savor excellent regional cuisine, fine wines, and the ambience of this popular restaurant close to the river.
🐾 All major cards

### 🍴 LE VIEUX BORDEAUX
**$$/$$$**
27 RUE BUHAN
TEL 05 56 52 94 26
www.le-vieux-bordeaux.com
Relax in this restaurant's leafy courtyard in the heart of the city and enjoy its good value and classic cuisine.
🕐 Closed Sun.–Mon. & 3 weeks in Aug. 🐾 All major cards

## BOULIAC

### 🏨 LE ST.-JAMES
🍴 **$$$$**
PLACE C HOLSTEIN
TEL 05 57 97 06 00
FAX 05 56 20 92 58
www.saintjames-bouliac.com
Original rustic buildings in a small village outside Bordeaux combine with the chic architectural design of Jean Nouvel in this unusual hotel. Home to the esteemed St. James restaurant, now with two

Michelin stars.
🕐 Restaurant closed Sat., Sun. & 3 weeks in Aug. 🐾 All major cards

## CAP-FERRET

### 🏨 DES PINS
**$ ✪✪**
RUE DE FAUVETTES
TEL 05 56 60 60 11
FAX 05 56 60 67 41
www.hotel-des-pins.fr
A small hotel converted from a theater with a huge glassed-in terrace, in a quiet part of town, set in gardens.
**(i)** 14 🕐 Closed Dec.–Feb. 🐎 🐾 MC, V

## CASTELNAU-DU-MÉDOC

### 🏨 CHÂTEAU DU FOULON
**$$**
TEL 05 56 58 20 18
FAX 05 56 58 23 43
www.au-chateau.com
An elegant white château set in a large park just outside the village. Breakfast en famille at the magnificent grand table. No restaurant.
**(i)** 4 + 4 suites **P** 🐾 Cash only

## ESPELETTE

### 🏨 EUZKADI
🍴 **$$**
285 KARRIKA NAGUSIA
TEL 05 59 93 91 88
FAX 05 59 53 90 19
www.hotel-restaurant-euzkadi.com
This hotel and restaurant in a typical Basque house prepares excellent Basque specialties.
🕐 Closed Mon.–Tues. in winter & all Nov.–Dec. 🌊 🐾 MC, V

## EUGÉNIE-LES-BAINS

### 🏨 LES PRÉS D'EUGÉNIE
🍴 **$$$$ ✪✪✪✪**
TEL 05 58 05 06 07

FAX 05 58 51 10 10
www.michelguerard.com
The empire of the legendary chef Michel Guérard, inventor of cuisine minceur and holder of three Michelin stars, it encompasses two hotels: Les Prés d'Eugénie and Le Couvent des Herbes, an 18th-century former convent. Two health spas, La Maison Rose and La Ferme aux Grives, complete the four establishments. All are individually decorated in exquisite taste. Restaurants serve both traditional and minceur cuisine, and there are luxurious spa facilities. Go for your health, your tastebuds, or both. Tennis.
**(i)** 60 rooms & 15 suites (all together) 🕐 Opening times vary; call ahead 🌊 🐾 All major cards

## LA ROCHELLE

### 🏨 LES BRISES
**$$ ✪✪✪**
CHEMIN DIGUE RICHELIEU
TEL 05 46 43 89 37
FAX 05 46 43 27 97
www.hotellesbrises.com
Close to the port with a fine terrace overlooking the sea.
**(i)** 50 **P** 🐾 AE, DC, MC, V

### 🏨 HOTEL RESIDENCE DE FRANCE
**$$ ✪✪✪✪**
43 RUE MINAGE
TEL 05 46 28 06 00
FAX 05 46 28 06 03
www.hotel-larochelle.com
Calm retreat in the center of old town, with shady courtyard and small pool. Stylish modern decor and artworks, and good local seafood dishes. Internet.
**(i)** 16 **P** 🐾 All major cards

## LIMOGES

### 🍴 LES PETITS VENTRES
**$/$$**
20 RUE DE LA BOUCHERIE
TEL 05 55 34 22 90

🐾 Nonsmoking  🐎 Air-conditioning  🏊 Indoor Pool  🌊 Outdoor Pool  🔱 Health Club  🐾 Credit Cards

www.les-petits-ventres.com
A 15th-century house with
Old World charm and a terrace where you dine on the
region's traditional cuisine. Try
*tête de veau* (calf's head) or the
*pot au feu.*
🕓 Closed Sun. & Mon., weeks in
Feb., May & Sept. 🚫 AE, MC, V

## MARGAUX

🏨 **LE PAVILLON
DE MARGAUX**
**$$** 〇〇〇
3 RUE GEORGES MANDEL
TEL 05 57 88 77 54
FAX 05 57 88 77 73
www.pavillonmargaux.com
Built in typical 19th-century
local style, this hotel has a
terrace surrounded by the
celebrated vineyards.
🛏 14 🅿 🕓 Closed Dec. 15–
Jan. 15 🚫 All major cards

🍴 **AUBERGE DE SAVOIE**
**$**
1 PLACE TRÉMOILLE
TEL 05 57 88 31 76
www.lesavoie.net
A good-value restaurant in
this wine town, specializing
in regional dishes such as a
quiche of *foie de canard et jus
de truffe.*
🕓 Closed Sun. & Mon. D & last 2
weeks in Feb. 🚫 DC, MC, V

## PAUILLAC

🏨 **CHÂTEAU**
🍴 **CORDEILLAN BAGES**
**$$$$** 〇〇〇〇
ROUTE DES CHÂTEAUX
TEL 05 56 59 24 24
FAX 05 56 59 01 89
www.cordeillanbages.com
An English country house–
style hotel with a Michelin
two-star restaurant. Home of
the École de Bordeaux, which
arranges wine coursess.
🛏 25 🅿 🕓 Closed early
Dec.–early Feb.; restaurant
closed Sat. L, Mon., & Tues.
🚫 All major cards

## POITIERS

🏨 **NOVOTEL
FUTUROSCOPE**
**$$** 〇〇〇
PORTES DU PARC
TEL 05 49 49 91 91
FAX 05 49 49 91 90
www.novotel.com
A modern hotel convenient to
the popular Futuroscope visual
technology park.
🛏 110 + 18 studios 🅿 🚫
🚫 All major cards

## ST.-ÉTIENNE-DE-BAÏGORRY

🏨 **ARCÉ**
**$$** 〇〇〇
TEL 05 59 37 40 14
FAX 05 59 37 40 27
www.hotel-arce.com
This mountain-village hotel
has been in the same family
for more than a hundred
years. A veranda sits out over
the river, and some rooms
have their own balconies.
Beamed sitting room, library,
and dining room with picture
windows. Tennis.
🛏 23 🕓 Closed mid-Nov.–
mid- March 🚫 🚫 All major
cards

## ST.-JEAN-DE-LUZ

🏨 **PARC VICTORIA**
🍴 **LES LIERRES**
**$$$$** 〇〇〇〇
5 RUE CÉPÉ
TEL 05 59 26 78 78
FAX 05 59 26 78 08
www.parcvictoria.com
A 19th-century villa with a
formal park and gardens. Luxu-
riously appointed rooms have
marble bathrooms, and some
balconies. The restaurant, Les
Lierres, has dining rooms in
thirties-style garden pavilions.
🛏 8 + 4 suites 🅿 🕓 Closed
mid-Nov.–mid-March 🚫 🚫 All
major cards

## CHEZ MATTIN
**$$**
63 RUE BAIGNOL, CIBORE
TEL 05 59 47 19 52
Rustic decor, Basque specialties, and a warm family
welcome. Sample the stuffed
peppers or Basque gâteau.
🕓 Closed Mon. & Jan.–Feb.
🚫 AE, MC, V

## ST.-JEAN-PIED-DE-PORT

🏨 **LES PYRÉNÉES**
🍴 **$$$$** 〇〇〇〇
19 PLACE DU GÉNÉRAL-
DE-GAULLE
TEL 05 59 37 01 01
FAX 05 59 37 18 97
www.hotel-les-pyrenees.com
An excellent hotel with a terrace. The restaurant (Michelin
two star) is well known for the
quality of its Basque/Gascon
cuisine. Excellent fish dishes
include langoustine, and they
do a fine gazpacho.
🛏 20 🅿 🕓 Restaurant closed
Mon. D in Nov.–March, Tues.
Oct.–June, 3 weeks in Jan. &
late Nov.–late Dec. 🚫 🚫 🚫
🚫 All major cards

## THE DORDOGNE & MIDI-PYRÉNÉES

## ALBI

🏨 **HOSTELLERIE
ST.-ANTOINE**
**$$/$$$** 〇〇〇〇
17 RUE ST.-ANTOINE
TEL 05 63 54 04 04
FAX 05 63 47 10 47
www.hotel-saint-antoine-albi
.com
A charming 18th-century inn
owned by the same family for
five generations. Most rooms
look out onto the garden.
🛏 44 🅿 🚫 🚫 🚫 All major
cards

🍴 **LE JARDIN DES QUATRE
SAISONS**
**$$**

19 BOULEVARD DE STRASBOURG
TEL 05 63 60 77 76
www.lejardindesquatresai
sons.fr
A restaurant of exceptional
quality and good value. Try
the terrine of escargots with
pig's feet and truffles, or the
roast pigeon with charlotte of
mushroom and rosemary.
🕐 Closed Mon. & Sun. D
⊗ AE, MC, V

## AUCH

### 🍴 FRANCE
**$$$/$$$$**
2 PLACE DE LA LIBÉRATION
TEL 05 62 61 71 71
Try the best of Gascon cook-
ing in this hotel-restaurant,
known for its promotion
of the region's cuisine and its
key elements of duck, goose,
garlic, and wine.
🛏 31 🕐 Closed Sun. D, Mon.,
& Tues. ⊗ All major cards

## BERGERAC

### 🏨 CHÂTEAU LES MERLES
### 🍴 $$$
TUILIERES, MOULEYDIER
TEL 05 53 63 13 12
FAX 05 53 63 13 45
www.lesmerles.com
A small 18th-century château
with stunning views; stylish
modern interior, and casual
but impeccable service from
Dutch owners. Fine cooking
includes on-site lessons.
🛏 12 + 2 suites + 1 apt. 🅿 🏊
⊗ All major cards

## BRANTÔME

### 🏨 LE MOULIN DE
### 🍴 L'ABBAYE
**$$$**
1 ROUTE DE BOURDEILLES
TEL 05 53 05 80 22
FAX 05 53 05 75 27
www.moulinabbaye.com
Dine on the terrace of this
lovely old mill, once the
house of Abbé Pierre de

Bourdeilles and now a hotel and
restaurant. Watch the Dronne
River roll by, and enjoy the
excellent cuisine: pigeon with
ceps, *foie gras de canard*, crème
brûlée with strawberries.
🅿 🕐 Closed Nov.–April, & L
except weekends ⊗ All major
cards

### 🏨 DOMAINE DE LA
ROSERAIE
**$$ ✪✪✪**
ROUTE D'ANGOULÊME
TEL 05 53 02 75 56
FAX 05 53 35 80 19
www.domaine-la-roseraie
.com
Renovated 17th-century hotel
just outside Brantôme, located
on nine acres (3.5 ha) of quiet
parkland. Breakfast in the rose
garden in summer; sit by the
open fire in winter.
🛏 7 + 1 suite 🕐 Closed mid-
Nov.–March 🏊 ⊗ All major
cards

## CAHORS

### 🍴 CLAUDE MARCO
**$$/$$$**
LAMAGDELAINE (4 MILES/6 KM
E OF CAHORS VIA D653)
TEL 05 65 35 30 64
www.restaurantmarco.com
An old *bergerie* where you can
eat inside beneath the vaulted
ceiling or out on the terrace.
Specialties at this Michelin
one-star restaurant include
*pot au feu* with duck or *filet
de boeuf* with morel mushrooms. Rooms available.
🛏 25 🕐 Closed Sun. D,
Mon. in winter, early Jan.–early
March, & 10 days in Oct. ⊗ AE,
MC, V

## CORDES

### 🏨 HOSTELLERIE DU VIEUX
### 🍴 CORDES
**$$**
RUE ST.-MICHEL
TEL 05 63 53 79 20
FAX 05 63 56 02 47

www.thuries.fr
Sit on the terrace in the shade
of an ancient wisteria at this
hotel-restaurant converted
from a 13th-century monas-
tery. Try authentic cassoulet or
delicious fish dishes.
🕐 Closed Tues. L, Sun. D, &
Mon. out of season ⊗ AE,
MC, V

## CUQ-TOULZA

### 🏨 CUQ EN TERRASSES
**$$/$$$**
TEL 05 63 82 54 00
FAX 05 63 82 54 11
www.cuqenterrasses.com
In a hilltop hamlet just outside
Cuq-Toulza, this former pres-
bytery is charmingly decorated
and has several terraces. Meals
by reservation only.
🛏 8 🅿 🕐 Closed Nov.–
March; restaurant closed Wed.
🏊 ⊗ All major cards

## DOMME

### 🏨 L'ESPLANADE
### 🍴 $$ ✪✪✪
TEL 05 53 28 31 41
FAX 05 53 28 49 92
www.esplanade-perigord.com
A quiet hotel within the fortifications of this historic *bastide*
town, with a terrace and lovely
views over the Dordogne
Valley. The Michelin one-star
restaurant makes good use
of local produce, particularly
truffles.
🛏 25 🕐 Closed early Nov.–
mid-Feb.; restaurant closed
Mon. except D in season ⊗ All
major cards

## FIGEAC

### 🍴 LA DÎNÉE DU VIGUIER
**$$**
4 RUE BOUTARIC
TEL 05 65 50 08 08
www.ladineeduviguier.fr
Le Dinée is the restaurant of
the hotel Viguier du Roy, a
château spanning the 12th to

---

18th centuries. Try gigot of monkfish spiked with truffles, the Quercy tart with morels, or the warm shrimp omelet. ⊕ Closed Mon. & Sun. D in winter ⬢ All major cards

## GRAMAT

### 🏨 CHÂTEAU DE 🍴 ROUMÉGOUSE
**$$/$$$ ✪✪✪✪**
ROUTE DE BRIVE
TEL 05 65 33 63 81
FAX 05 65 33 71 18
www.hotelsandchateaux.com
This romantic 19th-century château with its wooded parkland was a favorite with Charles de Gaulle. The rooms are charming, and there is even one in the tower. On fine evenings, dine on the terrace with river views.
ⓘ 16 ⊕ Closed Tues. except July–Aug. ⬛ ⬢ All major cards

## LES EYZIES-DE-TAYAC

### 🍴 LES GLYCINES
**$$**
ROUTE DE PÉRIGUEUX
TEL 05 53 06 97 07
A little auberge among greenery with a rustic interior and a terrace beside the river. Rooms available.
⊕ Closed Mon. L ⬢ AE, MC, V

## PÉRIGUEUX

### 🍴 HERCULE POIREAU
**$$**
2 RUE NATION
TEL 05 53 08 90 76
Dine on the best of Périgord cuisine beneath the low vaulted ceiling of this fine Renaissance building.
⊕ Closed Wed. & Tues. D in winter ⬢ MC, V

## PUYMIROL

### 🏨 MICHEL TRAMA
**🍴 $$$ ✪✪✪✪**

52 RUE ROYALE
TEL 05 53 95 31 46
FAX 05 53 95 33 80
www.aubergade.com
In the center of a fortified town, this 13th-century residence once belonged to the counts of Toulouse. The owner-chef, M. Trama, serves excellent cuisine that has won him three Michelin stars, and also offers a huge selection of cigars. Terraced garden. Rooms have Jacuzzis or massage showers.
ⓘ 11 🅿 🅂 ⊕ Closed L Mon. & Tues., & D Sun. & Mon. out of season ⬢ All major cards

## ROCAMADOUR

### 🏨 LES VIEILLES TOURS
**🍴 $ ✪✪**
ROUTE DE PAYRAC
(2 MILES/4 KM WEST OF ROCAMADOUR)
TEL 05 65 33 68 01
FAX 05 65 33 68 59
www.vieillestours-rocamadour.com
This partly 13th-century manor house makes a comfortable hotel. Good restaurant, too.
ⓘ 17 ⊕ Closed mid-Nov.– April ⬛ ⬢ AE, MC, V

### 🍴 SAINTE-MARIE
**$$**
PLACE DE SENHALS
TEL 05 65 33 63 07
www.hotel-sainte-marie.fr
A rustic restaurant with a terrace where you can dine on excellent local cuisine.
⊕ Closed Nov.–Easter ⬢ MC, V

## ST.-CÉRÉ

### 🏨 VILLA RIC
**🍴 $$$**
ROUTE DE LEYME
TEL 05 65 38 04 08
FAX 05 65 38 00 14
www.villaric.com
A small restaurant with a summer terrace, serving regional

---

## PRICES

**HOTELS**
An indication of the cost of a double room in the high season is given by $ signs.

| | |
|---|---|
| **$$$$$** | Over $400 |
| **$$$$** | $300–$400 |
| **$$$** | $200–$300 |
| **$$** | $100–$200 |
| **$** | Under $100 |

**RESTAURANTS**
An indication of the cost of a three-course meal without drinks is given by $ signs.

| | |
|---|---|
| **$$$$$** | Over $150 |
| **$$$$** | $100–$150 |
| **$$$** | $80–$100 |
| **$$** | $60–$80 |
| **$** | Under $60 |

cuisine. Some rooms.
ⓘ 5 ⊕ Closed mid-Nov.– March ⬛ ⬢ MC, V

## ST.-CIRQ-LAPOPIE

### 🏨 LA PELISSARIA
**$$ ✪✪✪**
LE BOURG
TEL 05 65 31 25 14
FAX 05 65 30 25 52
This popular hotel in a 13th-century building is perched on the edge of a hill village. Wonderful views.
ⓘ 8 + 2 suites ⊕ Only open July 23–Aug. 28 ⬛ ⬢ MC, V

### 🍴 AUBERGE DU SOMBRAL
**$$**
TEL 05 65 31 26 08
FAX 05 65 30 26 37
www.lesombrals.com
A peaceful old house and restaurant in the heart of this picturesque, medieval village.
⊕ Closed Sun.–Thurs. D, & Thurs. L out of season ⬢ MC, V

---

🏨 Hotel  🍴 Restaurant  ⓘ No. of Guest Rooms  🅿 Parking  🚇 Métro  ⊕ Closed  🛗 Elevator

## ST.-CYPRIEN-EN-PÉRIGORD

### 🏨 LA GRANDE MARQUE
**$ 😊😊**
MARNAC
TEL 05 53 31 61 63
FAX 05 53 28 39 55
www.lagrandemarque.fr
This 18th-century house on a hill with remarkable country views has rooms in the renovated former tobacco drying sheds. Dine on the shady terrace.
🛈 5 🍴 P 🕐 Closed Nov.–Easter 🔒 MC, V

## SARLAT-LA-CANÉDA

### 🍴 LA MADELEINE
**$$**
1 PLACE DE LA PETITE RIGAUDIE
TEL 05 53 59 10 41
A hotel-restaurant in Sarlat, the center of Périgord cuisine, which offers all the regional delicacies: goose, duck, ceps, truffles, and foie gras.
🕐 Closed mid- Nov.–mid-March, Mon. & Tues. L except July & Aug. 🔒 AE, MC, V

## SOUILLAC

### 🏨 CHÂTEAU DE LA TREYNE
**$$$/$$$$ 😊😊😊😊**
LA TREYNE
TEL 05 65 27 60 60
FAX 05 65 27 60 70
www.chateaudelatreyne.com
A charming white château surrounded by parkland above the Dordogne River. Amenities and activities include a restaurant, tennis, and canoeing.
🛈 14 + 2 suites P 🕐 Closed mid-Nov.–Easter 🏊 🔒 All major cards

## TOULOUSE

### 🏨 HOTEL GARONNE
**$$$$ 😊😊😊😊**
22 DESCENTE DE LA HALLE AUX

POISSONS
TEL 05 34 31 94 80
REST. 05 34 31 94 84
FAX 05 34 31 94 81
www.hotelgaronne.com
A handsome hotel by the river with Japanese-style chic at a price. Its vaulted Restaurant Le 19 opposite is good for sushi and steak tartare.
🕐 Closed most of Aug., Sat. L, Mon. L & Sun. 🔒 AE

### 🏨 BEAUX-ARTS
**$$$ 😊😊😊**
1 PLACE DU PONT NEUF
TEL 05 34 45 42 42
FAX 05 34 45 42 43
www.hoteldesbeauxarts.com
This 18th-century building beside the river has been a hotel for 100 years. No restaurant, but beneath the hotel is the lively Brasserie des Beaux-Arts.
🛈19 🔒 🔒 🔒 All major cards

### 🏨🍴 GRAND HÔTEL DE L'OPÉRA
**$$/$$$ 😊😊😊😊**
1 PLACE DU CAPITOLE
TEL 05 61 21 82 66
FAX 05 61 23 41 04
www.grand-hotel-opera.com
Centrally located, the hotel is in a courtyard hidden behind its two well-known restaurants. The Les Jardins de l'Opéra has seasonal specialties on its inventive menus. The Grand Café de l'Opéra serves light meals.
🛈 45 + 5 suites 🔒 Rooms 🎽 🔒 All major cards

### 🍴 LE CANTOU
**$$**
98 RUE VELASQUEZ
TEL 05 61 49 20 21
www.cantou.fr
A pretty restaurant where you can sample the best of regional cuisine, for example, fricassée of langoustines and scallops, or civet de canard with calf's foot.
🕐 Closed Sat. & Sun. & a week

in mid-Aug. and a week in early Jan. 🔒 All major cards

### 🍴 LE CANTINE DU CURÉ
**$**
2 RUE DES COUTELIERS
TEL 05 61 25 83 42
This cozy little restaurant in the old quarter near the river offers hearty peasant dishes like boeuf bourguignon at very reasonable prices.
🕐 Closed Sun.–Mon.
🔒 MC, V

## TRÉMOLAT

### 🏨🍴 LE VIEUX LOGIS
**$$$/$$$$ 😊😊😊**
TEL 05 53 22 80 06
FAX 05 53 22 84 89
www.vieux-logis.com
This village hotel with its charming mix of buildings has been in the same family for 400 years. The Michelin one-star restaurant serves versions of regional classics. The galleried dining room looks out onto the pretty garden.
🛈 18 P 🏊 🔒 All major cards

## THE PYRENEES

## ARREAU

### 🏨🍴 HOTEL D'ANGLETERRE
**$$$**
ROUTE LUCHON
TEL 05 62 98 63 30
FAX 05 62 98 69 66
www.hotel-angleterre-arreau.com
A charming old post house in a tiny slate-roofed village. Its restaurant has existed since the 19th century, its carré d'agneau and river trout favored by legendary mountaineer Sir Henry Russell.
🕐 Closed Mon., except July–Aug., Oct.–Dec., & April–May P 🏊 🔒 All major cards

## AX-LES-THERMES

### ▦ LE GRILLON
### 🍴 $$
RUE ST.-UDAUT
TEL 05 61 64 31 64
www.hotel-le-grillon.com
A hotel-restaurant up in the
mountains offering a terrace
with wonderful views. The
duck *magret* with honey is
recommended.
ℹ 71 🕒 Closed Tues. D, Wed.
(except holidays) 🅰 MC, V

## FOIX

### ▦ LONS
### $ 😊😊😊
6 PLACE GEORGES-DUTHIL
TEL 05 34 09 28 00
FAX 05 61 02 68 18
www.hotel-lons-foix.com
Situated next to the Ariège
River, this friendly hotel has
a terrace, a brasserie, and a
restaurant.
ℹ 40 🕒 Closed late Dec.–
mid-Jan. 🅰 All major cards

## GAVARNIE

### ▦ HOTEL COMPOSTELLE
### $
RUE DE L'EGLISE
TEL 05 62 92 49 43
www.compostellehotel.com
Small hotel on edge of the
village of Gavarnie with
magnificient views of the
cirque and waterfall. Proprietor Yvan is also a mountain
guide and can organize
expeditions.
🕒 Closed Oct.–Jan. 🅰 CB, V

## GÈDRE

### ▦ LA BRÈCHE DE ROLAND
### $ 😊😊
GÈDRE
TEL 05 62 92 48 54
FAX 05 62 92 46 05
www.pyrenees-hotel-breche
.com
An old mountain mansion,
in a village 5 miles (8 km)

north of Gavarnie. The hotel
has a garden and a terrace
where you can dine. The
owner can arrange trips
up into the mountains and
helicopter rides.
ℹ 28 🕒 Closed mid-Oct.–
Dec. 🅰 MC, V

## LIMOUX

### 🍴 MAISON DE LA BLANQUETTE
### $
46 BIS PROMENADE DU TIVOLI
TEL 04 68 31 01 63
A town restaurant with rustic
decor and a very good wine
selection, including, of course,
sparkling Limoux.
🕒 Closed Sun. D–Wed. 🅰 MC, V

## MIREPOIX

### ▦ LA MAISON DES CONSULS
### $$ 😊😊😊
6 PLACE DU MARÉCHAL LECLERC
TEL 05 61 68 81 81
FAX 05 61 68 81 15
www.maisondesconsuls.com
In the central square of a *bastide* town, this renovated 14th-
century house has historically
themed rooms overlooking
the medieval streets.
ℹ 8 🅿 🅰 All major cards

## ORION

### ▦ CHATEAU D'ORION
### $$$
ORION
TEL 05 59 65 07 74
FAX 05 59 65 08 21
An exquisite small château
overlooking rolling Bearn
countryside, lovingly restored
with original furniture, paintings, and meals served in
candlelit dining room.
🅿 🅰 No cards

## PAU

### ▦ GRAND HÔTEL DU COMMERCE
### $ 😊😊
9 RUE MARÉCHAL JOFFRE
TEL 05 59 27 24 40
FAX 05 59 83 81 74
A traditional hotel in the town
center close to the château,
with a good-value restaurant.
ℹ 51 🅰 All major cards

### ▦ PAU VILLA NAVARRE
### $
59 AVENUE TRESPOEY
TEL 05 59 14 65 65
FAX 05 59 14 65 64
www.villanavarre.fr
Atmosphere "très British"
in this superb villa, brought
back to 19th-century life with
leather armchairs and wood
paneling. Surrounded by a
large park with a pool and
views of the Pyrenees.
ℹ 26 🅿 🕒 Restaurant closed
Sun. D 🚇 🅰 All major cards

### 🍴 CHEZ PIERRE
### $$$
16 RUE LOUIS-BARTHOU
TEL 05 59 27 76 86
www.restaurant-chez-pierre.fr
An elegantly decorated town-
house restaurant. Try the langoustine ravioli with Madras
curry or veal with morels.
🕒 Closed Sat. L, Sun. (except
public hols.), Mon. L, 1 week
early Jan. 🅰 All major cards

## ST.-BERTRAND-DE-COMMINGES

### ▦ L'OPPIDUM
### $ 😊😊
RUE DE LA POSTE
TEL 05 61 88 33 50
FAX 05 61 95 94 04
A small hotel in the heart of
the medieval village, walking
distance to the cathedral.
ℹ 15 🕒 Closed Wed. & Nov.–Jan.
🅰 AE, MC, V

---

## 🍴 LUGDUNUM
**$$**
VALCABRÈRE
TEL 05 61 94 52 05
Reservations are essential for this unique and historic culinary experience. Sample recipes compiled by Apicius, a first-century Roman gastronome. Serves dishes such as boar or partridge with authentically spiced wines.
🕐 Closed Mon. & Tues. D
💳 MC, V

## ST.-GIRONS

### 🏨 EYCHENNE
### 🍴 **$$$ ⚫⚫⚫**
8 AVENUE PAUL-LAFFONT
TEL 05 61 04 04 50
FAX 05 61 96 07 20
www.ariege.com/hotel-eychenne
A beautiful old family-run hostelry with well-equipped rooms and a lovely garden. The restaurant serves traditional southwestern local cuisine; try monkfish with saffron or the confit de canard with ceps.
🛏 41 🕐 Closed Sun. D, Mon. (Nov.–March except public hols.), & late Dec.–end of Jan.
💳 All major cards

## ◼ SOUTH OF FRANCE

## CÔTE D'AZUR

## BEAULIEU-SUR-MER

### 🏨 LA RÉSERVE DE
### 🍴 BEAULIEU
### **$$$$$ ⚫⚫⚫⚫**
5 BOULEVARD DU MARÉCHAL LECLERC
TEL 04 93 01 00 01
FAX 04 93 01 28 99
www.reservebeaulieu.com
A fabulous Riviera hotel on the seafront, founded by the famous James Gordon Bennett, proprietor of the *New York Herald Tribune*. The restau-

---

rant, which has one Michelin star, specializes in fish.
🛏 33 🅿 🕐 Closed mid-Oct.–mid-Dec. 💺 Rooms 🖥 📺
💳 All major cards

## BIOT

### 🍴 LES TERRAILLERS
### **$$$/$$$$**
11 ROUTE DU CHEMIN-NEUF
TEL 04 93 65 01 59
www.lesterraillers.com
A large farmhouse restaurant south of Biot, with imaginative cuisine that has gained it one Michelin star. Try baby rabbit with *fines herbes* or foie gras ravioli with *fumet de morille*.
🕐 Closed Wed., Thurs., & Nov.
💺 💳 AE, MC, V

## CANNES

### 🏨 CARLTON
### INTERCONTINENTAL
### **$$$$$ ⚫⚫⚫⚫⚫**
58 LA CROISETTE
TEL 04 93 06 40 06
FAX 04 93 06 40 25
www.ichotelsgroup.com
A luxury hotel with a private beach and a terrace where film moguls make deals during the Cannes festival.
🛏 295 + 18 suites 🅿 💺 💺
💺 📺 💳 All major cards

### 🍴 LA SCALA
### **$$$**
HÔTEL NOGA HILTON, 50 BOULEVARD DE LA CROISETTE
TEL 04 92 99 70 93
A fashionable restaurant with a terrace overlooking the Mediterranean, serving a gourmet Italian menu. Specialties include risotto with artichokes and foie gras, and pigeon with cep ravioli.
💳 All major cards

### 🍴 LA MÈRE BESSON
### **$$/$$$**
13 RUE DES FRÈRES PRADIGNAC
TEL 04 93 39 59 24
A Cannes institution, this

---

popular little bistro serves a different fish dish every day.
🕐 Closed Sun. 💺 💺
💳 All major cards

## CAP D'ANTIBES

### 🏨 DU CAP-EDEN ROC
### **$$$$$ ⚫⚫⚫⚫⚫**
BOULEVARD KENNEDY
TEL 04 93 61 39 01
FAX 04 93 67 76 04
www.hotel-du-cap-eden-roc.com
Favored by Cannes film stars, this is the last word in luxury, especially the 1930s terrace and the pool hewn out of the rocks where Zelda Fitzgerald used to swim. Tennis.
🛏 121 + 9 suites 🅿 🕐 Closed Nov.–March 💺 🖥 📺
💳 All major cards

## HAUT-DE-CAGNES

### 🍴 JOSY-JO
### **$$$**
4 PLACE PLANASTEL
TEL 04 93 20 68 76
www.restaurant-josyjo.com
A bistro in the old town with rustic decor and a huge fireplace. Superb ingredients simply cooked such as peppers marinated in olive oil, and *petits farcis* (stuffed vegetables).
🕐 Closed Sat. L, Sun., & Dec.
💺 💳 AE, MC, V

## ÎLE DE PORQUEROLLES

### 🏨 LA MAS DU
### 🍴 LANGOUSTIER
### **$$$$ ⚫⚫⚫**
ÎLE DE PORQUEROLLES
TEL 04 94 58 30 09
FAX 04 94 58 36 02
www.langoustier.com
A luxury island hotel on a rocky position overlooking the sea, with a one-Michelin-star restaurant. Meals served in the garden. *Demi-pension* only.
🛏 44 + 5 suites 🕐 Closed Oct.–April 💳 All major cards

---

## JUAN-LES-PINS

### 🏨 DES MIMOSAS
**$$ ✪✪✪**
RUE PAULINE
TEL 04 93 61 04 16
FAX 04 92 93 06 46
www.hotelmimosas.com
A quiet, 19th-century house
with large modern rooms,
many with balconies, and a
shady garden. No restaurant.
ℹ 34 🅿 🕐 Closed Oct.–late
April 🔲 🔲 🔲 AE, MC, V

## MENTON

### 🍴 LE CAFÉ FIORI
**$$$$**
HOTEL LES AMBASSADEURS
3 RUE PARTOUNEAUX
TEL 04 93 28 75 75
A classic belle epoque hotel
in the center of town that has
been recently renovated with
an elegant airy terrace for
dining. The food is stylish, light
Mediterranean; try the sea
bass marinated with lemon,
basil, and avocado or the saf-
fron bouillabaisse.
🔲 All major cards

## MONACO: MONTE-CARLO

### 🏨 🍴 HERMITAGE
**$$$$$ ✪✪✪✪**
SQUARE BEAUMARCHAIS
TEL 00 377 98 06 40 00
FAX 00 377 98 06 59 70
www.montecarloresort.com
A luxurious belle epoque palace
with a huge, glass-domed win-
ter garden, opulent restaurant,
and terrace of cool marble.
ℹ 209 + 18 suites 🅿 🔲
🔲 🔲 🔲 All major cards

### 🍴 LOUIS XV
**$$$$$**
HÔTEL DE PARIS
PLACE DU CASINO
TEL 00 377 98 06 88 64
FAX 00 377 98 06 59 07
www.alain-ducasse.com

Monaco's most famous
and expensive restaurant, a
Michelin three-star establish-
ment presided over by the
celebrated Alain Ducasse. If
you need to look at the prices,
don't go. Typical dishes might
be Provençal vegetables with
black truffles, or pigeon with
*foie gras de canard.*
🕐 Closed Tues., Wed. (except D
mid-July–late Aug.), 2 weeks
Feb., & Dec. 🔲 All major cards

## MOUGINS

### 🍴 LE MOULIN DE MOUGINS
**$$$$$**
AVENUE NOTRE-DAME-DE-VIE
TEL 04 93 75 78 24
FAX 04 93 90 18 55
www.moulindemougins.com
This Michelin one-star restau-
rant with its sculpture-filled
garden, founded by Roger
Vergé—the chef celebrated for
his – (cuisine of the sun)—is
now run with equal panache
by Alain Lorca, former chef of
the Négresco in Nice.
🕐 Closed Mon. & Tues.
🔲 All major cards

## NICE

## SOMETHING SPECIAL

### 🏨 NÉGRESCO
The most famous and expen-
sive hotel in Nice. This mag-
nificent belle epoque building
on the Promenade des Anglais
has sumptuous furnishings and
impeccable service. As grand
as it gets—look for the vast
Baccarat chandelier.
**$$$$/$$$$$ ✪✪✪✪✪**
37 PROMENADE DES ANGLAIS
TEL 04 93 16 64 00
FAX 04 93 88 35 68
www.hotel-negresco-nice.com
ℹ 134 + 18 suites 🅿 🔲
🔲 🔲 🔲 All major cards

### 🏨 BEAU RIVAGE
**$$$/$$$$ ✪✪✪✪**
24 RUE ST.-FRANÇOIS-DE-PAULE
TEL 04 92 47 82 82
FAX 04 92 47 82 83
www.hotelnicebeaurivage
.com
Ideally located on the edge
of the old town and with
some views over the sea, this
superbly renovated large hotel
has its own private beach club.
It was here that Matisse stayed
on his first few visits to Nice.
ℹ 118 🔲 🔲 🔲 All major cards

### 🏨 HI-HOTEL
**$$$**
AVENUE DES FLEURS
TEL 04 97 07 26 26
FAX 04 97 07 26 27
www.hi-hotel.net
A boutique hotel with
post-modern design and
informal service offers
themed guest rooms for
music lovers, computer
freaks, and movie fans.
🔲 All major cards

🏨 Hotel 🍴 Restaurant ℹ No. of Guest Rooms 🅿 Parking 🚇 Métro 🕐 Closed 🛗 Elevator

### 🏨 LA PÉROUSE
**$$/$$$$** ○○○○
11 QUAI RAUBA-CAPÉU
TEL 04 93 62 34 63
FAX 04 93 62 59 41
www.hotel-la-perouse.com
For a sea view that won't
break the bank; flowery ter-
race and garden restaurant.
🛏 64 P 🅿 ⬛ 🅃 🅢
All major cards

### 🍴 LA MÉRENDA
**$$$**
4 RUE RAOUL BOSIO 06300
This tiny bistro is famous for
its traditional Niçois dishes:
stockfish, beignets, stuffed
sardines, beef daube. No
phone and no booking. Get
there early to find a table.
🕐 Closed Sat.–Sun. 🅢
🅢 No credit cards

### 🍴 LE COMPTOIR
**$$**
20 RUE ST.-FRANÇOIS-DE-PAULE
TEL 04 93 92 08 80
A 1930s style bar/restaurant,
particularly good for late-night
dining or for a light meal after
the opera.
🅢 AE, MC, V

### 🍴 LE SAFARI
**$$**
1 COURS SALEYA
TEL 04 93 80 18 44
www.restaurantsafari.fr
A big café with Mediterranean
blue shutters, close to the
market on Cours Saleya. Great
for alfresco dining. Try the
deep rich calamari, daube, or
*bagna cauda*, a hot anchovy dip
with raw vegetables.
🅢 All major cards

## ST.-JEAN-CAP-FERRAT

### 🏨🍴 GRAND HÔTEL DU CAP-FERRAT
**$$$$$** ○○○○○
BOULEVARD DU GÉNÉRAL-DE-
GAULLE
TEL 04 93 76 50 50

FAX 04 93 76 04 52
www.grand-hotel-cap-ferrat
.com
One of the Riviera's legendary grand hotels, secluded
in its own tropical gardens
overlooking the sea, with a
private funicular down to a
terrace and the seawater pool.
Magnificent interior furnishings and a Michelin one-star
restaurant. Tennis.
🛏 44 + 9 suites P 🅿 🅢 All
major cards

## ST.-PAUL-DE-VENCE

## SOMETHING SPECIAL

### 🏨🍴 COLOMBE D'OR
Dine on the terrace at
this celebrity-haunted hotel
restaurant amid a priceless
collection of art donated as
payment for meals and rooms
by Picasso, Calder, Braque,
and more. Try the serving of
15 hors d'oeuvres and the
soufflés. Reserve rooms in
advance.
**$$$/$$$$** ○○○
PLACE DES ORMEAUX/PLACE
DE GAULLE
TEL 04 93 32 80 02
FAX 04 93 32 77 70
www.la-colombe-dor.com
🛏 16 + 10 suites 🕐 Closed
Nov.–late Dec. 🅢 All major
cards

### 🏨🍴 LE ST.-PAUL
**$$$/$$$$** ○○○○
86 RUE GRANDE
TEL 04 93 32 65 25
FAX 04 93 32 52 94
www.lesaintpaul.com
A secluded, exquisitely
furnished 16th-century town
house, within the village
walls. With one-Michelin-star
restaurant.
🛏 15 + 3 suites 🕐 Closed Jan.
🅿 🅢 All major cards

## ST.-TROPEZ

### 🏨🍴 LE BYBLOS
**$$$$$** ○○○○○
AVENUE PAUL-SIGNAC
TEL 04 94 56 68 00
FAX 04 94 56 68 01
www.byblos.com
The famous hotel where
Mick Jagger married Bianca;
designed like a village with
sumptuous Moroccan decor,
a nightclub, and restaurants.
🛏 86 + 11 suites P 🅿 Closed
Nov.–March 🅿 ⬛ 🅃 🅢 All
major cards

### 🏨 VILLA MARIE
**$$$$$**
CHEMIN VAL RIAN, RAMATUELLE
TEL 04 94 97 40 22
FAX 04 94 97 37 55
www.villamarie.fr
Luxurious hotel in soft terra
cotta shades overlooking the
bay of Pampelonne, with its
own spa, pool with waterfall,
and terrace restaurant.
🕐 Closed Oct.–April P 🅿
⬛ 🅢 All major cards

### 🏨 LE YACA
**$$$$/$$$$$** ○○○○
1 BOULEVARD D'AUMALE
TEL 04 94 55 81 00
FAX 04 94 97 58 50
www.hotel-le-yaca.fr
An old Provençal house in the
town center, favored by Signac
and Colette, built around a
swimming pool and garden.
🛏 27 🕐 Closed mid-Oct.–
April 🅿 ⬛ 🅢 All major cards

### 🏨 LA PONCHE
**$$$$** ○○○○
PLACE RÉVELIN
TEL 04 94 97 02 53
FAX 04 94 97 78 61
www.laponche.com
A charming ensemble of
former fishermen's cottages
behind the port, with stylish,
surprisingly large guest rooms.
🛏 13 + 5 suites 🕐 Closed Dec.–
mid-Feb. 🅿 🅢 All major cards

**▮▮ CAFÉ SÉNÉQUIER**
$$
QUAI JEAN-JAURÈS
TEL 04 94 97 00 90
A favorite café on the port;
pricey but good for evening
aperitifs and watching
celeb-rities on yachts drink
theirs.
⊗ No credit cards

## VILLEFRANCHE-SUR-MER

**▮▮ LA MÈRE GERMAINE**
$$$
8 QUAI COURBET
TEL 04 91 90 63 63
www.meregermaine.com
A Vieux Port restaurant with
a new take on southern classics—bouillabaisse milkshake,
anyone? Inventive dishes,
good local wine list, and one
Michelin star.
🕒 Closed Sun., Mon., &
first 2 weeks in Aug. ⊗ AE,
MC, V

## PROVENCE

## AIX-EN-PROVENCE

**🏨 PIGONNET**
$$$/$$$$ ⭘⭘⭘⭘
5 AVENUE DU PIGONNET
TEL 04 42 59 02 90
FAX 04 42 59 47 77
www.hotelpigonnet.com
A provençal country house in
its own park, charmingly
embellished in the 1920s.
🛈 52 ▯ ⚙ ⛱ ▼ ⊗ All
major cards

**▮▮ LES DEUX GARÇONS**
$
COURS MIRABEAU
TEL 04 42 26 00 51
A classic terrace café on the
Cours Mirabeau, a favorite
with artists and intellectuals
since the 18th century.
⚙ ⊗ All major cards

## APT

**▮▮ AUBERGE DU LUBÉRON**
$$/$$$$
17 QUAI LÉON SAGY
TEL 04 90 74 12 50
Typical Provençal food in a
peaceful atmosphere, with
a terrace and garden. Try
the duck foie gras with fruit
confits; Lubéron lamb with
aubergine confits. Reservations
essential.
🕒 Closed Sun. in winter, Mon.
(except D in season), & Dec.
23–Jan. 15 ⊗ All major cards

## ARLES

**🏨 LE MAS DE PEINT**
$$$$ ⭘⭘⭘⭘
LE SAMBUC
TEL 04 90 97 20 62
FAX 04 90 97 22 20
www.masdepeint.com
Converted stables attached to
an old Camargue farmhouse.
Exquisite rooms have wooden
ceilings, white linen furnishings, and antiques. Home-
grown vegetables served.
🛈 8 + 2 suites ▯ 🕒 Closed
early Jan.–March ⚙ ⛱ ⊗ All
major cards

**🏨 GRAND HÔTEL
NORD PINUS**
$$$/$$$$$ ⭘⭘⭘⭘
14 PLACE DU FORUM
TEL 04 90 93 44 44
FAX 04 90 93 34 00
www.nord-pinus.com
Although brought up-to-date,
this luxury hotel has kept its
individuality. Traditional Pro-
vençal furniture. Popular with
bullfighters at festival time.
🛈 25 ▯ 🕒 Closed mid-Nov.–
mid-. Feb. ⚙ Rooms ⊗ All
major cards

**▮▮ LA GUEULE DE LOUP**
$$$
39 RUE DES ARÈNES
TEL 04 90 96 96 69
A wood-beamed restaurant

above the kitchen serves
Midi classics with an original
twist like the charlotte
d'agneau with aubergines
and red pepper coulis, or
tarte tatin of turnips with
foie gras and guinea fowl
with pears. It is popular, so
reserve.
🕒 Closed Jan., Sun., & Mon. L

**▮▮ CAFÉ LA NUIT**
$
PLACE DU FORUM
A favorite local café,
decorated to look as it was
in van Gogh's painting "Café
le Soir."
⊗ MC, V

## AVIGNON

**🏨 LA MIRANDE**
**▮▮ $$$$$ ⭘⭘⭘⭘**
4 PLACE AMIRANDE
TEL 04 90 85 93 93
FAX 04 90 86 26 85
www.la-mirande.fr
An 18th-century hotel close
to the Palais des Papes, with
luxurious rooms and tasteful
furnishings. The Michelin
one-star restaurant offers
Provençal specialties such as
flavorsome Lubéron lamb.
🛈 19 ▯ ⚙ ⊗ All major
cards

**🏨 L'EUROPE**
**▮▮ $$/$$$$$ ⭘⭘⭘⭘⭘**
12 PLACE CRILLON
TEL 04 90 14 76 76
FAX 04 90 14 76 71
www.heurope.com
Avignon's top hotel—even
Napoleon stayed here. The
grand entrance to this 16th-
century mansion leads onto
the peaceful terrace with
a fountain. The restaurant,
La Vieille Fontaine, lives
up to the splendor of the
establishment. Try courgette
flowers stuffed with
artichoke or roast sea bream
with tomato tart.
🛈 44 + 3 suites

P ⊕ Restaurant closed Mon.
L & all Sun. & 2 weeks in Aug.
⑤ 🍴 All major cards

## 🍴 AU PETIT BEDON
$$
70 RUE JOSEPH VERNET
TEL 04 90 82 33 98
A sweet homey restaurant
offering typical rustic Proven-
çal dishes like pumpkin soup,
veal with sage, and pear cake
and baked apple for dessert.
⊕ Closed Sun. & Mon. D
Oct.–Easter 🍴 MC, V

## CHÂTEAUNEUF-DU-PAPE

### 🏨 LA SOMMELLERIE
$ ❋❋❋
ROUTE DE ROQUEMAURE
TEL 04 90 83 50 00
FAX 04 90 83 51 85
www.la-sommellerie.fr
A charming 17th-century
bergerie situated among the
famous vineyards and now a
delightful small hotel.
🛏 14 ⊕ Closed Jan., Sun. D,
& Mon. Nov.–March 🍴 All
major cards

## GARGAS

### 🏨 LA COQUILLADE
### 🍴 $$$/$$$$
GARGAS
TEL 04 90 74 71 71
FAX 04 90 74 71 72
www.coquillade.fr
A wine domaine and hotel—a
hillside hamlet with panoramic
views over the Luberon,
surrounded by vineyards. Two
restaurants, cellar, chic high-
tech rooms, artworks, and eco-
logically designed gardens.
🛏 14 P ⊕ Closed Jan.–mid-
March 🏊 🍴 AE, MC, V

## GIGONDAS

### 🍴 LES FLORETS
$/$$$
TEL 04 90 65 85 01
FAX 04 90 65 83 80

www.hotel-lesflorets.com
An attractive, quiet restaurant
with Provençal decor and
a terrace. Choices include
monkfish braised with orange
butter, and lamb on a bed of
eggplant. Rooms available.
P ⊕ Closed Wed. & Jan.–March
🍴 All major cards

## GORDES

### 🏨 LA FERME DE LA HUPPE
$/$$
ROUTE D'APT LES POURQUIERS
TEL 04 90 72 12 25
FAX 04 90 72 01 83
www.lafermedelahuppe.com
In peaceful Lubéron countryside, a beautiful 18th-century
farm with an inner courtyard,
renovated in Provençal style.
🛏 8 P ⊕ Closed Nov.–March
⑤ Some rooms 🏊 🍴 AE, MC, V

### 🍴 LE MAS TOURTERON
$$$
CHEMIN ST.-BLAISE, LES IMBERTS
TEL 04 90 72 00 16
FAX 04 90 72 09 81
www.mastourteron.com
An old Provençal mas (farm-
house) with a walled garden
serving light, fresh, and imagi-
native cuisine using seasonal
products.
⊕ Closed Dec.–Feb. 🍴 All
major cards

## LES BAUX-DE-
## PROVENCE

### 🏨 LA BENVENGUDO
$$ ❋❋❋
1 MILE/2 KM S OF LES BAUX
TEL 04 90 54 32 54
FAX 04 90 54 42 58
www.benvengudo.fr
Tucked beneath the Alpilles
hills, a manor-hotel with an
elegant garden. The lounge
and dining room are in Provençal style; some rooms have
private terraces. Tennis.
🛏 20 + 3 suites P ⊕ Closed
Nov.–Feb. ⑤ Some rooms
🏊 🍴 AE, MC, V

### 🍴 OUSTAU DE
### BAUMANIÈRE
$$$$/$$$$$
TEL 04 90 54 33 07
www.oustaudebaumaniere
.com
A Michelin two-star restaurant
in an elegantly furnished 16th-
century building, famous for
its gigot d'agneau en croûte and
truffle ravioli.
⊕ Closed Jan.–Feb. & Tues. D–
Thurs. L Nov.–March
🍴 All major cards

## LOURMARIN

### 🏨 LE MAISON DU
### PARADOU
$$$$
2 ROUTE DE ST. ROCH
MAUSSANNE-LES-ALPILLES
TEL 04 90 54 65 46
FAX 04 90 54 85 83
www.maisondupardou.com
A chic boutique hotel run by
a British couple. Individual
styled rooms—one with its
own secret garden—and
high-tech facilities, including a
salon-library of films and giant
screen. Dinner (reservation
necessary) is served under
the pergola with views of the
Alpilles.
🛏 5 P 🏊 🍴 AE, MC, V

## MOUSTIERS-
## STE.-MARIE

### 🍴 LES SANTONS
$$$/$$$$
PLACE DE L'ÉGLISE
TEL 04 92 74 66 48
www.lessantons.com
A tiny restaurant, near the
Gorges du Verdon, famous for
its chicken in lavender honey.
⊕ Closed mid-Nov.–mid-Feb.
🍴 All major cards

## ORANGE

### 🍴 AUBERGE DE
### L'ORANGERIE
$$

4 PLACE DE L'ORMEAU, PIOLENC
TEL 04 90 29 59 88
FAX 04 90 29 67 74
www.orangerie.net
This 18th-century auberge with a charming stone-walled courtyard provides a traditional atmosphere for inventive cuisine, such as langoustine with truffle sauce and osso buco of langoustine.
🕒 Closed Mon., Tues. L, & Sun.
🚫 AE, MC, V

## STES.-MARIES-DE-LA-MER

🏨 **LE MAS DE LA FOUQUE**
**$$$$** ✪✪✪✪
ROUTE DU PETIT RHÔNE
TEL 04 90 97 81 02
FAX 04 90 97 96 84
www.masdelafouque.com
A traditional Camargue hotel. Large rooms with tiled floors and wooden beams have private terraces overlooking the lagoon and park.
ℹ️ 14 🅿️ 🕒 Closed Jan. 🎱
🚫 All major cards

## LANGUEDOC-ROUSSILLON

## BOUZIGUES

🍴 **LA CÔTE BLEUE**
**$$/$$$**
AVENUE LOUIS-TUDESQ
TEL 04 67 78 30 87
FAX 04 67 78 33 70
www.la-cote-bleue.fr
A large family restaurant overlooking the Bassin de Thau, which is the best place to sample the vast variety of shellfish found here: Mussels and langoustines are excellent, and do try the tiny sweet Bouzigues oysters.
🕒 Closed Wed. out of season, end of Nov., & Feb. holidays
🚫 AE, MC, V

## CARCASSONNE

🏨 **CITÉ**
**$$$$/$$$$$** ✪✪✪✪

PLACE DE L'ÉGLISE
TEL 04 68 71 98 71
FAX 04 68 71 50 15
www.hoteldelacite.com
A grand neo-Gothic hotel built into the ramparts of the old city, with its own garden and two restaurants.
ℹ️ 55 + 6 suites 🅿️ 🕒 Closed Dec. & mid-March 🏊 🚫 All major cards

🍴 **BRASSERIE LE DONJON**
**$**
2 RUE PORTE D'AUDE
TEL 04 68 25 95 72
FAX 04 68 25 06 60
www.brasserie-donjon.fr
An elegant restaurant in the middle of the old walled city serving such traditional dishes as cassoulet and foie gras.
🕒 Closed Sun. D Nov.–March
🚫 All major cards

## COLLIOURE

🏨 **CASA PARAIL**
**$/$$$** ✪✪✪
IMPASSE DES PALMIERS
TEL 04 68 82 05 81
FAX 04 68 82 52 10
www.hotel-casa-parail.com
A 19th-century Catalan villa set in a shady garden with palm trees and fountains—a peaceful haven in the town center. No restaurant.
ℹ️ 28 🅿️ 🕒 Closed Nov.–March 🏊 🎱 🚫 All major cards

🏨 **LES TEMPLIERS**
🍴 **$** ✪✪
12 QUAI DE L'AMIRAUTÉ
TEL 04 68 98 31 10
FAX 04 68 98 01 24
www.hotel-templiers.com
A hotel and restaurant in the old town near the harbor. Great seafood accompanied by Collioure wine. The hotel is famous for the artists who stayed here, including Matisse and Braque, and it retains its

---

## PRICES

**HOTELS**
An indication of the cost of a double room in the high season is given by $ signs.

| | |
|---|---|
| $$$$$ | Over $400 |
| $$$$ | $300–$400 |
| $$$ | $200–$300 |
| $$ | $100–$200 |
| $ | Under $100 |

**RESTAURANTS**
An indication of the cost of a three-course meal without drinks is given by $ signs.

| | |
|---|---|
| $$$$$ | Over $150 |
| $$$$ | $100–$150 |
| $$$ | $80–$100 |
| $$ | $60–$80 |
| $ | Under $60 |

---

authentic atmosphere.
ℹ️ 21 + 50 annex 🕒 Closed early Jan.–early Feb.; restaurant closed Sun. D & all Mon. in winter 🚫 AE, MC, V

## MOLITG-LES-BAINS

🏨 **CHÂTEAU DE**
🍴 **RIELL**
**$$$/$$$$** ✪✪✪✪
TEL 04 68 05 04 40
FAX 04 68 05 04 37
www.chateauderiell.com
A mock-Gothic château in the foothills of the Pyrenees with a view of Mont Canigou. Nearby spa. The restaurant serves Michel Guerard–style nouveau cuisine. Tennis.
ℹ️ 19 🅿️ 🕒 Closed Dec.–March 🏊 🚫 All major cards

## MONTPELLIER

🍴 **LE JARDIN DES SENS**
**$$$$/$$$$$**
11 AVENUE ST.-LAZARE

---

🏨 Hotel 🍴 Restaurant ℹ️ No. of Guest Rooms 🅿️ Parking 🚇 Métro 🕒 Closed 🛗 Elevator

TEL 04 99 58 38 38
FAX 04 99 58 38 39
www.jardindessens.com
A small, sophisticated,
Michelin two-star restaurant
with a garden in the middle
of Montpellier, celebrated for
its southern regional cooking.
🕐 Closed Mon. L, Wed. L, &
Sun. 🌐 All major cards

## NÎMES

### 🍴 L'ENCLOS DE LA
### FONTAINE
$$$
HÔTEL IMPERATOR,
QUAI DE LA FONTAINE
TEL 04 66 21 90 30
The restaurant of the Hôtel
Imperator is favored by bull-
fighters at *féria* time. Try local
specialties such as *brandade
de morue* (creamy salt cod),
*escabèche* (marinated fish), or
sea bass with fennel compôte.
🅿 📶 🌐 All major cards

### 🍴 LE LISITA
$$$
2 BOULEVARD DES ARENES
TEL 04 66 67 29 15
FAX 04 66 67 25 32
www.lelisita.com
Facing the Roman arena, an
elegant restaurant with a
tree-shaded terrace for stylish
southern cuisine; local speciali-
ties include *brandade* (salt cod)
roast pigeon, and strawberries
in Cevennes honey.
🕐 Closed Sun. & Mon. 🌐 AE,
MC, V

## PERPIGNAN

### 🍴 CASA SANSA
$$$
2 RUE FABRIQUE NADAL & 4 RUE
FABRIQUE COUVERTE
TEL 04 68 34 21 84
FAX 04 68 35 19 65
www.casa-sansa.fr
This Perpignan gastronomic
favorite is tucked away in a
tiny alley. It is an excellent
place to sample such flavorful

Catalan specialties as rabbit
with figs and beef daube with
orange.
🌐 CB, MC, V

### 🍴 LE FRANCE
$$
PLACE DE LA LOGE
TEL 04 68 51 61 71
This restaurant occupies one
of Perpignan's finest Renaissance buildings in the center
of the old town, now chicly
converted with terrace dining
for light Mediterranean-style
cuisine.
🌐 MC, V

## SÈTE

### 🏨 GRAND HÔTEL
$/$$ 🟠🟠🟠
17 QUAI MARÉCHAL DE LATTRE-
DE-TASSIGNY
TEL 04 67 74 71 77
FAX 04 67 74 29 27
www.legrandhotel
sete.com
A charming, classic belle
epoque hotel overlooking
the Sète's pretty Grand
Canal.
🛈 45 🅿 🕐 Closed early Jan.
& late July 📶 Rooms 🌐 All
major cards

# ◼ CORSICA

## BASTIA

### 🍴 LA CITADELLE
$$/$$$
6 RUE DRAGON
TEL 04 95 31 44 70
An old olive mill with a terrace
for alfresco dining on excellent
regional cuisine.
🕐 Closed Sun.–Mon. &
mid- Dec.–mid-Jan. 📶 🌐 All
major cards

## BONIFACIO

### 🏨 GENOVESE
$$$$/$$$$$ 🟠🟠🟠🟠
HAUTE VILLE

TEL 04 95 73 12 34
FAX 04 95 73 09 03
www.hotel-genovese.com
The former Foreign Legion
barracks in the old town has
been transformed into a modern,
luxury hotel. No restaurant.
🛈 14 🅿 🕐 Closed Jan.–Feb.
📶 🌊 🌐 AE, V

### 🍴 STELLA D'ORO
$$
7 RUE DORIA
TEL 04 95 73 03 63
A family-run restaurant with
rustic decor and a friendly
ambience. Try the stuffed
mussels or the bouillabaisse
(order in advance).
🕐 Closed Oct.–Easter 📶 🌐 All
major cards

## CALVI

### 🏨 AUBERGE
### 🍴 DE LA SIGNORIA
$$$/$$$$ 🟠🟠🟠
ROUTE DE FORÊT DE BONIFATO
TEL 04 95 65 93 00
FAX 04 95 65 38 77
www.hotel-la-signoria.com
A 17th-century house set peace-
fully in a park with pines, palms,
and orange trees to the south
of Calvi. A good restaurant with
terrace where you can dine by
candlelight. Tennis.
🛈 20 🅿 🕐 Closed mid-Oct.–
April 📶 Rooms 🌊 🌐 AF, MC, V

## PORTO-VECCHIO

### 🏨 GRAND HOTEL
### 🍴 CALA ROSSA
$$$/$$$$$ 🟠🟠🟠
PORTO-VECCHIO
TEL 04 95 71 61 51
FAX 04 95 71 60 11
www.cala-rossa.com
Northeast of Porto-Vecchio, a
very pleasant hotel with shady
trees, a flowery garden, terrace
on the beach, and a Michelin
one-star restaurant specializing
in fish dishes. Tennis.
🛈 49 🕐 Closed Jan.–March
📶 🌐 All major cards

---

🔲 Nonsmoking  📶 Air-conditioning  🏊 Indoor Pool  🌊 Outdoor Pool  🎽 Health Club  🌐 Credit Cards

# Shopping

Shopping is one of the great pleasures of a visit to France. From the smallest streets to the grandest city boulevards, French stores offer delectable displays of pastries, chocolates, and all manner of sweetmeats. Ordinary practical products are often beautifully designed and can make excellent presents: Stationery stores *(papeteries)* offer wonderful little notebooks and files, and *drogueries* (not drugstores but hardware stores) are Aladdin's caves of intriguing kitchen utensils and charming pottery. Town centers are now often car-free, with supermarkets and hypermarkets on the outskirts. These are ideal for bulk food shopping, often have a good selection of wine, and are also useful for buying stamps, newspapers, and gas.

## Markets

Markets are the best way to shop in France. Most places have a weekly market, and in bigger cities they may even be daily. They usually start early in the morning and close at noon—if you want the pick of the produce, go early. The livestock section is not for the tenderhearted, as cages full of live ducks, geese, and chickens wait to be carried home for dinner. Look for local delicacies such as cheese, honey, olives, charcuterie, spices, herbs, and special breads and cakes.

France also has numerous flea markets *(marchés aux puces* or *brocantes)* selling secondhand goods, antiques, and local curios.

## Dégustations

*Dégustation* means tasting. All over France, you will see signs inviting you to sample the local produce, particularly the wine. You are not obliged to buy, but it would be thought uncivil not to purchase at least one bottle.

## Opening Hours

Food stores, especially bakeries *(boulangeries)*, open early, around 7 a.m. Small stores and department stores *(grands magasins)* usually open at 9 a.m. Most stores close for lunch between noon and 2 or 3 p.m., staying open until 7 or 7:30 in the evening. Hypermarkets usually stay open all day until quite late. Many stores close on Mondays; food shops, and especially bakers, open on Sunday mornings.

## Payment

Supermarkets accept credit cards, but smaller stores often do not. Check the signs on the door before you go in. Some traders are reluctant to accept payment by American Express cards or travelers' checks.

## Exports

Most purchases include TVA (VAT or value-added tax) at a base rate running currently at 20.6 percent, rising to as high as 33 percent on luxury items. Visitors from outside the European Union may claim back TVA over a certain amount. Ask the store for a completed *bordereau* (export sales invoice), which must be shown, together with the goods, to customs officers when you leave the country. You then mail the form back to the retailer, who will refund the TVA—though this may take some time.

## What to Buy

The French are particularly good at luxuries such as lingerie, soap, cosmetics, perfume, chocolate, and delicious jam. Every region of France has its own special products that make irresistible souvenirs. Often these are gastronomic delights such as honey, herbs, cookies, foie gras, wine, brandies, or local liqueurs. Look, too, for local pottery, baskets, and fabrics.

The following is a list of regional products, with a selection of especially good places to buy in each region.

## ■ NORTHERN FRANCE

### Champagne

The big Champagne houses are in Reims or Épernay, and can be toured (see pp. 124 and 383–384). To buy Champagne, the following stores have good selections:
**La Vinocave** 45 place Drouet, Reims 51100, tel 03 26 40 60 07.
**Le Vintage** 3 cours Anatole France, Reims 51100, tel 03 26 40 40 00.

### Cheese

**Philippe Olivier** 43–45 rue Thiers, Boulogne-sur-Mer 62200, tel 03 21 31 94 74. Famous cheese store with hundreds of different cheeses.

### Chocolate

**Chocolaterie de Beussent** 66 Route de Desvres, Beussent 62170, tel 03 21 86 17 62, www.choco-france.com. Handmade chocolates.
**Chocolaterie Jean Trogneux** 1 rue Delambre, Amiens 80000, tel 03 22 71 17 17. Handmade

chocolates and macaroons.
**La Chocolaterie Thibaut** Zone
Artisanale, rue Max-Menu,
Pierry 51530, tel 03 26 51 58 04.
Handmade chocolates, including
chocolate Champagne corks filled
with *marc de Champagne*.

## Enamelware

**Société des Faienceries et Émaux
de Longwy** 3 rue Acacias, Longwy
54400, tel 03 82 24 30 94.
**Emaux Saint Jean l'Aigle** rue de
la Chiers, Herserange-Longwy
54400, tel 03 82 24 58 20.

## Foie Gras

**Traiteur Vincent** 11 rue des
Boulangers, Colmar 68000, tel 03
89 41 32 05.
**Jean Lutz** 5 rue du Chaudron,
Strasbourg 67000, tel 03 88 32
00 64.

## Glass

**Cristal Daum** Vannes-le-Chatel,
near Toul, tel 03 83 25 41 01.
**Terres d'Est** 1 rue de la Faience-
rie, Niderviller 57565, tel 03 87
23 80 04. Crystal products
**Espace Verre** rue de la Liberté,
Vannes-le-Chatel, near Toul,
tel 03 83 25 47 44.

## Markets

| | |
|---|---|
| Amiens | Wed. & Sat. |
| Beauvais | Wed. & Sat. |
| Boulogne-sur-Mer | Wed. & Sat. |
| Calais | Wed., Thurs., & Sat. |
| Colmar | Thurs. & Sat. |
| Langres | Fri. |
| Le Touquet | Mon.–Thurs. & Sat. |
| Lille | daily |
| Metz | Wed., Thurs., & Sat. |
| Nancy | Tues.–Sat. |
| Reims | daily |
| Strasbourg | Mon.–Sat. |
| Troyes | Sat. |

# ■ NORMANDY & BRITTANY

## Benedictine

**Palais Bénédictine** 110 rue
Alexandre-Le-Grand, Fecamp
76400, tel 02 35 10 26 10.
Taste and buy Benedictine liqueur.

## Calvados

**Christian Drouin Distilleries des
Fiefs Ste.-Anne**, Coudray-Rabut
14130, rel 02 31 64 30 05.
**Pierre Huet** Manoir la Brière des
Fontaines, Cambremer 14170, tel
02 31 63 01 09.

## Cheese

**Fromagerie Graindorge** 42 rue
Général-Lectere, tel 02 31 48 20
00, Livarot 14140, www.grain-
dorge.fr. Livarot cheese.
**Fromagerie Réaux** 1 rue des
Planquettes, Lessay 50430, tel 02
33 46 41 33. High-quality AOC
Camembert. Open Mon–Fri.
Visits by appointment.
**Domaine de St.-Hippolyte**
St.-Martin-de-la-Lieue 14100,
tel 02 31 31 30 68. Dairy farm.
Open daily May–Sept.

Several museums also offer sales
and tastings, including the Musée
du Fromage, Livarot; the Musée
du Fromage, Vimoutiers; and
La Ferme Président, the cheese
museum of Camembert.

## Cider

**Route du Cidre, Pays d'Auge** For
info about this route through
cider country: tel 02 31 63 08 87,
www.calvados-tourisme.com).
**La Ferme de Beuvron** Beuvron-
en-Auge 14430, Tel 02 31 79 29
19. Makers of cheese, Calvados,
and cider.

## Clothes

**Coopérative Maritime** Guilvinec
29730, Tel 02 98 58 10 31. Breton
fishermen's sweaters & other gear.

## Cookies

**Les Sources de l'Aven** 10 place
Paul Gauguin, Pont-Aven 29930,
tel 02 98 06 01 94. Homemade
butter cookies and Breton cake.

## Faience

**Faïencerie HB Henriot** 16 rue
Haute, Quimper 29337, Tel 02 98
90 09 36.

## Lace

**Musée des Beaux-Arts et de
la Dentelle** Cour Carrée de la
Dentelle, Alençon 61000, tel 02
33 32 40 07. Alençon lace

## Mustard & Other Food Specialties

**Épicerie Claude Olivier** 16 rue
St.-Jacques, Dieppe 76200, tel 02
35 84 22 55.

## Sea Salt

**La Salorge de Guérande** Buy
from roadside stands amid the
salt marshes south of Guérande.
**Les Salines de Guerande** Pradel
44350, tel 02 40 62 01 25.

## Markets

| | |
|---|---|
| Bayeux | Wed. & Sat. |
| Brest | daily |
| Caen | Fri. & Sun. |
| Concarneau | Mon. & Fri. |
| Dieppe | Tues., Thurs., & Sat. |
| Dinan | Thurs. |
| Honfleur | Sat. |
| Lorient | Sat. |
| Quimper | daily |
| Rennes | Tues.–Sun. |
| Rouen | Thurs.–Sun. |
| St.-Malo | Mon.–Sat. |
| Trouville-sur-Mer | Wed. & Sun. |
| Vannes | Wed. & Sat. |

**Apple fair** Ste.-Opportune-la-
Mare (north of Pont Audemer).
First Sunday of October.
**Camembert fair** South of Lisieux,
last Sun. in July.

Cider fair Caudebec-en-Caux. September.

# LOIRE VALLEY

## Baskets
Coopérative de Vannerie de Villaines 1 rue de la Cheneillère, Villaines-les-Rochers 37190, tel 02 47 45 43 03.

## Charcuterie
Charcuterie Hardouin Virage Gastronomique, Vouvray 37210, tel 02 47 40 40 40.

## Chocolates, Cookies, & Patisserie
La Chocolaterie Royale 53 rue Royale, Orléans 45000, tel 02 38 53 93 43.
La Petite Marquise 22 rue des Lices, Angers 49000, tel 02 41 87 43 01.
Chocolat Benoit 1 rue des Lices, Angers 49000, tel 02 41 88 94 52.

## Faience
Faïencerie de Gien place de la Victoire, Gien 45500, tel 02 38 67 00 05.
Faïenceries du Bourg-Joly 16 rue Carnot, Malicorne-sur-Sarthe 72270, tel 02 43 94 80 10.

## Wine & Spirits
Local maisons du vin will give information on tastings and on producers for direct sales.
Chateau de Montcontour 40 rue Carnot, Vouvray 37210, tel 03 80 22 35 47, www.vins-vouvray.com.
Maison des Vins du Pays Nantais Bellevue, La Haie-Fouassière 44690, tel 02 40 36 35 87.
Maison du Vin de l'Anjou 5 bis place Kennedy, Angers 49100, tel 02 41 88 81 13, www.vinsdeloire .fr.
Maison des Vin de Bourgueil Bourgueil 37140, tel 02 47 97 92 20, www.vinbourgueil.com.

*Cointreau*
Distillerie Cointreau St.-Barthé-lemy-d'Anjou 49124, Tel 02 41 31 50 50. Distillery tour.

## Markets
| | |
|---|---|
| Amboise | Fri. & Sun. |
| Angers | daily |
| Blois | Tues., Thurs., & Sat. |
| Bourges | Thurs.–Sun. |
| Chinon | Thurs. |
| Nantes | daily |
| Orléans | Tues.–Sun. |
| Saumur | Sat. |
| Tours | daily |

# CENTRAL FRANCE & THE ALPS

## Charcuterie
Charcuterie Raillard 4 rue Monge, Beaune 21200, tel 03 80 22 23 04.
Charcuterie Reynon 13 rue des Archers, Lyon 69000, tel 04 78 37 39 08.

## Cheese
Abbaye Notre-Dame de Cîteaux Cîteaux 21700, tel 03 80 61 34 28. Still produced by monks.
Coopérative Fromagerie d'Arbois rue des Fosses, Arbois 39600, tel 03 84 66 09 71.
Fromagerie Berthaut place Champ-de-Foire, Époisses 21460, tel 03 80 96 44 44.
Fromagerie René Richard Les Halles, 102 cours Lafayette, Lyon 69000, tel 04 78 62 30 78.
Les Caves Société Roquefort-sur-Soulzon 12250, tel 05 65 58 54 38. Tours through caves where the cheese is matured.

## Chocolate
Le Chocolatier d'Annecy 4 place-St. Francois-de-Sales, Annecy 74000, tel 04 50 45 12 08.
Pâtisserie-Chocolaterie Berna-chon 42 cours Franklin-Roosevelt, Lyon 69006, tel 04 78 24 37 98.

## Montélimar Nougat
Nougat Chabert et Guillot 1 rue André Ducatz, Montélimar 26200, tel 04 75 00 82 00.

## Mustard
Grey-Poupon Maille, 32 rue de la Liberté, Dijon 21000, tel 03 80 30 41 02.

## Olives
Coopérative Agricole du Nyonsais place Olivier-de-Serres, Nyons 26110, tel 04 75 26 95 00.

## Pain d'Épices
Mulot & Petitjean 13 place Bossuet, Dijon 21000, tel 03 80 30 07 10.

## Silk
L'Atelier de Soierie 33 rue Romarin, Lyon 69001, Tel 04 72 07 97 83.
La Boutique des Soyeux, 20 rue Romarin, Lyon 69005, near place des Terreaux, tel 04 78 39 96 67. For scarves from silk manufac-turers.

## Wine
*Beaujolais*
Les Routes des Vins Le Pays Villefranche-sur-Saône 69400, tel 04 74 07 27 50, www .villefranche-beaujolais.fr.
Le Hameau du Vin Romanèche-Thorins 71570, tel 03 85 35 02 64, www.hameauduvin.com. Wine museum & shop.

*Burgundy*
Marché aux Vins rue Nicolas-Rolin, Beaune 21200, tel 03 80 25 08 20. Tasting (charge).
Le Vigneron 6 rue d'Alsace, Beaune 21200, tel 03 80 22 68 21. Wine accessories.
Vins Beaune 40 rue Carnot, Beaune 21200, tel 03 80 22 35 47.

*Cassis*
Cassis Boudier 14 rue de Cluj,

Dijon 21007, tel 03 80 74 33 33.

*Chablis*
**La Chablisienne** 8 boulevard Pasteur, Chablis 89800, tel 03 86 42 89 89.

*Chartreuse*
**Les Caves de la Chartreuse** 10 boulevard Edgar-Kofler, Voiron 38500, tel 04 76 05 81 77.

*Jura*
**Societé de Viticulture du Jura** avenue du 44ème RI, Lons-le-Saunier 39016, tel 03 84 35 14 02.

*Mâcon*
**Maison du Vin** 520 avenue Maréchal de Lattre-de-Tassigny, Mâcon 71000, tel 03 85 22 91 11.
**Syndicat Viticole de Pouilly** 2 rue des Écoles, Pouilly-sur-Loire 58150, tel 03 86 39 06 83.

## Markets

| | |
|---|---|
| Aubusson | Sat. |
| Autun | Wed., Fri., & Sun. |
| Auxerre | Tues, & Fri. |
| Beaune | Wed. & Sat. |
| Besançon | Tues., Fri., & Sun. |
| Bourg-en-Bresse | Wed. & Sat. |
| Chablis | Sun. |
| Chambéry | Sat. |
| Clermont-Ferrand | Mon.–Sat. |
| Dijon | Tues., Fri., & Sat. |
| Grenoble | Tues.–Sun. |
| Le Puy-en-Velay | Sat. |
| Louhans | Mon. (Bresse poultry) |
| Lyon | Tues.–Sun. |
| Nyons | Thurs. |
| Vichy | Wed. |

## ■ SOUTHWEST FRANCE

## Basque Linen
**Jean Vier Basque Linen**
Carre-four des Cinq-Cantons, Bayonne 64100, Tel 05 59 59 16 18.

## Basque Berets
**Musée du Beret** place St. Roch, Nay 64800, tel 05 59 61 91 70.

## Bayonne Ham
**Maison Montauzer** 17 rue de la Salie, Bayonne 64100, tel 05 59 59 07 68.
**Pierre d'Ibaïalde** 41 rue des Cordeliers, Bayonne 64100, tel 05 59 25 65 30.

## Chocolate & Basque Caramels
**Chocolaterie Cazenave** 19 rue du Port-Neuf, Bayonne 64100, tel 05 59 59 03 16.
**Atelier du Chocolat** 1 rue Poste, Biarritz 64200, tel 05 59 24 47 05.

## Makhila
**Ainciart Bergara** Larressore 64480, tel 05 59 93 03 05. Traditional Basque walking sticks in wood, often silver-tipped.

## Porcelain
**Royal Limoges Magasin (factory shop)** 15 rue Victor Duray, Limoges 87000, www.royal-limoges.fr. See www.limoges-tourisme.com for more porcelain shops.

## Truffles, Foie Gras, & Confits
**Aux Armes du Périgord** 1 rue de la Liberté, Sarlat-la-Canéda 24200, tel 05 53 59 14 27.
**Conserverie Godard** Gourdon 46300, tel 05 65 41 03 97.
**La Ferme de Turnac** Domme 24150, tel 05 53 28 10 84.

**Le Gers Gourmet** Gayrin, St.-Germe 32400, tel 05 62 69 60 37.
**Pierre Champion** 21 rue Taillefer,
Périgueux 24004, tel 05 53 03 90 29.
**Pebeyre** 66 rue Frédéric-Suisse, Cahors 46000, tel 05 65 22 24 80.

## Wine & Spirits
For a good selection of Bordeaux wines try:
**L'Intendant** 2 allée de Tourny, Bordeaux 33000, Tel 05 56 43 26 39.
**La Vinothéque** 8 cours du 30 Juillet, Bordeaux 33000, Tel 05 56 52 32 05.

*Maisons du Vin*
**Maison des Sauternes** place de la Mairie, Sauternes 33210, tel 05 56 76 69 83.
**Maison des Vins de Graves** 61 cours Maréchal Foch, Podensac 33720, tel 05 56 27 09 25.
**Maison de Vins de Bergerac** 2 place du Dr. Cayla, Bergerac 24100, tel 05 53 63 57 55.
**Maison du Tourisme et du Vin** La Verrerie, Pauillac 33250, tel 05 56 59 03 08.
**Maison du Vin des Côtes de Blaye** 11 cours Vauban, Blaye 33390, tel 05 57 42 91 19.
**Maison du Vin des Côtes de Bourg** place de l'Éperon, Bourg 33710, tel 05 57 94 80 20.
**Maison du Vin de St.-Émilion** place Pierre, Meyrat, St.-Émilion 33330, tel 05 57 55 50 55.
**Syndicat Interprofessionel du Vin de Cahors** rue Mar. Joffre, Cahors 46000, tel 05 65 22 26 69.

*Armagnac*
**Jean-Gabriel Cénac** Domaine de Laubuchon, Manciet 32370, tel 05 62 08 50 29.
**Janneau Fils** avenue d'Aquitaine, Condom 32100, tel 05 62 28 24 77.

*Cognac*
**Cognac Otard** Château de Cognac, 127 boulevard Denfert-Rochereau, Cognac 16101, tel 05 45 36 88 88.

**Rémy Martin** 20 rue de la Société Vinicole, Cognac 16100, tel 05 45 35 76 66.

## Markets

| | |
|---|---|
| Auch | Thurs. & Sat. |
| Bayonne | Mon.–Sat. |
| Bergerac | Wed. & Sat. |
| Biarritz | Mon.–Sat. |
| Bordeaux | Mon.–Sat. |
| Brantôme | Fri. |
| Cahors | Wed. |
| Lalbenque | Mon. |
| (truffle market) | Dec.–March |
| Pauillac | Sat. |
| Périgueux | Wed. & Sat. |
| St.-Émilion | Sun. |
| St.-Jean-de-Luz | Tues. & Fri. |
| Sarlat-la-Canéda | Wed. & Sat. |
| Toulouse | daily |

# ■ SOUTH OF FRANCE & ■ CORSICA

## Anchovies
**Société Roque** 17 route d'Argelès, Collioure 66190, tel 04 68 82 04 99.

## Charcuterie
**La Maison du Saucisson d'Arles** 3 avenue de la République, St.-Martin-de-Crau 13310, tel 04 90 47 30 40.

## Espadrilles & Catalan Fabrics
**Les Toiles du Soleil** Le Village, St.-Laurent-de-Cerdans 66260, tel 04 68 39 50 02.

## Glassware
**Verrerie de Biot** chemin des Combes, Biot 06410, tel 04 93 65 03 00.

## Herbs
**L'Herbier en Provence** Montée la Castre, St.-Paul 06570, tel 04 93 32 91 51.

## Olives & Olive Oil
**Alziari** 14 rue St.-François-de-Paule, Nice 06000, tel 04 93 62 95 03.

**Moulin de la Brague** 2 route de Châteauneuf, Opio 06650, tel 04 93 77 23 03.

## Perfume
**Parfumerie Fragonard** 20 boulevard Fragonard, Grasse 06130, tel 04 93 40 12 04.

**Parfumerie Galimard** 73 route de Cannes, Grasse 06130, tel 04 93 70 36 22.

**Parfumerie Molinard** 60 boulevard Victor-Hugo, Grasse 06130, tel 04 93 36 01 62.

## Pottery
**Galerie Madoura** rue Suzanne Georges Ramiè, Vallauris 06220, tel 04 93 64 66 39.

**Moustiers-Ste.-Marie** Many potteries along route de Riez, Moustiers-Ste.-Marie 06430.

**Syndicat des Potiers** avenue Jean Gerbino, Vallauris 06220, tel 04 93 64 88 30.

## Provençal Fabrics
**Souleîado** 5 rue Joseph-Vernet, Avignon 84000, tel 04 90 86 32 05 (also in other locations including Nîmes & St.-Remy-de-Provence).

## Santons
**Arterra** 15 rue du Petit Puits, Marseille, tel 04 91 91 03 31. Christmas crib figurines.

## Wine
**Palais du Vin** Route de Perpignan, Narbonne 11100, tel 04 68 41 49 67.

**Costières de Nîmes** Maison des Costières, 19 place Aristide Briand, quai de la Fontaine, Nîmes 30900, tel 04 66 36 96 20.

**Caves des Vins de Fitou** Fitou 11510, tel 04 68 45 71 41.

**Maison de la Truffe et du Vin du Luberon** place de l'Horloge, Ménerbes 84560, tel 04 90 72 38 37.

**Domaine Tempier** 1802 chemin des Fanges, Le Plan du Castellet 83330, tel 04 94 98 70 21, www .domainetempier.com.

**Minervois** www.leminervois.com, tel 04 68 27 80 02.

**Vignerons de Beaumes-de-Venise** quartier Ravel, Beaumes-de-Venise 84190, tel 04 90 12 41 00.

## Corsican wine
**Vins de Corse** place St.-Nicolas, Bastia 20200, tel 09 95 31 24 94.

## Markets

| | |
|---|---|
| Aix-en-Provence | Tues.,Thurs., & Sat. |
| Apt | Sat. |
| Arles | Wed. & Sat. |
| Avignon | Tues.–Sun. |
| Cannes | daily |
| Carpentras | Fri. |
| Ceret | Sat. |
| Hyères | Sat. |
| L'Isle-sur-la-Sorgue | Thurs. & Sun. |
| Marseille | Fish market daily a.m., general & flea markets Tues.–Sun. |
| Montpellier | daily |
| Nice | Tues.–Sun., flea market Mon. |
| Orange | Thurs. |
| Perpignan | daily |
| St.-Rémy-de-Provence | Wed. |
| St.-Tropez | Tues. & Sat. |
| Tarascon | Tues. |

# Activities

Almost every possible kind of leisure activity can be pursued in France, and your preference may influence the regions you choose to visit. Most towns have excellent public swimming pools and sports facilities. The cities offer more worldly entertainments, from casinos to opera, and from nightclubs to local feast days. Within each region, we have indicated the best places or contacts for activities of particular interest, and listed the main festivals and events during the year. Below is a list of national numbers to contact for specific activities, some of which also have regional contacts. Local tourist offices will provide further information.

## Canoeing & Kayaking
Fédération Française du Canoë-Kayak 87 quai de la Marne, Joinville-le-Pont 94340, tel 01 45 11 08 50, ww.ffck.org.

## Cycling
Fédération Française du Cyclo-Tourisme 12 rue Louis Bertrand, Ivry-sur-Seine 94207, Tel 01 56 20 88 94, www.ffct.org.

## Golf
Fédération Française du Golf Levallois, For all courses in France, www.ffgolf.org.

## Hydrotherapy & Spas
Centre d'Informations Thermales 32 avenue de l'Opéra, Paris 75002, Tel 01 43 21 01 80.
Fédération Thermale et Climatique Française 71 rue Froidevaux, Paris 75014, tel 01 40 47 57 33, www.federationthermale.org.

## Mountain Climbing
Fédération Française de la Montagne et de l'Escalade 8 quai de la Marne, Paris 75019, Tel 01 40 18 75 50, www.ffme.fr.
Club Alpin Francais 24 avenue Laumiere, 75019 Paris, Tel 01 53 72 87 00, www.ffcam.fr. In mountain regions there are local clubs.

## Horseback Riding
Comité National de Tourisme Équestre For information on local riding centers, tel 02 54 94 46 80, www.tourisme-equestre.fr.

## Sailing
Fédération Française de Voile 17 rue Henri Bocquillon, Paris 75015, tel 01 40 60 37 00, www.ffvoile.org.

## Skiing
Fédération Française de Ski 50 rue des Marquisats, Annecy 74011, tel 04 50 51 40 34, www.ffs.fr.
Écoles de Ski Français 6 allée des Mitaillères, Meylan 38246, tel 04 76 90 67 36, www.esf.net.

## Underwater Sports
Fédération Française d'Études et de Sports Sous-Marins 24 quai de la Rive-Neuve, Marseille 13284, Tel 04 91 33 99 31, www.ffessm.fr.

## Walking
FFRP (Fédération Française de la Randonnée Pédestre) 64 rue de Dessous des Berges, Paris 75013, tel 01 44 89 93 90, www.ffrandonnee.fr.

## Waterskiing
Fédération Française du Ski Nautique, 9–11 rue du Borrego, Paris 75020, tel 01 53 20 19 19, www.ffsnw.fr.

## Tours & Organized Sightseeing
The Caisse Nationale des Monuments Historiques et des Sites publishes a map of historic routes (tel 01 44 61 20 00, www.monuments-nationaux.fr). Routes include cathedrals, parks and gardens, and castles, as well as specific historic routes. For information on private historical buildings, contact Demeure Historique (tel 01 55 42 60 00, www.demeure-historique.org).

For tours by bus, contact local information offices. Many sights offer guided tours, but are often only in French and can be lengthy.

## ■ NORTHERN FRANCE

### Alsace Wine Route
Maison des Vins d'Alsace, 12 avenue de la Foire aux Vins, Colmar 68012, tel 03 89 20 16 20.

### Champagne Tours
Most big Champagne houses have their cellars in Reims or Épernay and can be toured. Some of the château vineyards also have tours. It is always advisable to call first.

Lanson 66 rue de Courlancy, Reims 51100, Tel 03 26 78 50 50, www.lanson.fr. By appointment.
Moët et Chandon 20 avenue de Champagne, Épernay 51200, tel 03 26 51 20 00, www.moet.com. Fee.
Mumm 29 rue de Champ de Mars, Reims 51100, tel 03 26 49 59 70, www.mumm.com. Tours in several languages, tasting. Fee.
Piper-Heidsieck 51 boulevard Henry-Vasnier, Reims 51100, tel 03 26 84 43 44, www.piper-heidsieck.com.
Taittinger 9 place St.-Nicaise,

Reims 51100, Tel 03 26 85 45 35, www.taittinger.fr. Tours in French, English, and German. Fee.
**Veuve Clicquot** 1 place des Droits de l'Homme, Reims 51100, tel 03 26 89 53 90, www.veuve-clicquot.com.

## Main Events
*Sunday before Easter*
**Coulommiers** Wine & cheese fair
*May*
**Amiens** Carnival
*June*
**Chantilly** Horse races
*July*
**Boulogne-sur-Mer** Fish festival
**Douai** Festival of Giants
*August*
**Cambrai** Festival of giants
**Locon** Garlic fair
**Maroilles** Fête de la Flamiche (leek tart)
**Wimereux** Mussel festival
*September*
**Lille** Grand flea market and mussel festival *(braderie)*
*October*
**Neuilly-St.-Front** Apple fair
**St.-Augustin** Apple & cider festival

# ■ NORMANDY & BRITTANY

## Boat Trips
**Seine estuary** Promenade en Mer, Quai des passagers, Honfleur, tel 02 31 89 21 20, www.promenade-en-mer.com.
**Tourisme et Loîsirs Maritimes** Le Havre, tel 02 35 28 99 53.
**Les Sept Îles** Perros-Guirec, tel 02 96 91 10 00.

## Cycling
**Ligue de Basse-Normande** www.ffct-lbn.org. Cycling in Normandy.
**La Maison des Sports** Rennes, tel 02 99 54 67 52.

## Golf
**Ligue de Golf de Bretagne** Rennes, tel 02 99 31 68 80.

## Horseback Riding
**Domain Equestre** Tel 02 31 28 04 28, www.cabourg-equitation.com.
**Haras du Pin** (National Stud) Orne, www.chevalnormandie.com.

## Normandy Landings
**Normandy Landings** www.normandiememoire.com.
**Normandy Guide** www.normandy-guide.com. Tours in English.
**Private D-Day Tour** www.d-daytours.com.
**Normandy Tourism** www.normandie-tourisme.fr.
**Bayeux tourist office**, tel 02 31 51 28 28.
**Boat tours** www.bessin-normandie.com.
**Les Vedettes de Normandie** tel 02 31 43 86 12, lesvedettesdenormandie.fr. Orne canal boat tours.

## Oyster Route
**Association Ostreme** tel 02 97 42 04 66.

## Sea Fishing
**Trouville** tel 02 31 65 23 30.

## Thalassotherapy
(Sea-water treatment)
**Institut de Thalassotherapie** Arzon 56640, tel 02 97 53 49 00.
**Pornic Phytomer** Pornic 44210, tel 02 40 82 21 21.
**Thalassa Dinard** Dinard 35800, tel 02 99 16 78 10.
**Thermes Marin de St.-Malo** St.-Malo 35400, tel 02 99 40 75 75, www.thalassotherapy.com.

## Walking
www.ffrandonnee-haute-normandie.com, Tel 02 35 65 47 89, www.bretagne.ffrandonnee.fr.

## Main Events
**Normandy**
*May*
**Coutances** Jazz festival

**Mont-St.-Michel** Spring festival
**Rouen** Joan of Arc festival
*June*
**D-Day beaches** June 6
**Balleroy** Hot-air balloon meeting
*July*
**Le Havre** International regatta
**Mont-St.-Michel** Pilgrimage across the sands
*August*
**Cabourg** William the Conqueror procession
**Carteret** Festival of the Sea
**Deauville** Grand Prix, horse race
*September*
**Lessay** Holy Cross fair
**Lisieux** St. Thérèse festival
*September–October*
**Haras du Pin** Horse trials
**Brittany**
*May*
**Tréguier** Pardon of St. Yves
*July*
**Locronan** Petite or Grande Troménie
**Rennes** Les Tombées de la Nuit
**Vannes** Jazz festival
*August*
**Carnac** Menhir festival
**Concarneau** Festival of the Blue Nets
**Erquy** Festival of the Sea
**Lorient** Interceltic Festival
**Ste.-Anne-la-Palud** Grand Pardon
*September*
**Carnac** Pardon of St.-Cornély

# ■ LOIRE VALLEY

## Ballooning
**France Montgolfières** 24 rue Nationale, Montrichard 41400, tel 02 54 32 20 48, www.franceballoons.com.

## Canoeing & Kayaking
**Ligue Pays de la Loire de Canoë-Kayak** 75 ave du Lac de Maine, Angers 49000, Tel 02 41 73 86 10, www.canoekayakpaysdelaloire.fr.

## Cruises
**Bateaux Nantais** quai de la

Motte Rouge, Nantes, tel 02 40 14 51 14, www.bateaux-nantais.fr.

## Main Events

Most of the large châteaus have son et lumière (sound and light) performances.

*February*
**Angers** Honey fair
**Saumur** Wine festival
*May*
**Saumur** International Horse Show
**Orléans** Jeanne d'Arc festival
*May–June*
**Chambord** Festival de Chambord
*July*
**Amboise** Festival
**Chinon** Medieval market
**Doué La Fontaine** Rose festival
**Tours** Garlic and basil festival
*August*
**Rochefort sur Loire** Anjou folk festival
**Vouvray** Wine fair
*October*
**Azay-le-Rideau** Apple fair
**Bourgeuil** Chestnut fair

## ■ CENTRAL FRANCE & THE ALPS

### Ballooning
**Air Escargot** Remigny 71150, tel 03 85 87 12 30.

### Canals/Boating
**France Fluviale**, Vermenton 89270, tel 03 86 81 54 55, www.bourgogne-fluviale.com.

### Rock Climbing
**French Alpine Federation Club** www.clubalpin-rhone-alpes.com.
**Club Alpin Français Savoie** www.club-alpin-savoie.org.

### Silk Farm
**Ma Magnanerie** Lieu-dit Les Mazes, Vallon-Pont-d'Arc 07150, Tel 04 75 88 01 27. Restored silk farm *(magnanerie)* and museum.

### Skiing
**Bureau Info Montagne, Maison de Tourisme**, 3 rue Raoul Blanchard, Grenoble 38019, tel 04 76 42 45 90, fax 04 76 44 67 03, www.infos-montagne.com, www.skifrance.fr.

### Steam Trains
**Chemin de Fer du Haut-Rhône** Maison d'Accueil, Montalieu Vercieu 38390, tel 04 78 81 84 30, www.cft-hr.com.

### Walking
**Comité de la Côte d'Or** tel 03 80 63 64 60, www.cotedor-randonnee.com.
**Comité de Saône-et-Loire** Tournus, tel 03 85 09 15 08.
**Comité de l'Yonne** Auxerre, tel 03 86 52 61 82.

### Food & Wine Lessons & Tours
**Auberge de la Toison d'Or** Beaune, tel 03 80 22 29 62. Prepare a classic Burgundian menu.
**Burgundy on a Plate** tel 03 80 39 09 88, www.burgundyonaplate.com. Gourmet tours including access to winemakers.
**Caves de l'Abbaye** 20 rue Sylvestre Chauvelot, Beaune, tel 03 80 21 98 13, www.les-caves-abbaye.com. Tasting lunches with wine and complementary food.
**École des Vins de Bourgogne**, Beaune, Tel 03 80 26 35 10, www.ecoledesvins-bourgogne.com.

### Main Events
*Sunday before Palm Sunday*
**Nuits St.-George** Wine auction
*Maundy Thursday*
**Le Puy-en-Velay** Penitents procession by torchlight
*June*
**Villefranche-sur-Saône** Midsummer's night festivities
*July*
**Arbois** Wine festival
**Gannat** World folklore festival
**Le Puy-en-Velay** Marian procession
**Vienne** Jazz festival
*September*
**Mont Brouilly** Wine producers pilgrimage
*September–December*
Grape harvest throughout the region.
*October*
**Dijon** Annual gastronomic fair
*November*
**Bourg-en-Bresse** Gastronomic fair
**Beaune** Hospice wine auction
*December*
**Chablis** Wine festival
**Lyon** Festival of Light

## ■ SOUTHWEST FRANCE

The **Centre Loisirs Accueil du Périgord** offers information on horseback riding, kayaking, golf, and fishing, tel 05 53 35 50 24.

### Boat Trips on the Lot River
**Comité Départemental du Tourisme** 107 quai Cavaignac, Cahors 46001, tel 05 65 35 07 09, www.tourisme-lot.com.

### Gambling
**Casino de Biarritz** 1 avenue Édouard V11, Biarritz 64201, tel 05 59 22 77 77.
**Casino La Rochelle** allée du Mail, La Rochelle 17000, tel 05 46 34 12 75, www.lucienbarriere.com.

### Golf
**Golf de Biarritz** 2 avenue Edith Cavell, 64200 Biarritz, Tel 05 59 03 71 80, www.golf-biarritz.com.

### Skiing & Mountain Climbing in the Pyrenees
tel 05 62 56 70 00, www.lesPyrenees.net, www.tourisme-hautes-pyrenees.com.

## Surfing

**Fédération Française de Surf** Plage Nord, boulevard Front de Mer, Hossegor 40150, tel 05 58 43 55 88, www.surfingfrance.com.
**Lacanau Surf Club** tel 05 56 26 38 84, www.surflacanau.com.
**Surf sans Frontières** tel 05 56 03 27 60, www.ssf.fr.

## Tennis

**Biarritz Olympique** Parc des Sports d'Aguilera, Biarritz 64000, tel 05 59 01 64 64, www.bo-pb .com. Covered and outdoor courts.

## Thalassotherapy

**Institut Louison-Bobet** 11 rue Louison-Bobet, Biarritz 64200, tel 05 59 41 30 00, www.thalasso-thermale.com.
**Les Thermes Marins** 80 rue de Madrid, Biarritz 64200, tel 05 59 23 01 22, www.guide-thalasso.com.

## Walking

www.pyrenees-randonnee.com
**Randonnée Dordogne** Perigueux, tel 05 53 51 70 30, www.randon nee-dordogne.com.

## Wine Courses

**École du Vin** Château Loudenne, Médoc, St. Yzans, tel 05 56 09 05 03, www.medoc-bordeaux.com.

## Main Events

*Pentecost*
**La Rochelle** International sailing week
**Vic-Fezensac**. Bullfights
*June*
**St.-Jean-de-Luz** Fête de St.-Jean; torchlight procession, Basque festivities
*August*
**Marciac** Jazz festival
**Arcachon** Festival of the Sea
**Gujan-Mestras** Oyster fair
*September*
**Rocamadour** Torchlit Festival of the Assumption

**St.-Émilion** Grape harvest festival
*October*
**Nontron** Chestnut fair

# ■ SOUTH OF FRANCE & ■ CORSICA

## Casinos

**Le Casino** place du Casino, Monte-Carlo, Monaco, tel 00 377 98 06 21 21, www.montecarlocac sinos.com.
**Casino Ruhl**, Promenade des Anglais, Nice, tel 04 97 03 12 22.

## Horseback Riding

**Centre Équestre de la Ville de Marseille** 33 Traverse Carthage, Marseille, tel 04 91 73 72 94.
**Languedoc-Roussillon ATECREL** 14 rue des Logis, Loupian, Mèze 34140, tel 04 67 43 61 11, www .chevalsace.com.

## River Fishing

**Fédération Inter-départmentale de Peche et Pisciculture** 19 avenue Noël Franchini, Ajaccio 20000, tel 04 95 23 13 32.

## Sailing & Windsurfing

**Cannes Station de Voile** Port du Mourre Rouge, Cannes 06400, tel 04 92 18 88 88.
**Nautique 2000** Port Gallice, Juan-les-Pins 06160, Tel 04 93 61 20 01.
**Station Voile** place de la République, Port Bacarès, tel 04 68 86 16 56, www.portbarcares.com.

## Scuba Diving

**Federation Française d'Études et de Sports Sous-Marins** 24 quai Rive-Neuve, Marseille 13284, tel 04 91 33 99 31, www.ffessm.fr.

## Skiing

**Isola 2000 Alpes-Maritimes** Office de Tourisme, tel 04 93 23 15 15, www.isola2000.com.
**Font Romeu Pyreness** Office de Tourisme, tel 04 68 30 68 30.

## Walking

**Comité Départemental de la Randonnée Pédestre** 4 avenue de Verdun, Cagnes-sur-Mer, tel 04 93 20 74 73, www.cdrp06.org.
**Corsica** www.randonnee-corse .com

## Main Events

### Côte d'Azur
*February*
**Menton** Lemon Festival (Procession of the Golden Fruit)
*Shrove Tuesday*
**Nice** Carnival (2 weeks)
*May*
**Cannes** International Film Festival
**Monaco** Formula One Grand Prix
*July*
**Juan-les-Pins–Antibes** World Jazz Festival
**Nice** Jazz festival
### Provence
*May*
**Stes.-Maries-de-la-Mer** Le Pelerinage (Gypsy Pilgrimage)
*Whitsun*
**Nîmes** Feria (Whitsun Festival)
*June*
**Tarascon** Fête de la Tarasque
*July*
**Aix-en-Provence** International Festival of Opera & Music
**Arles** Feria bullfight season begins

### Languedoc–Roussillon
*Good Friday*
**Perpignan** Procession des Pénitents de la Sanch
*July*
**Montpellier** Dance Festival
**Carcassonne** Embrasement de la Cité
**Prades** Pablo Casals music festival (into August)
*September*
**Perpignan** Visa pour l'Image, Festival of Photojournalism

### Corsica
*Good Friday*
**Sarténe** Procession du Catenacciu

# Language Guide

## Useful words & phrases

### General
Yes *Oui*
No *Non*
Excuse me *Excusez-moi*
Hello *Bonjour*
Hi *Salut*
Please *S'il vous plaît*
Thank you (very much) *Merci (beaucoup)*
You're welcome *De rien*
Have a good day! *Bonne journée!*
OK *D'accord*
Goodbye *Au revoir*
Good night *Bonsoir*
here *ici*
there *là*
today *aujourd'hui*
yesterday *hier*
tomorrow *demain*
now *maintenant*
later *plus tard*
right away *tout de suite*
this morning *ce matin*
this afternoon *cet après-midi*
this evening *ce soir*
Do you speak English? *Parlez-vous anglais?*
I am American *Je suis Américain* (man); *je suis Américaine* (woman)
I don't understand *Je ne comprends pas*
Please speak more slowly *Parlez plus lentement, s'il vous plaît*
Where is...? *Où est...?*
I don't know *Je ne sais pas*
No problem *Ce n'est pas grave*
That's it *C'est ça*
Here it is *Voici*
There it is *Voilà*
What is your name? *Comment vous-appelez-vous?*
My name is... *Je m'appelle...*
Let's go *On y va*
At what time? *À quelle heure?*
When? *Quand?*
What time is it? *Quelle heure est-il?*

### In the hotel
Do you have...? *Avez-vous...?*
a single room *une chambre simple*
a double room *une chambre double*
with/without bathroom/shower *avec/sans salle de bain/douche*

### Help
I need a doctor/dentist *J'ai besoin d'un médecin/dentiste*
Can you help me? *Pouvez-vous m'aider?*
Where is the hospital? *Où est l'hôpital?*
Where is the police station? *Où est le commissariat?*

### Shopping
I'd like... *Je voudrais...*
How much is it? *C'est combien?*
Do you take credit cards? *Est-ce que vous acceptez les cartes de crédit?*
size (clothes) *la taille*
size (shoes) *la pointure*
cheap *bon marché*
expensive *cher*
Have you got...? *Avez vous...?*
I'll take it *Je le prends*
Anything else? *Avec ça?*
enough *assez*
too much *trop*
bill *la note*

### Shops
bakery *la boulangerie*
bookshop *la librairie*
chemist *la pharmacie*
delicatessen *la charcuterie/le traiteur*
department store *le grand magasin*
fishmonger *la poissonnerie*
grocery *l'alimentation/l'épicerie*
junk shop *la brocante*
library *la bibliothèque*
supermarket *le supermarché*
tobacconist *le tabac*

### At a restaurant
I'd like to order *Je voudrais commander*
Is service included? *Est-ce que le service est compris?*
I am on a diet *Je suis au régime*

### Sightseeing
visitor information office *office de tourisme* or *le syndicat d'initiative*
open *ouvert*
closed *fermé*
every day *tous les jours*
all year round *toute l'année*
all day long *toute la journée*
free *gratuit/libre*
abbey *l'abbaye* (f)
castle *le château*
church *l'église* (f)
museum *le musée*
staircase *l'escalier* (m)
tower *la tour* (La Tour Eiffel)
tour (walk or drive) *le tour*
town *la ville*
old town *la vieille ville*
Town Hall *Hôtel de Ville/la mairie*

# Menu Reader

See regional food sections for
recommended regional dishes.

*le petit déjeuner* breakfast
*le déjeuner* lunch
*le dîner* dinner
*menu à prix fixe* meal at set price
*le plat principal* main course
*carte des vins* wine list
*l'addition* the bill

## Les boissons drinks
*café* coffee
*déca/décaffeiné* decaffeinated
   coffee
*express/noir* espresso/black
*filtre* American filtered coffee
*thé* tea
*le lait* milk
*eau minérale* mineral water
*gazeux* fizzy
*limonade* fizzy lemon drink
*citron pressé* fresh lemon juice
   served with sugar
*bière* beer
*la carafe/le pichet* pitcher of tap
   water or wine
*la demi-carafe* half liter
*vin de maison* house wine
*vin de pays* local wine
*digestif* after-dinner drink

## Le repas the meal
*le pain* bread
*le poivre* pepper
*le sel* salt
*le sucre* sugar
*le potage* soup

## Meat dishes
*l'agneau* lamb
*le bifteck* steak
*saignant* rare
*bien cuit* well done
*entrecôte* rib steak
*faux-filet* sirloin steak
*blanquette* stew of veal, lamb,
   or chicken with creamy egg
   sauce
*boeuf à la mode* beef in red wine

with carrots & onions
*bourguignonne* cooked in red
   wine, onions, & mushrooms
*le canard* duck
*la carbonnade* stew of beef in beer
*le carré d'agneau* rack of lamb
*le cassoulet* stew of beans, sausages, pork, or duck
*le confit* duck or goose preserved
   in own fat
*le côte d'agneau* lamb chop
*le dinde* turkey
*le faisan* pheasant
*farci* stuffed
*le foie de veau* calf's liver
*le foie gras* liver of force-fed duck
   or goose
*le jambon* ham
*le lapin* rabbit
*le magret de canard* breast of duck
*l'oie* goose
*le porc* pork
*le pot-au-feu* casserole of beef &
   vegetables
*le poulet* chicken
*les rognons* kidneys
*rôti* roast
*le sanglier* wild boar
*la saucisse* fresh sausage
*le saucisson* salami
*le veau* veal

## Fish dishes
*l'anchois* anchovy
*l'anguille* eel
*la barbue* brill
*la bouillabaisse* fish soup
*le cabillaud* cod
*le coquillage* shellfish
*la coquille St.-Jacques* scallop
*la crevette* shrimp
*l'encornet* squid
*le flétan* halibut
*les fruits de mer* seafood
*le homard* lobster
*l'huître* oyster
*la lotte* monkfish
*la moule* mussel
*le saumon* salmon
*le thon* tuna
*la truite* trout

## Sauces
*américaine* white wine, tomatoes,
   butter, & Cognac
*bearnaise* egg, butter, wine, & herbs
*forestière* mushrooms & bacon
*hollandaise* egg, butter, & lemon
*meunière* butter, lemon, & parsley
*meurette* red wine sauce
*Mornay* cream, egg, & cheese
*Provençal* usually tomatoes, garlic,
   & olive oil

## Légumes vegetables
*l'artichaut* artichoke
*les asperges* asparagus
*l'aubergine* eggplant
*l'avocat* avocado
*le champignon* mushroom
*le cornichon* gherkin
*la courgette* zucchini
*le chou* cabbage
*le chou-fleur* cauliflower
*les crudités* raw vegetables
*les épinards* spinach
*les haricots verts* green beans
*les lentilles* lentils
*le maïs* corn
*l'oignon* onion
*le pois* pea
*le poivron* bell pepper
*les pommes de terre* potatoes
*les pommes frites* french fries
*la salade verte* green salad

## Fruits
*la cerise* cherry
*le citron* lemon
*le citron vert* lime
*la fraise* strawberry
*la framboise* raspberry
*le pamplemousse* grapefruit
*la pêche* peach
*la poire* pear
*la pomme* apple
*le raisin* grape

## Snacks
*le croque-monsieur* ham & cheese
   toasted sandwich
*le yaourt* yogurt

# INDEX

## ILLUSTRATIONS CREDITS

National Geographic
TRAVELER

# France

**Published by the National Geographic Society**
John M. Fahey, Jr., *Chairman of the Board,*
*and Chief Executive Officer*
Timothy T. Kelly, *President*
Declan Moore, *Executive Vice President;*
*President, Publishing*
Melina Gerosa Bellows, *Executive Vice President;*
*Chief Creative Officer, Books, Kids, and Family*

**Prepared by the Book Division**
Barbara Brownell Grogan, *Vice President*
*and Editor in Chief*
Jonathan Halling, *Design Director, Books*
*and Children's Publishing*
Marianne R. Koszorus, *Director of Design*
Barbara A. Noe, *Senior Editor*
Carl Mehler, *Director of Maps*
R. Gary Colbert, *Production Director*
Jennifer A. Thornton, *Managing Editor*
Meredith C. Wilcox, *Administrative Director,*
*Illustrations*

**Staff for This Book**
Sheila Buckmaster, *Project Editor*
Kay Kobor Hankins, *Art Director*
Mary Stephanos, Alison Kelman, *Text Editors*
Matt Propert, *Illustrations Editor*
Al Morrow, *Design Assistant*
Michael McNey and Mapping Specialists,
*Map Production*
Jack Brostrom, Rachel Jackson, Julie Woodruff,
*Contributors*

**Manufacturing and Quality Management**
Christopher A. Liedel, *Chief Financial Officer*
Phillip L. Schlosser, *Senior Vice President*
Chris Brown, *Technical Director*
Nicole Elliott, *Manager*
Rachel Faulise, *Manager*
Robert L. Barr, *Manager*

**National Geographic Traveler: France (Third Edition)**
**ISBN: 978-1-4262-0822-5**

First edition: Edited and designed by AA Publishing
(a trading name of Automobile Association Developments Limited, whose registered office is Norfolk House,
Priestley Road, Basingstoke, Hampshire, England RG24
9NY. Registered number: 1878835).

Printed in China

11/TS/1

The National Geographic Society is one of the world's
largest nonprofit scientific and educational organizations. Founded in 1888 to "increase and diffuse
geographic knowledge," the Society works to inspire
people to care about the planet. National Geographic
reflects the world through its magazines, television
programs, films, music and radio, books, DVDs, maps,
exhibitions, live events, school publishing programs,
interactive media and merchandise. *National Geographic*
magazine, the Society's official journal, published in
English and 33 local-language editions, is read by more
than 40 million people each month. The National
Geographic Channel reaches 370 million households
in 34 languages in 168 countries. National Geographic
Digital Media receives more than 15 million visitors a
month. National Geographic has funded more than
9,600 scientific research, conservation and exploration
projects and supports an education program promoting geography literacy.

For more information, please call 1-800-NGS LINE
(647-5463) or write to the following address:

National Geographic Society
1145 17th Street N.W.
Washington, D.C. 20036-4688 U.S.A.

Visit us online at www.nationalgeographic.com

For information about special discounts for bulk
purchases, please contact National Geographic
Books Special Sales: ngspecsales@ngs.org

For rights or permissions inquiries, please contact
National Geographic Books Subsidiary Rights:
ngbookrights@ngs.org

The Library of Congress has cataloged the first edition
as follows:
    The National Geographic traveler. France.
    p. cm. Includes index.
    ISBN 0-7922-7426-1
    1. France—Guidebooks 1. National Geographic
    Society (U.S.)
    II. Title: France
    DC16.N37 1999
    914.404'839—dc21        98-54974
                            CIP

The information in this book has been carefully
checked and to the best of our knowledge is accurate.
However, details are subject to change, and the
National Geographic Society cannot be responsible for
such changes, or for errors or omissions. Assessments
of sites, hotels, and restaurants are based on the
author's subjective opinions, which do not necessarily
reflect the publisher's opinion.

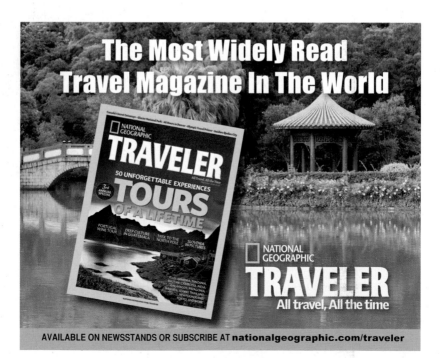